SCHOOLS AND SOCIETY

Fifth Edition

To the next generation, our grandchildren, Cosette, Chloe, Joseph, Daniel, Corinne, Hannah, Caleb, Kai, and Ayla Brynn

SCHOOLS AND SOCIETY

A Sociological Approach to Education

Fifth Edition

Editors

Jeanne H. Ballantine
Wright State University

Joan Z. Spade
The College at Brockport, State University of New York

Los Angeles | London | New Delhi
Singapore | Washington DC

Los Angeles | London | New Delhi
Singapore | Washington DC

FOR INFORMATION:

SAGE Publications, Inc.
2455 Teller Road
Thousand Oaks, California 91320
E-mail: order@sagepub.com

SAGE Publications Ltd.
1 Oliver's Yard
55 City Road
London EC1Y 1SP
United Kingdom

SAGE Publications India Pvt. Ltd.
B 1/I 1 Mohan Cooperative Industrial Area
Mathura Road, New Delhi 110 044
India

SAGE Publications Asia-Pacific Pte. Ltd.
3 Church Street
#10-04 Samsung Hub
Singapore 049483

Printed in the United States of America

Library of Congress Cataloging-in-Publication Data

A catalog record of this book is available from the Library of Congress.

9781452275833

This book is printed on acid-free paper.

Acquisitions Editor: Jeff Lasser
Editorial Assistant: Nick Pachelli
Production Editor: Brittany Bauhaus
Copy Editor: Melinda Masson
Typesetter: C&M Digitals (P) Ltd.
Proofreader: Jen Grubba
Cover Designer: Candice Harman
Marketing Manager: Erica DeLuca

14 15 16 17 18 10 9 8 7 6 5 4 3 2 1

CONTENTS

PREFACE

The challenge we struggled with as we selected material for this book was how to present sociology of education to students in a way that contains both a synopsis and a balanced picture of a complex field. As a result, we created this text to provide students with an overview of the scope, perspectives, and issues in the sociology of education. We drew on our many years of experience in researching, publishing, and teaching sociology of education. Our goal was to involve students by presenting well-rounded and provocative summaries of major areas in the field. Individual readings include a combination of classical foundations in the field, noted contemporary authors, and current issues most often discussed by instructors. The most frequently taught topics, according to 2004 survey data, are stratification, the social context of education, schools as organizations, and diversity in education (American Sociological Association, 2004). Issues related to these topics are addressed throughout the book.

Schools and Society is designed to appeal to both graduate and upper-level undergraduate students. The text is divided into 11 chapters that begin with introductions outlining issues in the topic area and summarizing how the readings that follow fit into the topic areas. The readings, written by leading scholars, are presented within a systematic framework that provides an overview of the field. These readings introduce major theoretical perspectives and include classic studies, current issues, and applications of knowledge to particular educational problems. Although this book is not about educational policy per se, many of the readings have practical and policy implications for education.

To accomplish the goal of presenting a comprehensive and theoretically balanced overview of the field, we selected readings that

1. illustrate major concepts, theoretical perspectives, and the complexity of education, including how to study it and how it has been studied;

2. blend classic studies with newer, sometimes controversial topics;

3. apply to students who are likely to take the course in various majors—sociology, education, and others;

4. exhibit writing at a level of sophistication appropriate to students in advanced undergraduate or graduate courses;

5. concentrate on materials drawn from a wide range of sources, including books, journals, scientific studies and reports, and commentaries; and

6. use the open systems approach to provide a framework for an overview of the field and analysis of a disparate group of topics.

The readings selected were tested for readability and interest level with graduate and undergraduate students. Those readings included were seen as useful and important contributions to understanding the field. Changes were made in both selections and the introductions to the readings as a result of students' comments. Each chapter begins with an introduction to show the interrelationships between the various issues in education. Each reading is preceded by introductory remarks and questions to guide students to key aspects of the article and to tie it to other articles.

NEW TO THIS EDITION

The fifth edition of *Schools and Society* introduces 20 new readings, plus revisions of 5 readings original to this book. Several of the new readings tap important issues in education today, including a piece on future approaches to education given changes in technology and another reading on international testing, both in Chapter 11. Chapters were reorganized to better portray the new materials in each section of the book, and some readings from the previous edition were moved to new chapters to reflect the new organizational structure. This reader can be used alone, with a text, or with other readings or monographs. The readings included are appropriate for a variety of courses focusing on the study of education, such as sociology of education, social foundations of education, social contexts of education, and the like. This book may be used in departments of sociology, education, social sciences, or others as appropriate.

REFERENCE

American Sociological Association. (2004). *Teaching sociology of education.* Washington, DC: Teaching Resources Center.

About the Editors

The editors, Jeanne Ballantine and Joan Spade, have known each other for many years through their involvement in the American Sociological Association (ASA) and Sociology of Education Section activities. This project started when Joan asked if Jeanne planned to update her reader. Thus, a collaboration began more than 12 years ago, with the two meeting in hotel rooms at conferences and visiting each other to develop and conceptualize this anthology. This collaboration continues with the publication of the fifth edition.

Jeanne H. Ballantine is professor emerita of sociology at Wright State University in Dayton, Ohio. She received an MA from Columbia University and a PhD from Indiana University, with a specialty in sociology of education. She has been teaching and writing for more than 35 years and has written or coauthored several texts, including *Sociology of Education: A Systematic Analysis*, *Teaching Sociology of Education*, *Sociological Footprints*, and *Our Social World: Introduction to Sociology*. She has also taught and published in other areas, including gender, global social issues, and teaching of sociology, and has been an active member of sociology of education organizations, including the ASA Section on Sociology of Education, the American Educational Research Association (AERA), and the International Sociological Association (ISA) Research Committee on Sociology of Education. She has won numerous awards, including the ASA Distinguished Contributions to Teaching Award.

Joan Z. Spade is professor emerita of sociology at The College at Brockport, State University of New York, in Brockport, New York. She received her MA from the University of Rochester and her PhD from the University of Buffalo. She has been teaching and writing in the field for more than 30 years, including a semester teaching in Budapest, Hungary, as a Fulbright Scholar; she is coeditor of *Implementing Educational Reform: Sociological Perspectives on Educational Policy* and coauthor of articles in sociology of education on stratification and grouping practices in education. She publishes in other areas, including gender and family, and is coeditor with Catherine G. Valentine of *The Kaleidoscope of Gender: Prisms, Patterns, and Possibilities*. She is a member of the ASA, including the ASA Section on Sociology of Education, the Eastern Sociological Society, and Sociologists for Women in Society.

INTRODUCTION

Schooling is ubiquitous in the world, making education a major institution in societies. Indeed, it is difficult to imagine any developed or developing society without a system of schools, from preschool to graduate level. Sociologists who study education examine schools from a variety of perspectives. The readings in this book introduce the primary sociological perspectives on educational systems and survey major issues in the field. The following illustrates some topics and questions addressed by sociologists of education:

What theories and research methods do sociologists of education use to obtain information? (Chapters 1 and 2)

What external social pressures and organizations affect the way we teach our children? (Chapter 3)

In what ways do the informal relationships and expectations in schools affect student learning and experiences in school? (Chapter 4)

What are roles and responsibilities of school administrators, teachers, and students? (Chapter 5)

How is the knowledge that we teach our children constructed and selected for our schools? (Chapter 6)

How do students' race, social class, and gender affect their school experiences and reflect systems of inequality in society? (Chapters 7 and 8)

How is higher education organized, and how has that system evolved? (Chapter 9)

How does the educational system in the United States compare to those in other countries? (Chapter 10)

What factors bring about changes in societies' schools and schooling? (Chapter 11)

We address these and many other questions by providing an overview of major theoretical perspectives in Chapter 1 and end by considering change and reform of educational institutions in Chapter 11. Throughout this book, readings look at how schools work, how they affect students and society, and how they might work differently. We look at the current condition of education and consider educational change and policy issues, all of which help us to understand the complex matrix of relationships and activities within schools. We hope this knowledge about educational issues will help you make more effective decisions as students, parents, taxpayers, and perhaps educators. After reading this book, you should have gained some understanding of the fields of sociology and education, what both fields contribute to the study of educational systems, and some specific educational issues of concern to sociologists and education professionals.

WHAT CAN SOCIOLOGISTS TELL US ABOUT EDUCATION?

Sociological analyses of education give us a deeper understanding of the form and purpose of education in a society and the interactions of people within educational organizations. Sociologists study structures and organizations of social systems, including education, family, religion, economics, politics, and health. Social institutions, such as education, constitute the major structural components of any society. Sociologists of education focus on the institution of education and the structure, processes, and interaction patterns within it. They also consider the surrounding context of the educational system including other institutions that influence the education our children receive. These aspects of education vary greatly across societies. In some societies, children learn their proper roles primarily by observing elders and imitating or modeling adult behavior. In other societies, children attend formal schools from a young age and learn the skills and knowledge needed for survival within the school and societal context.

Education and other institutions are interdependent in a society. Change in one brings change in others. For instance, a family's attitudes toward education will affect the child's school experience, as you will read in this book. Therefore, the sociological analysis of education is different from the approach taken by many people in society because sociologists begin by looking at the larger picture of society and the role that education plays in society rather than on individuals in that system. As a result, change in education is more likely to be based in structural rather than personal factors.

THE EDUCATIONAL SYSTEM

The analysis of educational systems falls into two main areas: process and structure. At whatever level of analysis we study the educational system of a society, processes are at work. These are the action parts of the system, bringing the structure alive. Examples of processes include teaching, learning, communication, and decision making, as well as those formal and informal activities that socialize students into their places in school and later life roles. These are the dynamic parts of the educational system.

However, we cannot ignore the structure of a system, including the hierarchy or roles people play—administrators, teachers, staff, parents, and, of course, students—as well as the organization of learning—classroom and school layout, types of schools, and structure of curriculum. Nor can we ignore the school's environment, which consists of groups, organizations, other institutions, and even the global society outside the school, all of which influence school functioning. For instance, politicians and other powerful people in society may put pressure on schools to select particular books (Chapter 6), communities may provide unequal academic opportunities to different groups of students (Chapter 7), and the federal and state political and economic structures shape policies and resources available to schools (Chapters 3, 4, 8, 9, 10, and 11). In short, no school exists in a vacuum. This open systems perspective is the uniting theme in this book.

THE OPEN SYSTEMS PERSPECTIVE

The open systems perspective looks at the educational system as a whole, integrated, dynamic entity. Unfortunately, most research studies focus on only parts of the whole system, and most theoretical perspectives have biases or limitations by focusing on one part. An open systems perspective is not a panacea for all the problems we face when trying to get the total picture, but this perspective can help us conceptualize a whole system and understand how the small pieces fit together into a working unity. The open systems perspective provides a useful way of visualizing many elements in the system; it helps to order observations and data and represents a generalized picture of complex interacting elements and sets of relationships. The perspective modeled in Figure I.1 refers to no one particular organization or theoretical perspective, but rather to the common characteristics of many educational settings.

Figure I.1 Open Systems Approach to Education

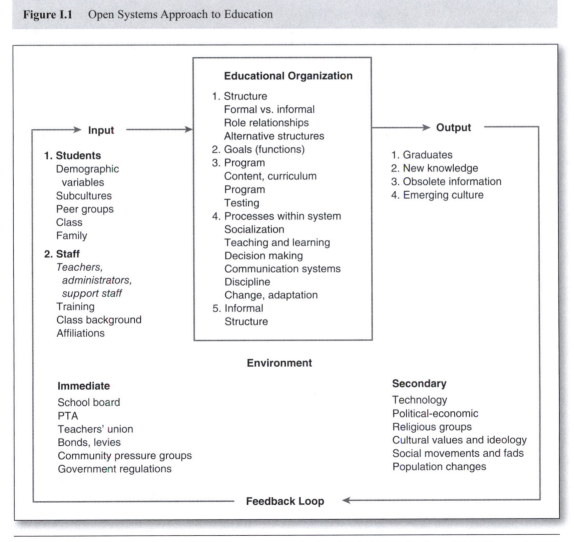

Note. From *The Sociology of Education: A Systematic Analysis* (7th ed., p. 21), by J. H. Ballantine and F. M. Hammack, 2012, Englewood Cliffs, NJ: Prentice Hall. Copyright 2012 by Pearson Education. Reprinted with permission.

Although this figure lists the component parts of a total system, it does not imply that one theory is better than another for explaining situations or events in the system. Neither does it suggest the best methodology to use in studying the system. The figure does allow you to visualize the parts you will read about in this book and help you to see where they fit and what relationship they bear to the system as a whole.

Figure I.1 shows the basic components or processes in any social system. These components are the organization, the environment, input, output, and feedback. In the following sections, we briefly discuss each of these parts as it relates to the educational system.

Step 1: Organization

Focus your attention on the center box, the organization. This refers to the center of activity and is generally the central concern for the researcher. This box can represent a society (such as the United States), an institution (such as the public education system), an organization (such as a particular school), a subsystem (such as a classroom), or an interaction (such as between teachers and students or between peers). For purposes of discussion, we shall refer to this as *the organization*. It is in the organization that many activities related to education take place, illustrating that the organization is more than structure, positions, roles, and functions. Within the organizational boundaries is a structure consisting of parts and subparts, positions and roles. Although we speak of the organization as though it were a living entity, we are really referring to the personnel who carry out the activities of the organization and make decisions about organizational action. The patterns of processes in the system bring the organization alive. Decision making and formulation of rules by key personnel, communication between members of the organization, socialization into positions in the organization, teaching in the classroom—these are among the many patterns of activities that are constantly taking place.

These patterns of processes do not take place in a vacuum. The decision makers holding positions and carrying out roles in the organization are constantly responding to demands from both inside and outside the organization. For example, the principal of a school must respond to many different constituencies, including federal, state, and local agencies; district personnel; parents; teachers; students; and even neighbors who live near the school. The boundaries of the organization are not solid but rather remain flexible and pliable in most systems to allow the system to respond to its environment. We call this *open boundaries*, or an open system.

Capturing the relationships in the school can tell us as much about its functioning as observing formal roles and structure. For example, students' experiences depend on their social class backgrounds, the responses of school staff to their behavior within schools, and the actions of students and staff that create school cultures.

Step 2: Environment

An open system implies that there is interaction between the patterns within the organizations and the environments outside the organizations. The environment refers to everything that surrounds the organization and influences it in some way. Typically the environment includes other surrounding systems. For schools, an important aspect of the environment is financial—where they get their money. What rules are imposed on schools is another critical factor, as schools exist within a maze of social, political, and legal expectations, such as the recent Race to the Top legislation. Another is the employment market and job skills needed at a particular time. For each school organization, the crucial factors in its environment will differ and change over time. Another important factor in the environment is family, and particularly the financial and other support families provide to schools and their children through their social class background. As described throughout the book, but particularly in Chapters 7 and 8, the social class context surrounding children has a strong influence on their academic achievement.

Organizations depend on their environments to meet many of their resource requirements and to obtain information. Every school and school district faces a different set of challenges from its environment. There are many necessary and desired interactions with the environment, and some that are not so pleasant. The interaction of the school with the environment takes place in our systems model in the form of input and output.

Step 3: Input

The organization receives input from the environment in such forms as information (including textbooks and classroom materials), raw materials, personnel, finances, and new ideas. Furthermore, persons who are members of the organization are also part of surrounding communities and bring into the organization influences from the environment.

Some environmental inputs are mandatory for the organization's survival; others vary in degree of importance. For most organizations, some inputs are undesirable but unavoidable: new legal restrictions, competition, or financial pressures. The organization can exert some control over inputs. For instance, schools have selection processes for new teachers, textbooks, and other curricular materials. Schools have less control over other inputs, such as which students they serve. Certain positions in the organization are held by personnel who act as buffers between the organization and its environment. For example, the secretary who answers the phone has a major controlling function, and so, too, in a very different manner, does the principal of a school.

Step 4: Output

Output refers to the material items and the nonmaterial ideas that leave the organization, such elements as completed products, wastes, information, evolving culture, and new technology. There may be personnel who bridge the gap between organizations and their environment. Personnel with responsibility for selling the organization's product serve this function, whether they work in a placement office for college graduates or in the central administrative offices of a school district creating newsletters and funding solicitations for local taxpayers and others.

The normal production of new knowledge in colleges and universities in the form of research papers and articles represents output from these educational institutions. As you will read in Chapter 6, despite the view that knowledge is produced within a well-organized structure, the process of producing knowledge is highly political and embedded within social relationships.

Step 5: Feedback

A key aspect of an open systems model is the process of feedback. This process implies that an organization's leaders are constantly learning about and adapting to changes and demands in the environment as a result of news they receive. For instance, the organizational personnel compare the current state of affairs with desired goals and environmental feedback to determine new courses of action. The feedback may be positive or negative, requiring differing responses. Top administrators of our educational institutions are, in many ways, managers of this system of feedback.

ORGANIZATION OF THE BOOK

The open systems perspective described above and in Figure I.1 can serve us in many ways. Not only does it provide an organizing framework for this book, but this perspective can also help to promote interdisciplinary study, as illustrated in many readings in this book. As Marvin Olsen (1978) has said:

> It is not a particular kind of social organization. It is an analytical model that can be applied to any instance of the process of social organization, from families to nation. . . . Nor is [it] a substantive theory—though it is sometimes spoken of as a theory in sociological literature. This model is a highly general, content-free conceptual framework within which any number of different substantive theories of social organization can be constructed. (p. 228)

A discussion of the fields of education and sociology must include numerous related fields: economics and school financing; political science, power, and policy issues; the family and child; church-state relationships; health and medical care for children; humanities and the arts; and the school's role in early childhood training, among others.

We structured this book to embrace the complexity of education, in terms of both what is studied and how it is studied, within the open systems perspective. Each chapter in the book focuses on illuminating aspects of the open systems perspective and contributing to an overview of educational systems. In selecting readings for the book, we sought to blend theory and classical readings with recent studies and current issues to provide background for current arguments as well as an understanding of new directions in sociology of education. Though we focus primarily on research within sociology of education, we also include relevant readings from other areas. The readings herein represent a broad range of topics in the field; however, an attempt to cover all areas is not possible because the topic of education is multifaceted and very complex. When we leave out topics, we try to address them briefly in the chapter introductions.

For each chapter, we provide an introduction to both the area of education being covered and the research in that area. Each reading also includes an introduction and questions for you to consider as you read. We encourage you to read individual chapters within the whole as exemplified by the open systems perspective presented in this introduction.

Chapter 1 presents an overview of major classical and contemporary theoretical perspectives to understanding educational systems—from functionalism to branches of conflict and interaction theory. These theoretical perspectives provide different explanations for why schools operate the way they do. This chapter provides the frameworks that are used to understand how schools work and to explain why things are as they are in schools.

Chapter 2 illustrates the relationship between theory and methods in sociology of education and provides examples of different methodological approaches. These approaches cover issues from microlevel to macrolevel analyses, from interaction between individuals to examinations of global systems. Readings discuss qualitative and quantitative approaches to understanding educational systems.

Chapter 3 moves to the environment, the larger context within which the educational system operates. The environment can influence the educational system through control of finances, law, public opinion, and attitudes toward schools.

Chapter 4 focuses on schools and educational systems as organizations including the formal and informal aspects of schools. This is Step 1 in the open systems model: what goes on within the educational organization. The readings provide a sample of the rich literature on formal and informal organizations and structures.

Chapter 5 also focuses inside the educational organization, but on the roles and responsibilities of administrators, teachers, and students. The readings illustrate several methods of research, including survey research, use of large data sets, and ethnography.

Chapter 6 considers what knowledge is presented in schools and how that knowledge is selected. These readings illustrate how the processes of determining curricula are affected by the cultural and environmental factors external to schools.

Chapter 7 delves into a key process in schools and societies—stratification by race, class, and gender. Readings explore how the stratification process in the larger society shapes the inputs and outputs as well as educational organizations themselves. This chapter examines inequalities of social stratification in schools and school-related relationships.

Chapter 8 looks at programs and policies established to bring equality and equity into educational systems. The attempts at equality and equity include laws, changes in school structures, and attempts to override the dynamics of inequality in society. However, as you will read, these efforts toward equality are not always successful. This chapter explores both the development of the reform efforts and the consequences.

Chapter 9 considers the top tiers of the educational system—higher education. The readings illustrate how this part of the educational system also includes both formal and informal structures and is reflected in the larger environment. Again, issues of inequality are addressed, both historically and in current contexts, as we consider the role of higher education in the United States and globally.

Chapter 10 illustrates that educational systems around the world are interrelated through the needs of the global community. Aspects of educational systems around the world are becoming increasingly similar. However, features of local and national environments also influence curricula, testing, and preparation of young people for their roles in a complex world.

Chapter 11 considers how educational systems change and may change in the future. It is important to understand how educational systems work. It is also important to understand why alternatives to current educational systems are difficult to design and implement.

As you read about the different parts of educational systems in this book, we hope you develop a deeper understanding of the role of education both in your life and in the society as a whole.

REFERENCES

Ballantine, J. H., & Hammack, F. M. (2012). *The sociology of education: A systematic approach* (7th ed.). Boston: Pearson Education.

Olsen, M. E. (1978). *The process of social organization: Power in social systems* (2nd ed.). New York: Holt, Rinehart, and Winston.

1

WHAT IS SOCIOLOGY OF EDUCATION?

Theoretical Perspectives

A whole new perspective on schools and education lies in the study of sociology of education. How sociologists understand education can contribute to informed decision making and change in educational institutions. Sociologists of education focus on *interactions* between people, structures that provide recurring organizations, and *processes* that bring the structures such as schools alive through teaching, learning, and communicating. As one of the major structural parts, or *institutions*, in society, education is a topic of interest to many sociologists. Some work in university departments teaching sociology or education, others work in government agencies, and others do research and advise school administrators. Whatever their role, sociologists of education provide valuable insights into the interactions, structures, and processes of educational systems. Sociologists of education examine many parts of educational systems, from interactions, classroom dynamics, and peer groups to school organizations and national and international systems of education.

Consider some of the following questions of interest to sociologists of education: What classroom and school settings are best for learning? How do peers affect children's achievement and ambitions? What classroom structures are most effective for children from different backgrounds? How do schools reflect the neighborhoods in which they are located? Does education "reproduce" the social class of students, and what effect does this have on children's futures? What is the relationship between education, religion, and political systems? How does access to technology affect students' learning and preparation for the future? How do nations compare on international educational tests? Is there a global curriculum? These are just a sampling of the many questions that make up the broad mandate for sociology of education, and it is a fascinating one. Sociologists place the study of education in a larger framework of interconnected institutions found in every society, including family, religion, politics, economics, and health, in addition to education. In this chapter we examine the basic building blocks for a sociological inquiry into education and the theories that are used to frame ways of thinking about education in society.

With a focus on studying people in groups, sociologists study a range of topics about educational systems. Chapters in this book focus on how sociologists study schools; the environment surrounding schools; the organization of schools and education; the roles people play in schools (teachers, students, administrators, and others); what we teach in schools; processes that take place in schools including those that result in unequal outcomes for students; how different racial/ethnic groups, genders, and social class backgrounds of students can affect educational outcomes; the system of higher education; and national and international comparisons of learning and achievement in different regions and countries. No other discipline has the broad approach and understanding provided by sociology of education.

THEORIES

Sociologists of education start with perspectives or *theories* that provide a framework to search for knowledge about education systems. Theories are attempts to explain and predict patterns and practices between individuals and in social systems, in this case educational systems. Theories are carefully structured explanations or arguments that are applied to real-life situations. Since theories are not descriptions of what is happening in schools but only carefully thought-out explanations of why things happen, we can apply more than one theory to explain educational phenomena. An understanding of several theoretical approaches gives us different ways of thinking about educational systems. Theories guide research and policy formation in the sociology of education and provide logical explanations for why things happen as they do, helping to explain, predict, and generalize about issues related to schools. It is from the theories and the resulting research that sociologists of education come to understand educational systems. This chapter provides an overview of sociological theories as they are related to sociology of education, followed by classical and contemporary readings on the major theories. These theories also appear in readings throughout the book.

Following the open systems model discussed in the Introduction enables us to visualize the school system and its relationships with other organizations in its social context, or environment. By visualizing the dynamics inside a school, we can use theories to explain various situations within schools, such as the roles individuals play in schools and interactions between administrators, teachers, students, and other staff; equal opportunity within individual school organizations; social class dynamics as played out between peers in schools; formal and informal dynamics within schools; and the organization of school systems.

WHAT YOU WILL FIND IN CHAPTER 1

The purpose of the first chapter is to introduce you to the sociology of education through some key perspectives and theories in the field. The first reading discusses the relationship between sociology and education, why it is useful to study the sociology of education, who has a stake in educational systems and why they are likely interested in the field, and questions asked by sociologists of education. The second reading, by the book's editors Jeanne Ballantine and Joan Spade, outlines early theories in sociology of education and how they have influenced contemporary theories and theorists. This provides an introduction to the remaining readings, which are original works in various theories of sociology of education.

Current sociological theories have a long history in sociological thought flowing from the early works of Émile Durkheim, Max Weber, and Karl Marx. The excerpts included in this chapter build upon their early ideas in attempting to understand the social world from the perspective of the "new" discipline of sociology in the early 1800s. Durkheim's study of the impact of the social system on maintaining order in society is considered the basis for functional theory.

An illustration of functional theory's application to education is found in the excerpt from a classical article by functionalist Talcott Parsons (1959) in the third reading in this chapter. This reading focuses on the workings of a school classroom and the roles performed by each position holder. In describing the functions of schools, Parsons focuses on the school class and its purposes in meeting the goals for schools. These activities contribute to socializing children into the expectations and knowledge needed for participation in society, preparing them for adult roles and contributing to a stable society.

Historically, the second major theoretical perspective to develop was conflict theory. It became a dominant theory in response to functional theory's focus on the need to preserve stability in society, sometimes at a cost to disadvantaged groups in society. Conflict theorists ask how schools contribute to unequal educational outcomes and distribution of people in stratification systems (such as social classes). A major issue for sociologists of education in the conflict tradition is the role education plays in maintaining the prestige, power, and economic and social position of the dominant groups in society. They contend that more powerful members of society maintain the most powerful positions in society, and the less powerful groups (often women, disadvantaged racial and ethnic groups, and lower social classes) are "allocated" to lower ranks.

Karl Marx and Max Weber set the stage for contemporary conflict theories, and the reading in this chapter by Randall Collins (1971) provides an example of this perspective applied to education. Classical conflict theorists argue that those who dominate capitalist economic systems also control other institutions in society, such as education. Capitalists use these institutions to maintain power and enhance their own profits, although not without resistance by some students and community groups. Collins also provides an overview of another approach to conflict theory, discussing the use of Weber's concept of "status groups." Weber points out the strong relationship between students' social class origins, their preparation in school, and the jobs they move into after school. Weber argued that schools teach and maintain particular "status cultures," that is, groups in society with similar interests and positions in the status hierarchy. Located in neighborhoods, schools are often rather homogeneous in their student bodies and teach to the local constituency, thus perpetuating status cultures in neighborhoods and communities.

Functional and conflict theorists have been debating how to explain what happens in schools since Marx, Weber, and Durkheim's times. Each function of education (discussed in the second reading) has generated controversy. For example, functionalists argue that schools prepare young members of society for their adult roles, thus allowing for the smooth functioning of society, whereas conflict theorists counter that the powerful members of society control access to the best educations, thus preparing only their children for the highest positions in society and retaining their positions of power.

The third major theoretical perspective in sociology of education is interaction theory, a microlevel theory that focuses on individual and small group experiences in the educational system: the processes and interactions that take place in schools. In *interaction* or *interpretive theory*, individuals are active players in shaping their experiences and cultures, and not merely shaped by societal forces. By studying the way participants in the process of schooling construct their realities, researchers can better understand the meaning of education for participants. The final reading by Ray Rist (1977) comes from the interaction theory tradition, and it focuses on *labeling theory*.

One important factor in the teaching and learning process is what teachers come to expect from their students. The concept of *self-fulfilling prophecy* applied to the classroom was made famous by Rosenthal and Jacobson's book *Pygmalion in the Classroom* (1968). They studied how teachers form judgments about their students and *label* them based on objective but also subjective factors, such as social class, appearance, and language patterns. The reading by Rist argues that utilizing labeling theory, and an outcome of labeling called the *self-fulfilling prophecy,* helps us to understand school processes from the standpoint of both teachers and students.

As you read about the theories presented in this chapter, try to picture the open systems perspective (discussed in the Introduction) with its many parts, activities, participants, structures, contexts or environments, and processes such as conflict. These readings provide an overview and examples of theoretical perspectives that will help you to understand the education system, interrelationships between parts, and many of the readings in the book that use these theories. In the following chapters, other parts of the open systems model are examined. Some readings take an institutional perspective, looking at how social structure affects the institution of education; others take a more microlevel focus on individuals, classrooms, and interactions in schools. All can be placed in the educational context of the open systems model, and all can be better understood with knowledge of the theories that are discussed in this chapter.

REFERENCES

Ballantine, J. H., & Hammack, F. M. (2012). *The sociology of education: A systematic analysis* (7th ed.). Boston: Pearson.

Collins, R. (1971). Functional and conflict theories of educational stratification. *American Sociological Review, 36*(6), 1002–1019.

Parsons, T. (1959). The school class as a social system: Some of its functions in American society. *Harvard Educational Review, 29*(4), 297–318.

Rist, R. C. (1977). On understanding the process of schooling: Contributions of labeling theory. In J. Karabel & A. H. Halsey (Eds.), *Power and ideology in education* (pp. 292–305). New York: Oxford University Press.

Rosenthal, R., & Jacobson, L. (1968). *Pygmalion in the classroom.* New York: Holt, Rinehart and Winston.

SOCIOLOGY OF EDUCATION

A Unique Perspective for Understanding Schools

Jeanne H. Ballantine and Floyd M. Hammack

For many readers, sociology of education is a new field of inquiry. It provides new perspectives on education for future teachers and administrators, parents, students, and policy makers. These first two articles lay the groundwork for understanding the importance of the sociological perspective and theories in researching schools and effective teaching and learning strategies. This reading focuses specifically on what sociologists of education study and how such research is useful in understanding schools in our society.

Questions to consider for this reading:

1. What can sociology contribute to our understanding of education?

2. Who can benefit from studying the sociology of education, and how?

3. What are some topics of importance to sociologists of education?

Education is a lifelong process. It begins the day we are born and ends the day we die. Found in every society, education comes in many forms, ranging from the "school of hard knocks" to formal institutional learning. The educational process occurs across societies from postindustrial to preindustrial communities, from rural to urban settings, and from youth to older persons. It encompasses all individuals in the world. How education takes place, how policies affect schools, and what works to educate young people are questions that sociologists of education tackle. While sociologists do not try to answer questions of right and wrong or good and bad, they do consider the state of education and the outcomes of certain policies.

SOCIOLOGY AND EDUCATION

Sociologists study people who interact in small to large group situations. Within this broad framework are many specialties and various ways of approaching sociological analysis. Within these specialty areas, sociologists study processes and structure of organizations and interactions between individuals and groups. A specialty within sociology is the study of institutions—established aspects of society that address common needs of people in society. Sociologists typically identify six major institutions as parts of societal structures: family, religion, education, politics, economics, and health. Formal, complex organizations, such as schools, are part of the

Source: From Jeanne H. Ballantine and Floyd M. Hammack. 2012 (revised). The Sociology of Education: A Systematic Analysis. 7th ed. Boston: Pearson.

institutional *structures* that carry out the needed work of societies. While these institutions are often studied separately, there is considerable overlap in terms of the workings of societies. The institution of education interacts and is interdependent with other institutions. For example, families' involvements in education affect children's educational achievements in school.

Processes, the action part of society, bring the institutional structures alive. The process of *stratification* sorts people within the social structure and, thus, defines their lifestyles and life chances. The process of *change* is ever-present and constantly forces schools and other organizations to adjust to new demands. And through the process of socialization in families and schools, children learn how to fit into society and what roles are expected of them. The processes of education *and learning* take place both formally in school settings and informally in our family, with peers, through media exposure, and by other influences in our lives. Not all children in the world receive a formal school education, but they all experience learning processes that prepare them for adult roles.

Sociology of education as a field is devoted to understanding what sociologists call the institution of education, including its structure, processes, and interactions. The subject matter of sociology of education ranges from one-on-one interactions of teachers and students to large educational systems of countries. By studying education systematically, sociologists offer insights to help guide policies for schools. Research on educational systems is guided by sociological theories, described further in this chapter, and studied using sociological methods, described in Chapter 2. Although sociology provides a unique and powerful set of tools to objectively explore the educational systems of societies, it may disappoint individuals who have an axe to grind or whose goal is to proselytize rather than objectively understand or explore. Sometimes simply raising certain questions is uncomfortable for those who think they "know the right answer." The goal of sociology of education is to objectively consider educational practices, structures of learning, beliefs, and important topics, whether controversial or not, to gain understanding of a system that affects us all.

Why Study Sociology of Education?

There are a number of answers to this question. Someday you may be a professional in the field of education or in a related field; you will be a taxpayer, if you aren't already; or you may be (or are) a parent with children in the school system. Right now you are a student involved in higher or continuing education, and that gives you further insight into why individuals study sociology of education. Think about why you are taking this class. You may be in pursuit of knowledge; this course may be required; you may need the credit; perhaps the teacher is supposed to be good; or it may simply fit into your schedule or fulfill a distribution requirement. If you are a sociology major, you are studying education as one of the major institutions of society; if you are an education major, sociology may give you a new or different perspective for understanding the foundations of education. Let's consider some personal reasons for studying sociology of education.

Teachers and Other Professionals. Study findings indicate that between 2008 and 2018, the most job openings, 597,000, for those with a bachelor's degree will be in elementary education (College Board, 2010). An estimated 3.5 million teachers are involved in public school education (U.S. Bureau of Labor Statistics, 2010–2011). Other college graduates teach in their respective academic fields or become involved with policy matters in the schools. Professionals in such fields as social work and business have regular contact with schools when dealing with clients and employees.

Taxpayers. Taxpayers play a major role in financing schools at all levels of education, including the money used to pay for physical plants, materials, salaries, and other essentials in the U.S. educational system. Revenues for schools come from local, state, and federal proceeds from sales, income, and property taxes. Considering differences among states as well as variations in U.S. school districts by median household income, the local contributions to schools range from 28% to 56%, and the federal contribution ranges from 3% to 12%. In 2012, the federal government's contribution to education was 3% ($121.1 billion), and projected 2013 expenditures were $118.1 billion. Compare this to 23% for defense spending in 2012 ($925.2 billion) (Chantrill, 2013).

Parents. Most adults in the United States are or will be parents. Even those who are not parents care about how schools are run. According to the Gallup polls on adult attitudes toward education, adults expect schools to teach basic skills, discipline children, and instill values and a sense of responsibility. The concerns of the American public regarding schools have shown a high level of consistency from year to year (see Table 1.1) (Bushaw & Lopez, 2012).

Lack of financial support and lack of discipline topped the list of problems seen by the public in 2012, with fighting/gang violence and drugs numbers 4 and 5 on the list. Parents need to make decisions regarding their children's education; an understanding of their attitudes about their school systems can be gained from a study of the sociology of education.

Table 1.1	What Do You Think Are The Biggest Problems That The Public Schools Of Your Community Must Deal With?

	National Totals 2012	Parent Totals 2012
1. Lack of financial support	35%	43%
2. Lack of discipline	8%	3%
3. Overcrowding	5%	6%
4. Fighting/gang violence	4%	5%
5. Drugs	2%	2%

Students. Grade school education is mandatory in most countries, and high school–level education is mandatory in developed countries and available in many developing countries. According to a study by Harvard University and the Asian Development Bank, only 6.7% of the world's population has a college degree (Huffington Post, 2010). In the United States, 87.7% of the population has a high school degree, 30.9% has a college degree, 8% has a master's degree, and 3% has a PhD (U.S. Census Bureau, 2012).

College attracts a wide variety of students with numerous incentives and goals for their educational experience. Understanding your own and others' goals will help you get the most from your education. For sociology majors, sociology of education provides a unique look at educational systems and their interdependence among other major institutions in society. For education majors, new insights can be gained by looking into the dynamic interactions both within educational settings and between the institution of education and other institutions in society. These insights should give education majors the ability to deal with complex organizational and interpersonal issues that confront teachers and administrators.

Policy Makers. Whether in political office voting on school allocations, in a school district on a school board making local decisions, or a company executive looking for educated graduates with needed skills, policy makers have a vested interest in the education schools provide and often have decision-making power.

Questions Asked by Sociologists of Education

As students, parents, and members of a community, we are constantly faced with a plethora of educational issues. Consider the following examples:

Are Our Children Safe in Schools? Among the most serious school problems noted in surveys of the American public are lack of discipline, fighting and gang violence, and drugs in schools. Yet, even with the recent school shootings, over 90% of the public believes school discipline is satisfactory (Bushaw & Lopez, 2012). National studies indicate that most students do not experience criminal victimization, and those who do are more likely to experience property crimes. Students in schools with gang members present express more concern about safety (Addington et al., 2002). The ultimate question is "Are our students safer in school than out of school?" The answer is that most studies conclude that schools are safe places for students.

Should Minimum Competency in Key Subjects Such as Reading and Math Be Required for High School Graduation? In many countries and some cities and states in the United States, students are required to take reading and math exams in order to enter high school and be graduated from it. The 2001 "No Child Left Behind" and current "Race to the Top" federal policies in the United States require all students to be tested at various times throughout their school years. Increasingly, states hold schools and teachers responsible for the academic competence of students who move through the system (Borman & Cotner, 2011). Tests are one way to hold schools accountable for students' progress. Yet, some educators and researchers question the value of requiring competency tests because they have little benefit for students who pass them and can harm students who do not pass (Warren & Grodsky, 2009).

What Type of Teachers and Classroom Environments Provide the Best Learning Experience for Children? Educators debate lecture versus experiential learning, and cooperative learning versus individualized instruction. Studies (e.g., Pescosolido & Aminzade, 1999) of effective teaching strategies provide information to help educators carry out their roles effectively. For example, research on the most effective size of classes and schools attempts to provide policy makers with data to inform decision making (Darling-Hammond, 2010; see also Biddle and Berliner in Chapter 2 [Reading 7]). What other classroom factors influence teaching and learning?

A review of the titles of articles in the premiere journal *Sociology of Education* provides an overview of current topics being studied in the field. For example, in the past few years researchers have explored immigrant education, gender inequality and gender income gaps, causes of academic failure, social class differences in college expectations and entrance, racial segregation in schools and educational attainment, higher education aspirations and enrollments, and the level of female and male participation in different academic fields. Looking through this book and other sociology of education resources will add to the list of questions asked by sociologists of education; they cover a fascinating array of topics. Sociological research knowledge sheds light on educational issues and thus helps teachers, citizens, and policy makers with the decision-making process. Multitudes of questions arise, and many of them are being studied around the world (see Box 1.1).

BOX 1.1

Current Research in the Sociology of Education

The following sampling of current research questions gives an idea of the wide range of subject matter:

1. If parents are involved in their children's schooling, are children more successful in school?

2. How effective are different teaching techniques, styles of learning, classroom organizations, and school and classroom size in teaching students of various types and abilities?

3. What are some community influences on the school, and how do these affect decision making in schools, especially as it relates to the school curriculum and socialization of the young?

4. Do teacher proficiency exams increase teaching quality?

5. Can minority students learn better or more in an integrated school?

6. Do schools perpetuate inequality?

7. Should religion be allowed in schools? What are practices around the world?

8. Does tracking (ability grouping) students help or hurt student learning?

9. Is the U.S. government policy "Race to the Top" having a positive or negative effect overall?

10. Do schools prepare students for the transition to work?

11. Who are the world's most prepared students according to international tests, and why?

12. Are some students overeducated for the employment opportunities that are available to them?

13. How does education affect income potential?

14. Does school choice produce better schools?

15. How does cultural capital affect academic achievement?

These and other topics are studied by sociologists of education. Many of these ideas are discussed in the following pages. Enjoy your trip into the sociology of education!

REFERENCES

Addington, L. A., Ruddy, S. A., Miller, A. K., Devoe, J. F., & Chandler, K. A. (2002, November). *Are America's schools safe? Students speak out.* Washington, DC: U.S. Department of Education, National Center for Education Statistics.

Borman, K. M., & Cotner, B. A. (2011). No Child Left Behind—and beyond: The federal government gets serious about accountability. In J. Ballantine & J. Spade (Eds.), *Schools and society: A sociological approach to education* (4th ed., pp. 100–106). Thousand Oaks, CA: Sage.

Bushaw, W. J., & Lopez, S. J. (2012, September). Public education in the United States: A nation divided. *Phi Delta Kappan, 94*(1), 9–26.

Chantrill, C. (2013). FY12 federal budget spending estimates for fiscal years 2011–2016. *U.S. Federal Budget Analyst.* Retrieved from www.usgovernmentspending.com/education_budget_2012_2.html

College Board. (2010, September 21). *Education Pays 2010* report shows college grads weather recession better than others. Retrieved from http://press.collegeboard.org/releases/2010/education-pays-2010-report-shows-college-graduates-weather-recession-better-others

Darling-Hammond, L. (2010). *The flat world and education: How America's commitment to equity will determine our future.* New York: Teachers College Press.

Huffington Post. (2010, May 19). 6.7% of world has college degree. Retrieved from http://www.huffingtonpost.com/2010/05/19/percent-of-world-with-col_n_581807.html

Pescosolido, B. A., & Aminzade, R. (Eds.). (1999). *The social worlds of higher education.* Thousand Oaks, CA: Pine Forge Press.

U.S. Bureau of Labor Statistics. (2012, March 29). Kindergarten and elementary school teachers. Occupational Outlook Handbook: 2010–2011. Retrieved from http://www.bls.gov/oco/ocos318.htm

U.S. Census Bureau. (2012). Education: Educational attainment. *The 2012 Statistical Abstract of the United States.* Retrieved from www.census.gov/compendia/statab/cats/education/educational_attainment.html

Warren, J. R., & Grodsky, E. (2009). Exit exams harm students who fail them—and don't benefit students who pass them. *Phi Delta Kappan, 90*(9), 645–649.

GETTING STARTED

Understanding Education Through Sociological Theory

Jeanne H. Ballantine and Joan Z. Spade

Each of us has opinions about schools. These opinions, particularly if held by people in powerful positions in society, often translate into policy decisions related to schools and votes on tax levies. Theories provide sociologists and policy makers with a choice of frameworks to view educational systems in more depth than simple opinions, and help us to understand the research that sheds light on what happens in schools, enabling informed decisions about school policies. In this reading, we outline key elements of several major theoretical approaches in sociology of education to provide multiple frames from which to view educational issues discussed in this book.

Questions to consider as you read this article:

1. How can theories in the sociology of education help us understand educational systems?

2. What are some research questions that microlevel and macrolevel theorists might address? How do they differ?

3. Think of a current issue in education that is of interest to you, and consider how the theories discussed in this reading would help to explain that issue.

To understand how education systems work—or don't work—social scientists develop theories providing logical, carefully structured arguments to explain schools and society. Theories together with research provide valuable insights into all parts of education. Those parts are represented by the open systems model discussed in the introduction to this book. Some theories have limited use, but others stand the test of time and have relevance beyond the immediate circumstances that generated them.

The purpose of this discussion is to review some of the leading theoretical approaches used in the sociology of education to develop questions about educational systems as a way to help organize discussion. The theories in this reading are divided into micro and macro levels of analysis. Microlevel explanations focus on the individual and interactions between individuals, such as how teachers, administrators, students, parents, or others perceive and respond to educational settings and how their responses shape interactions. For example, we can use microlevel

Revision of "Social Science Theories on Teachers, Teaching, and Educational Systems," in *The New International Handbook of Teachers and Teaching* (pp. 81–102), by A. G. Dworkin and L. J. Saha (Eds.), 2009, New York: Springer. Copyright 2009 by Springer. Adapted with permission.

theories to understand how teachers respond differently to some children based on their gender or the social class of their families. Macrolevel explanations, on the other hand, focus on the institution of education in societies and the world, and how schools fit into the larger social structure of societies. As such, macrolevel theorists might study why different educational structures emerge in different societies, looking at the role of schools in society as a whole. Our discussion of these theories begins with microlevel explanations and moves to macrolevel theoretical perspectives.

For over a half-century, *Why Johnny Can't Read* (Flesch, 1955) and numerous other books explored problems in school systems, from teachers' expectations of students to classroom dynamics and school policies such as tracking and testing. These issues continue to be debated today in both national and international contexts. We use the question of "why Johnny can't read" to illustrate the theories we introduce in this reading.

MICROLEVEL THEORIES OF EDUCATION

Efforts to understand why Johnny can't read are typically found at the micro level of analysis. They focus on interactions and experiences in the classroom between the student and others, often attributing failure to the students themselves, to their teachers, or to their home environments. *Interaction theorists* focus on the interpersonal dynamics of the situation and assume that individuals socially construct their lives based on the environments in which they find themselves. With origins in the field of social psychology, symbolic interaction theories link individuals with the symbols they use to understand the situations they are in. These symbols are developed and understood in their immediate social contexts, groups, and society. For example, the names students in each school or classroom call each other or the meanings they give to their schoolwork vary both within and between schools and are often linked to the social class backgrounds of students and their peers.

Nothing is taken for granted in interaction theory; what most people accept as given is questioned and studied. Thus, the question of why Johnny can't read begins with Johnny's "social construction of reality," as well as the socially constructed realities of his teachers, school administrators, parents, and others in his social world and embedded in all interactions Johnny has (Berger & Luckmann, 1963). Add to the puzzle complications of race, class, and gender, socially constructed categories themselves, and we have the context for symbolic interaction theory as illustrated in the reading by Morris in Chapter 7.

Interaction theories also focus on what teachers and students *do* in school. These theories grew from reactions to the macrolevel structural-functional and conflict theories, which focus on society and how schools as institutions fit into the big picture. The criticism is that macrolevel approaches miss the dynamics of everyday school interactions and life in classrooms that shape children's futures. Interaction theorists question things many people overlook, such as how students get labeled and tracked in schools; they ask questions about the most common, ordinary interactions between school participants. Sociologists of education using this approach are likely to focus on students' attitudes, values, and achievements, such as their motivations to do well in school; students' self-concepts; and how interactions between peers, students, teachers, and principals are shaped by the social class backgrounds of all participants.

Among the several approaches taken by interaction theorists are symbolic interaction, role theory, and labeling theory; dramaturgy and ethnomethodology; and phenomenological sociology. The following discussion gives an overview of some of these approaches.

Symbolic Interaction Theory

Symbols are the concepts or ideas that we use to frame our interactions. These concepts can be expressed by words or gestures; they define reality and affect our sense of self and the social hierarchies that surround us. As such, children are viewed as active participants in school and are, therefore, agents in creating the social reality in which they live. For example, popularity is a major issue for many children, especially in middle school years. Popularity is mostly a function of being visible and having everyone know who you are, but it also specifies a symbolic hierarchy of social power. Sometimes popularity is gained by representing the school in an athletic contest, by being attractive, or by being in a leadership position. The difficulty is that positions of popularity are scarce. Thus, competition is created, and some individuals are going to be "losers," with less social power, while a few others are "winners" in this socially defined popularity contest. Consider also the example of academic grouping. No matter what teachers or administrators call reading groups and different levels of English, mathematics, or science classes, children quickly learn whether they are "good" or "bad" students. Thus, symbols define students' and teachers' interactions—specifying who is "bright," "cooperative," "trouble," and so forth. Symbols define what experiences are "good" or "bad." In other words, symbols create our social reality.

Considerable inequality occurs in the symbols students bring with them to school. Children from families who cannot afford to purchase desired clothing or other status symbols are more likely to be the "losers." Those who "win" are more likely to have access to symbolic resources, including higher class–based language patterns and social experiences. The winners are given special privileges in the classroom or school. These students, who exude privilege in the symbols they bring with them, are more likely to develop leadership skills and generally feel good about themselves.

Symbolic interaction theory has its roots in the works of G. H. Mead and C. H. Cooley on the development of the self through social interaction, whether in school or in other areas of life. People within a culture generally interpret and define social situations in similar ways because they share experiences and expectations (Ballantine & Roberts, 2014). Students look to others, particularly their teachers, to understand their place in this culture. Common norms evolve to guide behavior. Students learn through interaction how they are different from others based on individual experiences, social class, and status.

Labeling Theory

Labeling theory is closely related to the symbolic interactionist perspective (Goffman, 1967). If Johnny is told often enough that he is stupid and can't do the work, the label of "stupid" can become a *self-fulfilling prophecy* as he comes to incorporate that label into his sense of self. Then, teachers and others who create and reinforce the label continue to respond to Johnny as if that symbol is an accurate reflection of his abilities. Using labeling theory, we can better understand how teachers' expectations based on students' race, class, ethnic background, gender, religion, or other characteristics affect students' self-perceptions and achievement levels.

Labeling theory helps us to understand how microlevel interactions in the school contribute to individuals' formations of their sense of self. Young people from 6 to 18 years old spend much of their time in school or school-related activities; therefore, *student* is a status that has enormous impact on how they see themselves. Interaction with others in school affects students' sense of self. The image that is reflected back to someone—as student or as teacher, for example—can begin to mold one's sense of competence, intelligence, and likability. The school creates a symbolic structure that influences how individuals make sense of their reality and interact with others. Official school positions such as president of the student council, lower-level reader, or athlete can become important elements of a student's sense of self.

The powerful interactions between labelers and labeled have been studied in schools. A classic study found that students in classrooms where the teachers were told that students in their classes were "late bloomers" and would "blossom" that year achieved much more academically than students in classrooms where the teacher had no expectations for students, even though students in both classrooms were similar in ability and potential (Rosenthal & Jacobson, 1968).

The process of labeling by assigning students to academic and nonacademic tracks and ability groups serves to reproduce inequalities in society. Low-income students are often placed in low-ability groups, which can become a "life sentence" affecting achievement and future opportunities. Interactions between participants in the school and classroom give insight into the labeling process. For example, in another classic study, Rist (1970, 1977) found that teachers formed expectations for students based on their race, class, ethnicity, and gender and that these expectations had long-term effects on students' achievement and sense of themselves. The result is that low-income students are more likely to be placed in lower-ability groups that do not reflect their actual ability (Rist, 1970, 1977; Sadovnik, 2007).

Outside-of-school statuses can be an important basis for interactions in schools. In addition to social class, gender is reinforced in social interactions in the classroom, as shown in research findings indicating that girls struggle more with self-esteem, especially in middle school, than do boys (AAUW Educational Foundation, 2001). Sadker and Sadker (1994) have found clear and distinct patterns in the way teachers interact with boys and girls in the classroom. Teachers tend to call on boys more, wait longer for boys' responses to questions, and expect boys to act out more in the classroom. Girls, on the other hand, are expected to be quiet and compliant, and teachers tend to do things for girls, rather than push them to succeed. Given how gendered expectations shape interactions in the classroom, it is not surprising that girls tend to struggle with self-esteem issues at adolescence. In Chapter 7, Roslyn Arlin Mickelson discusses gender differences in classrooms for boys and girls and how these differences are changing.

Furthermore, these patterns of gender and class differences vary by race and ethnicity (Carter, 2006; Grant, 2004). The point is that schools are powerful institutions, and the interactions within them heavily influence how children think about themselves and their futures. Students from different social classes, races, genders, and sexual orientations bring different orientations, patterns, and behaviors into the schools, resulting in unique symbolic and interactional experiences (see Rist in this chapter's readings).

Dramaturgy

Erving Goffman looked for connections between the micro levels and macro levels of sociology. Stemming from Durkheim's ideas of the importance of rituals and symbols in everyday life, the messages they transfer, and the collective conscience that develops from them, Goffman wrote that everyday interactions are based on codes or systems that represent rules of the larger society (Antikainen et al., 2010). He compared social life for individuals to front-stage and backstage behavior on which people perform differently depending on the impressions they wish to project to the audience (Goffman, 1959). Goffman's influence is also seen in the study of school interactions with his concepts of "encounters"—conscious and planned interaction (Goffman, 1990). As Johnny comes to school, he goes "on stage" and presents himself through his clothing and other symbols that he adopts. He attempts to manage the impressions he gives to others, including teachers and peers, in order to manipulate how they define him as he struggles with learning to read.

Rational Choice Theory

While rational choice theory does not ignore symbols and interactions, this theory focuses primarily on the assumption that there are costs and rewards involved in our individual decisions within the classroom and school. According to rational choice theory, if benefits outweigh costs, the individual is likely to act in order to continue receiving benefits. If costs outweigh benefits, the individual will seek other courses of action. In education, the question is how weighing of costs and benefits influences decisions about educational choices by students, teachers, and administrators in the conduct of school experiences.

For example, students who consider dropping out of school likely go through some analysis, comparing benefits of staying in school, such as ability to get a better job, with costs to themselves, for instance their battered self-esteem in schools. For Johnny, deciding whether to do what is necessary to learn to read or to focus on behaviors that gain him esteem in other areas may be part of his school day. Whether we would agree that individuals have assessed the costs and the benefits correctly is not the point; the issue is how individuals evaluate the benefits and costs at a given moment in making what theorists describe as a *rational choice* for them.

Rational choice theory can also be applied to the issue of teacher retention. Teachers have an extremely high dropout rate, with roughly half of all new teachers in the United States currently leaving the profession within 5 years (Lambert, 2006). Rational choice theorists would explain this in terms of the perceived costs—relatively low salary for a college graduate; minimal respect from parents, students, and administrators; long days for 9 months of the year; and little opportunity to participate in teaching- and job-related decisions (Dworkin, Saha, & Hill, 2003). Teachers compare these costs to the benefits of teaching—the feeling of making a contribution to society and helping children; time off in the summer; and enjoying aspects of teaching, coaching, or directing. When costs are seen as higher than benefits, teachers leave the profession, resulting in high teacher burnout and dropout rates (Dworkin, 2007; see the Dworkin and Tobe reading in Chapter 5). Rational choice theory extends interactionist theories and is useful as we try to understand decision making of individuals in schools.

MACROLEVEL THEORIES OF EDUCATION

Whereas microlevel theories focus on the individual's construction of reality in educational settings and interpersonal interactions between individuals and in small groups within schools, macrolevel explanations focus on larger societal and cultural systems. As such, schools as organizations, the processes of teaching and learning, and the interactions within schools and classrooms are viewed as part of larger social contexts (Brookover, Erickson, & McEvoy, 1996).

Functional Theory

Functional theory helps us to understand how education systems work and what purpose education serves in societies. While this is not a leading theory in sociology of education today, we describe it here because of its historical importance and influence on the field today, and because other theories arose as reactions to or modifications of functional theory. Functional theory starts with the assumption that education as an institution in society operates, along with other institutions, to facilitate the stability of society. There is a relationship between schools and other institutions in society, as all institutions must fulfill necessary societal functions to maintain society. Each part of a society—education, family, political and economic systems, health, religion—works together to create a functioning social system. Each part contributes necessary elements to the functioning and survival of the whole society, just as multiple parts of the body work together to keep us healthy and active. As such, in functional theory schools are analyzed in terms of their functions, or purposes, in the whole system (see the discussion of school functions below). The degree of interdependence among parts in the system relates to the degree of integration among these parts; all parts complement each other, and the assumption is that a smooth-running, stable system is well integrated. Shared values, or consensus, among members are important components of the system, as these help keep it in balance and working smoothly. In terms of why Johnny can't read, it may be that it is not important to society for Johnny to read, or it is simply not functional for all students to know how to read. Consider why this might be so.

Functional theories of education originated in the work of Émile Durkheim (1858–1917), who contributed a method for viewing schools and an explanation of how schools help to maintain order in societies. According to Durkheim, a major role of education in society was to create unity by providing a common moral code necessary for social cohesion in a society. Durkheim's major works in education were published in collections titled *Moral Education* (1925/1961), *The Evolution of Educational Thought* (1938/1977), and *Education and Society* (1903/1956), all written in the early 1900s. In these works, he set forth a definition of education that has guided the field.

In *Moral Education*, Durkheim outlined his beliefs about the function of schools and their relationship to society. Moral values are, for Durkheim, the foundation of the social order, and society is perpetuated through its educational institutions, which help instill values and a sense of moral order in the youngest members of society. In this work, he analyzed classrooms as "small societies," or agents of socialization, reflecting the moral order of the social system at that time. The school serves as an intermediary between the *affective morality* (or a morality related to emotion or feeling) of the family and the rigorous morality of society. Discipline is the morality of the classroom, and without it the classroom can become like an undisciplined mob, according to Durkheim. Because children learn to be social beings and develop appropriate social values through contact with others, schools are an important training ground for learning social skills and the "rules" of the larger society (instrumental skills), as opposed to the more emotional (affective) character of families. Functionalists also argue that the passing on of knowledge and behaviors is a primary function of schools, one necessary to maintain order and fill needed positions in society. Following Durkheim, sociologists see the transmission of moral and occupational education, discipline, and values as necessary for the survival of society. Thus, schools play a very important role in maintaining functioning of the larger society.

Durkheim was concerned primarily with value transmission for the stability of society. He did not consider the possible conflict between this stable view of the values and skills, and what is necessary for changing emerging industrial societies. He argued also that education should be under the control of the state, free from special interest groups; however, as we know, most governments are subject to influence from interest groups and changes in society, as you will read throughout this book. Talcott Parsons (1959) developed modern functional theory. He saw education as performing certain important tasks or "functions" for society, such as preparing young people for roles in a democratic society. Parsons argued that female elementary school teachers (he assumed all elementary school teachers should be female) play a role in transitioning children from the home and protection of mother to schools where a more impersonal female role socializes children to meet the less personal and more universal demands of society (Parsons, 1959). This linking of teachers to their role in the larger society is only one example of how functionalists have viewed the role of teachers (see the reading by Ingersoll and Merrill in Chapter 5).

Other functionalists argued that some degree of inequality is inevitable in society because the most challenging positions required attracting the most talented individuals who must spend time and money getting the necessary education to fill important roles in society. These theorists saw schools as part of a large system in which individuals who dedicate themselves to training for higher-level occupations would receive greater rewards in terms of income and prestige (Davis & Moore, 1945). This functional theory sees achievement in schools as based on merit, not one's status. Thus, the function of education is to support capitalism through the distribution of labor, allowing those with the most "merit" to achieve and fill higher-level positions in society.

Later functional theorists built on the base provided by Durkheim, Parsons, and others. For example, Dreeben (1968) considered the social organization of schools, while others examined the values taught in school and how these lead to greater societal consensus and preparation for one's role in society (Cookson & Sadovnik, 2002). To summarize, social scientists who research and interpret events from the functional perspective focus on the central functions of education for society as a whole (Ballantine & Hammack, 2012). We briefly summarize those functions as follows:

Socialization: Teaching Children to Be Members of Society. Most people remember their first day of elementary school, marking a transition between the warm, loving, accepting world of the family and a more impersonal school world that emphasizes discipline, knowledge, skills, responsibility, and obedience. In school, children learn that they must prove themselves; they are no longer accepted regardless of their behaviors as they were in their families. They must meet certain expectations and compete for attention and rewards. They also must prepare to participate in their society's political and economic systems, in which a literate populace is necessary to make informed decisions on issues. Citizens expect schools to respond to the constant changes in societies. In heterogeneous societies with diverse groups and cultures, school socialization helps to integrate immigrants by teaching them the language and customs of the larger society and by working to reduce intergroup tensions. This provides cohesion and order in society as a whole.

Teaching Children to Be Productive Members of Society. Societies use education to pass on values, skills, and knowledge necessary for survival. Sometimes this process occurs in formal classrooms, sometimes in informal places. For example, in West African villages children may have several years of formal education in a village school, but they learn future occupational roles informally by observing their elders in their families and by "playing" at the tasks they will soon undertake for survival. The girls help pound cassava root for the evening meal while boys build model boats and practice negotiating the waves. It is typically only the elite—sons and daughters of the rulers and the wealthy—who receive formal education beyond basic literacy in most traditional societies (Ballantine & Roberts, 2014). However, elders and family members in developed societies cannot teach all the skills necessary for survival. Formal schooling emerged to meet the needs of industrial and postindustrial societies, furnishing the specialized training required by rapidly growing and changing technology. Schools in industrialized societies play a major part in placing students into later work roles.

Selection and Training of Individuals for Positions in Society. Most people have taken standardized tests, received grades at the end of a term or year, and asked teachers to write recommendation letters. Functionalists see these activities as part of the selection process prevalent in competitive societies with formal education systems. Schools distribute credentials—grades, test scores, and degrees—that determine the college or job opportunities available to individuals in society, the fields of study individuals pursue, and ultimately individual status in society. For example, selection criteria determine who gets into the "best" colleges or even into college at all, thereby sealing one's place in society. As you will read later in this book, countries today are using standardized tests in a competition to provide the "best" education in our global society.

Promoting Change and Innovation. Institutions of higher education are expected to generate new knowledge, technology, and ideas, and to produce students with up-to-date skills and information required to lead industry and other key institutions in society. In a global age of computers and other electronic technology, critical thinking and analytical skills are essential as workers face issues that require problem solving rather than rote memorization. Thus, the curriculum must change to meet the needs of the social circumstances. Familiarity with technological equipment—computers, Internet resources, electronic library searches, and so forth—becomes a critical survival skill for individuals and society.

Colleges and universities are called on to provide ideas and innovations as well as skilled workers. Consider the example of India, which has top-ranked technical institutes training their graduates to meet changing world needs. These highly skilled graduates of India's colleges and universities are employed by companies around the world, including those from Europe and the United States, to process information and send it back the next morning. Thus, well-trained, efficient engineers and computer experts working in India for lower wages than in many developed countries have become an essential part of the global economy (Drori, 2006; Friedman, 2005).

Latent Functions of Education. In addition to these intended functions that are filled by schools, education provides unseen latent functions. These are unintended consequences of the educational process. For example, schools keep children off the streets until they can be absorbed into productive roles in society, serving an informal "baby-sitting" function. In fact, in the United States, children now stay in school well into their 20s, and the age at which they join the labor force or start families is much later than it was in previous generations. Schools also provide young people with a place to congregate, which fosters a youth culture of music, fashion, slang, dances, dating, and sometimes gangs. At the ages when social relationships are being established, especially with the opposite sex, colleges serve as "mating" and "matching" places for young adults. Education also weakens parental control over youth, helps them begin the move toward independence, and provides experiences in large, impersonal secondary groups (Ballantine & Roberts, 2014).

Functional theorists believe that when the above social functions are not adequately addressed, the educational system is ripe for change. The structure and the processes within the educational institution remain stable only if the basic functions of education in society are being met.

Functionalist arguments, therefore, look to how the structure of schooling "works" within the larger societal context. Understanding why Johnny can't read, thus, is not as important as understanding how Johnny's inability to read fits within the larger social order.

Conflict Theory

Conflict theorists challenge the functionalist assumptions that schools are ideologically and politically neutral and that schools operate based on meritocracy where each child is able to achieve to the highest level of his or her own ability so as to better meet the needs of society. Conflict theorists, instead, argue that inequality is based on one's position in the social system, not merit, and that schooling privileges some children and disadvantages others. There are several branches of conflict theory, which include different explanations of the role education systems play in maintaining inequality. Recent theories integrate ethnicity, race, and gender issues and add politics and culture to the traditional Marxist class and economic issues. In addition, issues of "reproduction and resistance" are recent additions to the conflict perspective. Origins of conflict theory are situated in the writings of Marx (1847/1955) and later Max Weber (1948a, 1948b, 1961).

In contrast to functional theory, conflict theory assumes a tension in society created by the competing interests of groups in society. Conflicts occur even when teachers, students, parents, and administrators agree on the rules. Each group obeys the rules even though the rules are not in their best interests because they may not see alternatives or may fear the consequences of not obeying. However, conflict theorists disagree on whether participants in the education system generally conform to the rules, rebel against them, or feel they have no choices. The roots of conflict thought are outlined below, and contemporary conflict theory, originating in the 1960s and 1970s, is discussed.

Karl Marx (1818–1883) was outraged over the social conditions of the exploited workers in the class system that resulted from early industrialization. He contended that the economic structure of industrialization, or what he called capitalism, created competing groups, the "haves" and the "have-nots," who lived in a constant state of tension (conflict) over resources that one had and the other wanted. The basis of this struggle is that the haves (or the owners of the means by which goods are produced in a society) control economic resources and thus have power, wealth, material goods, privilege (including access to the best schools and education), and influence. The have-nots (or the people who work for those who own the factories that produce goods in society) present a constant challenge as they seek a larger share of economic resources (wages) for their own survival. According to Marx, the haves often use coercive power and manipulation to hold society together. However, power can also be maintained by ideology—controlling ideas, or what people believe to be true. Conflict theorists view change as inevitable, as conflicts of interest should lead to the overthrow of existing power structures. Marx believed that class conflict would continue until the capitalist system of economic dominance was overthrown and replaced by a more equitable system. However, this revolution has yet to happen.

Marx argued that schools create and maintain inequality by teaching students an ideology that serves the interests of the rich and instills in students a sense of "false consciousness." That is, students in schools learn to accept the myth of meritocracy, that all have an equal chance of achieving. Those who buy into this ideology and fail often believe that their failure is due to their own shortcomings and lack of ability. Students learn to internalize their own lower position in society and their lowly fate, thus accepting a false consciousness and legitimizing the wealth and power of capitalists. Marx would also argue that the organization of schooling is set up in such a way that all students will not receive the same quality of education; thus, some students coming out of the educational system will work in factories for less pay.

Weber's Contributions to the Sociology of Education. Max Weber (1864–1920) was said to have argued with Marx's ghost because he believed that conflict in society was not based solely in economic relations as Marx had argued. Weber contended that inequalities and potential conflict were sustained in different distributions of status (prestige), power (ability to control others), and class (economic relations). While Weber also felt that conflict was a constant possibility, he focused more on power relationships between groups and differences in status that create a structure of inequality in societies.

Weber provided a less systematic treatment of education than Durkheim. His work in the field of sociology, however, has contributed to our understanding of many aspects of education. He is noted for his contributions to the understanding of bureaucracy and for the concept of *status groups*. In fact, he writes that the primary activity of schools is to teach particular "status cultures." Status cultures can be thought of as subcultures based on the social status of the group in society, such as working-class or upper-class culture. Each status group has its own set of symbols (e.g., sneakers that are "cool"), values (how important it is to go to college), and beliefs (whether studying and learning are important) that are known to the individuals in the group, but not fully understood or available to those outside the group. Power relationships and the conflicting interests of individuals and groups in society influence educational systems, for it is the interests and purposes of the dominant groups in society that shape the schools.

Weber (1961) spoke of the "tyranny of educational credentials" as a prerequisite for high-status positions, which thus maintains inequality in the social order of society. This theme is continued by Randall Collins (see his reading in this chapter), another conflict theorist following in Weber's tradition. Collins focuses on the increased requirements for higher-level positions used by more advantaged individuals to further their status (often called credentialism) (Collins, 1979). The rapid expansion of educational qualifications, faster than the number of jobs, has led to "credential inflation," yet these credentials are not necessary for most jobs. The result is that the credentials required for jobs keep increasing, further separating those who can afford the time and money to achieve these credentials and those who cannot.

Within the school there are "insiders" whose status culture, Weber believed, is reinforced through the school experience, and "outsiders" who face barriers to success in school. As we apply these ideas to school systems today to explain the situation of poor and minority students, and why Johnny can't read, the relevance of Weber's brand of conflict theory becomes evident. His theory deals with conflict, domination, and status groups struggling for wealth, power, and status in society. While education is used by individuals and society as a means to attain desired ends, it also creates unequal groups in society. Relating this to Karl Marx's writings on conflict theory, education produces a disciplined labor force for military, political, or other areas of control and exploitation by the elite. Status groups differ in property ownership; cultural status, such as social class or ethnic group membership; and power derived from positions in government or other organizations.

Weber, however, can also be considered a functionalist whose writings, using cross-cultural examples and exploring preindustrial and modern societies, shed light on the role of education in different societies at various time periods (Weber, 1948a). In preindustrial times, education served the primary purpose of training people to fit into a way of life and a particular station in society. With industrialization, however, new pressures faced education from upwardly mobile members of society vying for higher positions in the economic system. Educational institutions became increasingly important in training people for new roles in society (Weber, 1948b).

Conflict Theory Today. Marx and Weber set the stage for the many branches of conflict theory advocated by theorists today. Research from the conflict theorists' perspective tends to focus on those tensions created by power and conflict that ultimately cause change. Some conflict theorists, following from Marx's emphasis on the economic

structure of society, see mass public education as a tool of powerful capitalists to control the entrance into higher levels of education through the selection and allocation function. Marx argued that schools contributed to a "false consciousness," the equivalent of teaching students that the oppressive conditions that shape their lives cannot be changed. They must simply accept their situations, or even believe that they are not as worthy as others who are more powerful or have more advantages. Many conflict theorists believe that until society's economic and political systems are changed, school reform providing equal access to all children will be impossible (Bowles & Gintis, 1976).

Conflict theorists studying education systems point out that differences in the achievement of students are not based primarily on their ability or intelligence; rather, schools reflect the needs of the powerful, dominant groups in society and serve to perpetuate a capitalistic system that reproduces social classes. Teacher expectations based on characteristics of children, such as race and social class background, shape students' learning experiences and affect their achievements. For instance, teacher expectations may differ for poor students who have more limited language skills or speak with a dialect and lack middle-class dress, appearance, and manners. Some also argue that differential funding and resources for schools affect achievements of students. Poor and minority students are also more likely to be placed or tracked into lower reading and academic groups, placements that are hard to change. These groups are given different curricula. The higher-class students receive more mentally challenging curricula that prepare them to think creatively and make decisions, and the lower-class students experience less challenging curricula that prepare them for manual labor. They are more likely to lead students to drop out of school. All of the above factors make it harder for Johnny to learn to read and serve to reproduce inequalities in society as a whole.

Other theorists apply conflict theory arguments to the school and classroom level of analysis. For example, Willard Waller believes that schools are in a state of constant potential conflict and disequilibrium; teachers are threatened with the loss of their jobs because of lack of student discipline; academic authority is constantly threatened by students, parents, school boards, and alumni who represent other, often competing, interest groups in the system; and students are forced to go to schools, which they may consider oppressive and demeaning (Waller, 1932/1965). Although larger conflicts between groups in society may be the basis for these within-school patterns, the focus of some conflict theorists is not on these larger societal relationships. Many of these examples reinforce the concept of reproduction, discussed next.

Reproduction and Resistance Theories. In the second half of the 20th century, reproduction and resistance theories further expanded the ideas of conflict theories. The argument of cultural reproduction and resistance theories, very generally, is that those who dominate capitalistic systems mold individuals to suit their own purposes. These theorists examine how forms of culture passed on by families and schools end up shaping individuals' views of their worlds (Bowles & Gintis, 1976). The concept of *social reproduction* was developed in the late 1960s and early 1970s in Europe to explore the claim that schools actually *increase* inequality through the process of "teaching." At this time when equality was a central interest, the idea that schools might be contributing to societies' inequalities led to studies of the possibility that schools and families were actually perpetuating social class structures. Following from Marx, schools were viewed as part of a superstructure, along with family, politics, religion, culture, and economy, organized around the interests of the dominant capitalist group. The dominant group needs workers with good work habits, skills, and loyalty to produce products and services needed by capitalists in exchange for wages for their labor. Schools served the needs of the dominant group by teaching students their roles in society and perpetuating the belief that the system was a fair and merit-based way to select workers. For example, Bowles and Gintis's (1976) *correspondence theory* takes a macro view of schools, arguing that schools reproduce inequality and create class and power differences in societies. The reproduction process takes place through the student selection and allocation processes. These processes create hierarchies within schools and societies, socializing students into these hierarchies of power and domination, and legitimizing the hierarchies by claiming they are based on merit. Following the assumptions of Marx, Bowles and Gintis argue that school structure is based on the needs and standards of the dominant capitalist group in society and thus serves the purposes of that group. Students both bring into and take away different cultural competencies. The bottom line is that schools motivate higher-class students to achieve and decrease ambitions of others, creating a false consciousness (Apple, 1993, 1996).

Resistance theories go beyond social reproduction theories by arguing that teachers and students are not passive participants in the school process and that they do not always follow the expectations that result in social reproduction. For example, students may resist their socialization into certain roles in society (Willis, 1979), just as teachers do not have to accept their role in facilitating reproduction. Teachers may work with all students to give them more equal chances in the system. Teachers can empower students with curricula that are participatory, affective, problem solving, multicultural, democratic, interdisciplinary, and activist (Shor, 1986). Therefore, participants in schools are not necessarily passive actors in the reproduction of inequality.

CONTEMPORARY THEORIES IN SOCIOLOGY OF EDUCATION

Two concepts related to the development of reproduction and resistance theories are social capital and cultural capital. As you can see from the above, conflict theory started to move from strictly a macro/societal focus to more of a focus on interaction that maintains power and privilege. The concept of *cultural capital* was introduced in the 1970s primarily by Pierre Bourdieu (1973), and *social capital* was introduced by James S. Coleman (1988) in the late 1980s. These two concepts bridged macrolevel and microlevel explanations, attempting to understand how larger societal structures were maintained in day-to-day interactions.

Social capital refers to the social resources students bring to their education and future involvement in school or community. It results in building of networks and relationships students can use as contacts for future opportunities. Ultimately, these networks are connections that make achievement possible and connect individuals to the larger group. Several researchers have applied this concept to the study of students, teachers, and teaching. For instance, connections students make in elite private schools and alumni connections through private schools and colleges enhance future economic status. Coleman's concept of social capital was used to explain the role of schools in reproducing social class.

Bourdieu's *cultural capital* is used in many research studies today. Trained as a sociologist, anthropologist, and philosopher, Pierre Bourdieu (1931–2002) delved into education's influences on stratification and social class, trying to reconcile the influences of social structures on the subjective experiences of individuals. Among the many concepts attributed to Bourdieu and in use today are *cultural and symbolic capital, symbolic violence*, and *habitus* (Bourdieu, 1973). He saw individuals as having different cultural capital based on their social settings. *Social capital* (see above) included the sum of resources held by individuals or groups because of their respective contacts or networks. *Symbolic capital* referred to the prestige, honor, or attention an individual held. These were each sources of individual power. *Cultural capital* refers to cultural practices, including dress and mannerisms, language patterns and expressions, and knowledge of the world derived from life experiences such as visits to museums, all of which provide knowledge of

middle-class and upper-class culture; that is, the culture of schools. Cultural capital does not refer to knowing about "culture," commonly thought of in terms of art, music, and theater. Rather cultural capital allows students from middle and upper classes to use patterns of talking, common words, general knowledge, and values from their lives outside of school to fit into the patterns of interaction in school (Lareau, 1989). All individuals have cultural capital, and the form of cultural capital one has is generally related to one's social class background. A child who can speak the teacher's "language" is likely to fare better in school than one who has not been exposed to the cultural capital of the schools. Unfortunately, the cultural capital of children from working-class backgrounds is rarely valued in schools. Dominant groups pass on exposure to the dominant culture that their children take to school. Not only do their children know how schools work, but they also come to school with the knowledge of what to do to be successful there. Working-class children generally do not go to school with this advantage (Bourdieu & Passeron, 1977).

The important point here is that higher social, cultural, and symbolic capital result in more power for the holder. Over time these power relationships come to be seen by individuals as legitimate. Consider how working-class children in schools might see the educational success of middle-class children as "legitimate" because they work hard or have more natural ability, whereas these advantages are bestowed on middle-class and upper-class children because of their advantaged position in the social structure (Bourdieu & Passeron, 1977).

Cultural capital inadvertently is used by schools to reproduce inequality both in the interactions and in the structure of education. For example, different curricula in different tracks create a system of educational inequality for students. While the assignment of students to learning groups is supposed to be based on explicit criteria (merit) such as test scores or completion of previous work, in actuality cultural capital plays a considerable role in who is assigned to groups. As early as preschool, children experience different expectations from teachers (Lubeck, 1985). As noted earlier, Rist (1977) found that children were assigned to groups in kindergarten based on dress and speech patterns. Vanfossen, Jones, and Spade (1987) and Lucas (1999) found that family social class background was a strong predictor of the high school "track" in which students were placed. The end result is that students from working-class backgrounds end up learning more basic skills under strict rules because they are expected to cause problems in the classroom. Those from upper classes learn how to make decisions, be creative and autonomous, and prepare for college (Anyon, 1980; Miller, Kohn, & Schooler, 1985). And, students end up in networks within the learning groups they are placed in (see Ferrare reading in Chapter 7), further reinforcing their social and cultural capital advantages or disadvantages. At the college level, students are again tracked into two-year or four-year educations with differences in the curriculum, goals for educational outcomes, and economic results for students (Pincus, 1980, 2002). Therefore, schools end up perpetuating differences in cultural capital by maintaining groups in school that are generally homogeneous in terms of social class backgrounds. And, you thought Johnny couldn't read because he lacked the ability needed to read well!

Teachers also bring varying degrees of cultural capital to schools and classrooms. Some teachers come from working-class and middle-class backgrounds and bring that cultural capital to the education system, both in their own training and in how they teach others. However, in some cases, the students they teach may bring a different cultural capital to the classroom, cultural capital that is either higher or lower in the hierarchy of power and wealth. And, parents with higher cultural capital tend to be more involved in their children's schooling, more able to provide their children with stronger educational experiences, and more at ease with the cultural capital of the school (Lareau, 1989).

The concept of cultural capital has been used in a number of studies of schools and classrooms. Consider McLaren's (1989) study of his experiences as a middle-class white teacher teaching in an inner-city school, facing violence and hostile parents. The cultural capital mismatch he faced was one in which his middle-class cultural capital was ineffective in working with the children he taught. This situation is repeated over and over again because teachers, by the very fact that they have the credentials to teach, have adopted a cultural capital that is not compatible with the children they teach from economically disadvantaged neighborhoods.

Another study of social capital shows how resources in the family, community, and school serve as capital assets for improving student academic performance and psychological well-being (Schneider, 2002). This study points out that active involvement of parents at home with their children on homework and educational decisions can influence social capital and future opportunities. The reading in Chapter 9 by Portes and Fernández-Kelly further illustrates the value of cultural capital. They found that children of Mexican immigrants gained cultural capital in different ways, sometimes from people outside their families, to ensure that they went on to succeed in college. This study illustrates that the cultural capital children get from their social class backgrounds does not always have to hold them back. However, only a very few students in Portes and Fernández-Kelly's larger study actually made it to college and successful professional careers.

Code theory was developed around the same time as cultural capital. Code theory is presented in several volumes that lay out the sociolinguistic theory of language codes envisioned by Basil Bernstein (1924–2000). *Codes* refer to organizing principles used by members of a social group. The idea is that the language we use reflects and shapes the assumptions we hold about our relationship to a certain group. Our relationship with that group influences the way we use language.

Bernstein conceptualizes two types of codes—*restricted* and *elaborated*. Restricted codes are those we use with others who share the same knowledge base. It allows us to shortcut language because of assumptions and knowledge we share with those close to us. When we use restricted codes, our language is brief, and we expect the person or persons with whom we are speaking to fill in the rest of our meaning—for example, when we say, "Get that." With elaborated codes, on the other hand, we do not take shortcuts. Everything is spelled out in more detail to be sure the others understand what we are communicating (Bernstein, 1971). This form is used with people we do not know well and in formal speech, such as "Please pick up the hat on the table" (Littlejohn & Foss, 2007). People learn their place in the society by the language codes they use. The codes come to symbolize social identity.

As applied to schools, Bernstein was interested in the poor performance of working-class students, especially in language-based subjects. Though their scores in math-related classes were similar to the scores of middle-class students, lower performance in language signified to him a relation between social class and language. The result is that language codes aid in the social reproduction of class and differences in power, not only in school but also in politics and the workplace. Working-class children are at a disadvantage in schools because they do not share the dominant code of the middle-class and upper-class students. Even the curriculum and transmission of knowledge in schools reflect the dominant code. In trying to understand why Johnny can't read, it may be the codes he brings with him to the classroom.

Although code theory is used less often than cultural capital in understanding processes within schools, it provides an important perspective for us to think about as we study and try to understand inequality in educational achievement.

The last theoretical framework we discuss here is *feminist perspectives on education*. Feminist theorists have echoed the need to "hear" other voices in the education system, in particular women's voices, and to pay more attention to the situation of women (see discussion of "voice" in the pieces by Elizabeth J. Allan and Mary Madden in Chapter 2 and Rob Moore in Chapter 6). Much of the history of ideas is a history interpreted by

men, generally white men in the European tradition. Feminists see the world from a different perspective, one that represents a sometimes forgotten element in past theoretical interpretations of education systems, one in which women were essentially denied education for most of the history of the United States. They are still denied education in some countries of the world (see Lewis & Lockheed in Chapter 10 and 2006; Spender, 1987).

While there are many branches of feminist theory, we mention several general feminist ideas that influence the understanding of schools. Early writings on gender and schooling expressed the concern that girl students and female teachers faced certain injustices. Different theorists related inequalities faced by women to differential access, different treatment and exploitation, patriarchy, and male dominance. This led to examination of educational policy and how it affected girls, women, and their future opportunities (Dillabough & Arnot, 2002). Although women have made many gains in educational attainment over the past century, many inequalities remain. As late as 1994, Sadker and Sadker found that girls were treated differently in the classroom—that girls were not called upon as often as boys and essentially not challenged as much as boys in the same classrooms. This discrepancy in classroom treatment likely contributes to lower self-esteem for girls, and it may also explain why men are more likely to enter higher-paying, more prestigious careers because women are less likely to pursue mathematics and science degrees (see the reading by Roslyn Arlin Mickelson in Chapter 7).

Not all feminist scholarship on education focuses on describing gender inequalities. Feminist theory can be used to criticize school practices, such as the assumptions that schools use to connect to parents, but actually meaning mothers, to engage in their children's educational experiences. For example, Stambach and David (2005) argue that school choice programs operate on the gendered assumption about family and employment, implying that mothers should be involved in their children's education and schools. Even today, schools in many European countries send children home for an extended lunch hour during the middle of the day, making it difficult for mothers to work full-time. Much of feminist scholarship focuses on the critical perspective at the macro level with concern about gender issues in educational environments and reproduction of gender inequality in schools. Radical feminists also link their theory to practice, as is the case with critical theorists, resulting in connections between policy and research. Thus, feminist theory and pedagogy rely on "lived experience" and concerted efforts to change the system as it exists to disadvantage women and girls.

Early feminist theories of education were criticized for having a middle-class bias and not adequately recognizing issues of concern for women of color, women from other cultures, nontraditional gender and sexual orientations, different ethnic or global identities, or political persuasions. As a result, various branches of feminist theory of education have arisen (Weiner, 1997) to address gender issues as they intersect with other categories of difference and inequality. It is expected that these multiple feminisms will result in a variety of challenges to educational practices and systems in addressing the teaching and learning experiences of all young women.

These concerns have resulted in feminist theorists struggling to understand the intersection of different categories of difference and inequality. Students are treated not solely based on gender, but also based on race and ethnicity, social class background, and other categories of difference and inequality, such as sexual orientation. These categories intersect to create complex patterns of oppression and suppression not captured by either early feminist theories or other theories discussed in this reading. For example, research by Grant (2004) finds that teachers use black girls to run errands in the classroom and, with findings similar to Ferguson (2000), that black boys are viewed by teachers as "trouble" long before they do anything wrong. Gender alone does not explain fully the experiences of children across categories of difference and inequality.

Therefore, when trying to understand why Johnny can't read, we may want to consider effects of his gender and race.

CONCLUSION

There is a long and broad tradition of social science and sociological theories, beginning with the coining of the word *sociology* by Auguste Comte in 1838. These theories provide a range of explanations that can be used to examine issues and problems in educational systems in order to better understand the roles and activities in schools and society. All theories evolve. As described, interaction, functional, and conflict theories have gone through stages that attempted to explain the educational systems of the time and to react to previous theories that were inadequate to explain concerns of the education system. Recent trends see schools as "contested terrain" for determining curricula that meet diverse needs. How we think about the knowledge that is taught in schools is discussed in much greater detail in the articles by David Tyack and Rob Moore in Chapter 6, and as they illustrate, race, class, and gender issues have become dominant themes in this contested terrain.

In short, different theorists help us to think differently as we attempt to explain why schools work as they do. This broad range of theories presents many alternative ways of thinking about schools and is valuable as policy makers and researchers try to find solutions to the multitude of problems plaguing education today, in both developed and developing countries.

REFERENCES

American Association of University Women (AAUW) Educational Foundation. (2001). *Hostile hallways: Bullying, teasing, and sexual harassment in school.* Retrieved from http://www.aauw.org

Antikainen, A., Dworkin, A. G., Saha, L., Ballantine, J., Essacks, S., Teodoro, A., & Konstantinovshy, D. (2010). *The sociology of education.* Retrieved from http://www.sociopedia.isa

Anyon, J. (1980). Social class and the hidden curriculum of work. *Journal of Education, 162*(1), 67–92.

Apple, M. W. (1993). *Official knowledge: Democratic education in a conservative age.* New York: Routledge.

Apple, M. (1996). Power, meaning, and identity: Critical sociology of education in the United States. *British Journal of Sociology of Education, 17*(2), 125–144.

Ballantine, J., & Hammack, F. (2012). *The sociology of education, A systematic approach* (7th ed.). Upper Saddle River, NJ: Prentice-Hall.

Ballantine, J., & Roberts, K. (2014). *Our social world* (4th ed.). Thousand Oaks, CA: Sage.

Berger, P., & Luckmann, T. (1963). *The social construction of reality.* Garden City, NY: Doubleday.

Bernstein, B. (1971). *Class, codes, and control* (Vol. 1). London: Routledge & Kegan Paul.

Bourdieu, P. (1973). Cultural reproduction and social reproduction. In R. Brown (Ed.), *Knowledge, education, and cultural change* (pp. 71–112). London: Tavistock.

Bourdieu, P., & Passeron, J. C. (1977). *Reproduction in education, society and culture.* London: Sage.

Bowles, S., & Gintis, H. (1976). *Schooling in capitalist America.* New York: Basic Books.

Brookover, W. B., Erickson, E. L., & McEvoy, A. (1996). *Creating effective schools: An in-service program.* Holmes Beach, FL: Learning Publications.

Carter, P. L. (2006). Straddling boundaries: Identity, culture, and school. *Sociology of Education, 79*(4), 304–328.

Coleman, J. S. (1988). Social capital in the creation of human capital. *American Journal of Sociology, 94*, 95–120.

Collins, R. (1979). *The credential society.* New York: Academic Press.

Cookson, P. W., Jr., & Sadovnik, A. R. (2002). Functional theories of education. In D. L. Levinson, P. W. Cookson, Jr., & A. R. Sadovnik (Eds.), *Education and society: An encyclopedia* (pp. 267–271). New York: Routledge/Falmer.

Davis, K., & Moore, W. (1945). Some principles of stratification. *American Sociological Review, 10*(2), 242–245.

Dillabough, J., & Arnot, M. (2002). Sociology of education—Feminist perspectives: Continuity and contestation in the field. In D. L. Levinson, P. W. Cookson, Jr., & A. R. Sadovnik (Eds.), *Education and sociology: An encyclopedia* (pp. 571–585). New York: Routledge/Falmer.

Dreeben, R. (1968). *On what is learned in school.* Reading, MA: Addison-Wesley.

Drori, G. S. (2006). *Global e-litism: Digital technology, social inequality, and transnationality.* New York: Worth.

Durkheim, E. (1956). *Education and society* (S. D. Fox, Trans.). Glencoe, IL: Free Press. (Original work published 1903)

Durkheim, E. (1961). *Moral education* (E. K. Wilson & H. Schnurer, Trans.). Glencoe, IL: Free Press. (Original work published 1925)

Durkheim, E. (1977). *The evolution of educational thought* (P. Collins, Trans.). London: Routledge. (Original work published 1938)

Dworkin, A. G. (2007). School reform and teacher burnout: Issues of gender and gender tokenism. In B. Bank, S. Delamont, & C. Marshall (Eds.), *Gender and education: An encyclopedia* (pp. 69–78). Westport, CT: Greenwood.

Dworkin, A. G., Saha, L. J., & Hill, A. N. (2003). Teacher burnout and perceptions of a democratic school environment. *International Education Journal, 4*(2), 108–120.

Ferguson, A. A. (2000). *Bad boys: Public schools in the making of black masculinity.* Ann Arbor: University of Michigan Press.

Flesch, R. F. (1955). *Why Johnny can't read—and what you can do about it.* New York: Harper.

Friedman, T. L. (2005). *The world is flat: A brief history of the twenty-first century.* New York: Farrar, Straus and Giroux.

Goffman, E. (1959). *The presentation of self in everyday life.* New York: Anchor Books.

Goffman, E. (1967). *Interaction ritual.* Garden City, NY: Doubleday.

Goffman, E. (1990). *Asylums.* New York: Anchor Books.

Grant, L. (2004). Everyday schooling and the elaboration of race-gender stratification. In J. H. Ballantine & J. Z. Spade (Eds.), *Schools and society* (2nd ed., pp. 296–307). Belmont, CA: Wadsworth.

Lambert, L. (2006, May 9). Half of teachers quit in five years: Working conditions, low salaries cited. *Washington Post*, p. A7.

Lareau, A. (1989). *Home advantage.* Philadelphia: Falmer Press.

Lewis, M. A., & Lockheed, M. E. (2006). *Inexcusable absence: Why 60 million girls still aren't in school and what to do about it.* Washington, DC: Center for Global Development.

Littlejohn, S. W., & Foss, K. A. (2007). *Theories of human communication* (9th ed.). Belmont, CA: Cengage Learning.

Lubeck, S. (1985). *Sandbox society: Early education in black and white America.* London: Falmer Press.

Lucas, S. R. (1999). *Tracking inequality: Stratification and mobility in American high schools.* New York: Teachers College Press.

Marx, K. (1955). *The poverty of philosophy.* Moscow: Progress Publishers. (Original work published 1847)

McLaren, P. (1989). *Life in schools.* New York: Longman.

Miller, K. A., Kohn, M. L., & Schooler, C. (1985). Education self-direction and the cognitive functioning of students. *Social Forces, 63*(4), 923–944.

Parsons, T. (1959). The school as a social system. *Harvard Education Review, 29*(4), 297–318.

Pincus, F. L. (1980). The false promises of community colleges: Class conflict and vocational education. *Harvard Education Review, 50*(3), 332–361.

Pincus, F. L. (2002). Sociology of education: Marxist theories. In D. L. Levinson, P. W. Cookson, Jr., & A. R. Sadovnik (Eds.), *Education and sociology: An encyclopedia* (pp. 587–592). New York: Routledge/Falmer.

Rist, R. (1970). Student social class and teacher expectations: The self-fulfilling prophecy in ghetto education. *Harvard Education Review, 40*(3), 411–451.

Rist, R. (1977). On understanding the processes of schooling: The contributions of labeling theory. In J. Karabel & A. H. Halsey, *Power and ideology in education* (pp. 292–305). New York: Oxford University Press.

Rosenthal, R., & Jacobson, L. (1968). *Pygmalion in the classroom.* New York: Holt, Rinehart and Winston.

Sadker, M., & Sadker, D. (1994). *Failing at fairness: How our schools cheat girls.* New York: Simon & Schuster.

Sadovnik, A. R. (2007). Theory and research in the sociology of education. In A. R. Sadovnik (Ed.), *Sociology of education: A critical reader* (pp. 3–22). New York: Routledge.

Schneider, B. (2002). Social capital: A ubiquitous emerging conception. In D. L. Levinson, P. W. Cookson, Jr., & A. R. Sadovnik (Eds.), *Education and sociology: An encyclopedia* (pp. 545–550). New York: Routledge/Falmer.

Shor, I. (1986). *Culture wars: School and society in the conservative restoration, 1969–1984.* Boston: Routledge & Kegan Paul.

Spender, D. (1987). Education: The patriarchal paradigm and the response to feminism. In M. Arnot & G. Weiner (Eds.), *Gender and the politics of schooling* (pp. 143–154). London: Hutchinson.

Stambach, A., & David, M. (2005). Feminist theory and educational policy: How gender has been "involved" in family school choice debates. *Signs: Journal of Women in Culture and Society, 30*, 1633–1658.

Vanfossen, B. E., Jones, J. D., & Spade, J. Z. (1987). Curriculum tracking and status maintenance. *Sociology of Education, 60*(2), 104–122.

Waller, W. (1965). *Sociology of teaching.* New York: Russell and Russell. (Original work published 1932)

Weber, M. (1948a). The Chinese literati. In H. H. Gerth & C. Wright Mills (Eds.), *From Max Weber: Essays in sociology* (pp. 416–444). Abingdon, England: Routledge.

Weber, M. (1948b). The "rationalization" of education and training. In H. H. Gerth & C. Wright Mills (Eds.), *From Max Weber: Essays in sociology* (pp. 240–244). Abingdon, England: Routledge.

Weber, M. (1961). The three types of legitimate rule. In A. Etzioni (Ed.), *Complex organizations: A sociological reader* (pp. 4–14). New York: Holt, Rinehart and Winston.

Weiner, G. (1997). Feminisms and education. In A. H. Halsey, H. Laudner, P. Brown, & A. S. Wells (Eds.), *Education: Culture, economy, and society* (pp. 144–153). Oxford, England: Oxford University Press.

Willis, P. (1979). *Learning to labor: How working class kids get working class jobs.* Adlershot, Hampshire, England: Saxon House.

THE SCHOOL CLASS AS A SOCIAL SYSTEM

Talcott Parsons

Looking at the school classroom as a social system, Talcott Parsons provides an example of function-alist theory's approach to education. In these excerpts from a classic 1959 piece in the functionalist tradition, Parsons considers functions of schools that help hold society together, such as passing on knowledge and skills necessary for children to fit into society. In focusing on the school class, he looks at the function of school as facilitating socialization, preparing the young members of society for their adult roles. For example, schools sort students into college and noncollege groups early in the students' careers. Parsons also points out the relationships between family, peer groups, and schools. As you read his description of the school class, keep in mind the functional perspective and how it is presented in his discussion.

Questions to consider for this reading:

1. What functions of school are carried out in the classroom? How are they carried out?

2. How do family and family background interact with a child's school experience?

3. What factors affect the elementary child's achievement in school? How does achievement relate to future life chances?

4. How does the perspective presented in this reading compare to the discussion of functionalism as presented in the reading by Ballantine and Spade?

This essay will attempt to outline, if only sketchily, an analysis of the elementary and secondary school class as a social system, and the relation of its structure to its primary functions in the society as an agency of socialization and allocation. While it is important that the school class is normally part of the larger organization of a school, the class rather than the whole school will be the unit of analysis here, for it is recognized both by the school system and by the individual pupil as the place where the "business" of formal education actually takes place. In elementary schools, pupils of one grade are typically placed in a single "class" under one main teacher, but in the secondary school, and sometimes in the upper elementary grades, each pupil works on different subjects under different teachers; here the complex of classes participated in by the same pupil is the significant unit for our purposes.

From "The School Class as a Social System: Some of Its Functions in American Society," by T. Parsons, 1959, *Harvard Educational Review, 29*(4), pp. 297–318. Copyright 1959 by the President and Fellows of Harvard College. All rights reserved. Reprinted with permission.

THE PROBLEM: SOCIALIZATION AND SELECTION

Our main interest, then, is in a dual problem: first, of how the school class functions to internalize in its pupils both the commitments and capacities for successful performance of their future adult roles, and second, of how it functions to allocate these human resources within the role-structure of the adult society. The primary ways in which these two problems are interrelated will provide our main points of reference.

First, from the functional point of view the school class can be treated as an agency of socialization. That is to say, it is an agency through which individual personalities are trained to be motivationally and technically adequate to the performance of adult roles. It is not the sole such agency; the family, informal "peer groups," churches, and sundry voluntary organizations all play a part, as does actual on-the-job training. But, in the period extending from entry into first grade until entry into the labor force or marriage, the school class may be regarded as the focal socializing agency.

The socialization function may be summed up as the development in individuals of the commitments and capacities which are essential prerequisites of their future role-performance. Commitments may be broken down in turn into two components: commitment to the implementation of the broad values of society, and commitment to the performance of a specific type of role within the structure of society. Thus a person in a relatively humble occupation may be a "solid citizen" in the sense of commitment to honest work in that occupation, without an intensive and sophisticated concern with the implementation of society's higher-level values. Or conversely, someone else might object to the anchorage of the feminine role in marriage and the family on the grounds that such anchorage keeps society's total talent resources from being distributed equitably to business, government, and so on. Capacities can also be broken down into two components, the first being competence or the skill to perform the tasks involved in the individual's roles, and the second being "role-responsibility" or the capacity to live up to other people's expectations of the interpersonal behavior appropriate to these roles. Thus a mechanic as well as a doctor needs to have not only the basic "skills of his trade," but also the ability to behave responsibly toward those people with whom he is brought into contact in his work.

While on the one hand, the school class may be regarded as a primary agency by which these different components of commitments and capacities are generated, on the other hand, it is, from the point of view of the society, an agency of "manpower" allocation. It is well known that in American society there is a very high, and probably increasing, correlation between one's status level in the society and one's level of educational attainment. Both social status and educational level are obviously related to the occupational status which is attained. Now, as a result of the general process of both educational and occupational upgrading, completion of high school is increasingly coming to be the norm for minimum satisfactory educational attainment, and the most significant line for future occupational status has come to be drawn between members of an age-cohort who do and do not go to college.

We are interested, then, in what it is about the school class in our society that determines the distinction between the contingents of the age-cohort which do and do not go to college. Because of a tradition of localism and a rather pragmatic pluralism, there is apparently considerable variety among school systems of various cities and states. Although the situation in metropolitan Boston probably represents a more highly structured pattern than in many other parts of the country, it is probably not so extreme as to be misleading in its main features. There, though of course actual entry into college does not come until after graduation from high school, the main dividing line is between those who are and are not enrolled in the college preparatory course in high school; there is only a small amount of shifting either way after about the ninth grade when the decision is normally made. Furthermore, the evidence seems to be that by far the most important criterion of selection is the record of school performance in elementary school. These records are evaluated by teachers and principals, and there are few cases of entering the college preparatory course against their advice. It is therefore not stretching the evidence too far to say broadly that the primary selective process occurs through differential school performance in elementary school, and that the "seal" is put on it in junior high school.

The evidence also is that the selective process is genuinely assortative. As in virtually all comparable processes, ascriptive as well as achieved factors influence the outcome. In this case, the ascriptive factor is the socioeconomic status of the child's family, and the factor underlying his opportunity for achievement is his individual ability. In the study of 3,348 Boston high school boys on which these generalizations are based, each of these factors was quite highly correlated with planning college. For example, the percentages planning college, by father's occupation, were: 12 per cent for semi-skilled and unskilled, 19 per cent for skilled, 26 per cent for minor white collar, 52 per cent for middle white collar, and 80 per cent for major white collar. Likewise, intentions varied by ability (as measured by IQ), namely, 11 per cent for the lowest quintile, 17 per cent for the next, 24 per cent for the middle, 30 per cent for the next to the top, and 52 per cent for the highest. It should be noted also that within any ability quintile, the relationship of plans to father's occupation is seen. For example, within the very important top quintile in ability as measured, the range in college intentions was from 29 per cent for sons of laborers to 89 per cent for sons of major white collar persons.[1]

The essential points here seem to be that there is a relatively uniform criterion of selection operating to differentiate between the college and the non-college contingents, and that for a very important part of the cohort the operation of this criterion is not a "put-up job"—it is not simply a way of affirming a previously determined ascriptive status. To be sure, the high-status, high-ability boy is very likely indeed to go to college, and the low-status, low-ability boy is very unlikely to go. But the "cross-pressured" group for whom these two factors do not coincide[2] is of considerable importance.

Considerations like these lead me to conclude that the main process of differentiation (which from another point of view is selection) that occurs during elementary school takes place on a single main axis of achievement. Broadly, moreover, the differentiation leads up through high school to a bifurcation into college-goers and non-college-goers.

To assess the significance of this pattern, let us look at its place in the socialization of the individual. Entering the system of formal education is the child's first major step out of primary involvement in his family of orientation. Within the family certain foundations of his motivational system have been laid down. But the only characteristic fundamental to later roles which has clearly been "determined" and psychologically stamped in by that time is sex role. The postoedipal child enters the system of formal education clearly categorized as boy or girl, but beyond that his role is not yet differentiated. The process of selection, by which persons will select and be selected for categories of roles, is yet to take place.

On grounds which cannot be gone into here, it may be said that the most important single predispositional factor with which the child enters the school is his level of independence. By this is meant his level of self-sufficiency relative to guidance by adults, his capacity to take responsibility and to make his own decisions in coping with new and varying situations. This, like his sex role, he has as a function of his experience in the family.

The family is a collectivity within which the basic status-structure is ascribed in terms of biological position, that is, by generation, sex, and age. There are inevitably differences of performance relative to these, and they are rewarded and punished in ways that contribute to differential character formation. But these differences are not given the sanction of institutionalized social status. The school is the first socializing agency in the child's experience which institutionalizes a differentiation of status on nonbiological bases. Moreover, this is not an ascribed but an achieved status; it is the status "earned" by differential performance of the tasks set by the teacher, who is acting as an agent of the community's school system. Let us look at the structure of this situation.

THE STRUCTURE OF
THE ELEMENTARY SCHOOL CLASS

In accord with the generally wide variability of American institutions, and of course the basically local control of school systems, there is considerable variability of school situations, but broadly they have a single relatively well-marked framework.[3] Particularly in the primary part of the elementary grades, i.e., the first three grades, the basic pattern includes one main teacher for the class, who teaches all subjects and who is in charge of the class generally. Sometimes this early, and frequently in later grades, other teachers are brought in for a few special subjects, particularly gym, music, and art, but this does not alter the central position of the main teacher. This teacher is usually a woman.[4] The class is with this one teacher for the school year, but usually no longer.

The class, then, is composed of about 25 age peers of both sexes drawn from a relatively small geographical area—the neighborhood. Except for sex in certain respects, there is initially no formal basis for differentiation of status within the school class. The main structural differentiation develops gradually, on the single main axis indicated above as achievement. That the differentiation should occur on a single main axis is insured by four primary features of the situation. The first is the initial equalization of the "contestants'" status by age and by "family background," the neighborhood being typically much more homogeneous than is the whole society. The second circumstance is the imposition of a common set of tasks which is, compared to most other task areas, strikingly undifferentiated. The school situation is far more like a race in this respect than most role-performance situations. Third, there is the sharp polarization between the pupils in their initial

equality and the single teacher who is an adult and "represents" the adult world. And fourth, there is a relatively systematic process of evaluation of the pupils' performances. From the point of view of a pupil, this evaluation, particularly (though not exclusively) in the form of report card marks, constitutes reward and/or punishment for past performance; from the viewpoint of the school system acting as an allocating agency, it is a basis of selection for future status in society.

Two important sets of qualifications need to be kept in mind in interpreting this structural pattern, but I think these do not destroy the significance of its main outline. The first qualification is for variations in the formal organization and procedures of the school class itself. Here the most important kind of variation is that between relatively "traditional" schools and relatively "progressive" schools. The more traditional schools put more emphasis on discrete units of subject-matter, whereas the progressive type allows more "indirect" teaching through "projects" and broader topical interests where more than one bird can be killed with a stone. In progressive schools there is more emphasis on groups of pupils working together, compared to the traditional direct relation of the individual pupil to the teacher. This is related to the progressive emphasis on co-operation among the pupils rather than direct competition, to greater permissiveness as opposed to strictness of discipline, and to a de-emphasis on formal marking. In some schools one of these components will be more prominent, and in others, another. That it is, however, an important range of variation is clear. It has to do, I think, very largely with the independence-dependence training which is so important to early socialization in the family. My broad interpretation is that those people who emphasize independence training will tend to be those who favor relatively progressive education. The relation of support for progressive education to relatively high socioeconomic status and to "intellectual" interests and the like is well known. There is no contradiction between these emphases both on independence and on co-operation and group solidarity among pupils.

In the first instance this is because the main focus of the independence problem at these ages is vis-à-vis adults. However, it can also be said that the peer group, which here is built into the school class, is an indirect field of expression of dependency needs, displaced from adults.

The second set of qualifications concerns the "informal" aspects of the school class, which are always somewhat at variance with the formal expectations. For instance, the formal pattern of nondifferentiation between the sexes may be modified informally, for the very salience of the one-sex peer group at this age period means that there is bound to be considerable implicit recognition of it—for example, in the form of teachers' encouraging group competition between boys and girls. Still, the fact of coeducation and the attempt to treat both sexes alike in all the crucial formal respects remain the most important. Another problem raised by informal organization is the question of how far teachers can and do treat pupils particularistically in violation of the universalistic expectations of the school. When compared with other types of formal organizations, however, I think the extent of this discrepancy in elementary schools is seen to be not unusual. The school class is structured so that opportunity for particularistic treatment is severely limited. Because there are so many more children in a school class than in a family and [because] they are concentrated in a much narrower age range, the teacher has much less chance than does a parent to grant particularistic favors.

Bearing in mind these two sets of qualifications, it is still fair, I think, to conclude that the major characteristics of the elementary school class in this country are such as have been outlined. It should be especially emphasized that more or less progressive schools, even with their relative lack of emphasis on formal marking, do not constitute a separate pattern, but rather a variant tendency within the same pattern. A progressive teacher, like any other, will form opinions about the different merits of her pupils relative to the values and goals of the class and will communicate these valuations to them, informally if not formally. It is my impression that the extremer cases of playing down relative evaluation are confined to those upper-status schools where going to a "good" college is so fully taken for granted that for practical purposes it is an ascribed status. In other words, in interpreting these facts the selective function of the school class should be kept continually in the forefront of attention. Quite clearly its importance has not been decreasing; rather the contrary.

Notes

1. See table from this study in J. A. Kahl, *The American Class Structure* (New York: Rinehart & Co., 1953), p. 283. Data from a nationwide sample of high school students, published by the Educational Testing Service, show similar patterns of relationships. For example, the ETS study shows variation, by father's occupation, in proportion of high school seniors planning college, of from 35 per cent to 80 per cent for boys and 27 per cent to 79 per cent for girls (From *Background Factors Related to College Plans and College Enrollment Among High School Students* [Princeton, NJ: Educational Testing Service, 1957]).

2. There seem to be two main reasons why the high-status, low-ability group is not so important as its obverse. The first is that in a society of expanding educational and occupational opportunity the general trend is one of upgrading, and the social pressures to downward mobility are not as great as they would otherwise be. The second is that there are cushioning mechanisms which tend to protect the high-status boy who has difficulty "making the grade." He may be sent to a college with low academic standards, he may go to schools where the line between ability levels is not rigorously drawn, etc.

3. This discussion refers to public schools. Only about 13 per cent of all elementary and secondary school pupils attend non-public schools, with this proportion ranging from about 22 per cent in the Northeast to about 6 per cent in the South. U.S. Office of Education, Biennial Survey Education (*Biennial Survey of Education in the United States, 1954–56*, Washington: U.S. Government Printing Office, 1959, Chapter ii, "Statistics of State School Systems, 1955–56," Table 44, p. 114).

4. In 1955–56, 13 per cent of the public elementary school instructional staff in the United States were men (*Ibid.*, p. 7).

CONFLICT THEORY OF EDUCATIONAL STRATIFICATION

Randall Collins

Education prepares students for their positions and roles in society. In the excerpt that follows, Randall Collins relates education to occupations by using conflict theory, showing how students receive educations common to their status group. Similar to Max Weber's concept of status groups, these status groups correspond to the idea that schools prepare the young to fit an occupational position commensurate with their status in society. The type of education students receive seals their future status because their education is viewed as appropriate preparation for future jobs.

Questions to consider for this reading:

1. What is the meaning of *status groups,* and how are they related to the education of children?

2. What role does education play in preparation for membership in a status group?

3. According to Max Weber's conflict theory (see Ballantine and Spade's reading as well as this one), how are education and occupation related?

4. What is the role of conflict theory in Collins's discussion?

STATUS GROUPS

The basic units of society are associational groups sharing common cultures (or "subcultures"). The core of such groups is families and friends, but they may be extended to religious, educational, or ethnic communities. In general, they comprise all persons who share a sense of status equality based on participation in a common culture: styles of language, tastes in clothing and decor, manners and other ritual observances, conversational topics and styles, opinions and values, and preferences in sports, arts, and media. Participation in such cultural groups gives individuals their fundamental sense of identity, especially in contrast with members of other associational groups in whose everyday culture they cannot participate comfortably. Subjectively, status groups distinguish themselves from others in terms of categories of moral evaluation such as "honor," "taste," "breeding,"

From "Conflict Theory of Educational Stratification," by R. Collins, 1961, *American Sociological Review, 36*(6), pp. 1002–1019. Copyright 1961 by the American Sociological Association. Reprinted with permission.

"respectability," "propriety," "cultivation," "good fellows," "plain folks," etc. Thus the exclusion of persons who lack the ingroup culture is felt to be normatively legitimated.

There is no a priori determination of the number of status groups in a particular society, nor can the degree to which there is consensus on a rank order among them be stated in advance. These are not matters of definition, but empirical variations, the causes of which are subjects of other developments of the conflict theory of stratification. Status groups should be regarded as ideal types, without implication of necessarily distinct boundaries; the concepts remain useful even in the case where associational groupings and their status cultures are fluid and overlapping, as hypotheses about the conflicts among status groups may remain fruitful even under these circumstances. Status groups may be derived from a number of sources. Weber [1968] outlines three: (a) differences in life style based on economic situation (i.e., class); (b) differences in life situation based on power position; and (c) differences in life situation deriving directly from cultural conditions or institutions, such as geographical origin, ethnicity, religion, education, or intellectual or aesthetic cultures.

STRUGGLE FOR ADVANTAGE

There is a continual struggle in society for various "goods"—wealth, power, or prestige. We need make no assumption that every individual is motivated to maximize his rewards; however, since power and prestige are inherently scarce commodities, and wealth is often contingent upon them, the ambition of even a small proportion of persons for more than equal shares of these goods sets up an implicit counter-struggle on the part of others to avoid subjection and disesteem. Individuals may struggle with each other, but since individual identity is derived primarily from membership in a status group, and because the cohesion of status groups is a key resource in the struggle against others, the primary focus of struggle is between status groups rather than within them.

The struggle for wealth, power, and prestige is carried out primarily through organizations. There have been struggles throughout history among organizations controlled by different status groups, for military conquest, business advantage, or cultural (e.g., religious) hegemony, and intricate sorts of interorganizational alliances are possible. In the more complex societies, struggle between status groups is carried on in large part within organizations, as the status groups controlling an organization coerce, hire, or culturally manipulate others to carry out their wishes (as in, respectively, a conscript army, a business, or a church). Organizational research shows that the success of organizational elites in controlling their subordinates is quite variable. Under particular conditions, lower or middle members have considerable de facto power to avoid compliance, and even to change the course of the organizations (see Etzioni, 1961).

This opposing power from below is strengthened when subordinate members constitute a cohesive status group of their own; it is weakened when subordinates acquiesce in the values of the organization elite. Coincidence of ethnic and class boundaries produces the sharpest cultural distinctions. Thus, Catholics of immigrant origins have been the bulwarks of informal norms restricting work output in American firms run by WASPs, whereas Protestants of native rural backgrounds are the main "rate-busters" (Collins, Dalton, & Roy, 1946). Selection and manipulation of members in terms of status groups is thus a key weapon in intraorganizational struggles. In general, the organization elite selects its new members and key assistants from its own status group and makes an effort to secure lower-level employees who are at least indoctrinated to respect the cultural superiority of their status culture.

Once groups of employees of different status groups are formed at various positions (middle, lower, or laterally differentiated) in the organization, each of these groups may be expected to launch efforts to recruit more members of their own status group. This process is illustrated by conflicts among whites and blacks, Protestants and Catholics and Jews, Yankee, Irish and Italian, etc., found in American occupational life (Dalton, 1951; Hughes, 1949). These conflicts are based on ethnically or religiously founded status cultures; their intensity rises and falls with processes increasing or decreasing the cultural distinctiveness of these groups, and with the succession of advantages and disadvantages set by previous outcomes of these struggles which determine the organizational resources available for further struggle. Parallel processes of cultural conflict may be based on distinctive class as well as ethnic cultures.

EDUCATION AS STATUS CULTURE

The main activity of schools is to teach particular status cultures, both in and outside the classroom. In this light, any failure of schools to impart technical knowledge (although it may also be successful in this) is not important; schools primarily teach vocabulary and inflection, styles of dress, aesthetic tastes, values, and manners. The emphasis on sociability and athletics found in many schools is not extraneous but may be at the core of the status culture propagated by the schools. Where schools have a more academic or vocational emphasis, this emphasis may itself be the content of a particular status culture, providing sets of values, materials for conversation, and shared activities for an associational group making claims to a particular basis for status.

Insofar as a particular status group controls education, it may use it to foster control within work organizations. Educational requirements for employment can serve both to select new members for elite positions who share the elite culture and, at a lower level of education, to hire lower and middle employees who have acquired a general respect for these elite values and styles.

Tests of the Conflict Theory of Educational Stratification

The conflict theory in its general form is supported by evidence (1) that there are distinctions among status group cultures—based on both class and ethnicity—in modern societies (Kahl, 1957, pp. 127–156, 184–220); (2) that status groups tend to occupy different occupational positions within organizations (see data on ascription cited above); and (3) that occupants of different organizational positions struggle over power (Crozier, 1964; Dalton, 1959). The more specific tests called for here, however, are of the adequacy of conflict theory to explain the link between education and occupational stratification. Such tests may focus either on the proposed mechanism of occupational placement, or on the conditions for strong or weak links between education and occupation.

Education as a Mechanism of Occupational Placement

The mechanism proposed is that employers use education to select persons who have been socialized into the dominant status culture: for entrants to their own managerial ranks, into elite culture; for lower-level employees, into an attitude of respect for the dominant culture and the elite which carries it. This requires evidence that: (a) schools provide either training for the elite culture, or respect for it; and (b) employers use education as a means of selection for cultural attributes.

Historical and descriptive studies of schools support the generalization that they are places where particular status cultures are acquired, either from the teachers, from other students, or both. Schools are usually founded by powerful or autonomous status groups, either to provide an exclusive education for their own children, or to propagate respect for their cultural values. Until recently most schools were founded by religions, often in opposition to those founded by rival religions; throughout the 19th century, this rivalry was an important basis for the founding of large numbers of colleges in the U.S., and of the Catholic and Lutheran school systems. The public school system in the U.S. was founded mainly under the impetus of WASP elites with the purpose of teaching respect for Protestant and middle-class standards of cultural and religious propriety, especially in the face of Catholic, working-class immigration from Europe (Cremin, 1961; Curti, 1935). The content of public school education has consisted especially of middle-class, WASP culture ([Becker, 1961; Hess & Torney, 1967]; Waller, 1932, pp. 15–131).

At the elite level, private secondary schools for children of the WASP upper class were founded from the 1880s, when the mass indoctrination function of the growing public schools made them unsuitable as means of maintaining cohesion of the elite culture itself (Baltzell, 1958, pp. 327–372). These elite schools produce a distinctive personality type, characterized by adherence to a distinctive set of upper-class values and manners (McArthur, 1955). The cultural role of schools has been more closely studied in Britain (Bernstein, 1961; Weinberg, 1967) and in France (Bourdieu & Passeron, 1964), although Riesman and his colleagues (Jencks & Riesman, 1968; Riesman, 1958) have shown some of the cultural differences among prestige levels of colleges and universities in the United States.

Evidence that education has been used as a means of cultural selection may be found in several sources. Hollingshead's (1949, pp. 360–388) study of Elmtown school children, school dropouts, and community attitudes toward them suggests that employers use education as a means of selecting employees with middle-class attributes. A 1945–1946 survey of 240 employers in New Haven and Charlotte, N.C., indicated that they regarded education as a screening device for employees with desirable (middle-class) character and demeanor; white-collar positions particularly emphasized educational selection because these employees were considered most visible to outsiders (Noland & Bakke, 1949, pp. 20–63).

A survey of employers in nationally prominent corporations indicated that they regarded college degrees as important in hiring potential managers, not because they were thought to ensure technical skills, but rather to indicate "motivation" and "social experience" (Gordon & Howell, 1959,

p. 121). Business school training is similarly regarded, less as evidence of necessary training (as employers have been widely skeptical of the utility of this curriculum for most positions) than as an indication that the college graduate is committed to business attitudes. Thus, employers are more likely to refuse to hire liberal arts graduates if they come from a college which has a business school than if their college is without a business school (Gordon & Howell, 1959, pp. 84–87; see also Pierson, 1959, pp. 90–99). In the latter case, the students could be said not to have had a choice; but when both business and liberal arts courses are offered and the student chooses liberal arts, employers appear to take this as a rejection of business values.

Finally, a 1967 survey of 309 California organizations (Collins, 1971) found that educational requirements for white-collar workers were highest in organizations which placed the strongest emphasis on normative control over their employees. Normative control emphasis was indicated by (i) relative emphasis on the absence of police record for job applicants, (ii) relative emphasis on a record of job loyalty, and (iii) Etzioni's (1961) classification of organizations into those with high normative control emphasis (financial, professional services, government, and other public service organizations) and those with remunerative control emphasis (manufacturing, construction, and trade). These three indicators are highly interrelated, thus mutually validating their conceptualization as indicators of normative control emphasis. The relationship between normative control emphasis and educational requirements holds for managerial requirements and white-collar requirements generally, both including and excluding professional and technical positions. Normative control emphasis does not affect blue-collar education requirements. . . .

HISTORICAL CHANGE

The rise in educational requirements for employment throughout the last century may be explained using the conflict theory, and incorporating elements of the technical-functional theory into it at appropriate points. The principal dynamic has centered on changes in the supply of educated persons caused by the expansion of the school system, which was in turn shaped by three conditions:

Education has been associated with high economic and status position from the colonial period on through the twentieth century. The result was a popular demand for education as mobility opportunity. This demand has not been for vocational education at a terminal or commercial level, short of full university certification; the demand has rather focused on education giving entry into the elite status culture, and usually only those technically oriented schools have prospered which have most closely associated themselves with the sequence of education leading to (or from) the classical bachelor's degree (Collins, 1969, pp. 68–70, 86–87, 89, 96–101).

Political decentralization, separation of church and state, and competition among religious denominations have made founding schools and colleges in America relatively easy, and provided initial motivations of competition among communities and religious groups that moved them to do so. As a result, education at all levels expanded faster in America than anywhere else in the world. At the time of the Revolution, there were nine colleges in the colonies; in all of Europe, with a population forty times that of America, there were approximately sixty colleges. By 1880 there were 811 American colleges and universities; by 1966, there were 2,337. The United States not only began with the highest ratio of institutions of higher education to population in the world, but increased this lead steadily, for the number of European universities was not much greater by the twentieth century than in the eighteenth (Ben-David & Zloczower, 1962).

Technical changes also entered into the expansion of American education. As the evidence summarized above indicates: (a) Mass literacy is crucial for beginnings of full-scale industrialization, although demand for literacy could not have been important in the expansion of education beyond elementary levels. More importantly, (b) there is a mild trend toward the reduction in the proportion of unskilled jobs and an increase in the promotion of highly skilled (professional and technical) jobs as industrialism proceeds, accounting for 15% of the shift in educational levels in the twentieth century (Folger & Nam, 1964). (c) Technological change also brings about some upgrading in skill requirements of some continuing job positions, although the available evidence (Berg, 1970, pp. 38–60) refers only to the decade 1950–1960. Nevertheless, as Wilensky (1964) points out, there is no "professionalization of everyone," as most jobs do not require considerable technical knowledge on the order of that required of the engineer or the research scientist.

The existence of a relatively small group of experts in high-status positions, however, can have important effects on the structure of competition for mobility chances. In the United States, where democratic decentralization favors the use of schools (as well as government employment) as a kind of patronage for voter interests, the existence of even a small number of elite jobs fosters a demand for large-scale opportunities to acquire these positions. We thus have a "contest mobility" school system (Turner, 1960); it produced a widely educated populace because of the many dropouts who never achieve the elite level of schooling at which expert skills and/or high cultural status is acquired. In the process, the status value of American education has become diluted. Standards of respectability are always relative to the existing range of cultural differences. Once higher levels of education become recognized as an objective mark of elite status, and a moderate level of education as a mark of respectable middle-level status, increases in the supply of educated persons at given levels result in yet higher levels becoming recognized as superior, and previously superior levels become only average.

Thus, before the end of the nineteenth century, an elementary school or home education was no longer satisfactory for a middle-class gentleman; by the 1930s, a college degree was displacing the high school degree as the minimal standard of respectability; in the late 1960s, graduate school or specialized professional degrees were becoming necessary for initial entry to many middle-class positions, and high school graduation was becoming a standard for entry to manual laboring positions. Education has thus gradually become part of the status culture of classes far below the level of the original business and professional elites.

The increasing supply of educated persons . . . has made education a rising requirement of jobs . . . Led by the biggest and most prestigious organizations, employers have raised their educational requirements to maintain both the relative prestige of their own managerial ranks and the relative respectability of middle ranks. Education has become a legitimate standard in terms of which employers select employees, and employees compete with each other for promotion opportunities or for raised prestige in their continuing positions. With the attainment of a mass (now approaching universal) higher education system in modern America, the ideal or image of technical skill becomes the legitimating culture in terms of which the struggle for position goes on.

Higher educational requirements, and the higher level of educational credentials offered by individuals competing for positions in organizations, have in turn increased the demand for education by populace. The interaction between formal job requirements and informal status cultures has resulted in a spiral in which educational requirements and educational attainments become ever higher. As the struggle for mass educational opportunities enters new phases in the universities of today and perhaps in the graduate schools of the future, we may expect a further upgrading of educational requirements for employment. The mobilization of demands by minority groups for mobility opportunities through schooling can only contribute an extension of the prevailing pattern.

Conclusion

It has been argued that conflict theory provides an explanation of the principal dynamics of rising educational requirements for employment in America. Changes in the technical requirements

of jobs have caused more limited changes in particular jobs. The conditions of the interaction of these two determinants may be more closely studied.

Precise measures of changes in the actual technical skill requirements of jobs are as yet available only in rudimentary form. Few systematic studies show how much of particular job skills may be learned in practice, and how much must be acquired through school background. Close studies of what is actually learned in school, and how long it is retained, are rare. Organizational studies of how employers rate performance and decide upon promotions give a picture of relatively loose controls over the technical quality of employee performance, but this no doubt varies in particular types of jobs.

The most central lines of analysis for assessing the joint effects of status group conflict and technical requirements are those which compare the relative importance of education in different contexts. One such approach may take organization as the unit of analysis, comparing the educational requirements of organizations both to organizational technologies and to the status (including educational) background of organizational elites. Such analysis may also be applied to surveys of individual mobility, comparing the effects of education on mobility in different employment contexts, where the status group (and educational) background of employers varies in its fit with the educational culture of prospective employees. Such analysis of "old school tie" networks may also simultaneously test for the independent effect of the technical requirements of different sorts of jobs on the importance of education. International comparisons provide variations here in the fit between types of education and particular kinds of jobs which may not be available within any particular country.

The full elaboration of such analysis would give a more precise answer to the historical question of assigning weight to various factors in the changing place of education in the stratification of modern societies. At the same time, to state the conditions under which status groups vary in organizational power, including the power to emphasize or limit the importance of technical skills, would be to state the basic elements of a comprehensive explanatory theory of the forms of stratification.

REFERENCES

Baltzell, E. D. (1958). *An American business aristocracy.* New York: Macmillan.

Becker, H. S. (1961). Schools and systems of stratification. In A. H. Halsey, J. Floud, & C. A. Anderson (Eds.), *Education, economy, and society* (pp. 93–104). New York: Free Press.

Ben-David, J., & Zloczower, A. (1962). Universities and academic systems in modern societies. *European Journal of Sociology, 31,* 45–85.

Berg, I. (1970). *Education and jobs.* New York: Praeger.

Bernstein, B. (1961). Social class and linguistic development. In A. H. Halsey, J. Floud, & C. A. Anderson (Eds.), *Education, economy, and society* (pp. 288–314). New York: Free Press.

Bourdieu, P., & Passeron, J.-C. (1964). *Les heritiers: Les etudiants et la culture.* Paris: Les Editions de Minuit.

Collins, O., Dalton, M., & Roy, D. (1946). Restriction of output and social cleavage in industry. *Applied Anthropology, 5*(3), 1–14.

Collins, R. (1969). *Education and employment.* Unpublished doctoral dissertation, University of California, Berkeley.

Collins, R. (1971). *Educational requirements for employment: A comparative organizational study.* Unpublished manuscript.

Cremin, L. A. (1961). *The transformation of the school.* New York: Knopf.

Crozier, M. (1964). *The bureaucratic phenomenon.* Chicago: University of Chicago Press.

Curti, M. (1935). *The social ideas of American educators.* New York: Scribner's.

Dalton, M. (1951). Informal factors in career achievement. *American Journal of Sociology, 56*(5), 407–415.

Dalton, M. (1959). *Men who manage.* New York: Wiley.

Etzioni, A. (1961). *A comparative analysis of complex organizations.* New York: Free Press.

Folger, J. K., & Nam, C. B. (1964). Trends in education in relation to the occupational structure. *Sociology of Education, 38,* 19–33.

Gordon, R. A., & Howell, J. E. (1959). *Higher education for business.* New York: Columbia University Press.

Hess, R. D., & Torney, J. V. (1967). *The development of political attitudes in children.* Chicago: Aldine.

Hollingshead, A. B. (1949). *Elmtown's youth.* New York: Wiley.

Hughes, E. C. (1949). Queries concerning industry and society growing out of the study of ethnic relations in industry. *American Sociological Review, 14*(April), 211–220.

Jencks, C., & Riesman, D. (1968). *The academic revolution.* New York: Doubleday.

Kahl, J. A. (1957). *The American class structure.* New York: Rinehart.

McArthur, C. (1955). Personality differences between middle and upper classes. *Journal of Abnormal and Social Psychology, 50*(2), 247–254.

Noland, E. W., & Bakke, E. W. (1949). *Workers wanted.* New York: Harper.

Pierson, F. C. (1959). *The education of American businessmen.* New York: McGraw-Hill.

Riesman, D. (1958). *Constraint and variety in American education.* New York: Doubleday.

Turner, R. H. (1960). Sponsored and contest mobility and the school system. *American Sociological Review, 25*(6), 855–867.

Waller, W. (1932). *The sociology of teaching.* New York: Russell and Russell.

Weber, M. (1968). *Economy and society.* New York: Bedminster Press.

Weinberg, I. (1967). *The English public schools: The sociology of elite education.* New York: Atherton Press.

Wilensky, H. L. (1964). The professionalization of everyone? *American Journal of Sociology, 70*(2), 137–158.

ON UNDERSTANDING THE PROCESS OF SCHOOLING

The Contributions of Labeling Theory

Ray C. Rist

The final reading in this chapter on sociology of education and theory moves to the micro level, dealing with interactions between participants in schools. This is in contrast to the previous discussions of theories that more often dealt with large groups, educational systems, or even societal systems of education. Recall the discussion of interaction theory in the second reading in this chapter by Ballantine and Spade. Ray C. Rist goes into detail to describe labeling theory, one type of interaction theory. He first points out the value of labeling theory for understanding what is happening in schools. In the first part of this reading, Rist explains how teachers label students as bright or slow, and the consequences of these labels for the students in school and in the future. He explains the importance of understanding how and why individuals are labeled—who applied the label to whom—and the results for the labeled person. In applying this to school settings, Rist focuses on teacher expectations of students that are based on the labels given to a student. He also points out the research on the relationship between class, race, ethnicity, and labels. Often teachers expect less of lower-class children than they do of middle-class children. Finally, Rist explains the self-fulfilling prophecy as it applies to schools—the idea that teacher expectations of students influence the actual behavior of the students. Labeling theory and the self-fulfilling prophecy are commonly used theories in sociology of education studies of school interactions.

Questions to consider for this reading:

1. What is the importance of labeling theory for understanding interaction dynamics in schools?

2. Explain the relationship between labeling theory and self-fulfilling prophecy as they relate to students and classrooms.

3. Of what use do you feel labeling theory might be for understanding the relationship between teachers and students?

4. How does labeling theory overlap with some of the arguments in conflict theories discussed in this reading?

I. Becoming Deviant:
The Labeling Perspective

Those who have used labeling theory have been concerned with the study of *why* people are labeled, and *who* it is that labels them as someone who has committed one form or another of deviant behavior. In sharp contrast to the predominant approaches for the study of deviance, there is little concern in labeling theory with the motivational and characterological nature of the person who committed the act.

Deviance is understood, not as a quality of the person or as created by his actions, but instead as created by group definitions and reactions. It is a social judgment imposed by a social audience. As Becker (1963: 9) has argued:

> The central fact of deviance is that it is created by society. I do not mean this in the way it is ordinarily understood, in which the causes of deviance are located in the social situation of the deviant, or the social factors, which prompted his action. I mean, rather, that social groups create deviants by making the rules whose infraction constitute deviance, and by applying those rules to particular people and labeling them as outsiders. From this point of view, *deviance is not the quality of the act the person commits, but rather a consequence of the application by others of rules and sanctions to an "offender." The deviant is one to whom the label has been successfully applied. Deviant behavior is behavior that people so label* [emphasis added].

The labeling approach is insistent on the need for a shift in attention from an exclusive concern with the deviant individual to a major concern with the *process* by which the deviant label is applied. Again citing Becker (1964: 2):

> The labeling approach sees deviance always and everywhere as a process and interaction between at least two kinds of people: those who commit (or who are said to have committed) a deviant act, and the rest of the society, perhaps divided into several groups itself . . . One consequence is that we become much more interested in the process by which deviants are defined by the rest of the society, than in the nature of the deviant act itself.

The important questions, then, for Becker and others, are not of the genre to include, for example: Why do some individuals come to act out norm-violating behavior? Rather, the questions are of the following sort: Who applied the deviant label to whom? Whose rules shall prevail and be enforced? Under what circumstances is the deviant label successfully and unsuccessfully applied? How does a community decide what forms of conduct should be singled out for this kind of attention? What forms of behavior do persons in the social system consider deviant; how do they interpret such behavior; and what are the consequences of these interpretations for their reactions to individuals who are seen as manifesting such behavior? (See Akers, 1973.)

The labeling perspective rejects any assumption that a clear consensus exists as to what constitutes a norm violation—or for that matter, what constitutes a norm—within a complex and highly heterogeneous society. What comes to be determined as deviance and who comes to be determined as a deviant is the result of a variety of social contingencies influenced by who has the power to enforce such determinations. Deviance is thus problematic and subjectively given. The case for making the societal reaction to rule-breaking a major independent variable in studies of deviant behavior has been succinctly stated by Kitsuse (1964: 101):

> A sociological theory of deviance must focus specifically upon the interactions which not only define behaviors as deviant, but also organize and activate the application of sanctions by individuals, groups, or agencies. For in modern society, the socially significant differentiation of deviants from the nondeviant population is increasingly contingent upon circumstances of situation, place, social and personal biography, and the bureaucratically organized activities of agencies of social control.

Traditional notions of who is a deviant and what are the causes for such deviance are necessarily reworked. By emphasizing the processual nature of deviance, any particular deviant is seen to be a product of being caught, defined, segregated, labeled, and stigmatized. *This is one of the major thrusts of the labeling perspective—that forces of social control often produce the unintended consequence of making some persons defined as deviant even more confirmed as deviant because of the stigmatization of labeling. Thus, social reactions to deviance further deviant careers.* Erikson (1966) has even gone so far as to argue that a society will strive to maintain a certain level of deviance within itself as deviance is functional to clarifying group boundaries, providing scapegoats, clearing outgroups who can be the source of furthering ingroup solidarity, and the like.

The idea that social control may have the paradoxical effect of generating more of the very behavior it is designed to eradicate was first elaborated upon by Tannenbaum. He noted (1938: 21):

> The first dramatization of the "evil" which separates the child out of his group . . . plays a greater role in making the criminal than perhaps any other experience . . . He now lives in a different world. He has been tagged . . . The person becomes the thing he is described as being.

Likewise, Schur (1965: 4) writes:

> The societal reaction to the deviant then, is vital to an understanding of the deviance itself and a major element in—if not the cause of—the deviant behavior.

The focus on outcomes of social control mechanisms has led labeling theorists to devote considerable attention to the workings of organizations and agencies which function ostensibly to rehabilitate the violator or in other ways draw him back into conformity. Their critiques of prisons, mental hospitals, training schools, and other people-changing institutions suggest that the results of such institutions are frequently nearly the opposite of what they were theoretically designed to produce. These institutions are seen as mechanisms by which opportunities to withdraw from deviance are sealed off from the deviant, stigmatization occurs, and a new identity as a social "outsider" is generated. There thus emerges on the part of the person so labeled a new view of himself which is one of being irrevocably deviant.

This movement from one who has violated a norm to one who sees himself as a habitual norm violator is what Lemert (1972: 62) terms the transition from a primary to a secondary deviant. A primary deviant is one who holds to socially accepted roles, views himself as a nondeviant, and believes himself to be an insider. A primary deviant does not deny that he has violated some norm, and claims only that it is not characteristic of him as a person. A secondary deviant, on the other hand, is one who has reorganized his social-psychological characteristics around the deviant role. Lemert (1972: 62) writes:

> Secondary deviation refers to a special class of socially defined responses which people make to problems created by the societal reaction to their deviance. These problems . . . become central facts of existence for those experiencing them . . . Actions, which have these roles and self-attitudes as their referents make up secondary deviance. The secondary deviant . . . is a person whose life and identity are organized around the facts of deviance.

A person can commit repeated acts of primary deviation and never come to view himself or have others come to view him as a secondary deviant. Secondary deviation arises from the feedback whereby misconduct or deviation initiates social reaction to the behavior which then triggers further misconduct. Lemert (1951: 77) first described this process as follows:

> The sequence of interaction leading to secondary deviation is roughly as follows: (1) primary deviation; (2) societal penalties; (3) further primary deviation; (4) stronger penalties and rejections; (5) further deviations, perhaps with hostilities and resentments beginning to focus upon those doing the penalizing;

(6) crisis reached in the tolerance quotient, expressed in formal action by the community stigmatizing of the deviant; (7) strengthening of the deviant conduct as a reaction to the stigmatizing and penalties; and (8) ultimate acceptance of deviant social status and efforts at adjustment on the basis of the associated role.

Thus, when persons engage in deviant behavior they would not otherwise participate in and when they develop social roles they would not have developed save for the application of social control measures, the outcome is the emergence of secondary deviance. The fact of having been apprehended and labeled is the critical element in the subsequent construction of a deviant identity and pursuit of a deviant career.

II. The Origins of Labeling: Teacher Expectations

Labeling theory has significantly enhanced our understanding of the process of becoming deviant by shifting our attention from the deviant to the judges of deviance and the forces that affect their judgment. Such judgments are critical, for a recurrent decision made in all societies, and particularly frequent in advanced industrial societies, is that an individual has or has not mastered some body of information, or perhaps more basically, has or has not the capacity to master that information. These evaluations are made periodically as one moves through the institution of school and the consequences directly affect the opportunities to remain for an additional period. To be able to remain provides an option for mastering yet another body of information, and to be certified as having done so. As Ivan Illich (1971) has noted, it is in industrial societies that being perceived as a legitimate judge of such mastery has become restricted to those who carry the occupational role of "teacher." A major consequence of the professionalization of the role of teacher has been the ability to claim as a near exclusive decision whether mastery of

material has occurred. Such exclusionary decision-making enhances those in the role of "teacher" as they alone come to possess the authority to provide certification for credentials (Edgar, 1974).

Labeling theorists report that in making judgments of deviance, persons may employ information drawn from a variety of sources. Further, even persons within the same profession (therapists, for example) may make divergent use of the same material in arriving at an evaluative decision on the behavior of an individual. Among the sources of information available to labelers, two appear primary: first-hand information obtained from face-to-face interaction with the person they may ultimately label, and second-hand information obtained from other than direct interaction.

The corollary here to the activities of teachers should be apparent. Oftentimes, the evaluation by teachers (which may lead to the label of "bright," "slow," etc.) is based on first-hand information gained through face-to-face interaction during the course of the time the teacher and student spent together in the classroom. But a goodly amount of information about the student which informs the teacher's evaluation is second-hand information. For instance, comments from other teachers, test scores, prior report cards, permanent records, meetings with the parents, or evaluations from welfare agencies and psychological clinics are all potential informational sources. In a variation of the division between first-hand and second-hand sources of information, Johnson (1973) has suggested that there are three key determinants of teacher evaluations: student's prior performance, social status characteristics, and present performance. Prior performance would include information from cumulative records (grades, test scores, notes from past teachers or counselors, and outside evaluators) while social status and performance would be inferred and observed in the on-going context of the classroom.

What has been particularly captivating about the work of Rosenthal and Jacobson (1968) in this regard is their attempt to provide empirical justification for a truism considered self-evident by many in education: School achievement is not simply a matter of a child's native ability, but involves directly and inextricably the teacher as well. Described succinctly, their research involved a situation where, at the end of a school year, more than 500 students in a single elementary school were administered the "Harvard Test of Inflected Acquisition." In actuality this test was a standardized, relatively nonverbal test of intelligence, Flanagan's (1960) Test of General Ability (TOGA). The teachers were told that such a test would, with high predictive reliability, sort out those students who gave strong indication of being intellectual "spurters" or "bloomers" during the following academic year. Just before the beginning of school the following fall, the teachers were given lists with the names of between one and nine of their students. They were told that these students scored in the top twenty percent of the school on the test, though, of course, no factual basis for such determinations existed. A twenty percent subsample of the "special" students was selected for intensive analysis. Testing of the students at the end of the school year offered some evidence that these selected children did perform better than the nonselected.

The findings of Deutsch, Fishman, Kogan, North, and Whiteman (1964); Gibson (1965); Goslin and Glass (1967); McPherson (1966); and Pequignot (1966) all demonstrate the influence of standardized tests of intelligence and achievement on teachers' expectations. Goaldman (1971), in a review of the literature on the use of tests as a second-hand source of information for teachers, noted: "Although some of the research has been challenged, there is a basis for the belief that teachers at all levels are prejudiced by information they receive about a student's ability or character." Mehan (1971, 1974) has been concerned with the interaction between children who take tests and the teachers who administer them. He posits that testing is not the objective use of a measurement instrument, but the outcome of a set of interactional activities which are influenced by a variety of contingencies which ultimately manifest themselves in a reified "test score." Mehan suggests (1971):

> Standardized test performances are taken as an unquestioned, non-problematic reflection of the child's underlying ability. The authority of the test to measure the child's real ability is accepted by both teachers and other school officials. Test results are accepted without doubt as the correct and valid document of the child's ability.

Characteristics of children such as sex and race are immediately apparent to teachers. Likewise, indication of status can be quickly inferred from grooming, style of dress, need for free lunches, information on enrollment cards, discussion of family activities by children, and visits to the school by parents. One intriguing study recently reported in this area is that by two sociologists, Clifford and Walster (1973: 249). The substance of their study was described as follows:

> Our experiment was designed to determine what effect a student's physical attractiveness has on a teacher's expectations of the child's intellectual and social behavior. Our hypothesis was that a child's attractiveness strongly influences his teachers' judgments; the more attractive the child, the more biased in his favor we expect the teachers to be. The design required to test this hypothesis is a simple one: Teachers are given a standardized report card and an attached photograph. The report card includes an assessment of the child's academic performance as well as of his general social behavior. The attractiveness of the photos is experimentally varied. On the basis of this information, teachers are asked to state their expectations of the child's educational and social potential.

Based on the responses of 404 fifth grade teachers within the state of Missouri, Clifford and Walster concluded (1973: 255):

> There is little question but that the physical appearance of a student affected the expectations of the teachers we studied. Regardless of whether the pupil is a boy or girl, the child's physical attractiveness has an equally strong association with his teacher's reactions to him.

The variables of race and ethnicity have been documented, by Brown (1968), Davidson and Lang (1960), Jackson and Cosca (1974), and Rubovits and Maehr (1973), among others, as powerful factors in generating the expectations teachers hold of children. It has also been documented that teachers expect less of lower-class children than they do of middle-class children (cf. Becker, 1952; Deutsch, 1963; Leacock, 1969: Rist, 1970, 1973; Stein, 1971; Warner, Havighurst, & Loeb, 1944; Wilson, 1963). Douglas (1964), in a large-scale study of the tracking system used in British schools, found that children who were clean and neatly dressed in nice clothing and who came from what the teachers perceived as "better" homes, tended to be placed in higher tracks than their measured ability would predict. Further, when placed there they tended to stay and perform acceptably. Mackler (1969) studied schools in Harlem and found that children tended to stay in the tracks in which they were initially placed and that such placement was based on a variety of social considerations independent of measured ability. Doyle, Hancock, and Kifer (1971) and Palardy (1969) have shown teacher expectations for high performance in elementary grades to be stronger for girls than boys.

The on-going academic and interpersonal performance of the children may also serve as a potent source of expectations for teachers. Rowe (1969) found that teachers would wait longer for an answer from a student they believed to be a high achiever than for one from a student they believed to be a low achiever. Brophy and Good (1970) found that teachers were more likely to give perceived high achieving students a second chance to respond to an initial incorrect answer, and further, that high achievers were praised more frequently for success and criticized less for failure.

There is evidence that the expectations teachers hold for their students can be generated as early as the first few days of the school year and then remain stable over the months to follow (Rist, 1970, 1972, 1973; Willis, 1972). For example, I found during my three-year longitudinal and ethnographic study of a single, *de facto* segregated elementary school in the black community of St. Louis, that after only eight days of kindergarten, the teacher made permanent seating arrangements based on what she assumed were variations in academic capability. But no formal evaluation of the children had taken place. Instead, the assignments to the three tables were based on a number of socio-economic criteria as well as on early interaction patterns in the classroom. Thus, the placement of the children came to reflect the social class distinctions in the room—the poor children from public welfare families all sat at one table, the working-class children sat at another and the middle class at the third. I demonstrated how the teacher operationalized her expectations of these different groups of children in terms of her differentials of teaching time, her use of praise and control, and the extent of autonomy within the classroom. By following the same children through first and second grade as well, I was able to show that the initial patterns established by the kindergarten teacher came to be perpetuated year after year. By second grade, labels given by another teacher clearly reflected the reality each of the three groups experienced in the school. The top group was called the "Tigers," the middle group the "Cardinals," and the lowest group, the "Clowns." What had begun as a subjective evaluation and labeling by the teacher took on objective dimensions as the school proceeded to process the children on the basis of the distinctions made when they first began.

Taken together, these studies strongly imply that the notion of "teacher expectations" is multi-faceted and multi-dimensional. It appears that when teachers generate expectations about their students, they do so not only for reasons of academic or cognitive performance, but for their classroom interactional patterns as well. Furthermore, not only ascribed characteristics such as race, sex, class, or ethnicity are highly salient, interpersonal traits are also. Thus, the interrelatedness of the various attributes which ultimately blend together to generate the evaluation a teacher makes as to what can be expected from a particular student suggests the strength and tenacity of such subsequent labels as "bright" or "slow" or "trouble-maker" or "teacher's little helper." It is to the outcomes of the student's having one or another of these labels that we now turn.

III. AN OUTCOME OF LABELING: THE SELF-FULFILLING PROPHECY

W. I. Thomas, many years ago, set forth what has become a basic dictum of the social sciences when he observed, "If men define situations as real, they are real in their consequences." This is at the core of the self-fulfilling prophecy. An expectation which defines a situation comes to influence the actual behavior within the situation so as to produce what was initially assumed to be there. Merton (1968: 477) has elaborated on this concept and noted: "The self-fulfilling prophecy is, in the beginning, a *false* definition of the situation evoking a new behavior which makes the originally false conception come true" (emphasis in the original).

Here it is important to recall a basic tenet of labeling theory—that an individual does not become deviant simply by the commission of some act. As Becker (1963) stressed, deviance is not inherent in behavior *per se,* but in the application by others of rules and sanctions against one perceived as being an "offender." Thus, the only time one can accurately be termed a "deviant" is after the successful application of a label by a social audience. Thus, though many persons may commit norm violations, only select ones are subsequently labeled. The contingencies of race, class, sex, visibility of behavior, age, occupation, and who one's friends are all influence the outcome as to whether one is or is not labeled . . . Rosenthal and Jacobson's *Pygmalion in the Classroom* (1968) created wide interest in the notion of the self-fulfilling prophecy as a concept to explain differential performance by children in classrooms. Their findings suggested that the expectations teachers created about the children randomly selected as "intellectual bloomers" somehow caused the teachers to treat

them differently, with the result that the children really did perform better by the end of the year. Though the critics of this particular research (Snow, 1969; Taylor, 1970; Thorndike, 1968, 1969) and those who have been unsuccessful in replicating the findings (Claiborn, 1969) have leveled strong challenges to Rosenthal and Jacobson, the disagreements are typically related to methodology, procedure, and analysis rather than to the proposition that relations exist between expectations and behavior. In the context of a single student facing the authority and vested interests of a school administration and staff, the most likely outcome is that over time, the student will increasingly move towards conformity with the label the institution seeks to establish. Good and Brophy (1973: 75) have elaborated upon this process within the classroom as follows:

1. The teacher expects specific behavior and achievement from particular students.

2. Because of these different expectations, the teacher behaves differently toward the different students.

3. This teacher treatment tells each student what behavior and achievement the teacher expects from him and affects his self-concept, achievement motivation, and level of aspiration.

4. If this teacher treatment is consistent over time, and if the student does not actively resist or change it in some way, it will tend to shape his achievement and behavior. High-expectation students will be led to achieve at high levels, while the achievement of low-expectation students will decline.

5. With time, the student's achievement and behavior will conform more and more closely to that originally expected of him.

The fourth point in this sequence makes the crucial observation that teacher expectations are not automatically self-fulfilling. For the expectations of the teacher to become realized, both the teacher and the student must move toward a pattern of interaction where expectations are clearly communicated and the behavioral response is consonant with the expected patterns. The vulnerability of children to the dictates of adults in positions of power over them leaves the negotiations as to what evaluative definition will be tagged on the children more often than not in the hands of the powerful. As Max Weber himself stated, to have power is to be able to achieve one's ends, even in the face of resistance from others. When that resistance is manifested in school by children and is defined by teachers and administrators as truancy, recalcitrance, unruliness, and hostility, or conversely denied as a lack of motivation, intellectual apathy, sullenness, passivity, or withdrawal, the process is ready to be repeated and the options to escape further teacher definitions are increasingly removed.

POSTSCRIPT: BEYOND THE LOGJAM

This paper has argued that a fruitful convergence can be effected between the research being conducted on the self-fulfilling prophecy as a consequence of teacher expectations and the conceptual framework of labeling theory. The analysis of the outcomes of teacher expectations produces results highly similar to those found in the study of social deviance. Labels are applied to individuals which fundamentally shift their definitions of self and which further reinforce the behavior which had initially prompted the social reaction. The impact of the self-fulfilling prophecy in educational research is comparable to that found in the analysis of mental health clinics, asylums, prisons, juvenile homes, and other people-changing organizations. What the labeling perspective can provide to the study of educational outcomes as a result of the operationalization of teacher expectations is a model for the study of the *processes* by which the outcomes are produced. The detailing over time of the interactional patterns which lead to changes in self-definition and behavior within classrooms is sadly lacking in almost all of the expectation research to date . . .

To extend the research on the educational experiences of those students who are differentially labeled by teachers, what is needed is a theoretical framework which can clearly isolate the influences and effects of certain kinds of teacher reactions on certain types of students, producing certain typical outcomes. The labeling perspective appears particularly well-suited for this expansion of both research and theoretical development on teacher expectations by offering the basis for analysis at either a specific or a more general level. With the former, for example, there are areas of investigation related to (1) types of students perceived by teachers as prone to success or failure; (2) the kinds of reactions, based on their expectations, teachers have to different students; and (3) the effects of specific teacher reactions on specific student outcomes. At a more general level, fruitful lines of inquiry might include (1) the outcomes in the post-school world of having received a negative vs. a positive label within the school; (2) the influences of factors such as social class and race on the categories of expectations teachers hold; (3) how and why labels do emerge in schools as well as the phenomenological and structural meanings that are attached to them; and (4) whether there are means by which to modify or minimize the effects of school labeling processes on students.

Labeling theory provides a conceptual framework by which to understand the processes of transforming attitudes into behavior and the outcomes of having done so. To be able to detail the dynamics and influences within schools by which some children come to see themselves as successful and act as though they were, and to detail how others come to see themselves as failures and act accordingly, provides in the final analysis an opportunity to intervene so as to expand the numbers of winners and diminish the numbers of losers. For that reason above all others, labeling theory merits our attention.

REFERENCES

Akers, R. L. (1973). *Deviant behavior: A social learning approach*. Belmont, CA: Wadsworth.

Becker, H. S. (1952). Social class variations in the teacher-pupil relationship. *Journal of Educational Sociology, 25*(8), 451–465.

Becker, H. S. (1963). *Outsiders.* New York: Free Press.

Becker, H. S. (1964). *The other side.* New York: Free Press.

Brophy, J., & Good, T. (1970). Teachers' communications of differential expectations for children's classroom performance: Some behavioral data. *Journal of Educational Psychology, 61,* 365–374.

Brown, B. (1968). *The assessment of self-concept among four year old Negro and white children: A comparative study using the Brown-IDS Self-Concept Referents Test.* New York: Institute for Developmental Studies.

Claiborn, W. L. (1969). Expectancy in the classroom: A failure to replicate. *Journal of Educational Psychology, 60*(5), 377–383.

Clifford, M. M., & Walster, E. (1973). The effect of physical attractiveness on teacher expectations. *Sociology of Education, 46*(2), 248–258.

Davidson, H. H., & Lang, G. (1960). Children's perceptions of teachers' feelings toward them. *Journal of Experimental Education, 29*(2), 107–118.

Deutsch, M. (1963). The disadvantaged child and the learning process. In H. Passow (Ed.), *Education in depressed areas* (pp. 147–162). New York: Teachers College Press.

Deutsch, M., Fishman, J. A., Kogan, L., North, R., & Whiteman, M. (1964). Guidelines for testing minority group children. *Journal of Social Issues, 20*(2), 129–145.

Douglas, J. (1964). *The home and the school.* London: MacGibbon & Kee.

Doyle, W., Hancock, G., & Kifer, E. (1971). *Teachers' perceptions: Do they make a difference?* Paper presented at the meeting of the American Educational Research Association, New York.

Edgar, D. E. (1974). *The competent teacher.* Sydney, Australia: Angus & Robertson.

Erikson, K. T. (1966). *Wayward Puritans.* New York: Wiley.

Flanagan, J. C. (1960). *Test of general ability: Technical report.* Chicago: Science Research Associates.

Gibson, G. (1965). Aptitude tests. *Science, 149*(3684), 583.

Goaldman, L. (1971). Counseling methods and techniques: The use of tests. In L. C. Deighton (Ed.), *The encyclopedia of education.* New York: Macmillan.

Good, T., & Brophy, J. (1973). *Looking in classrooms.* New York: Harper & Row.

Goslin, D. A., & Glass, D. C. (1967). The social effects of standardized testing on American elementary schools. *Sociology of Education, 40,* 115–131.

Illich, I. (1971). *Deschooling society.* New York: Harper & Row.

Jackson, G., & Cosca, C. (1974). The inequality of educational opportunity in the southwest: An observational study of ethnically mixed classrooms. *American Educational Research Journal, 11*(3), 219–229.

Johnson, J. (1973). *On the interface between low-income urban black children and their teachers during the early school years: A position paper.* San Francisco: Far West Laboratory for Educational Research and Development.

Kitsuse, J. (1964). Societal reaction to deviant behavior: Problems of theory and method. In H. S. Becker (Ed.), *The other side.* New York: Free Press.

Leacock, E. (1969). *Teaching and learning in city schools.* New York: Basic Books.

Lemert, E. (1951). *Social pathology.* New York: McGraw-Hill.

Lemert, E. (1972). *Human deviance, social problems and social control.* Englewood Cliffs, NJ: Prentice-Hall.

Mackler, B. (1969). Grouping in the ghetto. *Education and Urban Society, 2*(1), 80–95.

McPherson, G. H. (1966). *The role-set of the elementary school teacher: A case study.* Unpublished doctoral dissertation, Columbia University, New York.

Mehan, H. B. (1971). *Accomplishing understanding in educational settings.* Unpublished doctoral dissertation, University of California, Santa Barbara.

Mehan, H. B. (1974). *Ethnomethodology and education.* Paper presented to the Sociology of Education Association conference, Pacific Grove, California.

Merton, R. K. (1968). Social problems and social theory. In R. Merton & R. Nisbet (Eds.), *Contemporary social problems* (pp. 697–737). New York: Harcourt, Brace & World.

Palardy, J. M. (1969). What teachers believe—what children achieve. *Elementary School Journal, 69,* 370–374.

Pequignot, H. (1966). L'equation personnelle du juge. *Semaine des Hopitaux, 14*(20), 4–11.

Rist, R. C. (1970). Student social class and teachers' expectations: The self-fulfilling prophecy in ghetto education. *Harvard Educational Review, 40,* 411–450.

Rist, R. C. (1972). Social distance and social inequality in a kindergarten classroom: An examination of the "cultural gap" hypothesis. *Urban Education, 7,* 241–260.

Rist, R. C. (1973). *The urban school: A factory for failure.* Cambridge: MIT Press.

Rosenthal, R., & Jacobson, L. (1968). *Pygmalion in the classroom.* New York: Holt, Rinehart and Winston.

Rowe, M. (1969). Science, silence, and sanctions. *Science and Children, 6*(6), 11–13.

Rubovits, P., & Maehr, M. L. (1973). Pygmalion black and white. *Journal of Personality and Social Psychology, 25*(2), 210–218.

Schur, E. (1965). *Crimes without victims.* Englewood Cliffs, NJ: Prentice Hall.

Snow, R. E. (1969). Unfinished Pygmalion. *Contemporary Psychology, 14*(4), 197–199.

Stein, A. (1971). Strategies for failure. *Harvard Educational Review, 41*(2), 158–204.

Tannenbaum, F. (1938). *Crime and the community.* New York: Columbia University Press.

Taylor, C. (1970). The expectations of Pygmalion's creators. *Educational Leadership, 28,* 161–164.

Thorndike, R. L. (1968). Review of *Pygmalion in the classroom. Educational Research Journal, 5*(4), 708–711.

Thorndike, R. L. (1969). But do you have to know how to tell time? *Educational Research Journal, 6,* 692.

Warner. W. L., Havighurst, R., & Loeb, M. B. (1944). *Who shall be educated?* New York: Harper & Row.

Willis, S. (1972). *Formation of teachers' expectations of student academic performance.* Unpublished doctoral dissertation, University of Texas at Austin.

Wilson, A. B. (1963). Social stratification and academic achievement. In H. Passow (Ed.), *Education in depressed areas* (pp. 217–236). New York: Teachers College.

Projects for Further Exploration

1. Using the basic ideas of the theoretical perspectives discussed in this chapter, consider two theoretical perspectives that you could use to help understand a specific situation that influenced your schooling. What are the strengths and weaknesses of each approach in explaining this situation?

2. Go to your library (or library's databases for searching journals) and find the most recent issue of *Sociology of Education*. Look at one or two articles in this journal, glancing through the first part of each article, and see if you can figure out which theoretical approach the authors used in their research.

3. Look around your current classroom and see if you can recognize any outward evidence of the theoretical arguments presented in this chapter. For example, are students all from the same social class background? If so, why? Is the curriculum structured for particular purposes in terms of maintaining social stability or the power structure in society? Discuss this with others in your class to see if you came up with similar examples and explanations.

2

STUDYING SCHOOLS

Research Methods in Education

In Chapter 1, we introduced some of the theories that social scientists and educators use to explain how schools work. However, theories are not descriptions of what is happening in schools; they are explanations that can be applied to what is happening. Research is used to see if the theories are supported in real educational institutions. Researchers use the theoretical explanations to formulate questions that are the basis for systematic examinations of schools. There are a variety of different ways to study schools, all of which offer valuable insights into education today.

The articles on education that you will read in this book and elsewhere depend on these different methods of social science research, offering unique pictures of what is happening in schools. Understanding the research methods used in articles you read is important because the methods used to collect data can influence the descriptions of what is happening in education, as illustrated in the article by Elizabeth J. Allan and Mary Madden. Furthermore, you may be in a position to work with research in education, and this chapter provides information on some of the techniques used.

So, let's get down to work! Social science research methods are a very large area to study, and we can only provide a brief overview here. These methods are often grouped into two large categories: quantitative and qualitative methods. We instinctively divide these two ways of collecting data based on the quantification of data using numbers. However, quantification of data can be used in qualitative as well as quantitative research. It is easier to distinguish between quantitative and qualitative methods if you focus on the way the data are collected, rather than the way the data are analyzed. For example, we can collect data on how students respond to new teaching innovation in a classroom by asking them to fill out a survey with questions. We might ask how much they have learned from using this new teaching innovation on a scale of 1 to 10 with 10 being "A great deal" and 1 being "Nothing." Or, we can go into the same classroom and observe the students in a lesson using this new teaching technique and draw conclusions from these observations. In the first instance, we are collecting data from the student that are already defined by what we know about the teaching innovation, and we can develop hypotheses and measures such as those using the numbers 1 to 10, which can be used later in a quantitative analysis. This is referred to as deductive analysis: We develop our research study based upon what we know of the subject. In the second instance, we begin by observing and then develop a way of analyzing what we see. This is referred to as inductive analysis. For the most part, quantitative methods use data that are collected and coded prior to quantitative analysis, whereas qualitative methods may use some quantification, but any quantification emerges from the process of analyzing the data during their collection or after they have been collected. Researchers who use quantitative data spend a great deal of time before collecting the data organizing the ways in which they will collect their data based upon prior studies and what they know of the subject, whereas researchers using qualitative methods rely more on observation and, thus, develop an understanding of the subject with emerging analysis.

Let's consider an example testing Bernstein's theory of *restricted and elaborated codes* (described in Chapter 1) using quantitative and qualitative methods. Using a quantitative research design, we can develop a survey instrument with quantifiable measures of social class as well as measures of elaborated and restricted codes that Bernstein developed in his theory. Of course, we would spend a lot of time developing these measures, but if the measures are valid, we can easily give them to thousands of individuals, thus testing Bernstein's theory. On the other hand, we could also go into upper-class, middle-class, and working-class schools and observe classrooms to see how children respond to materials taught in schools. Although the classrooms cannot be identical—that would be impossible to find—we pick our classrooms carefully to study the same age and same subject matter and perhaps even the same area of the country. Then we may discover some interesting differences that may or may not support Bernstein's theory about the use of elaborated and restricted codes varying by the social class background of children in classrooms. The first reading in this chapter by Allan and Madden provides an excellent example of how quantitative and qualitative methods can be used to study an issue in education, in their case the "chilly climate" for women on college campuses.

With this basic distinction between qualitative and quantitative research designs in mind, and an understanding that there are many variations that fall within these two categories, we move to describing in greater detail the nuances of these two approaches.

ISSUES IN QUANTITATIVE METHODS

Every research method has advantages and disadvantages, and quantitative methods are no exception. One major advantage of using quantitative methodology is that you can study a very large group of individuals or educational institutions. The coding of data before you begin, as represented by various forms of surveys (Internet, mail, or in-person), facilitates the use of larger numbers of individuals or groups in the research. Of course we cannot study everyone whom we wish to study, so we select a sample from the larger population, ideally using random selection. Large random samples are likely to lead to more representative samples. Selecting a sample that is representative of the group you are studying is critical to being able to generalize your findings to a larger population. A large sample, however, does not always guarantee a representative sample. Therefore, as you read research studies, it is important that you understand how samples are selected. For instance, in our example above, would you have more confidence in a sample of 100,000 students whom teachers selected from schools in upper-class, middle-class, and working-class districts, or a smaller sample of students, selected randomly by the researchers, from schools in neighborhoods of differing social class? Sampling is an important step in quantitative research method design, and it is important to understand how researchers obtain their samples.

In addition to sampling in research designs that use quantitative methods, researchers must pay special attention to how they ask questions about those things that they wish to measure. One issue is whether the questions are valid measures of that which is being studied. For example, does the measurement of school achievement reflect what the students in the study are actually achieving in school? Another question is whether the measure is reliable. That is, if you gave the same question to the same person at another time, would you get the same answer? Needless to say, invalid and unreliable measures do not help us to understand how schools work. Therefore, researchers work hard to develop accurate measures. As a result, you want to look carefully at the way concepts are measured in the studies you read.

Another issue that comes up in quantitative research is that of *causation*. In a cross-sectional survey of a group of students done at one point in time, it is difficult to say that one thing caused another. For example, in a survey of students looking at dropping out of school, would the correlation between dropping out and grades indicate that low grades *caused* the students in the study to drop out? Or could dropping out have resulted in low grades because the students left before the end of the year? Or could family issues such as illness or sudden homelessness have interfered with some students' academic work and led to both poor grades and the students dropping out? It is not always possible to figure out what happened unless you have data from more than one point in time.

Longitudinal studies are helpful in determining causation because data are collected over time. It is much better if data are collected from the same individuals over time. By collecting data this way, it is possible to follow patterns in the individuals' lives and identify things that may predict later outcomes. It would be easier to assess why students drop out in 12th grade if you also had information from these students in earlier years.

Some quantitative data are collected by large research organizations and made available to researchers to analyze. Most of these large data sets are carefully designed longitudinal studies based on random samples of all students in the United States. Many of these data sets were collected by the National Center for Education Statistics (NCES), part of the U.S. Department of Education. Beginning in 1972, NCES began collecting longitudinal survey data starting with high school seniors (NLS-72). In 1980, NCES began collecting data from high school sophomores and seniors, a data set called High School and Beyond (HS&B). In 1988, another study was begun beginning with eighth graders (NELS-88). In 1990 and 1993, the Beginning Postsecondary Students Longitudinal Study and the Baccalaureate and Beyond Longitudinal Study began to follow postsecondary students (Schmidt, 2002). Individuals who completed the original survey are typically followed up with every two years—not a small task as the samples are drawn to be representative of the entire United States, and some of these data sets include data from more than 30,000 individuals at two or more points in time (Schmidt, 2002).

A recent large data set collected by NCES (in collaboration with other federal agencies and organizations) is the Early Childhood Longitudinal Study program. This includes three longitudinal studies. One is a representative sample of the kindergarten class of 1998–1999 (ECLS-K) and the other of the birth cohort of 14,000 children born in the year 2001 (ECLS-B). NCES expects the two studies to "provide detailed information on children's health, early care and early school experiences" (NCES, 2010). The ECLS-K began in the fall of 1998 with a nationally representative sample of approximately 21,000 kindergarteners. These children will be followed with testing in the fall and spring from kindergarten through fifth grade and then again in eighth grade. The birth cohort in ECLS-B will be followed yearly until the children are in kindergarten (NCES, 2010). NCES recently began a third study in 2010–2011 of the kindergarten cohort that year. Imagine the value of these large, longitudinal data sets for researchers. Therefore, don't be surprised if the methods sections of articles in this book list data collected by NCES or another agency.

The second reading in this chapter is by Bruce J. Biddle and David C. Berliner and reviews mostly quantitative research on the effects of class size on students. While these researchers' findings are very important, pay special attention to their discussion of the various studies they examined and their detailed description of the longitudinal research on class size. This is a very interesting introduction to both the research on class size and the issues surrounding quantitative research.

The last reading in this chapter, by Gerald W. Bracey, warns us to use caution when confronted with numbers. Although statistics are a normal part of analyzing quantitative data, Bracey provides excellent guidelines for reading those numbers so as not to be tricked by an argument that is "backed up by statistics."

ISSUES IN QUALITATIVE METHODS

As noted previously, qualitative methods, sometimes referred to as ethnographies, are also used to study education. And, as noted, qualitative methods rely primarily on observation or open interviews, but can also use other techniques such as the focus groups used in the reading by Allan and Madden. Qualitative researchers typically do not spend a lot of time worrying about sampling methods, as virtually no qualitative studies use random samples. Nor do qualitative researchers have to worry about the accuracy or reliability of their measures, because they don't create measures ahead of time. Instead, most qualitative research begins with finding a site to observe or individuals to interview who fit the kinds of questions the researcher has in mind. For example, for the first reading in this chapter, Allan and Madden collected data by writing down observations of what women said in the focus groups they conducted on one college campus. As you will see, their qualitative data analysis did not involve any statistics, but rather involved quotations from and summaries of their observations.

Many researchers analyze their data as they begin their observations and continue to analyze the notes and materials for some time afterward. It is likely that data collected using qualitative methods are more "valid" than quantitative data because researchers are reporting what they say from multiple observations and directly from the sources. However, it is not as easy to make a statement about what causes what when collecting qualitative data because, unlike quantitative analyses, a researcher cannot possibly observe as many people using qualitative methods, and it is possible that the very question a researcher goes out to study may change in the course of the observations, as Edward W. Morris reports in a reading in Chapter 7. In addition to this article by Morris, and the Allan and Madden reading in this chapter, there are many more examples of qualitative research in this book.

At the close of this chapter, we hope you are better prepared to understand the basis for knowledge claims that you find in the readings in this book and in other research on education that you encounter. Understanding the types of methods researchers use to do their studies is important in being a good consumer of knowledge. For example, although you may get a deep understanding of a topic with an article that used qualitative techniques, it is not a good idea to generalize beyond the setting observed. However, ideas can be taken from that qualitative study, using deductive reasoning, and often are used to create a survey of a larger population and develop questions and causal statements (called *hypotheses*) that can be tested on a large number of individuals across settings through inductive reasoning. After reading this chapter, you will have some basic information about the theories and methods that sociologists use to explore educational systems as portrayed by the open systems model discussed in the introduction.

REFERENCES

National Center for Education Statistics (NCES). (2010). *Surveys and programs.* Retrieved from http://nces.ed.gov/surveys/SurveyGroups.asp?Group=3

Schmidt, C. (2002). Longitudinal studies data collection program. In D. L. Levinson, P. W. Cookson, Jr., & A. R. Sadovnik (Eds.), *Education and sociology: An encyclopedia* (pp. 409–420). New York: Routledge Falmer.

CHILLY CLASSROOMS FOR FEMALE UNDERGRADUATE STUDENTS

A Question of Method?

Elizabeth J. Allan and Mary Madden

Equal opportunity for girls and women in education has been an issue of debate for some time in sociology of education as discussed in the reading by Roslyn Arlin Mickelson in Chapter 7. This reading by Elizabeth J. Allen and Mary Madden illustrates how the method used by researchers in the analysis of issues can affect the conclusions one draws from the analyses. Consider the strengths and weaknesses of quantitative and qualitative research discussed in the introduction to this chapter as you read through their discussion of their use of both methods in studying this important topic. Unfortunately, we could not include the theory they used to develop their research questions as we wanted your focus in this reading to be on the methods alone, but good research requires combining theory, including results from previous research studies, with methodological rigor to add to our understanding of educational issues.

Questions to consider for this reading:

1. What problems with quantitative research identified in the introduction to this chapter can you see in this description of the research on the "chilly climate"?

2. What problems with qualitative research identified in the introduction to this chapter can you see in this description of the research on the "chilly climate"?

3. In terms of the topic of this reading, "chilly climate," which methodology do you think produces the most accurate and valid results?

Despite relatively widespread claims of "chilly climates," several studies have concluded that evidence of chilly climates for women in postsecondary classrooms is thin (Constantinople, Cornelius, & Gray, 1988) or no longer relevant (Drew & Work, 1998). These studies relied primarily on quantitative data (e.g., frequencies of behavior recorded through observation and self-report surveys with closed-ended questions) to reach these conclusions. Classroom climate researchers and scholars who study gender have argued that many "chilling" behaviors may go unacknowledged because they reflect socially accepted patterns of communication (Brady & Eisler, 1999; Hall & Sandler, 1982; Sadker & Sadker, 1994; Sandler,

Silverberg, & Hall, 1996; Valian, 1998). If this is accurate, findings derived from quantitative data alone may not be best suited to drawing conclusions about the existence or nonexistence of "chilly climates" in classrooms where socially accepted norms of communication may obscure behaviors typically identified as "chilling." The study of classroom climates is an important indicator of educational quality, not only for women but also for other historically disadvantaged groups. Thus, it is crucial that conclusions about classroom climates be accurately reported so that, if problems do exist, appropriate responses can be implemented.

* * *

RESEARCH DESIGN

Research Questions

This study was designed to explore the question of whether or not research findings, claiming that chilly classrooms no longer exist in postsecondary education, are conclusions based largely upon methods of data collection and therefore, subject to change depending on the research methods employed. The following questions were used as a guide for this investigation:

1. Do quantitative data lead us to conclude that chilly classroom climates exist for undergraduates in selected fields of study?

   a. Are there differences in perceptions of chilly classroom climates for women depending on the gender enrollment pattern of their field of study?

2. Do qualitative data lead us to conclude that chilly classroom climates exist in the selected fields of study measured in question one?

   a. Are there differences in perceptions of chilly classroom climates for women depending on the gender enrollment pattern of their field of study?

3. Do different research methods lead us to draw different conclusions about chilly climates for women in classrooms?

Defining Chilly Climate

Drawn from the literature on classroom climates, the operational definition of chilly classroom climate used for this study was "a psychological climate in which students of one sex are valued differently and therefore treated differently than are students of the opposite sex" (Serex & Townsend, 1999, p. 528).

Data Sources and Methods

This study was conducted with female undergraduate juniors or seniors in six different fields of study[1] at a research university in the northeast. The fields of study were selected based on the following enrollment patterns: (a) those where men comprised the majority of students, (b) those where women comprised the majority of students, and (c) fields of study where the enrollment of men and women was more evenly distributed.

For purpose of comparison, both quantitative and qualitative methods of data collection were employed to investigate female undergraduate students' experiences of both overt and subtle behaviors that characterize chilly classroom climates for women. Our focus was on student perceptions of classroom experiences across time within a particular field of study rather than in a single course.

The first method, an electronic self-report anonymous survey, was developed based on the chilly climate literature, including a sample questionnaire provided by Sandler et al. (1996). Closed-ended questions were designed to elicit the frequency with which a student had experienced particular behaviors. Participants were asked .to respond using a 4-point scale where "never" was equal to 1, "rarely" was equal to 2, "sometimes" was equal to 3, and "often" was equal to 4. The survey questions were designed to elicit perceptions about behaviors found to be characteristic of chilly climates. For instance, scholarship related to gendered communication patterns has indicated that men are more likely to interrupt in conversations than are women (Coates, 1998; Tannen, 1990). Thus, the survey asked women to report on the extent to which they perceive they are interrupted by men in classroom discussions. The survey also included several open-ended questions to provide opportunities for respondents to offer clarifying comments.

An invitation to complete the survey was emailed to randomly selected female students in the six fields of study, including business, elementary education, engineering, physical education and kinesiology, English and journalism,[2] and psychology. Business and engineering had a male majority in student enrollment; elementary education and psychology had female majority enrollment; and English and journalism, and physical education and kinesiology, had approximately equal enrollments. The response rate was 41% ($N = 394$) with relatively equal proportions received from each field of study.

The Web-based survey was anonymous, but respondents were invited to submit their name for entry into a raffle. Drawing from this list, we invited students by email to participate in a focus group. Focus groups were organized around each field of study with the exception of physical education and kinesiology, which did not have adequate participation. Six focus groups were held with a total of 20 participants (three groups representing fields with male-majority enrollments, two with female-majority enrollments, and one with balanced distribution). Focus groups were 90–120 minutes in duration, facilitated by the investigators, audio-taped, and transcribed for analysis.

Quantitative Analysis

Frequencies were calculated for each survey item. Seven scales were created to represent constructs found to contribute to chilly classroom climates (Sandler et al., 1996). Variables describing student and faculty behaviors were assigned to scales based upon face validity. Each scale consisted of three to eight items. Cronbach's alpha was used to measure the reliability of scales. [Authors' note: To review items used for the scales, see original article.]

Three scales categorized student behaviors. The first scale, *behaviors of male classmates* ($\alpha = .80$), consisted of six questions related to the frequency with which male classmates dominate discussion, space, and "collaborative" activities. The second scale, *silencing behaviors* ($\alpha = .86$), consisted of eight variables related to students' self-censoring in class due to discomfort as well as derogatory comments about women from other students. The third scale of student behaviors, *sexually offensive behaviors* ($\alpha = .85$), consisted of five questions regarding sexually suggestive humor, sexual remarks, leering, and sexual or physical contact.

Items related to faculty behaviors characteristic of chilly classroom climates for women were divided into four scales. The first of these scales, *stereotyping women* ($\alpha = .67$), consisted of three items related to stereotypical expectations and portrayal of women by faculty. The second scale, which measured faculty behaviors that contribute to chilly classroom climates, *encouraging men more than women* ($\alpha = .78$), consisted of three items related to faculty focusing more attention and encouragement on men in the classroom. The third scale, *dismissing and demeaning women* ($\alpha = .87$), consisted of eight items related to faculty behaviors that fail to take women seriously, send messages that women and their contributions are not valued, and use sexist language and materials. And the last scale, *sexually inappropriate behaviors* ($\alpha = .74$), consisted of three items related to subtle and overt sexual behaviors of faculty. Mean scores and standard deviations were computed for each scale. If the mean score of the scale was equivalent to or greater than 2.5 (the midpoint), indicating the behaviors occurred more often than "rarely," authors considered the construct to be a contributing factor to a chilly classroom for women.

Respondents were assigned to one of three groups based on the gender enrollment pattern of their field of study (female majority, male majority, or proportional male/female enrollment). One-way ANOVAs were conducted to determine if these groups differed in their ratings of classroom climate. Significant differences between groups were examined using post-hoc tests (Scheffe's).

Qualitative Analysis

Responses to open-ended questions from the survey and data collected via focus groups were analyzed using established methods of qualitative inquiry, including coding and categorizing processes that use both inductive and deductive approaches (Miles & Huberman, 1984). A deductive analytic approach was also used in response to the research questions "Do qualitative data lead us to conclude that chilly classroom climates exist in the selected fields of study?" and "Are there differences in perceptions of chilly classroom climates for women depending on the gender enrollment pattern of their field of study?"

Based on the literature about chilly classroom climates in postsecondary education (Sandler et al., 1996), we looked specifically for confirming and disconfirming evidence of the following: encouragement and/or discouragement; valuing women's contributions; defining women by their sexuality and/or unwanted sexual attention; female representation/inclusion in the curriculum; reinforcing traditional or stereotypical views of women and gender roles; questioning women's competence; gender differences related to space, time, and attention; and gender differences related to peer interactions.

Each of these categories served as a theme in the deductive coding process. Once all data were coded by category, they were also tagged with a code identifying whether the source of the behavior was attributed to male peers, faculty, or female peers. In some cases, data units were tagged with multiple "source" codes. Finally, in an effort to explore further if the data could provide insights as to why quantitative and qualitative methodologies might lead to different findings, a third layer of coding focused on the types of explanations offered by participants in relation to chilly classroom behaviors. The themes generated through this process included denial, minimizing, trivializing, blaming women, meritocracy, and sexism. We explore these further in the Discussion section of this article.

FINDINGS

Quantitative Findings

Quantitative survey data portrayed a complex picture of the classroom climate. The frequency rates for individual variables suggested that chilly classroom climates existed for a portion of survey respondents. Eleven of the 19 student behaviors and one of 16 faculty behaviors were reported to occur sometimes or often by 25% or more of women responding to the survey. The following is a list of these behaviors and the percentage of women that reported their occurrence at least sometimes: men taking over leadership in a small group activity (58%); sexually suggestive stories, jokes, or humor (55%); men taking up more class time or space (41%); censoring themselves in classes because they felt uncomfortable (40%); disparaging remarks about women's behaviors (37%); being interrupted by men (35%); sexual remarks, including discussion about personal or sexual matters (34%); body language such as staring, leering, or sexual gestures (33%); men ignoring their ideas or input (28%); pressure to avoid being seen as a supporter of women's issues (25%); and disparaging remarks about women's roles or career interests (25%). Faculty paying attention to the most talkative students who are male was reported to occur sometimes or often by 43% of the women.

When data were reduced to scales to represent constructs that contribute to chilly classroom climates, descriptive statistics indicated that women in this study rarely experienced the behaviors. Mean ratings on scales representing student behaviors characteristic of chilly classroom climates—behaviors of male classmates ($M = 1.99$), silencing behaviors ($M = 1.81$), and sexually offensive behaviors ($M = 1.87$)—indicated that these rarely occur. One-way ANO-VAs . . . show that there were no differences in *silencing behaviors* or *sexually offensive behaviors* scales based on the gender enrollment pattern of respondents' fields of study. There was a difference in reporting of *male behaviors* contributing to chilly classroom climates based on gender enrollment patterns. Fields of study with a male majority reported a higher occurrence of behaviors characteristic of a chilly climate. However, it is possible that male behaviors were identified as occurring more frequently in male-majority fields simply because there were more men in these classrooms.

Mean ratings of the four scales representing faculty behaviors that contribute to chilly climate—stereotyping women ($M = 1.41$), encouraging men more than women ($M = 1.82$), dismissing or demeaning women ($M = 1.36$), and sexually inappropriate behaviors ($M = 1.38$)—indicated that students perceived these faculty behaviors as occurring less than rarely. A one-way ANOVA . . . revealed no differences between students from fields of study with differing gender enrollment patterns regarding faculty behaviors that encourage men more than women or that are sexually inappropriate. However, significant differences were found on scales that measure behaviors related to stereotyping of women and dismissing and demeaning women. Respondents in female-majority fields reported a significantly higher occurrence of behaviors on both of these scales than did respondents in male-majority fields. This finding can be supported by gender schema and privilege frameworks that explain how chilling practices can be produced in classrooms regardless of the sex of the instructor. It may also be a reflection of the faculty/instructors in these particular fields at this institution. Further attention to this dynamic is needed in future studies.

Finally, respondents were asked to rate overall classroom environment for women using a 3-point scale ranging from 1 (*very supportive*) to 3 (*not at all supportive*). The mean rating of 1.42 indicates that respondents characterized the classroom climate as very supportive to somewhat supportive, with no significant differences between groups.

Qualitative Findings

Qualitative data indicated that behaviors characteristic of chilly classroom climates occurred across groups regardless of enrollment pattern. The data reflected some differences in the magnitude of specific types of behaviors; however, none of the groups were exempt from reporting chilly classroom behaviors. We describe qualitative data according to the primary themes that emerged in the analysis, including discouragement, invisibility, time and space, questioning women's competence, and defining women by their sexuality. While data we share here focus specifically on behaviors characteristic of chilly classroom climates, some participants who reported these experiences also described feeling "comfortable" and "equal" in their classrooms. We begin by discussing the data related to academic discouragement. . . .

Discouragement: "I just got the sense that . . . he was trying to drive the women away."

Women enrolled in male-majority fields reported experiencing the most overt forms of discouragement by faculty, as exemplified by the above quotation from a female engineering major. Not all students reported feeling as though their instructors or peers discouraged them, and for those who did, the overt behaviors were often isolated to one or two faculty members. Often, the discouraging behaviors were of a more subtle nature. For instance, one participant described a certain professor who favored men over women, explaining that this faculty member would call on male students more frequently than he would call on female students during class sessions. She said he would "take their comments over ours toward the discussion; we'd say something, he'd just kind of pass [us] over. If a guy said something, he'd have to stop and discuss it." . . .

Sometimes the examples were more reflective of female students' feelings of discouragement resulting from the perceived absence of faculty guidance or intervention. For example, a participant from a field with proportional male and female enrollment reported the following:

I had a physics lab a couple of years ago that was a horrible experience for me because I wanted to be an equal partner in the lab with the men in my group but they were . . . I mean it's horrible to say that they were far superior to me in terms of doing that work and I tried my darndest, but in a sense I had to relinquish some of the control to them because it's not my field and I tried so hard and I participated as much as I could, but I was really just a shadow and that was very frustrating . . . feeling dumb in a situation like that, feeling like I knew that I should have been able to do it as well, but really couldn't.

Other times, examples were reflective of female students' discouragement resulting from the attitudes and behaviors of their male peers. For instance, when describing her experience as a female civil engineering major in a lab setting, one student summed up the attitude of her male classmates as "they don't let you do crap." She elaborated, "Even if you show up in overalls and a t-shirt and you're like, I'm ready," the response is "no." Another participant shared similar experiences with male peers in a male-majority classroom:

Yeah, it's funny because when I was growing up I was the youngest kid of three girls, and so my dad taught me a lot about tools, fixing cars, things like that, so I feel very capable and comfortable but I don't think anyone who would meet me would really expect that because I don't volunteer that kind of information 'cause it's not really that important so they just assume that I can't do things.

These examples provide a snapshot of some of the types of gendered behaviors that can contribute to classroom environments where faculty and male peers have discouraged female students. These incidents of "discouragement" differ from other types of chilling behaviors in that they were plainly seen and interpreted as discouraging by female students participating in this study.

Invisibility and Marginalization: "It's like 'hello.' Didn't I just say that 10 minutes ago?"

While the previous examples portray some of the more overt types of behaviors that discourage women and contribute to chilly classroom climates, the greater share of participant comments reflected behaviors of a more subtle nature. For instance, some women reported feeling they are disregarded by male peers in their classrooms, as a participant from a male-majority field explained: "We got put into groups to do a project. . . . We had to pick an organization . . . and the guys would not even consider my topics. . . . They wouldn't even listen to my suggestions and I totally felt like I was completely ignored." Others described similar experiences of male students who "talk over" and "overpower female students" in classroom discussions, especially in small group discussions where faculty members are less likely to be facilitating the dialogue. For example, a second participant from a male-majority field reported:

I noticed that . . . when I was working in a group, I couldn't even make a suggestion of something to do and the males would just like overlook it and pretend you didn't even say anything. . . . Then one of them would say it maybe just like 10 minutes later, and everybody would say, "Oh, yeah, that's a good idea." . . . But it seems like it doesn't matter if it's coming from a female.

Another student from a male-majority field described similar feelings about male peers in class group work: "But that also has a lot to do with the men taking over when I'm trying to do something in a lab. It's the same thing. It could be that they just want to make their points."

Another factor involved in chilly classroom climates is the lack of representation and inclusion of women in the curriculum, in classroom activities, or in both. Students in all disciplinary groups commented on this aspect and offered a variety of examples and interpretations. . . .

One English major (a field with proportional male and female enrollment) reported that, when asked why the syllabus in a literary theory course did not include any works by female authors, her professor replied, "There wasn't any writing from females back then on this particular topic." While women's access to education and print media has indeed been limited during particular historical periods, the professor offered no further explanation, leaving this student and others in the class to presume women did not contribute anything worth studying or that women did not influence the historical development of literary theory in any significant way. Similarly, a participant from a female-majority field commented that she understood times were different for women "like in the 1800s," but she felt that her instructors "should mention some more of the women from back then and what they did" because "I'm sure they had great ideas."

These examples provide a glimpse of the ways in which female students reported being ignored or marginalized by having their own contributions to class discussion overlooked or by the lack of women's contributions included in the formal curriculum. Participants also reported other ways in which they were marginalized in classrooms. For instance, they described examples of male peers taking up more of the professor's time and attention in the classroom. When asked to comment on interactions with male peers in the classroom, one student from a male-majority field exclaimed, "I'm interrupted all the time and it really bothers me a lot!" Other students shared similar experiences. . . .

Like the findings related to overt discouragement of female students, participants who were enrolled in male-majority fields provided the greater share of examples related to feelings of invisibility and marginalization in the classroom. Nevertheless, even women enrolled in female-majority fields reported that such behaviors occur.

Questioning Women's Competence: "He was like, 'you can't lift that; you're a girl.'"

Stereotypical views of gender roles emerged as a prominent theme in the analysis of focus group data for this study. Comments related to this characteristic of chilly classroom climates

cut across fields of study, but they were most pronounced in the fields with a male majority. For example, one student reported being the only female student in a lab group where one of the students "took cheap shots all semester." She elaborated, "I had no idea why, just . . . making comments, saying I couldn't do it because I was a girl. We were doing concrete testing. . . . He was like, 'you can't lift that; you're a girl.'" In other instances, students reported that their male peers questioned their capability or their motivations for joining a field with a majority of men. Referring to her male peers in such a field, one student reported, "They just assume I can't do things." When asked why her male peers would assume this, she explained,

> I don't know, I like to wear girly clothes. . . . I'm a feminine girl and I don't really deny it so I guess that infers that I'm not comfortable dealing with grease and getting my hands dirty when in fact, I love doing stuff like that.

Another student recounted similar experiences, saying she gets the "oh you're a girl look" and explaining, "It's second nature for guys to want to protect you or want to control what's going on, and you know, I'm not going to fight that initially." . . .

Interestingly, at the same time female students' competence is called into question based on stereotypical views of gender, these stereotypes are also used to justify women's responsibility for doing a greater share of the work. Related to group work especially, participants in this investigation reported they are often expected to shoulder the greater burden of responsibility for keeping group members on task and ensuring they follow through with assignments. For example, one participant from a male-majority field shared that group projects were a place where she saw gender differences playing out:

> When I get into those [group projects] in classes, it always seems like all the guys want me to be the smart one of the group . . . because I was just kind of quiet in class and take my notes.

Another participant described being the only woman in a group of 11 students assigned to work on a course project in which she was delegated to be the "leader." When we probed further to inquire what the term *leader* meant in this context, she replied that there was no specific role; rather, it was just that "nobody [else] has the motivation . . . just nobody has the ambition or desire to organize this." She described how the professor asked her to take on this role since he knew "it would get done." In this case, the term *leader* might be understood as a substitute for a group secretary. Similarly, when asked about group work, another participant commented, "The guys are always less prepared." . . .

This student further explained her experience of taking on the role of group leader/secretary,

> Nobody . . . none of the guys got it to me on time. One of them didn't even send it to me until like two hours before class the next day. And then when he sent me his part of the paper, it was horrible. Not to be mean, but it sucked. And so then I'm trying to put a paper together, completely redo the whole thing and after putting in all this effort, you know we get like a 70 or something on the paper and when I put in all that effort and I still get the same grade as them, that's when it's hard.

References to traditional gender roles not only were made with regard to male attitudes toward women, but also occasionally reflected women's internalization of traditional gender roles and sometimes revealed their discomfort with and/or (mis)understandings about equity for women. For example, a participant from a male-majority field commented: "There's reverse prejudice in some instances . . . like we have the women's something center right? Is there a men's resource center? I'm more scared of those feminists than I am of men."

Heterosexism—the centrality of heterosexuality and the implicit perception that it is the only normal way of expressing one's sexuality—may be another factor to consider in making sense of the data from this study. Because of heterosexism and homophobia, those who do identify as (or are perceived to be) gay, lesbian, bisexual, or transgendered are often subject to harassment, ridicule, and marginalization. In a climate where heterosexism and sexism work in tandem to privilege heterosexuality as the norm, stereotypes of feminism abound, and some young women fear their real and/or perceived association with feminism may be mistakenly interpreted as anti-male and/or identification as a lesbian (Hogeland, 1994). This dynamic emerged in our conversations as several students in different focus groups shared worries that classmates might perceive them to be lesbians if they were to voice their concerns about the absence of women in the curriculum. In another instance, a focus group participant from a female-majority field described a classroom exercise in a class where the professor was explaining "3D imagery or something . . . and he was passing around [a device] . . . to see 3D . . . and it was really of naked women." He said, "'the women (students) might not want to look at this.' . . . If I looked at it, I felt like other people might think I was a lesbian or something." She continued, "I did look at it quickly just to see what he was talking about. . . . It kind of made me feel uncomfortable because I was looking at it wondering what people were thinking of me."

Defining Women by their Sexuality: "Dazed look on their face . . . ga ga eyes"

Another characteristic of chilly classroom climates is the tendency for women to be evaluated "more on the basis of their attractiveness, sexuality, and personality than their intellectual competence and abilities" (Sandler et al., 1996, p. 15). Participants in this investigation described these types of behaviors as well. While several students relayed experiences they characterized as inappropriate, other students described behaviors that were more subtle to them, but not without power to affect the climate of the classroom. For instance, one student relayed her experience in a predominantly male classroom,

> If I have ever noticed a difference in gender, it's when there's someone standing in front of the class. . . . There's an attractive young lady up there, you can kind of see them getting squirmy in their

seats. . . . if there is like a cute girl up there, they're definitely not listening to her at all. There is a dazed look on their face.

She elaborated on how this affects her personally when she's in a class where students have to make many presentations, "we have to dress up. . . . You know, and I'm always like, okay I'm standing up in front of 60 boys; what am I going to wear?"

Related to faculty behaviors, a number of students described instances where professors or instructors used sexual humor, innuendo, and explicit sexual attention, making students uncomfortable. A participant from a field of study with proportional male/female enrollment reported the following example:[3]

Yeah, he's very outrageous in the classroom. He makes women get up and dance. There was one girl in class who was a dancer and she was very into it. He just egged on all this weird gender stuff in the classroom. . . . There were times when I was really mad because he put people in situations that they . . . put me in situations that I didn't feel comfortable being in, but also I had to watch other people and a lot of the men, they were into that. They responded to him on that level, I think, and they wanted to talk about what they thought about women and assumptions and things. And some of the girls, like the girl who wanted to dance in the class, got off on it. . . . it wasn't appropriate in a writing classroom, I don't think. . . . He alienated quite a few of us.

Another participant, from a male-majority field, described the following experience: "One professor would come up behind me while seated and grab my shoulders or occasionally he would lean in toward my neck and comment on how good I smelled." Other participants provided further examples . . .

Some participants echoed the perception that the male professors they described were relying upon sexually suggestive comments and jokes to develop rapport with students—to be seen as "cool." Some reported being confused by such experiences; others said they were "shocked," "uncomfortable," and "humiliated." Some students clearly differentiated humor used by some faculty members as "sexual, but not sexist."

Discussion

This study grew out of a desire to investigate whether the choice of data collection methods could help to explain why some researchers studying classroom climates for undergraduate women reach differing conclusions about the existence of a chilly climate. Drawing conclusions about the presence of chilly classroom climates for women in this investigation gave rise to some thought-provoking questions.

It is conceivable that markedly different conclusions could be drawn based on the data generated from this investigation. If conclusions were drawn from frequency data alone, some researchers could assert that at least 25% of female undergraduate students at this institution experience chilly classroom climates. If conclusions were drawn from mean values derived from the scales in this investigation, some might conclude that chilly classroom climates are rare. However, if researchers drew conclusions based on the qualitative data alone (from open-ended survey comments and focus groups), they could assert that chilly classroom climates are not uncommon to female undergraduate students at this institution. They could conclude not only that chilly classroom climates persist but also that the magnitude of the problem is quite disturbing. Based on this investigation, it is clear that data collection and methods of analysis are important factors to consider when evaluating claims about classroom climates for girls/women. Further, data concerning gender and classroom climates can be interpreted quite differently depending upon a researcher's conceptual framework guiding analytic and interpretive decision making.

As is typically the case, data analysis for this study involved a series of choices and decisions. First, we made a decision to reduce data into scales that measured constructs related to chilly classroom climates. This approach is supported by the contention that chilly classroom climates for women result from an accumulation of overt and subtle discriminatory behaviors. Related variables were merged to create scales, and descriptive statistics were used to analyze these scales. Subsequently, we were faced with a decision to determine a cut-off point for a mean value indicative of a chilly climate. We decided that if the mean value indicated the set of behaviors had occurred more than "rarely," this would be sufficient to suggest the presence of chilly classroom climates. This series of decisions about how to analyze and interpret data from this investigation led us to conclude that chilly classroom climates are rare at the institution under investigation. Yet the net result of these decisions obscures the experiences of roughly one quarter of the undergraduate women who completed the survey. These women reported that 11 of 19 student behaviors and 1 of 16 faculty behaviors known to contribute to chilly classroom climates occurred at least sometimes.

What proportion of women must report chilly classroom behaviors before we conclude that such environments are indeed inhospitable for women? The answer to this question may vary according to a researcher's perspective. Drawing the conclusion (from survey data) that chilly classroom climates did not exist, when 25% of survey respondents identified chilling behaviors in their classrooms, was troubling to us. Discounting these behaviors because a larger proportion of women do not report them might be compared to suggesting that the presence of sexual violence is not a problem for women on college campuses because a majority of women are not direct victims of this violence.[4] Such an assertion fails to recognize the way in which the presence of sexual violence can circumscribe women's lives by creating a climate in which they are regularly reminded of the potential to experience such violence directly and adjust their daily lives accordingly. In a similar way, even women who have not been the direct recipients of chilly classroom behaviors may have witnessed them directed toward others in their classrooms or may have heard about such experiences from friends. These "ripple effects" of chilly classroom behaviors also contribute to creating inhospitable classroom climates for female students.

Valian's (1998) delineation of gender schemas, or the normalization of differential treatment on the basis of gender, is another factor to be considered while interpreting data from this study. Sadker and Sadker (1994) documented unintentional gender bias in school classrooms. Often, these gender-biased behaviors were difficult for teachers and students to identify precisely because the behaviors contributing to gender-bias reflected taken-for-granted gender norms that are rarely called into question (Valian, 1998). Similarly, it is conceivable that many participants in this study do not regularly question taken-for-granted gender norms in society. This lack of critical consciousness related to gender norms and sex inequality creates a dilemma in drawing conclusions from data analyzed via surveys or focus group discussions. As the literature related to gender norms makes clear, many of the behaviors characteristic of "chilly climates" reflect socially accepted patterns of communication. As such, it is not uncommon for many types of discriminatory behaviors to be interpreted as "normal" and/or justified in order to fit them into an acceptable or comfortable worldview (Johnson, 1997; Valian, 1998).

Similar to challenges experienced in efforts to promote anti-racist consciousness, Hogeland (1994) has described some barriers to adopting a feminist consciousness for girls and young women, including fear of complexity, fear of thinking, fear of change, fear of politics, and fear of anger. Acknowledging the reality of sexism can be deeply troubling, as it requires reframing one's worldview. . . .

Numerous scholars have described the cultural "myth of meritocracy" (Johnson, 2001; Mantsios, 2001; McNamee & Miller, 2004) as a substantial impediment to acknowledging a wide range of discriminatory practices. Operating within this mythical framework, individuals are firmly rooted in seeing social life as fair and equitable—with one's station in life primarily a measure of the individual's work ethic rather than of race, class, gender/sex (and other types of) privilege, and discrimination in society. This discourse emerged in the thinking of a number of study participants who felt that if students simply worked hard they would succeed. . . .

Gender schemas, heterosexism, the discourse of meritocracy, and fear of feminism may help to explain impediments to acknowledging and understanding chilly classroom and gender-biased behaviors. As such, it seems prudent that these be considered in determining which methodological approaches to employ when studying gender dynamics of classroom climates. In this investigation, the focus group method and the open-ended survey questions elicited different kinds of data than the quantitative portion of the survey elicited. This outcome aligns with perspectives shared by Madriz (2000) and others who claim the collectivist dynamic of focus groups are particularly helpful for uncovering the realities of women's daily experiences. . . .

Further, researchers also have acknowledged how the collective nature of the focus group method may mitigate the influence of the interviewer by shifting power away from the researcher and toward the group (Kitzinger & Barbour, 1999; Wilkinson, 1999a, 1999b), fostering "free expression of ideas, encouraging the members of the group to speak up," and empowering participants by validating their voices and experiences (Madriz, 2000, p. 838).

While strengths of the focus group method, as Madriz (2000) and others describe, may make it well suited to collecting data on classroom climates, it is not without limitations. One criticism of focus group data is that group dynamics may introduce bias or may potentially skew the data. However, Marshall and Rossman (1999) point out that an implicit assumption of the focus group method is that individual attitudes and beliefs are not formed in isolation. Krueger and Casey (2000) assert that participant interactions in focus group interviews enhance data quality, as "participants tend to provide checks and balances on each other, which weeds out false or extreme views" (Patton, 2002, p. 386).

In this investigation, the collective nature of the focus groups appeared to contribute to participants' recollection of classroom behaviors. For instance, in several cases where students came to the focus group with the expressed intent of reporting the *absence* of any gender-biased behaviors in their classrooms, they later described one, or sometimes numerous, instances of chilly classroom behaviors that they had "forgotten" until hearing another participant describe a similar experience. Over the course of our facilitation of the focus groups, we began to recognize a pattern in the cadence of the group discussions beginning with very little dialogue—sometimes silence—which shifted over the 60–90 minute period. The progression was usually sparked when one participant described an experience that resonated with others in the group, who then proceeded to detail classroom experiences they previously neglected to identify as "chilly."

Limitations and Soundness of the Investigation

The sample was drawn from a single institution with the survey distributed to a randomly selected group of female students (except in engineering, where all female students received a survey due to limited numbers of women in that field of study). Despite this, we had very little control over who, within that sample, chose to respond; consequently, some bias may be inherent in the self-selection of respondents.

Focus group participation averaged 3–4 students per group. These participants were invited from those students who completed the Web-based survey and who had indicated a willingness to be contacted for further participation in the study. It could be argued that these participants might over-represent survey respondents who reported chilly classroom climates. However, it is possible the converse is true in this case. For example, in four of the six focus groups held for this study, at least one of the participants explicitly articulated that her interest in participating was solely to communicate that gender bias *did not* exist in her field of study.

In any research project, potential researcher bias should be considered throughout the investigation. As Denzin and Lincoln (2000) have pointed out, researchers are multicultural subjects and as such, their particular conceptions of self and others may influence the design and analysis of an investigation. As White, middle-class, academic women, we came to this study with particular interests and experiences shaping our perceptions of the research problem. Recognizing our potential biases, we implemented a number of strategies designed to promote trustworthiness of findings, including researcher reflexivity, peer debriefing, and negative case analysis (Merriam, 2002).

In light of this, we worked to promote the soundness and validity of the findings through careful attention to detail, triangulation of data sources, and methods of analysis. We expect the findings to provide insights and assertions that are transferable to other settings and that can serve as a guide for further inquiry and more careful evaluation of research claims about classroom climates. . . .

NOTES

1. We use the term "field of study" in reference to students' major area of study including both academic disciplines such as psychology or professional fields such as engineering.

2. English and journalism students were grouped to represent one field of study in order to increase the sample size to be comparable to the other fields of study participating in this investigation.

3. The university had a sexual harassment policy at the time of this study, though it was not referenced by any of the students in this investigation.

4. According to Fisher, Cullen, and Turner (2000), 27.7 per 1,000 college women are victims of attempted or completed rapes.

REFERENCES

Brady, K. L., & Eisler, R. M. (1999). Sex and gender equity in the college classroom: A quantitative analysis of faculty-student interactions and perceptions. *Journal of Educational Psychology,* *9*(1), 127–145.

Coates, J. (Ed.). (1998). *Language and gender: A reader.* Malden, MA: Blackwell.

Constantinople, A., Cornelius, R., & Gray, J. (1988). The chilly climate: Fact or artifact? *The Journal of Higher Education, 59,* 527–550.

Denzin, N. K., & Lincoln, Y. S. (2000). The discipline and practice of qualitative research. In N. K. Denzin & Y. S. Lincoln (Eds.), *Handbook of qualitative research* (2nd ed., pp. 1–28). Thousand Oaks, CA: Sage.

Drew, T. L., & Work, G. G. (1998). Gender-based differences in perception of experiences in higher education: Gaining a broader perspective. *The Journal of Higher Education, 69,* 542–555.

Fisher, B. S., Cullen, F. T., & Turner, M. G. (2000). *The sexual victimization of college women* (Research Report). Washington, DC: U.S. Department of Justice.

Hall, R., & Sandler, B. (1982). *The classroom climate: A chilly one for women?* Washington, DC: Project on the Status and Education of Women, Association of American Colleges.

Hogeland, L. M. (1994, November/December). Fear of feminism: Why young women get the willies. *Ms. Magazine,* 18–21.

Johnson, A. G. (1997). *The gender knot: Unraveling our patriarchal legacy.* Philadelphia: Temple University Press.

Johnson, A. G. (2001). *Power, privilege and difference.* Mountain View, CA: Mayfield.

Kitzinger, J., & Barbour, R. S. (1999). Introduction: The challenge and promise of focus groups. In R. S. Barbour & J. Kitzinger (Eds.), *Developing focus group research: Politics, theory and practice* (pp. 1–20). London: Sage.

Krueger, R. A., & Casey, M. A. (2000). *Focus groups: A practical guide for applied research.* Thousand Oaks, CA: Sage.

Madriz, E. (2000). Focus groups in feminist research. In N. K. Denzin & Y. S. Lincoln (Eds.), *Handbook of qualitative research* (2nd ed., pp. 835–850). Thousand Oaks, CA: Sage.

Mantsios, G. (2001). Class in America: Myths and realities. In P. S. Rothenberg (Ed.), *Race, class, and gender in the United States* (5th ed., pp. 168–182). New York: Worth.

Marshall, C., & Rossman, G. (1999). *Designing qualitative research* (3rd ed.). Beverly Hills, CA: Sage.

McNamee, S. J., & Miller, R. K. (2004). *The meritoc-racy myth.* Lanham, MD: Rowman & Littlefield.

Merriam, S. B. (2002). Introduction to qualitative research. In S. B. Merriam (Ed.), *Qualitative research in practice: Examples for discussion and analysis* (pp. 1–33). San Francisco: Jossey-Bass.

Miles, M., & Huberman, A. (1984). *Qualitative data analysis: A sourcebook of new methods.* Beverly Hills, CA: Sage.

Patton, M. Q. (2002). *Qualitative research and evalu-ation methods.* Beverly Hills, CA: Sage.

Sadker, M., & Sadker, D. (1994). *Failing at fairness: How our schools cheat girls.* New York: Touchstone.

Sandler, B. R., Silverberg, L., & Hall, R. M. (1996). *The chilly classroom climate: A guide to improve the education of women.* Washington, DC: National Association of Women in Education.

Serex, C. P., & Townsend, B. K. (1999). Student per-ceptions of chilling practices in sex-atypical majors. *Research in Higher Education, 40*(5), 527–538.

Tannen, D. (1990). *You just don't understand: Women and men in conversation.* New York: HarperCollins.

Valian, V. (1998). *Why so slow? The advancement of women.* Cambridge, MA: MIT Press.

Wilkinson, S. (1999a). Focus groups: A feminist method. *Psychology of Women Quarterly, 23,* 221–244.

Wilkinson, S. (1999b). How useful are focus groups in feminist research? In R. Barbour & J. Kitzinger (Eds.), *Developing focus group research: Politics, theory and practice* (pp. 64–78). London: Sage.

Small Class Size and Its Effects

Bruce J. Biddle and David C. Berliner

Debates over ideal class size have pitted policy makers and politicians against each other, and stimulated many researchers to study the issue. Politicians argue for larger versus smaller schools based on "the research," but the research presents a mixed picture. The question that is sometimes overlooked is the effect of large versus small classrooms on equality of educational opportunity, especially in overcrowded schools and classes. Biddle and Berliner present an overview of research and projects addressing size issues, especially the relationship of size to achievement of students. This study provides an overview of the advantages and disadvantages of using quantitative research to support policy issues on this important topic, the impact of class size on equal opportunity of academic achievement.

Questions to consider for this reading:

1. What does research show about class size and achievement?

2. What problems with quantitative research identified in the introduction to this chapter can you see in this description of the research on class size?

3. What features of quantitative research do the authors identify that lead to stronger studies on the effects of class size?

Studies of the impact of class size on student achievement may be more plentiful than for any other issue in education. Although one might expect this huge research effort to yield clear answers about the effects of class size, sharp disagreements about these studies' findings have persisted.

Advocacy groups take opposite stances. The American Federation of Teachers, for example, asserts that

taken together, these studies provide compelling evidence that reducing class size, particularly for younger children, will have a positive effect on student achievement. (Murphy & Rosenberg, 1998, p. 3)

The Heritage Foundation, by contrast, claims that "there's no evidence that smaller class sizes alone lead to higher student achievement" (Rees & Johnson, 2000).

Reviewers of class size studies also disagree. One study contends that "large reductions in school class size promise learning benefits of a magnitude commonly believed not within the power of educators to achieve" (Glass, Cahen, Smith, & Filby, 1982, p. 50), whereas another claims that "the evidence does not offer much reason to expect a systematic effect from overall class size reduction policies" (Hanushek, 1999, p. 158).

That the American Federation of Teachers and the Heritage Foundation sponsor conflicting judgments is easy to understand. But why have reviewers come to such divergent views about the research on class size, and what does the evidence really say?

EARLY SMALL FIELD EXPERIMENTS

To answer these questions, we must look at several research traditions, beginning with early experiments on class size. Experiments have always been a popular research technique because investigators can assign their subjects randomly to different conditions and then compare the results of those conditions—and this human intervention can appear to provide information about causes and effects. Experiments on class size, however, are nearly always done in field settings—schools—where uncontrolled events can undermine the research and effect results.

Small experimental studies on the effects of class size began to appear in the 1920s, and scores of them emerged subsequently. In the 1960s, informal reviews of these efforts generally concluded that differences in class size generated little to no effect. By the late 1970s, however, a more sophisticated research method, meta-analysis, had been invented, which facilitated the statistical assembly of results from small-but-similar studies to estimate effects for the studies' populations. Reviewers quickly applied meta-analysis to results from early experiments in class size (Educational Research Service, 1980; Glass et al., 1982; Glass & Smith, 1979; Hedges & Stock, 1983) and eventually emerged with a consensus that short-term exposure to small classes generates—usually minor—gains in students' achievement and that those gains are greater in the early grades, in classrooms with fewer than 20 students, and for students from groups that are traditionally disadvantaged in education.

Most of these early class size experiments, however, had involved small samples, short-term exposures to small classes, only one measure of student success, and a single education context (such as one school or school district). Poor designs had also made results of some studies questionable. Researchers needed to use different strategies to ascertain the effects of long-term exposure to small classes and to assess whether the advantages of early exposure to small classes would generalize to other successes and be sustainable.

SURVEYS

Survey research has provided evidence on the effects of class size by analyzing naturally occurring differences in schools and classrooms and by asking whether these differences are associated with student outcomes.

Well-designed surveys can offer evidence about the impact of variables that experiments cannot manipulate—such as gender, minority status, and childhood poverty—but survey research cannot easily establish relationships between causes and effects. For example, if a survey examines a sample of schools where average class size varies and discovers that those schools with smaller classes also have higher levels of student achievement, has the survey ascertained that class size generated achievement? Hardly. Those schools with smaller classes might also have had more qualified teachers, better equipment, more up-to-date curriculums, newer school buildings, more students from affluent homes, or a more supportive community environment—factors that may also have helped generate higher levels of achievement. To use survey data to make the case for a causal relation between class size and student outcomes, then, researchers must use statistical processes that control for the competing effects of other variables.

Serious surveys of education achievement in the United States began in the 1960s with the famous Coleman report (Coleman et al., 1966).

Written by authors with impressive reputations and released with great fanfare, this massive, federally funded study involved a national sample and took on many issues then facing education. Today, most people remember the report for its startling claim that student achievement is almost totally influenced by the students' families and peers and not by the characteristics of their schools. This claim was widely accepted—indeed, was greeted with dismay by educators and endorsed with enthusiasm by fiscal conservatives—despite flaws in the report's methods that were noted by thoughtful critics.

Since then, researchers have conducted surveys to establish whether differences in school funding or in the reforms that funds can buy—such as small class sizes—are associated with desired education outcomes. Most of these surveys, usually designed by economists, have involved questionable design features and small samples that did not represent the wide range of U.S. schools, classrooms, or students . . .

Fortunately, a few well-designed, large-scale surveys have investigated class size directly (see, for example, Elliott, 1998; Ferguson, 1991; Ferguson & Ladd, 1996; Wenglinsky, 1997). These studies concluded that long-term exposure to small classes in the early grades can be associated with student achievement; that the extra gains that such exposure generates may be substantial; and that such gains may not appear with exposure to small classes in the upper grades or at the secondary school levels.

TRIAL PROGRAMS AND LARGE FIELD EXPERIMENTS

Other types of small class research have addressed some of the shortcomings of early experiments and surveys. In the 1980s, state legislatures in the United States began political debates about the effects of small class size, and some states began trial programs or large-scale field experiments . . .

Tennessee's Project STAR

Such an experiment shortly appeared in Tennessee's Project STAR (Student/Teacher Achievement Ratio), arguably the largest and best-designed field experiment ever undertaken in education (Finn & Achilles, 1990; Finn, Gerber, Achilles, & Boyd-Zaharias, 2001; Folger, 1989; Grissmer, 1999; Krueger, 1999, 2000; Krueger & Whitmore, 2001; Mosteller, 1995; Nye, Hedges, & Konstantopoulos, 1999).

In the mid-1980s, the Tennessee legislature funded a four-year study to compare the achievement of early-grade students assigned randomly to one of three conditions: *standard classes* (with one certificated teacher and more than 20 students); *supplemented classes* (with one teacher and a full-time, noncertificated teacher's aide); and *small classes* (with one teacher and about 15 students). The study began with students entering kindergarten in 1985 and called for each student to attend the same type of class for four years. To control variables, the study asked each participating school to sponsor all three types of classes and to assign students and teachers randomly to each type. Participating teachers received no prior training for the type of class they were to teach.

The project invited all the state's primary schools to be in the study, but each participating school had to agree to remain in the program for four years; to have the class *rooms* needed for the project; and to have at least 57 kindergarten students so that all three types of classes could be set up. Participating schools received no additional support other than funds to hire additional teachers and aides. These constraints meant that troubled schools and those that disapproved of the study—and schools that were too small, crowded, or underfunded—would not participate in the STAR program, so the sample for the first year involved "only" 79 schools, 328 classrooms, and about 6,300 students. Those schools came from all corners of the state, however, and represented urban, inner-city, suburban, and rural school districts. The sample population included majority students, a sizable number of African

American students, and students receiving free school lunches.

At the beginning of each year of the study, the sample population changed somewhat. Some participating students had moved away, been required to repeat kindergarten, or left the study because of poor health. Other families moved into the districts served by STAR schools, however, and their children filled the vacant seats. Also, because attending kindergarten was not then mandatory in Tennessee, some new students entered the STAR program in the 1st grade.

In addition, some parents tried to move their children from one type of STAR class to another, but administrators allowed only a few students to move from a standard class to a supplemented class or vice versa. By the end of the study, then, some students had been exposed to a STAR class for four years, but others had spent a shorter time in such classes. These shifts might have biased STAR results, but Alan Krueger's careful analysis (1999) concluded that such bias was minimal.

Near the end of each year, STAR students took the Stanford Achievement Test battery and received separate scores for reading, word-study skills, and mathematics. Results from these tests were similar for students who were in the standard and supplemented classes, indicating that the presence of untrained aides in supplemented classes did *not* contribute to improving student achievement. Results for small classes were sharply different, however, with long-term exposure to small classes generating substantially higher levels of achievement and with gains becoming greater the longer that students were in small classes. . . .

STAR investigators found that the students in small classes were 0.5 months ahead of the other students by the end of kindergarten, 1.9 months ahead at the end of 1st grade, 5.6 months ahead in 2nd grade, and 7.1 months ahead by the end of 3rd grade. The achievement advantages were smaller, although still impressive, for students who were only exposed to one, two, or three years of small classes. STAR investigators found similar (although not identical) results for word-study skills and mathematics.

Small-class advantages appeared for all types of students participating in the study. The gains were similar for boys and girls, but they were greater for impoverished students, African American students, and students from inner-city schools—groups that are traditionally disadvantaged in education.

These initial STAR findings were impressive, but would students who had been exposed to small classes in the early grades retain their extra gains when they entered standard size classes in 4th grade? To answer this question, the Tennessee legislature authorized a second study to examine STAR student outcomes during subsequent years of schooling.

At the end of each year, until they were in the 12th grade in 1997–1998, these students took the Comprehensive Tests of Basic Skills and received scores in reading, mathematics, science, and social science. The results showed that average students who had attended small classes were months ahead of those from standard classes for each topic assessed at each grade level. Figure 7.1 displays results from some of these tests, showing, for example, that when typical students who had attended small classes in the early grades reached grade 8, they were 4.1 months ahead in reading, 3.4 months ahead in mathematics, 4.3 months ahead in science, and 4.8 months ahead in social science.

Students who had attended small classes also enjoyed other advantages in the upper grades. They earned better grades on average, and fewer dropped out or had to repeat a year. And when they reached high school, more small class students opted to learn foreign languages, study advanced-level courses, and take the ACT and SAT college entrance examinations. More graduated from high school and were in the top 25 percent of their classes. Moreover, initial published results suggest that these upper-grade effects were again larger for students who are traditionally disadvantaged in education. . . .

[O]f students who opted to take the ACT or SAT exams as high school seniors, roughly 44 percent of those from small classes took one or both of these tests, whereas only 40 percent of

Figure 7.1 Average Months of Grade-Equivalent Advantage in Achievement Scores for Students Who Experienced One or More Years of Small Classes

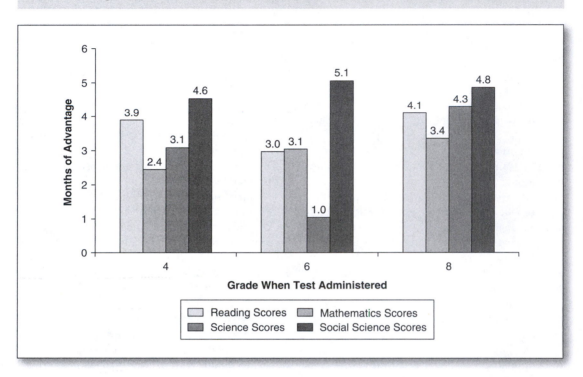

those from standard classes did so. The difference, however, was far greater for African American students. Instruction in small classes during the early grades had eliminated more than half of the traditional disadvantages that African American students have displayed in participation rates in the ACT and SAT testing programs.

Taken together, findings from the STAR project have been impressive, but they are not necessarily definitive. The STAR student sample did not quite match the U.S. population, for example, because very few Hispanic, Native American, and immigrant (non-English-speaking) families were living in Tennessee in the middle-1980s. Also, news about the greater achievement gains of small classes leaked out early during the STAR project, and one wonders how this may have affected participating teachers and why parents whose children were in other types of

classes did not then demand that their children be reassigned to small classes. Finally, the STAR schools had volunteered to participate, suggesting that the teachers and principals in those schools may have had strong interests in trying innovative ideas. Questions such as these should not cause us to reject the findings from the STAR project, but we should keep in mind that this was a single study and that, as always, other evidence is needed to increase certainty about class size effects . . .

Like Project STAR, the SAGE program (Wisconsin's Student Achievement Guarantee in Education Program) studied schools that had volunteered for the program and provided them with sufficient funds to hire additional teachers. The SAGE program, however, involved more Hispanic, Asian, and Native American students than had the STAR project.

After the announcement of findings from the initial effort, the Wisconsin legislature extended the SAGE program to other primary schools in the state. Therefore, what began as a small trial project has now blossomed into a statewide program that makes small classes in the early grades available for schools serving needy students.

The California Class Size Reduction Program

In 1996, California began a class size reduction program that has been far more controversial than such programs elsewhere. In earlier years, California had experienced many social problems, and major measures of achievement ranked California schools last in the United States. That year, however, a fiscal windfall became available, and then-governor Pete Wilson announced that primary schools would receive $650 annually for each student (an amount later increased to $800) if they would agree to reduce class sizes in the early grades from the statewide average of more than 28 students to not more than 20 students in each class (Hymon, 1997; Korostoff, 1998; Stecher, Bohrnstedt, Kirst, McRobbie, & Williams, 2001).

Several problems quickly surfaced. First, the California definition of a small class was larger than the size recommended in other studies. In fact, the size of small classes in California matched the size of standard classes in some other states. On the other hand, some California schools had been coping with 30–40 students in each classroom in the early grades, so a reduction to 20 students constituted an improvement.

The second problem was that the program's per-student funding was inadequate. Contrast the SAGE program's additional $2,000 for each student with the $650 or $800 offered by California. Nevertheless, the lure of additional funding proved seductive, and most California school districts applied to participate. This inadequate funding imposed serious consequences on poorer school districts, which had to abolish other needed activities to afford hiring teachers for smaller classes. In effect, then, the program created rather than solved problems for underfunded school districts.

In addition, when the California program began, many of its primary schools were overcrowded, and the state was suffering from a shortage of well-trained, certificated teachers. To cope with the lack of space, some schools created spaces for smaller classes by cannibalizing other needed facilities such as special education quarters, child care centers, music and art rooms, computer laboratories, libraries, gymnasiums, or teachers' lounges. Other schools had to tap into their operating budgets to buy portable classrooms, resulting in delays in paying for badly needed curricular materials or repairs for deteriorating school buildings. And to staff their smaller classes, many schools had to hire teachers without certification or prior training.

So far, results from the California program have been only modest. Informal evidence suggests that most students, parents, and teachers are pleased with their schools' smaller classes. And comparisons between the measured achievements of 3rd grade students from districts that did and did not participate in the early phases of the program have indicated minor advantages for California's smaller classes. These effects, however, have been smaller than those reported for the STAR and SAGE programs.

In many ways, the California initiative has provided a near-textbook case of how a state should *not* reduce class size. After failing to conduct a trial program, California adopted an inadequate definition of class size, committed insufficient funds to the initiative, and ignored serious problems of overcrowding and teacher shortages. This example should remind us that small classes are not a panacea for education. To be effective, programs for reducing class size need careful planning and consideration of the needs and strengths of existing school systems.

WHAT WE NOW KNOW ABOUT SMALL CLASSES

What should we conclude about the effects of small classes? Although the results of individual studies are always questionable, a host of different studies suggest several conclusions.

- When planned thoughtfully and funded adequately, small classes in the early grades generate substantial gains for students, and those extra gains are greater the longer students are exposed to those classes.
- Extra gains from small classes in the early grades are larger when the class has fewer than 20 students.
- Extra gains from small classes in the early grades occur in a variety of academic disciplines and for both traditional measures of student achievement and other indicators of student success.
- Students whose classes are small in the early grades retain their gains in standard size classrooms and in the upper grades, middle school, and high school.
- All types of students gain from small classes in the early grades, but gains are greater for students who have traditionally been disadvantaged in education.
- Initial results indicate that students who have traditionally been disadvantaged in education carry greater small-class, early-grade gains forward into the upper grades and beyond.
- The extra gains associated with small classes in the early grades seem to apply equally to boys and girls.
- Evidence for the possible advantages of small classes in the upper grades and high school is inconclusive.

TENTATIVE THEORIES

Why should reducing class size have such impressive effects in the early grades? Theories about this phenomenon have fallen largely into two camps.

Most theorists focus on the teacher, reasoning that small classes work their magic because the small class context improves interactions between the teacher and individual students. In the early grades, students first learn the rules of standard classroom culture and form ideas about whether they can cope with education. Many students have difficulty with these tasks, and interactions with a teacher on a one-to-one basis—a process more likely to take place when the class is small—help the students cope. In addition, teachers in small classes have higher morale, which enables them to provide a more supportive environment for initial student learning. Learning how to cope well with school is crucial to success in education, and those students who solve this task when young will thereafter carry broad advantages—more effective habits and positive self-concepts—that serve them well in later years of education and work.

The need to master this task confronts all students, but doing so is often a more daunting challenge for students who come from impoverished homes, ethnic groups that have suffered from discrimination or are unfamiliar with U.S. classroom culture, or urban communities where home and community problems interfere with education. Thus, students from such backgrounds have traditionally had more difficulty coping with classroom education, and they are more likely to be helped by a reduction in class size.

This theory also helps explain why reductions in class size in the upper grades may not generate significant advantages. Older students normally have learned to cope with standard classrooms and have developed either effective or ineffective attitudes concerning academic subjects—and these attitudes are not likely to change just because of a reduction in class size.

The theory also suggests a caution. Students are likely to learn more and develop better attitudes toward education if they are exposed to well-trained and enthusiastic teachers, appropriate and challenging curriculums, and physical environments in their classrooms and schools that support learning. If conditions such as these are not also present, then reducing class size in the early grades will presumably have little impact. Thus, when planning programs for reducing class size, we should also think about the professional development of the teachers who will participate in them and the educational and physical contexts in which those programs will be placed.

A second group of theories designed to account for a class size effect focuses on the classroom environment and student conduct rather than on the teacher. We know that discipline and classroom management problems interfere with subject-matter instruction. Theories in this group argue that these problems are less evident in small classes and that students in small classes are more likely to be engaged in learning. Moreover, teacher stress is reduced in small classes, so teachers in the small class context can provide more support for student learning. Studies have also found that small instructional groups can provide an environment for learning that is quite different from that of the large classroom. Small instructional groups can create supportive contexts where learning is less competitive and students are encouraged to form supportive relationships with one another.

Theories such as these suggest that the small class environment is structurally different from that of the large class. Less time is spent on management and more time is spent on instruction, students participate at higher levels, teachers are able to provide more support for learning, and students have more positive relationships. Such processes should lead both to greater subject-matter learning and to more positive attitudes about education among students, with more substantial effects in the early grades and for those groups that are traditionally disadvantaged in education.

These two theories are not mutually exclusive. On the contrary, both may provide partial insights into what happens in small classes and why small class environments help so many students. Collecting other types of evidence to assess such theories directly would be useful, particularly observational studies that compare the details of interaction in early-grade classes of various sizes and surveys of the attitudes and self-concepts of students who have been exposed to classes of different sizes. Unfortunately, good studies of these effects have been hard to find.

POLICY IMPLICATIONS AND ACTIONS

Given the strength of findings from research on small classes, why haven't those findings provoked more reform efforts? Although many state legislatures have debated or begun reform initiatives related to class size, most primary schools in the United States today do not operate under policies that mandate small classes for early grades. Why not?

This lack of attention has several causes, among them ignorance about the issue, confusion about the results of class size research and ineffective dissemination of those results, prejudices against poor and minority students, the politicizing of debates about class size effects and their implications, and practical problems associated with adopting small classes.

Recent debates about class size have become quite partisan in the United States, with Democrats generally favoring class size reductions and Republicans remaining hostile to them. Responding to President Bill Clinton's 1998 State of the Union address, the U.S. Congress set up a modest program, aimed at urban school districts with high concentrations of poverty, which provided funds for hiring additional teachers during the 1999 and 2000 fiscal years. This program enabled some districts to reduce class sizes in the early grades, and informal results from those cities indicated gains in student achievement.

Republicans have been lukewarm about extending this program—some apparently believing that it is ineffective or is merely a scheme to enhance the coffers of teacher's unions—and have welcomed President George W. Bush's call for an alternative federal program focused on high-stakes achievement tests and using results from those tests to apply sanctions to schools if they do not perform adequately.

The major problems standing in the way of reducing class sizes, however, are often practical ones. In many cases, cutting class sizes means hiring more teachers. With the looming shortage of qualified teachers, recruiting more teachers may be even more difficult than finding the funds to pay their salaries. Further, many schools would have to find or create extra rooms to house the additional classes created by small class programs, which would require either modifying school buildings or acquiring temporary classroom structures.

In many cases, meeting such needs would mean increasing the size of public school budgets, a step abhorred by fiscal conservatives and those who are critical of public education. The latter have argued that other reforms would cost less and be more effective than reducing class sizes. In response to such claims, various studies have estimated the costs of class size reduction programs or compared their estimated costs with those of other proposed reforms. Unfortunately, studies of this type must make questionable assumptions, so the results of their efforts have not been persuasive.

Nevertheless, reducing the size of classes for students in the early grades often requires additional funds. All students would reap sizable education benefits and long-lasting advantages, however, and students from educationally disadvantaged groups would benefit even more. Indeed, if we are to judge by available evidence, no other education reform has yet been studied that would provide such striking benefits. Debates about reducing class sizes, then, are disputes about values. If citizens are truly committed to providing a quality public education and a level playing field for all students regardless of background, they will find the funds needed to reduce class size.

References

Coleman, J. S., Campbell, E. Q., Hobson, C. J., McPartland, J., Mood, A. M., Weinfield, F. D., & York, R. L. (1966). *Equality of educational opportunity*. Washington, DC: U.S. Government Printing Office.

Educational Research Service. (1980). Class size research: A critique of recent meta-analyses. *Phi Delta Kappan, 70*(December), 239–241.

Elliott, M. (1998). School finance and opportunities to learn: Does money well spent enhance students' achievement? *Sociology of Education, 71*(3), 223–245.

Ferguson, R. F. (1991). Paying for public education: New evidence on how and why money matters. *Harvard Journal on Legislation, 28*(2), 465–498.

Ferguson, R. F., & Ladd, H. F. (1996). How and why money matters: An analysis of Alabama schools. In H. F. Ladd (Ed.), *Holding schools accountable: Performance-based reform in education* (pp. 256–298). Washington, DC: Brookings Institution.

Finn, J. D., & Achilles, C. M. (1990). Answers and questions about class size: A statewide experiment. *American Educational Research Journal, 27*(3), 557–577.

Finn, J. D., Gerber, B., Achilles, C. M., & Boyd-Zaharias, J. (2001). The enduring effects of small classes. *Teachers College Record, 103*(1), 145–183.

Folger, J. (Ed.). (1989). Project STAR and class size policy (Special issue). *Peabody Journal of Education, 67*(1).

Glass, G. V., Cahen, L. S., Smith, M. L., & Filby, N. N. (1982). *School class size: Research and policy*. Beverly Hills, CA: Sage.

Glass, G. V., & Smith, M. L. (1979). Meta-analysis of research on class size and achievement. *Educational Evaluation and Policy Analysis, 1*(1), 2–16.

Grissmer, D. (Ed.). (1999). Class size: Issues and new findings [Special issue]. *Educational Evaluation and Policy Analysis, 21*(2).

Hanushek, E. A. (1999). Some findings from an independent investigation of the Tennessee STAR experiment and from other investigations of class size effects. *Education Evaluation & Policy Analysis, 21*(2), 143–163.

Hedges, L. V., & Stock, W. (1983). The effects of class size: An examination of rival hypotheses. *American Educational Research Journal, 20*(1), 63–85.

Hymon, S. (1997). A lesson in classroom size reduction: Administrators nationwide can learn from California's classroom size reduction plan and how districts implemented it. *School Planning & Management, 36*(7), 18–23, 26.

Korostoff, M. (1998). Tackling California's class size reduction policy initiative: An up close and personal account of how teachers and learners responded. *International Journal of Educational Research, 29*(8), 797–807.

Krueger, A. B. (1999). Experimental estimates of education production functions. *The Quarterly Journal of Economics, 114*(2), 497–532.

Krueger, A. B. (2000). *Economic considerations and class size* (Working paper #447). Princeton, NJ: Princeton University, Industrial Relations Section.

Krueger, A. B., & Whitmore, D. M. (2001). The effect of attending a small class in the early grades on college-test taking and middle school test results: Evidence from Project STAR. *Economic Journal, 111,* 1–28.

Mosteller, F. (1995). The Tennessee study of class size in the early school grades. *The Future of Children, 5*(2), 113–127.

Murphy, D., & Rosenberg, B. (1998, June). *Recent research shows major benefits of small class size* (Educational Issues Policy Brief No. 3). Washington, DC: American Federation of Teachers.

Nye, B., Hedges, L. V., & Konstantopoulos, S. (1999). The long-term effects of small classes: A five-year follow-up of the Tennessee class size experiment. *Educational Evaluation and Policy Analysis, 21,* 127–42.

Rees, N. S., & Johnson, K. (2000, May 30). A lesson in smaller class sizes. *Heritage Views 2000.* Retrieved from http://www.heritage.org/views/2000/ed053000.html

Stecher, B., Bohrnstedt, G., Kirst, M., McRobbie, J., & Williams, T. (2001). Class-size reduction in California: A story of hope, promise, and unintended consequences. *Phi Delta Kappan, 82*(9), 670–674.

Wenglinsky, H. (1997). How money matters: The effect of school district spending on academic achievement. *Sociology of Education, 70*(3), 221–237.

How to Avoid Statistical Traps

Gerald W. Bracey

How to Lie With Statistics and *Damned Lies and Statistics* are two books that point out the complications in interpreting the meaning of statistics. Data do not always support the conclusions drawn in research and reports, yet parents, educators, and policy makers rely on statistics to make sense of the educational scene and trends. Statistics are an essential part of quantitative methods because they are used to summarize data collected to test theories and to determine if the data collected from a sample are representative of the larger population that one would like to generalize to. Thus, as Bracey illustrates, knowing how to interpret statistics is crucial for understanding research on schools.

Questions to consider for this reading:

1. What role do statistics play in helping researchers understand educational systems?

2. Why is it important to have more than one statistical result?

3. What does Bracey recommend we do to ensure more accuracy in research results?

There are three kinds of lies: lies, damned lies, and statistics. This quote from Benjamin Disraeli, Prime Minister of England under Queen Victoria, demonstrates that the field of statistics has needed to defend its honor since its inception in Europe centuries ago.

The original term for statistics, *political arithmetic* (Best, 2001), might be more accurate. Statistics are rarely neutral. Those who collect them have a purpose—sometimes benign, sometimes not—and translate the information to serve that purpose. For example, some people, including representatives of the pharmaceutical industry, say that statistics reveal an "obesity crisis" in the United States. Other people, including some financed by the food industry, allege that the "obesity crisis" is a false alarm spread by drug companies that want the standards for diseases constantly made stricter so that they can define more people as patients and sell them expensive drugs. It's true that the numbers accepted as indications of high cholesterol, high blood pressure, and high blood sugar have all become much lower in the last decade.

Contradictory claims like these may be one reason why people say that you can prove anything with statistics. You can't, but people will certainly try to prove their particular viewpoints by using only those numbers that serve their purposes.

More Than One Number

You need more than one statistic to get a full picture of just about anything. Educators whose performance is being judged solely by annual standardized test scores will appreciate this point.

As I was writing this, an article in *The New York Times* gave three statistics for various nations' greenhouse gas emissions: total emissions, per capita emissions, and emissions per industrial output (Barringer, 2006). Using total emissions, the United States is number one by far, with China second and Russia third. Using per capita emissions, the United States is still number one and Russia is still third, but Canada is second. (China has lots of people and is still largely a rural nation despite its rapid urbanization.) Using industrial output, Russia is first, China second, and the United States fifth. (Russian and Chinese industries are not as clean as U.S. industries.)

Which statistic is best? All of them together. Using only one would be like evaluating a center fielder only on his batting average or a quarterback only on yards gained per pass. You need more than one statistic to paint a complete picture.

Similarly, a recent e-mailer asked me whether a preschool program, which produced a four-month gain in vocabulary and math and cost $6,000 per kid per year, was worth it. I said that I couldn't tell. For one thing, the program likely produced health, socialization, and other outcomes besides the two mentioned. In addition, the real value of the program might not be clear for years: It took long-term evaluations of the outcomes of the Perry Preschool Project and the Chicago Family Centers project to establish that society gained about $7 for every dollar invested in these programs (Berrueta-Clement, Schweinhart, Barnett, Epstein, & Weikart, 1984; Reynolds, 2001).

Principles of Data Interpretation

Despite the limitations of individual statistics and public cynicism about being able to prove anything, people remain remarkably trusting when it comes to statistics. Best (2001) observes that "Most of the time, most people simply accept statistics without question" (p. 4). This acceptance would be dangerous at any time, but given today's polarized politicization of education (and virtually everything else), it is particularly hazardous now. Educators can avoid this danger by following some basic principles of data interpretation.

Go Back to the Data

Many people call the National Commission on Excellence in Education's 1983 report *A Nation at Risk* "the paper *Sputnik*" because it focused attention on education in the same way *Sputnik* did in 1954. Some still refer to it today as a "landmark" study. It's a landmark, all right: a golden treasury of selected, spun, distorted, and even manufactured statistics.

After opening with a blast of Cold-Warrior rhetoric, the good commissioners listed 13 indicators of the "risk," all referring to test scores. For example, "Over half the population of gifted students do not match their tested ability with comparable achievement in school." Given that achievement tests at the time were the principal means of selecting kids for gifted and talented programs, how could this possibly be true? When I sought an answer from some commissioners and their staff members, no one could remember where this statistic came from. How convenient.

Another statistic was, "Average tested achievement of students graduating from college is also lower." The United States has no program to test students graduating from college that would yield a statistic showing their "average tested achievement." What on earth could this mean? These examples illustrate a vital principle of data interpretation: If you find a statement the least bit suspect, ask to see the raw data.

Beware of Selectivity

Some of the other indicators in *A Nation at Risk* illustrate perhaps the most common misuse of statistics: selecting a statistic that, although accurate in itself, paints an incomplete and misleading picture. For instance, the report claimed that "there was a steady decline in science achievement scores of U.S. 17-year-olds as measured by national assessments in 1969, 1973, and 1977." This was true.

But the statement refers only to science, and only to 17-year-olds. What about the 9- and 13-year-olds also tested in national assessments? No "steady decline" in science for them. What about math? What about reading? No hint of any decline in either subject for any of the three age groups (National Center for Education Statistics [NCES], 2000).

The commissioners had nine trend lines available from NCES data (three ages times three subjects). Only one could be used to support crisis rhetoric, and that was the only one the commissioners mentioned.

Compare Rhetoric With the Numbers

Perhaps the most dangerous statistic is the one that Joel Best calls the *mutant* statistic. This statistic begins life as a legitimate datum, but mutates into something new and wrong. Best (2001) gives the example of the claim, widely circulated, that 150,000 women die in the United States each year from anorexia. The U.S. Census Bureau's *Statistical Abstract of the United States* shows that 55,000 women ages 15–44 die each year of all causes. Even if anorexia had killed all 55,000, given that anorexia mostly affects young women, it is unlikely that we can find another 95,000 anorexia victims younger than 15 and older than 44. In fact, the proper statistic is that 150,000 women *suffer* from anorexia—and even this number is probably a bit inflated because it was produced by an activist group attempting to call attention to the problem.

Mutant statistics afflict education data as well. *Washington Post* pundit George Will wrote in one column that almost half of Chicago's public school teachers sent their own children to private schools (Will, 1993a). This was true. The figure was 43 percent at the time, and that was the highest proportion in the United States. (Religion figured strongly in the Chicago teachers' decisions.) But over a period of six months, Will's neurons replaced "Chicago" with "the nation"; in another column, he wrote, "Nationally about half of urban public school teachers with school-age children send their children to private schools" (Will, 1993b). This was not true. According to data from the 2000 census, 17.5 percent of all urban families and 21.5 percent of urban public school teachers send their children to private schools. The rate ranges from 43.8 percent of teachers in the Philadelphia/Camden metro area down to 1.7 percent in Oklahoma City. In 21 of these top 50 cities, teachers use private schools less than urban families do (Doyle, DeSchryver, & Diepold, 2004).

Will's brain might have been addled by the work of Denis Doyle, whose reports using data from the 1980, 1990, and 2000 censuses have promoted the idea that public school teachers do send their kids to private schools in larger numbers than the general public does (Doyle, 1995; Doyle, DeSchryver, & Diepold, 2004; Doyle & Hartle, 1986). Doyle refers to teachers as "connoisseurs" of education, implying that if they send their kids to private schools, they must know something that the rest of us don't. He writes,

> With teachers choosing private schools, the truth is self-evident: While they work in public schools, they choose private schools for their own children because they believe they are better. (Doyle, 1995)

This statement creates the impression that all public school teachers in all types of communities use private schools. But if we look beyond the rhetoric to the actual statistics, we find these figures for the United States as a whole (Doyle, 1995; Doyle, DeSchryver, & Diepold, 2004):

	Teachers	General public
1990	12.1%	13.1%
2000	10.6%	12.1%

The numbers show that teachers made less use of private schools than the general public did. What's more, despite all the lionization of private schools and the demonization of public schools during the 1990s, a smaller proportion of both teachers and the general public had children in private schools in 2000 than in 1990.

Make Sure That Groups Are Comparable

The statistics on the percentages of children sent to private schools point to another principle of data interpretation: When comparing groups, make sure the groups are comparable. Teachers and the general public are not comparable. Teachers are more likely to have at least a bachelor's degree and less likely to live below the poverty line. We need to consider the implications of these and similar factors before we draw conclusions about the two groups' public school–private school choices.

This principle often comes into play in figuring out the impact of high-stakes graduation tests. In 2004, Massachusetts announced that 96 percent of its seniors had passed the state test and would graduate. This was true, but it was true only for people who had begun the 2003–2004 school year as seniors and who were still in school. Many in the class of 2004 were no longer present and accounted for. When that cohort of students started 9th grade, it contained 78,000 students; by the time it reached 12th grade, there were only 60,000. Eighteen thousand students had decamped (Wheelock, 2004).

We don't know what happened to these students. Some, of course, left the state and might well have passed the test and graduated if they had remained. But others were retained in grade and were no longer in the class of 2004. Some failed and dropped out or sought a General Equivalency Diploma. If we look at how many who started as 9th graders in the class of 2004 eventually graduated, we find rates ranging from 54 percent for Latino students to 80 percent for white students (Wheelock, 2004). We can't draw an accurate conclusion about the effects of high school graduation exams unless we consider all the groups, including those that did not graduate on time.

Know the Difference Between Rates and Scores

The Massachusetts example also illustrates another principle of data interpretation: Be aware of whether you are dealing with rates or scores. The two metrics can paint very different pictures of a situation. These days, most states are reporting some kind of rate: percent passing, percent proficient, or percent meeting state standards. But if we focus only on the proficiency cutoff, it doesn't matter whether the student exceeds it by one question or 40. We're looking at how many kids can jump over the barrier, not at how high they jump.

Moreover, using passing rates instead of scores can obscure the fact that the white-minority achievement gap may be increasing. Consider the theoretical data in Figure 8.1. If we look only at passing rates, black students have reduced the gap from 40 percent to 30 percent. But if we look at scores, the gap has actually increased from 16 points to 24 points.

This discrepancy might not be so important if the passing score actually meant something in terms of performance in the real world. But it doesn't. These passing scores are totally arbitrary. Some readers might recall that in my recent report on the condition of public education (Bracey, 2005), I awarded a Golden Apple to a student in Ohio because he refused to take the Ohio Proficiency Tests. It was not his act of defiance that garnered him a prize; it was the reasons he gave:

In 13 years of testing, Ohio has failed to conduct any studies linking scores on the proficiency test to college acceptance rates, dropout rates, college

Figure 8.1   Pass Rates and Average Scores Tell a Different Story

Pass rate—Gap closed by 10 points		
	2004	**2005**
Black students	60%	70%
White students	100%	100%
Gap	40	30
Average scores—Gap increased by 8 points		
	2004	**2005**
Black students	62	68
White students	78	92
Gap	16	24

These are hypothetical data. Score needed to pass = 60.

grades, income levels, incarceration rates, scores on military recruiting tests, or any other similar statistic. [The student was admitted to several colleges.] (p. 140)

Do the Arithmetic

Here's a final principle of data interpretation to examine on your own: Do the arithmetic. In 1995, an article in an education periodical (not *Educational Leadership*) stated that "Every year since 1950, the number of American children gunned down has doubled." Sit down with a calculator and a sheet of paper on which you write in one column the years from 1950 to 1994. Then assume that one child was "gunned down" in 1950 and let the figure double for each successive year. Have fun.

REFERENCES

Barringer, F. (2006, January 26). United States ranks 28th on environment, a new study says. *The New York Times,* p. A3.

Berrueta-Clement, J. R., Schweinhart, L. J., Barnett, W. S., Epstein, A. S., & Weikart, D. P. (1984). *Changed lives: The effects of the Perry preschool program on youths through age 19.* Ypsilanti, MI: High/Scope Press.

Best, J. (2001). *Damned lies and statistics: Untangling numbers from the media, politicians, and activists.* Berkeley: University of California Press.

Bracey, G. W. (2005). The fifteenth Bracey report on the condition of public education. *Phi Delta Kappan, 87*(2), 138–153.

Doyle, D. P. (1995). *Where connoisseurs send their children to school.* Washington, DC: Center for Education Reform.

Doyle, D. P., DeSchryver, D. A., & Diepold, B. (2004, September 7). *Where do public school teachers send their kids to school?* Washington, DC: Thomas B. Fordham Institute. Retrieved from http://www.edexcellence.net/foundation/publication/publication.cfm?id=333

Doyle, D. P., & Hartle, T. W. (1986). *Where public school teachers send their children to school: A preliminary analysis.* Washington, DC: American Enterprise Institute.

Huff, G. (1993). *How to lie with statistics.* New York: Norton.

National Center for Education Statistics (NCES). (2000). *NAEP 1999 trends in academic progress* (Report No. NCES-2000–469). Washington, DC: Author.

National Commission on Excellence in Education. (1983). *A nation at risk.* Washington, DC: Author. Retrieved from http://www.ed.gov/pubs/NatAtRisk

Reynolds, A. J. (2001, May/June). *Age 21 benefit cost analysis of the Chicago child-parent center program.* Paper presented to the Society for Prevention Research, Madison, Wisconsin.

Wheelock, A. (2004, June 8). *Massachusetts department of education "progress report" inflates "pass rates" for the class of 2004.* Retrieved from http://www.massparents.org/news/2004/passrate_2004.htm

Will, G. F. (1993a, March 7). When the state fails its citizens. *The Washington Post,* p. C7.

Will, G. F. (1993b, Aug. 26). Taking back education. *The Washington Post,* p. A27.

Projects for Further Exploration

1. As you read the articles in this book, keep a list of which methodology is used in each, even if a full discussion of the methods is not included in each one. This should sharpen your ability to evaluate information.

2. Pick a reading from this book that you find particularly interesting and do a library search for another article on the same topic. If possible, compare different methodologies to see if they come up with similar findings.

3. Do a library search for *"class size"* (use quotation marks around it) and *achievement* to see if the articles you find correspond to the arguments made in the article by Biddle and Berliner in this chapter.

3

Schooling in a Social Context

Educational Environments

With an introduction to theories and methods (Chapters 1 and 2) used to study educational systems, we can now begin our study of actual schools. We start by examining the contexts (environments) that surround schools and affect how schools work. No education system exists in a vacuum. In this chapter we consider the *environment* as the part of the open systems model (discussed in the Introduction) that influences schools from outside school walls. If schools ignore the environment in which they are located, they do so at their own peril. Results could be loss of financing, accreditation, and community support. To focus only on what happens behind the closed doors of the school or classroom misses the total picture of the educational system. Changing values in society and the community, political and economic constraints, home environments of students and school personnel, business and technology, special-interest groups, and other external influences affect what happens within school walls. In addition, the social context or environment helps to define the purpose, meaning, functions, and limitations of education.

Each of the readings in this section provides an example of the educational system's environment. The first reading considers political involvement in educational systems. John W. Meyer and Brian Rowan discuss the institution of education as it operates in the larger political context. In most countries, control of schools is in the hands of the national political system. The dominant goal of governments is to incorporate students into society by meeting the educational and skill needs of the society. To find schools that are entities independent of or separate from the state is rare. In their classic book from which the first reading in this chapter comes, Meyer and Rowan discuss the United States, a country that allows a degree of local control, "decoupling" schools from some external federal political and environmental pressures. The authors use the term *decoupling* to describe the discrepancy between what schools do and how schools and their environments evaluate the outcomes. In practice, U.S. schools are organized to meet different internal and external pressures. Decoupling serves the purpose of protecting local schools from too much external scrutiny, resulting in more autonomy at the local level and little evidence of ineffectiveness, conflict, or inconsistency. Furthermore, decoupling occurs with the tacit agreement of all players, from the community to school personnel. Because schools cannot ignore important aspects of their environments, especially those that are necessary for support and even survival, we consider several environmental factors and how they can influence educational settings: the participants in schools, the public, families, technology, governments, religion, and other institutions. For example, each of *the participants* in a school brings values, beliefs, attitudes, abilities, and behaviors into the school. Add home dynamics (including what each participant had for breakfast!), and we have a picture of some of the environmental complexities brought by participants that affect schools. For example, students are processed in the school system. They are required to attend school to learn skills and knowledge that are necessary for success in the world outside school. Teachers and administrative staff members are also participants. Participants bring in unique characteristics. They differ in age and educational background, and they can differ in social class background, factors that can add complexity to school interactions.

In addition, *the public* holds attitudes on school policies, curriculum, and funding. Attitudes reflect opinions of the parents who send their children to school, of community members who pay taxes to support schools, and of many political and religious interest groups that express their feelings about school policies. The significance of public opinion is that school policies and support for schools often reflect attitudes of the community. Each year the Phi Delta Kappa/Gallup Poll of the Public's Attitudes Toward the Public Schools surveys a sample of more than 1,000 U.S. adults on questions related to school issues. Responses to the survey indicate areas of most concern to the public and opinions on current issues. In 2013, key issues and attitudes included lack of financial support, lack of discipline, overcrowded schools, lack of parental support, testing regulations, fighting, difficulty getting good teachers, and use of drugs. These public attitudes influence passage of levies and are the focus of other demands on schools (Bushaw & Lopez, 2013, p. 20).

Parents and *family* have direct interest in what their children are learning, and parents can be quite vocal about agendas for their children's schooling. Some schools require parental participation for students to attend, and many educational policy makers point out the value of parental involvement in and outside of school. However, how, when, and why parents are involved is important in determining the impact involvement will have on individual children's achievement (Pomerantz, Moorman, & Litwack, 2007).

One example of an area of research for sociologists of education has been the effects of parental involvement in children's homework. Especially in elementary and high school, positive involvement can be effective in raising achievement; the effectiveness even varies by subject matter (Patall, Cooper, & Robinson, 2008). After-school and summer experiences of children are also directly related to student achievement. Students with higher socioeconomic status tend to have experiences that enhance their academic performance. Music lessons, sports lessons, camps, or visits to museums influence their achievement (Alexander, Entwisle, & Olson, 2007; Bennett, Litz, & Jayaram, 2012; Epstein, 1987, 1988).

Children who come from poor families start out with a strike against them in their efforts to achieve in school. In the second article, Pedro A. Noguera discusses the problems faced by children raised in poverty and presents an approach that can break the cycle of poverty and improve the children's learning environment.

Technology also affects what students and teachers bring into the school setting as well as what the schools teach students. Most studies of computer access and school achievement confirm that technology improves student achievement (North Central Regional Educational Laboratory, 2010). Yet keeping up to date with technology is a challenge for budget-strapped schools and busy teachers. Almost all schools have Internet access, but the use of computers differs by the socioeconomic composition of schools (Purcell, Heaps, Buchanan, & Friedrich, 2013). The digital divide reflects the community socioeconomic differences (Attewell, 2001).

Because all *institutions* in society are interrelated, influence and pressure on schools often come from all other institutions in the educational environment. *Federal, state, and local government institutions* play a major role in the educational environment and in policy decisions, in part because the money they provide to schools is essential to operations. In the Race to the Top policies of the Obama administration, expectations are laid out for schools and districts, such as the requirement that schoolchildren pass proficiency tests; failure to do so places a red failing mark on the school district. These practices can disadvantage schools with high numbers of children living in poverty, especially immigrants and refugees (Winerip, 2010). Two of the articles in this section discuss government as an environmental influence on schools. Over half of the state governments require high school exit exams, although their effect on curriculum and student achievement is mixed as discussed in this chapter's third reading by John Robert Warren and Eric Grodsky. The funding for schools is based on federal and state government mandates, discussed in the next reading by Augustina H. Reyes and Gloria M. Rodriguez on patterns of school funding.

An example of another institution that causes conflict for schools is *religion*. Separation of church and state has been a guiding principle supporting freedom of religious practice since the founding of the United States. Yet where to draw the line has been a bone of contention in many communities. The line is challenged in discussions of what constitutes school prayer; whether to allow released time for religious classes in public schools; what support from taxpayer monies can legally be spent on parochial school students for transportation, free meals, counseling, and other services; what standards private parochial schools should meet; and what curriculum and textbooks to use, especially when the topics are related to religious beliefs such as creationism. In the final reading, Edwin C. Darden discusses the influence of religion and the courts on educational systems.

Another example of the influence on school environments is the relationship between the *economic institution—business enterprises—*and schools. To what extent should schools be influenced by pressures from the business community? Should businesses have a say in what schools teach? After all, they are the main source of jobs for students on completion of schooling. Many argue no, that education should remain independent of external influences with profit motives. One concern related to business interests and schools has been the advertising that crept into the hallways and classrooms. From soft drink companies providing incentives to schools to have their products be the only choice on school campuses to labels of popular consumer items found in textbooks, on book covers, and on clothing worn to school, business ventures have subtly inserted themselves into our schools. Many schools are now eliminating soda and candy machines due to concerns from parents and governmental agencies about the health and obesity of children.

The importance of any particular part of the environment changes over time. For example, when the school needs to pass a levy to obtain operating funds, the voters become a highly salient community. When school administrators face pressure from teachers' unions at contract time, their negotiations take on high salience. At other times, voters or unions take a secondary position in importance compared to other pressing issues in the environment at the time.

The readings in this chapter present examples of environmental influences and constraints on what happens in schools and classrooms and how the environment affects educational achievement. The bottom line is whether schools are preparing children to be productive members of society, a question that we discuss throughout this book and that is of much debate among experts, researchers, and the various public constituencies of schools.

REFERENCES

Alexander, K. L., Entwisle, D. R., & Olson, L. S. (2007). Lasting consequences of the summer learning gap. *American Sociological Review, 72*(2), 167–177.

Attewell, P. (2001). The first and second digital divides. *Sociology of Education, 74*(3), 252–259.

Bennett, P. R., Lutz, A. C., & Jayaram, L. (2012). Beyond the schoolyard: The role of parenting logics, financial resources, and social institutions in the social class gap in structured activity participation. *Sociology of Education, 85*(1), 131–157.

Bushaw, W. J., & Lopez, S. J. (2013). The 45th annual Phi Delta Kappa/Gallup Poll of the Public's Attitudes Toward the Public Schools: Which way do we go? *Phi Delta Kappan, 95*(1), 9–25.

Epstein, J. (1987). *Target: An examination of parallel school and family structures that promote student motivation and achievement* (Report 6). Baltimore: Johns Hopkins University, Center for Research on Elementary and Middle Schools.

Epstein, J. (1988). Effects on student achievement of teachers' practices of parent involvement. In S. B. Silvem (Ed.), *Literacy through family, community, and school interaction* (pp. 261–276). Greenwich, CT: JAI Press.

Natriello, G. (2006). *Bridging the second digital divide: What can sociologists of education contribute?* New York: EdLab, Teachers College, Columbia University.

North Central Regional Educational Laboratory. (2010). *Critical issue: Technology: A catalyst for teaching and learning in the classroom.* Retrieved from http://www.ncrel.org/sdrs/areas/issues/methods/technlgy/te600.htm

Patall, E. A., Cooper, H., & Robinson, J. C. (2008). Parent involvement in homework: A research synthesis. *Review of Educational Research, 78*(4), 1039–1101.

Pomerantz, E. M., Moorman, E. A., & Litwack, S. D. (2007). The how, whom, and why of parents' involvement in children's academic lives: More is not always better. *Review of Educational Research, 77*(3), 373–410.

Purcell, K., Heaps, A., Buchanan, J., & Friedrich, L. (2013). *How teachers are using technology at home and in their classrooms.* Washington, DC: Pew Research Center.

Van Dijk, J., & Hacker, K. (2003). The digital divide as a complex and dynamic phenomenon. *The Information Society, 19,* 315–326.

Winerip, M. (2010, July 18). A popular principal, wounded by government's good intentions. *The New York Times.* Retrieved from http://www.nytimes.com/2010/07/19/education/19winerip.html

THE STRUCTURE OF EDUCATIONAL ORGANIZATIONS

John W. Meyer and Brian Rowan

To begin our exploration of the social context of educational systems, John W. Meyer and Brian Rowan present a macrolevel interpretation of the school in modern society. Schools serve individual, family, and societal needs, and in many societies they are controlled by centralized political authorities. By preparing youth for positions in the social class and economic stratification systems, educational bureaucracies serve the societies in which they are located. Educational systems prepare and credential individuals for participation in society, especially postindustrial corporate information society. By meeting the expectations of external political and corporate organizations, schools gain legitimacy and resources to carry out their missions and to be innovative. Whereas educational systems and authority in most societies are centralized, the U.S. system is decentralized, with controls at the local and state levels. This means that educators are less secure in their positions because they are beholden to sometimes-conflicting local interests.

Questions to consider for this reading:

1. How do schools serve the needs of the political and corporate sectors of society?

2. What theoretical approach or approaches relate most closely to the ideas in this reading?

3. How does credentialing link schools to other institutions in society, such as family and the economy?

THE ORGANIZATION OF SCHOOLING: ANOTHER INTERPRETATION

The explanation developed here begins with the context in which educational organizations are presently found. Modern education today takes place in large-scale, public bureaucracies. The rise of this kind of educational system is closely related to the worldwide trend of national development. The first step in our argument, therefore, is to relate national development to the organization of education.

The Growth of Corporate Schooling

[W]e know that bureaucratic schooling has not arisen from a need to coordinate and standardize instruction, for this is precisely what

From *The Structure of Educational Organizations: Environments and Organizations* (pp. 217–221), by J. Meyer and B. Rowan, 1978, New York: John Wiley & Sons. Copyright 1978 by John Meyer and Brian Rowan. Reprinted with permission.

modern American educational organizations do not do. Nor do these bureaucratic organizations merely fund and administer an exchange between educational professionals and families needing educational services. Educational bureaucracies present themselves not as units servicing education but as organizations that embody educational purposes in their collective structure. A theory of their emergence and dominance should explain why these bureaucracies assume jurisdiction over educational instruction. The most plausible explanation is that modern schools produce education for society, not for individuals or families. In the nineteenth and twentieth centuries, national societies everywhere took over the function of defining and managing the socialization of their citizen personnel (Coombs, 1968; Meyer & Rubinson, 1975; Ramirez, 1974). In national societies, education is both a right and duty of citizenship (Bendix, 1964). It also becomes an important way of gaining status and respect (for example, see Blau & Duncan, 1967). For reasons that do not require elaborate discussion here, education becomes the central agency defining personnel—both citizen and elite—for the modern state and economy.

Since World War II, the trend toward corporate control of education has intensified. As nation-states have consolidated their control over a growing number of elements of social life, they have established educational systems to incorporate citizens into the political, economic, and status order of society. This incorporation is managed by a large public bureaucracy that uniformly extends its standardization and authority through all localities. Thus, educational organizations have come to be increasingly structured by centers of political authority (Meyer & Rubinson, 1975). Bailyn (1960), Field (1972), Katz (1968), and Tyack (1974) describe the steps of this process in pre-twentieth-century American history. First local, and later national, elites became concerned with the social control of peripheral citizen groups—who need control precisely because they are citizens. At first, the rural New Englanders who escaped from the control of clergy and town community (Bailyn,

1960), then the Irish immigrants (Field, 1972; Katz, 1968), and finally the great waves of nineteenth century immigration (Tyack, 1974) created the pressures to control, standardize, and coordinate the educational system. As these steps progressed, the impetus to organize schooling on a large scale—to certify and classify pupils, to certify teachers, to accredit schools, and to control formal curriculum—gained force.

The growth of corporate control of education has major implications for educational organizations. As citizen personnel are increasingly sorted and allocated to positions in the social structure on the basis of classified or certified educational properties, the ritual classifications of education—type of student, topic, teacher, or school—come to have substantial value in what might be called the societal identity "market." A workable identity market presupposes a standardized, trustworthy currency of social typifications that is free from local anomalies. Uniform categories of instruction are therefore developed, and there is a detailed elaboration of the standardized and certified properties comprising an educational identity.

The result of this social expansion of education is a basic change in social structure. Education comes to consist, not of a series of private arrangements between teachers and students, but rather of a set of standardized public credentials used to incorporate citizen personnel into society. Society and its stratification system come to be composed of a series of typifications having educational meaning—ordinary citizens are presumed to have basic literacy. Strata above ordinary citizens are composed of high school and college graduates. The upper levels contain credentialed professionals, such as doctors and lawyers.

Thus, as societies and nation-states use education to define their basic categories of personnel, a large-scale educational bureaucracy emerges to standardize and manage the production of these categories. The credentials that give individuals status and membership in the wider collectivity must come under collective control. Such collective control would not be necessary if instruction were conceived of as a merely private matter between individuals and teachers. But, as educational organizations emerge as the credentialing agency of modern society and as modern citizens see their educational and corporate identities linked—that is, as education becomes the theory of personnel in modern society—it is consequently standardized and controlled.

Society thus becomes "schooled" (Illich, 1971). Education comes to be understood by corporate actors according to the schooling rule: Education is a certified teacher teaching a standardized curricular topic to a registered student in an accredited school. The nature of schooling is thus socially defined by reference to a set of standardized categories the legitimacy of which is publicly shared. As the categories and credentials of schooling gain importance in allocation and membership processes, the public comes to expect that they will be controlled and standardized. The large-scale public bureaucracy created to achieve this standardization is now normatively constrained by the expectations of the schooling rule. To a large degree, then, education is coordinated by shared social understandings that define the roles, topics, and contents of educational organizations.

The Organizational Management of Standardized Classifications

The political consolidation of society and the importance of education for the allocation of people to positions in the economic and stratification system explain the rise of large-scale educational bureaucracies. These processes also explain why educational organizations focus so tightly on the ritual classifications of education. Educational organizations are created to produce schooling for corporate society. They create standard types of graduates from standard categories of pupils using standard types of teachers and topics. As their purposes and structures are defined and institutionalized in the rules, norms, and ideologies of the wider society, the legitimacy of schools and their ability to

mobilize resources depend on maintaining congruence between their structure and these socially shared categorical understandings of education (Dowling & Pfeffer, 1975; Meyer & Rowan, 1977; Parsons, 1956).

Consider this matter from the viewpoint of any rational college president or school superintendent. The whole school will dissolve in conflict and illegitimacy if the internal and external understanding of its accredited status is in doubt: If it has too few Ph.D.'s or properly credentialed teachers on its faculty, it may face reputational, accreditational, or even legal problems. If it has one too many "economics" courses and one too few "history" courses (leave aside their actual content), similar disasters may occur as the school falls short of externally imposed accrediting standards. No matter what they have learned, graduates may have difficulty finding jobs. No matter what the school teaches, it may not be capable of recruiting funds or teachers. Thus, the creation of institutionalized rules defining and standardizing education creates a system in which schools come to be somewhat at the mercy of the ritual classifications. Failure to incorporate certified personnel or to organize instruction around the topics outlined in accreditation rules can bring conflict and illegitimacy.

At the same time, the creation of institutionalized rules provides educational organizations with enormous resources. First, the credentials, classifications, and categories of schooling constitute a language that facilitates exchange between school and society. Social agencies often provide local schools with "categorical funding" to support the instruction of culturally disadvantaged or educationally handicapped students or to support programs in bilingual or vocational education. Second, schools can exploit the system of credentials and classifications in order to gain prestige. They can carefully attend to the social evaluations of worth given to particular ritual classifications and can maximize their honorific worth by hiring prestigious faculty, by incorporating programs that are publicly defined as "innovative," or by upgrading their status from junior college to four-year college. Finally, the school relies on the ritual classifications to provide order. Social actors derive their identities from the socially defined categories of education and become committed to upholding these identities within the context of their school activities. To the degree that actors take on the obligation to be [a part of the system] (Goffman, 1967), the whole educational system retains its plausibility.

In modern society, then, educational organizations have good reason to tightly control properties defined by the wider social order. By incorporating externally defined types of instruction, teachers, and students into their formal structure, schools avoid illegitimacy and discreditation. At the same time, they gain important benefits. In schools using socially agreed-on classifications, participants become committed to the organization. This is especially true when these classifications have high prestige (McCall & Simmons, 1966). And, by labeling students or instructional programs so that they conform to institutionally supported programs, schools obtain financial resources. In short, the rewards for attending to external understandings are an increased ability to mobilize societal resources for organizational purposes.

The Avoidance of Evaluation and Inspection

We have explained why schools attend to ritual classifications, but we have not explained why they do not attend (as organizations) to instruction. There are two [primary] ways that instructional activities can be controlled in modern education bureaucracies. First, many of the properties of educational identities may be certified in terms of examinations. Second, many of the ritual classifications involve a reorganization of educational activity, and some school systems organize an inspection system to make sure these implications are carried through. Thus, two basic kinds of instructional controls are available to educational organizations—the certification of status by testing, and/or the inspection of instructional activity to ensure conformity to rules.

Our explanation of the loose control of instruction in U.S. school systems must in part focus on specific features of U.S. society, since most other societies have educational bureaucracies that assignment to a classification such as student, graduate, or teacher is determined by various tests, most often controlled by national ministries of education. Also, national inspectors are often employed to attempt to make sure that teachers and schools conform to national standards of practice, regardless of the educational outcome. Thus, in most societies the state, through a ministry of education, controls systems of inspection or examination that manage the ritual categories of education by controlling either output or instructional procedure (Ramirez, 1974; Rubinson, 1974).

In American society, tests are used in profusion. However, most of these tests are neither national nor organizational but, rather, are devices of the individual teacher. The results seldom leave the classroom and are rarely used to measure instructional output. In the United States, the most common national tests that attempt to standardize local output differences—the Scholastic Aptitude Test (SAT) and the Graduate Record Examination (GRE)—are creatures of private organization. Further, only the New York State Board of Regents examination approximates (and at that in a pale way) an attempt to standardize curriculum throughout a political unit by using an examination system.

The apparent explanation for this lack of central control of instruction in American education is the decentralization of the system. Schools are in large part locally controlled and locally funded. While higher levels of authority in state and federal bureaucracies have made many attempts to impose evaluative standards on the educational system, the pressures of continued localism defeat them; category systems that delegate certification or evaluation rights to the schools themselves are retained. The reason for this is clear. A national evaluation system would define almost all the children in some communities as successes and almost all those in others as failures. This could work in a nationally controlled system, but it is much too dangerous in a system that depends on legitimating itself in and obtaining resources from local populations. Why, for instance, should the state of Mississippi join in a national credentialing system that might define a great proportion of its schools and graduates as failures? It is safer to adapt the substantive standards of what constitutes, say, a high school graduate to local circumstances and to specify in state laws only categories at some remove from substantive competence.

There is yet another way in which the institutional pattern of localism reduces organizational controls over instruction. In the United States, the legitimacy of local control in some measure deprofessionalizes school administrators at all levels (in contrast to European models). They do not carry with them the authority of the central, national, professional, and bureaucratic structures and the elaborate ideological backing such authority brings with it. American administrators must compromise and must further lose purely professional authority by acknowledging their compromised role. They do not have tenure, and their survival is dependent on laypersons in the community, not professionals. Their educational authority of office is, therefore, lower than that of their European counterparts, especially in areas dealing with central educational matters such as instruction and curriculum. This situation is precisely analogous to the "red" versus "expert" conflict found in many organizations in communist societies, where organizational managers must often act contrary to their expert opinion in order to follow the party line. The profusion of local pressures in American society turns school administrators into "reds" as it were . . .

OVERVIEW OF THE ARGUMENT

With the growth of corporate society, especially the growth of nation-states, education comes into exchange with society. Schooling—the bureaucratic standardization of ritual classifications—emerges and becomes the dominant form of educational organization. Schools become organized in relation to these ritual categories in order to gain support and legitimacy. In America, the local and pluralistic control of schools causes these classifications to have little impact on the actual instructional activities of local schools. Thus the official classifications of education, although enforced in public respects, are decoupled from actual activity and can contain a good deal of internal inconsistency without harm. As a result, American schools in practice contain multiple realities, each organized with respect to different internal or exogenous pressures. These multiple realities conflict so little because they are buffered from each other by the logic of confidence that runs through the system.

In this fashion, educational organizations have enjoyed enormous success and have managed to satisfy an extraordinary range of external and internal constituents. The standardized categories of American society and its stratification system are maintained, while the practical desires of local community constituents and the wishes of teachers, who are highly satisfied with their jobs, are also catered to. As new constituents rise up and make new demands, these pressures can be accommodated within certain parts of the system with minimal impact on other parts. A great deal of adaptation and change can occur without disrupting actual activity. And, conversely, the activities of teachers and pupils can change a good deal, even though the abstract categories have remained constant.

REFERENCES

Bailyn, B. (1960). *Education in the forming of American society*. Chapel Hill: University of North Carolina Press.

Bendix, R. (1964). *Nation building and citizenship*. New York: Wiley.

Blau, P. M., & Duncan, O. D. (1967). *The American occupational structure*. New York: Wiley.

Coombs, P. H. (1968). *The world educational crisis*. New York: Oxford University Press.

Dowling, J., & Pfeffer, J. (1975). Organizational legitimacy: Social values and organizational behavior. *Pacific Sociological Review, 18*(1), 122–136.

Field, A. (1972). *Educational reform and manufacturing development, Massachusetts 1837–1865* (Unpublished doctoral dissertation). University of California, Berkeley.

Goffman, E. (1967). *Interaction ritual*. Garden City, NY: Doubleday.

Illich, I. (1971). *Deschooling society*. New York: Harper & Row.

Katz, M. (1968). *The irony of early school reform*. Boston: Beacon.

McCall, G. J., & Simmons, J. L. (1966). *Identities and interactions*. New York: Free Press.

Meyer, J. W., & Rowan, B. (1977). Institutionalized organizations: Formal structure as myth and ceremony. *American Journal of Sociology, 83*(2), 340–363.

Meyer, J. W., & Rubinson, R. (1975). Education and political development. *Review of Research in Education, 3,* 134–162.

Parsons, T. (1956). Suggestions for a sociological approach to the theory of organizations. *Administrative Science Quarterly, 1*(1), 63–85.

Ramirez, F. O. (1974). *Societal corporateness and status conferral* (Unpublished doctoral dissertation). Stanford University: Palo Alto, California.

Rubinson, R. (1974). *The political construction of education* (Unpublished doctoral dissertation). Stanford University: Palo Alto, California.

Tyack, D. B. (1974). *The one best system*. Cambridge, MA: Harvard University Press.

A Broader and Bolder Approach Uses Education to Break the Cycle of Poverty

Pedro A. Noguera

The social environment including the neighborhood and family that is the background for some children is not conducive to learning. So argues Pedro A. Noguera. While some school policy makers base policy on the idea that every child can learn and should be encouraged to learn regardless of circumstances, others including Noguera argue that poverty and related social conditions affect children's ability to learn. Middle-class children are more likely to receive external academic and social support from parents and communities. Where poverty is endemic and children face issues of poor health, safety, and lack of parental support, learning is more difficult.

Noguera describes a reform plan called Broader, Bolder Approach (BBA) that is directed at some of the issues of concern for children growing up in poverty. A guiding principle behind the reforms is that the community and schools must work together to meet student needs.

Questions to consider for this reading:

1. Why is it not enough to say that "all children can learn"?

2. What are three factors that affect the learning of children in poverty?

3. How does the Broader, Bolder Approach propose to provide educational opportunity for children in poverty?

Recognizing that poverty has a profound influence on academic outcomes is not a new idea. In fact, a large body of research over several decades has shown that poor children face enormous education challenges specifically related to poverty (Coleman et al., 1966; Rothstein, 2004). However, recently it's become fashionable for policy makers and reformers to criticize anyone who points to poverty as an obstacle to learning and higher achievement. Loudly proclaiming "no excuses," these reformers claim that large numbers of ineffective classroom teachers, not poverty, are the real obstacles to improving academic outcomes for poor children. While it is absolutely the case that poor children need dedicated, passionate, and effective teachers and principals to be successful, there is no evidence that even the best schools can overcome the effects of poverty on their own. However, a growing number of "reformers" steadfastly make this assertion, and these individuals have enormous influence over education policy.

From "A Broader and Bolder Approach Uses Education to Break the Cycle of Poverty," by Pedro A. Noguera, 2011, *Phi Delta Kappan, 93*(3), pp. 9–14. Reprinted with permission. Copyright November 2011 by Phi Delta Kappa International. All rights reserved. Reprinted by permission.

In an op-ed piece in *The Washington Post* last year [2010], Joel Klein, former New York City Schools chancellor, Michael Lomax, chief executive of the United Negro College Fund, and Janet Murguía, president and chief executive of the National Council of La Raza, wrote:

> In the debate over how to fix American public education, many believe that schools alone cannot overcome the impact that economic disadvantage has on a child, that life outcomes are fixed by poverty and family circumstances, and that education doesn't work until other problems are solved. This theory is, in some ways, comforting for educators.
>
> After all, if schools make only a marginal difference, we can stop faulting ourselves for failing to make them work well for millions of children . . . Problem is, the theory is wrong. It's hard to know how wrong—because we haven't yet tried to make the changes that would tell us—but plenty of evidence demonstrates that schools can make an enormous difference despite the challenges presented by poverty and family background (Klein, Lomax, & Murguía, 2010).

While it might seem encouraging for education and civil rights leaders to assert that poverty isn't an obstacle to higher student achievement, the evidence does not support such claims. Over 50 years, numerous studies have documented how poverty and related social conditions (e.g., lack of access to health care, early childhood education, stable housing, etc.) affect child development and student achievement. The research never suggests that poor children are incapable of learning or that poverty itself should be regarded as a learning disability. Rather, research suggests that poor children encounter obstacles that often adversely affect their development and learning outcomes. To ignore this reality and make bold assertions that all children can achieve while doing nothing to address the outside-of-school challenges they face is neither fair nor a sound basis for developing public policy.

Despite compelling evidence that education policy must devise ways to at least mitigate the harmful effects of poverty on student achievement and child development, most state and federal policies have failed to do so. However, there is growing awareness among a number of educators, mayors, and policy advocates of the need to do so based on the realization that a great deal can be done to counter the effects of poverty on children's lives and their education.

POVERTY INFLUENCES LEARNING

A substantial body of evidence shows that concentrated poverty in urban neighborhoods and the adverse social conditions that typically accompany it affect the performance of students and of schools in at least three important ways.

#1. External support: Academic and social support is less available to students outside of school.

Sociologist James Coleman (1998) coined the term "social closure" to describe the mutually reinforcing partnerships between parents and schools in healthy schools and communities. Coleman found that supportive relationships between parents and teachers promote and strengthen values and norms that positively influence student achievement. He also said such relationships serve as an essential ingredient of school success.

In her research on parents, sociologist Annette Lareau (2003) found that middle-class parents provide their children with a broad assortment of advantages (e.g., access to private tutors, summer enrichment camps, homework support, etc.) that improve the likelihood of academic success, while poor parents were typically less able to provide this type of support. Moreover, in inner-city communities, social closure between parents and schools is generally weak or even nonexistent because racial and class differences contribute to a lack of trust (Noguera, 2003; Lawrence-Lightfoot, 2003). Instead of working together to benefit children, schools in poor communities frequently experience difficulty in getting parents involved at school and are more likely to experience antagonism and even hostility with the parents they serve, particularly at schools with a long history of poor performance.

#2. Environmental obstacles: Adverse conditions influence students' health, safety, and well-being, which invariably influence learning.

In cities and towns where poverty is concentrated, rates of inter-personal violence tend to be higher, health indicators tend to be more negative, stress and overall psychological and emotional well-being tends to be substantially worse (Kirp 2011; Noguera 2003). This is due to the lack of services as well as what sociologist William Julius Wilson has described as a "concentration effect" (1987). A substantial body of research has shown that the quality of life and the overall health of children in poor neighborhoods are substantially lower than for middle-class children. Not surprisingly, these conditions influence academic and developmental outcomes (Adelman & Taylor, 1999; Syme, 2004; Eccles & Gootman, 2002). Without the resources to support children or a strategy to protect children from the harmful effects of dangerous and even toxic conditions in their communities (Greenberg & Schneider, 1996), schools can be overwhelmed. Not surprisingly, the inability to respond to the nonacademic needs of their students often compromises the ability of schools to meet the academic needs. For example, several studies on federally funded Head Start programs have shown that the benefits of early childhood education are often undermined when children don't receive ongoing support, both in and outside of school, after they enter kindergarten (RAND, 2007). Similarly, a study on the long-term consequences of infant exposure to substance abuse has shown that such children are no more likely to experience school failure than nonaffected children from the same neighborhoods; the harmful effects of the environment can be as devastating as early exposure to drugs (RAND, 2007).

#3. Negative social capital: Adverse conditions undermine the ability of parents and schools to influence the character of schools and ensure that they serve their interests.

Adverse environmental conditions in poor communities, such as violence and substance abuse, tend to negatively influence the ability of parents and schools to develop the social capital to draw upon local resources to further student learning and promote healthy development. In middle-class communities, schools often draw on community resources to augment services they either can't afford or simply can't provide. In fact, real estate agents often use the viability and attractiveness of local schools as a selling point to attract homebuyers.

In contrast, schools in high-poverty communities often function in isolation from other community organizations and agencies (churches, social service agencies, recreation centers, etc.), either because school staff lack relationships with these groups or because they perceive the neighborhood as hostile and potentially dangerous. If residents perceive the school as undesirable, residents who can will go out of their way to avoid sending their children there. Sociologist Lois Wacquant (2002) has argued that, in many poor urban areas, public schools become negative assets that actually undermine the well-being of their communities. Even though public schools are often the most stable social institutions in poor neighborhoods (largely because of public funding), when they function poorly because they're overwhelmed by the needs of their students, they may become formidable obstacles to neighborhood improvement and stability (Noguera, 2003).

None of this means poverty is destiny, or that the obstacles are so significant that they can't be overcome. There are many inspiring examples of poor children who manage to overcome obstacles related to poverty to achieve success in life. But these individuals are always the exceptions. More often than not, when the obstacles confronting poor communities are ignored, efforts to help students achieve and schools improve are less effective.

MITIGATING THE EFFECTS OF POVERTY

While expecting a single school to counter the effects of poverty on its own is unrealistic, a small but growing number of American schools are finding ways to reduce some of the effects. Mitigation is not the same as solving a problem, but it's nonetheless an important strategy for schools to employ.

In Newark, N.J., for example, the Broader, Bolder Approach (BBA) reform plan is developing a comprehensive school reform strategy. Operating in seven schools in Newark's Central Ward (six kindergarten through 8th-grade schools and one large comprehensive high school), BBA has introduced school-based interventions that are responsive to the issues and challenges. Through these interventions, social services, and a concerted effort to increase civic engagement, BBA is working to ensure that environmental hardships related to poverty don't undermine efforts to transform schools. With funding from the Ford, Victoria, and Prudential foundations, the BBA effort commenced two years before the $100-million donation from Facebook's Mark Zuckerberg came to Newark.

BBA is working to:

- Expand learning opportunities for students through quality early childhood education and by extending the traditional school day;
- Enrich the curriculum through enhanced literacy development in all content areas and greater emphasis on project-based learning; and
- Build critical partnerships that will strengthen the capacity of schools to respond to student needs and enable community interests to come together so parents and their allies can hold schools and their leaders accountable for academic outcomes.

The BBA strategy draws on research that suggests a more comprehensive approach is needed to increase academic outcomes for poor students and to improve schools that serve them (Blaue & Currie, 2006; Comer, 1988; Dryfoos, 1993; Rothstein, 2004; Waldfogel & Lahaie, 2007). The community schools movement, which provides students (and often their families) with access to mental health and other social supports at school sites is but one example of how service organizations have partnered with schools in high-poverty urban areas to

address the social needs of children (Dryfoos, Quinn, & Barkin, 2005). In a recent book, David Kirp (2011) cites the full service schools developed by the Children's Aid Society and Communities in Schools as models that have helped schools meet both the academic and nonacademic needs of children. A growing body of research shows that when schools can offer students access to a variety of social services (e.g., licensed social workers or psychologists, nurse practitioners, or dental services), academic and developmental outcomes for children can improve (Darling-Hammond, 2010). Similarly, research shows that extending the school day before and after traditional school hours, as well as requiring students to attend school on Saturdays and lengthening the school year, can have a tremendous impact on achievement (Kirp, 2011). When carried out in tandem, these practices enable schools to meet many of the needs that typically undermine student learning and child development.

SCHOOL REFORM IS COMMUNITY REFORM

Newark has embraced BBA because there is a growing awareness that the city needs new strategies for developing its human capital before it can experience sustained economic and social renaissance. Transforming schools so they're more effective in providing young people in Newark with an education that can make it possible for them to participate fully in the economic rebirth of the city is widely recognized as essential.

Improving Newark schools will enable the city to address many of the social and economic challenges that have prevented residents from experiencing a superior quality of life. Specifically, the BBA strategy aims at combining research-based education strategies with school-based social services, after-school programs, and interventions to increase the capacity of schools to respond to issues that are endemic to the social and environmental context (e.g., the need for health, nutrition, jobs, safety, etc.). The assumption is that such a full-service approach would enable Newark schools to better meet student needs.

The BBA strategy is based on the theory that improving the schools could spur economic development and improve the quality of life for a greater number of residents. Though this proposition has never been tested at such a large scale before, the theory behind BBA is based on the recognition that education is both a *cause* of many of the problems that plague the city and a potential *solution* to those problems.

BBA seeks to transform schools by creating a series of strategic partnerships between schools, businesses, universities, hospitals, local government, and an array of neighborhood-based service organizations. Such partnerships are designed to increase local support for schools and enhance the social capital of students and their families. Policy advocates of civic capacity building have argued that providing schools with substantial increases in external support is the most cost-effective means of delivering the resources and support they need. The theory holds that such support will lead to greater accountability, better functioning schools, and higher levels of student achievement.

A combination of social, economic, and political problems has historically constrained efforts to improve Newark schools. These problems are also at the root of many of the current challenges confronting its residents. Social isolation and economic marginalization (Wilson, 1987) have an enormous influence upon employment opportunities, health and welfare, aspirations and behavior, and the non-cognitive traits typically associated with academic success (Bryk et al., 2010). Experience in Newark (and several other cities) has shown that when education reforms fail to consider how environmental factors influence students and schools, sustainable improvements in student academic outcomes are difficult to achieve (Noguera, 2003; Payne, 2008; Rothstein, 2004). The BBA strategy seeks to mitigate the detrimental effects of the environment by developing the

capacity of schools to respond to student needs and by drawing on support and resources from local institutions.

The BBA strategy also seeks to transform how urban public schools typically serve low-income children of color and their families. In many low-income urban communities, complacency, low expectations, disorder, and dysfunction are endemic to the public schools. In such schools, failure has been normalized (Noguera, 2008), and change often seems impossible. In *Getting What We Ask For* (1984), sociologist Charles Payne points out that schools with a track record of failure often rationalize failure as the inevitable consequence of serving impoverished children. Years of failure in Newark schools have had similar effects upon many of its staff. In Newark, the normalization of failure can be seen in high absentee rates of staff, tolerance of student absenteeism and tardiness, and a lack of attention when implementing interventions and programs designed to help students. BBA will attempt to counter these trends by working with parents and community organizations to support schools and hold them accountable. . . .

Clearly, it is too early to declare victory or to proclaim the BBA strategy an unqualified success. However, it is also clear that the NCLB [No Child Left Behind] strategy of using high-stakes testing to apply pressure on students and schools hasn't worked, and more of the same under a new name (Race to the Top) is unlikely to bring significant improvements in student achievement, if contextual issues like poverty continue to be ignored. American policy makers and reformers must be willing to accept the obvious: School reform efforts can't ignore the effects of poverty on children's lives or on the performance of schools. What we need is a more holistic strategy, one that makes it possible for schools that serve the most disadvantaged children to meet their academic and social needs so that they can overcome a track record of failure. The BBA strategy can't do this by itself. It must be combined with state and federal reforms that promote enriched learning environments, that make it possible to attract and retain excellent teachers, and that create clear criteria for accountability of all stakeholders in the education process—educators, parents, and students.

REFERENCES

Adelman, H.S. & Taylor, L. (1999). Mental health in schools and system restructuring. *Clinical Psychology Review, 19* (2), 137–163.

Blaue, D. & Currie J. (2006). Preschool, day care, and after-school care: Who's minding the kids? In E. Hanushek & F. Welch (Eds.), *Handbook on the Economics of Education*. Amsterdam, The Netherlands: North Holland.

Bryk, A.S., Sebring, P.B., Allensworth, E., Luppescu, S., & Easton, J.Q. (2010). *Organizing schools for improvement: Lessons from Chicago*. Chicago, IL: University of Chicago Press.

Coleman, J., Campbell, E., Hobson, C., McPartland, J., Mood, A., Weinfeld, F., & Yonk, R. (1966). *Equality of educational opportunity*. Washington, DC: U.S. Department of Health, Education, and Welfare, Office of Education.

Coleman, J.S. (1998). *Foundations of social theory*. Cambridge, MA: Harvard University Press.

Comer, J.P. (1988). Educating poor minority children. *Scientific American, 259* (5), 24–30.

Darling-Hammond, L. (2010). *The flat world and education: How America's commitment to equity will determine our future*. New York, NY: Teachers College Press.

Dryfoos, J. (1993). Schools as places for health, mental health, and social services. *Teachers College Record, 94* (3), 540–567.

Dryfoos, J.G., Quinn, J., & Barkin, C. (2005). *Community schools in action: Lessons from a decade of practice*. New York, NY: Oxford Press.

Eccles, J.S. & Gootman, J. (2002). *Community programs to promote youth development*. Washington DC: National Academy Press.

Greenberg, M. & Schneider, D. (1996). *Environmentally devastated neighborhoods: Perceptions, policies, and realities*. New Brunswick, NJ: Rutgers University Press.

Kirp, D. (2011). *Kids first: Five big ideas for transforming children's lives and America's future*. New York, NY: Perseus.

Klein, J., Lomax, M., & Murguía, J. (2010, April 9). Why great teachers matter to low-income students. *The Washington Post*.

Lareau, A. (2003). *Unequal childhoods: Class, race, and family life*. Berkeley and Los Angeles, CA: University of California Press.

Lawrence-Lightfoot, S. (2003). *The essential conversation: What parents and teachers can learn from each other*. New York, NY: Ballantine.

Noguera, P. (2003). *City schools and the American dream: Reclaiming the promise of public education*. New York, NY: Teachers College Press.

Noguera, P. (2008). *The trouble with black boys and other reflections on race, equity, and the future of public education*. San Francisco, CA: Wiley & Sons.

Payne, C. (1984). *Getting what we ask for: The ambiguity of success and failure in urban education*. Santa Barbara, CA: Greenwood Publishing.

Payne, C. (2008). *So much reform, so little change: The persistence of failure in urban schools*. Cambridge, MA: Harvard Education Press.

RAND. (2007). *The proven benefits of early childhood education*. Washington, DC: Author.

Rothstein, R. (2004). *Class and schools: Using social, economic, and educational reform to close the black-white achievement gap*. Washington, DC: Economic Policy Institute.

Syme, S.L. (2004). Social determinants of health: The community as empowered partner. *Public Health Research, Practice, and Policy, 1* (1), 1–4.

Wacquant, L. (2002). Taking Bourdieu into the field. *Berkeley Journal of Sociology, 46*, 180–186.

Waldfogel, J. & Lahaie, G. (2007). The role of preschool and after-school policies in improving the school achievement of children of immigrants. In J.E. Lansford, K. Deater-Deckard, & M.H. Bornstein (Eds.), *Immigrant families in contemporary society*. New York, NY: Guilford Press.

Wilson, W.J. (1987). *The truly disadvantaged: The inner city, the underclass, and public policy*. Chicago, IL: University of Chicago Press.

EXIT EXAMS HARM STUDENTS WHO FAIL THEM—AND DON'T BENEFIT STUDENTS WHO PASS THEM

John Robert Warren and Eric Grodsky

A major part of government institution policies such as Race to the Top and Blueprint for Reform is examinations, usually mandated by state or federal agencies with a price tag attached for noncompliance. At various points in students' careers, they are given achievement exams to see if they are on grade level. Many states are also requiring expensive exit exams for students to graduate with a high school degree; currently approximately two in three U.S. students will have to pass an exit exam to graduate. In most cases the goal is to be sure students have mastered the knowledge expected by the time they graduate from high school, and that they have not just slid through high school without mastering basic skills. Among the problems pointed out by critics of exit exams are that these exams result in some students dropping out of school and others not being able to graduate. However, few alternatives to failure are offered for these students who slip through the net. Also, the curriculum in states with tests often changes to accommodate the material being tested, thus cutting time spent on other valuable subjects such as physical education, art, and music. The authors studied the effects of exit exams on students and report some surprising findings, as outlined in the following reading.

Questions to consider for this reading:

1. Why do the authors indicate that exit exams help no one?

2. Do exit exams really lower graduation rates? Why or why not?

3. Do exit exams improve learning or preparation for work?

A generation ago, high school students earned their diplomas by showing up for classes, keeping up their grades, and staying out of trouble. Since the late 1970s, a growing number of states have also required aspiring graduates to pass "exit exams"—standardized tests that assess mastery of basic skills—in order to graduate. This spring, about two in three American high school students will have to pass an exit exam on their way to earning their diplomas.

After evaluating the effects of high school exit exams on a variety of student outcomes using nationally representative data spanning nearly 30 years, we conclude that exit exams hurt students who fail them without benefiting students who pass them—or the taxpayers who pay for developing, implementing, and scoring them. Exit exams are just challenging enough to reduce the graduation rate but not challenging enough to have measurable consequences for how much students learn or for how prepared they are for life after high school. Political pragmatism rather than academic benchmarks have led states to implement fundamentally flawed exit exam policies. Policy makers should either revamp exit exams to be sufficiently challenging to make a real difference for how much students learn or abandon them altogether.

ARGUING ABOUT EXIT EXAMS

Proponents of exit exam policies say too many students simply get credit for "seat time," graduating without basic literacy and numeracy skills. With the decline in manufacturing and growth of the information economy, architects of exit exam policies have sought to bolster the value of the diploma. Supporters say these policies have increased pressure on students, parents, teachers, and school systems to boost academic achievement and to better prepare young people for college and the global economy.

Critics contend that such policies are fundamentally counterproductive and unfair. First, they assert, exit exams deny diplomas to some students and lead others to drop out of high school without offering much in the way of improved academic outcomes. Second, exit exams force educators to narrow the curriculum by "teaching to the test," neglecting to devote adequate time to subjects not covered on the exit exam. Third, these policies are expensive to develop, implement, and score, diverting resources from instruction. Finally, critics argue that these policies are unfair to students who haven't had sufficient opportunity to master the tested material, either because of disabilities or limited English proficiency or because of inequities in educational resources.

Besides the similarity of the rhetoric and claims for and against exit exam policies over

time and across states, these debates have also typically proceeded in the absence of sound empirical evidence on either side.

DO EXIT EXAMS LOWER GRADUATION RATES?

At first glance, it seems obvious that exit exam policies should reduce high school graduation rates, at least during the initial years of their implementation. By design, these policies deny diplomas to students who don't meet basic proficiency standards in core curricular areas and who, presumably, would have earned diplomas before the exit exam requirement.

On the other hand, there are reasons to suppose that exit exams may have very minimal consequences for graduation rates. First, it may be that the only students who can't exceed the low bar imposed by exit exam policies would have dropped out anyway. Second, it may be that the basic proficiency standards set by most states are so low that nearly all students who continue in high school through their senior year would eventually be able to meet those standards. Third, schools and districts may "game the system" to artificially increase test scores and graduation rates by selectively exempting students for whom exit exams would present a serious barrier to graduation.

Our analyses indicate that state exit exams reduce high school graduation rates (Warren, Jenkins, & Kulick, 2006). In states with "minimum competency" exit exams (assessing mastery of material that students should learn before 9th grade), graduation rates decline by about one percentage point. In states with "higher competency" exit exams, graduation rates decline by about two percentage points. Nationally, each percentage point reduction in the graduation rate means about 35,000 fewer young people leave high school with a diploma each year.

Exit exams have a greater impact on graduation rates in states that are more racially/ethnically diverse and have higher rates of poverty. This doesn't necessarily mean exit exams increase dropout rates of disadvantaged students more than advantaged students, but it is consistent with that claim.

Do Exit Exams Improve How Much Students Learn?

Exit exams deny diplomas to some students, but they may also increase the academic achievement of others by raising the bar. If diploma recipients learn more than they would have in the absence of exit exams, exit exams are redistributive rather than capricious. They may increase the rewards to those who succeed as well as the costs to those who fail. However, surprisingly little empirical research has investigated the impact of state exit exams on students' proficiency in core academic subjects.

Data from the long-term trend component of the National Assessment of Educational Progress (or LTT NAEP) help answer this question (Grodsky, Warren, & Kalogrides, [2009]). LTT NAEP includes a set of achievement test items that are the same from year to year in order to allow for methodologically sound assessments of trends over time in reading, mathematics, and science achievement. In combination with the detailed information that we collected about exit exam policies in each state, we asked whether exit exams increased the reading and math achievement of students between 1971 and 2004. Beyond asking whether exit exams improved *average* levels of achievement in reading and math, we also asked whether exit exams improved the achievement of students closer to the top and the bottom of the achievement distribution. Exit exams might do the most to improve the achievement of marginal students and the least to improve the reading or math test scores of already high-achieving students. We also asked whether exit exams matter more or less for racial/ethnic minority students and for students from different social class backgrounds.

We found no evidence for any effect of exit exams (minimum competency *or* higher competency) on reading or math achievement at the mean or at any of several cut-points of the achievement distribution. These results hold for 13-year-olds and for 17-year-olds and don't vary across racial/ethnic or social class backgrounds, undermining claims of disparate impact.

Do Exit Exams Prepare Students for Work?

Although exit exams have no discernable effects for reading or math achievement, could exit exams still affect graduates' employment prospects and wages? Employers, like many other members of the public, may *believe* exit exams have increased the academic achievement of high school graduates. Employers of relatively less skilled workers—that is, those without a college education—generally value such traits as trustworthiness, reliability, and sound work ethics at least as much as they value academic skills in reading and math. Exit exams may signal to employers that diploma holders are able to follow through on a more rigorous set of high school graduation requirements and thus certify that graduates possess the noncognitive skills that employers value.

If exit exams produce graduates who are better prepared for work, then we should expect lower unemployment rates and higher wages among young people who passed exit exams to obtain their diplomas. These effects should be most pronounced among young people who don't go on to college; the effects of postsecondary training and credentials are probably much larger than any effect of exit exams.

We use data from the 1980 through 2000 U.S. Censuses and from the 1984 through 2002 Current Population Surveys to evaluate the labor market returns to exit exams (Warren, Grodsky, & Lee, 2008). Both data sources include large, nationally representative samples of American young people. We limited our focus to 20- to 23-year-olds with no college education (and along the way we found that exit exams have no bearing on 20- to 23-year-olds' chances of having attended college). Young high school graduates who obtained their diplomas in exit exam states fared no better in the labor market than their peers who obtained their diplomas in other states. These findings held in states with minimum competency exit exams and in states with higher competency exit exams. They also held for students from different racial/ethnic backgrounds.

HOW DID WE GET HERE? LESSONS FROM FLORIDA AND CALIFORNIA

Our research suggests that exit exams fail to improve either academic achievement or early labor market outcomes. At the same time, the direct costs of developing, implementing, and scoring exams, as well as the indirect costs of denying diplomas to thousands of otherwise eligible students each year, are substantial. How is it that 23 states (and counting) have implemented policies that appear to do such harm without doing any good?

The answer has more to do with political pragmatism than sound policy. Consider the history of exit exam policies in Florida and California. There, as in other states, exit exam policies were shaped by fears of unacceptably high exam failure rates, resulting in concerns about lowered graduation rates and legal challenges on behalf of various classes of students. These factors may very well minimize the potential benefits and costs of exit exams.

Florida tried to adopt an exit exam beginning with the graduating classes of 1979, but the exam was quickly challenged in court. In *Debra P. v. Turlington,* attorneys representing 10 African-American students argued that the test was racially biased and imposed without adequate notice. The U.S. District Court sided with the plaintiffs, delaying implementation of the exit exam requirement until the 1982–83 school year and compelling the state to demonstrate the instructional validity of the test, which it did. The class of 1983 was the first cohort of Florida students required to pass a high school exit exam. Florida revised and first administered a more difficult version of its exit exam in October 1994, first affecting students in the class of 1996.

Not surprisingly, far fewer students did well on the more difficult Florida exit exam. Two months after first administering and scoring the revised exit exam in fall 1994, the Florida Department of Education opted to set the passing threshold at the point on the test score distribution that would guarantee that the same percentage of students failed the revised (more difficult) exam as failed the previous year's (less difficult) exam. In the end, the state based decisions about which students had "mastered" key curricular materials on fear of politically unacceptable failure rates.

The California High School Exit Exam (CAHSEE) was originally scheduled to go into effect for the class of 2004. In the face of very high failure rates—just under half of the class of 2004 had passed both components of the exam by summer 2003—the state Board of Education voted unanimously to postpone the exit exam as a graduation requirement until the class of 2006. At that time, the board also opted to revise the CAHSEE, making the mathematics portion of the exam easier in order to ensure that the failure rate was lower.

As in Florida and other states, plaintiffs challenged California's exit exam in the courts based on claims that the state had inadequately prepared racial/ethnic minority and economically disadvantaged students for the exit exam. Weeks before the class of 2006 was to graduate, a superior court judge struck down the CAHSEE on these grounds. The CAHSEE was eventually upheld after a series of appeals.

This same basic pattern of exit exam policy evolution has played out in a number of states. States begin by setting moderate to high standards and then spend hundreds of thousands of dollars designing exit exams that purport to hold students to these standards. In short order, however, high failure rates and much-publicized legal challenges test the political will of policy makers to hold students to these standards. In the end, politics wins over principle and the exit exam, the passing threshold, or both are altered to increase the share of students who pass the exam. In the end, most states set the bar for passing exit exams at a point too low to make a real difference for academic achievement or workplace preparedness but just high enough to prevent a modest number of would-be graduates from obtaining diplomas.

Where Do We Go From Here?

State exit exams harm students who fail them and provide no discernable benefits to students who pass them. Obviously, states didn't intend to implement ineffective and punitive education policies. Exit exam policies are broken, and states should either fix them or get rid of them, but either option requires a political will that is in scarce supply among policy makers and politicians.

To fix exit exams, states would need to set substantially higher standards for passage—requiring mastery of more challenging and advanced curricular materials—and actually hold students to those standards. While educationally sound, the cost of raising standards would be daunting, especially in the current fiscal climate. More students will be initially unprepared to meet these higher standards, which means states will need to devote more time, money, and other resources to preparation and remediation. Such policies will reduce high school graduation rates, at least in the short term. The social costs of denying greater numbers of would-be graduates their high school diplomas should not be born lightly. The high school diploma is now a prerequisite for social and economic success in American society.

If states abandon exit exams, they would be on sound scientific ground. Many researchers question the wisdom of basing something as important as the decision about which students deserve diplomas on the score from a single standardized test. The ethics of high school exit exams are questionable at best. According to the American Educational Research Association (2000, p. 378), "Decisions that affect individual students' life chances or educational opportunities should not be made on the basis of test scores

alone." As noted above, there are also persistent concerns about the disparate impact of such policies. However, public opinion determines the outcomes of elections, not science. Anyone with the courage to advocate for abolishing high school exit exams would likely be portrayed as "soft on education."

Conclusion

We came to our work on exit exams not as policy advocates but as researchers. We believed that the claims proponents made about the benefits of high school exit exams were just as plausible as those made by opponents of those policies. We still believe that arguments in favor of exit exams as policy levers may have merit. However, arguments in favor of the exit exam polices in place today do not. Exit exams, as currently implemented, appear to have real downsides and none of their purported upsides. After a quarter of a century of experience with exit exams, states have reached a crossroads. The policies that we have now aren't working. It's time to try something else.

References

American Educational Research Association (AERA). (2000). *Position statement on high-stakes testing in pre-K–12 education.* Retrieved from http://www.aera.net/?id=378

Grodsky, E., Warren, J. R., & Kalogrides, D. (2009). State high school exit examinations and NAEP long-term trends in reading and mathematics, 1971–2004. *Educational Policy, 24,* 589–614.

Warren, J. R., Grodsky, E., & Lee, J. C. (2008). State high school exit examinations and post-secondary labor market outcomes. *Sociology of Education, 81*(1), 77–107.

Warren, J. R., Jenkins, K. N., & Kulick, R. (2006). High school exit examinations and state-level completion and GED rates, 1973–2000. *Educational Evaluation and Policy Analysis, 28*(2), 131–152.

School Finance

Raising Questions for Urban Schools

Augustina H. Reyes and Gloria M. Rodriguez

The economic environment of schools is as important as the political environment discussed in the previous articles on federal policies such as Race to the Top and the Blueprint for Reform, especially exit exams. Educational systems would not exist were there not funding from local and state taxes and federal allocations for special initiatives and programs, plus parent tuition for private schools and funding for special school events. Even bake sales and chili cook-offs help raise funds for school activities. Augustina H. Reyes and Gloria M. Rodriguez discuss funding options, structures, and systems used in school districts. The purpose of this reading is to provide insight into another crucial aspect of the education system's environment. Although funding formulas are established to cover needs of schools and school districts, equalization so that basic levels of funding are available for different school districts has been an ongoing concern and cause for judicial actions.

Questions to consider for this reading:

1. Explain the basic school funding structures discussed in the reading.

2. Why can funding structures result in inequality of educational opportunity?

3. If you were to design a funding structure for schools, what would be the components?

School finance drives policy and practice in public education, yet most citizens and some practitioners know very little about how their schools are funded. The purpose of this article is to address the financial issues related to urban schools and the challenge of balancing expectations of higher levels of education with the values of equity, efficiency, and economic growth.

In school finance theory and policy, there are a number of terms and concepts that are commonly used to discuss the mechanisms for directing funds to public schools. This section provides a brief definition of each term or concept and discussion of how it is used in policy and theoretical treatments of school finance issues.

One key component of any state or local system of school finance is *revenues*. Revenues are the dollars that are generated by either fees for various services or taxes on certain goods and services. At the state level, revenues are largely produced from a variety of taxes that are levied on things such as income, the sale of merchandise, and capital gains. To a lesser degree, states also collect fees for licensing, professional certificates, and so forth. Revenues are distributed to local governments and school districts and referred to according to the level of government from which they originated. For example, all school districts will generally have some combination of revenues from local, state, and federal sources, and they can either be referred to by source or by program (e.g., State Compensatory Education or Federal Title I). Over the past 30 years, there has been considerable legal, legislative, and grassroots activity to address the disparities that exist among districts in terms of the revenues they are able to generate from property taxes. Indeed, the interdistrict variations in property wealth disparities have been at the crux of most school finance equity cases . . . State policies designed to ameliorate the disparities among school districts in terms of property tax revenues generated are referred to as *equalization policies.*

Equalization policies include state methods for ensuring that there is provision for a basic level of educational funding supported by a combination of local and state revenues. In cases where large disparities exist relative to the local property tax revenue-raising capacity among districts, the state provides funding for school districts in an inverse relationship to their capacity to raise revenues. By doing so, states are able to ensure that low-property-wealth districts have access to at least a basic minimum level of funding for their schools, while high-property-wealth districts are able to maintain their basic funding from primarily locally raised revenues.

Very often, the starting point for figuring the available funding for schools is the foundation program or base amount that is allotted at a minimum basic level of funding for schools. In some cases, states may include a variety of adjustments to the funding distributed to districts based on factors that relate to either higher costs of education or variations in student needs among districts. States may use average daily attendance (ADA) or average daily membership (ADM) to distribute foundation funds. ADA systems tend to favor stable suburban school districts with students who attend school regularly, have access to health care (which promotes healthy children), and [have] role models that instill the economic importance of an education. ADA penalizes urban schools with large numbers of low-income students who have less access to health care; consequently, they experience lower attendance. For example, a state constitution may provide originating language guiding the state legislature or other agency to ensure that each district receive a flat grant or equal dollar figure in total or per pupil. The flat grant usually reflects the starting point of the funding available for all districts within a given state.

Additionally, the state may add funding to support the additional costs associated with transportation, special educational services, and so forth. Such adjustments may be made using an index or using weighted pupils, the latter of which is a method for counting students eligible for special services in a way that reflects the additional costs associated with providing them with a basic education. Although a state or district may determine the amount that reflects a minimum basic education, the student with special educational needs is typically assigned a weight that indicates the extra costs associated with his or her education. For example, it may be determined that a student who is eligible for certain extraeducational services costs twice as much to educate as a student who is not eligible. Such a student would count as two students in a weighted pupil system.

The funding most states distribute to local school districts is typically some balance of local, state, and federal support, with the latter often filtering through state-level structures. In cases where the local share is nearly or completely nonexistent, it is referred to as *full-state funding.* This means that the revenues that schools use to support their operations are composed virtually or entirely from state-collected taxes, fees, and other sources. The concept of full-state funding is also used to describe situations where, because of equalization efforts at the state level, local districts are no longer able to exert the same control over the generation, distribution, or expenditure of such funds.

The intricate mechanisms that determine the level of funding that public schools receive are referred to as *funding formulas*. Indeed, the structures used to systematically determine how much and what sources of funding districts and schools receive are generally very complex sets of mathematical operations grouped together and applied as a formula. The mathematical operations involve each of the different types of adjustments, upward and downward, that reflect the various factors that are acknowledged as necessary in appropriately distributing available funding to local school districts that exhibit wide variation in characteristics and challenges.

As mentioned above, revenues that states receive are, in turn, distributed to school districts for support of local educational services. When the revenues are distributed to districts, they are referred to as *district revenues*. Several factors can affect the level and variation of available district revenues. For example, in most states, revenues are distributed to districts based on some measure of students in attendance the previous year, including actual attendance or ADA (the methods used to determine how many students a district can count for funding purposes can likewise vary significantly). This is why, for many educators, attendance in school is such a huge concern—indeed, it drives district revenues to a great degree in many finance systems.

Within state school finance systems, considerable attention is paid to the tax policies that help to support reforms to ensure increased equity in the distribution of funding to school districts. In particular, one concept that has been useful to policy makers is the notion *of district power equalization*. District power equalization refers to state policies or structures that intervene in situations where large disparities exist in the property tax revenue-raising capacity among school districts. The idea is to enable districts with lower capacity to raise property tax revenues, especially in cases where the average property values are significantly lower than in other districts, and to benefit from policies that enable them to more easily generate property tax revenues. Another term that is often used to refer to district power equalization is *guaranteed tax base*, where states ensure that districts can generate property tax revenues as though they had access to higher average property values.

One key component associated with a policy of district power equalization or guaranteed tax base is *guaranteed tax yield*. The guaranteed tax yield feature is tied to a district's taxpayers' willingness to tax themselves at higher levels to generate sufficient support for local schools. Under some state finance schemes, when a district's taxpayers approve a certain tax rate, this enacts a policy that guarantees a certain yield (level of revenues), given a certain tax rate, regardless of the average property wealth in the district. Typically, such features are applied only to lower property wealth districts using a very specific property value threshold to qualify for participation. In addition, the guaranteed yield is usually stated in dollar terms tied to specific tax rates. For example, in a given state system, low-property-wealth districts may have the option of taxing themselves at a slightly higher rate per $1,000 of property wealth, which, in turn, generates a set dollar amount in yield for every extra percentage of tax rate levied. That is, if a district taxes itself at $1.55 per $1,000 of property value and the guaranteed tax yield is enacted above a rate of $1.50 per $1,000, the district would enjoy the enhanced yield guaranteed for the additional $.05 levied. In this way, districts are able to generate extra revenues at the margin that would reflect higher average property values in the absence of the guaranteed tax yield.

Finally, another concept that is often used in the distribution of funding to schools is the *categorical program*. Categorical programs, also referred to as targeted programs, are designed to address either a particular or targeted educational policy goal or the special needs of a category of eligible student populations. Very often, the existence of categorical programs within a school finance formula reflects an acknowledgement by policy makers that additional resources are needed in districts with several schools exhibiting certain characteristics or serving students with certain special needs. In other instances, the categorical programs through which resources are distributed to districts fall outside of the regular state school finance formula and are therefore under the scrutiny of other parties, such as the federal U.S. Department of Education. Some categorical programs operate as entitlements, meaning that the dollars follow the students who qualify under the programs' guidelines. In other cases, categorical programs are doled out to schools on a competitive basis, requiring a carefully presented school district (or state) proposal for the use of funds to advance the particular purposes of the program.

RELIGION IN THE SCHOOLS

Edwin C. Darden

Each institution in society—family, religion, government, economics, health—is part of the educational environment. We have already pointed out influences of family, government (exams), and economics (financing schools), and in this reading we turn to the role of religion in society and schools. In some countries the two go together, with public schools representing the official religion of the country. In other countries there is strict separation of church and state. This distinction has been controversial in the United States with its multiethnic and religious population. The questions that come before the courts are what crosses the line of separation. Edwin C. Darden explains the dilemma and some court cases and rulings that affect this separation of church and state.

Questions to consider for this reading:

1. How does the separation of church and state reflect the educational environment?

2. What are some ways in which this separation has been controversial?

3. Do you see solutions to the controversies described in this article?

Nearly every religion has a version of the Golden Rule: Do unto others as you would have them do unto you.

Yet, school districts find themselves increasingly confronted by individuals and organizations that use religion aggressively—wielding it like a sword to poke others whose behavior or beliefs fall short of their spiritual standard. In the opposite corner are groups like Americans United for Separation of Church and State and the American Civil Liberties Union that file lawsuits to prevent religion in schools.

The clash has widespread legal implications. Religiously motivated people can cloak themselves in the First Amendment's free exercise clause and then bolster their claim by adding a First Amendment free speech right. School districts, by contrast, often see a Constitutional duty to be neutral—which translates to strenuously avoiding favoritism toward a single group, or religion in general.

Sixteen words from the First Amendment to the U.S. Constitution are the guide: "Congress shall make no law respecting an establishment of religion or prohibiting the free exercise thereof." That phrase has been interpreted to represent an intentional design by the nation's founders to ensure that religion is a matter of personal conscience. Therefore, school districts may not use their power to unfairly persuade, and citizens hold the right to freely express beliefs or to reject religion entirely. Some observers describe the idea as the right to be free from religion.

If only it were that simple.

Because the U.S. Constitution is involved, conflicts about schools and religion are decided in federal court. But, instead of creating bright-line rules that give educators clear boundaries about what is and isn't permissible, litigation has produced a barrage of contradictory rulings. The resulting hodgepodge has created massive confusion in its wake and forces educators to parse fine-point distinctions that can tie top flight lawyers in knots.

ESTABLISHMENT V. FREE EXERCISE

In the last decade, courts have more readily viewed religious speech (e.g., clothing, flyers, and symbols) the same as any other kind of speech and dubbed neutrality efforts as discrimination *against* religion. When Establishment Clause concerns are pitted against the First Amendment Free Exercise Clause in combination with "free speech" rights, the free exercise/free speech twosome usually wins. The U.S. Constitution's Establishment Clause cautions school systems (as government entities) against embracing religion, while the Free Exercise Clause gives individuals the right to express religious devotion. The First Amendment free speech right forbids government from squelching unpopular, dissenting or, in this case, religious speech.

These rulings by federal judges have emboldened religious advocates to rely on the courts to advance their perspective. Quickest into the fray are a variety of vocal and well-funded religious organizations that actively seek cases where courts can approve of a cozier relationship between schools and religion.

No disrespect intended toward those who make devoutness a part of their daily life. True believers are often sincere and well-meaning individuals who want to see their views reinforced in the classroom or seek an unimpeded opportunity to convince others to believe likewise.

The flip side is that school districts and building officials have the responsibility of maintaining neutrality by creating an environment that allows believers and nonbelievers to coexist without one having to endorse or adhere to the other's beliefs.

Sorting it all out, however, can leave a teacher, superintendent, or board member quite flummoxed. With little consistency in the law, educators are forced to make on-the-spot judgments—and to hope for the best when the lawsuit comes.

DISTRICTS ON THE DEFENSE

Trouble can arrive from many different directions. Here are a few examples:

TEACHERS

In March 2012, the U.S. Supreme Court refused to hear *Johnson v. Poway Unified School District,* a California case involving a high school calculus teacher who adorned his room with banners that read, "In God We Trust"; "One Nation Under God"; "God Bless America"; and "God Shed His Grace on Thee."

Bradley Johnson argued that the banners were patriotic expressions and no different from the Declaration of Independence. The appeals court disagreed. "Because the speech at issue owes its existence to Johnson's position as a teacher, Poway acted well within constitutional limits in ordering [him] not to speak in a manner it did not desire," the Court explained.

PARENTS

In 2009, the 3rd U.S. Circuit Court of Appeals ruled against a Pennsylvania mom who sought to read passages from the Bible in her son's kindergarten class during a show-and-tell activity.

In *Busch v. Marple Newton School District,* the court reasoned that Bible reading "unquestionably conveys a strong sense of spiritual and moral authority." The court noted that " . . . the audience is involuntary and very young." The U.S. Supreme Court declined to hear an appeal in the case.

The case earned friend-of-the-court support from the Alliance Defense Fund (ADF) on the mom's side. The Anti-Defamation League, the American Jewish Congress, Americans United for Separation of Church & State, and the Pennsylvania and National School Boards Associations supported the school.

STUDENTS

In Fairfax County, Va., a 12th-grade student sought service credits for being a Sunday school teacher. She needed the credits to maintain membership in the National Honor Society. School officials refused to apply them, citing district policy requiring "a secular [nonreligious] purpose" to earn service-learning points.

The Fairfax County School District, caught in a nationwide media storm and facing a lawsuit by the above-mentioned ADF, yielded. The 175,000-student system settled the litigation in May 2012 by reinstating the student's credits and agreeing to revise the policy.

The "secular purpose" words echo the landmark 1971 U.S. Supreme Court case *Lemon v. Kurtzman.* Under *Lemon*, courts rely on three questions to weigh alleged Establishment Clause violations: Is there a secular purpose? Does the government action advance or inhibit religion? Does it cause excessive government entanglement?

The *Lemon* test has been disparaged by justices in the 41 years since, but has not been formally overturned. Instead, two other legal yardsticks have swayed decisions about schools and religion: the "coercion" and the "endorsement" tests. The coercion test asks whether students are a captive audience and feel coerced by religious sentiment. The endorsement test focuses on whether school districts are validating religion.

In another student-related issue, the U.S. Supreme Court recently refused a case from Plano, Texas. In *Morgan v. Swanson*, the 5th U.S. Circuit Court of Appeals shielded principals from financial liability after they prevented students from distributing pencils and candy canes with sayings like, "Jesus loves me, this I know, for the Bible tells me so," and "Jesus is the Reason for the Season."

Principals can be held liable for actions violating well-established Constitutional rights. But not this time, said the court. " . . . The general state of the law in this area is abstruse, complicated, and subject to great debate among jurists."

Outside Organizations

The 8th U.S. Circuit Court of Appeals approved Missouri's Lee's Summit R-7 School District's policy to restrict youth community group's access to "backpack flyers" at the beginning of the school year. The Victory Through Jesus Sports Ministry Foundation sued in 2011 claiming religious discrimination and a free speech right to promote "sports evangelism" summer soccer camps.

Victory Through Jesus lost the case. The court ruled that the policy was within the board's discretion and did not provide "unbridled discretion" to discriminate against religion.

With religion advocates and opponents squaring off nationwide and with schools in the middle, these legal battles are likely to continue for a long time.

Perhaps the U.S. Supreme Court . . . will take a case or two that starts to untangle the intricate legal web they've woven. For school systems—where educators must exercise judgments about religion regularly—the state of confusion serves mostly in practice to deceive.

Projects for Further Exploration

1. Using an academic database, look up *student* and *"out of school" learning*. Relate this to family, social class, and community influences.

2. After reading the selections in this chapter, construct an interview form that includes various environmental influences on schools. Now interview a superintendent, a principal, or several teachers in a school district in your area to learn how environmental (social context) factors influence them and the decision-making processes in the district. If you interviewed individuals in different school roles, how did their answers differ? Projects in later chapters will ask you to collect additional data on this school district.

3. As a part of the educational environment, how do you or might you influence what happens in schools?

4

SCHOOLS AS ORGANIZATIONS

Formal and Informal Education

The bell rings, lockers slam, conversations end, and classroom doors shut as the school day begins. We are all familiar with these signs that the formal school day is about to start. Schools provide the framework for meeting certain goals of societies and preparing young people for future statuses and roles. School organizations, just as other organizations, have formally stated goals, criteria for membership, a hierarchy of roles and relationships, and a number of informal goals, such as friendship and sharing of interests. Although individual schools around the world share a number of similarities in their structures and roles, they also have their own distinct personalities.

This chapter examines the formal and informal organization of schools: the structure, stated goals, and what "really" happens in schools. Organizationally, schools are divided into classrooms, the day into periods, teachers into subject areas and ranks, and students into groups by grades or performance results on examinations (Hurn, 1993; Parsons, 1959). Like other *formal organizations,* schools have memberships composed of individuals holding different status positions necessary to carry out the functions and goals of the school. Each position holder has certain roles to perform—administrating, teaching, learning, and providing support functions such as driving the bus and preparing the meals. These activities are the processes of schools, the means to meet school goals.

The broad functions and goals of schools are common knowledge and shared by many people. However, there is often conflict over how to carry out those functions and goals—how to organize schools, what curriculum to teach, what courses to offer, and how to best prepare all students for society. As discussed in the previous chapter, conflicts can also occur between schools and their environments; between the school and school board; with different interest groups in communities such as religious, political, parental, or other groups; and between schools and the state or federal government. These conflicting goals can be seen in readings throughout the text.

Although the organizational goals of schools call for educating all students, not all students meet the requirements for passing to the next grade level or for graduating, especially when exams are administered to promote and graduate students. Grade retention of students has consequences, including informal effects on student friendships, feelings of alienation, misconduct in schools, and futility resulting in dropping out (Demanet & Van Houtte, 2012). However, to give up on the students—that is, to "fire" them—would be to lose societal resources. Therefore, schools cannot be run by the same rules and under the same efficiency model as business organizations. Schools are expected, according to their goals, to prepare students for the next stage in their lives by transmitting shared knowledge, skills, societal values, and ideals; fostering cognitive and emotional growth; and sorting and selecting students into different categories—college material, gifted, talented, slow, rebellious, and so forth—with consequences for future adult status.

Many organizational proposals have been put forth to improve student outcomes. Discussion about how to make schools more effective for student achievement stimulates social science research. An example of these proposals is to reduce class size. The controversy is over the cost of smaller classes and whether smaller classes really produce more learning and better outcomes (Chingos & Whitehurst, 2011; Honig, 2009). The reading by Bruce J. Biddle and David C. Berliner in Chapter 2 reviews studies of class size and the impact of class size on student learning, considering the effect of size on school organizations and processes of teaching and learning. Linda Darling-Hammond's reading in Chapter 8 also discusses class size, as well as a number of other school practices that can result in improving school quality.

Another example of attempts to improve student outcomes is the charter school movement; it provides possibilities for school districts to try new organizational structures. The success of these "independent" public schools is mixed to negative, and the organizational models controversial (Credo, 2013). The search for more effective school organizations continues. For example, the reading in Chapter 8 by Linda A. Renzulli and Vincent J. Roscigno discusses the growth of charter schools.

The readings in this chapter discuss educational organizations from large educational systems to individual classrooms. To begin our exploration of schools as organizations, Rebecca Barr and Robert Dreeben focus on schools and classrooms. Their reading covers events that take place in schools, the division of labor in schools, the roles of participants, the organization of classrooms, and how time structures the day in schools and classrooms.

Part of the formal organization of education is local school boards; their role is to translate the broad mandates from state and federal government into policies to meet the goals of the local district. Debates continue over the role of local school boards in determining the organization of schools and whether states, local governments, or even city governments should take control of schools. The role of the school board in school organization is discussed in the reading by Michael A. Resnick and Anne L. Bryant, organization leaders in the National School Boards Association.

Behind the formal organization, rules, classroom and school size and structure, and goal statements is another layer to explore—*the informal system*, or what really happens in schools. Whenever you enter a classroom, especially for the first time, interact with peers or teachers, or determine what you really need to do for a class, you are dealing with the informal system.

Students learn both the formal and informal systems, each quite important to understanding how schools work. In fact, Philip Jackson (1968) argues that success in school requires mastery of both systems, even though there are contradictions between them. Students who have problems in school are often the ones who have not learned to balance the two systems or to negotiate the contradictions. The "hidden curriculum," as labeled by Snyder (1971) in his book by the same name, defines this system as "implicit demands (as opposed to the explicit obligations of the visible curriculum) that are found in every learning institution and which students have to find out and respond to in order to survive within it" (p. 6). These unwritten regulations and unintended consequences are an education in themselves and determine how we learn to cope with the unspoken expectations in life. Conflict theorists, as described in Chapter 1, see in the hidden curriculum a social control and power element that reproduces the social class of students. Working-class students find that they are not fully integrated into the educational system; they learn to cope with boredom in school, which prepares them for the boredom of future jobs. Consider the following examples.

Several of the best-known studies of the informal system use qualitative methods in which the researchers immerse themselves in the school settings to observe the more subtle workings of schools and messages students receive from schools. The not-so-obvious aspects of the informal system of schooling include these subtle messages and power relationships inherent in any system. These aspects of schooling cannot be studied by looking at lists of goals, school documents, descriptions of role responsibilities, or recorded test scores. In fact, most studies of the informal system are ethnographies (see Chapter 2), or carefully documented observations of interactions, behaviors, and the atmosphere in schools that record the "school climate." The reading by Megan M. Holland (see Chapter 8) describes how this informal system works to include or exclude minority students in an integrated high school.

In studying aspects of the informal system in her ethnographic study of classrooms including interviews with teachers in eight diverse settings, Mary Haywood Metz (1990) found a "common script" in schools. All the schools were recognizably similar in many respects, but she found clear differences in the way the script was carried out based on the dominant social-class background of the students and the informal system this created in the schools. Sociologists who study education ask numerous questions about the role of the informal system in selection and allocation of students: how students and teachers learn to cope with the expectations of school; feelings about themselves and others that students bring to school and develop in school; the classroom and school climate, or culture; and power relationships in schools between teachers, students, and peers.

School climate, or culture, which makes up one aspect of the informal system, refers to several parts of the school experience: the interactions that result from grouping students, the resistance of some students to schooling, and teachers' expectations of students that affect their achievement levels. Factors inside and outside the school influence school climate (Ballantine & Hammack, 2012; Demanet & Van Houtte, 2011). Sociologists refer to the school value climate, learning climate, and power dynamics, among other types of climate. For instance, "effective schools" studies consider both the formal and informal systems in schools, making recommendations on how to change school climate to make schools more conducive to learning for all children (Brookover, Erickson, & McEvoy, 1996). These studies measure school climate by considering teacher expectations, academic norms, students' sense of futility (giving up on school), role definitions, grouping patterns, and instructional practices.

In a now classic ethnography, Paul Willis (1979) describes the activities of two groups of English students, the "lads" and the "ear'oles." The lads experience an informal hidden curriculum that reinforces their working-class status and prepares them for factory work. The ear'oles suck up the knowledge from teachers in preparation for further education and success in higher-level professional jobs in the work world. The lads show resistance to school in their "counterschool culture" and create a "shop-floor culture" of chauvinism, toughness, and machismo to cope with the unpleasant situations they face in the middle-class school culture and hidden curriculum. In another ethnography, Jay MacLeod (2008) provides a vivid description of two groups of kids from a poor Chicago housing project and their experiences negotiating the educational system. He talks about the differences in the groups, one group of boys with high aspirations and the other whose members have given up on the system, and how those differences are influenced by the messages and experiences they receive in the informal system of the school. Unfortunately, in both the Willis and MacLeod studies, whether they give up or have high aspirations, all students tend to have trouble succeeding in life in general.

Two articles in this chapter look at what goes on in the informal school interactions and organizations, and their importance for the overall understanding of organization in educational systems. At the classroom level of organization and bridging the formal and informal school classroom, David Diehl and Daniel A. McFarland report on their research about the development of routines and rituals in classrooms through the informal interaction between students and teachers. These routines and rituals result in organizational patterns that make for an ordered classroom, they describe.

Another reading in this chapter by Harry L. Gracey continues the ethnographic tradition by taking us through the lives of children experiencing the informal system of education, starting with kindergarten. Students learn both the formal and informal rules of the classroom from their earliest experiences in schools. Gracey describes a day in the life of a kindergarten class for the teacher and the students. He points out both the formal lesson plans and time schedule and the informal learning that takes place in lessons about punctuality, obedience, respect, and other rules that govern the informal aspects of the classroom. This illustrates the interaction between formal goals of schools and informal lessons learned by children from teachers and peers to prepare them to move to the next levels of schooling.

Anthony S. Bryk's reading concludes the chapter on "schools as organizations" with a discussion of organizing schools for improvement, comparing school organizations that work with those that don't work. Based on a large study of Chicago schools, he points out the essential elements for school improvement and how these can lead to better student achievement. After studying these readings, you should have a clearer idea of what the formal organization of schools means, what sociologists of education look for in the formal organization of schools, and the importance of informal systems in schools.

REFERENCES

Ballantine, J., & Hammack, F. (2012). *The sociology of education: A systematic approach* (7th ed.). Upper Saddle River, NJ: Prentice Hall.

Brookover, W., Erickson, F. J., & McEvoy, A. W. (1996). *Creating effective schools: An in-service program.* Holmes Beach, FL: Learning Publications.

Chingos, M. M., & Whitehurst, G. J. (2011). Class size: What research says and what it means for state policy. *Brookings Institution*, May 11. Retrieved from http://brookings.edu/research/papers/2011/05/11-class-size-whitehurst-chingos

Credo. (2013). Charter school growth and replication. *Center for Research on Education Outcomes*, January 30. Retrieved from http://credo.stanford.edu/

Demanet, J., & Van Houtte, M. (2011). Social-ethnic school composition and school misconduct: Does sense of futility clarify the picture? *Sociological Spectrum, 31,* 224–256.

Demanet, J., & Van Houtte, M. (2012). Grade retention and its association with school misconduct in adolescence: A multilevel approach. *School Effectiveness and School Improvement, 24*(4), 417–434.

Honig, M. I. (2009). No small thing: School district central office bureaucracies and the implementation of new small autonomous schools initiatives. *American Educational Research Journal, 46*(2), 387–422. Retrieved from http://aerj.aera.net

Hurn, C. J. (1993). *The limits and possibilities of schooling: An introduction to sociology of education* (3rd ed.). Boston: Allyn & Bacon.

Jackson, P. E. (1968). *Life in classrooms.* New York: Holt, Rinehart and Winston.

MacLeod, J. (2008). *Ain't no makin' it: Leveled aspirations in a low-income neighborhood* (2nd ed.). Boulder, CO: Westview Press.

Metz, M. H. (1990). Real school: A universal drama amidst disparate experience. In D. E. Mitchell & M. E. Goertz (Eds.), *Education politics for the new century: The 20th anniversary yearbook of the politics of education association* (pp. 75–92). London: Falmer Press.

Parsons, T. (1959). The school class as a social system: Some of its functions in American society. *Harvard Educational Review, 29*(4), 297–318.

Snyder, B. R. (1971). *The hidden curriculum.* New York: Alfred A. Knopf.

Willis, P. (1979). *Learning to labor: How working class kids get working class jobs.* Aldershot, Hampshire, England: Saxon House.

HOW SCHOOLS WORK

Rebecca Barr and Robert Dreeben

In this excerpt from Rebecca Barr and Robert Dreeben's book, *How Schools Work*, the authors discuss the functioning of schools and classrooms. They examine different levels of organization in school districts from district offices to instructional groups in classrooms; they identify distinct events that take place in each unit, and how what happens in one unit affects others. They also discuss the roles and division of labor among some participants. Within classrooms there are instructional groups, often by ability level of students. Organization of time is another determinant of how schools work. From the length of the class period and day to the number of days in a year, the way time is structured affects opportunities to learn. The importance of this excerpt is in providing the methods and framework needed to understand the organization of educational systems and how schools work. The reading provides an example of the levels of analysis in the open systems model.

Questions to consider for this reading:

1. What are topics to consider and methods that can be used to study how schools work?

2. How does this article relate to the open systems model and levels of organization?

3. What is the division of labor that influences classroom activities, directly and indirectly, and how does this relate to a school system with which you are familiar?

Our formulation begins with the idea that school systems are organizations that like others can be readily subject to sociological analysis. In all organizations labor is divided, which means that different activities are carried out in the different parts and that the parts are connected to each other in a coherent way. The parts of school systems are very familiar. They consist of a central administration with jurisdiction over a school district as well as local administrations situated in each school with responsibility for what happens therein. The business of schooling, mainly instruction, takes place in classrooms run by teachers; and teachers preside not only over classes but over parts of them as well when they rely upon grouped forms of instruction. We will show how the work that gets done in district offices, schools, classes, and instructional groups is different in character, that these separate jurisdictions are locations for carrying on different sorts of activities. Indeed, this proposition is true for teachers as classroom instructors and as group instructors in that teachers do different things in organizing a class from what they do while instructing subgroups within it. Part of the answer to our question of how schools work, then, is to be found by identifying the distinct events happening at each level of school system organization. A second part of the answer can be found by discovering how the events characteristic of one level influence those taking place at another. It would be a strange organization indeed if the parts were hermetically sealed off from each other; if, for example, what the principal did had no bearing on what teachers did and if what teachers did made no difference for what students did and learned. Yet it is precisely the failure to come up with satisfactory answers to these questions that has caused so much grief in our understanding of educational effects. The answer must come from identifying correctly what the activities are and from being able to trace their antecedents and effects across pathways that connect one level to another.

The third part of the answer pertains not so much to what to look for as it does to how to look for it. School systems, like other forms of social existence, are characterized by variability. We can learn about their workings by attending to the different ways that comparable parts act: different schools in the same system, different classes in the same school, different groups in the same class. What can vary in these levels of school organization is the way in which resources are allocated, transformed, and used. A particular resource, like books, may be purchased by the district office. All fourth grade mathematics texts, for example, can then be distributed to each elementary school, thence to be stocked in each fourth grade class. Thus, a simple process of resource transmission takes place. From there, teachers in the same school may use the text in almost identical ways or in vastly different ways depending on how they organize their instructional programs. The program itself determines the instructional use, and hence the meaning, of the resource. Accordingly, insofar as the school is no more than a transmission belt for

transporting books from the district office to the classroom, school-by-school comparisons will show similar activities. Class-by-class comparisons in textbook use, however, might show sharp contrasts. Depending upon the nature of those class contrasts, they may average out to show no school differences or bunch up to show marked school differences. In either case, it is the comparison of events at the same level—school and class in these examples—that tells us what is going on.

The Formulation

Levels of Organization

Labor in school systems is divided; it is differentiated by task into different organizational levels in a hierarchical arrangement. While we customarily think about hierarchies as pertaining to relations of authority, rank, and power, they not only are manifestations of stratification and status distinction, but also represent organizational differentiation, a manifestation of labor being specialized and other resources distributed to different locations, of the elements of production having been both separated and tied together in some workable arrangement. We are concerned here with hierarchy in this latter sense.

In an educational division of labor, school systems comprise several levels of administrative and staff officers as well as "production" workers occupying positions with district, school, and classroom jurisdictions. In addition, school systems are differentiated according to the resources they use, such as time and physical objects—like books—that constitute instructional materials. As we shall indicate shortly, time is a resource that has meaning at all levels of the hierarchy, but its meaning has different manifestations at each level. Textbooks, by contrast, are productive resources only inside classrooms. School systems also contain one additional element: students who are both the clients of the organization, the intended beneficiaries of its services, and, because schools are engaged in effecting change in children, productive resources in their own right because they participate directly and actively in their own learning.

When organizations are differentiated, it is because their parts make distinct contributions to the overall productive enterprise. This means that people located hierarchically at different places perform different kinds of activities; it also means that resources come into play in different ways depending upon where they are utilized in the productive process. A complete formulation of school production, therefore, should identify all relevant combinations of people, time, and material resources at each hierarchical level.

More specifically, school systems characteristically contain a managerial component responsible for centralized financial, personnel, procurement, plant maintenance, and supervisory functions applicable to all their constituent elements. This component is also engaged in direct dealings with agencies of the federal and state governments as well as with locally based interest groups and units of municipal government. Activities occurring at this managerial level have nothing directly to do with running schools or teaching students but rather are concerned with the acquisition of resources, with general supervision, and with the maintenance of relations with the surrounding community including suppliers of labor. We refer to this as the district level of organization; its jurisdiction includes all schools in the district.

Even though districts are divided into levels (elementary and secondary) related to the ages of students, and some are also divided into geographical areas as well as functional units, we are primarily concerned—at the next lower hierarchical level—with schools. Contrary to conventional belief, schools are not organizational units of instruction. They are structures akin to switching yards where children within a given age range and from a designated geographical area are assigned to teachers who bring them into contact with approved learning materials, specified as being appropriate to age or ability, during certain allotted periods of time. Schools deal in potentialities; they assemble a supply of teachers, of students, and of resources over a given period of time. Their central activities are the assignment of children to specific teachers, the allocation of learning materials to classrooms, the arrangement of a schedule so that all children in the school can be allotted an appropriate amount of time to spend on subjects in the curriculum, and the integration of grades so that work completed in one represents adequate preparation for the next.

These activities are the primary responsibility of school principals; they are core functions peculiar to the school level of organization. This is so because decisions affecting the fate of all classrooms in a school are not likely to be left to individuals (teachers) who have in mind primarily classroom interests rather than whole school interests and whose self-interest puts them in a poor position to settle disputes among equals. Nor are they likely to be left to district-wide administrators, whose locations can be too remote and jurisdictions too widespread to allow them to make informed decisions about local school events.

While these decisions constitute the peculiar core activities of school level administration, they by no means exhaust the responsibilities of school administrators, which frequently include such matters as planning curriculum; establishing disciplinary standards; and making school policies for homework, decorum in public places, and the like. But while such concerns are frequently characteristic of school administration, they are not peculiar to it because district-wide administrators and teachers also participate in them at the school level in fulfilling responsibilities within their own respective jurisdictions.

While instruction is not the business of the school, it is the business of classrooms and of teachers responsible for the direct engagement of students in learning activities. Aggregations of children are assigned to specific teachers who direct their activities and bring them into immediate contact with various sorts of learning materials. These activities are more than potentialities because children's active engagement working with teachers and materials is what enables them to learn.

Because classes contain diverse aggregations of children, it is not automatic that the instruction appropriate for one member of the aggregation will be appropriate for another. Hence, teachers in the lower grades characteristically create an additional level of suborganization to manage activities not easily handled in a grouping as large as the class. For example, in primary grade reading, there are suborganizations called instructional groups that represent still another level of organizational differentiation.

Finally, there are individual students. It is only individuals who work on tasks, and it is only they who learn; so that while work tasks might be set for all students in the class or in a group, the individual members vary in how much work they do and in how much they learn.

We argue here not only that school systems can be described by their constituent organizational levels, but that the events, activities, and organizational forms found at each level should be seen as addressing distinct as well as partially overlapping agendas. Districts, schools, classes, and instructional groups are structurally differentiated from each other; and what is more they make different contributions to the overall operation of the school system. We recognize that not all schools have precisely the same organizational pattern. In the upper elementary grades, for example, formalized instructional groups characteristically used for primary level reading might or might not be employed; and in secondary schools, which lack self-contained classrooms, a departmental level of organization usually appears as does formal tracking that distinguishes students largely on the basis of ability within schools but not within classes. Despite these variations, the general principle of differentiated structures and agendas holds.

Linkages Between Levels

If organizational levels are as distinct as this analysis suggests, how is it possible to think about a coherent production process for the whole school district organization? How should the connections between levels be formulated? We contend that each level of a school system has its own core productive agenda even though certain activities are performed at more than one level. That is, productive events of differing character occur at each level to effect outcomes that are themselves characteristic of each level. For example, a school outcome becomes a productive condition in classes yielding in turn a class outcome; the class outcome in turn becomes a productive element for instructional groups yielding a group outcome; and so on. We see, then, a set of nested hierarchical layers, each having a conditional and contributory relation to events and outcomes occurring at adjacent ones.

Consider an example of how levels of organization are connected to each other to constitute school production. As we observed earlier, classroom characteristics do not directly affect individual learning; they influence the formation of instructional groups. This might seem to be a strange statement since everyone knows that classroom teachers are responsible for instructing all children in a class. However, the teacher's job, we maintain, is first to transform an aggregation of children into an arrangement suitable for establishing an instructional program. In first grade reading, this usually means creating instructional reading groups. Hence, before any instruction takes place, decisions are made about how to arrange the class; whether to teach everyone together in one group, as in recitation; whether to establish subgroups in which only some children work intensively with the teacher while the others proceed by themselves with little supervision; whether to set everyone to work independently at their desks to perform at their own rate such more or less individualized tasks as are contained in workbooks.

The results of these classroom decisions are not instructional, nor do they appear as individual learning. They are alternative grouping arrangements which should be thought of as class outcomes, or values. We must draw a distinction between what teachers do in organizing classes for instruction and the instruction they actually provide for the groupings of children that make up classroom organization. Down the road, those grouping arrangements influence individual learning through a chain of connections consisting of instructional activities. Individual learning, however, is not itself a class outcome. As our story unfolds, we will show how class grouping arrangements determine certain characteristics of the groups composing them, in particular the level of children's ability characteristic of each classroom group. As it turns out, this level of ability is a direct determinant of certain instructional activities undertaken by teachers, who treat differently composed groups in different ways.

One form this treatment takes is the amount of material covered, which we construe as an outcome, or value, created by instructional groups. (Note again: individual learning is not a group outcome any more than it is a class outcome.) Then, depending on how much material children cover over a given span of time, in combination with their own characteristics, they learn proportionally more or less. In sum, group arrangements are the value created at the class level, coverage the value at the group level, and learning the value at the individual level. Note particularly that the activities and outcomes characteristic of each level are qualitatively distinct—grouping, coverage, learning—and that they are linked together in a coherent manner.

Most readers will have recognized that we have been describing aspects of the familiar phenomenon of ability grouping, but not in a familiar way. Instead of simply distinguishing students according to whether they belong to homogeneous or heterogeneous groups, which is the usual (and not very illuminating) way of studying grouping, we have tried to identify distinct though related activities that refer to sets of decisions that constitute class organization, grouped instruction, and individual learning.

This brief analysis shows the concatenation of distinct activities that constitute and surround classroom instruction. An implication of this analysis is that we can take any single educationally relevant resource and trace its manifestations across several hierarchical levels of school system organization. To illustrate the logic of the formulation, we will consider here the resource of time.

A school district administration makes three kinds of decisions about time. The first reveals its responsibilities of law enforcement to the state: the schools must remain open for a stipulated number of days to qualify for state aid. While this enforcement of state law places an outside limit on time available for teaching, it does not bear directly on teaching, instruction, or learning. Furthermore, when the length of the academic year is combined with a determination about the length of the school day, the second type of district decision is made: how much time teachers (and other employees) will work as part of a contractual agreement with suppliers of labor. The third type of decision pertains to when the schools will start and finish each academic year, open and close each day, and recess for vacations, decisions that determine when and whether parents can leave the household for work and arrange for the care of very young children. Basic time considerations, then, at the district level of organization are tied up with law enforcement, labor contracts, and the integration of the school system with households in the community; and district outcomes can be defined in these terms.

School systems, of course, do not hire teachers in general, but teachers who instruct in particular subjects in secondary schools and in a variety of basic skills in elementary schools. Hiring teachers by subject and skill presumes that curricular priorities have been established, which means that decisions have been made about how much time will be devoted to each segment of the curriculum: to English, mathematics, science, foreign languages, and so on, in secondary schools; to reading, arithmetic, science, social studies, and so on, in elementary schools. At the level of schools, these decisions become manifest in the time schedule, a formal statement written in fine-grained time units of how much time will be devoted to each subject matter and to extracurricular pursuits.

The school schedule is really a political document that acknowledges the influences of administrative directives and the preferences of teachers and parents expressing varying views about the welfare of the student body, of individual students, and of different types of students. It embodies past decisions about how much ordinary instruction there will be, in which subjects, at which more or less desirable times, and in which more or less desirable places. It expresses how segregated or desegregated classes will be in response to higher level administrative directives as well as the integration of the handicapped in regular and special classes. These resultant priorities conventionally expressed in the time schedule are an outcome of school level organization.

The curricular priorities expressed in the school time schedule represent temporal constraints upon the work of teachers in classrooms. While in secondary schools the order of classes throughout the day is established by the schedule itself, in elementary schools the teachers themselves arrange activities within the confines of daily time allotments, deciding which activities come earliest in the day, which next, and which last, with some flexibility about how long each successive activity will last. In addition to determining which activities take place during the "better" and "worse" times of the day, teachers also establish, within school guidelines and across parts of the curriculum (reading, arithmetic, science), how long instruction will last in each of a variety of classroom formats (whole class, grouped, individual instruction) and how much time gets wasted through interruptions, poor planning, and transitions between activities. At the classroom level, then, teachers allocate time in ways that bear directly upon instruction by determining the amount of time that students will have available for productive work in various subject areas.

Finally, given the time that teachers make available for productive work, students then decide how much of that time to use and to waste, and in so doing influence the amount they will learn.

What we have done here is to trace the allocation of time through the layers of school system organization to show how it takes on different manifestations as district, school, class, and individual phenomena. We have also shown how the nature of time at one level becomes a time condition for events occurring at the next lower level.

What our formulation does is very simple. It locates productive activities at all levels of the school system that in more common but less precise parlance are known as administration and teaching. It also states that productive activities specific to levels produce outcomes specific to levels. Accordingly, we distinguish carefully between the productive processes that constitute the working of school organization from the outcomes, or values, produced by those processes. They are not the same thing, although they have commonly been confused in discussions about educational effects. The distinction between production and value not only is important conceptually, but provides a principle that ties the parts of the levels of school organization into a coherent pattern.

The formulation also carries us some distance in thinking about how the effectiveness of schools should be viewed. The common practice of using individual achievement (or aggregations of individual achievement) as a primary index to gauge whether schools are productive is of limited value because there are other outcomes that are the direct result of productive processes occurring at higher levels of school system organization. There is no question that achievement is an important outcome at the individual level; it may or may not be an important outcome at other levels, as our previous analyses of time and grouping indicate. Perhaps, for example, the properly understood outcome of instructional groups is a group-specific rate of covering learning materials or the amount of time a teacher makes available for instruction, outcomes that when considered at the individual level are properly construed as conditions of learning. An important class level outcome may be the creation of an appropriate grouping arrangement or the establishment of a productive time schedule, both of which are conditions bearing on the nature of group instruction.

Similarly, at the school level, the important outcomes may be the allocation of time to curricular areas that makes enough time available for basic skill subjects, an assignment of teachers to classes that makes the most appropriate use of their talents or that provides equitable work loads, or the appropriate coordination of skill subjects from year to year so that children are prepared for the work of the succeeding grade. At the district level, perhaps negotiating labor contracts that satisfy employees, administrators, and the taxpayers, or having a satisfactory book and materials procurement policy represent significant outcomes.

SCHOOL BOARDS

Why American Education Needs Them

Michael A. Resnick and Anne L. Bryant

The formal organizational structure of educational systems includes many levels, from federal and state funding and mandates to local schools and classrooms in which teaching and learning take place. Each level has a role to play in meeting the overall goals of schooling in a society. However, this complexity raises the question of where decisions are made and who should make decisions about school policies and operations. Traditionally, local control of schools takes place through school boards, elected to represent the views of community citizens. However, these boards have come under fire as governments and citizens look for explanations for why many schools fail children. Some large school districts have shifted to mayoral control—with mixed results. Michael A. Resnick and Anne L. Bryant, leaders in the National School Boards Association, address the importance of school boards to create a link between communities and their schools, to interpret state and federal mandates, and to ensure local oversight of education.

Questions to consider for this reading:

1. Who should make decisions for schools, and why? Locally elected school boards? Mayors of cities? Other decision makers?

2. What impact do state and federal governments have on local board decision makers?

3. What role do school boards play in the organization of local community schools?

Everyone thinks that they know what's best for schools because they have had a school experience. The public wants their voices heard inside the schoolhouse walls. They want to know that their tax dollars are being spent effectively and responsibly. They want to know that children in their communities are receiving a world-class education. They want to know that someone is accountable for what happens in classrooms. And the ones who are accountable are the members of the local school board. . . .

Although states and the federal government are becoming increasingly involved in education, public education remains a local enterprise. It represents a community's culture and values, which in turn are reflected in our schools. What works in one district doesn't necessarily translate to others.

From "School Boards: Why American Education Needs Them," by Michael A. Resnick and Anne L. Bryant, 2010, *Phi Delta Kappan, 91*(6), pp. 11–14. Copyright 2010 by Phi Delta Kappa International. All rights reserved. Reprinted by permission.

Increasingly, local school boards are charged with ensuring that broader state and federal education requirements are met while translating local values and priorities into policies to meet the goals and aspirations of parents, taxpayers, and local businesses. By engaging their communities (parents, businesses, civic and religious groups, and community members), school boards create a culture that supports schools in their main mission: raising student achievement.

Across the country, school boards are successfully doing just that while performing a variety of key governance functions, such as setting academic goals, priorities, and policies; empowering the superintendent; and providing on-the-ground oversight and accountability for results.

In recent years, the chronically weak performance of several high-profile urban districts has led to some form of mayoral takeover or operational influence when school boards could not muster the necessary leadership to overcome educational challenges in their schools and the larger community. While a relative handful in number, the attention given to these districts has caused some to wrongly conclude that the nation's 14,350 school boards overall might not be needed or equipped to provide a 21st-century education.

So, the questions raised are: Why do we have school boards? What do we lose without them? and What are they doing that tells us they are up to the task?

MAKING THE CONNECTION

One major and increasingly important purpose for having school boards is to connect the federal and state levels, as well as local educators, with the real and diverse world of local people in a way that is close to the community, accountable to it, and which has the authority to act. Mayors and county officials can use their clout to rally the community behind the schools, but these officials are unlikely to provide the knowledge,

focus, commitment, or on-going accessibility that school boards do. After all, mayors run cities with a myriad of priorities to fulfill, including the needs of the majority of voters who don't have children in school. If education becomes a department of city or county government, what are the chances that education in the long run will get the attention it deserves? Elected school boards were created for the singularity of their purpose and accountability.

The demands of education have changed, and so has the operation of today's school boards. Go to school board meetings and witness the time devoted to student achievement issues, including newer approaches to goal setting, budget and policy development, and program evaluation. Look at the use of data and the level of reports given and discussed.

At the board level and in other meetings, board members work closely with their local community on issues of importance. Similarly, look at the conferences school board members are attending and the resources they're using to sharpen their knowledge around student achievement. Critics of school boards too often lack knowledge of the successful leadership that today's school boards provide through their changed substantive focus and governing method.

For example, in 1999, the National School Boards Association (NSBA) launched its Key Work of School Boards program, a year-round governance process used by many U.S. school boards. Specifically, the Key Work is aimed at increasing student achievement through effective board practices in goal setting, policy and resource alignment, evaluation, accountability, and fostering a climate for success (Gemberling, Smith, and Villani 2009).

With support from the Bill & Melinda Gates Foundation, NSBA is developing a school board training program for data-driven decision making that reflects the Obama Administration's Race to the Top program. Likewise, state school boards associations have developed hands-on programs to help boards meet a wide range of challenges through effective governance.

TAKING THE LEAD FOR STUDENTS

Beyond good decision making, do school boards perform special leadership functions that make a difference in raising student achievement? Evidence from Iowa suggests that they do.

Since 1999, the Iowa Lighthouse Study has interviewed and surveyed hundreds of school district leaders and school board members in an effort to answer that question (Iowa Association of School Boards 2000). Examined were districts that were comparable in socioeconomic makeup and finances but which had vastly different student achievement. One of the study's key findings was that low-performing school districts had a self-fulfilling prophecy of low expectations by school staff and students. By contrast, high-performing school districts had climates of success specifically established by the board through expectations of students and staff, including the accountability and resources provided by the board and the community support that the board garnered for the schools.

In these high-performing districts, the boards and superintendent had strong team relationships, including a constructive oversight process for setting goals and evaluating results to drive the staff's work. Not surprisingly school boards had a different view of the school district's accountability and responsibility than did the school staff, and that difference can add to the climate for success.

School boards have a long history as a cornerstone of democracy. Attend any school board meeting and you'll see communities having their say. Board members take their work home—and to grocery stores, soccer games, and gas stations—because they're never off duty. They can't be—they live in the communities where they serve, allowing for easy access and input from those who put them into office.

E-mails, phone calls, PTA meetings, and other regular communications are part of the job in a way that can't be matched by mayors or distant state agencies. Given their proximity to the community and their singularity of purpose, school boards are not only uniquely positioned to hear the community, but to proactively engage the community as well.

No magic bullet exists for this, but the Key Work of School Boards encourages communication and transparency as critical pieces of the puzzle. Inviting key stakeholders and the public to the table, whether at public school board meetings or in other ways, creates a culture of collaboration that aids school board success. By building strong relationships, school boards can actively engage key stakeholders and grow support for their schools.

School boards give parents a mechanism for engaging in decisions that directly affect their children. This ability to engage allows parents to effect change and feel invested not only in their children's schools, but in the child's education as a whole. This cannot help but affect student achievement.

Having school boards that engage the public also pays off in passing tax and bond referenda. Debates over local funding measures frequently become high-profile community discussions about the direction of education in the local schools. Those debates also include the majority of people who don't have school-age children. They provide a means to balance local control and priorities with those of the state and federal levels. To pass these measures, typically school board members, and not professional staff, reach out to stakeholders—business leaders, parents, teachers, religious and community groups—to demonstrate how the use of taxpayer dollars will strengthen the schools and their community.

As education becomes more centralized at the state and federal levels, providing communities with opportunities to talk with policy makers and influence policy matters will become even more important. Anything less risks alienating parents and other community members from the schools. It also risks shuffling off decisions to other levels of government that are not as knowledgeable—or caring—about a school district's plans or the community's desires. To meet these goals, school boards are well positioned with the perspective, knowledge of their schools, and authority to represent the system as a whole.

Furthermore, school boards make decisions in public, not behind closed doors or by executive fiat. The requirement that decisions occur through a majority vote helps ensure that a board consider a variety of options, debate proposals, and consider differing viewpoints—including voices from the community, not just from the school board.

BOARDS ARE UP TO THE TASK

Even in sound economic times, budgets and funding are at the core of the issues facing school boards. In times of financial stress, funding and budgeting become even more urgently tied to what schools are able to deliver. Add to this the increased numbers of poor and underserved children, immigrant students who may not speak English, and the diversion of tax dollars from public schools to other purposes. Unlike school board members, legislators and mayors address a variety of issues in their scope as government officials. Education issues are the heart of what school board members do, and they make decisions accordingly without the burden of partisan politics.

Schools also are human institutions. Parents entrust their children to schools for six hours a day, 180 days a year and expect schools to provide a safe environment that also supports their broader development of skills, interests, character, and values. School boards must respond to diverse and varied communities, as well as set broader education and social policies and practices that address specific interests of their communities. They must also provide oversight to ensure that their policies are met. . . .

CONCLUSION

Schools can't exist in a vacuum. They're a critical part of their communities and they must engage those communities in order to thrive. The responsibility for drawing community and business leaders, parents, civic groups, and the public into the schools falls squarely on the shoulders of the local school board. To go about the business of running schools and educating children, the local school board must engage with the community, listen to its concerns, and enact policies and strategies that make the most of the local community's resources and culture.

Just as schools are human institutions, so are school boards. They aren't any more infallible than mayors, state legislators, presidents—or nondemocratically governed institutions. The institution of school boards should not be eliminated because of the performance of some chronically weak boards.

At the same time, we should not excuse the performance of such boards. Given the value that school boards bring to the education process, the better way to address this is by changing a weak board's leadership through the electoral process and by strengthening those boards through the various governance resources that can be made available to them—just as we do for other governing bodies in both the public and the private sector.

In sum, if local school boards were eliminated, it wouldn't be long before communities would try to reinvent them. School boards, as an institution, make our schools stronger and better equipped to educate the 50 million children in our nation's public schools.

REFERENCES

Gemberling, Katheryn W., Carl W. Smith, and Joseph S. Villani, eds. *The Key Work of School Boards Guidebook,* 2nd ed. Alexandria, Va.: National School Boards Association, 2009.

Iowa Association of School Boards. "IASB's Lighthouse Study: School Boards and Student Achievement." *Iowa School Board Compass* 5, no. 2 (Fall 2000): 4.

National School Boards Association/Council of Urban Boards of Education. "Norfolk; Developing World-Class Schools." *Urban Advocate* (October 2006): 2–3.

National School Boards Association/Council of Urban Boards of Education. "Atlanta Public Schools." *Urban Advocate* (October 2009): 3.

CLASSROOM ORDERING AND THE
SITUATIONAL IMPERATIVES OF ROUTINE AND RITUAL

David Diehl and Daniel A. McFarland

A classroom without order is like a mob—and not much can be accomplished (Durkheim, 1911/1961). Much of the teaching and learning in schools takes place in classrooms where teachers and students establish routines and rituals that result in order in the classroom. As authors David Diehl and Daniel A. McFarland (2012) put it, classroom order comes from the coordination of "interaction into institutionalized patterns (routine) and the validation of participants' identities (ritual)" (p. 326). Informal classroom interaction patterns result in formal routines. In a major study of 601 high school classrooms, the authors analyze interactions between students and teachers to determine how classroom organization is formed from interactions, and how the resulting organization affects classroom dynamics and learning. The analysis in this article is complex and moves the understanding of interaction and its effects on group order to a new level. We have not included the detailed methodology with discussions of how the research was conducted and theories used such as sociolinguistic studies and ethnographies, but we encourage you to go to the original article to learn about the sophisticated methods used to study interactions. This reading connects the microlevel interactions in classrooms with mesolevel school and classroom organization. The interactions and rituals in the classroom determine the classroom order. It looks at how individual student and teacher needs and ideas work together with classroom groups to result in routines. These routines change depending on each type of interaction and activity in the classroom, whether group work, discussion, free time, student presentations, audiovisual presentations, recitation, seatwork, lecture, or exams. The authors do not support one type of teaching (traditional lecture and teacher-controlled class vs. student-centered class) based on their study, but rather indicate that a mix of pedagogical or teaching methods is desirable.

Questions to consider for this reading:

1. According to the authors, how is order established in classrooms?

2. How might understanding the role of interaction in establishing routines and rituals be useful?

3. How do the open systems model and levels of analysis from micro to macro help us understand classroom order?

Creating and maintaining order in the classroom is a central concern for educators (Waller 1932; Metz 1978; Boocock 1978; Bossert 1979; Mehan 1979; Doyle 1986; McNeil 1986; Stodolsky 1988; Cazden 1988; Nystrand 1997; Gamoran and Kelly 2003). Despite the best efforts of teachers, however, research from diverse perspectives has shown that disruption and defiance are ubiquitous and seemingly unavoidable (MacBeth 1990:192). It is unclear why some classes are more orderly than others and why disorder can arise and recede even within individual class periods. Fundamental aspects of classroom teaching and learning remain obscure without a better understanding of how teachers and students construct, and are molded by, the social context they jointly enact through moment-by-moment social transactions (Wells 1993).

We address this lacuna through two theoretical and empirical elaborations. The first is to regard interactional order as a multidimensional phenomenon. Following Goffman, we relate order as meeting two requirements, namely, those of routine and ritual (cf. system and normative requirements, Goffman 1981:14–15; 1983). For an encounter to be comprehensible, participants must coordinate according to some collective routine. In classrooms, this entails the mobilization of participants into and across stable interactional configurations associated with particular academic activities (Goffman 1981:137). For an encounter to be embraced and valued, participants must conduct interpersonal rituals demonstrating concord and a sense of collective goodwill. In classrooms, this entails the ratification of valued identities (Goffman 1981:266). While situational anchors of routine and ritual can reinforce one another, in crowded classroom settings there arises a tension between efforts to coordinate the group and to ratify identities.

Our second elaboration is to regard interactional order as a situated phenomenon. By this we mean that the problem of classroom order changes from moment to moment. As teachers move their classes through different academic activities, the structures and expectations for interaction shift, as do the means by which routine and ritual requirements of interaction are accomplished. Most practitioners negotiate these dynamics and tensions via ongoing talk and communication. However, discursive moves seldom have the same effect on every situation. As most educators can attest, declarative statements and jokes have different effects on the enactment of lectures and group work activities. To study this situated nature of classroom order, we identify proxies for interactional stability (routine) and concord (ritual) within the overall network of moment-to-moment discourse. By treating individual acts of communication within institutionalized activities as the building blocks of classroom order (Goffman 1981; Wells 1999; Butts 2008), we are able to offer a novel comparison of the dynamic patterns of interactions (and their effects) across a multitude of diverse classrooms, class periods, and class lessons. . . .

ROUTINE AND RITUAL: DUAL REQUIREMENTS FOR CLASSROOM ORDERING

Our work can be located within an ongoing effort to understand variation in classroom order at increasingly fine-grained levels of analysis. Pioneering work on the social order of schooling was primarily concerned with providing a generalizable description of the interaction dynamics between teachers and students rather than explaining variation within classrooms. The result was a view of classroom order shaped by a ubiquitous tension between the different interests and motivations of teachers and students as well as the incompatible demands of the teaching profession itself (Waller 1932; Bidwell 1965; Lortie 1975).

Building off of this work, midcentury sociology of education began to offer explanations for variations in the teacher-student tension between classrooms. This work identified numerous sources of interclassroom differences that affected interaction, including teacher styles and dispositions (Brookover 1945; Cogan 1956) as well as the culture (Gordon 1957; Coleman 1961) and composition (Dreeben and Barr 1988) of the student body. In this work variation arises from differences in how teachers and students consistently enact their institutional roles. Following the general trend of post-Parsonian sociology in the 1960s, however, sociolinguists and interactionists shifted focus inward toward language, micro-processes, and variations within classrooms.

Sociolinguists, for their part, paid close attention to conversational dynamics and began to document routinized (generally dyadic) turn-taking structures in activities such as recitation and group work (Mehan 1979; Erickson 1982; Stodolsky 1988). Interactionists, in contrast, drew on ethnographies to illuminate the ongoing negotiation of control and defiance in the classroom (Jackson 1968; Metz 1978; Pace 2006). Both streams of research focused on moment-to-moment dynamics of interaction, but each offered a fundamentally different conception of the nature of classroom order and how to research it.

The study of these two aspects of social order—the formal structure of talk and the ongoing negotiation of identities—has remained largely disconnected in the sociological literature. One exception is in Goffman's work on what he called the "interaction order" (Goffman 1967, 1981, 1983). Goffman argued that interaction is multidimensional and that the individual has multiple obligations to and interests in maintaining order (Goffman 1983:5). To that end, the actor uses various strategies and techniques to ensure his or her own proper involvement as well as the proper involvement of others (Goffman 1967:115). Doing so entails meeting both routine (system) and ritual (normative) requirements of interaction (Goffman 1981:14–15). Problematically, however, Goffman did not adequately delineate between these two central features of situated order, nor did he provide means for studying them (Schegloff 1988). Part of our aim in this work is to address both of these shortcomings.

First, the *requirement of routine* concerns rendering interactional exchanges into recursive and predictable configurations based on a working agreement about "what is going on here" (Goffman 1974; 1981). The most important organizing conventions in classrooms are academic activities and the typified sets of relations, orientations, and discourses they entail (Erickson 1982; Doyle and Carter 1984; Stodolsky 1988). Activities provide routinized features such as the opening and closing of communication channels, the distribution of turns, and communication rules for bystanders (Goffman 1981). In a classroom discussion, for example, students follow teacher-defined and enforced rules for legitimate talk, generally taking the floor and speaking only once given permission to do so. . . .

In classrooms, the successful accomplishment of ritual interaction creates a shared sense of respect, or goodwill, between teachers and students (Dreeben 1970; Bidwell 2005). Interpersonal goodwill often is marked by subjective and experiential factors that are difficult to observe. Therefore, teachers and students mostly infer the presence of goodwill from overt acts of compliance and defiance (Kelman 1961). The absence of defiance in social encounters can be referred to as the behavioral expression of concord. To be clear, concord is not synonymous with the subjective experience of classroom goodwill. In the first part of our empirical analysis, we address concord as an observable feature of interaction patterns, and in the second part, we look at goodwill as a feature of subjective experience reported on surveys.

As with routine, meeting ritual requirements of interaction has a positive effect on teaching and learning. Students, for their part, defy authority when they feel their character has been imputed in a demeaning way (Lawrence et al. 1984:122). Teachers, in turn, feel student defiance threatens their institutional identity and devalues the investment of time and energy they put into an activity (Lawrence et al. 1984:121; McFarland 2001, 2004). When there is classroom goodwill, interactions are characterized by warmth and respect, and with those come lower levels of disruptive behaviors (Battistich et al. 1997), higher levels of on-task behavior (Marzano, Marzano, and Pickering 2003), and greater intellectual risk taking (Murray and Greenberg 2000).

The Variable Relationship between Stability and Concord. Classrooms are crowded settings where a multiplicity of doings and interests come into and fall out of focus over the course of a lesson (Jackson 1968; McFarland 2005). In the flux of affairs, situational requirements of coordination and identity are variably catered to and met. This means that there are two distinct ways that disorder can arise: through either problems related to instability in activity structures or challenges to concord. How any particular communicative act relates to these interactional anchors depends, however, on the nature of the activity within which it takes place.

This conceptualization emphasizes the nature of participation, or the way that individuals align or orient themselves toward the activity and its rules and expectations for speaking, listening, and turn taking (Erickson 2004). Sociolinguists have long described the pattern of these alignments and orientations as the participation framework of an activity (Goffman 1981). These frameworks define interpersonal expectations and obligations such that everyone is called on to adopt particular interaction roles or participation statuses (e.g., speaker or hearer). These participation statuses are then arranged in such a way as to form a larger pattern. When recursively enacted, it becomes a recognized, guiding framework to which everyone adheres (Gee 1999). This is true for both academic activities prescribed by the teacher and informal activities initiated by students (e.g., gossip in Eder and Enke 1991). The successful cueing of an activity's participation framework, the mobilization of classroom participants into the activity, and its stable reenactment over time are quite an accomplishment.

From this perspective, the basic empirical units out of which classroom order is generated are discrete communicative events (i.e., utterances) produced by one actor and directed toward one or more targets (Butts 2008: 158). Adapting the language of Goffman (1981), we refer to these as discursive "moves." Actors use discursive moves to present particular orientations toward each other and toward shared interaction (see "footings" in Goffman 1981). These moves can commence interactional alignments, which in turn lead to larger changes in the structural configuration of group communication (Goodwin 1998; Gibson 2003).

Teachers use discourse to manage the timing and sequencing of interactions to strike a balance between coercion and engendering voluntary participation that allows them to mobilize students in and out of the participation framework of academic activities (Kounin 1970; McFarland 2004). Students, for their part, also use discourse both to align with academic activities and to resist them, all the while asserting and expressing valued identities (Alpert 1991; McFarland 2001). The overall picture is one of an ongoing struggle about positions in the classroom network of talk (Grenfell 1998) as distinct activity frameworks are cued via discourse and ensuing patterns of association form and fall (see Figure 16.1 for a schematic and Supplemental Online Materials for a network movie demonstrating pattern switches at http://soe.sagepub.com/content/85/4/326/suppl/DC1).

* * *

DISCUSSION

In summary, we present multiple findings about social order in classrooms. Our analyses reveal the multidimensional and situated nature of classroom order. First, we find a strong relation between temporality and classroom order that is consistent with prior qualitative work and reinforces the validity of our models. Second, we find that most of the variance in stability and concord occurs within classroom contexts and their moments. As such, the primary issue of classroom order is often situational. Third, we find that activities often dictate the overall levels of stability and concord in participant behaviors and that they often work at cross-purposes. Activities that require greater interactivity and

Figure 16.1 Percentage of Activities Students Consider Boring

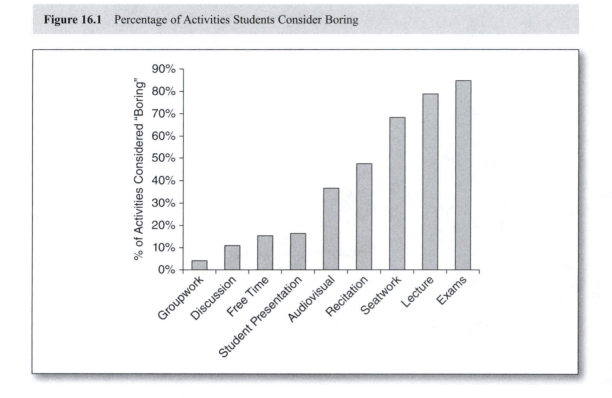

distribute attention evenly are harder to stabilize but less conflictual. By contrast, activities that are less interactive and focus attention unevenly are easier to stabilize and acquire compliance (but not goodwill). Fourth, we find that the stability and concord within activities entail situated usage of discursive moves. The use of a joke in lectures and seatwork, for example, has different effects on the stability and concord in those particular situations. . . .

Our analyses of task duration find that in general, stable and concordant activities last longer. The relationship is weaker, however, for activities such as tests and videos that have more rigid starting and ending times. When the degree of interactivity is high and/or attention is centralized on the teacher, activities are more sensitive to issues of stability. The influence of concord, in contrast, is weaker in activities wherein students have the opportunity to engage in decentralized conversations. Next, we

find that teacher attitudes respond to issues of stability and student attitudes to issues of concord. Such biases reflect a central tendency across lessons. Teachers adopt more transmittal formats of instruction that diminish interactivity and centralize attention on themselves so that collective mobilization and compliance occurs. This places students in a consistently nonactive role and devalues identity. What we learn is that our analyses of concord in part A may often reflect compliance more than goodwill and that we need to take into account participants' attitudes. Once we do, we see that teachers want more than mere compliance; they want stability with student role embracement.

CONCLUSION

In this article, we have attempted to reconceptualize the problem of classroom social order. Prior

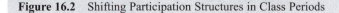

Figure 16.2 Shifting Participation Structures in Class Periods

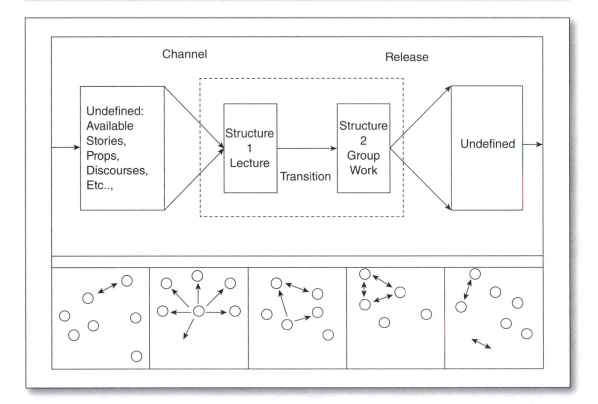

work in the sociology of education explains classroom order in terms of factors that are static across classroom moments, such as the composition of students (Dreeben and Barr 1988; McFarland 2001) and characteristics of teachers (Pianta and Hamre 2009), the mismatch between adolescent and academic cultures (Willis 1977; Woods 1983), and the organizational features of the classroom setting (McFarland 2005). In contrast, we have located important interactional dynamics between teachers and students within the discursively constructed structures of classroom situations themselves. In doing so we build off of Goffman's insight that "the proper study of interaction is not the individual and his psychology, but rather the syntactical relations among acts of different persons mutually present to one another . . . not, then,

men and their moments. Rather, moments and their men" (Goffman 1967:3).

In the classroom, this means seeing the motivations and interests of students and teachers not as essential features of their characters or roles but rather as the result of their shifting positions in changing activity structures and discourse (see Figure 16.2).

In this view, problems and perturbations in classroom order are largely a function of the interrelation of discourse and task in particular social situations. Each activity and form of talk cues different participation statuses, and with those come different experiences and obligations for stability and concord. By altering the task and the discursive cues, the situation changes, and another arrangement of participation statuses arises along with different potential affronts to activity and self (i.e., routine and ritual). It is only in the consistent selection of activities such as recitation, lecture, and seatwork that classroom actors take up orientations toward one another and a more abstract sense of the institutional roles of teacher and student forms.

One might infer from our results that the best course for educators interested in improving experience for students is to shift focus away from stability and routine and toward building concord and ritual in the classroom. Similar prescriptions were made with student-centered instruction and youth empowerment (Swidler 1979; Cohen and Lotan 1997). Opposite prescriptions are made by traditionalists arguing centralized activities have greater returns to achievement (Adams and Engelmann 1996). The findings of this article, however, suggest that any either-or prescription is problematic. Successful situations must be "worked," and interactional requirements must be balanced so as best to accomplish collective mobilization and rapport. This suggests part of the reason reform efforts arguing for one direction over another tend not to succeed. Rather than pitting the efficacy of traditional and progressive pedagogies against each other, then, researchers should be investigating how different patterns in the usage of types of academic activities create variable classroom experiences. Instead of promoting single instructional formats, the research presented here suggests educators may want to consider the alternation of divergent forms. Using decentralized and centralized tasks in cycles may meet situational requirements of routine and ritual in an oscillating manner. . . .

[T]he data used here remain unparalleled in education research and offer a novel glimpse into the interactional construction of classroom social order. Future research would do well to look at how planned changes in classroom practices reshape the interrelation of routine and ritual features of interaction, often in unintentional ways. Studying the dynamics laid out in this article during instances of reform can offer a new way of studying the failure or success of change

efforts. Future work should look at the same activities across a wide range of school settings and grades. Doing so would provide new and important perspectives on some of the most central questions in the sociology of education including the processes through which students are socialized into school practices and the micro-interactional sources of inequality and differences in educational outcomes.

References

Adams, Gary and Siegfried Engelmann. 1996. *Research on Direct Instruction: 25 Years beyond DISTAR.* Seattle, WA: Educational Achievement Systems.

Alpert, Bracha. 1991. "Students' Resistance in the Classroom." *Anthropology and Education Quarterly* 22(4): 350–66.

Battistich, Victor, Daniel Solomon, Marilyn Watson, and Eric Schaps. 1997. "Caring School Communities." *Educational Psychologist* 32(3): 137–51.

Bidwell, Charles E. 1965. "The School as a Formal Organization." Pp. 972–1022 in *Handbook of Organizations,* edited by James P. March. Chicago: Rand McNally.

Bidwell, Charles E. 2005. "A Sociological Agenda for Research on Education." Pp. 15–36 in *The Social Organization of Schooling,* edited by Larry Hedges and Barbara Schneider. New York: Russell Sage.

Boocock, Sarane. 1978. "The Social Organization of the Classroom." *Annual Review of Sociology* 4: 1–28.

Bossert, Steven T. 1979. *Tasks and Social Relationships in Classrooms.* New York: Cambridge University Press.

Brookover, Wilbur. 1945. "The Relation of Social Factors to Teaching Ability." *Journal of Experimental Education* 13(4): 191–205.

Butts, Carter T. 2008. "A Relational Event Framework for Social Action." *Sociological Methodology* 38(1): 155–200.

Cazden, Courtney B. 1988. *Classroom Discourse.* Portsmouth, NH: Heinemann.

Cogan, Morris L. 1956. "Theory and Design of a Study of Teacher-Pupil Interaction." *Harvard Educational Review* 26(4): 315–42.

Cohen, Elizabeth G. and Rachel A. Lotan. 1997. *Working for Equity in Heterogeneous Classrooms: Sociological Theory in Practice.* Sociology of Education Series. New York: Teachers College Press.

Coleman, James. 1961. *The Adolescent Society: The Social Life of the Teenager and Its Impact on Education.* New York: Free Press of Glencoe.

Doyle, Walter. 1986. "Classroom Organization and Management." Pp. 392–431 in *Handbook of Research on Teaching,* edited by M. C. Wittrock. New York: Macmillan.

Doyle, Walter and Kathy Carter. 1984. "Academic Tasks in Classrooms." *Curriculum Inquiry* 14(2): 129–49.

Dreeben, Robert. 1970. *The Nature of Teaching.* Glenview, IL: Scott Foresman.

Dreeben, Robert and Rebecca Barr. 1988. "Classroom Composition and the Design of Instruction." *Sociology of Education* 61(3): 129–42.

Durkheim, Emile. 1961. *Moral Education,* translated by Everett K. Wilson & Herman Schnurer. Glencoe, IL: Free Press. (Original work published 1911)

Eder, Donna and Janet Enke. 1991. "The Structure of Gossip: Opportunities and Constraints on Collective Expression amongst Adolescents." *American Sociological Review* 56(4): 494–508.

Erickson, Frederick. 1982. "Classroom Discourse as Improvisation: Relationships between Academic Task Structure and Social Participation Structure in Lessons." Pp. 153–81 in *Communicating in the Classroom,* edited by L. C. Wilkinson. New York: Academic.

Erickson, Frederick. 2004. *Talk and Social Theory: Ecologies of Speaking and Listening in Everyday Life.* Malden, MA: Polity Press.

Gamoran, Adam and Scan Kelly. 2003. "On What Is Learned in School to How Schools Work: Learning and Teaching in Secondary School English Classrooms." Pp. 109–26 in *Stability and Change in American Education: Structure, Processes and Outcomes,* edited by Maureen T. Hallinan, Adam Gamoran, Warren Kubitschek, and Tom Loveless. Clinton Corners, NY: Eliot Werner.

Gee, John Paul. 1999. *An Introduction to Discourse Analysis: Theory and Method.* New York: Routledge.

Gibson, David R. 2003. "Participation Shifts: Order and Differentiation in Group Conversation." *Social Forces* 81(4): 1335–80.

Goffman, Erving. 1967. *Interaction Ritual: Essays on Face-to-face Behavior.* New York: Pantheon.

Goffman, Erving. 1974. *Frame Analysis: An Essay on the Organization of Experience.* New York: Harper and Row.

Goffman, Erving. 1981. *Forms of Talk.* Philadelphia: University of Pennsylvania Press.

Goffman, Erving. 1983. "Presidential Address: The Interaction Order." *American Sociological Review* 48(1): 1–17.

Goodwin, Marjorie H. 1998. "Games of Stance: Conflict and Footing in Hopscotch." Pp. 23–46 in *Kid's Talk: Strategic Language Use in Later Childhood,* edited by Susan Hoyle and Carolyn Temple Adger. New York: Oxford University Press.

Gordon, Calvin Wayne. 1957. *The Social System of the High School: A Study in the Sociology of Adolescence.* Glencoe, IL: Free Press.

Grenfell, Michael. 1998. "Language in the Classroom." Pp. 71–88 in *Bourdieu and Education,* edited by Michael Grenfell and David James. Bristol, PA: Falmer Press.

Jackson, Philip W. 1968. *In Life in Classrooms.* Oxford, England: Routledge.

Kelman, Herbert C. 1961. "Processes of Opinion Change." *Public Opinion Quarterly* 25(1): 57–78.

Kounin, Jacob S. 1970. *Discipline and Group Management in Classrooms.* New York: Holt, Rinehart and Winston.

Lawrence, Jean, David Steed, and Pamela Young. 1984. *Disruptive Children: Disruptive Schools?* New York: Croom Helm.

Lortie, Dan. 1975. *Schoolteacher: A Sociological Study.* Chicago: University of Chicago Press.

MacBeth, Douglas H. 1990. "Classroom Order as Practical Action: The Making and Un-making of a Quiet Reproach." *British Journal of Sociology of Education* 11(2): 189–214.

Marzano, Robert J., Jana Marzano, and Deborah Pickering. 2003. *Classroom Management That Works: Research-based Strategies for Every Teacher.* Alexandria, VA: ASCD.

McFarland, Daniel A. 2001. "Student Resistance: How the Formal and Informal Organization of Classrooms Facilitate Everyday Forms of Student Defiance." *American Journal of Sociology* 107(3): 612–78.

McFarland, Daniel A. 2004. "Resistance as a Social Drama: A Study of Change-oriented Encounters." *American Journal of Sociology* 109(6): 1249–1318.

McFarland, Daniel A. 2005. "Why Work When You Can Play?" Pp. 147–74 in *The Social Organization of Schooling,* edited by Larry V. Hedges and Barbara L. Schneider. New York: Russell Sage.

McNeil, Linda M. 1986. *Contradictions of Control: School Structure and School Knowledge.* New York: Routledge.

Mehan, Hugh. 1979. *Learning Lessons: Social Organization in the Classroom.* Cambridge, MA: Harvard University Press.

Metz, Mary. 1978. *Classrooms and Corridors: A Study of Authority in American Secondary Schools.* Berkeley: University of California Press.

Murray, Christopher and Mark Greenberg. 2000. "Children's Relationship with Teachers and Bonds with School: An Investigation of Patterns and Correlates in Middle Childhood." *Journal of School Psychology* 38(5): 423–45.

Nystrand, Martin. 1997. *Opening Dialogue: Understanding the Dynamics of Language and Learning in the English Classroom.* With Adam Gamoran, Robert Kachur, and Catherine Prendergast. New York: Teachers College Press.

Pace, Judith L. 2006. "Saving (and Losing) Face, Race, and Authority in 9th Grade English Class." Pp. 87–112 in *Classroom Authority: Theory, Research, and Practice,* edited by Judith L. Pace and A. Hemmings. Mahwah, NJ: Lawrence Erlbaum.

Pianta, Robert C. and Bridget K. Hamre. 2009. "Conceptualization, Measurement, and Improvement of Classroom Processes: Standardized Observation Can Leverage Capacity." *Educational Researcher* 38(2): 109–19.

Schegloff, Emanuel A. 1988. "Goffman and the Analysis of Conversation." Pp. 89–135 in *Erving Goffman: Exploring the Interaction Order,* edited by Paul Drew and Anthony Wootton. Oxford, England: Polity Press.

Stodolsky, Susan S. 1988. *The Subject Matters: Classroom Activity in Math and Social Studies.* Chicago: University of Chicago Press.

Swidler, Ann. 1979. *Organizations without Authority: Dilemmas of Social Control in Free Schools.* Cambridge, MA: Harvard University Press.

Waller, Willard. 1932. *The Sociology of Teaching.* Chicago: University of Chicago Press.

Wells, Gordon C. 1993. Reevaluating the IRF Sequence: A Proposal for the Articulation of Theories of Activity and Discourse for the Analysis of Teaching and Learning in the Classroom." *Linguistics and Education* 5(1): 1–37.

Wells, Gordon C. 1999. *Dialogic Inquiry: Towards a Sociocultural Practice and Theory of Education.* New York: Cambridge University Press.

Willis, Paul E. 1977. *Learning to Labor: How Working Class Kids Get Working Class Jobs.* New York: Columbia University Press.

Woods, Peter. 1983. *Sociology and the School: An Interactionist Viewpoint.* Boston: Routledge and Kegan Paul.

READING 17

LEARNING THE STUDENT ROLE

Kindergarten as Academic Boot Camp

Harry L. Gracey

The organizational structure of schools cannot be studied in isolation from the roles of individuals holding positions within the system. Part of the informal organization includes messages students learn about their expected roles. Bridging Chapter 4 on organizations and Chapter 5 on roles is Harry L. Gracey's classic discussion of young students learning their roles within the organizational structure. In his complete article, Gracey describes the socialization process into the role of "student" by documenting the organizational structure of the classroom and a day in the life of a kindergarten teacher and class. New initiates to formal schooling learn the expectations of school so that they will fit into the educational system and later into the world of work. In these excerpts from this classic article, some of the references may seem a bit old-fashioned; however, the article conveys a powerful message about the way students are socialized in school and for what purposes.

Questions to consider for this reading:

1. What are the formal and informal organizational structures of kindergarten classrooms, and what role do they play in preparing kindergarten students for the next stages of school life?

2. Taking the message about learning the student role, how is this role perpetuated and expanded through other levels of schooling?

3. How might functional and conflict theorists described in Chapter 1 interpret the processes taking place in kindergarten?

Education must be considered one of the major institutions of social life today. Along with the family and organized religion, however, it is a "secondary institution," one in which people are prepared for life in society as it is presently organized. The main dimensions of modern life, that is, the nature of society as a whole, are determined principally by the "primary institutions," which today are the economy, the political system, and the military establishment. Education has been defined by sociologists, classical and contemporary, as an institution which serves society by socializing people into it through a formalized, standardized procedure. At the beginning of this century, Emile Durkheim told student teachers at the University of Paris that education "consists of a methodical socialization of the younger generation." He went on to add:

> It is the influence exercised by adult generations on those that are not ready for social life. Its object is to arouse and to develop in the child a certain number of physical, intellectual, and moral states that are demanded of him by the political society as a whole and by the special milieu for which he is specifically destined. To the egotistic and asocial being that has just been born, [society] must as rapidly as possible add another capable of leading a moral and social life. Such is the work of education.[1]

"The education process," Durkheim said, "is above all the means by which society perpetually recreates the conditions of its very existence."[2] The contemporary educational sociologist, Wilbur Brookover, offers a similar formulation in his recent textbook definition of education.

> Actually, therefore, in the broadest sense education is synonymous with socialization. It includes any social behavior that assists in the induction of the child into membership in the society or any behavior by which the society perpetuates itself through the next generation.[3]

The educational institution is, then, one of the ways in which society is perpetuated through the systematic socialization of the young, while the nature of the society which is being perpetuated—its organization and operation, its values, beliefs, and ways of living—is determined by the primary institutions. The educational system, like other secondary institutions, serves the society which is created by the operation of the economy, the political system, and the military establishment. Schools, the social organizations of the educational institution, are today for the most part large bureaucracies run by specially trained and certified people. There are few places left in modern societies where formal teaching and learning is carried on in small, isolated groups, like the rural, one-room schoolhouses of the last century. Schools are large, formal organizations which tend to be parts of larger organizations, local community school districts. These school districts are

bureaucratically organized and their operations are supervised by state and local governments. In this context, as Brookover says:

> The term education is used . . . to refer to a system of schools, in which specifically designated persons are expected to teach children and youth certain types of acceptable behavior. The school system becomes a unit in the total social structure and is recognized by the members of the society as a separate social institution. Within this structure a portion of the total socialization process occurs.[4]

Education is the part of the socialization process which takes place in the schools; and these are, more and more today, bureaucracies within bureaucracies.

Kindergarten is generally conceived by educators as a year of preparation for school. It is thought of as a year in which small children, five or six years old, are prepared socially and emotionally for the academic learning which will take place over the next twelve years. It is expected that a foundation of behavior and attitudes will be laid in kindergarten on which the children can acquire the skills and knowledge they will be taught in the grades. A booklet prepared for parents by the staff of a suburban New York school system says that the kindergarten experience will stimulate the child's desire to learn and cultivate the skills he will need for learning in the rest of his school career. It claims that the child will find opportunities for physical growth, for satisfying his "need for self-expression," acquire some knowledge, and provide opportunities for creative activity. It concludes, "The most important benefit that your five-year-old will receive from kindergarten is the opportunity to live and grow happily and purposefully with others in a small society." The kindergarten teachers in one of the elementary schools in this community, one we shall call the Wilbur Wright School, said their goals were to see that the children "grew" in all ways: physically, of course, emotionally, socially, and academically. They said they wanted children to like school as a result of their kindergarten experiences and that they wanted them to learn to get along with others.

None of these goals, however, is unique to kindergarten; each of them is held to some extent by teachers in the other six grades at Wright School. And growth would occur, but differently, even if the child did not attend school. The children already know how to get along with others, in their families and their play groups. The unique job of the kindergarten in the educational division of labor seems rather to be teaching children the student role. The student role is the repertoire of behavior and attitudes regarded by educators as appropriate to children in school. Observation in the kindergartens of the Wilbur Wright School revealed a great variety of activities through which children are shown and then drilled in the behavior and attitudes defined as appropriate for school and thereby induced to learn the role of student. Observations of the kindergartens and interviews with the teachers both pointed to the teaching and learning of classroom routines as the main element of the student role. The teachers expended most of their efforts, for the first half of the year at least, in training the children to follow the routines which teachers created. The children were, in a very real sense, drilled in tasks and activities created by the teachers for their own purposes and beginning and ending quite arbitrarily (from the child's point of view) at the command of the teacher. One teacher remarked that she hated September, because during the first month "everything has to be done rigidly, and repeatedly, until they know exactly what they're supposed to do." However, "by January," she said, "they know exactly what to do [during the day] and I don't have to be after them all the time." Classroom routines were introduced gradually from the beginning of the year in all the kindergartens, and the children were drilled in them as long as was necessary to achieve regular compliance. By the end of the school year, the successful kindergarten teacher has a well-organized group of children. They follow classroom routines automatically, having learned all the command signals and the expected responses to them. They have, in our terms, learned the student role.

* * *

TRAINING FOR LEARNING AND FOR LIFE

The children [at the Wright School] learned to go through routines and to follow orders with unquestioning obedience, even when these make no sense to them. They have been disciplined to do as they are told by an authoritative person without significant protest. Edith Kerr [the teacher] has developed this discipline in the children by creating and enforcing a rigid social structure in the classroom through which she effectively controls the behavior of most of the children for most of the school day. The "living with others in a small society" which the school pamphlet tells parents is the most important thing the children will learn in kindergarten can be seen now in its operational meaning, which is learning to live by the routines imposed by the school. This learning appears to be the principal content of the student role.

Children who submit to school-imposed discipline and come to identify with it, so that being a "good student" comes to be an important part of their developing identities, become the good students by the school's definitions. Those who submit to the routines of the school but do not come to identify with them will be adequate students who find the more important part of their identities elsewhere, such as in the play group outside school. Children who refuse to submit to the school routines are rebels, who become known as "bad students" and often "problem children" in the school, for they do not learn the academic curriculum, and their behavior is often disruptive in the classroom. Today schools engage clinical psychologists in part to help teachers deal with such children.

[It is interesting to look at Edith Kerr's] kindergarten at Wright School [and] to ask how the children learn this role of student—come to accept school-imposed routines—and what, exactly, it involves in terms of behavior and attitudes. The most prominent features of the classroom are its physical and social structures. The room is carefully furnished and arranged in ways adults feel will interest children. The play store and play kitchen in the back of the room, for example, imply that children are interested in mimicking these activities of the adult world. The only space left for the children to create something of their own is the empty center of the room, and the materials at their disposal are the blocks, whose use causes anxiety on the part of the teacher. The room, being carefully organized physically by the adults, leaves little room for the creation of physical organization on the part of the children.

The social structure created by Edith is a far more powerful and subtle force for fitting the children to the student role. This structure is established by the very rigid and tightly controlled set of rituals and routines through which the children are put during the day. There is first the rigid "locating procedure" in which the children are asked to find themselves in terms of the month, date, day of the week, and the number of the class who are present and absent. This puts them solidly in the real world as defined by adults. The day is then divided into six periods whose activities are for the most part determined by the teacher. In Edith's kindergarten the children went through Serious Time, which opens the school day, Sharing Time, Play Time (which in clear weather would be spent outside), Work Time, Clean-up Time, after which they have their milk, and Rest Time after which they go home. The teacher has programmed activities for each of these times.

Occasionally the class is allowed limited discretion to choose between proffered activities, such as stories or records, but original ideas for activities are never solicited from them. Opportunity for free individual action is open only once in the day, during the part of Work Time left after the general class assignment has been completed (on the day reported, the class

assignment was drawing animal pictures for the absent Mark). Spontaneous interests or observations from the children are never developed by the teacher. It seems that her schedule just does not allow room for developing such unplanned events. During Sharing Time, for example, the child who brought a bird's nest told Edith, in reply to her question of what kind of bird made it, "My friend says it's a rain bird." Edith does not think to ask about this bird, probably because the answer is "childish," that is, not given in accepted adult categories of birds. The children then express great interest in an object in the nest, but the teacher ignores this interest, probably because the object is uninteresting to her. The soldiers from "Babes in Toyland" strike a responsive note in the children, but this is not used for a discussion of any kind. The soldiers are treated in the same way as objects which bring little interest from the children. Finally, at the end of Sharing Time the child-world of perception literally erupts in the class with the recollection of "the spooky house" at the zoo. Apparently this made more of an impression on the children than did any of the animals, but Edith is unable to make any sense of it for herself. The tightly imposed order of the class begins to break down as the children discover a universe of discourse of their own and begin talking excitedly with one another. The teacher is effectively excluded from this child's world of perception and for a moment she fails to dominate the classroom situation. She reasserts control, however, by taking the children to the next activity she has planned for the day. It seems never to have occurred to Edith that there might be a meaningful learning experience for the children in re-creating the "spooky house" in the classroom. It seems fair to say that this would have offered an exercise in spontaneous self-expression and an opportunity for real creativity on the part of the children. Instead, they are taken through a canned animal imitation procedure, an activity which they apparently enjoy, but which is also imposed upon them rather than created by them.

While children's perceptions of the world and opportunities for genuine spontaneity and creativity are being systematically eliminated from the kindergarten, unquestioned obedience to authority and rote learning of meaningless material are being encouraged. When the children are called to line up in the center of the room they ask "Why?" and "What for?" as they are in the very process of complying. They have learned to go smoothly through a programmed day, regardless of whether parts of the program make any sense to them or not. Here the student role involves what might be called "doing what you're told and never mind why." Activities which might "make sense" to the children are effectively ruled out, and they are forced or induced to participate in activities which may be "senseless," such as calisthenics.

At the same time the children are being taught by rote meaningless sounds in the ritual oaths and songs, such as the Lord's Prayer, the Pledge to the Flag, and "America." As they go through the grades children learn more and more of the sounds of these ritual oaths, but the fact that they have often learned meaningless sounds rather than meaningful statements is shown when they are asked to write these out in the sixth grade; they write them as groups of sounds rather than as a series of words, according to the sixth grade teachers at Wright School. Probably much learning in the elementary grades is of this character, that is, having no intrinsic meaning to the children, but rather being tasks inexplicably required of them by authoritative adults. Listening to sixth grade children read social studies reports, for example, in which they have copied material from encyclopedias about a particular country, an observer often gets the feeling that he is watching an activity which has no intrinsic meaning for the child. The child who reads, "Switzerland grows wheat and cows and grass and makes a lot of cheese" knows the dictionary meaning of each of these words but may very well have no conception at all of this "thing" called Switzerland. He is simply carrying out a task assigned by the teacher because it is assigned, and this may be its only "meaning" for him.

Another type of learning which takes place in kindergarten is seen in children who take advantage of the "holes" in the adult social structure to create activities of their own, during Work Time or out-of-doors during Play Time. Here the children are learning to carve out a small world of their own within the world created by adults. They very quickly learn that if they keep within permissible limits of noise and action they can play much as they please. Small groups of children formed during the year in Edith's kindergarten who played together at these times, developing semi-independent little groups in which they created their own worlds in the interstices of the adult-imposed physical and social world. These groups remind the sociological observer very much of the so-called "informal groups" which adults develop in factories and offices of large bureaucracies.[5] Here, too, within authoritatively imposed social organizations people find "holes" to create little subworlds which support informal, friendly, unofficial behavior. Forming and participating in such groups seems to be as much part of the student role as it is of the role of bureaucrat.

The kindergarten has been conceived of here as the year in which children are prepared for their schooling by learning the role of student. In the classrooms of the rest of the school grades, the children will be asked to submit to systems and routines imposed by the teachers and the curriculum. The days will be much like those of kindergarten, except that academic subjects will be substituted for the activities of the kindergarten. Once out of the school system, young adults will more than likely find themselves working in large-scale bureaucratic organizations, perhaps on the assembly line in the factory, perhaps in the paper routines of the white collar occupations, where they will be required to submit to rigid routines imposed by "the company" which may make little sense to them. Those who can operate well in this situation will be successful bureaucratic functionaries. Kindergarten, therefore, can be seen as preparing children not only for participation in the bureaucratic organization of large modern school systems, but also for the large-scale occupational bureaucracies of modern society.

Notes

1. Durkheim, E. (1956). *Sociology and education* (pp. 71–72). New York: Free Press.

2. Ibid., p. 123.

3. Brookover, W. (1957). *The sociology of education* (p. 4). New York: American Book.

4. Ibid., p. 6.

5. See, for example, Blau, P. M. (1956). *Bureaucracy in modern society* (Chapter 3). New York: Random House.

ORGANIZING SCHOOLS FOR IMPROVEMENT

Anthony S. Bryk

Two of the worst schools in Chicago make efforts to raise student achievement. One is impressively successful, but one fails. What is the difference? In the final article in this chapter, Anthony S. Bryk addresses organizational differences between schools that succeed and those that fail, using findings from a major study of hundreds of elementary schools in which the researchers identified five essential supports for school improvement. These five essential supports touch on many aspects of school organization and relations to parents and community, the environment surrounding schools. The author reminds us that schools are complex organizations with many subsystems that must be considered in efforts to improve teaching and learning for students.

Questions to consider for this reading:

1. How do the five essential supports for school improvement work to help schools?

2. How do these five essential supports relate to levels of organization described by Barr and Dreeben in the first reading?

3. What are some challenges that we might encounter when applying these five essential supports to effect school reform?

Alexander Elementary School and Hancock Elementary School began the 1990s as two of the worst schools in Chicago in terms of math and reading achievement. Only two miles apart, the schools are in bordering neighborhoods and appear similar in many ways. Both enrolled nearly 100% minority students from families considered low income.

During the 1990s, both launched an array of initiatives aimed at boosting student achievement. Hancock moved impressively forward, while Alexander barely moved the needle on improvement. How did Hancock "beat the odds" while Alexander failed to do so?

This puzzle led us to undertake a systematic longitudinal investigation of *hundreds* of elementary schools in Chicago, just like Alexander and Hancock. Beginning in 1990, the Consortium on Chicago School Research initiated an intensive longitudinal study of the internal workings and external community conditions that distinguished improving elementary schools from those that failed to improve. That unique 15-year database allowed us to develop, test, and validate a framework of essential supports for school improvement. These data provided an extraordinary window to examine the complex interplay of how schools are organized and interact with the local community to alter dramatically the odds for improving student achievement. The lessons learned offer guidance for teachers, parents, principals, superintendents, and civic leaders in their efforts to improve schools across the country.

FIVE ESSENTIAL SUPPORTS FOR SCHOOL IMPROVEMENT

Students' academic learning occurs principally in classrooms as students interact with teachers around subject matter. How we organize and operate a school has a major effect on the instructional exchanges in its classrooms. Put simply, whether classroom learning proceeds depends in large measure on how the school as a social context supports teaching and sustains student engagement. Through our research, we identified five organizational features of schools that interact with life inside classrooms and are essential to advancing student achievement.

1. **Coherent instructional guidance system**. Schools in which student learning improves have coherent instructional guidance systems that articulate the what and how of instruction. The learning tasks posed for students are key here, as are the assessments that make manifest what students actually need to know and provide feedback to inform subsequent instruction. Coordinated with this are the materials, tools, and instructional routines shared across a faculty that scaffold instruction. Although individual teachers may have substantial discretion in how they use these resources, the efficacy of individual teacher efforts depends on the quality of the supports and the local community of practice that forms around their use and refinement.

2. **Professional capacity**. Schooling is a human-resource-intensive enterprise. Schools are only as good as the quality of faculty, the professional development that supports their learning, and the faculty's capacity to work together to improve instruction. This support directs our attention to a school's ability to recruit and retain capable staff, the efficacy of performance feedback and professional development, and the social resources within a staff to work together to solve local problems.

3. **Strong parent-community-school ties**. The disconnect between local school professionals and the parents and community that a school is intended to serve is a persistent concern in many urban contexts. The absence of vital ties is a problem; their presence is a multifaceted resource for improvement. The quality of these ties links directly to students' motivation and school participation and can provide a critical resource for classrooms.

4. **Student-centered learning climate**. All adults in a school community forge a climate that enables students to think of themselves as learners. At a minimum, improving schools establish a safe and orderly environment—the most basic prerequisite for learning. They endorse ambitious academic work coupled with support for each student. The combination allows students to believe in themselves, to persist, and ultimately to achieve.

5. **Leadership drives change**. Principals in improving schools engage in a dynamic interplay of instructional and inclusive-facilitative leadership. On the instructional side, school leaders influence local activity around core instructional programs, supplemental academic and social supports, and the hiring and development of staff. They establish strategic priorities for using resources and buffer externalities that might distract from coherent reform. Working in tandem with this, principals build relationships across the school community. Improving teaching and learning places demands on these relationships. In carrying out their daily activities, school leaders advance instrumental objectives while also trying to enlist teachers in the change effort. In

the process, principals cultivate a growing cadre of leaders (teachers, parents, and community members) who can help expand the reach of this work and share overall responsibility for improvement.

Using extensive survey data collected by the consortium from teachers, principals, and students, we were able to develop school indicators for each of the five essential supports, chart changes in these indicators over time, and then relate these organizational conditions to subsequent changes in student attendance and learning gains in reading and mathematics. Among our findings:

- Schools with strong indicators on most supports were 10 times more likely to improve than schools with weak supports.
- Half of the schools strong on most supports improved substantially in reading.
- Not a single school weak on most supports improved in mathematics.
- A material weakness in any one support, sustained over several years, undermined other change efforts, and improvement rarely resulted.

This statistical evidence affords a strong warrant that how we organize schools is critical for student achievement. Improving schools entails coherent, orchestrated action across all five essential supports. Put simply, there is no one silver bullet.

DYNAMICS OF IMPROVEMENT

Schools are complex organizations consisting of multiple interacting subsystems (that is, the five essential organizational supports). Personal and social considerations mix deeply in the day-to-day workings of a school. These interactions are bound by various rules, roles, and prevailing practices that, in combination with technical resources, constitute schools as formal organizations. In a sense, almost everything interacts with everything else. That means that a true picture of what enables some schools to improve and others to stagnate requires identifying the critical interconnections among the five essential supports: *How do these five essential supports function together to substantially change the odds for enhancing student engagement and academic learning?*

Schools that improved student attendance over time strengthened their ties to parents and community and used these ties as a core resource for enhancing safety and order across the school. This growing sense of routine and security further combined with a better-aligned curriculum that continually exposed students to new tasks and ideas. Engaging pedagogy afforded students active learning roles in the classroom. High-quality professional development aimed to enhance teachers' capacity to orchestrate such activity under the trying circumstances that most confront daily. When this combination of conditions existed, the basic recipe for improving student attendance was activated.

In terms of the organizational mechanisms influencing academic achievement, this can be told in two contrasting stories. Schools that stagnated—no learning improvement over several years—were characterized by clear weaknesses in their instructional guidance system. They had poor curriculum alignment coupled with relatively little emphasis on active student engagement in learning. These instructional weaknesses combined with weak faculty commitments to the school, to innovation, and to working together as a professional community. Undergirding all of this were anemic school-parent-community ties.

In contrast, schools in which student learning improved used high-quality professional development as a key instrument for change. They had maximum leverage when these opportunities for teachers occurred in a supportive environment (that is, a school-based professional community) and when teaching was guided by a common, coherent, and aligned instructional system. Undergirding all of this, in turn, was a solid base of parent-community-school ties.

Leadership drives change in the four other organizational supports—but the actual execution of improvement is more organic and dynamic. Good teachers advance high-quality instruction, but developing good teachers and retaining them in a particular school depends on supportive school leadership and positive work relations with colleagues. Meaningful parent and community involvement can be a resource for solving problems of safety and order; but, in a reciprocal fashion, these ties are likely to be stronger in safe and orderly schools. This reciprocity carries over to leadership as the driver for change. While a principal commands formal authority to effect changes in the four other organizational supports, a school with some strengths in these four supports is also easier to lead.

Arguing for the significance of one individual support over another is tempting, but we ultimately came to view the five supports as an organized system of elements in dynamic interaction with one another. As such, primary value lies in their integration and mutual reinforcement. In this sense, school development is much like baking a cake. By analogy, you need an appropriate mix of flour, sugar, eggs, oil, baking powder, and flavoring to produce a light, delicious cake. Without sugar, it will be tasteless. Without eggs or baking powder, the cake will be flat and chewy. Marginal changes in a single ingredient—for example, a bit more flour, large versus extra-large eggs—may not have noticeable effects. But, if one ingredient is absent, it is just not a cake.

Similarly, strong local leadership acting on the four other organizational elements constitutes the essential ingredients for spurring school development. Broad-based instructional change and improved student learning entail coordinated action across these various domains. Correspondingly, student outcomes are likely to stagnate if a material weakness persists in any of the supports. The ensemble of supports is what's essential for improvement. Taken together, they constitute the core organizational ingredients for advancing student engagement and achievement . . .

Unrecognized Challenges

In many recent discussions about school reform, ideas about parent involvement and school community contexts fade into the background. Some school reform advocates believe only instruction and instructional leadership matter. This perspective assumes that a school's social and personal connections with local families and communities play a small role in reform. Our evidence, however, offers a strong challenge. To be sure, instruction matters—a lot. But social context matters too. We have documented that strength across all five essential supports, including parent-school-community ties, is critical for improvement to occur in all kinds of urban schools. Unfortunately, we have also learned that this organizational development is much harder to initiate and sustain in some community contexts than others.

As data accumulated in Chicago and school-by-school trends in attendance and student learning gains became clear, a complex pattern of results emerged. Improving schools could be found in all kinds of neighborhoods varying by socioeconomic and racial/ethnic composition. Stagnating schools, in contrast, piled up in very poor, racially isolated African-American neighborhoods. We became haunted by the question, "Why? What made reform so much more difficult to advance in some school communities?"

Our analyses led us to two different answers. First, the social capital of a neighborhood is a significant resource for improving its local school. We found that the latter was much more likely in neighborhoods where residents had a history of working together. In contrast, the absence of such collective efficacy in the surrounding community increased the likelihood that a troubled school would continue to stagnate. Correspondingly, communities with strong institutions, especially religious institutions, were more supportive contexts for school improvement. These institutions afford a network of social ties that can be appropriated for other purposes, such as improving schools. They also create connections that can bring new outside resources into isolated neighborhoods.

So, differences among neighborhoods in their bonding and bridging social capital help explain why the essential supports were more likely to develop in some neighborhoods than others. But this was only a partial answer for a subset of the school communities.

A second mechanism was also at work. We found that the proportion of children who were living under extraordinary circumstances—neglect and abuse, homeless, foster care, domestic violence—also created a significant barrier to improvement in some schools. To be clear, these students were learning at about the same rates as their classmates in whatever school they were enrolled. So, the learning gains for these particular students were not depressing the overall results for their schools. But the odds of school stagnation soared when a concentration of these students appeared in the same place. On balance, schools are principally about teaching and learning, not solving all of the social problems of a community. However, when palpable personal and social needs walk through doors every day, school staff can't be expected to ignore those needs. Our evidence suggests that when the proportion of these needs remains high and pressing, the capacity of a school staff to sustain attention to developing the five essential supports falls by the wayside. A few schools managed to succeed under these circumstances, but most did not.

In sum, a nettlesome problem came into focus on improving student learning to truly disadvantaged communities where social capital is scarce and human need sometimes overwhelming. These schools face a "three-strike" problem. Not only are the schools highly stressed organizations, but they exist in challenged communities and confront an extraordinary density of human needs every day.

Our findings about schooling in truly disadvantaged communities offer a sobering antidote to a heady political rhetoric of "beating the odds" and "no excuses." To be sure, we believe that all schools can and must improve. Such claims represent our highest, most noble aspirations for our children, our schools, and systems of schools. They are ideas worthy of our beliefs and action. But there are also facts, sometimes brutal facts. Not all school communities start out in the same place and confront the same problems. Unless we recognize this, unless we understand more deeply the dynamics of school stagnation, especially in our most neglected communities, we seem bound to repeat the failures of the past.

Our concluding point is straightforward—it is hard to improve what we do not understand.

We need more attention on how to improve schools in these specific contexts. All plausible ideas for educational improvement deserve serious consideration. Absent systematic analysis of not only where we succeed but also where and why we fail, we will continue to relegate many of our students and their teachers to a similar fate.

Projects for Further Exploration

1. To gain a better understanding of schools as organizations in the United States, select indicators from the reading by Barr and Dreeben, or from others in this chapter. Using the webpages in the Appendix, go to your state website and find school report card data. Locate a data set that allows you to compare schools in your area using at least two of these indicators. There may also be information about schools on your state webpage.

2. The reading by Bryk in this chapter discusses ways to improve schools. Find a case study of a school that has improved its achievement levels on tests and graduation rates and describe what factors have made the difference. Compare this with the information provided by Bryk. Case examples can be found in Chicago, Annapolis, and other cities.

3. Replicate the study by Gracey on the organization of the kindergarten classroom. Observe a nursery school or kindergarten class and keep notes on your observations. Write a summary that describes the lessons taught, the organization of the classroom, and the organizational structure in the teacher's lesson plan, plus activities and interactions in the classroom.

4. Discuss the organizational structure of a school district with which you are familiar, from federal and state influences, to local school boards and school administration, to the classrooms.

5

ROLES AND RESPONSIBILITIES

Administrators, Teachers, and Students

Organizations provide the structure and goals for education, but people run organizations. For educational systems, that involves people both inside and outside the organization. Outside influences on schools were discussed in Chapters 3 and 4 where we explored some of the external people and organizations that influence schools, such as parents and local businesses. In this chapter we focus on positions individuals hold in schools and the responsibilities, or roles, that go with those positions. For example, principals are responsible for the management of the local school buildings, their roles put them in the middle between superintendents, school boards, and community members on the one hand and teachers, staff, and students on the other. Principals must negotiate solutions to differences between these other participants. Who has influence over what happens in schools is based in part on the social, cultural, and economic capital held by school leaders (Spillane, Hallett, & Diamond, 2003). Decisions on policies, practices, and reforms in schools come from leaders, often the principals. The roles and responsibilities of principals are discussed in the first reading, which consists of excerpts from Dan C. Lortie's book, *School Principal* (2009).

The total number of public school teachers is more than 3.2 million (Center for Education Reform, 2012; National Center for Education Statistics [NCES], 2010, Table 62). The number of public school teachers has risen at a greater rate than that of students in the past 10 years, resulting in a decline in student-teacher ratios from 17 to 15.7 students per teacher (NCES, 2010, Table 67). In addition, 5 million people served as professional, administrative, and support staff in schools and colleges.

Many sociologists of education have focused on the roles of teachers in educational organizations. Three readings in this chapter review what makes successful teachers, who teachers are, what conditions they face, how much control they have in their jobs, and dissatisfaction and burnout resulting from, among other things, lack of control. In their reading in this chapter, Richard M. Ingersoll and Elizabeth Merrill discuss the criteria for professional status, when teachers meet these criteria, and where they fall short.

Anthony Gary Dworkin and Pamela F. Tobe in the next reading in this chapter examine the effects of changing school accountability standards, federal and state mandates, school safety, and student misbehavior on teachers' trust, job satisfaction, and burnout. Teachers have direct contact with the children they are educating. Although they are responsible for their students, teachers are not free to make many decisions or act autonomously. This presents a dilemma for many teachers, who feel they should have power to make decisions for the children they teach (Dworkin, 2007). Lack of control is one factor leading to teacher burnout (Dworkin, Saha, & Hill, 2002). The degree of trust that teachers have in their job security, the challenges to their competence from the standards-based accountability movement, and suspicions from school critics of teacher incompetence have resulted in a higher rate of teacher burnout. In addition, average teachers' salaries have held steady at around $50,000 for the past few years (NCES, 2010, Table 79), not rising with inflation.

Because teachers are the front line in the classroom and are the main adults interacting with students, their influence has a major impact on the way students feel about their school experiences. If students like school and have supportive teachers, they have fewer disciplinary problems and higher achievement, plus they are less likely to drop out of school. The reading by Jannick Demanet and Mieke Van Houtte addresses the interaction between the roles of teachers and peers in students' success in school, and the role of the school-as-community in student success versus misconduct and dropping out. Using sociology of education perspectives such as school-as-community combined with sociology of deviance perspectives of differential association, who the student bonds with (peers, teachers, and others) plays a major role in the student's level of misconduct.

A latent function of schools is that they provide a gathering place for young people of similar ages. They facilitate the formation of peer groups that influence how the formal goals of schools are carried out or rejected. Students' experiences in schools vary greatly depending on their socioeconomic backgrounds, the school climate, and their roles in the school classroom and after-school activities. Some are leaders, some are followers; some are jocks, some are brains; some succeed, some fail. The informal aspects of schools discussed in Chapter 4 have great influence on students' experiences and the roles they take on in school.

Probably the most difficult problem in schools, and one about which the public is most concerned, is violence, even though schools are one of the safest places for students to be (Addington, Ruddy, Miller, DeVoe, & Chandler, 2002). Some of this violence is brought into schools from the external environment by gang members. Some violence comes from isolated or alienated students, a cause made apparent by recent school shootings. Whatever the source, violence is perceived by the public and school personnel alike as a severe problem for schools, and debates about how to deal with school violence are the subject matter of many conferences. Violence finds its roots in the climate of schools. In their reading, David R. Dupper and Nancy Meyer-Adams illustrate the importance of school climate, in particular environments of intimidation and fear from bullying, in which some students have intolerable experiences. They suggest possible ways to change these toxic school climates.

When the education system fails students or students fail in the education system, policy analysts ask why and what can be done to correct the problem. Research tells us many of the factors resulting in students dropping out of school. They include high turnover of students and teachers; lack of school resources; problems with school structure including student-teacher ratios and school size; quality of teachers; teacher-student relations; students' feelings of failure or futility; and student characteristics and composition (Rumberger & Thomas, 2000). In addition, most dropouts have low attendance rates or failing grades—or both. One-third are lost in ninth grade. Approximately 1.3 million students do not graduate each year. More than half of these are students of color, and students from low-income families are seven times more likely to drop out of high school than students from high-income families. Nearly half of the U.S. dropouts come from the lowest-performing 12% of the nation's high schools, about 2,000 schools (Alliance for Excellent Education, 2010). In the last reading, Russell W. Rumberger discusses the situation of students for whom the educational system does not work. These "at risk" students and dropouts face reduced opportunities in life and are a considerable cost to society.

All of the readings in this section touch on aspects of roles held by participants in school systems. They also relate to both the formal and the informal school systems. Keep both the formal and informal organizations, plus the roles of participants in these organizations, in mind as you read other parts of this book and in your contacts with educational institutions.

REFERENCES

Addington, L. A., Ruddy, S. A., Miller, A. K., DeVoe, J. F., & Chandler, K. A. (2002, November). *Are America's schools safe? Students speak out* (U.S. Department of Commerce, National Technical Information Service, Technical Report, NTIS PB2003-101473, pp. 79–81). Washington, DC: U.S. Department of Education, National Center for Education Statistics.

Alliance for Excellent Education. (2010). *High school dropouts in America: Fact sheet.* Washington, DC: Author.

Center for Education Reform. (2012). *K–12 facts: Total public school teachers.* Retrieved June 13, 2013, from www.edreform.com/2012/04/k-12-facts/

Dworkin, A. G. (2007). School reform and teacher burnout: Issues of gender and gender tokenism. In B. Banks, S. Delamont, & C. Marshall (Eds.), *Gender and education: An encyclopedia* (pp. 69–78). New York: Greenwood Press.

Dworkin, A. G., Saha, L. J., & Hill, A. N. (2002). *Teacher burnout and perceptions of a democratic school environment.* Unpublished manuscript.

Lortie, D. C. (2009). *School principal: Managing in public.* Chicago: University of Chicago Press.

National Center for Education Statistics (NCES). (2010). Total number of teachers in public elementary and secondary schools, Tables 62, 67, and 79. *Digest of Education Statistics.* Washington, DC: U.S. Department of Education. Retrieved June 13, 2013, from http://nces.ed.gov/programs/digest/

Rumberger, R. W., & Thomas, S. L. (2000). The distribution of dropout and turnover rates among urban and suburban high schools. *Sociology of Education, 73*(1), 39–67.

Spillane, J. P., Hallett, T., & Diamond, J. B. (2003). Forms of capital and the construction of leadership: Instructional leadership in urban elementary schools. *Sociology of Education, 76*(1), 1–17.

School Principal

Complications and Complexities

Dan C. Lortie

The school principal holds an administrative role in the middle between government, school boards, and superintendents and teachers, staff, and students. Principals are the leaders of schools, and as such shape the culture of their schools. Schools have stronger cultures when principals are adaptable, motivate members of the school community, are cooperative and innovative, resolve conflicts, and effectively achieve their goals (Louis & Wahlstrom, 2011). Their roles involve balancing demands of multiple internal and external constituencies. The constraints and pressures on schools often fall to the principal to negotiate. In this excerpt from the newest edition of an old classic on school principals, Dan C. Lortie reviews the challenges elementary school principals face. Among the daily ongoing challenges are scarcity of time, interruptions to work, maintaining safety, and paperwork. More complex tasks include teacher evaluations and supervision, and problems or mistakes that need to be rectified. In their leadership positions, principals need to set the tone for the school. This reading provides an overview of the complex role of principals in schools.

Questions to consider for this reading:

1. In what ways is the role of principal a balancing act?

2. What are some ongoing challenges faced by principals in their day-to-day work?

3. With whom must principals interact in their roles as middle managers?

COMPLICATIONS AND COMPLEXITIES

What is hard about being an elementary principal? What is the downside? We will look at conditions that complicate the day, tasks that principals find difficult and/or dislike, and, finally, trouble that can strike as they go about doing their work. The progression in the discussion is from the least to the most serious challenges elementary principals face.

COMPLICATING CONDITIONS

Certain of the conditions under which principals work make that work more challenging than it might otherwise be. Although no single problem is limited to the principalship, the combination of challenges may well be unique.

The Scarcity of Time

"What do you do all day long?" people ask my friend the Chicago principal. The questioners point out that since the children are dispersed among classrooms and supervised by teachers, she must surely have a lot of time on her hands. Perhaps memory plays a part in their raising the question; my informal inquiries, including discussion with persons who work in schools, suggest that many have little idea of how their elementary principals spent their time. There is irony, therefore, in the fact that principals express a lot of anxiety about not having enough time, of feeling constant pressure as they try to complete their work. We mentioned earlier that classroom teachers have designated responsibilities that prevent them from being free to assist the principal in doing organizational jobs. That low "assignability" of staff members contributes to the long list of duties principals have to handle (McPherson, Salley, & Baehr, 1975). Empirical studies have pointed out that the principal's day tends to be fractured into numerous activities, which, on average, last only a few minutes (Peterson, 1977). This fragmentation of time, although not unique to school managers, is probably exacerbated by the nature of managerial work in schools (Mintzberg, 1973). Part of the difficulty lies in the fact that school officials find it difficult to persuade board members and the public at large to spend money on administrative assistance for principals.

What other aspects of the job produce principals' sense of time deprivation? There seem to be several. One is the rigidity of school schedules—the length of the day and number of weeks and the total time schools may operate—are all specified in advance and are extremely resistant to change. Whatever is going to be accomplished has to be done within the rigid parameters of overall schedules set by state authorities and specified by school district authorities. Collective bargaining has added to that rigidity by placing distinct limits on the amount of time that principals can ask teachers to meet outside regular school hours. Other causes grow out of the nature of principal tasks and their definition as public service, both of which limit the amount of time principals can use as they see fit. All compress the working day.

A lack of time flexibility is built into some of the major sets of tasks faced by principals, particularly, for example, in the responsibility to evaluate staff members. This area is highly formalized, an approach that is reinforced by the anxiety of officials to avoid legal action and the need to respect specifics worked out in collective bargaining contracts.

The steps in teacher evaluation illustrate how formalization reduces the control principals have over their time. Although districts differ in their specific requirements (e.g., how many members of the faculty to evaluate each year), the process normally demands many hours. The prescribed steps must be taken in a set order and, once initiated, must proceed at an appropriate pace: delays complicate communication and add anxiety for those being evaluated. Each step takes time—a preparatory conference between the principal and the teacher, observation in the classroom, writing up observations, and a conference to share the evaluation with the teacher. Tension can run high, for the results are entered in the teacher's permanent file. Principals quickly discover how prickly the process can be, leading them to adhere closely to district rules in case teachers who are dissatisfied with their evaluations fault them on procedural grounds (perhaps through the union) or central officials reprimand them for flouting district policies and practices. These rigidly prescribed sequences can stretch over many days during the academic year, particularly in schools with large faculties and/or in districts with particularly stringent procedures. Principals, as we shall see, express numerous doubts about evaluation; some of their dissatisfaction lies in the bureaucratic rigidities involved and the time spent at the expense of activities they consider more important.

On Interruption

Although research on managerial time indicates that interactions tend to come fast and often, there are respects in which principals are probably more vulnerable to interruption than is the case in many other organizational settings. Like middle managers in general, it is difficult for principals to resist demands from higher ranked officials; school heads complain that they are sidetracked by sudden deadlines for information and/or requests to attend meetings on matters in which they have little interest. In addition, the norms of public service deny them the right to privacy so prevalent in corporate affairs. Unlike the situation in private sector, it is difficult to erect barriers to limit access from their customers. Not for them, for example, are the elaborate, recorded responses to telephone calls found in businesses, which constrain access to officers by steering callers to "customer service representatives." In schools, however, to be seen as unresponsive to parents is a serious matter. In addition, many principals maintain an "open door" to teachers, a practice that is consistent with the emphasis we have seen on sustaining the approval and support of faculty members.

One way to underscore the weakness of barriers between principals and the public at large is to consider the scope of potential intervention by "customers" up to and including intervention in the processes of production. There are retail chains (e.g., Sears Roebuck) that control the manufacturing processes of some of the products they sell either through factory ownership or specifications in contracts with suppliers. Such retail firms deal with complaints in a routine fashion, usually by replacing products or refunding the dissatisfied customer's money. They would hardly agree, however, to a retail customer visiting and suggesting changes in the manufacture of, let's say, a washing machine—incredulity would greet any such request. Compare that, however, to the situation of a principal where parents insist that their child be transferred to another class, a demand that penetrates to the core of instructional practice. Granting the request may alienate not

only one faculty member but, depending on the circumstances, other teachers as well. Simple rejection of parental requests ("That is none of your business") is not among the responses available to the principal. In fact, a parent who continues to be dissatisfied can appeal to officials in central office. Similar contrasts can be made, of course, to the ability of surgeons and other high-status professionals to restrict client influence on how they do their work.

The Maintenance of Order and Safety

The principal is a front-line supervisor with custodial responsibility (in loco parentis) for hundreds of young children. President Harry Truman's placard saying "the buck stops here" would be appropriate on the principal's desk, particularly in regard to maintaining good order and student safety. The principal serves as backup for teachers who need assistance in maintaining control and who refer individual students for final decisions. There are also occasions when the principal acts as the immediate supervisor of students, such as in the lunchroom or halls and play areas, which may not be supervised by teachers.

Outbursts of student misbehavior can be sudden and unpredictable—effective responses may demand immediate attention and allow little time for deliberation. The same applies, of course, to dealing with accidents in which a student is hurt. The risk of legal liability intensifies official concern, particularly if parents become alarmed and are ready to blame the school for injuries sustained by the children. Other tasks, even when interrupting them is costly, must be put aside. Principal work is marked by such unpredictable urgencies.

It is important to bear in mind the behavioral volatility of children, to recall that they are only gradually socialized into complying with the norms of orderly behavior which can usually be taken for granted among adults. Those charged with supervising children learn that lapses in adult control can produce disorder and that keeping order requires the physical presence of adults. That need results in "pinning down" many staff members and by reducing their mobility, also limiting the range of tasks they might otherwise undertake and preventing the formation of a more refined division of labor. It is another factor that affects the "assignability" of those who report to the principal.

Paperwork

The interviews make it clear that principals see various types of desk work as a constant, unremitting pressure on their time, a pressure many detest. If done at the office, it cuts off contact with teachers and students, but if taken home, affects relationships within the family. Some of the tasks result from the principal being the only (official) manager in the school who consequently has responsibility for overseeing the ordering and distribution of supplies, monitoring cash revenues, etc. Superintendents and boards also expect the principal to report on whatever information they consider relevant and urgent at a particular time—in addition, of course, to maintaining regular records such as attendance figures, which affect state revenues to the district. State and federal surveys are routinely shunted to principals who see such duties as contributing nothing to the instruction of their students. A small number of suburban principals mentioned that they had secretaries or assistants they could entrust with much of the paperwork; nationwide, there was a similar lack of help.

There are subjective costs in having to spend considerable amounts of time doing paperwork—tasks that are not only disliked but that block action on other tasks that are felt to be more urgent, important, or interesting. The load of paperwork also intensifies the principals' sense of too little time.

COMPLEX TASKS

One is hard put to think of any occupation that has no difficult or even distasteful tasks that have to be done. They may be difficult to do well or intrinsically complex. When we bear in mind that school management is fundamentally interactive in nature, it is not surprising that the major complexities that emerge focus on relationships with other people. Two questions that provoked talk about such difficulties will be discussed here; the first asked what aspect of the work is most difficult to do well and the second inquired into any mistakes the principal had made during the previous year. . . . Unrewarding tasks are difficult in a particular way; dealing with them requires mobilizing energy without the hope of pleasure and at the expense of tasks that are rewarding.

Challenges at the Core

The most frequent responses dealing with difficult tasks focus on the core of the principal's instructional responsibilities—that is, the formal evaluation and supervision of faculty members (Table 19.1). Within that large category, we find two central sources of difficulty: the lack of confidence principals have in the evaluative procedures they are required to use and the resistance teachers show to evaluation and to making whatever changes are proposed by the principal. (Less frequent but closely related responses include dismissing teachers, principal dislike of the evaluative process, and sustaining teacher morale.)

Principals mention several problems in evaluating teachers and using the assessments they make to supervise their work. The process, they say, is "too subjective." The appropriate criteria are not clear, and/or there is not enough time to visit classrooms and make solid judgments. ("It's hard to define what you are looking for and to get it across" [Male, 52].) Two kinds of uncertainty are evident—"How do I know what is best?" and "Do I have enough information to make a good judgment?" There are issues, then, in regard to the appropriateness of available standards and doubts about the empirical basis for their judgments.

Some principals felt caught between boards and superintendents who wanted corroboration for

Table 19.1   Most Difficult Task

	M	% Total M
A. Evaluation and supervision of teachers		
Weaknesses of evaluation process	31	27%
Dealing with teacher resistance	22	19%
Principal dislikes process	5	4%
Dismissing teachers disturbing	4	4%
Sustaining teacher morale	2	2%
Subtotal	64	56%
B. Other tasks		
Paperwork and "administrivia"	12	11%
Deciding without adequate knowledge	7	6%
Dealing with parents (resistant, angry)	6	5%
Resolving conflicts	5	4%
Living with time constraints	4	4%
Student discipline	3	3%
Miscellaneous (1 mention each)	12	11%
Subtotal	49	44%
Total mentions (N = 107)	113	100%

assumption they perceived in evaluative procedures, namely, that there is only one right way to teach. Others reported that central office required them to use forms with specific and limited choices that constrained the quality of their judgments. Principals may, moreover, be required to state conclusions when unsure of their diagnoses; for example, they may not understand why a teacher is having particular problems and what steps might correct them. Recall, however, that principals, whatever their misgivings, have no choice in this matter—they must complete and submit formal evaluations; private reservations must be set aside and formal procedures carried out.

Given the variety of bases for discomfort mentioned by principals, it appears that being required to do formal evaluations imposes interpersonal and emotional "costs" on a substantial number of principals. Yet no respondent called for serious revision of the process or its elimination; it may be that despite those costs, principals see their evaluative responsibilities as supporting their authority in technical and professional realms. It concretizes the right of the principal to evaluate teacher behavior and to propose changes in their classroom activity; it underlines the important part played by principals in the district "chain of command." In a context of many limits on their authority, it remains valued by principals despite the problems it creates; the responses, taken together, point to considerable ambivalence toward the responsibility to evaluate teachers.

A substantial proportion of the principals' responses (19%) referred to the lack of cooperation shown by teachers when told to make changes in their behavior. The word "threatened" appears often in such responses, with principals varying in how broadly they apply the term to teachers— some generalize broadly while others restrict such references to a few. There are times when teacher resistance is portrayed sympathetically and times when it is not. Assisting teachers with some problems may face built-in difficulties, such as helping teachers to develop more control in the classroom.

I was against ranking teachers when I was a teacher and I still am. (Male, 35)

possible dismissal and teachers who wanted supportive evaluations; the first called for cool and detailed critiques, the second for more generous appraisals. Other principals saw a contradiction between representing evaluation as pedagogical assistance while, in fact, using it as the basis for retention or dismissal. Some principals rejected the

The teacher union protects mediocrity. (Male, 61)

The more you intercede the more the children disrespect the teacher. (Female, 50)

Some principals mention the need for tact, the importance of taking teacher sensitivities into account. Whatever the specifics, teachers are not portrayed as welcoming evaluation and the supervision growing out of it. One of the challenges facing principals, therefore, is to exercise their instructional authority in ways that do not alienate the members of their faculties.

You have to keep a positive rapport with the person you are evaluating. Trying to get adults to change is a hell of a lot harder than getting children to change. (Male, 49)

The other responses to this question point to the variety of difficulties principals associate with their work. They may disdain the seemingly endless paperwork and administrative duties they define as trivial, and they are hard-pressed to maintain the energy to perform tasks that bore them or that seem unimportant. Some regretted their lack of knowledge: ignorance of cleaning techniques hampered one principal in supervising custodians, a former physical education teacher found it hard to cope with the academic curriculum, and another principal who knew little about budget matters had trouble dealing with the central office business manager. It can be taxing to interact with angry parents or those, at another extreme, who show little interest in what is happening to their children. Conflict, time constraints, and discipline problems round out the list of difficult tasks and situations.

What general observations can we derive from these responses? Two appear to be clear. Principals face considerable uncertainty in the course of their daily activities, uncertainty that makes their work harder; they are often unsure about the standards they should use and the reliability or validity of their judgments. The second overall theme is relational complexity. Teachers can and do fail to respond to the professional judgments of the principal. Parents produce

unpredicted outbursts while students may exhibit puzzling and/or defiant behavior. Complexities around interaction account for a large proportion of the difficulties they mention. If their efforts to resolve problems with parents and subordinates fail, principals may be left with chronically dissatisfied parents and/or embittered faculty members, an unhappy and career-threatening state of affairs. Time and again we see principals emphasize the importance of good working relationships; at the same time, it is also evident that they cannot count on them to prevail.

Mistakes

Mistakes are, of course, considerably more likely to occur in difficult rather than easy situations; for that reason, they are cited here as another indicator of the particular tasks that principals find difficult to perform. Respondents were asked to talk about any mistakes they had made in the recent past. Seventy-one percent were ready to respond with actions they regretted or actions they wished they had taken and did not (Table 19.2).

The responses to this question are, in interesting ways, similar to those we just examined. Respondents ready to concede mistakes link most of them to day-in, day-out relationships; they connected 68% of the mistakes to interactions with others. Of those 61 relational errors, teachers stand out as the major source (32/61 of $N = 52\%$). The latter divide almost equally between employment issues of hiring and firing ($M = 14$) and problems that arise in the day-to-day management of faculty members ($M = 18$). The following quotation is a strong instance.

I have one teacher I think is crappy. I say some things, and weigh it. I wish she would take early retirement. I wish it, but I don't say it. I put kids in her classroom every year. Would I put my own kid in her classroom? No. I've been guilty for 22 years of not being able to get rid of bad teachers. (Male, 47)

This respondent is not alone in citing reluctance to let teachers go as a mistake. In nine of

Table 19.2 Types of Mistakes

	M	% Total M
1. Relational errors		
Teachers		
Managing faculty	18	20
Hiring and firing	14	16
Subtotal	32	36
Noncertified staff		
Hiring and firing	3	3
Parents		
Public relations	8	9
Allocation time and energy	2	2
Subtotal	10	11
Students		
Helped more	7	8
Disciplinary action	2	2
Subtotal	9	10
Central office		
Pushed harder	4	5
Avoided anger	2	2
Informed better	1	1
Subtotal	7	8
Subtotal of relational errors	61	68 (r.e.)
2. Other allocations of time and energy		
Instructional program	10	11
Other	3	3
Subtotal	13	14
3. Career-related regrets	3	3
4. Miscellaneous (1 mention each)	11	13
Grand Total mentions	88	98 (r.e.)
(N = 80/112: 71%)		

fourteen references to teachers, the principals regretted not having arranged their dismissal; the remaining five principals mentioned hiring teachers who did not work out. (The three mistakes with noncertified employees were also regrets about waiting too long to dismiss them.) Decisions about employment, and particularly the reluctance to dismiss staff members, can produce remorse. The most frequent regrets arise from omissions, from not acting rather than from acting too boldly; the others were based on poor predictions about how teachers would perform.

The responses classified under "managing faculty" include a variety of mistakes that can be made in supervising teachers. They must be assigned to particular classes, a process that can and does go wrong. There are issues with no clear answers. How should one use one's scarce resources of time and attention? Should one emphasize better performance from teachers, including more training opportunities, or devote more time and effort to increasing rapport with them? One principal may regret not going along with teacher preferences and another regret not having resisted them more strongly. Some principals may rue expressing anger at an uncooperative teacher where others wished they had not ignored the feelings of, and not helping, a new group of teachers displaced from a school that was closed. The perplexing choices involved in exercising authority in achieving an effective balance between "consideration" and "thrust," to quote terms used by Andrew Halpin (Halpin & Croft, 1963), are potential sources of remorse.

The mistakes made with parents consist almost entirely of not according them enough attention or not doing well in relating to them. You can be "too confrontational" said one, a sentiment voiced by two others as well who criticized themselves for being too "testy" and "authoritarian" with parents. Others regret mistakes such as being late in providing information about school changes and being slow to defuse the concerns of some parents. One idea summarizes these responses: the wise principal pays close attention to the parents of students and works hard to keep them well-informed and satisfied. Failure to do so can be costly.

Professional consciences are voiced when principals talk about mistakes with students; while two wish they had been somewhat sterner in disciplinary matters, others regretted occasions when they might have done more to help. Examples include the failure to seek outside expertise in a particular case, not fighting to prevent students from having to compete in an unfair (as she saw it) district competition and, in one tragic case, not trying harder to prevent a student from committing suicide. These mistakes exemplify what can be an important aspect of the principal's moral concerns—the obligation to serve as the defender of, and advocate for, the students in his or her charge.

Mistakes vis-à-vis central office differ. Some say they should have pushed harder against central office decisions; a few regret occasions when they displayed negative feelings toward superordinates and their decisions.

Finally 14% of those mentions derive from what principals later see as poor judgments in allocating their own time and energy—mostly, insufficient attention devoted to instructional matters. Principals are exposed continuously to the idea that they should exercise "educational leadership," an injunction from authorities who do not necessarily accompany it with permission to slight competing obligations. Some look back, it seems, and blame themselves when they have not met whatever time and energy standards they associate with instructional leadership. One principal's regrets were echoed by others as well:

> Strengths for me are conferences, public relations, communications. Up to this year I have not concentrated on curriculum as much as I should have, perhaps. I want to mesh the two better. I'm not sure if it can be done, but I would like to. (Female, 40)

To summarize, the responses to our two questions on task difficulties undermine any view of the work of elementary principals as straightforward and uncomplicated. The difficulties they described arose in the central responsibilities laid on them, responsibilities, as we have seen, that included aims and relationships they considered important, for example, the oversight and improvement of instruction provided by faculty members. Substantial numbers doubted their own ability to make solid judgments on the quality of teacher performance; similar numbers found teachers did not respond affirmatively to their direction on how to improve their work.

Asked about mistakes they had made, these principals faulted themselves primarily in their managerial decisions in employment matters and where they chose to focus their attention and energy. They were too slow to dismiss ineffective teachers; they made mistakes in how they organized the work of their subordinates. Some did not, as they see it, do a good job in relating to parents and handling their relationship with central office. While none said they put too much emphasis on instructional matters, over a tenth wished they had concentrated more on teaching and learning. Some felt, after the fact, that they had not honored their obligation to take proper care of their students. It seems that recriminations come readily for these men and women—recriminations that grow out of the uncertainties and relational complexities that inhere in their work.

REFERENCES

Halpin, A. W., & Croft, D. B. (1963). *The organizational climate of schools.* Chicago: Midwest Administration Center, University of Chicago.

Louis, K. S., & Wahlstrom, L. (2011). Principals as cultural leaders. *Phi Delta Kappan,* 92(5), 52–56.

McPherson, R. B., Salley, C., & Baehr, M. F. (1975). *A national occupational analysis of the school principalship.* Chicago: Industrial Relations Center, University of Chicago.

Mintzberg, H. (1973). *The nature of managerial work.* New York: Harper & Row.

Peterson, K. D. (1977). The principal's task. *Administrator's Notebook, 26*(8), 1–4.

READING 20

THE STATUS OF TEACHING AS A PROFESSION

Richard M. Ingersoll and Elizabeth Merrill

Teachers are often considered the backbone of schools; without them there would be no school. Thus, understanding teachers' roles is key to understanding the educational system. Discussions of organizations often include information about the roles people occupy within them. One aspect of roles that distinguishes organizations is the type of workers they employ. Professionals have a high degree of control over their work environments, high prestige, and relatively high compensation compared to nonprofessionals. This designation is not without controversy, and it is often at the foundation of many labor disputes. Whether teachers qualify as professionals is one of these debates. Richard M. Ingersoll and Elizabeth Merrill evaluate the criteria of professionalization as they apply to teachers and conclude that teachers generally fall into a category called "semi-professionals."

Questions to consider for this reading:

1. What criteria differentiate professionals from other types of workers?

2. Where do teachers meet or fall short of these criteria?

3. Will teachers ever gain professional status?

Professionalization has long been a source of both hope and frustration for teachers. Since early in the 20th century, educators have repeatedly sought to promote the view that elementary and secondary teaching is a highly complex kind of work, requiring specialized knowledge and skill and deserving of the same status and standing as traditional professions, like law and medicine. This movement to professionalize teaching has, however, been marked by both confusion and contention, much of which centers on what it means to be a profession and to professionalize a particular kind of work. To some, the essence of a profession is advanced training, and hence the way to best professionalize teaching is to upgrade teachers' knowledge and skills through professional development. For others, the essence of a profession lies in the attitudes individual practitioners hold toward their work. In this view, the best way to professionalize teaching is to instill an ethos of public service and high standards—a sense of professionalism—among teachers. For even others, the focus is on the organizational conditions under which teachers work; in this view, the best way to professionalize teaching is to improve teachers' working conditions. As a result of this wide range of emphases, it is often unclear whether education critics and reformers are referring to the same things when they discuss professionalization in teaching (Labaree, 1992, 2004; Lortie, 1969, 1975).

Although education reformers often disagree over what is meant by profession, professionalism, and professionalization, students of occupations, notably sociologists, do not. The study of work, occupations, and professions has been an important topic in sociology for decades, and researchers in this subfield have developed what is known as the professional model—a series of organizational and occupational characteristics associated with professions and professionals and, hence, useful to distinguish professions and professionals from other kinds of work and workers (Abbott, 1988; Etzioni, 1969; Freidson, 1986, 2001; Hughes, 1965; Larson, 1977; Starr, 1982). These include rigorous training and licensing requirements, positive working conditions, an active professional organization or association, substantial workplace authority, relatively high compensation, and high prestige. From this viewpoint, occupations can be assessed according to the degree to which they do or do not exhibit the characteristics of the professional model. The established or "traditional" professions—law, medicine, university teaching, architecture, science, and engineering, in particular—are usually regarded as the strongest examples of the professional model. There are, of course, large variations both between and within these professions in the degree to which they exhibit the professional model. Moreover, most professions have been and are currently undergoing change in the degree to which they exhibit the attributes of the professional model, that is, in their degree of professionalization or deprofessionalization (Freidson, 2001; Simpson & Simpson, 1983).

Sociologists have also been careful to distinguish professionalization from professionalism. The former refers to the degree to which occupations exhibit the structural or sociological attributes, characteristics, and criteria identified with the professional model. The latter refers to the attitudinal or psychological attributes of those who are considered to be, or aspire to be considered as, professionals. From the latter perspective, a professional is someone who is not an amateur, but is committed to a career and to public service. Although professionalism is often considered part of the professionalization process, sociologists do not consider it a reliable indicator of the professional model. Members of established professions do not necessarily exhibit a higher degree of the attitudes associated with professionalism than do those in less professionalized occupations. For instance, those with a strong service orientation—who place more importance on helping others and contributing to society and less importance on material rewards such as income and status—are less likely to be found in some of the traditional professions, such as law, and more likely to be found in occupations such as nursing and teaching that traditionally have not been categorized as full professions (Ingersoll, 2003; Kohn & Schooler, 1983; Rosenberg, 1981).

This chapter attempts to theoretically and empirically ground the debate over the status of teaching as a profession. Our purpose is neither explanatory nor evaluative. We do not seek to provide a historical account of the sources behind teachers' status, nor do we seek to assess the benefits and costs, advantages, and disadvantages of professionalization. Moreover, our purpose is not normative; while we personally feel teaching should be treated as a profession, our purpose here is analytic and descriptive. Our objective is to define and describe teaching's occupational status. The focus of this analysis is on professionalization or the characteristics of school workplaces and teaching staffs, and not on professionalism or the attitudes of individual teachers. Our primary point is that much of the educational discussion and literature on teaching as a profession has overlooked some of the most basic characteristics that sociologists have used to distinguish professions from other kinds of occupations. We empirically ground the subject by presenting a range of representative data from the best sources available. From these data we developed a series of indicators of the traditional characteristics of the professional model and used them to assess the professionalization of teaching. These include:

1. Credential and licensing levels

2. Induction and mentoring programs for entrants

3. Professional development support, opportunities, and participation

4. Specialization

5. Authority over decision making

6. Compensation levels

7. Prestige and occupational social standing

These, of course, are not the only characteristics used to define professions, nor are they the only kinds of criteria used to distinguish or to classify work and occupations in general. But they are among the most widely used indicators of professions and professionals and are the subject of much discussion in reference to teachers and schools.

In background analyses of these empirical indicators, we have found large differences in professionalization among different kinds of schools. Consistent with other research on school organization, we found school sector (public/private) and poverty level, in particular, to be the most significant factors related to professionalization (Ingersoll, 1997, 2003).

Below, we will briefly describe each of the classic indicators of professionalization we examined, and then we will summarize what the data tell us about levels of professionalization in teaching and, where possible, the extent to which it varies across these above different types of schools.

How Professionalized Is Teaching?

Credentials

To sociologists, the underlying and most important quality distinguishing professions from other kinds of occupations is the degree of expertise and complexity involved in the work itself. In this view, professional work involves highly complex sets of skills, intellectual functioning, and knowledge that are not easily acquired and not widely held. For this reason, professions are often referred to as the "knowledge-based" occupations. But even if laypeople were to acquire these complex sets of skills and knowledge, rarely would they be able to practice as professionals. Entry into professions requires credentials. That is, entry into professions typically requires a license, which is obtained only after completion of an officially sanctioned training program and passage of examinations. Indeed, it is illegal to do many kinds of work, professional and not, from plumbing and hairstyling to law and medicine, without a license.

These credentials serve as screening or "gatekeeping" devices. Their rationale is protection of the interests of the public by ensuring that practitioners hold an agreed-upon level of knowledge and skill, and by filtering out those with substandard levels of knowledge and skill. The importance of such credentials is evidenced by the practice, commonly used by professionals, such as physicians, dentists, architects, and attorneys, of prominently displaying official documentation of their credentials in their offices.

Given the importance of credentials to professions, not surprisingly, upgrading the licensing requirements for new teachers has been an important issue in school reform. (Licenses for teachers are known as teaching certificates and are issued by states.) But it has also been a source of contention. On one side are those who argue that entry into teaching should be more highly restricted, as in traditional professions. From this viewpoint, efforts to upgrade certification requirements for new teachers will help upgrade the quality and qualifications of teachers and teaching.

On the other side are those who argue that entry into teaching should be eased. Proponents of this view have pushed a range of initiatives, all of which involve a loosening of the entry gates: programs designed to entice professionals into midcareer changes to teaching; alternative certification programs, whereby college graduates can postpone formal education training, obtain an emergency teaching certificate, and begin teaching immediately; and Peace Corps–like programs, such as Teach for America, which seek to lure the "best and brightest" into understaffed schools. These alternative routes into the occupation claim the same rationale as the more restrictive traditional credential routes—enhanced recruitment of talented candidates into teaching—but the ultimate consequence of such initiatives, intended or not, can be deprofessionalization. That is, traditional professions rarely resort to loosening licensing standards to recruit and retain quality practitioners.

Conflict over the ease of entry into teaching is reflected in the degree to which employed teachers actually hold a full state-approved certificate. The data (the first row in Table 20.1) show that most, but not all, teachers in public districts do, indeed, hold full teaching certificates. In contrast, teachers in private schools are far less inclined to hold a full license to teach; just under half of private school teachers do so. This reflects different standards in public-private state regulations; many states do not require private school teachers to hold state certification (Tryneski, 2007). It also contrasts sharply with traditional professions. Hospitals, whether they are public or for-profit, for instance, would rarely hire unlicensed doctors and nurses to fill regular physician and licensed nurse positions (Simpson & Simpson, 1983).

This does not mean, of course, that private schools are not selective in who they hire as teachers. Private schools can, indeed, often be very selective in their choice of teaching candidates, but they far less frequently use licensing criteria associated with professions. They are, however, not uniform in this indicator of professionalization. There are distinct differences in the use of these hiring criteria among private schools, depending upon their orientation. Catholic schools, in particular, are far more likely than other private schools to require certificates and tests of their new hires.

Induction

In addition to initial formal training and preparation, professional work typically requires extensive training for new practitioners upon entry. Such training is designed to pick up where pre-employment training has left off. That is, while credentials and examinations in many professions are usually designed to ensure that new entrants have a minimum or basic level of knowledge and skill, induction programs for practitioners are designed to augment this basic level of knowledge and skill. As a result, entry to professions typically involves both formal and informal mechanisms of induction—internships, apprenticeships, or mentoring programs. Sometimes these periods of induction can be prolonged and intensive, as in the case of physicians' internships. The objective of such programs and practices is to aid new practitioners in adjusting to the environment, to familiarize them with the concrete realities of their jobs and also to provide a second opportunity to filter out those with substandard levels of skill and knowledge.

In teaching, mentoring, apprenticeship, and induction programs have been the subject of much discussion among reformers. The teaching occupation has long been plagued by high attrition rates among newcomers (Ingersoll, 2012), and, reformers argue, one of the best ways to increase the efficacy and retention of new teachers is to better assist them in coping with the practicalities of teaching, of managing groups of students, and of adjusting to the school environment.

The data suggest these attempts at professionalization have had some success: Over the past decade the numbers of schools with assistance programs has increased. Our background analysis of the data shows that in 1990–1991 in the public sector about one half of first-year teachers participated in formal induction programs of one sort or another. By 2007–2008 this had increased to over 90% (see Table 20.1). The proportion of beginning teachers in private schools who participated in formal induction programs has been lower than that for public schools, but this percentage has dramatically increased over the past two decades. However, the data also show that induction programs vary widely in the number and kinds of activities and supports they include. The most comprehensive include a wide range of components, such as mentoring by veterans, structured planning time with teachers in one's field, orientation seminars, regular communication with an administrator, a reduced course load,

Table 20.1 Level of Teacher Professionalization in Schools, by Type of School

	Public	Public Low Poverty	Public High Poverty	Private
Credentials				
% teachers with full or regular certification	93	93	91	49
Induction				
% beginning teachers participating in induction program	93	94	93	77
Professional development				
% schools providing teachers with time for professional development activities	98	98	97	85
% teachers participating in professional organization activities	94	93	96	83
% teachers receiving funding for professional development activities	66	69	64	64
Specialization				
Mean % in-field teaching	77	81	71	58
Authority				
Over teacher hiring				
% with influential board	23	18	25	28
% with influential district staff	32	29	33	–
% with influential principal	91	92	88	94
% with influential faculty	27	27	27	33
Over teacher evaluation				
% with influential board	13	11	15	16
% with influential district staff	26	27	28	–
% with influential principal	94	93	94	95
% with influential faculty	19	22	20	18
Compensation				
% with retirement plan	88	87	90	57
Mean starting salary ($)	33,567	37,116	32,616	26,920
Mean maximum salary ($)	62,231	73,695	57,610	47,108

Source: Original analyses by the authors of the U.S. Department of Education's nationally representative *Schools and Staffing Survey* (SASS). To date, six independent cycles of SASS have been completed: 1987–1988, 1990–1991, 1993–1994, 1999–2000, 2003–2004, and 2007–2008 (see Tourkin et al., 2010). The SASS data presented here are primarily from the 2007–2008 cycle, with the exception of the second and third indicators of teacher professional development, from the 2003–2004 SASS, and the indicator of in-field teaching, from the 1993–1994 SASS. Low poverty refers to schools where 10% or less of the students receive publicly funded free or reduced price lunches. High poverty refers to schools where more than 50% do so.

and a classroom assistant. Moreover, importantly a growing body of empirical research has shown that induction has positive effects on beginners' classroom teaching practices, on their retention, and on their students' academic achievement (Ingersoll & Strong, 2011).

Professional Development

Beyond both preservice basic training and mentoring for beginners, professions typically require ongoing in-service technical development and growth on the part of practitioners throughout their careers. The assumption is that achieving a professional-level mastery of complex skills and knowledge is a prolonged and continuous process and, moreover, that professionals must continually update their skills, as the body of technology, skill, and knowledge advances. As a result, professionals typically belong to associations and organizations that, among other things, provide mechanisms, such as periodic conferences, publications, and workshops, for the dissemination of knowledge and skill to members. Moreover, professionalized workplaces typically both require and provide support for employee development. These include on-site workshops, financial support for conferences, course work, skill development, and sabbaticals.

Professional development has been one of the most frequently discussed and advocated teacher reforms in recent years. Again, the data present a picture of success in the provision of support for, and teacher use of, professional development.

Data on three indicators of teacher professional development are displayed in Table 20.1: the percentage of schools that provided professional development programs for the teaching staff during regular school hours; the percentage of teachers who participated in workshops, seminars, or conferences provided by their school or by external professional associations or organizations; and the percentage of teachers who received financial support for college tuition, fees, or travel expenses for participation

in external conferences or workshops during that school year.

What is striking about the data on professional development is the consistency across schools. Most schools, both public and private, provide professional development, most teachers participate in workshops or activities either sponsored by their schools or sponsored by external professional organizations, and most teachers also receive financial support of some sort for external professional development activities. These data are an impressive set of indicators of this aspect of professionalization. However, they, of course, do not tell us about the quality or length of these professional development programs and activities.

Specialization

Given the importance of expertise to professions, it naturally follows that one of the most fundamental attributes of professions is specialization—professionals are not generalists, amateurs, or dilettantes, but possess expertise over a specific body of knowledge and skill. Few employers or organizations would require heart doctors to deliver babies, real estate lawyers to defend criminal cases, chemical engineers to design bridges, or sociology professors to teach English. The assumption behind this is that because such traditional professions require a great deal of skill, training, and expertise, specialization is considered necessary and good. In contrast, the other part of the assumption is that nonprofessions and semiskilled or low-skill occupations require far less skill, training, and expertise than traditional professions, and hence specialization is assumed less necessary.

Despite the centrality of specialization to professionalization, there has been little recognition of its importance among education reformers, even among proponents of teacher professionalization. Indeed, some school reformers have argued that teacher specialization, especially at the elementary school level, is a step backward for education because it does not address the needs of the "whole child," unduly fragments the educational process, and hence contributes to the alienation of students (e.g., Sizer, 1992).

To assess the degree of specialization in teaching and the degree to which teachers are treated as professionals with expertise in a specialty, we examine the phenomenon known as out-of-field teaching—the extent to which teachers are assigned to teach subjects that do not match their fields of specialty and training. Out-of-field teaching is an important but little understood problem. It is misunderstood because it is usually confused with teacher training. Most researchers and reformers assume, wrongly, that out-of-field teaching is due to a lack of training or preparation on the part of teachers. The source of out-of-field teaching lies not in a lack of education or training on the part of teachers, but in a lack of fit between teachers' fields of preparation and their teaching assignments. Out-of-field teaching is a result of misassignment—when school principals assign teachers to teach subjects in which they have little background. It is important because otherwise-qualified teachers may become highly unqualified when assigned out of their fields of specialty.

Assessing the extent of in-field or out-of-field teaching is one way of assessing the importance of professional specialization in the occupation of teaching—it provides a measure of the extent to which teachers are treated as if they are semi-skilled or low-skill workers whose work does not require much specialized expertise or, alternatively, as if they are professionals whose work requires expertise in a specialty. Table 20.1 presents a measure of in-field/out-of-field teaching—the average percentage of secondary-level classes in which teachers do have at least a college minor in the fields taught—we have developed (Ingersoll, 1999).

The data show that an emphasis on specialization in one's area of expertise often does not hold in secondary-level teaching. Teachers at the secondary school level are assigned to teach a substantial portion of their weekly class schedules out of their fields of specialty. For example, in public schools, teachers, on average, spend only about three quarters of their time teaching in fields in which they have a college major or even a minor. This lack of specialization is more widespread in high-poverty schools. But, again, these comparisons are overshadowed by public-private differences.

Private school teachers are far more often assigned to teach subjects out of their fields of training than are public school teachers—just over half of a private school teacher's schedule is in fields for which the teacher has basic training. However, there are differences among private schools (not shown here). Teachers in nonsectarian private schools have higher levels of in-field teaching than do teachers in other private schools. On average, teachers in nonsectarian schools spend about two thirds of their schedules teaching in field; in contrast, in-field levels in religious private schools are lower—about half their class loads.

Authority

Professionals are considered experts in whom substantial authority is vested, and professions are marked by a large degree of self-governance. The rationale behind professional authority is to place substantial levels of control into the hands of the experts—those who are closest to and most knowledgeable of the work. Professions, for example, exert substantial control over the curriculum, admissions, and accreditation of professional training schools; set and enforce behavioral and ethical standards for practitioners; and exert substantial control over who their future colleagues are to be. Sometimes this control is exerted through professional organizations. For instance, gaining control over (and sharply limiting) medical school admissions by the American Medical Association was a crucial factor in the rise of medicine from a lower-status occupation to one of the pinnacle professions (Starr, 1982). Other times control is exerted directly in workplaces, and as a result, professionalized employees often have authority approaching senior management when it comes to organizational decisions surrounding their work. In the case of hospitals, physicians traditionally were the senior management. Academics, for another example, often have substantially more control than university administrators over the hiring of new colleagues and, through the institution of peer review, over the evaluation and promotion of members and, hence, over the ongoing content and character of the work of the profession.

The distribution of power, authority, and control in schools is one of the most important issues in contemporary education research and policy. Indeed, this issue lies at the crux of many current reforms, such as teacher empowerment, site-based management, charter schools, and school restructuring. But it is also a source of contention. Some hold that schools are overly decentralized organizations in which teachers have too much workplace autonomy and discretion. Others hold the opposite—that schools are overly centralized in which teachers have too little influence over school operations. Part of this confusion arises because of differences in the domain analyzed; most focus on how much autonomy teachers have in their classrooms over the choice of their texts or teaching techniques. Others focus on how much power faculties collectively wield over school-wide decision making, such as budgets (Ingersoll, 2003). Here we focus on faculty influence over two issues traditionally controlled by professionals—peer hiring and peer evaluation.

Table 20.1 displays the frequency of schools in which principals report the school board, the district staff if in the public sector, the faculty, and the principals themselves to have substantial decision-making influence over two activities— staff evaluation and hiring. The data paint a picture of a steep organizational-level hierarchy, with principals at the top.

Overall, principals clearly view themselves as powerful actors in reference to decisions concerning teacher evaluation and hiring and view teachers as among the least powerful actors. In comparison to principals, boards and district staff far less frequently have authority over these school decisions, at least from the viewpoint of principals. In every kind of school, principals report faculty to be influential far less often than they are themselves. Teachers are also less often influential than district staff over these issues. However, in comparison to school boards, teachers' professional authority is more often higher in both public and private schools.

Consistent with conventional wisdom, the hierarchy in some ways is less steep in affluent than in poor public schools; faculty in poor schools are less often reported to be influential, especially over hiring, and boards are more often influential. But, especially over hiring, private school teachers are less often empowered than those in public schools, counter to conventional wisdom that private school teachers are delegated more workplace influence than public school teachers (e.g., Chubb & Moe, 1989).

Compensation

Professionals typically are well compensated and are provided with relatively high salary and benefit levels throughout their career span. The assumption is that, given the lengthy training and the complexity of the knowledge and skills required, relatively high levels of compensation are necessary to recruit and retain capable and motivated individuals.

Teacher salaries have been a much discussed topic amongst teacher reformers. But, unfortunately, data on teacher salaries have often been misleading. Teacher salary analyses typically focus on the average salary levels of teachers of particular types or in particular jurisdictions. Comparing average teacher salaries for different kinds of teachers or schools can be misleading because teacher salary levels are often standardized according to a uniform salary schedule, based on the education levels and years of experience of the teachers. Especially with an aging teaching workforce, it is unclear if differences in average salary levels are due to real differences in the compensation offered to comparable teachers by different schools, or are due to differences in the experience and education levels of the teachers employed. That is, schools with older teachers may appear to offer better salaries, when in fact they do not.

A more effective method of comparison across schools is to compare the normal salaries paid by schools to teachers at common points in their careers. Start-of-career salary levels provide some indication of how well particular kinds of workplaces are able to compete for the pool of capable individuals. End-of-career salary levels provide some indication of the ability of particular kinds of workplaces to retain and motivate capable individuals. The ratio between starting salaries and end-of-career salaries provides some indication of the extent of opportunity for promotion, and the range of monetary rewards available to employees as they advance through their careers.

Table 20.1 shows data on the normal starting and maximum teacher salaries offered in different kinds of districts or schools in the 2007–2008 school year. Of course, salary data such as these quickly get "old" due to inflation. However, our analysis is concerned not with absolute salary values, but with comparisons—which have shown little change over time. We make four comparisons: how salaries vary across different types of schools; the ratio between teachers' start-of-career and end-of-career salaries; how beginning teachers' salaries compare with those of other recent college graduates; and, finally, how teachers' annual salaries compare to those in other occupations. These are revealing comparisons to make and get at the status of teaching as a profession. Data on the provision of retirement benefits are also displayed.

Consistent with conventional wisdom (Kozol, 1991), there are differences in the compensation afforded to teachers in public schools. In particular, public schools serving high-poverty communities pay less than schools in more affluent communities. But the differences between public and private schools are even greater. Teachers in private schools are paid far less than teachers in public schools, and also are less likely to be provided with a retirement plan by their school. The average starting salary for an individual with a bachelor's degree and no teaching experience was about 25% more in public schools than in private schools. Moreover, the public-private salary gap widens as teachers progress through their careers. The average maximum salary (the highest possible salary offered) for public school teachers was more than 30% more than for private school teachers. We also found that among private schools, there are large differences in compensation. Non-Catholic religious private schools pay their starting teachers a salary that is just above the official federal poverty line. Teachers' salaries, in both public and private schools, are also "frontloaded." The ratio of teachers' end-of-career to start-of-career salaries in Table 20.1 is less than 2 to 1. This is far less than for many other occupations and traditional professions. Frontloading suggests limited opportunity for financial gains, can undermine long-term commitment to an occupation, and can make teaching less attractive as a career (Lortie, 1975).

In order to place teachers' salaries in perspective, it is useful to compare them to the salaries earned in other lines of work. Traditionally teachers have long been called the "economic proletarians of the professions" (Mills, 1951), and the data bear this out. Different data sources have long documented that the salaries of new college graduates who have become teachers are considerably below those of new college graduates who chose many other occupations. For instance, data from the nationally representative *Baccalaureate and Beyond Longitudinal Study* show the average salary (one year after graduation) for 2,000 college graduates who became teachers was below the average for all college grads, 10% less than for those working as editors or reporters, one third less than for those who entered the military, 37% less than for those in sales jobs, and almost 90% less than the average starting salary of their classmates who took computer programming jobs.

These differences remain throughout the career span. For instance, data collected by the Bureau of Labor Statistics show that the average annual salaries of teachers were far below those of professionals, such as college professors, scientists, pilots, veterinarians, accountants, pharmacists, architects, and lawyers.

Prestige

Professions are high-status, high-prestige occupations. In other words, they are respected and envied. Prestige and status, unlike salary, power, or professional development, at first glance, might seem very difficult to empirically assess because they are highly subjective. But, like other attitudes, public perceptions of which kinds of occupations are more or less prestigious can be assessed, and indeed, for more than 50 years, sociologists have studied how the public evaluates the relative prestige of occupations. Table 20.2 presents some of the results from the best-known studies of occupational prestige.

These data are useful to illustrate how the status of teaching compares to other occupations and also to compare the relative status of different levels of teaching. The data clearly show that, as expected, the traditional professions are very prestigious. Teaching, like many of the other female-dominated occupations, is rated in the middle. Teaching is less prestigious than law, medicine, and engineering, but it is more prestigious than most blue-collar work, such as truck driving, and pink-collar work, such as secretarial work. The status of teaching also changed slightly from the early 1970s to the late 1980s. Both elementary and secondary teaching went up in prestige, but kindergarten and preschool teaching went down. The result is a distinct status hierarchy within the teaching occupation; secondary teachers are slightly higher status than

Table 20.2   Relative Prestige of Selected Occupations (ranked by 1972 scores)

Occupation	Score 1972	Score 1989	Occupation	Score 1972	Score 1989
Physicians	82	86	Funeral directors	52	49
Professors	78	74	Athletes	51	65
Lawyers	76	75	Bank tellers	50	43
Judges	76	71	Police	48	60
Physicists and astronomers	74	73	Secretaries	46	46
Dentists	74	72	Mail carriers/postal service	42	47
Architects	71	73	Plumbers	41	45
Aerospace engineers	71	72	Tailors	41	42
Psychologists	71	69	Carpenters	40	39
Chemists	69	73	Barbers	38	36
Clergy	69	69	Bakers	34	35

(Continued)

Table 20.2 (Continued)

Occupation	Score 1972	Score 1989	Occupation	Score 1972	Score 1989
Chemical engineers	67	73	Truck drivers	32	30
Secondary school teachers	63	66	Cashiers	31	29
Registered nurses	62	66	Painters/construction/maintenance	30	34
Elementary school teachers	60	64	Cooks	26	31
Authors	60	63	Waiters and waitresses	20	28
Pre-K/kindergarten teachers	60	55	Maids	18	20
Actors and directors	55	58	Garbage collectors	17	28
Librarians	55	54	Janitors/cleaners	16	22
Social workers	52	52			

Source: From *General Social Survey*, 1972 and 1989, Washington, DC: U.S. Census Bureau. Reprinted with permission. See Davis & Smith (1996).

elementary teachers. Both are substantially higher status than kindergarten and preschool teachers.

IMPLICATIONS

This chapter attempts to ground the ongoing debate over teacher professionalization by evaluating teaching according to a series of classic criteria used to distinguish professions from other kinds of work. The data show that, on the one hand, almost all elementary and secondary schools do exhibit some of the important characteristics of professionalized workplaces. On the other hand, and despite numerous reform initiatives, almost all schools lack or fall short on many of the key characteristics associated with professionalization. Clearly, teaching continues to be treated as, at best, a "semi-profession" (Etzioni, 1969; Lortie, 1969, 1975).

But there are also large variations in the degree of professionalization, depending on the type of school. Consistent with conventional wisdom, low-income schools are, in a number of ways, less professionalized than are the more affluent public schools. The most striking differences are those between public and private schools. The teaching job in private schools is in some important ways less professionalized than in public schools. Moreover, there are distinct differences within the private sector, often overlooked in public-private comparisons. Our background analyses show that in most ways, the least professionalized of schools are non-Catholic religious private schools. This has important implications for current school reform and policy. It suggests there may be an overlooked but fundamental clash between teacher professionalization and school privatization reforms, such as some school choice initiatives. It also suggests that privatization may lead to an unintended consequence—the further deprofessionalization of teaching.

These data raise some obvious questions. What difference does professionalization make for those in schools? What are the implications of variations among schools in professionalization? To be sure, research and reform concerned with teacher professionalization typically assume that professionalization is highly beneficial to teachers, schools, and students. The rationale underlying this view is that upgrading the teaching occupation will lead to improvements in the motivation, job satisfaction, and efficacy of teachers, which, in turn, will lead to improvements in teachers' performance, which will ultimately lead to improvements in student learning. If we accept this assumption—in other words if we assume that professionalization attracts capable recruits to an occupation, fosters their expertise and commitment, and, ultimately, provides assurance to the public of quality service to the public—then these data do not yield a reassuring portrait of the teaching occupation.

This logic and these assumptions seem reasonable enough. Indeed, equivalent arguments are regularly used by proponents of professionalization in any number of other occupations and also by defenders of the status quo in the traditional professions. However, just as in other occupations and professions, very little empirical research has ever been done to test such claims. It is difficult to find, for instance, empirical research examining the direct effects of the relatively high levels of training, power, compensation, and prestige accorded to physicians and professors.

It is important, however, to ask these kinds of questions because proponents of professionalization, in teaching and elsewhere, ignore an important stream of literature in the sociology of work, occupations, and professions that illuminates the downside to professionalization. For instance, medicine, long considered among the pinnacle professions and the clearest example of work that has successfully become professionalized over the past century, has been the subject of a great deal of criticism. The focus of this criticism is the negative consequences of the power and privilege of professionalization—monopolistic control over medical knowledge and the supply of practitioners, antagonism toward alternative medical approaches, and a power imbalance in the physician-client relationship (e.g., Abbott, 1988; Freidson, 1986; Starr, 1982). From this viewpoint, professionalization in medicine has brought many benefits, but it also incurs costs. The implication of this line of thought is that it is important to distinguish both the benefits and costs of professionalization and also to specify to whom both of these apply.

In other follow-up research projects, we and colleagues have analyzed the effects of various indicators of professionalization on teachers themselves—specifically their engagement or commitment to teaching; on conflict in schools; and on teachers' actual rates of retention and turnover (see, e.g., Ingersoll, 1997, 2003, 2012; Ingersoll & May, 2012). We found that most of the above indicators of professionalization do, indeed, positively affect teacher commitment, school climate, and teacher retention. Several, however, particularly stood out for their strong effects: faculty autonomy and decision-making influence; the effectiveness of assistance for new teachers; and teachers' salaries and benefits.

References

Abbott, A. (1988). *The system of professions: An essay on the division of expert labor*. Chicago: University of Chicago Press.

Chubb, J. E., & Moe, T. M. (1989). *Politics, markets, and America's schools*. Washington, DC: Brookings Institution.

Davis, J., & Smith, T. (1996). *General social surveys, 1972–1996: Cumulative codebook*. Chicago: National Opinion Research Center.

Etzioni, A. (Ed.). (1969). *The semi-professions and their organizations: Teachers, nurses, and social workers*. New York: Free Press.

Freidson, E. (1986). *Professional powers: A study in the institutionalization of formal knowledge*. Chicago: University of Chicago Press.

Freidson, E. (2001). *Professionalism: The third logic.* Chicago: University of Chicago Press.

Hughes, E. (1965). Professions. In K. Lynn & the editors of Daedalus (Eds.), *The professions in America* (pp. 1–14). Boston: Houghton Mifflin.

Ingersoll, R. (1997). *Teacher professionalization and teacher commitment: A multilevel analysis.* Washington, DC: National Center for Education Statistics.

Ingersoll, R. (1999). The problem of underqualified teachers in American secondary schools. *Educational Researcher, 28*(2), 26–37.

Ingersoll, R. (2003). *Who controls teachers' work? Power and accountability in America's schools.* Cambridge, MA: Harvard University Press.

Ingersoll, R. (2012). Beginning teacher induction: What the data tell us. *Phi Delta Kappan, 93*(8), 47–51.

Ingersoll, R., & May, H. (2012). The magnitude, destinations and determinants of mathematics and science teacher turnover. *Educational Evaluation and Policy Analysis, 34*(4), 435–464.

Ingersoll, R., & Strong, M. (2011). The impact of induction and mentoring for beginning teachers: A critical review of the research. *Review of Educational Research, 81*(2), 201–233.

Kohn, M., & Schooler, C. (1983). *Work and personality.* Norwood, NJ: Ablex.

Kozol, J. (1991). *Savage inequalities.* New York: HarperCollins.

Labaree, D. (1992). Power, knowledge, and the rationalization of teaching: A genealogy of the movement to professionalize teaching. *Harvard Educational Review, 62,* 123–154.

Labaree, D. (2004). *The trouble with ed schools.* New Haven, CT: Yale University Press.

Larson, M. (1977). *The rise of professionalism: A sociological analysis.* Berkeley: University of California Press.

Lortie, D. (1969). The balance of control and autonomy in elementary school teaching. In A. Etzioni (Ed.), *The semi-professions and their organizations: Teachers, nurses and social workers* (pp. 1–53). New York: Free Press.

Lortie, D. (1975). *School teacher.* Chicago: University of Chicago Press.

Mills, C. W. (1951). *White collar.* New York: Oxford University Press.

Rosenberg, M. (1981). *Occupations and values.* New York: Arno Press.

Simpson, I., & Simpson, R. (1983). *Research in the sociology of work.* Greenwich, CT: JAI Press.

Sizer, T. (1992). *Horace's compromise: The dilemma of the American high school.* Boston: Houghton Mifflin.

Starr, P. (1982). *The social transformation of American medicine.* New York: Basic Books.

Tourkin, S., Thomas, T., Swaim, N., Cox, S., Parmer, R., Jackson, B., Cole, C., & Zhang, B. (2010). *Documentation for the 2007–08 Schools and Staffing Survey* (NCES 2010-332). Washington, DC: National Center for Education Statistics, U.S. Department of Education.

Tryneski, J. (2007). *Requirements for certification of teachers, counselors, librarians, administrators for elementary and secondary schools* (71st ed.). Chicago: University of Chicago Press.

DOES SCHOOL ACCOUNTABILITY ALTER TEACHER TRUST AND PROMOTE BURNOUT?

Anthony Gary Dworkin and Pamela F. Tobe

Teachers often feel bombarded, blamed for everything from students' low test scores to holding negative attitudes toward poor children. Recent governmental plans to improve education call for teacher accountability, implying a lack of trust and confidence in teachers' abilities. Actions related to accountability in turn result in low morale and ultimately teachers leaving the classroom due to burnout, one result of accountability measures. Threats to teacher security if they do not improve student learning and test scores put added pressure on teachers. These challenges have resulted in high stress for teachers. Even their autonomy to run their classes is being challenged. In order to avoid teacher burnout, teachers need to feel trusted by their peers, administration, and parents of students. Such issues as safety, support, and appreciation reduce burnout. Anthony Gary Dworkin and Pamela F. Tobe report on factors that affect trust and burnout.

Questions to consider for this reading:

1. What problems cause teacher burnout?

2. Why do teachers feel a lack of trust and confidence from their administrators, the public, and government officials?

3. What might be done to increase trust and reduce teacher burnout?

The effectiveness of public education depends upon a hierarchy of trust relationships. Parents must trust school districts, school administrators, and teachers with the welfare and education of their children. School personnel, in turn, expect parents to bring their children to school ready and able to learn. Teachers expect their efforts and expertise to be valued and respected by parents as well as school administrators. Finally, stakeholders must trust the public and government officials to value the contributions of school personnel and trust them sufficiently to educate society's next generation. Breaks in the trusting relationships jeopardize the well-being of the educational process and limit the capacity of schooling to adapt to social change in a globalizing world (Bryk & Schneider, 2002; Forsyth, Barnes, & Adams, 2006; Tschannen-Moran & Hoy, 2000).

The national movement toward greater school accountability, including the mandate for high-stakes testing, plays a dominant role in the shaping and maintenance of trust relationships. Accountability mandates affect the morale of school actors, often because their implementation alters vulnerabilities of actors and tests the extent to which actors view one another as trustworthy (i.e., benevolent, reliable, competent, honest, and open [Tschannen-Moran & Hoy, 2000]). The present chapter explores the longitudinal effects of changing school accountability mandates on teacher morale and burnout and its relationship with teacher trust of school administrators, colleagues, students, and the parents of their students. The mandates have increasingly altered teachers' expectations about their job security and, therefore, challenged the level of trust that teachers have in those whose performances affect their fate and compensation.

TRUST

Building on Coleman's work on social capital, Bryk and Schneider (2002) examined two forms of relational trust: organic and contractual. For Bryk and Schneider (2002), "Organic trust is predicated on the more or less unquestioning beliefs of individuals in the moral authority of a particular social institution, and characterizes closed, small-scale societies" (p. 16). Trust is interwoven into the very fabric of social relations, and its violation is met with outrage and even severe sanctions (Blau, 1964; Durkheim, 1893/1964; Homans, 1961).

Contractual trust, by contrast, is vested in more bureaucratic and formally defined relationships in which the parties require the force of law to ensure mutual compliance with agreed-to expectations. "A contract defines basic actions to be taken by the parties involved. The terms of the contract explicitly spell out a scope of work to be undertaken by the parties involved, or a product or service to be delivered" (Bryk & Schneider, 2002, p. 17). Because of its specificity, the task of determining whether the terms of a contract have been met or violated is relatively simple. Violation of the terms of the contract is likely to be met with lawsuits. In modern, complex societies, both organic and contractual trusts are present in most relationships, although there is a predominance of contractual trust. Difficulties often arise when individuals view contractual work relations as if they were based on organic trust. Thus, relations that are specified in contract and occur in bureaucratic settings are overly interpreted as based on a common moral and emotional footing. Violations of the terms of a contract are thus seen as betrayal.

The shift from organic to contractual trust, caused by an increasingly more invasive school accountability system, has heightened the magnitude of teacher burnout. Prior to externally based accountability, the mutual understanding between teachers and school districts was that teachers would provide instruction in the best interests of their students, and districts in turn offered job security (after a probationary period) and autonomy in the classroom. This understanding constituted a loosely coupled system (Weick, 1976). Only when there was clear evidence of incompetence or that a teacher failed to consider the best interests of children would districts intervene.

Contractual trust, however, demands accountability and specifies often severe consequences for its violation. Contractual trust assumes that teachers are motivated by self-interest at the expense of their students. Therefore, the state, acting on behalf of its citizens, must monitor teacher behaviors and test their continued competence, often based on the result of students' standardized tests scores. Ironically, the basis for contractual trust relies on distrust of the individual.

Due to their scale and diversity, large urban schools are often characterized by the lack of interpersonal connectedness, which jeopardizes the development of supportive and trusting relationships. Further, large schools are frequently organizationally complex, which requires interdependence, but may make relationships problematic. The result is a diminished sense of connectedness and a proportional increase in burnout and distrust. In turn, teachers may relate to parents more negatively, diminishing parental involvement with a corresponding lack of support for student learning at home.

When class and cultural differences exist between teachers and others in the school (especially students and their parents), it is likely that teachers will assume that there is also a lack of shared educational values. The perceived lack of shared values in this diverse environment reduces the confidence in the abilities and intentions of others, including doubts regarding the competence, reliability, and belief in the good intentions of others (central to organic trust).

SCHOOL ACCOUNTABILITY AND THE MODIFIED SOCIAL CONTRACT

Until the standards-based school accountability movement, teaching offered a guarantee that assumed that unless a serious offense was committed, teachers had lifetime employment and relative autonomy within their classroom. Under the new accountability system, teachers no longer have classroom autonomy, they have a specified curriculum, and their employment is no longer secure. The result has been increasing levels of teacher burnout and changes in the nature of the relationships between teachers and other stakeholders within the school system.

The standards-based school accountability movement can trace its origins to the release of the report *A Nation at Risk* (1983) by the National Commission on Excellence in Education during the Reagan administration. The report held that the nation was at risk of failing to remain competitive against other economies of the world because the nation's students were deficient in science, mathematics, and an array of other skills linked to a globally competitive labor force. Recently, Dworkin and Tobe (2012a) chronicled the waves of school reforms that followed the 1983 commission report, including *America 2000* in the first Bush administration, *Goals 2000* in the Clinton administration, *No Child Left Behind (NCLB)* in the younger Bush administration, and *Race to the Top* in the current Obama administration.

No Child Left Behind and Race to the Top incorporate increasing standardized passing criteria for subgroups of students (based on ethnicity, poverty status, and home language status) to judge school and teacher performances. Low performances resulted in the right of students to change schools and could result in school closure and the termination of the current teaching and administrative staff.

School accountability systems assume that schools and school personnel will not assess their performance and cannot adequately evaluate their students' learning. Schools can only be evaluated by externally imposed standardized testing, which in turn can evaluate teacher competence. External accountability systems are premised upon the assumption that the school system will not act in the best interests of its students without external coercion (Dworkin & Tobe, 2012b). Externally imposed mandates, with severe consequences for failure to attain specified goals, convert organic trust to contractual trust. This conversion has become a precipitating factor in the growth of teacher burnout.

TEACHER BURNOUT

Psychologists tend to view burnout in terms of personal failures to adequately cope with stress, but as a sociological concept, burnout is explained in terms of structural and organizational causes. Stress can still be a precipitating factor in teacher burnout, but from the sociological view the causal elements operate within the organization of schooling, the policies that dictate how teachers are appraised, and how they are expected to conduct themselves within their teaching role. Accountability systems that hold teachers responsible for the learning outcomes of their students in settings where teachers have little control over their students' nonclassroom activities create structural barriers that deprive teachers of their sense of control over outcomes.

Both psychological and sociological models of burnout view job-related stressors as an essential component, and the accountability system precipitates job stress. Increased job stress diminishes teacher trust of students, coworkers, and administrators. Distrust becomes cyclical. In fact, Dworkin, Saha, and Hill (2003) noted that especially in high-poverty schools, neither the teachers nor the principals are willing to place their personal fate in the hands of their students and their students' parents, and therefore they adopt pedagogical styles that leave little to student initiative and reject democratic schooling. Job satisfaction for teachers is thus jeopardized.

PREDICTORS OF TEACHER BURNOUT

Job Stress. Preservice teachers come to expect through their training that they will be accorded professional respect. They often feel that teaching is a calling and that their students will accept them and participate in their education. Their experiences can be at odds with their expectations, as they face resource shortages, disrespect from students and parents, and an unreceptive work environment. Added to the gap between expectations and experience are the additional stressors associated with the accountability system.

Safe Schools. Compared with safe schools, schools that are characterized by drug and gang problems, disruptive students, and bullying create additional stressors that adversely affect teacher morale and a sense of trust. Thus, an unsafe school is likely to have depressed test scores among all students, resulting in elevated teacher stress due to fear of negative job appraisals, increased burnout, and diminished trust among individuals within the school. Schools that are persistently dangerous under NCLB can be deemed INOI (In Need of Improvement) and can face sanctions, including school closings. Vettenburg (2002) noted how teachers who feel unsafe in their workplace have difficulty focusing their attention on teaching, and the stress associated with the perception of physical danger diminishes their commitment to their students and their work. It is therefore expected that, in relatively unsafe schools, teacher burnout will be higher and that, as the accountability system changes from minimally threatening to severe (e.g., school closings and staff terminations), burnout levels among the teaching staff will increase. In comparison, safe schools will have lower burnout scores and lower levels of job stress.

Principal and Peer Support. Principals and coworkers provide support systems that reduce teacher burnout (Blasé, 2009; Dworkin, 1987, 2009; Saros & Saros, 1992). Lack of support from principals is associated with a strong relationship between job stress and teacher burnout. Peer support is also associated with reduced teacher burnout; however, Dworkin, Haney, Dworkin, and Telschow (1990) found that only when the principal was supportive would peer support significantly diminish burnout. The threat of school closure under accountability systems may place principals under greater stress, leading them to be less trusting of their staff. Teachers' attempts to support coworkers under a stress-laden environment are likely to be unsuccessful.

DATA AND CONTEXT

The data used in the current study are drawn from a single, large school district in the Houston metropolitan area. The students from the district generally come from families living in poverty (82% of the students are on free or reduced lunch status) and are overwhelmingly minority group members (Latino, African American, and Asian American). The total student body numbers over 60,000, and the teaching staff exceeds 4,000 individuals.

The 2002 teacher data set was enumerated in the early spring, soon after the passage of No Child Left Behind, but before any of the accountability details were made public or implemented. Although Texas had a working accountability system with student testing and the evaluation of schools in place for several years, there was little evidence to suggest that low student performance would have consequences for teachers or schools within the state at the time of the 2002 survey. Stress levels were nonetheless higher than they were a decade earlier (see Dworkin, 2009) in part because the data were collected within four months of 9/11 and three months after the beginning of the war in Afghanistan. Thus, the social context in which the survey was conducted remained with numerous stressors. The 2002 data set consisted of 2,869 surveys of K–12 teachers.

The 2004 survey was also administered during the spring semester. While No Child Left Behind had specified consequences for teachers and schools when student failure resulted in schools and districts not meeting their adequate yearly progress (AYP) goals, AYP passage standards were still relatively low in the 2003–2004 academic year. Accountability in Texas generally was high stakes for students, but teacher terminations for schools that failed to meet AYP goals remained minimal. In reality, few if any teachers lost their jobs due to low student achievement in Texas schools. The 2004 survey consisted of the responses of 1,771 K–12 teachers.

The data collection in 2009 follows the U.S. economic crisis that occurred the fall semester before. Although many teachers experienced some decline in the value of their savings, the state retirement fund seemed to be healthy, and most teachers could continue to assume that their jobs were also safe. Teacher layoffs were not yet an issue in early 2009; thus, most teachers remained somewhat cynical about risks to job security. The 2009 sample consisted of 1,825 teachers in Grades K–12.

The Texas Legislature meets every other year and passes biennial budgets. The Legislature met in late spring 2009 and generally imposed budget cuts in programs and the reduction of overhead. The surveyed district pledged not to lay off teachers but focused on increasing efficiency in all services and used attrition. Thus, by 2010 there was only moderate evidence that the schools would experience budget shortfalls large enough to result in the termination of programs and layoffs of teachers. The 2010 survey reflects the continued belief by teachers that their jobs were secure, despite the mandates of No Child Left Behind for schools that failed to meet their AYP objectives. Many urban schools in Texas began to incorporate value-added models based on student test scores to assess teacher performance. High student gain scores drove additional compensation for some teachers, while lower gain scores resulted in no additional compensation. Many teacher organizations challenged the validity of the process and the calculation of value-added. Nevertheless, the accountability system resulted in no clear evidence that teachers were losing their jobs. A total of 1,560 K–12 teachers participated in the 2010 survey.

The pledge by conservatives in the Texas government not to raise taxes resulted in substantial cuts in the funding of many Texas agencies. Education suffered more than other sectors of the state economy. In 2011, the Texas Legislature and the governor addressed the shortfall in funding for state agencies by significantly reducing the state education budget. In 2010–2011 the budget cuts led to the use of low student performance as a reason for teacher layoffs. Reductions in per-student funding of Texas public schools amounted to a loss of more than $5.4 billion over the biennium, and by 2012, Texas public schools lost more than 25,000 positions, including nearly 11,000 teaching jobs as reported in the Houston media. The Houston-area school districts lost nearly 3,000 teaching positions, some due to attrition (failure to fill jobs after teachers leave) and some due to the termination of programs. The school district surveyed had a reduction in workforce of 6%, mainly through attrition, but had a resultant increase in class sizes.

Consequently, teachers in the 2012 survey finally recognized that the threats to job security under NCLB and the Texas accountability system were becoming a reality. School districts rely on principals to make the initial recommendations for program closures and staff layoffs, as well as the relationship between teachers and principals, and the content of teacher-principal trust was modified due to financial constraints. The sample of K–12 teachers surveyed in 2012 consisted of 1,575 individuals.

RESEARCH QUESTIONS

This data analysis addresses two central issues: (1) How have changes in school accountability since the inception of NCLB affected teacher burnout, and (2) have changes in the accountability system altered the capacity of teacher support systems (trust of principals, colleagues, and parents) to limit burnout?

Does the level of burnout change with increased employment jeopardy? Similarly, social factors heighten risks to the safety of teachers or increase their workload (including class sizes), and will these social factors be reflected in changes in the level of teacher burnout? Furthermore, how does increasing risks to job security, caused by changes in the accountability system and the economic downturn, affect the relative explanatory power of individual predictors of teacher burnout?

RESULTS

Changes in Burnout Levels

Burnout is measured using a 10-item scale used by Dworkin and his colleagues since 1987. Burnout is computed using a statistical procedure called *factor analysis,* which extracts a common (latent) theme from a correlation matrix based upon the 10 items. The results of factor analysis are scale scores in z-score format with a mean of zero and a standard deviation of one. Positive scores indicate more burnout than negative scores.

The factor analysis was computed across all years because scale values are likely to change depending upon the particular attitudes and experiences of the teachers each year, thereby causing some patterns of responses to the burnout items to have different scale values at one time or another. All 10 items used in the burnout scale across the five time periods were therefore pooled resulting in a common scale that permits comparisons by year. The same procedure was conducted on the items that make up the predictors of burnout (job stress, unsafe school, trust of principal, trust of peers, trust of students and their parents). Presented in Table 21.1 are the means and standard deviations for the burnout scale scores and each predictor of burnout for samples collected between 2002 and 2012.

Table 21.1   Means and Standard Deviations of Burnout and Its Predictors

Year		Burnout	Job Stress	Safe Schools	Principal Trust	Peer Trust	Student & Parent Trust
2002	Mean	.036	−.347	.028	.162	.114	−.222
	S. D.	.960	.882	.960	.792	.777	.953
2004	Mean	−.133	−.367	.073	.190	.125	.324
	S. D.	.985	.869	.966	.847	.751	.990
2009	Mean	−.189	.075	.207	.204	.195	.407
	S. D.	.958	.957	.940	.797	.724	.997
2010	Mean	−.011	.286	−.056	−.053	.119	.468
	S. D.	.999	1.002	1.013	.861	.771	.956
2012	Mean	.241	.500	−.275	−.674	−.667	−.378
	S. D.	1.085	1.030	1.020	1.455	1.696	.788

Burnout. Tests of the significance of differences among the mean burnout scores demonstrated there were three groups of years. The years 2004 and 2009 had lower mean burnout scores than did the other years. Further, there were no differences between 2002 and 2010, but they had higher mean burnout scores than 2004 and 2009. Finally, the year 2012 had significantly higher mean burnout scores than any other year.

In 2002 teachers were anticipating changes that might occur once accountability under NCLB was implemented. There may also have been some added stress associated with 9/11 that had occurred early in the prior semester. Once teachers realized that the changes associated with NCLB would not result in terminations or school closures, the 2004 burnout levels declined.

Although the national economic recession had begun in 2008 and was even more severe in 2009, teachers in Houston were not experiencing downsizing of school districts or campuses. By spring 2010, the economy had affected the Houston labor market. Despite the fact that teacher layoffs were not yet occurring, districts were asked by the state legislature to trim their budgets and economize. Burnout was slightly higher than in 2009. When layoffs occurred in 2011 and 2012, the level of burnout rose significantly to a mean substantially higher than had been seen before.

Predictors of Burnout. Table 21.1 also displays the means and standard deviations of the burnout predictors across the five time periods. Tests of significance yielded the following results. The mean scores for the predictors followed a similar pattern as was found for burnout. Job stress was significantly higher in 2012 than any other year, followed by 2010. Other years had significantly lower mean scores for stress. Safe schools were seen as highest in 2009 and lowest in 2012, followed by 2010. School safety was compromised by budget cuts and increased class sizes in 2012. Efforts to economize in 2010, including reductions to district budgets for police protection, resulted in perceived threats to school safety.

Principal trust was significantly lower in 2012 than in any other year, followed by 2010, and

significantly higher in 2002, 2004, and 2009. Peer trust was also lowest in 2012 and highest in 2009. Finally, student and parent trust was minimal in 2012, and higher in 2004, 2009, and 2010.

Table 21.2 presents standardized regression coefficients for the predictors of burnout, including the three trust measures, for each of the years, permitting comparisons of the relative effect size of each predictor. Statistically significant standardized predictors are displayed in boldface.

Across the five time periods the adjusted R^2 varied from .337 to .532. Job stress has become an increasingly powerful predictor since 2009. Initially regression analyses included teacher demographics including years of education, race, and gender. These variables did not attain statistical significance in any year and are not included in the present analysis.

The key constructed variables of safe school, job stress, and peer trust *had a significant effect each year* on teacher burnout. Tests of statistical significance revealed changes in the explanatory power of the predictors over time. Principal trust declined steadily from 2004 with a precipitous drop in 2012, while trust of peers steadily increased from 2004 to 2012. Student and parent trust dropped in 2009 and was not significant in 2012.

Prior research has shown that stress is usually the strongest single predictor of burnout, and this has certainly been the case since 2009. In 2002 and 2004 stress had less of an effect than any of the trust measures. Safe school reduced burnout in all years but had a stronger effect in 2002 and 2012.

The declining relationship between principal trust and burnout is likely the consequence of the budget cuts and the mandate from school districts that principals initiate cuts in their programs and staff. Furthermore, the continued tenure of principals relies on improvements in student achievement and meeting AYP goals under NCLB. Principals are under more stress than they experienced prior to the current levels of school accountability, which makes them less able to be supportive of their faculty. Relationships between principals and teachers were initially based on organic trust, but have shifted to

Table 21.2 Effect of Predictors on Teacher Burnout Across Years (standardized regression coefficients)

Predictors	Beta 2002	Beta 2004	Beta 2009	Beta 2010	Beta 2012
Job Stress	**.096**	**.064**	**.303**	**.388**	**.397**
Safe School	**−.280**	**−.210**	**−.158**	**−.225**	**−.294**
Principal Trust	**−.195**	**−.249**	**−.230**	**−.219**	**−.108**
Peer Trust	**−.117**	**−.086**	**−.100**	**−.117**	**−.152**
Student & Parent Trust	**−.148**	**−.282**	**−.248**	−.053	−.002
Grade Level	**−.052**	**−.044**	−.027	.042	.026
Constant Sig.	**.240**	**.123**	.029	−.192	−.129
Adjusted R^2 =	**.337**	**.468**	**.532**	**.482**	**.479**
Statistically significant predictors ($p < .05$) are in **bold**.
Years of *Education, Race,* and *Gender* were not significant contributors.

a more contractual form of trust (Lee, Dietrich, & Smith, 1991), weakening the principal's ability to provide support.

Peer trust remained a modest but significant factor in reducing teacher burnout throughout the time periods. However, as the capacity of principal trust to reduce burnout declined, peer trust increased its beneficial effect on burnout. This may be a result of the recognition by teachers that they all share a common fate. Their supportiveness is social and emotional, but unlike that of the principal who is also an evaluator, peers cannot effectively save one another's jobs.

Student and parent trust is significant except in 2012. The effects of declining school funding and the school accountability system have merged to alter the social contract between both teachers and students, and teachers and parents. Prior to, and in the earlier years of, the accountability system student achievement had little effect on teacher job security. Now, however, teachers' careers are dependent upon the test scores of their students rather than the teachers' own sense of competence. The accountability system forces teachers to rely on students, whose

abilities they doubt and over whom they have very little control, to ensure continued employment. Parents are seen as essential in supporting student achievement. In urban and economically disadvantaged public schools, teachers rarely believe that parents provide adequate support. Similar to the quandary involving students, parental support is perceived as out of teachers' control but still influential in determining teaching effectiveness.

Discussion

Teacher burnout levels appear to be sensitive to changes in the accountability system, as well as funding levels, which challenge job security, increased class sizes, and the perceived level of school safety. The accountability system in Texas and the escalating AYP expectations for student performance mandated by NCLB and Race to the Top have heightened stress levels for teachers as well as rates of burnout. The accountability system specifies school closures and job terminations as outcomes of continued low student performance. For many years, closures and terminations did not occur, leading teachers to question the risks associated with the accountability system. Following the state's budgetary crisis and budget cuts, job risks became a reality, and the social contract between schools and teachers ensuring job security has been voided and replaced with a labor contract with an *at will* clause (no employment security).

The standards-based school accountability movement in the United States has altered the understandings the various school stakeholders had with one another. Teachers are no longer trading lower pay for job security (compared with the business sector); they are recipients of both lower pay and job insecurity. Additionally, the terms of their contract with society changed. Their own efforts no longer determine how well they were appraised; rather the efforts of their students on externally created, standardized tests are assessed.

Trust that was more organic in nature existed between stakeholders, especially among principals and teachers, in the years prior to the accountability movement. Teachers believed they could rely upon the support of their principals when confronted by parents, the community, and district administrators. The externally based accountability system shifted the balance toward more contractual trust, where both principals and teachers were subject to threat. In a system in which personal relationships are supplanted by legal-rationalism involving contracting partners, external threats leave participants with few resources for real support or trust.

It must be realized that the dichotomy between organic and contractual trust is based upon an *ideal typology*. No school system is purely one or the other even under the most rigorous accountability system. However, the relative importance of contractual trust over organic trust has shifted.

The accountability system since the 1980s has been based upon a suspicion of teacher incompetence and administrator negligence; in essence, it is based upon distrust. Threats of punishment for poor performance are assumed to motivate teachers, administrators, and even students to perform better (Dworkin, 2008). However, such threats merely increase levels of burnout among school personnel and diminish their sense of trust. As Forsyth et al. (2006) and Hoy and Tarter (2004) each have demonstrated, effective school improvements are predicated on a climate of trust and a sense of justice. Accountability systems that emphasize punishments destroy trust, exacerbate burnout, and defeat the intended goals of that system. Clearly, school accountability has had the effect across the data sets of diminishing teacher trust relationships, the support they provide, and increasing teacher burnout.

REFERENCES

Blasé, J. (2009). School administrator mistreatment of teachers. In L. J. Saha & A. G. Dworkin (Eds.), *International handbook on teachers and teaching* (pp. 433–448). New York: Springer Science and Business Media.

Blau, P. M. (1964). *Exchange and power in social life.* New York: Wiley.

Bryk, A. S., & Schneider, B. (2002). *Trust in schools: A core resource for improvement.* Rose Series in Sociology. New York: Russell Sage Foundation.

Durkheim, E. (1964). *The division of labor in society* (George Simpson, trans.). New York: Free Press. (Original work published 1893)

Dworkin, A. G. (1987). *Teacher burnout in the public schools: Structural causes and consequences for children.* Albany: State University of New York Press.

Dworkin, A. G. (2008). School accountability and the standards-based reform movement: Some unintended consequences of education policies. *International Journal of Contemporary Sociology, 45*(2), 11–31.

Dworkin, A. G. (2009). Teacher burnout and teacher resilience: Assessing the impacts of the school accountability movement. In L. J. Saha & A. G. Dworkin (Eds.), *New international handbook of teachers and teaching* (pp. 491–509). New York: Springer.

Dworkin, A. G., Haney, A., Dworkin, R. J., & Telschow, R. L. (1990). Stress and illness behavior among urban public school teachers. *Education Administration Quarterly, 9,* 159–171.

Dworkin, A. G., Saha, L. J., & Hill, A. N. (2003). Teacher burnout and perceptions of a democratic school environment. *International Education Journal, 4*(2), 108–120.

Dworkin, G., & Tobe, P. (2012a). The expanded federal role in US public schools: The structural forces of globalization, immigration and demographic change. In C. Kassimeris & M. Vryonides (Eds.), *The politics of education.* New York: Routledge.

Dworkin, G., & Tobe, P. (2012b). Teacher burnout in an era of school accountability and student misbehavior. In J. H. Ballantine & J. Z. Spade (Eds.), *Schools and society* (3rd ed.). Belmont, CA: Wadsworth Thompson Learning.

Forsyth, P. B., Barnes, L. L. B., & Adams, C. M. (2006). Trust effectiveness patterns in schools. *Journal of Educational Administration, 44*(2), 122–141.

Homans, G. C. (1961). *Social behavior: Its elementary forms.* New York: Harcourt, Brace and World.

Hoy, W. K., & Tarter, C. J. (2004). Organizational justice in schools: No justice without trust. *International Journal of Educational Management, 18*(4), 250–259.

Lee, V. E., Dietrich, R. F., & Smith, J. B. (1991). The effect of the social organization of school on teacher efficacy and satisfaction. *Sociology of Education, 64*(3), 190–208.

National Commission on Excellence in Education. (1983). *A nation at risk: The imperative for educational reform.* Washington, DC: U.S. Department of Education.

Saros, J. C., & Saros, A. M. (1992). Social support in teacher burnout. *Journal of Educational Administration, 30*(1), 55–69.

Tschannen-Moran, M., & Hoy, W. K. (2000). A multidisciplinary analysis of the nature: Meaning, and measurement of trust. *Review of Educational Research, 70*(4), 547–593.

Vettenburg, N. (2002) Unsafe feelings among teachers. *Journal of School Violence, 1*(4), 33–49.

Weick, K. E. (1976). Education systems as loosely coupled systems. *Administrative Science Quarterly, 21,* 1–19.

School Belonging and School Misconduct

The Differing Role of Teacher and Peer Attachment

Jannick Demanet and Mieke Van Houtte

Students' success in school depends on more than their intellectual ability. To cooperate with the goals of school and achieve to their maximum capacity, students need to feel a part of the learning process, comply with the school rules, and not drop out. Jannick Demanet and Mieke Van Houtte discuss factors that result in student success and cooperation versus misconduct (minor forms of deviance such as rule-breaking, cheating on tests, skipping school, and arriving late for school). One theory of student success is that the *school-as-community*, or school cohesion, results in students having a sense of belonging to the school community; this belonging results in their integration into the school and improved chances for success. Another theory is that a student's *individual bonding* with caring teachers and peers has a greater effect on deviance than school cohesion. The more students perceive that teachers are supportive and that they belong to a peer group, the less likely they are to engage in misconduct. Both explanations help us understand why some students misbehave, though this study found more support for the theory that individual bonding with teachers and peers results in more success and less misconduct. The importance is to understand what factors lead to lack of involvement in school and potential for misconduct and dropping out.

Questions to consider for this reading:

1. What is meant by student misconduct, and how might it affect student and school success?

2. What factors enter into student learning in addition to ability?

3. What might school planners learn from this article in order to reduce misconduct and increase chances for students to stay in school and succeed?

Introduction

A recurrent theme within educational and adolescent research is the explanation of school misbehavior (e.g. Freidenfelt Liljeberg et al. 2011). A popular explanation revolves around the schools-as-communities perspective (Battistich et al. 1995), a broad line of inquiry advocating that schools should be organized as caring school communities. In such caring

From "School Belonging and School Misconduct: The Differing Role of Teacher and Peer Attachment," by Jannick Demanet and Mieke Van Houtte, 2012, *Journal of Youth and Adolescence, 41*(4), pp. 499–514. Copyright © Springer/CCC.

communities, students feel emotionally connected to their peers, teachers, and school, which, among other beneficial outcomes, fosters less school misconduct in students (Battistich and Hom 1997). However, researchers are still unsure whether the preventive effects of belonging act at the individual or the school level. While some scholars state that the beneficial effects of school belonging result from students' personal feelings (Wehlage et al. 1990; Goodenow 1993), others hold that, in order to combat school deviancy, efforts should be made to establish cohesion between actors at the school level (Bryk and Driscoll 1988; Battistich et al. 1995). However, few studies have tested specifically whether the effects of school belonging act at the individual or the school level. Therefore, the first aim of this study is to assess the relative contribution of feelings of belonging at the school level—that is school cohesion—and at the individual level in preventing school misconduct.

Researchers from the schools-as-communities perspective also state that attachment to different actors at school and the school itself impedes school deviancy. However, while studies have established that feelings of school belonging (Dornbusch et al. 2001) and teacher attachment (Freidenfelt Liljeberg et al. 2011) are associated with lower rates of deviant behavior, research in this tradition has yet to investigate whether attachment to peers is related in the same way to school misconduct. The schools-as-communities perspective currently draws, in regard to its expectations concerning deviancy, on insights from early social control theory (Hirschi 1969), a theoretical approach that expects all strong social bonds to prevent delinquency. However, this theoretical approach failed to address the role of deviant peer influences (Erickson et al. 2000). In fact, research shows that peers can cause each other to break school rules, especially in the case of cohesive friendship bonds between deviant peers (Kandel 1978; Wellman and Frank 2001; Espelage et al. 2003). It is important to consider these different sources of attachment—school, teachers, and peers—together, to gain insight in

the unique role played by each in preventing or promoting school misconduct. The few studies that have incorporated both teachers and peers as sources of support relate this to achievement (Klem and Connell 2004), smoking (Karcher and Finn 2005), and other health-risk behaviors (McNeely and Falci 2004). These find higher teacher support to advance achievement and impede health-risk behaviors, and higher peer support to yield a higher likelihood of smoking and engaging in other health-risk behavior. In our study, a specific aim is to incorporate peer attachment, teacher support and general school belonging and test their relative contribution to school deviancy. Contrary to earlier studies on school deviancy, which deal with student delinquency (e.g. Crosnoe 2002), we focus on school misconduct, a minor form of deviancy, consisting of rule-breaking behavior such as cheating on tests, skipping lessons, and arriving late at school (e.g., Stewart 2003; Demanet and Van Houtte 2011), as we can imagine that peer and teacher attachment is more likely to influence minor forms of rule-breaking behavior than delinquency at school. Hence, we operationalize feelings of school belonging multi-dimensionally, discerning three aspects—general school belonging, peer attachment and perceived teacher support—to test whether these three dimensions relate differently to school misconduct.

In a third contribution to the schools-as-communities perspective, we embed all this within the social context of schools. Researchers state that receiving support prevents school deviancy even more effectively in disadvantaged schools (Battistich et al. 1995), but evidence concerning this is mixed. In the current study, we focus on two indicators of disadvantage in schools, namely the Socioeconomic Status (SES) composition and the ethnic composition (Demanet and Van Houtte 2011). Hence, our third research question is whether the relationships between general school belonging, peer attachment and perceived teacher support are stronger in schools with a lower SES composition, and schools where immigrants are overrepresented. As such, our study tries to find evidence for a long-held claim that supporting students in disadvantaged schools has even more beneficial effects, because these students often lack such sources of support outside the school context.

The Schools-As-Communities Perspective

The schools-as-communities perspective is a popular viewpoint in educational research. Barber and Olsen (1997) emphasized three aspects of adolescent socialization: connection to significant others, regulation of behavior, and psychological autonomy. The schools-as-communities perspective focuses on the first, stating that schools fulfill their socialization function best when organized as caring communities (Battistich et al. 1995). Such school communities are defined in diverging ways, but scholars put forward common elements (see Battistich et al. 1997, p. 137). Broadly stated, communal schools make students feel emotionally connected to one another—i.e., they feel attached (see Libbey 2004, p. 274)—and feel respected and helped by their peers and teachers—in other words, they perceive themselves as supported (see Libbey 2004, p. 281). In communal schools, students are made to feel at home at school. Furthermore, students in caring school communities feel that they make important contributions: hence, they are given a certain amount of influence in the school's activities and decision-making process. Lastly, in such schools, there is some sort of common value system (Battistich et al. 1997). Communal schools yield a wide array of positive effects in their students, including higher school enjoyment, academic achievement, and less school disruption (Battistich et al. 1995; Battistich and Hom 1997).

The preventive effect of school bonding on deviancy has been replicated in many studies. Dornbusch et al. (2001) showed in a longitudinal study that school attachment reduces the overall frequency, prevalence, and initiation of deviant involvement, and that this association held across males and females, different community contexts and regardless of ethnic groups.

Another longitudinal study distinguished between three forms of student engagement at school—emotional, behavioral, and cognitive engagement—confirming that emotional engagement had strong preventive effects on the occurrence of delinquency (Hirschfield and Gasper 2011). In an influential study, Finn (1989) proposed the participation-identification model, which highlights the role of identification with and participation in school in preventing school dropout, and, as dropout is linked to other problem behavior (see Finn 1989, p. 118), also school misconduct. The preventive effect of establishing strong social and emotional connections at school on student deviancy is thus well-established in research. . . .

The Role of Peer Attachment in Adolescence

Although the schools-as-communities perspective holds that all strong social bonds prevent school misconduct, there are reasons to think that peer bonds in adolescence are unlikely to have the same effect. In stating that bonding prevents disruptive behavior, the schools-as-communities perspective echoes the premises of the earliest version of control theory (Hirschi 1969). This theory holds that all individuals are inclined to deviancy, but having strong social bonds to others prevents its manifestation. Hirschi (1969) applied his view to adolescents, asserting that they must have strong bonds with school, parents and peers in order to behave properly. . . .

Deviant students tend to choose each other as friends, but they also influence each other to commit deviant acts (Bendixen et al. 2006). It is noteworthy that influence occurs especially when friendship bonds with deviant peers are quite cohesive. Deviant peer influence has been explained by differential association theory (Sutherland and Cressey 1978), which states that deviancy is learned from others who support deviancy as justifiable behavior. Therefore, having close bonds with others will increase the chances of being deviant, that is, when these others endorse deviancy.

It is likely that antisocial values will prevail in adolescent peer groups. Research indeed shows that peer norms in adolescence tend to favor minor forms of deviancy (Moffitt 1993; Agnew 2003; Allen et al. 2005). Authors argue that while youngsters are biologically mature, they are not allowed to fulfill social roles with complete adult privileges and responsibilities, creating a maturity gap. Adolescents thus have been viewed as endorsing deviancy as a way to show autonomy. As students are socialized into the norms held by the majority of their peers (Allen et al. 2005), and socialization especially occurs in cohesive friendship relationships (Sutherland and Cressey 1978), higher peer attachment in adolescence can be conducive to school misconduct. In the schools-as-communities perspective, then, it may be essential to consider the possible deviance-yielding effect of cohesive bonds between youngsters.

The Context of Communal Effects

Researchers suggest that bonding impedes school misconduct most in disadvantaged schools (Battistich et al. 1995; Battistich and Hom 1997). This is not to say that school misconduct is more prevalent there, only that supporting students in such schools makes a larger difference. This occurs because advantaged students are likely to have sources of support outside of school (Battistich et al. 1995). For disadvantaged students, external sources of support are less prevalent (Stanton-Salazar and Dornbush 1995). Therefore, for them, receiving support at school has a major impact. Testing this, Battistich et al. (1995) confirmed that belonging had more positive effects on school and class enjoyment in poorer schools. Battistich and Hom (1997), however, showed that this does not apply to school delinquency, as feelings of communality were more preventive in low and moderate poverty schools than in high poverty ones. At the neighborhood level, scholars have found no evidence for this assertion

(Dornbusch et al. 2001). Hence, scholars have provided mixed evidence to the claim that enhancing school belonging should be even more beneficial in poorer schools.

Next to poverty, a school's concentration of different ethnic groups also can create a disadvantaged situation in that school. It has been shown that students achieve less in schools with a high concentration of migrant or ethnic minority students (Felouzis 2003; Rumberger and Palardy 2005). Moreover, teachers in those schools report job dissatisfaction, lower academic expectations, and more difficulty establishing relationships with students (Freeman et al. 1999). Importantly, some research has demonstrated that these disadvantages are entirely due to the poor socioeconomic context of these schools (e.g. Rumberger and Palardy 2005). Ultimately, students in such schools *perceive* the school as more disadvantaged, and expect less from their academic career (Bankston and Caldas 1996).

* * *

Discussion

School deviance is a widely studied topic in adolescent research. One of the most influential explanations for the occurrence of school misbehavior is offered by the schools-as-communities perspective (Battistich et al. 1995), which states that preventing school deviancy requires that students feel part of a caring school community and have meaningful and supportive relationships to actors at school (Battistich and Hom 1997). In the present study, we built on this perspective in three ways. While most researchers contend that feelings of belonging have important preventive effects on school misbehavior (e.g. Dornbusch et al. 2001), opinions are divided whether efforts should be directed at transforming the school into a community by building cohesion between actors at the school level (Battistich et al. 1995), or whether it is more efficient to impact students' personal feelings of belonging

(Goodenow 1993) in order to prevent school misconduct. While some studies in the past have indeed pointed to the multilevel nature of the sense of belonging to school, no study has yet investigated the relative importance of school-level cohesion versus individual feelings of peer, teacher, and school attachment in relation to school misconduct. Moreover, in this article, we investigated whether the schools-as-communities perspective should distinguish between the different actors bonded with at school. Regarding school deviancy, the perspective currently is based largely on early control theory (Hirschi 1969), a theoretical approach that has neglected the characteristics of the actor involved in the bonding. Differential association theory (Sutherland and Cressey 1978), on the contrary, states that closer peer relationships might generate more deviancy if antisocial socialization occurs in the friendship group. This is likely in adolescence, as deviancy is accepted by a certain number of adolescents as a valid form of behavior (Allen et al. 2005). Led by this theoretical exploration, we expected peer attachment to relate differently to school misconduct than general school belonging and perceived teacher support. In a third contribution to the schools-as-communities perspective, we investigated a long-held claim by researchers that providing students with supportive relationships should impact those students even more in disadvantaged school contexts (Battistich et al. 1995). However, especially in the case of deviancy, this claim has received mixed empirical support. In the current study, we considered the SES composition and the ethnic composition of schools as indicators of school disadvantage (Demanet and Van Houtte 2011), to investigate whether feelings of support were indeed more strongly related to less school misconduct in schools with a lower mean SES and a higher proportion of minority students.

To assess the first research question, namely what the relative importance is of school-level cohesion versus individual feelings of belonging, we tested whether the association of school cohesion is maintained when controlling for three aspects of students' sense of belonging—peer attachment, perceived teacher support, and general school belonging. We found that, in association to school misconduct, individual bonding seems more important than overall school cohesion, as no relation of school cohesion is seen once the three aspects of individual belonging are taken into account. . . .

Regarding the second research question, our results show that, while higher school belonging and perceived teacher support are related to less school misconduct, greater peer attachment was associated to more school misconduct. It is noteworthy that the association between peer attachment and school misconduct only showed up when we controlled for general school belonging and perceived teacher support, meaning that both characteristics buffer the relation of peer attachment with school misconduct. This occurs because students who feel bonded to their school and teachers generally perceive a high degree of peer attachment as well. Students who are bonded to all three sources are less deviant than others, because the preventive effect of teacher support and school belonging overshadows the deviance-generating effect of their high peer attachment. However, students lacking teacher support and school belonging miss this suppression effect, so that the deviance-yielding effect of peer attachment is free to occur. Hence, for students feeling attached to their peers, yet lacking teacher and school bonding, more misconduct can be expected. . . .

In response to the third research question, we found no evidence for the claim that supportive relationships should be related even more strongly to school misconduct in disadvantaged schools: none of the cross-level interaction effects were significant. This concurs with research relating this to neighborhood disadvantage (Dornbusch et al. 2001). A possible explanation for the lack of support found for this claim is that having supportive relationships is not more beneficial for all students in disadvantaged schools. As described above, the rationale for interaction effects is that disadvantaged students will benefit disproportionally from school communality because they have less social capital outside of school. Hence, this does not apply to advantaged students in disadvantaged schools. It is possible, then, that supportive relationships are more beneficial for disadvantaged students, whatever the school context they enroll in, than for advantaged students. . . .

In summary, our study's main finding is that, although associations appear to be small, bonding with different actors at school can have mixed connections to deviant behavior. This contradicts early control theory, on which the schools-as-communities perspective, with reference to school deviancy, is now largely based. Following the addition of differential association theory to the early version of control theory, we argue that it is vital to account for the characteristics of the actors with whom the student bonds, and especially whether they endorse deviancy or not. It seems important to incorporate this in the schools-as-communities perspective. Furthermore, our results support earlier findings that receiving teacher support yields multiple positive outcomes for students, including less involvement in health-risk behavior (West et al. 2004), and higher engagement and achievement (Klem and Connell 2004). Hence, we contribute to the evidence base showing that schools should be organized as caring communities. Adults at school play a large role in this, as they are responsible for making all students, even the disruptive and poor achieving ones, feel at home at school.

REFERENCES

Agnew, R. (2003). An integrated theory of the adolescent peak in offending. *Youth and Society, 34,* 263–299.

Allen, J. P., Porter, M. R., McFarland, F. C., Marsh, P., & McElhaney, K. B. (2005). The two faces of adolescents' success with peers: Adolescent popularity, social adaptation, and deviant behavior. *Child Development, 76,* 747–760.

Barber, B. K., & Olsen, J. A. (1997). Socialization in context: Connection, regulation, and autonomy in the family, school, and neighborhood, and with peers. *Journal of Adolescent Research, 12,* 287–315.

Barber, B. K., & Schluterman, J. M. (2008). Connectedness in the lives of children and adolescents: A call for greater conceptual clarity. *Journal of Adolescent Health, 43,* 209–216.

Battistich, V., & Hom, A. (1997). The relationship between students' sense of their school as a community and their involvement in problem behaviors. *American Journal of Public Health, 87,* 1997–2001.

Battistich, V., Solomon, D., Kim, D. I., Watson, M., & Schaps. E. (1995). Schools as communities, poverty levels of student populations, and students attitudes, motives, and performance: A multilevel analysis. *American Educational Research Journal, 32,* 627–658.

Battistich, V., Solomon, D., Watson, M., & Schaps, E. (1997). Caring school communities. *Educational Psychologist, 32,* 137–151.

Bendixen, M., Endersen, I. M., & Olweus, D. (2006). Joining and leaving gangs: Selection and facilitation effects on self-reported antisocial behaviour in early adolescence. *European Journal of Criminology, 3,* 85–114.

Bryk, R., & Driscoll, D. (1988). *The high school as community: Contextual influences and consequences for students and teachers.* Madison: Center for Educational Research Wisconsin.

Crosnoe, R. (2002). High school curriculum track, and adolescent association with delinquent friends. *Journal of Adolescent Research, 17,* 143–167.

Demanet, J., & Van Houtte, M. (2011). Social-ethnic school compositions and school misconduct: Does sense of facility clarify the picture? *Sociological Spectrum, 31,* 224–256.

Dornbusch, S. M., Erickson, K. G., Laird, J., & Wong, C. A. (2001). The relation of family and school attachment to adolescent deviance in diverse groups and communities. *Journal of Adolescent Research, 16,* 396–322.

Erickson, K G., Crosnoe, R., & Dornbusch, S. M (2000). A social process in model of adolescent deviance: Combining social control and differential association perspectives. *Journal of Youth and Adolescence, 29,* 395–425.

Espelage, D. L., Holt, M. K., & Henkel, R. R. (2003). Examination of peer-group contextual effects on aggression during early adolescence. *Child Development, 74,* 205–220.

Felouzis, G. (2003). La ségrégation ethnique au collége et ses conséquences [Ethnic segregation at secondary school and its consequences]. *Revue Française de Sociologie, 44,* 413–447.

Finn, J. D. (1989). Withdrawing from school. *Review of Educational Research, 59,* 117–142.

Freeman, D. J., Brookhart, S. M., & Loadman, W. E. (1999). Realities of teaching in racially/ethnically diverse schools: Feedback from entry-level teachers. *Urban Education, 34,* 89–114.

Freidenfelt Liljeberg, J., Eklund, J. M., Väfors Fritz, M., & af Klinteberg, B. (2011). Poor school bonding and delinquency over time: Bidirectional effects and sex differences. *Journal of Adolescence, 34,* 1–9.

Goodenow, C. (1993). The psychological sense of school membership among adolescents: Scale development and educational correlates. *Psychology in the Schools, 30,* 79–90.

Hirschfield, P. J., & Gasper, J. (2011). The relationship between school engagement and delinquency in late childhood and early adolescence. *Journal of Youth and Adolescence, 40,* 3–22.

Hirschi, T. (1969). *Causes of delinquency.* Berkeley: University of California Press.

Kandel, D. B. (1978). Homophily, selection, and socialization in adolescent friendships. *American Journal of Sociology, 84,* 427–456.

Klem, A. M., & Connell, J. P. (2004). Relationships matter: Linking teacher support to student engagement and achievement. *Journal of School Health, 74,* 262–273.

Libbey, H. P. (2004). Measuring student relationships to school: Attachment, bonding, connectedness, and engagement. *Journal of School Health, 74,* 274–283.

McNeely, C., & Falci, C. (2004). School connectedness and the transition into and out of health-risk behaviour among adolescents: A comparison of social belonging and teacher support. *Journal of School Health, 74,* 284–292.

Moffitt, T. E. (1993). Adolescence-limited and life-course-persistent antisocial-behavior: A developmental taxonomy. *Psychological Review, 100,* 674–701.

Rumberger, R. W., & Palardy, G. J. (2005). Does segregation still matter? The impact of student composition on academic achievement in high school. *Teachers College Record, 107,* 1999–2045.

Stanton-Salazar, R. D., & Dornbush, S. M. (1995). Social capital and the reproduction of inequality: Information networks among Mexican-origin high school students. *Sociology of Education, 68,* 116–135.

Stewart, E. A. (2003). School social bonds, school climate, and school misbehavior: A multilevel analysis. *Justice Quarterly, 20,* 575–604.

Sutherland, E., & Cressey, D. (1978). *Criminology.* Philadelphia: Lippincot.

Wehlage, G., Rutter, R., Smith, G., Lesko, N., & Fernandez, R. (1990). *Reducing the risk: Schools as communities of support.* Philadelphia: Falmer.

Wellman, B., & Frank, K. (2001). Network capital in a multilevel world: Getting support from personal communities. In N. Lin, K. Cook, & R. S. Burt (Eds.), *Social capital: Theory and research* (pp. 233–274). New York: Walter de Gruyter, Inc.

West, P., Sweeting, H., & Leyland, A. (2004). School effects on pupils' health behaviours: Evidence in support of the health promoting school. *Research Papers in Education, 19,* 261–291.

READING 23

Low-Level Violence

A Neglected Aspect of School Culture

David R. Dupper and Nancy Meyer-Adams

Recent stories of students committing suicide because they have been bullied and harassed in school have brought increased attention to low-level violence in schools. However, bullying does not make the headlines like school shootings and other violent crimes in schools. In reality, schools are among the safest places for young people to gather (Addington, Ruddy, Miller, DeVoe, & Chandler, 2002). What doesn't make the headlines are the millions of "little" acts of harassment and violence that leave some children afraid to go to school, tormented by peers and teachers, and lacking in self-esteem. These informal aspects of the school system affect students' ability to concentrate and achieve, and can result in anger, alienation, and hostile school environments. David R. Dupper and Nancy Meyer-Adams address several common forms of low-level violence. In this early article on school violence, the authors suggest ways to create more positive school culture and climate.

Questions to consider for this reading:

1. Why is low-level violence often neglected by news media and the public?

2. How can the low-level violence discussed by the authors affect student performance in school?

3. What can be done to change the culture of schools, particularly as new technologies change the form and anonymity of harassment?

April, Age 13

Her mother said her daughter was being bullied and the ringleader was a popular girl who had targeted her for some unknown reason. Some kids called her fat, while others threw things at her and pushed her around, [and] they even ridiculed her with rumors that she stuffed tissue in her bra. April took it all to heart. Faced with the prospect of juvenile detention as a truant or returning to a school to face taunting classmates, April decided against both. On Valentine's Day, she went into her bedroom, shut the door and hanged herself with a belt ("Faced With 'Go to Jail' or 'Go to School,'" 2000).

School shootings over the past several years, especially the carnage at Columbine High School in Littleton, Colorado, have propelled the issues of school violence prevention and school safety to the forefront in communities across the United States. Although high-level school violence (e.g., murder, rape, possession of weapons) is a serious problem that grabs the headlines and the public's attention, it is relatively rare (Astor, Vargas, Pitner, & Meyer, 1999; Centers for Disease Control and Prevention, 1998; Hyman & Snook, 1999; Kachur et al., 1996). In fact "there was a 40% decline in school-associated violent deaths between school years 1997–98 and 1998–99" (Brooks, Schiraldi, & Ziedenberg, 2000, p. 3). Unfortunately, relatively little attention has been paid to low-level or underlying forms of violence that occur in most secondary schools every day. The heartbreaking story of April illustrates the need to focus much more attention on low-level school violence such as bullying, peer sexual harassment, victimization based on known or presumed gay or lesbian sexual orientation, and the psychological maltreatment of students by teachers. Research over the past decade has shown that these forms of school violence, although not as overtly serious as weapons offenses, occur with greater frequency than most believe and have a profound impact on students' mental health and school performance (Elliott, Hamburg, & Williams, 1998).

BULLYING

Bullying refers to unprovoked physical or psychological abuse of an individual by one or a group of students over time to create an ongoing pattern of harassment and abuse (Batsche & Knoff, 1994; Hoover, Oliver, & Thomson, 1993; Olweus, 1991). It comprises direct behaviors (e.g., teasing, taunting, threatening, hitting, and stealing) and indirect behaviors (e.g., causing a student to be socially isolated by spreading rumors) (Smith & Sharp, 1994). Bullying victimization is estimated to affect 15% to 20% of the U.S. student population, with verbal teasing and intimidation being its most common form and boys reported to be victims at a higher

rate than girls (Furlong, Chung, Bates, & Morrison, 1995). A study found that 88% of secondary school students reported having observed bullying and 76.8% stated that they had been a victim of bullying at school (Hoover, Oliver, & Hazler, 1992). Bullying appears to peak in the middle school and junior high years (Batsche & Knoff, 1994). Students are bullied at school for a variety of reasons. These include girls being viewed by their peers as physically unattractive or not dressing stylishly, girls being physically well developed or not "fitting in" in some other way, boys not fitting a stereotypic macho male image, students having a different religion, students wearing unique or unusual clothes, [and] students having physical weaknesses and/or being different in appearance (Furlong et al., 1995; Shakeshift et al., 1995).

The act of bullying has long-term implications for both victims and perpetrators. Negative impacts of chronic victimization include increased rates of truancy and dropping out as well as difficult psychosocial and psychosexual relationships (Hazler, Hoover, & Oliver, 1991). Hazler (1994) found that the impact of bullying on its victims includes a loss of self-esteem and feelings of isolation which, according to new research, can last into adulthood. He stated that

> their grades may suffer because their attention is being drawn away from learning. Being repeatedly victimized may push even "good kids" to extremes, such as starting fights or bringing weapons to school to exact vengeance on their tormentors, [and] even students and adults who are witnesses are affected [in that] they must deal with the lowered self-esteem and loss of control that accompanies feeling unsafe and unable to take action. The result is children and adults who do all they can to avoid recognizing when someone else is being hurt. (p. 39)

It is harmful to those who witness peer harassment if this harassment is tacitly approved of and not acted upon by school personnel. For example, youth who are not direct victims of violence at school "may be victimized by the chronic presence of violence" (American Psychological Association, 1993, p. 42). "Students who must think about avoiding harm at school are diverting energy that should be expended on learning" (Chandler, Nolin, & Davies, 1995, p. 5). Bullies whose behavior is allowed to continue are 5 times more likely than their classmates to wind up in juvenile court, to be convicted of crimes, and, when they become adults, to have children with aggression problems (Hazler, 1994). A recent report that examined the profiles of school shooters concluded that in 66% of the cases, "the attackers felt persecuted, bullied, threatened, attacked or injured by others prior to the incident" and that a number of attackers had experienced longstanding and severe bullying and that "the experience of bullying appeared to play a major role in motivating the attack at school" (Vossekuil, Reddy, Fein, Borum, & Modzeleski, 2000, p. 7). Olweus (1993) found that 60% of students characterized as bullies in Grades 6 to 9 had at least one criminal conviction by age 24.

Peer Sexual Harassment

The problem of peer sexual harassment appears to be pervasive in U.S. schools. A survey of 1,600 White, African American, and Hispanic students in Grades 8 through 11 sponsored by the American Association of University Women (AAUW) (1993) found that 85% of girls and 76% of boys reported experiencing some form of sexual harassment in school. Of that total, 25% reported being targeted "often." The types of peer sexual harassment in the AAUW study ranged from nonphysical forms (e.g., making sexual comments, spreading sexual rumors, flashing) to physical forms (e.g., touching, grabbing, pinching). The most common form of harassment, reported by 65% of girls and 42% of boys, was being the target of sexual comments, jokes, gestures, or looks. The second most common form of harassment was being touched, grabbed, or pinched in a sexual way. The AAUW study found that a child's first experience of sexual harassment is most likely to occur in middle or junior high school and that girls suffer more negative effects as a result of peer sexual

harassment than boys. For example, girls reported "not wanting to go to school" (33%), "not wanting to talk as much in class" (32%), and "finding it hard to pay attention in school" (28%) as outcomes of being sexually harassed at school. Additionally, 64% of girls reported experiencing "embarrassment," 52% reported feeling "self-conscious," and 43% of girls reported feeling less sure or less confident of themselves as a result of sexual harassment. Perhaps the most disturbing finding in the AAUW study was the response of students who engaged in sexually harassing behaviors at school. The majority of these perpetrators responded, "It's just part of school life," "A lot of people do it," "It's no big deal" (AAUW, 1993). Moreover, this indifference appears to extend to school personnel, because teachers and other school staff rarely, if ever, intervene to stop peer sexual harassment in schools (Batsche & Knoff, 1994; Hoover et al., 1992; Shakeshift et al., 1995; Stein, 1995). For example, in a study conducted by Shakeshift et al. (1995), a female respondent stated, "In science class, the boys snap our bras. The [male] teacher doesn't really care. He doesn't say anything [and] the boys just laugh" (p. 42).

Victimization Based on Known or Presumed Gay or Lesbian Sexual Orientation

Victimization based on known or presumed gay or lesbian sexual orientation is the most common form of bias-related violence in the United States (Pilkington & D'Augelli, 1995). Being called gay or lesbian was the most disturbing form of unwanted behavior for boys (86%), and "being called gay would be more upsetting to boys than actual physical abuse" (AAUW, 1993, p. 23). In 1999, the Gay, Lesbian and Straight Education Network (GLSEN) conducted a survey of 496 lesbian, gay, bisexual, and transgender (LGBT) youth from 32 states. The authors of this survey found that over 91.4% of LGBT youth reported that they sometimes or frequently hear homophobic remarks (e.g., "faggot," "dyke," "queer") in their school. Homophobic remarks seem to be pervasive in schools. For example, the Massachusetts Governor's Commission on Gay and Lesbian Youth (1993) found that 97% of students in public high schools reported hearing homophobic remarks from their peers on a regular basis. This harassment often extends beyond verbal abuse. Pilkington and D'Augelli (1995) found that 22% of the males and 29% of the females reported having been physically hurt by another student because of their sexual orientation.

As is the case in peer sexual harassment, school personnel rarely intervene when students are victimized based on known or presumed gay or lesbian sexual orientation. For example, almost half the youth in the GLSEN (1999) study reported that someone intervened only some of the time, and one third reported that no one ever intervened in these circumstances. Compounding this problem is a finding by Sears (1992) that two thirds of guidance counselors harbored negative feelings toward gay and lesbian persons, less than 20% have received any training on serving gay and lesbian students, and only 25% consider themselves "highly competent" in serving gay and lesbian youth. Beyond their indifference and lack of training is the fact that school personnel are often perpetrators themselves. For example, almost 37% of respondents in the GLSEN (1999) study and over 53% of students in the Massachusetts Governor's Commission on Gay and Lesbian Youth study (1993) reported that they hear homophobic remarks from faculty or school staff. Given these findings, it is not surprising that gay and lesbian students keep their sexual orientation hidden from teachers and school counselors.

Victimization based on known or presumed gay or lesbian sexual orientation has a detrimental impact on the mental health and school performance of victims. Nearly half of the youth in the GLSEN (1999) study reported that they did not feel safe in their school because they are gay, lesbian, bisexual, or transgender. Furthermore, Krivascka, Savin-Williams, and Slater (as cited in Elia, 1993) reported that 80% of gays and lesbians had declining school performance,

almost 40% had problems with truancy, and 30% had dropped out of school. Gays and lesbians also attempt suicide 2 to 7 times more frequently than heterosexual comparison groups (Saunders & Valente, 1987). In their survey of 194 lesbian, gay, and bisexual youth between the ages of 15 and 21, Pilkington and D'Augelli (1995) found that "approximately one-third of the males (30%) and females (35%) reported that being harassed or verbally abused in school currently limits their openness about their sexual orientation" (p. 44).

PSYCHOLOGICAL MALTREATMENT OF STUDENTS BY TEACHERS

Although emotional maltreatment of students by teachers "receives little pedagogical, psychological, or legal attention, data based on case studies, anecdotal reports, and some beginning research suggest that [the] psychological maltreatment [of students by teachers] may occur in schools more often than many think" (Hyman & Perone, 1998, p. 21). Psychological maltreatment of students by teachers and other adults in authority consists of discipline and control techniques that are based on fear and intimidation (Brassard, Hart, & Germaine, 1987). Too many teachers use screaming, sarcasm, threats, and ridicule to control students in their classroom (Hyman, 1997). Sakowski (1993) found that students who are psychologically maltreated exhibited behavior problems and poor interpersonal competencies. According to Hyman (1997), "Although psychological maltreatment is believed to occur more often than other forms of abuse [in schools], it is difficult to determine rate of occurrence in specific regions or schools, because schools are not anxious to investigate their own malfeasance" (p. 331).

BUILDING A MORE POSITIVE SCHOOL CULTURE AND CLIMATE

According to Davila and Willower (1996), in each individual school there is a culture that is owned by that school that embodies its values, norms, and beliefs. Additionally, each school has distinct yet overlapping climates that exist for the students, the faculty, and the staff. These climates play a critical role in the everyday performance and attitudes of these individuals and how these individuals can work together as a team to build a strong, positive culture in their school's environment. A school's culture and climate are important because we know that they significantly affect and influence students' behavior and learning (Wang, Haertel, & Walberg, 1997). Hamilton and Richardson (1995) defined a school's culture as "the beliefs and expectations apparent in a school's daily routine, including how colleagues interact with each other . . . culture is the socially shared and transmitted knowledge of what is and what ought to be symbolized in act and artifact" (p. 369). Freiberg and Stein (1999) stated that

> school climate is the heart and soul of a school. It is about that essence of a school that leads a child, a teacher, an administrator, [or] a staff member to love the school and to look forward to being there each school day. The climate of a school can foster resilience or become a risk factor in the lives of people who work and learn in a place called school. (p. 11)

Culture affects students through the norms that drive behavior in a school environment, and climate reflects the perceptions that students have of the impact of that environment on their own well-being (Brown & Leigh, 1996; Glisson, 2000).

Stolp (1995) contends that

> students work harder, attend school more often, and have stronger academic skills in schools with strong communities and student violence decreases in communal organizations . . . teachers work harder and enjoy their work more in an environment that puts social bonds above individual success . . . school community positively affects school culture. (p. 14)

Not only does a culture of low-level violence place students at risk, but it also deprives them of the opportunity to benefit from the educational opportunities a school provides.

PROGRAMS DESIGNED TO CHANGE THE CULTURE AND CLIMATE OF SCHOOLS

Based on our review, it is evident that bullying, peer sexual harassment, victimization based on known or presumed gay or lesbian sexual orientation, and the psychological maltreatment of students by teachers are problems that must be addressed in any comprehensive school violence prevention program. One way of reducing low-level, underlying violence in schools is to build a more positive school culture and climate. Interventions must be designed to change or modify the culture and climate of a school so that schools become safe havens and sanctuaries for all children and youth; places where teachers, students, administrators, parents, support staff, [and] all feel invited to participate and welcome and share a psychological sense of community. The culture of a school must reflect a place where children and youth want to be, places they will respect. A recent publication by the National Association of Attorneys General (1999) concludes that research indicates that a supportive school climate is the most important step in ensuring that schools provide a safe and welcome environment for all students. Hansen and Childs (1998) stated that working toward a positive school climate involves "dedicated individuals [who] are making conscious efforts to enhance and enrich the culture and conditions in the school so that teachers can teach better and students can learn more" (p. 14).

Several programs have focused on building a more positive school culture and climate. These include the Bullying Prevention Program (Olweus, 1991, 1993), the School Development Program (Comer, 1988), and the Positive Action Through Holistic Education (PATHE) (Gottfredson, 1986). Of these, the Office of Juvenile Justice and Delinquency Prevention (OJJDP) has recognized the Bullying Prevention Program as one of its 10

Blueprint Programs that ha[ve] been shown to be effective in preventing violence. Based on a large-scale study conducted in Norway in the early 1980s, the Bullying Prevention Program was shown to result in a substantial reduction in boys' and girls' reports of bullying and victimization; a significant reduction in students' reports of general antisocial behavior such as vandalism, fighting, theft, and truancy; and significant improvements in the "social climate" of the class, as reflected in students' reports of improved order and discipline, more positive social relationships, and a more positive attitude toward schoolwork and school (Olweus & Limber, 1999). More information about the School Development Program and PATHE Program may be found in the OJJDP publication "School and Community Interventions to Prevent Serious and Violent Offending."

Recently, two schools in California have been highlighted as a result of their efforts to reduce school violence by changing the culture and climate of the school. Epstein (1998) described Oakland's Emiliano Zapata Street Academy as "a public high school where there are no fights, no security guards, no metal detectors, no guns, and the police department visits to ticket meter violations rather than arrest students. It is like a 'private academy for poor kids'" (p. 1). Epstein goes on to describe four core components of this school: (a) This is a school of "tight relationships," where every staff member is a "consulting teacher" for 15 to 20 students. The teacher meets with his or her students twice a day to check on academic performance and behavior and responds immediately to problems by calling a parent or conferring with another student if there are conflicts—problems are not allowed to fester and grow! Even verbal altercations are taken seriously, and students are not sent back to class until they have worked out a solution. (b) This is a school that espouses multiculturalism—the staff's ethnic composition mirrors that of students and many staff live in the community. Racism is explicitly discussed and there is a stern response to cross-racial disrespect among students. (c) This is a small school with a closed campus. It treats its students as whole human beings; students tell teachers what is actually happening in their lives. (d) This is a school that is self-renewing, creating teachers who get better every year instead of burning out. According to Epstein, "teachers have enormous latitude in creating new teaching methods and procedures, but the school's leader is demanding of everyone, including herself, when it comes to meeting student needs" (p. 1).

Ruenzel (1997) described another school in California that is focusing on changing its culture and climate to reduce school violence. Ginger Hovenic, the principal of Clear View Elementary School, believes that a vital school culture is the "foundation for all learning that takes place in the classroom" (p. 1). In this school, 595 students speak 26 native languages, and 200 are from low-income families (Ruenzel, 1997). Hovenic and her teachers attempted to create a school environment where all children felt welcome and no child would fall between the cracks. In the end, she and her teachers came up with a variation of homerooms, something they call "families," and it has become the central feature of the school culture. According to Ruenzel, each family consists of two dozen students randomly drawn from every grade in her K–6 school. Students remain in the same family and with the same teacher until they go on to middle school. The families meet for an hour each week. They celebrate birthdays and holidays together, they go on outings, and keep hefty family scrapbooks. They take part in a number of social projects such as collecting food and clothing for families and helping out needier children in the school. The Peace Patrol involves student volunteers trained in the art of negotiation, wearing blue jackets and carrying clipboards, patrolling school grounds and mediating disputes before they spiral out of control. Part of the school culture is that kids get sent to the principal only for having done something positive. Parents are involved by attending a town meeting at the beginning of each year, where they are encouraged to pose questions and voice concerns; the principal also hosts regular coffees with parents throughout the school year to keep them up to date on the full range of school matters; routine parent conferences are not led by teachers but by students, who present their work to their parents. Teachers are encouraged to dream and scheme together about new things they can try—this type of collaboration takes time, so every Thursday afternoon, 2 hours are set aside for teachers to discuss everything from books they have read to workshops they are thinking of attending. They also discuss students who need academic help—with the aid of computer-generated spreadsheets that provide a statistical picture of each student's academic performance. Teacher evaluation is also a collaborative effort. Although neither of these programs has been formally evaluated, they each offer some promising ideas and directions for school personnel interested in reducing low-level violence in the schools they serve.

RECOMMENDATIONS

To prevent or reduce low-level, underlying violence in schools, we recommend that school personnel focus on changing a school's culture and climate by implementing interventions based on the following assumptions:

- Every individual should have the right to be spared oppression and repeated, intentional humiliation in school as well as in society at large. Schools must send a strong message to students and staff that all forms of low-level violence are inappropriate and that adults will actively intervene in all instances of low-level violence and that those who fail to recognize and stop low-level forms of violence as they occur actually promote violence.
- Because many school personnel do not acknowledge that low-level violence is a serious problem, it is essential that a needs assessment be conducted and all school personnel be informed about the extent of bullying, peer sexual harassment, victimization based on known or presumed gay or lesbian sexual orientation in their school, and the psychological maltreatment of students by teachers and other school staff. If ignored, low-level violence in

schools can jeopardize students' academic achievement, undermine their physical and emotional well-being, and may provoke retaliatory violence.
- The best way to reduce low-level forms of school violence is to create a school culture and climate characterized by warmth, tolerance, positive responses to diversity, sensitivity to others' views, cooperative interactions among students, teachers, and school staff, and an environment that expects and reinforces appropriate behavior. In cases of violations of limits and rules, nonhostile, nonphysical sanctions should be consistently applied.
- Homophobia makes schools unsafe for all students, not only for those who are gay and lesbian. Antigay prejudice and homophobia can make any student who defies the narrowly defined gender roles a target for violence and harassment. A concerted effort is required to address homophobic attitudes among school personnel.
- Rather than focusing on the perpetrators or victims alone, effective interventions must happen at multiple levels, concurrently. These multiple levels include school-level interventions (e.g., conflict resolution and diversity training workshops for teachers and school staff), classroom-level interventions (e.g., regularly scheduled classroom meetings during which students and teachers engage in discussion, role-playing, and creative activities related to preventing all forms of low-level violence), and individual-level interventions (e.g., formation of discussion groups for victims of low-level violence).

The middle and junior high grades (6 through 8) are a critical time for intervention and should receive highest priority.

CONCLUSIONS

The pervasiveness of low-level school violence in the forms of bullying, peer sexual harassment, victimization based on sexual orientation, and the psychological maltreatment of students by teachers must be acknowledged and addressed in a more preventive and proactive manner. School personnel must assume a leadership role in conceiving and implementing interventions designed to change the culture and climate of schools to reduce low-level violence.

References

Addington, L. A., Ruddy, S. A., Miller, A. K., DeVoe, J. F., & Chandler, K. A. (2002). *Are America's schools safe? Students speak out*. Washington, DC: National Center for Education Statistics, U.S. Department of Education.

American Association of University Women (AAUW). (1993). *Hostile hallways: The AAUW survey on sexual harassment in America's schools*. Washington, DC: Author.

American Psychological Association. (1993). Violence and youth: Psychology's response. Volume I. *Summary report of the American Psychological Association Commission on Violence and Youth*. Washington, DC: Author.

Astor, R. A., Vargas, L. A., Pitner, R., & Meyer, H. A. (1999). School violence: Research, theory, and practice. In J. M. Jenson & M. O. Howard (Eds.), *Youth violence: Current research and recent practice innovations* (pp. 139–171). Washington, DC: National Association of Social Workers Press.

Batsche, G. M., & Knoff, H. M. (1994). Bullies and their victims: Understanding a pervasive problem in the schools. *School Psychology Review, 23*(2), 165–174.

Brassard, M., Hart, S., & Germaine, B. (1987). *Psychological mistreatment of children and youth*. Elmsford, NY: Pergamon Press.

Brooks, K., Schiraldi, V., & Ziedenberg, J. (2000). *School house hype: Two years later.* Washington, DC: Justice Policy Institute and Children's Law Center.

Brown, S. P., & Leigh, T. W. (1996). A new look at psychological climate and its relationship to job involvement, effort, and performance. *Journal of Applied Psychology, 81*(4), 358–368.

Cantalano, R. F., Loeber, R., & McKinney, K. C. (1999). *School and community interventions to prevent serious violent offending* (Juvenile Justice Bulletin). Washington, DC: U.S. Department of Justice, Office of Juvenile Justice and Delinquency Prevention.

Centers for Disease Control and Prevention. (1998). *Youth risk behavior surveillance—United States,* *1997* (Morbidity and mortality weekly report, 47(SS-3), U.S. Department of Health and Human Services). Washington, DC: Author.

Chandler, K., Nolin, M. J., & Davies, E. (1995). *Student strategies to avoid harm at school* (National Center for Education Statistics 95–203). Rockville, MD: Westat.

Comer, J. P. (1988). Educating poor minority children. *Scientific American, 259*(5), 42–48.

Davila, A., & Willower, D. J. (1996). Organizational culture in a Mexican school: Lessons for reform. *International Journal of Educational Reform, 5*(4), 438–443.

Elia, J. P. (1993). Homophobia in the high school: A problem in need of a resolution. *The High School Journal, 77,* 177–185.

Elliott, D. S., Hamburg, B., & Williams, K. R. (1998). Violence in American schools: An overview. In D. S. Elliott, B. A. Hamburg, & K. R. Williams (Eds.), *Violence in American schools* (pp. 3–28). New York: Cambridge University Press.

Epstein, K. K. (1998, March 4). An urban high school with no violence. *Education Week on the Web.* Retrieved from http://www.edweek.org/ew/1998/25epstei.h17

Faced with "go to jail" or "go to school, get beat up," 13-year-old hangs herself. (2000, February 19). *Knoxville News-Sentinel,* p. A-6.

Freiberg, H. J., & Stein, T. A. (1999). Measuring, improving and sustaining healthy learning environments. In H. J. Freiberg (Ed.), *School climate: Measuring, improving and sustaining healthy learning environments* (pp. 11–29). London: Falmer Press.

Furlong, M. J., Chung, A., Bates, M., & Morrison, R. L. (1995). Who are the victims of school violence? A comparison of student non-victims and multi-victims. *Education and Treatment of Children, 18*(3), 282–298.

Gay, Lesbian and Straight Education Network (GLSEN). (1999). *GLESN's national school climate survey: Lesbian, gay, bisexual and transgender students and their experiences in school.* Retrieved from http://www.glsen.org/pages/sections/news/natlnews/1999/sep/survey

Glisson, C. (2000). Organizational climate and culture. In R. Patti (Ed.), *The handbook of social welfare* (pp. 195–218). Thousand Oaks, CA: Sage.

Gottfredson, D. C. (1986). An empirical test of school-based environmental and individual interventions to reduce the risk of delinquent behavior. *Criminology, 24*(4), 705–731.

Hamilton, M. L., & Richardson, V. (1995). Effects of the culture in two schools on the process and outcomes of staff development. *Elementary School Journal, 95*(4), 367–385.

Hansen, J. M., & Childs, J. (1998). Creating a school where people like to be. *Educational Leadership, 56*(1), 14–17.

Hazler, R. J. (1994). Bullying breeds violence: You can stop it. *Learning, 22*(6), 38–41.

Hazler, R. J., Hoover. J. H., & Oliver, R. (1991). Student perceptions of victimization by bullies in school. *Journal of Humanistic Education and Development, 29*(4), 143–150.

Hoover, J. H., Oliver, R., & Hazler, R. L. (1992). Bullying: Perceptions of adolescent victims in the midwestern USA. *Social Psychology International, 13,* 5–16.

Hoover, J. H., Oliver, R. L., & Thomson, K. A. (1993). Perceived victimization by school bullies: New research and future directions. *Journal of Humanistic Education and Development, 32*(2), 76–84.

Hyman, I. A. (1997). *School discipline and school violence*. Boston: Allyn & Bacon.

Hyman, I. A., & Perone, D. C. (1998). The other side of school violence: Educator policies and practices that may contribute to student misbehavior. *Journal of School Psychology, 36*(1), 7–27.

Hyman, I. A., & Snook, P. A. (1999). *Dangerous schools: What we can do about the physical and emotional abuse of our children*. San Francisco: Jossey-Bass.

Kachur, P., Stennies, G., Powell, K., Modzeleski, W., Stephens, R., Murphy, R., . . . Lowry, R. (1996). School-associated violent deaths in the United States, 1992 to 1994. *Journal of the American Medical Association, 275,* 1729–1733.

Massachusetts Governor's Commission on Gay and Lesbian Youth. (1993). *Making schools safe for gay and lesbian youth: Report of the Massachusetts Governor's Commission on Gay and Lesbian Youth*. Boston: Author.

National Association of Attorneys General. (1999). *Protecting students from harassment and hate crime*. Washington, DC: U.S. Department of Education, Office for Civil Rights.

Olweus, D. (1991). Bully/victim problems among schoolchildren: Basic facts and effects of a school based intervention program. In D. J. Pepler & K. H. Rubin (Eds.), *The development and treatment of childhood aggression* (pp. 411–448). Hillsdale, NJ: Lawrence Erlbaum.

Olweus, D. (1993). *Bullying at school*. Oxford, England: Basil Blackwell.

Olweus, D., & Limber, S. (1999). *Blueprints for violence prevention: Bullying prevention program*. Boulder, CO: Institute of Behavioral Science, University of Colorado.

Pilkington, N. W., & D'Augelli, A. R. (1995). Victimization of lesbian, gay, and bisexual youth in community settings. *Journal of Community Psychology, 23,* 34–56.

Ruenzel, D. (1997). One school that can. *Education Week on the Web*. Retrieved from http://www .edweek.org/ew/1998/25epstei.h17

Sakowski, L. (1993). *A study of pre- and post-trauma adjustment in corporally punished students* (Unpublished doctoral dissertation). Temple University, Philadelphia.

Saunders, J. M., & Valente, S. M. (1987). Suicide risk among gay men and lesbians: A review. *Death Studies, 11*(1), 1–23.

Sears, J. (1992). Educators, homosexuality, and homosexual students: Are personal feelings related to professional beliefs? *Journal of Homosexuality, 22*(3/4), 29–80.

Shakeshift, C., Barber, E., Hergenrother, M., Johnson, Y. M., Mandel, L. S., & Sawyer, J. (1995). Peer harassment in schools. *Journal for a Just and Caring Education, 1,* 30–44.

Smith, P. K., & Sharp, S. (1994). *School bullying: Insights and perspectives*. London: Routledge. Retrieved from ERIC Database (ED 387 223).

Stein, N. (1995). Sexual harassment in school: The public performance of gendered violence. *Harvard Educational Review, 65*(2), 145–162.

Stolp, S. (1995). *Every school a community: The academic value of strong social bonds among staff and students*. Eugene: Oregon School Study Council.

Vossekuil, B., Reddy, M., Fein, R., Borum, R., & Modzeleski, W. (2000). *USSS safe school initiative: An interim report on the prevention of targeted violence in schools*. Washington, DC: U.S. Secret Service, National Threat Assessment Center.

Wang, M. C., Haertel, G. D., & Walberg, H. J. (1997). Learning influences. In H. J. Walberg & G. D. Haertel (Eds.), *Psychology and educational practice* (pp. 199–211). Berkeley, CA: McCuthan.

Dropping Out

Why Students Drop Out of High School and What Can Be Done About It

Russell W. Rumberger

Misconduct in schools, failure to engage in the academic program, negative peer influence, retention in the previous grade, and other factors discussed in this and the previous article can result in students' sense of futility and dropping out. Russell W. Rumberger lays out the dropout statistics in the United States and reasons students drop out, both individual and contextual. Concerns about the situation for dropouts include the costs to dropouts and society. The author cites evidence for the negative outcomes for dropouts versus graduates: Dropouts in comparison with graduates experience poorer health, lower life expectancy, more likelihood of criminal activity and incarceration, and dependence on public assistance. Therefore, efforts to reduce dropout rates would likely reduce economic problems and negative social outcomes.

Questions to consider for this reading:

1. What are some individual and contextual factors that result in students dropping out of school, and what are the effects on dropouts?

2. Considering the readings on student dropouts, what might be done to reduce the number of students leaving school as dropouts?

3. What are issues faced by teachers, and what causes burnout?

Introduction

Cesar entered Hacienda Middle School in the Los Angeles School District in the sixth grade. He lived with his mother and three younger siblings in a garage that was divided into sleeping quarters and a makeshift kitchen with no running water. His mother, who spoke only Spanish, supported the family by working long hours at a minimum-wage job.

During the first semester of seventh grade, Cesar failed every class, in part due to poor attendance and not completing assignments. But by the end of seventh grade, with the assistance of a dropout prevention project at the school, Cesar was able to pass two of his six classes.

With the support of the dropout prevention project, his grades continued to improve. Yet, as he entered eighth grade, Cesar was spending more time after school away from home and on the

From *Dropping Out: Why Students Drop Out of High School and What Can Be Done About It,* by Russell W. Rumberger, 2011, pp. 1–7, 9–11. Cambridge, MA: Harvard University Press.

streets. He began to wear gang-related attire and hairstyles, although he denied gang involvement.

Teachers began to respond to him more positively as his grades improved, but because he did not change his "appearance," school administrators did not seem to change their earlier negative perceptions about him.

Two weeks into his last semester of eighth grade, Cesar got into a fight and kicked a younger student. Because of this incident, Cesar was given what the school district called an "opportunity transfer." However, no apparent effort was made by the school to see that Cesar actually enrolled in the new school, nor [did they endeavor to confirm] that he attended.

Cesar stopped attending school in eighth grade. He became a school dropout.

Public high schools in the United States reported that 607,789 students dropped out in 2008–09.[1] An even higher number fails to graduate. *Education Week*, the nation's leading education periodical, estimates that 1.3 million students from the high school class of 2010 failed to graduate.[2] This means that the nation's schools are losing more than 7,000 students each school day. And these figures do not count students like Cesar who drop out *before* reaching ninth grade. Altogether, the U.S. Census estimates that in October 2010 there were almost 28 million dropouts age eighteen and over in the United States.[3]

While these figures are sizeable, the magnitude of the problem is better understood when expressed as a rate that reflects the proportion of students who drop out of high school. The 607,789 students who dropped out of high school in 2008–09 represent more than 4 percent of all students enrolled in grades 9–12.[4] The 1.3 million students from the high school class of 2010 who failed to graduate represent 30 percent of the 4.3 million students enrolled in the ninth grade in 2006.[5]

Yet dropout rates tell only part of the story. It is also important to consider *graduation rates,* which reflect the proportion of students who actually graduate from high school. The two rates are not directly related. Students who drop out can still graduate at a later time, while students who never quit school still may not graduate. To graduate, students must earn a high school diploma, but some students earn alternative diplomas by taking state or national examinations. Students who earn these alternative diplomas are not considered graduates, but they also are not considered dropouts.

Dropout and graduation rates vary widely among various populations of students. For example, *Education Week* estimates that in the nation as a whole, 69 percent of all students who entered high school in the fall of 2003 graduated in 2007. But only 56 percent of Hispanics and 54 percent of blacks from that class graduated in 2007, compared to 81 percent of Asians and 77 percent of whites.[6] Among the almost 400,000 students with disabilities who left school in 2006–07, only 56 percent graduated with a diploma.[7] Dropout rates in the two-year period from 2002 to 2004 were twice as high for tenth-grade students whose native language was not English, compared to native English speakers.[8]

Similar disparities exist among districts and schools. *Education Week* estimates that the high school graduation rate for the class of 2007 among the nation's fifty largest school districts ranged from 40 percent in Clark County, Nevada, to 83 percent in Montgomery County, Maryland.[9] One study of Chicago's eighty-six public high schools found that the graduation rates over a four-year period for students who entered the ninth grade in 2000 varied from a low of 27 percent to a high of 90 percent![10]

Not only is the graduation rate in the United States generally low and highly variable, but it also appears to be getting worse. Nobel economist James Heckman examined the various sources of data used to calculate dropout and graduation rates and, after correcting for errors in previous calculations, concluded that:

- The high school graduation rate is lower than the federal government reports.
- It is lower today than it was forty years ago.
- Disparities in graduation rates among racial and ethnic minorities have not improved over the past thirty-five years.[11] . . .

The national concern for dropouts is reflected in numerous studies and programs focusing on this issue at the national, state, and local levels. Since 1988, the federal government alone has spent more than $300 million on dropout prevention programs.[12] Many states have enacted their own programs to assist local schools and districts in addressing this issue. And research on school dropouts has increased dramatically over the past decade.

But why is there so much concern?

There are a number of reasons. One is economic. Dropping out of school is costly both for dropouts themselves and for society as a whole. First, dropouts have difficulty finding jobs. Government data show that only 31 percent of students who dropped out of school in the 2009–10 school year were employed the following October.[13] America's recent economic recession has been particularly hard on dropouts: in December 2010 only 44 percent of high school dropouts sixteen to twenty-four years of age were employed, compared to 60 percent of high school completers who were not enrolled in school.[14]

Second, even if they find a job, dropouts earn substantially less than high school graduates. In 2008, the median annual earnings of high school dropouts working full-time over an entire year were 22 percent less than those of high school graduates.[15] Over their working lives, dropouts earn $260,000 less than high school graduates.[16] Dropouts' poor economic outcomes are due in part to their low levels of education; yet dropouts can, and sometimes do, return to school. Almost two-thirds of eighth-grade students who dropped out of school before their originally scheduled graduation date in 1992 completed either a regular high school diploma (19 percent) or a GED or alternative certificate (43 percent) by the year 2000.[17] And dropouts who earned a high school diploma were more likely to enroll in postsecondary education than students who did not complete high school (60 percent versus 15 percent).[18] Nonetheless, dropouts as a group are much less likely to enroll in postsecondary education than high school graduates, even though most states allow dropouts to enroll in community colleges

without a high school diploma. Thus, dropouts' poor economic prospects are due not simply to the fact that they fail to finish high school, but also to their continued underinvestment in education over their lifetime.

Dropouts experience other negative outcomes.[19] They have poorer health and higher rates of mortality than high school graduates; they are more likely than graduates to engage in criminal behavior and be incarcerated over their lifetimes. For instance, black male dropouts have a 60 percent probability of being incarcerated over their lifetime, a rate three times higher than for black male graduates.[20] Dropouts are also more likely to require public assistance and are less likely to vote. Although the observed relationship between dropping out and these economic and social outcomes does not necessarily imply a causal relationship, a growing body of research evidence has demonstrated one. This suggests that efforts to reduce dropout rates would, in fact, reduce these negative economic and social outcomes.

The negative outcomes from dropouts generate huge social costs to citizens and taxpayers. Federal, state, and local governments collect fewer taxes from dropouts. The government also subsidizes the poorer health, higher criminal activity, and increased public assistance of dropouts. One recent study estimated that each new high school graduate would generate more than $200,000 in government savings, and that cutting in half the dropout rate from a single group of twenty-year-olds would save taxpayers more than $45 billion.[21]

A second reason for the growing concern about the dropout problem is demographic. The proportion of students who are racial, ethnic, and linguistic minorities, who come from poor families, and who live in single-parent households— all factors that research has shown are associated with school failure and dropping out—is increasing in the nation's schools.[22] The most profound change is the growth of the Hispanic school-age population, which is projected to grow from 11 million in 2006 to 28 million in 2050, an increase of 166 percent, while the non-Hispanic school-age population is projected to increase by just 4 percent over this same period.[23] Because the rate of high school failure is higher among Hispanics and it improved more slowly in the 1990s than for whites and blacks, the increasing proportion of Hispanics in the school-age population could increase the overall number of dropouts even with marginal improvements in the dropout rate.

A third reason is the growing push for accountability in the nation's public schools that has produced policies to end social promotion (the practice of promoting a student to the next grade level despite low achievement) and to institute high school exit exams that could increase number of students who fail to complete high school.[24]

A final reason for widespread concern over dropping out is that it is related to a host of other social problems facing adolescents today. As noted by the Forum on Adolescence, created by the National Institute of Medicine and the National Research Council to bring authoritative, nonpartisan research to bear on policy issues facing adolescents and their families:

> One of the important insights to emerge from scientific inquiry into adolescence in the past two decades is that problem behaviors, as well as health-enhancing ones, tend to cluster in the same individual, and these behaviors tend to reinforce one another. Crime, dropping out of school, teenage pregnancy and childbearing, and drug abuse typically are considered separately, but in the real world they often occur together. Teenagers who drink and smoke are more likely to initiate sex earlier than their peers; those who engage in these behavior patterns often have a history of difficulties in school.[25]

If students face such a bleak future by dropping out of school, why do they do it? The question defies an easy answer.

Dropouts themselves report a wide variety of reasons for leaving school, including those related to school, family, and work.[26] The most specific reasons cited by tenth graders who dropped out in 2002 were "missed too many school days" (44 percent); "thought it would be easier to get a GED" (41 percent); "getting poor grades/failing

school" (38 percent); "did not like school" (37 percent); and "could not keep up with schoolwork" (32 percent). But these reasons do not reveal the underlying causes of why students quit school, particularly those causes or factors in elementary or middle school that may have contributed to students' attitudes, behaviors, and school performance immediately preceding their decision to leave school. Moreover, if many factors contribute to this phenomenon over a long period of time, it is virtually impossible to demonstrate a causal connection between any single factor and the decision to quit school.

Although for the most part existing research is unable to identify unique causes, a vast empirical research literature has examined numerous predictors of dropping out of and graduating from high school. The empirical research comes from a number of social science disciplines and has identified two types of factors: (1) individual factors associated with students themselves, such as their attitudes, behaviors, school performance, and prior experiences; and (2) contextual factors found in students' families, schools, and communities.

Individual Factors. The research has identified a wide variety of individual factors that are associated with dropping out. Attitudes and behaviors during high school predict dropping out. Dropout rates are higher among students who have low educational and occupational aspirations. Absenteeism, misbehavior in school, and pregnancy are also related to dropping out. Finally, poor academic achievement is a strong predictor of dropping out. Together, these factors support the idea that dropping out is influenced by both the social and the academic experiences of students in high school. . . .

[T]here is a growing body of research that has identified an array of factors in families, schools, and communities that affect a child's likelihood of dropping out of school.[27]

Contextual Factors. Among the three types of contextual factors, families are the most critical. Family background is widely recognized as the single most important contributor to success in school. Socioeconomic status, most commonly measured by *parental education and family income*, is a powerful predictor of school achievement and dropout behavior. Parental education influences students' aspirations and educational support (e.g., help with homework), while family income provides resources to support their children's education, including access to better quality schools, after-school and summer school programs, and support for learning within the home (e.g., computers). In addition, students whose parents monitor and regulate their activities, provide emotional support, encourage independent decision-making (practicing what is known as *authoritative parenting style*), and are generally more involved in their schooling are less likely to drop out.[28] Additionally, students living in single-parent homes and with stepfamilies are more likely to drop out of school than students in two-parent families.

Schools are a second contextual factor. It is widely acknowledged that schools exert powerful influences on student achievement, including dropout rates. Four types of school characteristics influence student performance, including the propensity to drop out or to graduate:

1. *Social composition*, such as the characteristics of students attending the schools, particularly the socioeconomic composition of the student body.

2. *Structural characteristics*, such as size, location, and school control (public traditional, public charter, private).

3. *School resources*, such as funding, teacher quality, and the student—teacher.

4. *Policies and practices*, such as the academic and social climate.

School characteristics influence dropout behavior in two ways. One way is indirectly, by creating conditions that influence student engagement, which can lead to students' *voluntarily* withdrawing from school due to boredom, poor attendance, or low achievement. Another way is directly, through explicit policies and conscious decisions by school

personnel that lead to students' *involuntarily* withdrawing from school. Schools may enact rules and/or take actions in response to low grades, poor attendance, misbehavior (such as zero-tolerance policies), or exceeding the compulsory schooling age that lead to suspensions, expulsions, or forced transfers. This form of withdrawal is school-initiated and contrasts with the student-initiated form mentioned previously. Some schools, for example, contribute to students' involuntary departure from school by systematically excluding and discharging "troublemakers" and other problematic students.[29]

In addition to families and schools, communities and peer groups can influence students' withdrawal from school. Differences in neighborhood characteristics help explain disparities in dropout rates among communities, apart from the influence of families.[30] Some neighborhoods, particularly those with high concentrations of African-Americans, are communities of concentrated disadvantage with extremely high levels of joblessness, family instability, poor health, substance abuse, poverty, welfare dependency, and crime.[31] Disadvantaged communities may influence child and adolescent development through the lack of resources (playgrounds and parks, after-school programs) or negative peer influences.[32] Community residents may also influence parenting practices over and above parental education and income. Students living in poor communities may also be more likely to have dropouts as friends, which increases the likelihood of dropping out of school.

Settings are important in influencing dropout behavior, but similar settings also affect individuals differently. Why is it that some students persist in school while living in poor families or attending "bad" schools? These different outcomes arise not only because of so-called objective differences in individuals—intelligence, race, or family situation—but also because of how individuals view or interpret their conditions. Thus, dropping out of school cannot be understood simply by studying the conditions of families and schools, or even the behaviors of students, but must also be understood by studying the views and interpretations of those conditions and behaviors by dropouts themselves. Anthropological studies of dropouts are based on this premise.

Finally, understanding why students drop out requires looking at school experiences and performance over a long period of time. Dropping out is more of a process than an event. Students don't suddenly drop out of school. Many dropouts show patterns of early school failure—disruptive behavior, failing grades, repeating a grade—that eventually lead them to give up or be pushed out, [as] Cesar was.[33]

NOTES

1. Robert Stillwell, Jennifer Sable, and Chris Plotts, *Public School Graduates and Dropouts from the Common Core Data: School Year 2008–09* (NCES 2011-312) (Washington, DC: National Center for Education Statistics, U.S. Department of Education, 2011), http://nces.ed.gov/Pubsearch/Pubsinfo.Asp? Pubid=2011312 (accessed May 9, 2011), table 4.

2. "Diplomas Count 2010: Graduation by the Numbers: Putting Data to Work for Student Success," *Education Week*, June 10, 2010, www.edweek.org/ Ew/Toc/2010/06/10/Index.html (accessed August 28, 2010), 25.

3. Thomas D. Snyder and Sally A. Dillow, *Digest of Education Statistics 2010* (NCES 2011-015) (Washington, DC: National Center for Education Statistics, U.S. Department of Education, 2011), http:// nces.ed.gov/Pubsearch/Pubsinfo.Asp?Pubid=2011015 (accessed May 9, 2011), table 9.

4. Stillwell, Sable, and Plotts, *Public School Graduates*, table 4.

5. Snyder and Dillow, *Digest of Education Statistics 2010,* table 37.

6. "Diplomas Count 2010," 24.

7. Special-education students are entitled to receive services for a specified number of years, often until they reach age twenty-one. They may exit school at that time with a regular diploma, an alternative diploma, a certificate of attendance, or no certificate. See Snyder and Dillow, *Digest of Education Statistics 2010,* table 117.

8. Russell W. Rumberger, *Tenth Grade Dropout Rates by Native Language, Race/Ethnicity, and Socioeconomic Status* (Santa Barbara: University of California Notes to Pages 2–4 Linguistic Minority Research Institute, 2006), http://lmri.ucsb.edu/ Publications (accessed January 17, 2011), figure 1.

9. "Diplomas Count 2010," 25.

10. Elaine Allensworth, *Graduation and Dropout Trends in Chicago: A Look at Cohorts of Students from 1991 through 2004* (Chicago: Consortium on Chicago School Research, 2005), http://ccsr.uchicago.edu/content/ publications.php?pub_id=61&list=t (accessed January 17, 2011), table 5.1.

11. James J. Heckman and Paul A. Lafontaine, "The American High School Graduation Rate: Trends and Levels," *Review of Economics and Statistics 92* (2010): 244–262.

12. The largest of these was the School Dropout Demonstration Assistance Program (SDDAP), which funded $294 million in targeted and school reform programs from 1989 to 1996. An evaluation of the last and largest phase of the program found that most programs had little impact on reducing dropout rates. See Mark Dynarski and Philip Gleason, *How Can We Help? What We Have Learned from Federal Dropout-Prevention Programs* (Princeton, NJ: Mathematica Policy Research, 1998).

13. *College Enrollment and Work Activity of 2010 High School Graduates* (Washington, DC: U.S. Department of Labor, Bureau of Labor Statistics, 2011), www.bls.gov/schedule/archives/all_nr.htm#HSGEC (accessed May, 2011), table 1.

14. *Labor Force Statistics from the Current Population Survey* (Washington, DC: Bureau of Labor Statistics, U.S. Department of Labor, 2010), www.bls .gov/Cps/Tables.Htm#Nempstat_M (accessed January 17, 2011), table A-16.

15. Susan Aud et al., *The Condition of Education 2010* (NCES 2010-028) (Washington, DC: National Center for Education Statistics, 2010), http://nces.ed .gov/pubsearch/pubsinfo.asp?pubid=2010028 (accessed January 17, 2011), table A-17-1.

16. Cecilia E. Rouse, "Consequences for the Labor Market," in *The Price We Pay: Economic and Social Consequences of Inadequate Education,* ed. C. R. Belfield and H. M. Levin (Washington, DC: Brookings Institution Press, 2007), 99–141. Rouse estimates that if dropouts who completed high school attended college at rates similar to those of high school graduates, the difference would exceed $550,000.

17. Susan Rotermund, *Education and Economic Consequences for Students Who Drop Out of High School,* Statistical Brief 5 (Santa Barbara: California Dropout Research Project, University of California, 2007), http://cdrp.ucsb.edu/Dropouts/Pubs_Statbriefs. Htm#5 (accessed January 17, 2011), figure 1.

18. Ibid., Figure 2.

19. Clive Belfield and Harry M. Levin, eds., *The Price We Pay: Economic and Social Consequences of Inadequate Education* (Washington, DC: Brookings Institution Press, 2007)

20. Becky Pettit and Bruce Western, "Mass Imprisonment and the Life Course: Race and Class Inequality in U.S. Incarceration," *American Sociological Review 69* (2004): 151–169.

21. Henry M. Levin and Clive R. Belfield, "Educational Interventions to Raise High School Graduation Rates," in *The Price We Pay: Economic and Social Consequences of Inadequate Education,* ed. C. R. Belfield and H. M. Levin (Washington, DC: Brookings Institution Press, 2007), 177–199, 194.

22. Aud et al., *The Condition of Education 2010.*

23. Rick Fry and Felisa Gonzales, *One-in-Five and Growing Fast: A Profile of Hispanic Public School Students* (Washington, DC: Pew Hispanic Center, 2008), http://pewhispanic.org/Files/Reports/92.Pdf (accessed January 17, 2011), i.

24. Russell W. Rumberger and Sun Ah Lim, *Why Students Drop Out of School: A Review of 25 Years of Research* (Santa Barbara: California Dropout Research Project, University of California, 2008), http://cdrp.ucsb.edu/Dropouts/Pubs_Reports.Htm#15 (accessed January 17, 2011).

25. Michele D. Kipke, ed., *Risks and Opportunities: Synthesis of Studies on Adolescence*, National Research Council and Institute of Medicine, Forum on Adolescence (Washington, DC: National Academic Press, 1999), 11–12.

26. Susan Rotermund, *Why Students Drop Out of High School: Comparisons from Three National Surveys,* Statistical Brief 2 (Santa Barbara: California Dropout Research Project, University of California, 2007), http://cdrp.ucsb.edu/Dropouts/Pubs_Statbriefs.Htm#2 (accessed January 17, 2011). See also John M. Bridgeland, John J. DiIulio Jr., and Karen Burke Morison, *The Silent Epidemic: Perspectives on High School Dropouts* (Washington, DC: Civil Enterprises, 2006).

27. See Rumberger and Lim, *Why Students Drop Out of School.* Rumberger and Lim reviewed 203 empirical studies from academic journals published over the 25-year period from 1983 to 2007. The summary in the text is based on that review.

28. Russell W. Rumberger, Rita Ghatak, Gary Poulos, Philip L. Ritter, and Stanford M. Dornbusch, "Family Influences on Dropout Behavior in One California High School," *Sociology of Education* 63 (1990): 283–299; Rumberger, "Dropping Out of Middle School."

29. Michelle Fine, *Framing Dropouts: Notes on the Politics of an Urban Public High School* (Albany: State University of New York Press, 1991); Carolyn Riehl, "Labeling and Letting Go: An Organizational Analysis of How High School Students Are Discharged as Dropouts," in *Research in Sociology of Education and Socialization,* ed. A. M. Pallas (New York: JAI Press, 1999), 231–268.

30. Rebecca L. Clark, *Neighborhood Effects on Dropping Out of School Among Teenage Boys* (Washington, DC: The Urban Institute); Jonathan Crane, "The Epidemic Theory of Ghettos and Neighborhood Effects on Dropping Out and Teenage Childbearing," *American Journal of Sociology* 96 (1991): 1226–1259.

31. Robert J. Sampson, Jeffrey D. Morenoff, and Thomas Gannon-Rowley, "Assessing 'Neighborhood Effects': Social Processes and New Directions in Research," *Annual Review of Sociology* 28 (2002): 443–478.

32. Tama Leventhal and Jeanne Brooks-Gunn, "The Neighborhoods They Live in: The Effects of Neighborhood Residence on Child and Adolescent Outcomes," *Psychological Bulletin* 126 (2000): 309–337; Maureen T. Hallinan and Richard A. Williams, "Students' Characteristics and the Peer-influence Process," *Sociology of Education* 63 (1990): 122–132; William J. Wilson, *The Truly Disadvantaged: The Inner City, the Underclass, and Public Policy* (Chicago: The University of Chicago Press, 1987).

33. Karl L. Alexander, Doris R. Entwisle, and Nadir S. Kabbini, "The Dropout Process in Life Course Perspective: Early Risk Factors at Home and School," *Teachers College Record* 103 (2001): 760–882; Byron L. Barrington and Bryan Hendricks, "Differentiating Characteristics of High School Graduates, Dropouts, and Nongraduates," *Journal of Educational Research* 82 (1989): 309–319; Robert B. Cairns, Beverley D. Cairns, and Holly J. Necherman, "Early School Dropout: Configurations and Determinants," *Child Development* 60 (1989): 1437–1452; Margaret E. Ensminger and Anita L. Slusacick, "Paths to High School Graduation or Dropout: A Longitudinal Study of a First-Grade Cohort," *Sociology of Education* 65 (1992): 95–113; Helen E. Garnier, Judith A. Stein, and Jennifer K. Jacobs, "The Process of Dropping Out of High School: A 19-Year Perspective," *American Educational Research Journal* 34 (1997): 395–419; Melissa Roderick, *The Path to Dropping Out* (Westport, CT: Auburn House, 1993).

Projects for Further Exploration

1. Using variables from the first reading on principals, plan and carry out an interview with a principal and write up your findings about the role of the principal. How closely do your interview findings coincide with Lortie's discussion of the principal's role?

2. Using an academic database, find the latest data on a topic related to teachers' roles that was described in the reading by Ingersoll and Merrill on the status of teaching. Restrict your search to refereed journals.

3. Using an academic database, pick one variable, such as student feelings of belonging or misconduct, that might influence students' achievements and performance in school. Look up that variable in an advanced search with both school and achievement and find studies that explain the influence on student achievement. Some examples of variables you might consider are substance abuse, bullying, school violence, student employment, gang membership, absenteeism, participation in sports or extracurricular activities, and cliques.

6

WHAT WE TEACH IN SCHOOLS

Knowledge for What and for Whom?

Knowledge is the base of all education. Without knowledge to impart to students there would be no justification for schools, even though education fills many other functions in a society. Knowledge and knowing are basic social elements in all societies. The first reading in this chapter is a provocative piece by Rob Moore that examines how sociologists study knowledge. The other two readings in this chapter examine the social construction of knowledge and how it comes to be taught and learned in schools. What knowledge is appropriate and what knowledge is included in the curriculum are determined by a number of both input and output factors as illustrated in the open systems model. For example, social reproduction theorists would argue that the knowledge taught in schools reflects the perspectives and views of those in power in society and the outputs are the appropriate knowledge for one's station in life, thus reproducing the social class structure. The study of knowledge provides another way of thinking about how social forces shape what is taught in our schools.

Researchers often consider the social context of educational institutions and people's educational experiences and trajectories. Rarely, however, do they consider what is meant by knowledge or how it comes to be taught and learned. When we consider knowledge, we assume that there are truths and that our educational systems are teaching those truths. The readings in this chapter make us think about these assumptions. Indeed, the reading by David Tyack suggests the knowledge that we teach in schools is negotiated within a variety of social and political constraints—for example, religious beliefs and political philosophies—thus the social construction of knowledge is very much a part of the process of education in society. Tyack's analysis of history textbooks suggests that knowledge is created in society, particularly by those in power. Moore, however, argues that there is a truth that can be taught, while at the same time not denying a great deal of inequality in our educational systems.

In this introduction, we explore different approaches, both past and present, that theorists have used to study knowledge. One way to view knowledge is to investigate it as a characteristic of persons—such as viewing someone as knowledgeable or smart (Swidler & Arditi, 1994). Knowledge can be seen as a private good, something that one uses to enhance oneself or one's status in life. However, some societies see knowledge as a public good that can be used to benefit society as a whole; that is, Thomas Jefferson once argued that in order to have a good, working democracy, the populace must be educated.

As discussed in Chapter 1, functionalists emphasize that schools are expected to produce individuals with the capabilities, attitudes, and orientations necessary to function in society. Thus, knowledge is viewed as a component of our everyday world—something that frames people's expectations for themselves and others. All of these approaches to knowledge affect schools; each perspective views knowledge as something that individuals use to interpret their worlds, something that shapes their orientations to others and their place in institutions in society such as schools and work.

Theories also relate to the production of knowledge (Swidler & Arditi, 1994). These theorists see the role of authority and power in knowledge production as part of a stratification process that maintains and reproduces inequality. As Tyack discusses in the second reading in this chapter, knowledge is sold to schools, and textbooks are the final product in the production of knowledge. However, the process by which knowledge is sold to schools is very complex, as Tyack describes, with many segments of the population influencing what is contained in the final "product" or the textbook that our children read. He discusses the blandness of history textbooks that is the result of the political pressure on textbook companies to produce textbooks that appeal to, and can be sold to, everyone and offend no one. Ideally, we should all be able to agree on one common core of knowledge, as Moore would like to see; however, in reality, that rarely happens. Current efforts to develop a common curriculum are ongoing, and more successful in countries outside the United States, as discussed by Ben Levin, Robert B. Schwartz, and Adam Gamoran in the reading in Chapter 11.

Another approach to studying knowledge focuses on the authority to define it and examines the organizational practices that shape knowledge as well as the structure and relations of power (Swidler & Arditi, 1994). This approach focuses on the development and use of authority, who gets to define what is "knowledge." The structure producing knowledge is important here, including the level of the social organization of knowledge or the power of the individuals within that organization. For example, knowledge is now situated in colleges and universities in developed countries, and there are structures defining who is "knowledgeable." Yet, in other societies at different times, knowledge was embedded in the church, and those knowledgeable were clerics. At the more macro level of social organization, the production of knowledge within this framework is embedded in how society is organized to define legitimate authority. In our society, we define knowledge within the context of formal institutions, as opposed to apprenticeships or applied learning. Therefore, college professors in civil engineering have more authority in defining how bridges are to be built than the contractors who put up the bridges.

If we further examine the organizational structure of knowledge, we can focus on an analysis of the gatekeepers who work to generate and select knowledge. It is not surprising to find that many of the major scientific advances in history were discovered years before they were acknowledged as "discoveries." Thomas S. Kuhn, in a classic book on *The Structure of Scientific Revolutions* (1970), developed the idea of shared paradigms within the scientific community. That is, prestigious scholars and scholars at prestigious universities, often the same people, have the authority to define what is known within their disciplines. They share paradigms of what is known and are generally unwilling to have their paradigms challenged. Kuhn argued that "normal science" seeks confirmation, not disconfirmation of its theories. Because scientists are more concerned about maintaining their forms of knowledge than with discovering new forms of knowledge, a significant number of disconfirming findings must occur before gatekeepers allow new forms of knowledge to be recognized.

Pierre Bourdieu takes a different approach, examining how power creates knowledge or how those in power can manipulate knowledge (Swidler & Arditi, 1994; see also Moore's criticism of this approach in this chapter). In this explanation, those who hold power in society also shape knowledge. Individuals with *cultural capital* fit the expectations of those in power in schools and, thus, have more power themselves. This is because they both understand and have access to the social and cultural artifacts and knowledge that are most valued in society. In fact, individuals get to define knowledge and can create ideologies or belief systems that support and maintain their positions of power. Powerful people may be involved in financing the organizations or politicians that support these individuals in their causes, which would support Bourdieu's argument that the rich and powerful manipulate knowledge (Swidler & Arditi, 1994). How it is that textbooks are developed to portray knowledge that reflects some people's worldview and not others' is a multilayered social puzzle, reflected in textbook boycotts and bans on books in schools dating back to the 1950s and 1960s, with an increase in censorship activities beginning in the 1980s (DelFattore, 1992). Tyack in the second reading in this chapter defines this as a political struggle.

DelFattore (1992) and others argue that undue influence on textbook publishing leads to the "dumbing of America" because publishers are pressured to present "knowledge" that is acceptable to many diverse audiences. She, as does Tyack in this chapter, describes states where textbooks are purchased at the state level for all students. Decision making is consolidated as administrators in these states either set down standards for textbook publishers or refuse to adopt textbooks unless they have the option of rewriting sections of the books of which they do not approve (DelFattore, 1992). The decision of what textbook to purchase is highly profitable for the publisher whose textbook is selected. As a result, the selection process in a very few states shapes textbooks for the remaining states. Knowledge, therefore, as Tyack argues, is oftentimes embedded in politics rather than education.

A growing body of literature on pedagogy, or the process of teaching, addresses these concerns at all levels of education. Initially the focus of this literature was on introducing knowledge of women and other cultures into classrooms. Advocates of multiculturalism and feminism focus not simply on inclusion of women and nonmajority groups into the curriculum but also on the ways in which these groups are presented. These groups are part of the political pressure to shape textbooks.

Another concern in the sociology of knowledge includes the effect of new technologies or the mode of delivery of knowledge. Technology has been growing at a pace far faster than ever before in history (Tyack & Cuban, 1995). Swidler and Arditi (1994) discuss the impact of moveable type and the printed book on the social construction of knowledge. There is less theoretical speculation about the changes that current technologies may have on the way we formulate knowledge. Cyberspace is a large frontier that enters the classroom both formally and informally as more and more students from preschool through college own and use computers. Wenglinsky (2005/2006) argued that the computer-to-student ratio went from 1 to 20 in 1990 to 1 to 5 at the end of that decade, creating a revolution in how knowledge was delivered to students in the classroom. He used national data to assess the impact of the use of technology on student achievement and found that students did better when computers were used for higher-order thinking such as to write papers and generate ideas rather than for drill and practice exercises (Wenglinsky, 2005/2006). Therefore, the technology itself is not as important as how it is used in the classroom. Whether technology transforms the way we think and use knowledge is still open to question. Tyack and Cuban (1995) feel that technology and computers may be the innovations that could change education in the future. However, many questions remain. Our final reading in this book by Paul Hill and Mike Johnston looks at future classrooms as seen through new technologies. We will just have to wait to see if knowledge becomes more anonymous when it comes to us through a computer and whether teaching and learning will respond to technology's speeding up the process of generating knowledge.

Technology is not the only potential controversy in terms of how knowledge is constructed in classrooms. The reading by Harold Wenglinsky in this chapter discusses the impact of testing for accountability on the way knowledge is taught (do we teach basic facts or critical thinking?) and the effects of teaching methods on learning. This is also discussed in the Levin, Schwartz, and Gamoran reading in Chapter 11. While the subjects taught may be the same, standardized tests can shape the way materials are presented to students and ultimately affect the depth of understanding of what we learn in school.

At the conclusion of this chapter, we hope you are more aware of the complexity in the process of constructing and presenting knowledge and the impact of those processes on how we define the reality of children. An important part of the social organization of knowledge is that knowledge is perceived to be legitimate and provides a shared understanding of a common world. Although this seems to be a simple and straightforward matter, the readings in this chapter point to many problems and difficulties in defining what knowledge is legitimate.

REFERENCES

DelFattore, J. (1992). *What Johnny shouldn't read: Textbook censorship in America*. New Haven, CT: Yale University Press.

Kuhn, T. S. (1970). *The structure of scientific revolutions* (2nd ed., enl.). Chicago: University of Chicago Press.

McEneaney, E. H., & Meyer, J. W. (2000). The content of the curriculum: An institutional perspective. In M. T. Hallinan (Ed.), *Handbook of the sociology of education* (pp. 189–211). New York: Kluwer Academic/Plenum.

Swidler, A., & Arditi, J. (1994). The new sociology of knowledge. *Annual Review of Sociology, 20,* 305–329.

Tyack, D., & Cuban, L. (1995). *Tinkering toward utopia: A century of public school reform*. Cambridge, MA: Harvard University Press.

Wenglinsky, H. (2005/2006). Technology and achievement: The bottom line. *Educational Leadership, 63*(4), 29–32.

BEING SOCIOLOGICAL ABOUT KNOWLEDGE

Setting the Agenda

Rob Moore

Is there a truth, or objective knowledge? Epistemology is the study of knowledge, and Rob Moore in this chapter takes a more epistemological approach as he challenges the sociological approach to knowledge. Moore briefly reviews the problems that occur with sociological analyses of knowledge, which see knowledge as relative to the social context, or reflecting the position and experience of individuals. He argues for a slightly different approach that, while recognizing inequality in society and unequal access to knowledge, also believes that equality can be achieved if efforts shift to find a more objective knowledge. If "knowledge" is objective and can be presented in a way that is accessible to all, then he believes inequality in society can be reduced. This reading is an excerpt from Moore's book, *Toward the Sociology of Truth*, which will offer you many challenges in the way you think about knowledge.

Questions to consider for this reading:

1. Why does Moore argue against the sociological approach to knowledge?

2. Is there a possibility of eliminating cultural aspects from the knowledge we learn?

3. Is the knowledge we learn in schools truth, and if not, what is it?

[The] general problems of sociology and knowledge are in some ways intensified in the sociology of education. Here the questions, "what is knowledge and how is it made?" are supplemented by "how is it transmitted and acquired and, so, distributed in society?" In this manner, questions of knowledge become associated with questions of social inequality and difference. Some social groups get more or better knowledge than others and as a consequence some groups end up with greater opportunities, wealth and status than others. Hence, sociological questions about knowledge frequently become ideological and political. Being sociological about knowledge is to examine the relationship between knowledge and social inequality and, behind that, power.

Educational knowledge is, as it were, seen as "doubly" constructed—a curriculum is socially constructed from knowledge that has itself already been socially constructed. But because, for constructionist approaches, this prior knowledge cannot provide an *epistemological* basis for the curriculum arrangements, such arrangements are ultimately arbitrary and reflect power relations in society. The manner in which the sociology of education is sociological about knowledge, then, has important implications for approaches to school knowledge and how educational reform is seen, or "misrecognized," as a means of promoting greater equality of opportunity and social justice. Because of the reductive nature of the sociological approach adopted, knowledge relations in themselves are treated as epistemologically arbitrary. In the final analysis they reflect (more or less directly) the broader social relations of society. A person's place in the organization of knowledge is a function of their place in the social order and to learn the organization of knowledge is to learn the social order. . . . This is the common logic of reproduction theories.

If it is the case that the organization of knowledge is epistemologically arbitrary in that it is *entirely* reducible to power relations, but socially non-arbitrary in that it *necessarily* expresses those relations . . . and the interests and standpoint of the dominant social group, then it follows that the way to radically change the social order of education would be to radically change the knowledge order of education (though how, within the parameters of such a theory, this could ever be possible remains a vexed problem). Within the mainstream of educational reform it was this type of thinking that played a part in fuelling comprehensivization, progressivism, mixed ability teaching, integrated studies and the curriculum innovations. . . .

Across the spectrum, certain aspects of these reform movements share in common, despite other fundamental differences, a deep hostility to knowledge in a strong epistemological form and any sense of knowledge as having an inner necessity that gives it an autonomous structure in its own right. It is important to stress, here, that this is no less true for certain sorts of "traditionalist" defenders of a subject-based curriculum. They do not defend it on epistemological grounds, but on the basis that it embodies *traditional* wisdom, values and authority and constitutes a distinct *culture*. Hence, there is a wide range of ideologically contrasting critiques that attempt to restructure the organization of knowledge in ways that are held to be capable of bringing about changes in the educational and social relations between groups. Between them they construct a view of knowledge as something that is plastic and pliable and can be pulled around in all directions. The curriculum can be remodelled into shapes that are held to be the cultural profiles of different groups: the masculinist form of science moulded into a girl-friendly shape, Eurocentric history into multicultural history, the literary canon into popular culture, the scholarly and detached into the relevant and technically instrumental or certain aspects of each combined to represent the "British way of life." Knowledge has no inner power to resist; different people and interests can do with it as they wish. It has no form or structure other than that imposed upon it from without—the only question is, "who wins the battle to shape it in their own image?" Not *what* knowledge, but *whose* knowledge, not which *truths*, but whose *power*?

THE LIMITATIONS OF REFORM AND THE PROBLEMS OF EXPLANATION

The approach of the sociology of education as described above and its relationship to educational change reflects a preoccupation with issues of education and social justice. Sociology of education has seen its primary task as identifying sources of education-related inequality and promoting those changes, at various levels, that might alleviate those inequalities. Similarly, educational reform has historically been concerned with changes that will increase equality of opportunity in education and beyond and, to varying degrees, in different periods, the sociology of education has supported and/or critiqued those reforms. In both cases, there are more or less explicit assumptions or claims about "causality"—this inequality is a result of *x*, if we change *x* to *y* we will achieve the desired result, *z*. . . . However, the evidence suggests more puzzles than it does answers or solutions and this situation, I feel, requires a radical rethink about how the sociology of education has tended to approach these issues for some long time now.

The most striking example of such a puzzle is that of class differences in educational attainment. The outstanding fact in education over the past 50 years is that, despite all the substantial reforms that have taken place, class differentials have remained unchanged (Goldthorpe 2000). This fact is of major significance for sociology generally as it raises fundamental issues for social scientific explanation. If we note that Britain is not unique in this way, then the historical and comparative laboratory presents us with a major challenge. To be quite clear: the *average* absolute level of education has risen consistently, but equally for all classes, hence *relative* differences have remained unchanged (though it is the case in England that the bottom 20 per cent of pupils have not raised their level in the same way). This raises serious issues about the relationship between the kinds of things that were changed through successive waves of educational reform and the kinds of things that are responsible for class differences in educational attainment. Clearly the kinds of things changed and the changes made have had no strong effects in relation to class *differentials* in education. . . .

should improve their chances. It is this kind of explanation and approach to educational change that could be called into question by puzzles and anomalies such as those above. It will be argued that the sociology of education has been disproportionately preoccupied with "culture effects," but that the evidence indicates that the actual effectivity of such factors is relatively weak in terms of the production of social differences in educational *outcomes*.

This is not to reject outright the undoubted influence of "culture effects" in education (in terms of the cultural capital of home background or the *habitus* of educational institutions, for instance), but to suggest that, in their various forms, they do not account for *enough* of what needs accounting for. Nor is it to ignore "structure effects" associated with macro forces such as increasing social inequality and the reduction in rates of social mobility over the past 25 years—though these issues are not to be addressed to any great degree here. . . . [T]here is a third kind of effect that has been virtually ignored completely: that of *knowledge* and this is largely because "culturalist" approaches have tended to be actively hostile to the idea of knowledge as a strong category in its own right. . . . To a significant degree, macro and micro approaches to the study of education have come to be viewed as constituting different *paradigms* and, hence, as incommensurable rather than complementary, and knowledge as a distinct category has been in effect invisible for a long time. The principle aim of this work is to recover "knowledge."

THE CULTURAL TURN

In broad terms, sociological accounts and attempts at explanation have tended to concentrate on *cultural* aspects of educational organization and processes such as the selectively alienating effects of a "middle-class" curriculum or its "sexist" or "ethnocentric" features. These things are seen as contributing to the under-attainment of various groups and changing them

KNOWLEDGE, LEARNING, SOCIETY

Within the sociology of education the theory of knowledge is at the same time, in a broad sense, a theory of *learning*. Different groups are held to learn (or *fail* to learn) as they do because of the way in which knowledge is organized and presented to them. Working class children, for instance, are held to be alienated by a narrowly academic "middle-class" curriculum, girls by androcentrism, and non-Western ethnic minorities by Eurocentrism. Social differentiation in education is a function of the organization of knowledge and the manner in which that organization is itself a reflection of the inequalities of the social order. Changing the organization of knowledge should induce change in both the other dimensions. But this has not been realized.

Within the arena of public debate, progressive attempts to make educational success more widely available to disadvantaged groups through progressive "culturalist" reforms, often come up against the charge of dumbing-down and of lowering of standards and the undermining of traditional values. The peculiarity about these often-fierce debates about school knowledge is that *knowledge* is actually the absent party in that there is no *theory* of knowledge itself: knowledge *as* knowledge. . . .

There are two important points to be taken from this. The first is the distinction between, "chang[ing] the underlying structuring principles of the school, curriculum or classroom to match the code already possessed by these pupils, or develop[ing] ways of providing those pupils with the key to the code enabling success within those contexts." The former is what I am calling the "culturalist" approach whereas the later points towards "knowledge effects." The other is that of the difficulty of addressing this second option: that this, "requires acknowledging the differential status of different forms of knowledge, an admission considered beyond the pale in much contemporary social science"; that is, that some knowledge is *objectively* better than others.

Given the dominant view of what being sociological about knowledge entails, it is easy to see why acknowledging the differential status of different forms of knowledge is "beyond the pale." If the hierarchy of knowledge is always seen as a representation of social hierarchy then to say that some knowledge is better than others is to say that some people are better than others—to elevate the perspectives and experiences of some groups over others. For a sociology of education that has seen its primary purpose as promoting social justice by revealing the social bases (and *biases*) of knowledge, to *defend* established knowledge is to reinforce entrenched social inequalities. In these terms, epistemological relativism is the equivalent of social equalitarianism. It is very important to note, here, that lurking behind this reflex is the assumption that knowledge is the same thing as *experience*. It is this reflex that lies behind certain calls to make knowledge "inclusive"; that is, not to provide equal access to the best knowledge, but to include all "knowledge(s)" (experience) on an equal basis. The logic of standpoint reductionism is that the dominant form of knowledge represents the perspective of the dominant group—its experience of the world from its particular place in the social order and in terms of its interest. It is the social construction of "reality" from a particular point of view. In this manner it is *necessarily* exclusive because only those within that standpoint can have that knowledge (experience) and the power to impose it.

Alternatively, in a different way, it can be argued, instead, that the dominant groups have *privileged access* to the best knowledge, in ways that can marginalize other groups, rather than having imposed their *particular* knowledge as "the best." . . .

[T]he possibility that *increased* stratification in knowledge (on the basis of epistemological principles) could support *reduced* stratification in society by facilitating access by disadvantaged groups to cognitively powerful knowledge codes through forms of pedagogy appropriate to the knowledge rather than through ones *presumed* to be appropriate to the cultural codes of different groups of pupils. This raises the key issue of the relationship between a *realist* rather than a constructionist, theory of knowledge and pedagogy. Within the sociology of education this requires a shift from a preoccupation with culture effects to knowledge effects and to ways of promoting greater equality of access to the *objectively* best knowledge.

The crucial shift in orientation outlined above might be difficult to achieve because for the currently dominant and deeply entrenched approach that has been described so far there can be no such thing as "best" knowledge, no means of *objectively* differentiating in knowledge because to do so is to do no more than introduce invidious distinctions between groups. Inclusion on this basis comes to mean the critical unmasking, debunking or deconstruction of the "dominant" form of knowledge in such a way that *all* knowledge, i.e. forms of experience, become equal in that *none* are privileged. However, in the array of perspectives that emerges, each is equal but each is also exclusive unto itself because each is incommensurable with all others because specialized to and authorized by its particular experiential base. There is no knowledge, only a plurality of *knowledges* or "voices."

* * *

THE TRUTH ABOUT TRUTHFULNESS

The above is not so much an argument *against* what I have called the dominant way of being sociological about knowledge, rather it is directing attention to the way in which the inherent inconsistencies or antinomies of its "epistemology" not only fatally undermine its own analyses, but systematically deflect attention away from what should be the central focus: knowledge *as* knowledge rather than simply a reflex or relay of some external power. . . .

This internal relationship has been powerfully explored by the philosopher, Bernard Williams, in his book (2002), *Truth and Truthfulness*. He begins by saying that, "Two currents of ideas are very prominent in modern thought and culture. On the one hand, there is an intense commitment to truthfulness—or, at any rate, a pervasive suspiciousness, a readiness against being fooled, an eagerness to see through appearances to the real structures and motives that lie behind them" (ibid. p. 1). In these terms, our way of being sociological about knowledge has been preoccupied with "truthfulness," with seeing through appearances: the "reflex against deceptiveness" (ibid. p. 1). But, he argues, "there is an equally pervasive suspicion about truth itself . . ." so that, ironically, "The desire for truthfulness drives a process of criticism which weakens the assurance that there is any secure or unqualifiedly stateable truth" (ibid.). . . .

The sociology of *truthfulness* calls for a sociology of *truth* as its necessary foundation. Being sociological about knowledge is to "do" a sociology of truth—but what is it that is being *done*. We begin to address this question by taking seriously the "*internal ordering of symbolic forms*." Williams poses the question: "Can the notions of truth and truthfulness be intellectually stabilized, in such a way that what we understand about truth and our chances of arriving at it can be made to fit with our need for truthfulness?" (ibid. p. 3). . . .

[He argues] that postmodern relativism is as much a threat to Truth as absolutist forms of certainty—*the* truth lies in the zone between the two, within a quantum of tolerance between their extremes: *in media res*. The relativizers tend to take for granted that their position is *benign* and tolerant.

BIBLIOGRAPHY

Goldthorpe, J. (2000), *On Sociology*. Oxford: Oxford University Press.
Williams, B. (2002), *Truth and Truthfulness*. Princeton: Princeton University Press.

MONUMENTS BETWEEN COVERS

The Politics of Textbooks

David Tyack

A historian of education, David Tyack turns his attention to examining the factions that have shaped the content of history textbooks in the United States. Beginning with censorship of ideas from competing politicians in the colonial United States, he highlights the various historical struggles over the content of history textbooks. This reading gives more attention to the debate as to whether to view knowledge from an epistemological (philosophical study of the production of true or adequate knowledge) versus a historical, political, or sociological examination of knowledge.

Questions to consider for this reading:

1. Is there a "truth" that should be contained in history textbooks? If so, why is it so difficult to publish the "truth" and make it interesting?

2. What social forces influenced the criticism of the content of history textbooks during different historical periods?

3. Do you agree with Tyack when he states that there need not be "one state-approved set of truths"? As such, do you think he agrees or disagrees with Moore in the first reading in this chapter?

Why are history textbooks so controversial when they are, by most accounts, so dull (Schudson, 1994)? People have generally wanted history texts to tell the official truth about the past. The search for a lowest common civic denominator has often resulted in terminal blandness, but even then critics have argued that texts did not get the public truth right. Textbooks resemble stone monuments. Designed to commemorate and *re-present* emblematic figures, events, and ideas—and thus to create common bonds—they may instead arouse dissent.

By law, many states have mandated that history textbooks be nonpartisan in politics and nonsectarian in religion (Pierce, 1926). Publishers have found a consensual approach a smart commercial strategy, for disaffected citizens would not buy their books. Advertisements for the McGuffey Readers—which sold more than 120 million copies—assured potential customers that the books contained nothing offensive to any

From "Monuments Between Covers: The Politics of Textbooks" by David Tyack, 1999, *American Behavioral Scientist, 42*(6), pp. 922–930. Copyright © Sage Publications.

religion, political persuasion, or section of the country. In their tone of solemn certainty, early textbooks resembled catechisms of political correctness (old version), and even some recent history texts have a catechetical flavor. "Those of us who grew up in the fifties," recalls historian Frances Fitzgerald (1979), "believed in the permanence of our American-history textbooks. . . . Those texts were the truth of things; they were American history. They were weighty volumes. They spoke in measured cadences: imperturbable, humorless, and as distant as Chinese emperors" (p. 7).

For two centuries, Americans have generally agreed that there was a public truth that should be taught to the young, but they have repeatedly and ardently disagreed about what that truth was. In 1915, Florida legislators attacked "the so-called histories" of the Confederacy written by Northerners and offered a prize to the author who best told the "True and Correct History" (Pierce, 1926, pp. 66–67). The South had lost the Civil War but was determined not to lose this battle. They would have their own textbooks just as they had their own monuments of the War for Southern Independence. Eight decades later, a popular book bore the title *Lies My Teacher Told Me: Everything Your American History Textbook Got Wrong* (Loewen, 1995). It gave an opposite account of White supremacy.

No Golden Age of Consensus

Amid recent contention over multiculturalism and culture wars, some imagine a golden age in the past when there was only one story to tell about American origins and destiny. But no such consensus ever existed among Americans in all their variety. The Philadelphia riots of the 1840s over the Bible as textbook make most disputes over multiculturalism today look like minuets. For two centuries, citizens in their associations of many kinds—religious, ethnic, gendered, economic, regional, racial, and fraternal—have contested with one another about what story to tell. In status-group politics, citizens sought to enhance

their own standing in the society and their representation in the public culture.

In a nation so diverse socially and economically, and with such a rich array of associations, it would have been surprising if there had not been conflict about the official truths of the textbooks. Irish complained in the 1850s that histories were anti-Catholic and in the 1920s that histories were too Anglophile. Southerners protested Yankee bias. The National Association for the Advancement of Colored People (NAACP), beginning early in the 20th century, demonstrated that Blacks were either ignored or stereotyped in textbooks. The American Legion and the Daughters of the American Revolution enthusiastically pursued "the Americanization of America." Business leaders attacked the "socialistic" message in Harold Rugg's books. And labor leaders argued that unions were invisible in the textbooks. Most of the protesters—and for that matter, the textbook writers—were White prosperous males. Issues of race and gender, so salient in textbook critiques of the 1960s, arose infrequently before that time (Pierce, 1930, 1933).

As the ranks of professional historians swelled in the 20th century, historians themselves wrote textbooks and lobbied for their own brand of civic orthodoxy and historical truth in the public schools. But the American Legion and other superpatriotic groups believed that history was too important to leave to the historians. As Walter Lippmann (1928) argued in *American Inquisitors,* both these loyalty police and professional historians in the 1920s shared a commitment to truth even when they energetically disputed what that truth was.

Between the two world wars, conservative textbook lobbies like the American Bar Association, the Daughters of the American Revolution, and the National Association of Manufacturers commanded considerable political clout in legislatures and local school districts. They successfully lobbied for laws requiring the teaching of American history and the Constitution. Occasionally, members of groups like the Knights of Columbus sought to represent the views of recent immigrants (Zimmerman, in press). In the past generation, outsider groups have attended to textbooks as they sought to achieve social justice through social movements. Organizations of feminists, African Americans, Native Americans, and Latinos have lobbied against distortions and omissions in textbooks. Meanwhile, religious concerns have persisted, as Muslims and Jews have protested negative stereotypes, and fundamentalists have complained about humanist indoctrination in the texts.

Textbook critics used various techniques to influence the public truths taught in textbooks. They lobbied state legislatures to prescribe or proscribe content (in the 1920s, Oregon banned history books that spoke ill of the Founding Fathers). They vetted texts according to certain criteria (e.g., secular humanism or gender bias) and publicized the results in public hearings and the media. Critics pressed lawsuits. The American Legion used its national magazine and local posts to keep track of patriotism in the schools. Politicians sometimes joined forces with ethnic associations, as in Mayor Thompson's Chicago of the 1920s, to make textbook bias a campaign issue and vote-getter (Pierce, 1933).

How much did these various protest groups and legislative lobbies actually change textbooks? It is hard to say, but scholars have found some discernable shifts in tone and content (Fedyck, 1980; Fitzgerald, 1979). The Confederate veterans and Southern historians who protested Yankee prejudices in accounts of Reconstruction contributed to a pro-White-Southern shift in textbooks in the early 20th century (no doubt publishers also wanted to add the South to their national market). Powerful groups of loyalty police during World War I and the cold war contributed to the fervid patriotism of the texts in those years. The civil rights and feminist movements of the 1960s and 1970s increased the attention textbooks paid to minorities and women, though often in a bland and additive rather than transformative fashion (Tetrault, 1986).

EPISODES IN THE POLITICS OF TRUTH

A variety of forces have triggered conflict over textbooks in American history: wars, immigration and other demographic shifts, religious conflicts, fears of subversion, and changing political philosophies and conceptions of citizenship. The aims of the textbook critics have differed, as have their strategies and achievements. But most activists shared these two common convictions: that textbooks should represent public truth and that existing textbooks had not gotten that truth right.

The educational intellectuals of the Revolutionary period agreed that correct political doctrines should be taught to the young and that leaders should exercise eternal vigilance against errors that could destroy liberty. If the young imbibed the wrong ideas, the republic itself was in danger. Thus, correct textbooks became essential in creating republican citizens, both leaders and followers. Noah Webster, avatar of homogenization, included catechisms of morality and civics in his famous spellers. Benjamin Rush, signer of the Declaration of Independence, wanted texts to give children heroes to emulate. Although he had not admired George Washington's conduct of the war, he thought it unwise to suggest that the Founding Fathers had faults, for "their *supposed* talents and virtues . . . will serve the cause of patriotism" (Rush, 1951, p. 388). Although Jefferson was a passionate advocate of religious and intellectual freedom, he thought it best to prescribe the political texts used at the University of Virginia and to expurgate the Tory passages in Hume's history. The republic was safe only insofar as republicans learned the same political principles. Of course, the political principles Jefferson wanted to teach were hardly those of Federalist opponents like Joseph Story, who wrote his own text to contradict Jeffersonian errors and instill an alternate version of truth (Tyack, 1966).

In the middle third of the 19th century, the crusaders who spread the common school across the nation thought that the textbook should teach the ideological *unum* that would bind together a diverse nation. Differences of class, ethnicity, race, region, religion, and political philosophy split the nation. Reformers like Horace Mann argued that the public school could counteract such fragmentation only by teaching nonsectarian and politically neutral knowledge, a common denominator of moral and civic instruction (Messerli, 1972). In constitutions and statutes, many states banned sectarian and partisan textbooks in the public schools.

For a time it seemed that religious controversies could be held at bay at the schoolhouse door. Mann and other school promoters had a simple set of propositions to justify the use of the Bible for "nonsectarian" moral instruction: The purpose of the common school is to train upright citizens; moral training of this sort must be based on religion; religion rests on the Bible; therefore, the teacher can accomplish nonsectarian moral instruction only by reading the Bible without comment. Some orthodox Protestants feared that Mann was thereby sneaking his Unitarianism into the public school, but in many parts of the country, this supposedly nonsectarian compromise, with the Bible as textbook, satisfied most citizens. One reason was that the Protestant-Republican ideology of the time so thoroughly blended politics and religion, piety and patriotism. Millennial reformers believed that the United States was literally God's country (Elson, 1964).

But Catholics disagreed, for they saw Mann's solution as sneaky pan-Protestant aggression and anti-Catholic propaganda. Proper moral instruction required the Catholic (Douay) Bible and authoritative interpretation by the priest. If anyone needed proof that the schools were anti-Catholic, said Irish activists, all they needed to do was to look at some of the textbooks used in places like Boston or New York that featured Catholics as the anti-Christ. What's more, the textbooks arranged nationalities in a hierarchy and described the Irish in despicable terms. How could one compromise with contempt (Cross, 1965)?

In the second half of the 19th century, Catholics developed their own parochial schools where they no longer felt like outsiders and where their children could learn the truth from their own textbooks in history. The story of Irish-American history told there was heroic, and the Puritans lost the luster the Yankee texts gave them.

Like the Catholic/Protestant differences that found their way into textbooks, the split between North and South on slavery could not be papered over, even in textbooks that specialized in avoiding controversy. Southerners protested in the 1850s that their children were forced to learn from books written by Yankees hostile to slavery and Southern culture. When the Civil War came, Southerners produced a few books of their own, and by the end of the century Confederate veterans lobbied for laws (like the one in Florida) requiring that textbooks give a "true account" of the War for Southern Independence. Meanwhile, the Grand Army of the Republic pressed for its own truthful text and erected monuments to the War of the Great Rebellion. Little common denominator there (Pierce, 1930, 1933).

By the turn of the century, educational policy makers and text writers were no longer so concerned about sectional and religious conflict. Time was ripe for a new kind of progress in education, they believed, a period of scientific efficiency and moral uplift. History could document progress and give guidance to the present.

But all was not well: The massive immigration of "new immigrants" from southeastern Europe threatened this progress. They were such unpromising material, many educational leaders complained. These newcomers were illiterate, easily misled by agitators, and unaccustomed to Anglo-Saxon concepts of justice and representative government. Such stereotypes of immigrants often found their way into the textbooks their children read—no celebration of cultural pluralism or self-esteem there. But most textbooks, like most educators, did show faith that the newcomers might one day prove themselves worthy of taking part in American progress (Fass, 1989).

During World War I, conservative noneducators came to dominate policy talk about Americanization and to portray loyalty not as something assumed but as imposed on "foreigners." Employers grew panicked when immigrant labor organizers spoke to workers in Polish, Italian, or Serbian. When World War I broke out, civic leaders spoke of domestic fifth columns. As the Red scare spread, schoolchildren were even enlisted to inform on disloyal neighbors, and the word *alien* took on a distinctly unfriendly ring. The "Americanization of America" became a motto of the loyalty police (Hartmann, 1948; McClymer, 1982).

The climate of opinion, then, was favorable to a whole host of conservative activists who sought to use public schools, and specifically textbooks in American history, as instruments to enforce their own notions of patriotism. Organizations like the American Legion, the Daughters of the American Revolution, the American Bar Association, the National Association of Manufacturers, and the National Security Council lobbied successfully in state capitols for teachers' loyalty oaths, instruction in English only, and mandatory courses in the Constitution and American history, and even sponsored their own textbooks for use in schools. Agencies of the federal government helped to coordinate these efforts and actually wrote textbooks for Americanizing immigrants (so much for local control in that era of mobilization). In this superheated patriotic atmosphere, history became an ally in the crusade. Historians eagerly rewrote school histories to illustrate the evils of the Huns and the virtues of our friends, the English.

The war was hardly over when the pro-British version of official truth became anathema. Irish and German ethnic associations and groups like the Knights of Columbus attacked the historians and their textbooks as un-American because they exalted the British. Aside from the Irish joy in pulling the lion's tail, there were many immigrant associations resentful of the demand for Anglo conformity during the war years. Critics attacked one historian because he said that the British had "returned courageously to the attack" at Bunker Hill. Tongue-in-cheek, he changed the textbook to declare that "three times the cowardly British" went back into battle (Fitzgerald, 1979, p. 35). The American Legion attacked David Muzzey,

the most popular text writer of the 1920s, as an English-sympathizer.

In the 1930s and 1940s, a number of textbooks began to shift to a more inclusive and welcoming attitude toward the "strangers." Experts on "Americanization," many of them second-generation immigrants themselves, came to realize that insulting the "new immigrants" was no way to absorb them into the society and that public schools were too often wedges between parents and children. Negative stereotypes of the "new immigrants" began to give way to positive textbook images of their contributions. Wartime movies in the 1940s, with their "foxhole pluralism" of ethnically mixed troops, echoed the celebration of diversity often found in the textbooks of the 1930s and 1940s (Fedyck, 1980; Tyack, 1993).

A leader in cultural pluralism in the curriculum was Rachel Davis DuBois. The American Legion denounced her, which no doubt helped her multicultural cause in some circles. Individual Black activists like W.E.B. DuBois (no relation to Rachel) and organizations like the NAACP worked to improve textbook representations of African Americans. Harold Rugg wrote an influential series of social studies textbooks that took a very different view of the "Americanization of America" from the Anglo-centered views of most 1920s texts. He saw Americanism as the enlargement of social justice, welcomed cultural diversity as a virtue not a threat, and adopted a more inclusive concept of citizenship that welcomed the underdog and the outsider to the pages of his texts (Olneck, 1990).

Rugg's broad definition of Americanism and his left-liberal views on the economy made him the bête noire of conservatives in the Hearst Press, various business organizations, and patriotic societies. They wanted history to reflect traditional interpretations of the nation-state. Their well-publicized attacks on Rugg effectively destroyed the market for his liberal textbooks (Fitzgerald, 1979). When Senator McCarthy tried in the 1950s to root out subversive people and subversive ideas, in education and elsewhere, he had plenty of precedent. Efforts to police loyalty have been common in periods of stress like World War I and the cold war, and some textbooks from each era reflected the prevailing draconian definitions of patriotism.

Criticism of textbooks in the 1960s and 1970s came increasingly from the left of the political spectrum, although the right was still organized and vocal. Activists in the civil rights and feminist movements complained that the public truths of the textbooks were radically wrong for they omitted or distorted the experience of excluded and oppressed groups. History was not just a story of the exploits of White male politicians and generals (Apple [& Christian-Smith], 1991; Cornbleth & Waugh, 1995; Schlesinger, 1991).

Demands for representation in texts coincided with the flourishing of social history "from the bottom up." Once marginal as fields of inquiry, African American and women's history have entered the mainstream of historical scholarship. The history of immigration and the working class have also enjoyed a resurgence. Scholars wishing to develop multicultural approaches in American history gained rich resources on which to draw (Nash, 1995).

Traditionally sensitive to criticism, not to say timid about it, textbook publishers have rapidly added images and stories about women and minorities. Scholars and activists have complained, however, that previously excluded groups have appeared not as main characters in the narrative but as figures in sidebars and illustrations. Surveys of high school textbooks have generally found that the development of the nation-state is still the master narrative in most books. And an ingenious study by historian Michael Frisch (1989) shows that the old icons (like George Washington, Betsy Ross, and Abraham Lincoln) are the people who spring to the minds of his college students when they are asked to free associate about historical figures through the Civil War.

WHITHER TEXTBOOKS?

Today a noisy confusion reigns about what stories the textbooks should tell. Worries abound about old truths betrayed and new truths ignored. Many groups want to vet or veto what children learn, and it is unclear what roles teachers, parents, ethnic groups, historians, and others should play (Schlesinger, 1991). Tempers rise. In New York debates over a multicultural curriculum, Catherine Cornbleth and Dexter Waugh (1995) observed, "Both sides engaged in a rhetoric of crisis, doom, and salvation" (p. 79).

In the United States, unlike most other nations, private agencies—publishing companies—create and sell textbooks. Thus, commerce plays an important part in deciding which historical truths shall be official. So does politics (Schudson, 1994), for public agencies decide which textbooks to adopt (about half of the states delegate text adoption to local districts, and the rest use some form of state adoption). For all the conventionality of the product, the actual production and sale of textbooks is a somewhat risky business. It is very expensive to create and print textbooks, and the market (the various agencies that actually decide which to adopt) is hard to predict. In addition, at any time some citizens are likely to protest whatever messages the texts send (Fitzgerald, 1979; Tyson-Bernstein, 1988).

Thus, it is not surprising that textbooks beget textbooks. To control risk, companies find it wise to copy successes. It has been easier to add to the master narrative than to rethink it [and] easier to incorporate new content into a safe and profitable formula than to create new accounts. Old icons (Washington) remain, but publishers respond to new demands by multiplying new state-approved truths. Current American history textbooks are enormous: 888 pages, on average (Loewen, 1995, p. 279). Publishers often seek to neutralize or anticipate criticisms by adding topics.

The traditional American fear of centralized power, salient today in debates over national standards and tests, has resulted in a strange patchwork of agencies and associations—textbook companies, state and local governments, lobby groups of many persuasions—to choose and monitor the public truths taught in the texts (Delfattore, 1992). One of the most rapid ways of changing what students learn in American schools is to transform the textbooks, but the present Rube Goldberg system of creating and selecting textbooks makes such reforms very difficult although occasionally fine texts do appear (Stille, 1998).

What might be some strategies to cope with the cross-cutting demands on history textbooks? These are some possibilities:

- muddling through with modest improvements,
- turning over the task of writing textbooks to experts,
- giving parents choices about what their children learn,
- subsidizing ethnic and racial groups to write their own group-centered books, as in Afrocentric programs, or
- devising texts that depart from the model of state-approved truths and embrace instead multiple perspectives. . . .

Those are some current ways of coping with choices about textbooks. In earlier times, decisions seemed simpler. Noah Webster was so certain about how to produce good citizens that he wrote a political catechism to accompany his texts. David Muzzey assumed that political and military history—read, White males running the polity—was the stuff of history. But today, the scholarly subfields of social history blossom, while many previously ignored groups demand a place in the public culture. History today is hardly a catechism. Instead, it resembles pieces of a sprawling novel with diverse characters and fascinating subplots waiting for an author to weave into a broader narrative.

REFERENCES

Apple, M., & Christian-Smith, L. (Eds.). (1991). *The politics of the textbook*. New York: Routledge.

Cornbleth, C., & Waugh, D. (1995). *The great speckled bird: Multicultural politics and education policymaking*. New York: St. Martin's.

Cross, R. (1965). The origins of the Catholic parochial schools in America. *American Benedictine Review, 16,* 194–209.

Delfattore, J. (1992). *What Johnny shouldn't read: Textbook censorship in America*. New Haven, CT: Yale University Press.

Elson, R. M. (1964). *Guardians of tradition: American schoolbooks of the nineteenth century*. Lincoln: University of Nebraska Press.

Fass, P. S. (1989). *Outside in: Minorities and the transformation of American education*. New York: Oxford University Press.

Fedyck, M. (1980). *Conceptions of citizenship and nationality in high school American history textbooks, 1913–1977*. Unpublished doctoral dissertation, Columbia University.

Fitzgerald, F. (1979). *America revised: History schoolbooks in the twentieth century*. New York: Vintage.

Frisch, M. (1989). American history and the structures of collective memory: A modest exercise in empirical iconography. *Journal of American History, 75,* 1130–1155.

Hartmann, E. G. (1948). *The movement to Americanize the immigrant*. New York: Columbia University Press.

Lippmann, W. (1928). *American inquisitors: A commentary on Dayton and Chicago*. New York: Macmillan.

Loewen, J. W. (1995). *Lies my teacher told me: Everything your American history textbook got wrong*. New York: Touchstone.

McClymer, J. F. (1982). The Americanization movement and the education of the foreign-born adult, 1914–25. In B. J. Weiss (Ed.), *American education and the European immigrant: 1840–1940* (pp. 96–116). Urbana: University of Illinois Press.

Messerli, J. (1972). *Horace Mann: A biography*. New York: Knopf.

Nash, G. B. (1995). American history reconsidered: Asking new questions about the past. In D. Ravitch & M. A. Vinovskis (Eds.), *Learning from the past: What history teaches about school reform* (pp. 135–166). Baltimore: Johns Hopkins University Press.

Olneck, M. R. (1990). The recurring dream: Symbolism and ideology in intercultural and multicultural education. *American Journal of Education, 99,* 147–174.

Pierce, B. L. (1926). *Public opinion and the teaching of history in the United States*. New York: Knopf.

Pierce, B. L. (1930). *Civic attitudes in American school textbooks*. Chicago: University of Chicago Press.

Pierce, B. L. (1933). *Citizens' organizations and the civic training of youth.* New York: Charles Scribner's Sons.

Rush, B. (1951). *Letters of Benjamin Rush* (L. H. Butterfield, Ed., Vol. 1). Princeton, NJ: Princeton University Press.

Schlesinger, A. M., Jr. (1991). *The disuniting of America.* Knoxville, TN: Whittle Direct Books.

Schudson, M. (1994). Textbook politics. *Journal of Communication, 44,* 43–51.

Stille, A. (1998, June 11). The betrayal of history. *New York Review of Books,* pp. 15–20.

Tetrault, M. K. (1986). Thinking about women: The case of United States history textbooks. *History Teacher, 19,* 211–262.

Tyack, D. (1966). Forming the national character: Paradox in the thought of the revolutionary generation. *Harvard Educational Review, 36,* 29–41.

Tyack, D. (1993). Constructing differences: Historical perspectives on schooling and social diversity. *Teachers College Record, 95,* 8–34.

Tyson-Bernstein, H. (1988). *A conspiracy of good intentions: America's textbook fiasco.* Washington, DC: Council for Basic Education.

Zimmerman, J. (in press). Educational history from the bottom up: Exploring popular influences upon the American curriculum, 1890–1954. *Teachers College Record.*

FACTS OR CRITICAL THINKING SKILLS?

What NAEP Results Say

Harold Wenglinsky

This reading by Harold Wenglinsky examines the role of teaching practices on what knowledge is presented. The debate between teaching basic skills and teaching critical thinking is not new, but it has become more heated with the No Child Left Behind (NCLB) and Race to the Top legislations' emphasis on accountability. Although the National Assessment of Educational Progress (NAEP) that measures factual learning has been around since 1969, the new federal government emphasis on accountability uses other methods of evaluation that emphasize basic skills rather than critical thinking.

Questions to consider for this reading:

1. What national and local factors influence how knowledge is presented in schools?

2. What difference does it make if students learn basic skills rather than critical thinking?

3. Will the current focus on changing testing to assess basic skills influence the type of knowledge presented in schools or only the presentation of the knowledge?

In the past 30 years, policymakers and educators have debated whether schooling should emphasize facts or critical thinking skills. Proponents of the first view argue that students need to know when the Civil War happened before they can accurately interpret its causes. Proponents of the second view counter that students will soon forget the exact dates of the Battle of Chancellorsville, but they will probably remember the insights that they gain from studying the battle's causes, leadership, military reasoning, and human costs.

State policymakers have responded to the shifting debate. Thus, the California legislature has gone back and forth between emphasizing phonics and whole language approaches in its reading curriculum. Maryland emphasizes critical thinking skills in its state standards and tests; just across the Potomac River, Virginia emphasizes basic facts.

For the most part, however, this debate has not been informed by actual empirical data. Fortunately, the National Assessment of Educational Progress (NAEP) offers relevant information. Administered every year or two since 1969 in various subjects—including mathematics, science, reading, and civics—the NAEP assessments are taken by representative samples of 4th, 8th, and 12th graders throughout the United States (U.S. Department of Education, 2000). Because each student takes only a small subset of the examination, the full examination can cover a substantial breadth and depth of material. Test items include both multiple-choice responses and more complex written responses so that they assess both basic skills and critical thinking skills. In addition to the test, students and their teachers and school administrators also fill out questionnaires that furnish information about student and teacher backgrounds and the instructional practices used in the classroom. By measuring the relationships between specific instructional practices and student performance, we can use NAEP data to compare the effectiveness of teaching for meaning with that of teaching basic skills. Using advanced statistical techniques, we can even take into account the potential influence of student achievement, thus isolating the effects of instruction oriented to teaching for meaning.

When we examine various analyses, some published and some unpublished (Wenglinsky, 2000, 2002, 2003), a clear pattern emerges from the data: Across subjects, teaching for meaning is associated with higher NAEP test scores. Although students must learn basic skills and facts at some point, these results suggest that instruction emphasizing advanced reasoning skills promotes high student performance.

MATH AND SCIENCE: EARLY TEACHING FOR MEANING

In mathematics, some educators advocate teaching students basic skills, such as the times tables,

and reinforcing those skills through drill and practice. Others advocate teaching students mathematical reasoning, such as the principles behind algorithms for multiplication and division, and emphasizing such complex topics as data analysis and probability early in the curriculum. The NAEP data supports the latter approach. Among U.S. 4th and 8th graders, teaching that emphasizes higher-order thinking skills, project-based learning, opportunities to solve problems that have multiple solutions, [and] such hands-on techniques as using manipulatives were all associated with higher performance on the mathematics NAEP. Such methods reflect the idea that learning mathematics is an iterative process, rather than a linear process in which students progress from simple facts to more complicated ones (McLauglin & Talbert, 1993).

The Trends in International Mathematics and Science Study (TIMSS) provides further evidence. Stigler and Hiebert (1999), analyzing videotapes of classes in the United States, Germany, and Japan, found that the Japanese 8th grade teachers were more likely to emphasize critical thinking by having students fashion their own solutions to problems and by introducing advanced material (for example, algebra) at a relatively early stage. And overall, Japanese students outperformed their U.S. and German counterparts in mathematics.

In science, the curricular debate has been between those who advocate teaching students the facts of science and those who emphasize hands-on activities that allow students to explore theory. Basic skills advocates do not necessarily object to the use of hands-on activities, but they assign them a different role, in which the teacher defines laboratory procedures and students carry them out to demonstrate, for example, what happens when heat is placed under a balloon.

The NAEP data again suggest the benefits of teaching for meaning. Students tended to score higher on the 4th grade and 8th grade NAEP science tests when they had experienced science instruction centered on projects in which they took a high degree of initiative. Traditional activities, such as completing worksheets and reading primarily from textbooks, seemed to have no positive effect.

READING AND CIVICS: A MORE LINEAR PICTURE

In contrast to the NAEP results for math and science, the results in the humanities demonstrate the benefits of a more linear approach to teaching.

In reading, one debate has centered on how students should learn to identify words and develop fluency, and a second debate has centered on how students should develop reading comprehension. The first debate has played itself out in the reading wars between phonics and whole language advocates. The phonics approach emphasizes teaching students to sound out words, whereas whole language emphasizes identifying unfamiliar words from their context. Because the NAEP does not test students until grade 4, its results shed little light on this first debate. Reports by the National Reading Panel (2000) and the National Research Council (Snow, Burns, & Griffin, 1998) have supposedly resolved the issue in favor of a balanced approach that focuses on phonics but leaves some room for contextual approaches (although some reading researchers question the reports' findings).

The second debate—regarding reading comprehension—has not been fully engaged. Some scholars have simply staked out positions on reading comprehension analogous to their position on word identification and fluency. Yet here, NAEP scores do offer some guidance—and they strongly suggest that when it comes to comprehension, basic skills approaches are inappropriate.

In both 4th and 8th grades, NAEP scores in comprehension favor teaching for meaning. Students tended to perform better on NAEP comprehension questions when they had experienced instruction in metacognitive skills (drawing meaning from text by asking questions, summarizing the work, identifying key themes, and thinking critically about the author's purpose and

whether that purpose was achieved). In addition, students' comprehension was higher when they had been exposed to "real" texts—books and stories rather than short passages in basal readers. Finally, students improved their comprehension skills by reading literature and then writing about that literature, which gave them the opportunity to apply their metacognitive skills.

Thus, it appears that learning to read follows a linear trajectory. Previous studies suggest that students first need to learn the basic skills from phonics to sound out words and develop fluency. Once they have done that, however, the NAEP scores indicate that students should move on to develop reasoning skills and critical thinking skills in order to comprehend texts.

In civics, the story is also linear. The debate in civics centers on whether students should learn facts about the government through textbooks and homework or through more hands-on civics activities, such as community service. The NAEP data indicate that the 4th graders, on the other hand, benefit both from reading textbooks and such hands-on activities as service learning. Thus, in the case of civics, students will likely do best with a developmental model in which they begin by learning the content and then go on to make sense of it through civic practice.

BASIC SKILLS AND TEACHING FOR MEANING IN PARTNERSHIP

These analyses of NAEP results suggest that although basic skills have their place in pedagogy, critical thinking skills are essential. In mathematics and science at both the 4th and 8th grade levels, practices that emphasize critical thinking skills are associated with higher student achievement, whereas practices that emphasize basic skills are not. Apparently, students more effectively learn simple content, such as the times tables, if they understand the conceptual framework that lies behind that content. Educators do not need to choose between basic and advanced skills in math and science, but we should introduce advanced skills early to motivate students to learn the basic algorithms—which, let's face it, are not very interesting in and of themselves.

In the humanities, on the other hand, the data suggest the value of a more linear process. Students should not begin their school lives as readers developing their own rules for spelling or creating their own vernacular language. But once they know how to take language from the page, students need opportunities to construct sense out of text by interpreting it, writing about it, and reflecting on what they have written. Similarly, civics students need to know what the branches of government do, what freedoms the Bill of Rights protects, and how to influence their elected officials. Once students have learned these facts, however, they need to put their knowledge into practice by performing community service activities, going on field trips, and communicating with elected officials on matters important to them. . . .

IMPLICATIONS FOR POLICYMAKERS AND EDUCATORS

These empirical findings about the importance of teaching for meaning suggest certain actions that public officials and education administrators need to take.

At the school level, principals need to encourage their teachers to spend more time teaching for meaning across subject areas—especially in math and science in the early grades. In the humanities, students may need to learn basic skills in reading and civics in elementary school. But by the time students reach middle school, teaching for meaning becomes crucial.

Unfortunately, school principals and superintendents may have difficulty moving in this direction because federal policy now intervenes in state and local curriculum choices in favor of basic skills and against teaching for meaning. The No Child Left Behind Act (NCLB) constitutes an unprecedented level of federal involvement in education.

NCLB's goals are highly laudable. Despite the complaints of many educators, creating a national infrastructure that holds schools accountable for the performance of their students and sanctions schools for a pattern of repeated failure is an appropriate role for the federal government. When the states demonstrated their inability during the Great Depression to provide social insurance and welfare benefits to their unemployed and elderly, and when states were unwilling during the civil rights era to educate black and white students together, federal intervention became necessary. These days, where the states have demonstrated their inability to educate our children well—particularly minority children and those living in poverty—the federal government is again obligated to act. Only the federal government can create a common yardstick for measuring performance and take actions against states that do not make the fiscal effort to provide good schools for all students. My own state of New York provides a case in point: Education in New York City and other urban systems is woefully underfunded, and as a result, school and teacher quality is manifestly lacking. In the sense of holding states accountable, then, NCLB could do some good.

But NCLB has overextended itself. It has moved beyond accountability for student achievement results by providing professional development funds that exclusively support a basic skills approach. To qualify for the funds, such cities as New York—which desperately need money—must teach a basic skills curriculum across the board. In addition, the federal government is rewriting the NAEP so that the tests will reflect a greater emphasis on basic skills instead of their current balance between basic and higher-order skills. By squeezing out critical thinking skills, these actions put the cognitive development of our students at risk.

Many education leaders oppose NCLB on the wrong grounds. They should embrace the notion of being held accountable for the achievement of their students but demand autonomy in how to improve that achievement. And as the NAEP data suggest, the best way for school leaders to raise student achievement is by placing more emphasis on teaching for meaning.

REFERENCES

McLauglin, M. W., & Talbert, J. E. (1993). Introduction: New visions of teaching. In M. W. McLauglin & J. E. Talbert (Eds.), *Teaching for understanding* (pp. 1–10). San Francisco: Jossey-Bass.

National Reading Panel. (2000). *Teaching children to read: An evidence based assessment of the scientific research literature on reading and its implications for reading instruction.* Washington, DC: National Institute of Child Health and Human Development.

Snow, C. E., Burns, M. S., & Griffin, P. (Eds.). (1998). *Preventing reading difficulties in young children.* Washington, DC: Committee on Prevention of Reading Difficulties in Young Children.

Stigler, J. W., & Hiebert, J. (1999). *The teaching gap: Best ideas from the world's teachers for improving education in the classroom.* New York: Free Press.

U.S. Department of Education. (2000). *Trends in academic progress: Three decades of student performance.* Washington, DC: Author.

Wenglinsky, H. (2000). *How teaching matters: Bringing the classroom back into discussions of teacher quality.* Princeton, NJ: Educational Testing Service.

Wenglinsky, H. (2002). How schools matter: The link between teacher classroom practices and student academic performance. *Education Policy Analysis Archives, 10*(12).

Wenglinsky, H. (2003). Using large-scale research to gauge the impact of instructional practices on student reading comprehension: An exploratory study. *Education Policy Analysis Archives, 11*(19).

Projects for Further Exploration

1. Try to find one or two history textbooks. Do you agree with Tyack that they are bland? Can you see some of the social/cultural influences that he argues have shaped the knowledge presented in these textbooks?

2. Using the web, see if you can find out more about the publication of textbooks. That is, check out a major publisher to see how many textbooks are sold (e.g., a fourth-grade reading series) and how that publisher markets the textbooks.

3. Examine textbooks from public schools in your area and ask whether the information presented is geared toward exploring ideas or reciting the cultural character of this country. Do these textbooks provide an opportunity for creative exploration or a focus on test-taking as described by Wenglinsky in the reading in this chapter?

7

WHO GETS AHEAD?

Race, Class, and Gender in Education

Sorting people into categories and ranking those categories are processes that pervade all institutions, including education systems. Social stratification has been a central concern for sociologists of education. In this chapter we explore the role that education plays in stratifying individuals and groups in society and within schools. Although issues of stratification are discussed throughout this book, this chapter focuses on the ways schools stratify by race, class, and gender, while readings in Chapter 8 describe attempts to alleviate inequality in schools. Unfortunately, space does not permit us to explore all inequalities, such as the prejudice and discrimination in schools for students with alternative sexual identities (Pascoe, 2007) and those whose body types and learning styles do not fit the "norm" (physical and cognitive differences). As you study the readings in this chapter and in Chapter 8, we encourage you to examine parallels between the ways different groups are treated in schools and to consider how and why inequality exists in education. In doing so, you will develop a deeper understanding of the role schools play in maintaining inequality at the micro and macro levels.

Let's stop to take a look at America's schools by examining class, race, and gender compositions. First, while it would seem that the proportion of males and females in schools should be similar to the population as a whole—49.2% male to 50.8% female (U.S. Census Bureau, 2011)—this is not the case. The relatively even sex ratio changes as students move through the school system, with boys (7.7%) more likely than girls (6.5%) to drop out of high school (National Center for Education Statistics [NCES], 2012b). Women are more likely to graduate college at all degree levels (NCES, 2012c)—bachelor's degrees (57.4% of women vs. 42.6% of men), master's degrees (62.6% vs. 37.4%), and doctoral degrees (53.3% vs. 46.7%). This is a change in the gender distribution of higher education degrees, and some people are concerned about boys not achieving as much as girls in schools as Roslyn Arlin Mickelson discusses in her reading in this chapter.

There are concerns as well about educational outcomes related to racial/ethnic and social class differences. The U.S. Census Bureau (2012) reports that, in 2009, the number of children living in poverty varied widely by race—13.4% white, 42.1% black, and 33% Hispanic. The percentage graduating from high school varies by race. The U.S. Department of Education (NCES, 2012b) reports that, in 2008, the percentage of individuals 16 through 24 years old dropping out of high school was 5.0% for whites (non-Hispanic), 7.3% for blacks, and 13.6% for Hispanics. The rates of college completion for individuals 25 to 29 years old are also distressing. In 2011, the percentage of 25- to 28-year-olds with bachelor's degrees was much higher for whites (31.1%) and Asian/Pacific Islanders (39.8%) than for blacks (16.1%) and Hispanics (10.1%) (NCES, 2012a). Clearly these figures suggest considerable inequality in American education.

Sociologists focus on inequality in education. This inequality comes in a variety of forms, as you will soon see. However, the end result is always to give advantage to one group over another or put some children at a distinct disadvantage in what might otherwise be an equal playing field. Caroline Hodges Persell discusses various explanations for racial inequality in school. The readings by John R. Logan, Elisabeta Minca, and Sinem Adar; Joseph J. Ferrare; and Pamela R. Bennett, Amy C. Lutz, and Lakshmi Jayaram focus on social class as a barrier to equal educational opportunities. The reading by Roslyn Arlin Mickelson adds to this discussion by examining gender as well as race and social class differences in educational experiences. Edward W. Morris's reading also illustrates the interaction of race, class, and gender in his study of students' experiences in a rural school. Clearly, improving academic achievement for *all* individuals is very complex.

Stratification in schools has been studied either at the school level or by examining the effects on individuals. At the school level, researchers study stratification within schools or between schools. The Logan, Minca, and Adar reading attempts to explain between-school differences in educational achievement. Stratification between schools refers to the different educational experiences offered in different schools and includes the placement of students within certain courses or curriculum tracks, as well as structures that exclude or discourage some groups of students from programs or curricula. Ferrare's reading in this chapter looks at within-school differences in educational experiences.

One of the primary methods of within-school stratification affecting students across race and social class is the process of curriculum tracking described in the Ferrare reading. Curriculum tracking is a structural feature of schools in which students take classes at different levels of difficulty. Different classes on the same topic are offered at differing levels of difficulty for some classes, as Ferrare describes; these classes determine the next course a student will take in the sequence of courses in that topic. However, Ferrare also examines opportunities that are open or denied by students' selection of nonrequired courses.

Mentioned in this chapter are the large number of quantitative studies that define or examine the effects of tracking on students. Vanfossen, Jones, and Spade (1987) categorize the early research on the effects of tracking on status maintenance into three categories. One category of research looked at the effects of tracking in maintaining social-class status from generation to generation. The second category assumed that tracking was based on ability; therefore, differential treatment in tracks is unrelated to social mobility. The third category of research concluded that the relationship between tracking and status maintenance is "irrelevant, because tracking in high school does not have a significant impact upon achievement, values, and educational outcomes" (Vanfossen et al., 1987, p. 105). The first explanation is most likely. When children enter middle school, they are placed in ability groups based on achievement test scores; however, such placement is not based on academic factors alone (Dauber, Alexander, & Entwisle, 1996). This trajectory of ability grouping is reinforced as children enter high school. The correlation between social class and track placement is too strong to be explained away by chance. Although some lower-class students end up in more challenging tracks, many others do not. Assignment to a lower track typically exposes a student to less rigorous instructional methods along with less challenging curricula (Gamoran, Nystrand, Berends, & LePore, 1995). Tracking students into lower-level curriculum is also related to attachment to school, level of self-esteem, and more limited views of future opportunities (Vanfossen et al., 1987). Some of the more recent research on tracking focuses on defining tracking itself. Indeed, the procedure is more complicated than simply assigning students to academic or vocational programs of study, as envisioned at the beginning of the 20th century. The idea of differential courses of study was introduced at that time as one of many efforts to tailor schools to the needs of a society dealing with nascent industrialization and an influx of immigrants (Oakes, 1985; Tyack & Cuban, 1995). By 1970, the organization of tracking became less rigid as schools allowed students to select their own courses (see also discussion of horizontal courses in Ferrare's reading in this chapter). Powell, Farrar, and Cohen (1985) called this array of choices the "shopping mall high school." Samuel Lucas (1999) describes the variations in patterns of course-taking across subjects that exist today, which continue to be organized in a hierarchical level of knowledge presentation tailored to different ability levels.

Most of the more recent literature in this area attempts to understand the effects of tracking on students' academic achievements and orientations toward school. Grouping students by ability or tracking begins in elementary school, disadvantaging children from lower-income families long before they enter the middle school. Children from lower-income families not only do not "catch up" to their wealthier peers in elementary school, but they fall further behind throughout the school years. Alexander, Entwisle, and Olson (2007) followed students over a period of time and found that lower-income children experience a "summer setback" in achievement, whereas their peers from higher-income families actually show gains on achievement tests over the summer when they are away from school because they are exposed to more academic-enhancing experiences during their time off. The reading in this chapter by Bennett, Lutz, and Jayaram adds to our understanding of how social class influences children's educational outcomes by examining the influence of social class on how time is spent outside of school. They provide data from interviews with parents detailing the parents' orientations toward afterschool activities for their children and explore cultural and structural explanations for why some children are not afforded the same opportunities as others in their after-school activities. Thus, the influence of social class is not only strong in predicting academic achievement, but it is also complex.

The reading by Morris in this chapter focuses on aspects of within-school stratification, looking at the microlevel or interactional factors that shape children's schooling and life experiences. Persell also describes the interpersonal interactions that create inequalities within schools, reviewing various explanations for racial differences in achievement outcomes. As the readings by Morris and Persell illustrate, families can have a significant impact on the direction of their children's schooling; however, teachers' expectations based upon the gender and racial and social class backgrounds of children can also influence learning.

The reading by Mickelson further examines gender differences within schools, as well as the unequal payoffs of education for females and males across race and social class. These processes are subtle, yet they have a substantial impact on the ultimate success of women and minority students. These readings illustrate how the stratification process occurs in different school contexts and is reinforced by teachers, peers, and others in the process of educating our children.

The following readings are meant to provide you with a better understanding of the mechanisms that segregate students both between and within schools in terms of curriculum and learning experiences. This differential treatment results in unequal educational and occupational opportunities for students across social class, race and ethnicity, and gender.

References

Alexander, K. I., Entwisle, D. R., & Olson, L. S. (2007). Lasting consequences of the summer learning gap. *American Sociological Review, 72*(2), 167–168, 175–177.

Dauber, S. L., Alexander, K. L., & Entwisle, D. R. (1996). Tracking and transitions through the middle grades: Channeling educational trajectories. *Sociology of Education, 69*(4), 290–307.

Gamoran, A., Nystrand, M., Berends, M., & LePore, P. C. (1995). An organizational analysis of the effects of ability grouping. *American Educational Research Journal, 32*(4), 687–715.

Lucas, S. R. (1999). *Tracking inequality: Stratification and mobility in American high schools*. New York: Teachers College Press.

National Center for Education Statistics. (2010). *Fast facts: What is the percentage of degrees conferred by sex and race?* Washington, DC: U.S. Department of Education. Retrieved from http://nces.ed.gov/fastfacts/display.asp?id=72

National Center for Education Statistics. (2012a). *Digest of education statistics: Table 9*. Washington, DC: U.S. Department of Education. Retrieved from http://nces.ed.gov/programs/digest/d11/tables/dt11_009.asp

National Center for Education Statistics. (2012b). *Digest of education statistics: Table 128*. Washington, DC: U.S. Department of Education. Retrieved from http://nces.ed.gov/programs/digest/d12/tables/dt12_128.asp

National Center for Education Statistics. (2012c). *Fast facts: Degrees conferred by sex and race*. Washington, DC: U.S. Department of Education. Retrieved from http://nces.ed.gov/fastfacts/display.asp?id=72

Oakes, J. (1985). *Keeping track: How schools structure inequality*. New Haven, CT: Yale University Press.

Pascoe, C. J. (2007). *Dude, you're a fag: Masculinity and sexuality in high school*. Berkeley: University of California Press.

Powell, A. G., Farrar, E., & Cohen, D. K. (1985). *The shopping mall high school: Winners and losers in the educational marketplace*. Boston: Houghton Mifflin.

Tyack, D., & Cuban, L. (1995). *Tinkering toward utopia: A century of public school reform*. Cambridge, MA: Harvard University Press.

U.S. Census Bureau. (2011). *Age and sex composition in the United States: 2011—Table 1*. Washington, DC: Author. Retrieved from https://www.census.gov/population/age/data/2011comp.html

U.S. Census Bureau. (2012). *Statistical abstract of the United States: 2012—Table 712*. Washington, DC: Author. Retrieved from http://www.census.gov/compendia/statab/2012/tables/12s0712.pdf

Vanfossen, B. E., Jones, J. D., & Spade, J. Z. (1987). Curriculum tracking and status maintenance. *Sociology of Education, 60*(2), 104–122.

The Geography of Inequality

Why Separate Means Unequal in American Public Schools

John R. Logan, Elisabeta Minca, and Sinem Adar

There are many possible explanations for why some children achieve and others do not, but one fact we cannot overlook is that schools in the United States still are segregated despite school integration efforts following the landmark 1954 Supreme Court decision *Brown v. Board of Education of Topeka, Kansas.* It stated that racially separated schools are "inherently unequal." Many argue today that schools have since "resegregated," and the racial distribution of schools in the United States is just as segregated as it was in 1954. In this reading, John R. Logan, Elisabeta Minca, and Sinem Adar revisit the question of whether differences in academic achievement outcomes are related to the racial and social class composition of schools. They consider the current situation, looking more analytically at the patterns of school segregation in the United States today.

Questions to consider for this reading:

1. What factors contribute to our schools being segregated by race?

2. Why does the racial composition of a school matter in predicting the school's academic achievement?

3. Why won't the Race to the Top policy of closing underperforming schools likely increase the academic achievement of black and Hispanic students?

The principal question raised by most research on racial segregation in schools is whether children of different racial and ethnic backgrounds attend different schools. Many studies have traced trends in segregation, which persists at fairly high levels despite substantial desegregation of schools in the 1970s in the wake of the *Brown* decision (Clotfelter 2004; Logan, Oakley, and Stowell 2008). While documenting trends, researchers emphasize that segregation is important not only because it separates children but because it leaves minority children in inferior schools (Orfield and Yun 1999). If many children are being "left behind" in public schools, one hard fact is that those children are disproportionately minorities. Yet until recently it has not

From "The Geography of Inequality: Why Separate Means Unequal in American Public Schools," by John R. Logan, Elisabeta Minca, and Sinem Adar, 2012, *Sociology of Education, 85*(3), pp. 287–301. Published by Sage Publications on behalf of the American Sociological Association. Copyright © ASA/Sage.

been possible to measure these inequalities at a national level. That is our purpose here. We ask what schools minority children attend and how those schools are performing.

The assumption is that, all else equal, it is advantageous to attend a school where more students are successful. This is why, for example, the No Child Left Behind Act (NCLB) signed into law in 2002 introduced mechanisms to identify "failing schools" (Borman et al. 2004). We take advantage of the testing requirements of that legislation to offer a national-level accounting of the performance disparities in the schools attended by white and minority children. We then explore the sources of these disparities, examining what kinds of schools children of different races and ethnicities are attending and how various school characteristics are associated with overall school performance.

There is no doubt about the extent of racial and ethnic disparities in educational outcomes for individual students (Jencks and Phillips 1998; Hallinan 2001; Henderson 2002; Maruyama 2003; Rumberger and Palardy 2005). One review of recent results from the National Assessment of Educational Progress (NAEP) showed that nationwide only 54 percent of black students, compared with 87 percent of white students, performed at or above the basic level on the 2003 eighth-grade reading exam (Stiefel, Schwartz, and Chellman 2008:527). Dropout rates are much higher among black and Hispanic students than among white and Asian students (Mickelson 2003). It is less clear how these differences may be related to the characteristics of the schools that children attend. There has long been a suspicion that school segregation is somehow a factor. In the landmark 1954 case of *Brown v. Board of Education of Topeka,* the U.S. Supreme Court officially declared that the "separate but equal" doctrine established 58 years earlier in *Plessy v. Ferguson* had no place in the field of public education (Whitman 1998). Racially segregated schools, according to the court, were inherently unequal. There was little empirical basis at the time for this claim. We provide new evidence based on school performance on standardized tests, taking into account racial composition as well as other school characteristics such as poverty; location in a central city, suburban, or nonmetropolitan setting; and the demographic composition of local residents.

WHAT SCHOOLS DO MINORITY STUDENTS ATTEND?

It is widely reported that minority students attend worse schools than non-Hispanic whites do (Bankston and Caldas 1998; Roscigno 1998), although few studies have had direct measures of school-level outcomes. An exception is the study by Crosnoe (2005), which analyzed data on a national sample of kindergarten students, finding that Mexican kindergarteners were in schools with more minorities, higher student poverty levels, lower teacher experience, larger size, and worse community locations than white and Asian students were, even after controlling for individual-level characteristics that might have been expected to produce such disparities. Hanushek and Rivkin (2009), drawing on the extensive database of the Texas Schools Project, found that black students attend schools with a less experienced teaching staff than do white students and that this factor has a significant impact on widening black–white performance differentials between elementary and middle school.

There is more evidence that minority children are more likely [than white children] to be in high-poverty schools. Saporito and Sohoni (2007) found that unlike the typical white child, who attends a public school in which most of the children are above the poverty line, the typical black or Hispanic child attends a public school in which most of the children are below the poverty line. Orfield and Lee (2005) pointed out that more than 60 percent of black and Hispanic students attend high-poverty schools (defined as more than 50 percent poor). Only 18 percent of white students and 30 percent of Asian students attend high-poverty schools. Logan (2002) reported that non-Hispanic whites on average attended public elementary schools where 30 percent of students qualified for free or reduced price lunches, compared with 65 percent for schools attended by the average black student and 66 percent for the average Hispanic student.

Black and Hispanic students are also more likely to attend city schools. The 24 largest central cities (with 4.5 million students) have enrollments that are more than 70 percent black and Hispanic (Orfield and Lee 2005). In 20 of these districts, the student population is 90 percent black.

WHICH SCHOOLS HAVE HIGHER STUDENT PERFORMANCE?

A considerable literature examines how various aspects of the school population, the school district, and school organization affect learning outcomes. Several key factors are highly interrelated: the racial/ethnic composition of the school, poverty level, location in the central city or suburbs, and immigration. In addition, some research has focused on how schools are organized: their size and grade levels. The most sophisticated studies use multilevel analyses, evaluating contextual effects on individual children's outcomes after controlling for their personal characteristics. For our purpose, even simpler designs based on school-level data are relevant.

Many scholars have sought to evaluate the effect of racial segregation on performance (Mercer & Scout 1974; Wells and Crain 1994; Armor 1995; Schofield 1995; Orfield and Eaton 1996; Cutler and Glaeser 1997; Rumberger and Palardy 2005; Bilfulco and Ladd 2006). Several studies suggest a direct and independent effect of racial composition on student performance. Bankston and Caldas (1996, 1997) and Rumberger and Williams (1992) showed that minority concentration is associated with lower achievement on standardized tests. Academic outcomes are generally better for blacks in racially integrated schools (Dawkins and Braddock 1994; Armor

2002). Stiefel et al. (2008) found that the achievement gap between white and nonwhite schoolchildren is greatest between racially segregated schools. Card and Rothstein (2005) concluded that segregation continues to be a major obstacle to equal educational opportunities for minority children and a source of gaps in academic achievement.

Of course the racial composition of schools is strongly correlated with other school characteristics, such as class composition. The classic study of school effects, the Coleman Report (Coleman et al. 1966), provided evidence that the racial isolation of black children in majority minority schools is associated with lower academic achievement. But Coleman demonstrated that these racial differences were primarily attributable to socioeconomic differences between races. He argued that predominantly white schools tended to enroll students from higher socioeconomic backgrounds and it was for this reason that the academic performance of these schools was better than that of predominantly minority schools. He found, in short, that apparent contextual effects were really compositional (see also Hauser, Sewell, and Alwin 1976). If there was a contextual effect, in Coleman's view, it was the effect of class composition. A recent study of this question (Chaplin 2002) found that the concentration of poverty within a school is negatively associated with student performance and later outcomes, even after controlling for a student's own family background (see also a number of prior studies, including Chubb and Moe 1990; Jencks and Mayer 1990; Gamoran 1996; Lee and Smith 1997).

Another relevant factor is metropolitan location, which is related to both racial and class composition and strongly associated with educational outcomes. For example, Swanson (2008) found that high school graduation rates are 15 percentage points lower in the nation's urban schools than in schools located in the suburbs. And in 12 cities, 9 of which are in the Northeast and Midwest, the city–suburban graduation gap exceeds 25 percentage points. In addition to the contextual effects of concentrated poverty, it is argued that poor central city schools are more likely to have inadequate resources and funding, as well as a less qualified teaching staff, compared with schools in suburban school systems (Eaddy et al. 2003; Hochschild and Scovronick 2003).

There has been considerable discussion of whether immigration has an independent effect on school performance, apart from the observed differences related to the Hispanic and Asian shares of the student population. Most studies have been conducted at the individual level, but they have clear implications for school-level relationships. Immigration appears to be a positive factor, as immigrant youth or those with immigrant parents tend to perform better than otherwise similar native-born students (Fuglini 1997; Zhou and Bankston 1998; Portes and Rumbaut 2001; Glick and White 2003). Schwartz and Stiefel (2006) reported an immigrant advantage over native-born students on test scores in New York City. A subsequent analysis (Conger, Schwartz, and Stiefel 2007) found that immigrant students also have higher attendance rates and are less likely to be enrolled in special education classes. Scholars point to strong traditional family and community ties among some immigrant groups and a strong emphasis on education as a means of advancement as protective factors (Portes and Zhou 1993; Zhou and Bankston 1998).

* * *

DISCUSSION AND CONCLUSION

This is the first national-level study at all grade levels to look beyond the racial segregation of schools to the question of inequalities in the performance of schools that children of different races and ethnicities attend. Our concern is the geography of opportunity. We have no information on group-specific test scores. Rather, we are identifying the schools that children are taught in. In the unlikely event that school test scores are a function only of the ability or willingness to learn of the students who attend them, these results would have little interest. However, our assumption is that attending a school in the 60th percentile of the distribution provides a significant advantage for the educational future of a child in comparison to attending a school in the 35th percentile. And that is the order of magnitude of differences that we find here. Public schools are not only separate but also unequal.

The key result is the simple accounting of disparities presented . . . Disparities are clear already in the elementary grades, where black, Hispanic, and Native American children attend schools that are on average at the 35th to 40th percentile of performance compared with other schools in the same state. White and Asian children are in schools at close to the 60th percentile. The degree of disparity is not much different at higher grades, and there is almost no change across grades in relative reading scores. At higher grade levels there is noticeable improvement in mathematics scores in the schools attended by Hispanics, Asians, and Native Americans, which could result from the larger attendance zones of middle and high schools. But this trend is not found for blacks.

The multivariate analyses provide more information about the sources of these disparities, which are deeply rooted in differences that are linked to race. Because we are working with cross-sectional data with no information on educational processes within schools, the results should be viewed as descriptive of patterns rather than as an effort to find the causes of differences. Our first step, the latent cluster analysis, is a search for patterns in the data. It leads us to identify six types of schools. This result is more complex than the simple model of affluent-white-suburban versus poor-minority-central-city schools, although that dichotomy is part of the story. We found three kinds of high-poverty schools. One of these is disproportionately located in central cities, although a considerable share is also in suburbs, and it is more Hispanic than black. Another is more heavily black but is quite mixed in location. The third type of high-poverty school is also in mixed locations, and this type is also mixed in racial composition. What most distinguishes this third type of school from other high-poverty schools is that nearly three-quarters of Native American children attend this type. These three types of high-poverty schools are the usual venue for minority children; together, they account for about 27 percent of white students in public elementary schools across the nation and 29 percent of Asian students, but a very large majority of black, Hispanic, and Native American students.

The remaining three school types all have lower levels of poverty, but they differ among themselves in other respects. Closest to the stereotype of white exclusion is the second cluster, schools that are nearly 90 percent white, lowest in poverty, and predominantly in suburbs. Another similar type, the fifth cluster, is even more exclusively white but is most commonly found in nonmetropolitan areas. Nonmetropolitan schools tend to be overlooked in the segregation literature, but they are an important component of the educational system. More challenging to the usual stereotype is the fourth cluster. It represents relatively affluent and disproportionately suburban schools with a clear white majority but with nontrivial shares of other groups. These are the schools where black and Hispanic students are likely to find more access to educational advantage, and they are also the schools where most white and Asian students have opportunities to encounter other groups. About a quarter of white students and nearly half of Asian students attend these schools. A quarter of Native Americans are also found here. But less than 10 percent of black and Hispanic students have access to this resource.

The implications of this pattern of segregation across types of schools are brought home in the analysis of predictors of school performance. Consider first the finding that the racial composition of schools matters in itself—schools with more minorities do worse. Because race and poverty are highly correlated in the United States, we would expect some racial differences even if race in itself did not matter. However, we find substantial race differences even after controlling for poverty and other factors. One interpretation

is the one put forward by the Supreme Court, that segregation alone creates inequality. Another is that minority students under current social conditions bring down a school's average test score. If that were true, creating more diverse schools would improve school quality for minorities at the expense of whites. Yet another possibility is that parents of white children take into account both the race and class composition of schools and their reputation for performance when deciding where to live and that their selectivity contributes to the disparities that we have measured. In that case, of course, one would have to explain why black and Hispanic parents do not make the same calculations. Possibly they have fewer choices, even taking into account their own income and education (a point often made in the literature on residential segregation).

Poverty has as large an effect as the black or Hispanic share of students. This could also be a simple compositional effect—poor students (perhaps because of their home or neighborhood situation or parental background) are known to perform worse than students from affluent families. It could also be a contextual effect, as some other studies have suggested—the overall composition of the school could affect all students, or high-poverty schools might in some cases have fewer educational resources. But regardless of the reason, this finding implies that, independent of racial segregation, class segregation is associated with a lower quality of school available to minority students. It supports the view of some policy analysts that race-neutral school assignment based on equalizing the class composition of schools could have strong positive effects. Here, too, such a policy could have a negative impact on students who are currently in advantaged positions.

Family background in the community is another powerful factor, but our results show that adults' educational levels matter much more than issues of family disruption. Another community characteristic, the percentage foreign born, has no significant positive or negative effect. This finding should alleviate concerns about whether immigration itself is a risk factor for schools. We might expect these variables to work more strongly at the individual level, if we knew the performance of each child and had information on his or her parents' immigration status, education, or marital situation.

Finally there is no evidence that metropolitan location independently affects school performance. Low-performing schools may be found in every zone of the metropolis, depending on the other factors identified here. This result is a reminder of the increasing heterogeneity of suburban regions, where the disparities between communities can be as great as the overall difference between city and suburb.

Taken together, these data show that racial inequalities in education are large and deeply entrenched in the society. When *typical* black, Hispanic, and Native American children are assigned to schools that perform so much below the median, few can be in above-average schools and a substantial share are in schools well below the 30th percentile. Attacking this pattern by focusing on a few low-achieving schools (the NCLB [No Child Left Behind] policy to close failing schools at the very bottom of the distribution) can have only marginal results. To drive this point home, we have calculated a simulation of what the distribution of students would be across schools under a scenario that represents a very successful implementation of NCLB school closures. . . . Suppose we could close all the schools that perform under the 10th percentile. Suppose we could reassign these students to other schools in proportion to white students' presence in the remaining schools. This would be a stunning change because black, Hispanic, and Native American children would gain much greater access to the resources of predominantly white schools. More than a quarter of them would be in schools that are currently above the 80th percentile.

So what is the result? Less than 20 percent of white and Asian students but about 35 percent of black and Hispanic students would still be in schools below the 31st percentile. About 15 percent of black and Hispanic students but close to 30 percent of white and Asian students would be in schools above the 81st percentile. This is because the disparities across groups not only are the result of minorities' concentration in the worst schools but are found across the whole distribution of "non-failing" schools. The simulation is simply a way to emphasize the depth of disparities.

Aside from dealing with failing schools, trends in residential segregation will not soon move many black children into more diverse neighborhood schools, and residential changes are exacerbating rather than solving the isolation of Hispanic children. Since progress in school desegregation has come to a halt in most parts of the country, partly due to the strong boundaries between school districts, and court rulings are creating obstacles to existing desegregation plans, there is little chance for improvement from this source. Efforts at equalization of poverty rates across schools, which could make a strong contribution, will also run up against the barrier of district boundaries. Decades after the *Brown v. Board* desegregation order, separate and unequal continues to be the pattern in American public education.

REFERENCES

Armor, D. J. 1995. *Forced Justice: School Desegregation and the Law*. New York: Oxford University Press.

Armor, D. J. 2002. "Desegregation and Academic Achievement." Pp. 147–88 in *School Desegregation in the 21st Century,* edited by C. H. Rossell, D. Armor, and H. Walberg. Westport, CT: Praeger.

Bankston, C. and S. Caldas. 1996. "Majority African American Schools and Social Injustice: The Influence of de Facto Segregation on Academic Achievement." *Social Forces* 75(2):535–55.

Bankston, C. and S. Caldas. 1997. "The American School Dilemma: Race and Scholastic Performance." *Sociological Quarterly* 383:423–29.

Bankston, C. L., III and S. J. Caldas. 1998. "Race, Poverty, Family Structure, and the Inequality of Schools." *Sociological Spectrum* 18:55–76.

Bilfulco, R. and H. Ladd 2006. "School Choice, Racial Segregation, and Test-score Gaps: Evidence from

North Carolina's Charter School Program." *Journal of Policy Analysis and Management* 261:31–56.

Borman, K., T. Eitle, D. Michael, D. Eitle, R. Lee, L. Johnson, D. Cobb-Roberts, S. Dorn, and B. Shircliffe. 2004. "Accountability in a Post-desegregation Era: The Continuing Significance of Racial Segregation in Florida's Schools." *American Educational Research Journal* 413:605–31.

Card, D. and J. Rothstein. 2005. "Racial Segregation and the Black–White Test Score Gap." Working Paper No. 109, Center for Economic Policy Studies, Princeton University. Princeton, NJ.

Chaplin, D. 2002. "Estimating the Impact of Economic Integration." Pp. 87–113 in *Divided We Fail: Coming Together through Public School Choice*. New York: Century Foundation Press.

Chubb, J. E. and T. M. Moe. 1990. *Politics, Markets and America's Schools*. Washington, DC: Brookings Institution.

Clotfelter, C. T. 2004. *After* Brown*: The Rise and Retreat of School Desegregation*. Princeton, NJ: Princeton University Press.

Coleman, J. S., E. Campbell, C. Hobson, J. McPartland, A. Mood, F. D. Weinfield, and R. York. 1966. *Equality of Educational Opportunity*. Washington, DC: U.S. Government Printing Office.

Conger, D., A. E. Schwartz, and L. Stiefel. 2007. "Immigrant and Native-born Differences in School Stability and Special Education: Evidence from New York City." *International Migration Review* 41:403–32.

Crosnoe, R. 2005. "Double Disadvantage or Signs of Resilience? The Elementary School Contexts of Children from Mexican Immigrant Families." *American Educational Research Journal* 42:269–303.

Cutler, D. and E. Glaeser. 1997. "Are Ghettos Good or Bad?" *Journal of Economics* 112(3):827–47.

Dawkins, M. and J. Braddock. 1994. "The Continuing Significance of Desegregation: School Racial Composition and African American Inclusion in American Society." *Journal of Negro Education* 63(3):394–405.

Eaddy, R., C. Sawyer, K. Shimizu, R. McIlwain, S. Wood, D. Segal, and K. Stockton. 2003. *Residential Segregation, Poverty, and Racism: Obstacles to America's Great Society*. Washington, DC: Lawyers' Committee for Civil Rights Under Law.

Fuglini, A. J. 1997. "The Academic Achievement of Immigrants from Adolescent Families: The Roles of Family Background, Attitudes, and Behavior." *Child Development* 682:351–63.

Gamoran, A. 1996. "Effects of Schooling on Children and Families." Pp. 107–14 in *Family-School Links: How Do They Affect Educational Outcomes?* edited by A. Booth and J. F. Dunn. Hillsdale, NJ: Erlbaum.

Glick, J. E. and M. J. White. 2003. "The Academic Trajectories of Immigrant Youths: Analysis within and across Cohorts." *Demography* 40(4):759–83.

Hallinan, M. T. 2001. "Sociological Perspectives on Black–White Inequalities in American Schooling." *Sociology of Education* 74:50–70.

Hanushek, E. and S. Rivkin. 2009. "Harming the Best: How Schools Affect the Black–White Achievement Gap." *Journal of Policy Analysis and Management* 28(3):366–93.

Hauser, R., W. Sewell, and D. Alwin. 1976. "High School Effects on Achievement." Pp. 309–42 in *Schooling and Achievement in American Society*, edited by W. Sewell, R. Hauser, and D. Featherman. London: Academic Press.

Henderson, W. D. 2002. "Demography and Desegregation in the Cleveland Public Schools: Toward a Comprehensive Theory of Educational Failure and Success." *Review of Law and Social Change* 26(4):460–568.

Hochschild, J. and N. Scovronick. 2003. *The American Dream and the Public Schools*. New York: Oxford University Press.

Jencks, C. and E. Mayer. 1990. "The Social Consequences of Growing Up in a Poor Neighborhood." Pp. 111–86 in *Inner-city Poverty in the United States*, edited by L. E. Lynn Jr. & M. G. H. McGeary. Washington, DC: National Academy Press.

Jencks, C. and M. Phillips, eds. 1998. *The Black–White Test Score Gap*. Washington, DC: Brookings Institution.

Lee, V. and J. Smith. 1997. "High School Size: Which Works Best and for Whom?" *Educational Evaluation and Policy Analysis* 19(3):205–27.

Logan, J. 2002. "Choosing Segregation: Racial Imbalance in American Public Schools, 1990–2000." Report of the Lewis Mumford Center, March 29. Retrieved on 5 December 2011 from (http://www.s4.brown.edu/cen2000/SchoolPop/SPReport/SPDownload.pdf.

Logan, J., D. Oakley, and J. Stowell. 2008. "School Segregation in Metropolitan Regions, 1970–2000: The Impacts of Policy Choices on Public Education." *American Journal of Sociology* 113(6):1611–44.

Maruyama, G. 2003. "Disparities in Educational Opportunities and Outcomes: What Do We Know and What Can We Do?" *Journal of Social Issues* 59(3):653–76.

Mercer, J. and T. Scout. 1974. "The Relationship between School Desegregation and Changes in the Racial Composition of California School Districts 1963–73." University of California, Riverside. Unpublished paper.

Mickelson, R. 2003. "When Are Racial Disparities in Education the Result of Racial Discrimination? A Social Science Perspective." *Teachers College Record* 105(6):1052–86.

Orfield, G. and S. Eaton. 1996. *Dismantling Desegregation: The Quiet Reversal of* Brown v. Board of Education. New York: New Press.

Orfield, G. and C. Lee. 2005. *Why Segregation Matters: Poverty and Educational Inequality.* Cambridge, MA: Civil Rights Project at Harvard University.

Orfield, G. and J. Yun. 1999. *Resegregation in American Schools.* Cambridge. MA: Civil Rights Project at Harvard University. Retrieved December 14, 2010 http://course.cas.sc.edu/germanyk/post1945/materials/orfield_Resegregation_American_Schools99.pdf

Portes, A. and R. Rumbaut. 2001. *Legacies: The Story of the Immigrant Second Generation.* Berkeley: University of California Press.

Portes, A. and M. Zhou. 1993. "The New Second Generation: Segmented Assimilation and Its Variants." *Annals of the American Academy of Political and Social Science* 530:74–96.

Roscigno, V. 1998. "Race and the Reproduction of Educational Disadvantage." *Social Forces* 76:1033–60.

Rumberger, R. and G. Palardy. G. 2005. "Does Segregation Still Matter? The Impact of Student Composition on Academic Achievement in High School." *Teachers College Record* 107(9):1999–2045.

Rumberger, R. and J. Williams. 1992. "The Impact of Racial and Ethnic Segregation on the Achievement Gap in California High Schools." *Educational Evaluation and Policy Analysis* 14(4):377–96.

Saporito, S. and D. Sohoni. 2007. "Mapping Educational Inequality: Concentrations of Poverty among Poor and Minority Students in Public Schools." *Social Forces* 85(3):1227–53.

Schofield, J. 1995. "Review of Research on School Desegregation's Impact on Elementary and Secondary School Students." Pp. 597–617 in *Handbook of Research on Multicultural Education,* edited by J. A. Banks and C. A. McGee-Banks. New York: McMillan.

Schwartz, A. E. and L. Stiefel. 2006. "Is There a Nativity Gap? New Evidence on the Academic Performance of Immigrant Students." *Education Finance and Policy* 11:17–49.

Stiefel, L., A. Schwartz, and C. Chellman. 2008. "So Many Children Left Behind: Segregation and the Impact of Subgroup Reporting in No Child Left Behind on the Racial Test Score Gap." *Educational Policy* 21:527–41.

Swanson, C. 2008. *Cities in Crisis: A Special Analytic Report on High School Graduation.* Washington, DC: Editorial Projects in Education Research Center.

Wells, A. and R. Crain. 1994. "Perpetuation Theory and the Long-term Effects of School Desegregation." *Review of Educational Research* 64:531–55.

Whitman, M. 1998. *The Irony of Desegregation Law 1955–1995.* Princeton, NJ: Markus Wiener.

Zhou, M. and C. L. Bankston, III. 1998. *Growing Up American: How Vietnamese Children Adapt to Life in the United States.* New York: Russell Sage Foundation.

READING 29

THE DUALITY OF COURSES AND STUDENTS

A Field-Theoretic Analysis of Secondary School Course-Taking

Joseph J. Ferrare

While the first reading in this chapter addressed between-school inequalities, this reading by Joseph J. Ferrare looks to within-school inequalities in course-taking patterns. Using a complicated methodology that simultaneously examines the patterns of course-taking of individual students and the patterns of students in courses, Ferrare examines schools both structurally (vertical sequencing of courses within different academic tracks) and horizontally (courses that are not distributed along a vertical axis, or those that can be taken at any time without following a sequence of levels of difficulty such as art, business, keyboarding, music, or computer science). Interestingly, he finds that students tend to congregate in the same classes (space) with other students, segregated by social class in patterns of course-taking. Thus, there are structures and spaces within schools that also create inequalities in learning opportunities.

Questions to consider for this reading:

1. Describe how the mathematics or science courses were organized vertically in your high school. That is, what was the sequence of the courses in these subjects that you were required to take?

2. Thinking back to your own high school career, which combination of course-taking patterns did you take—vertical (the courses you were required to take) and horizontal (the courses you chose to take)?

3. Given the patterns that Ferrare describes, what might high schools do to encourage students to take more rigorous courses?

Courses serve as an important medium through which students become affiliated at specific places and times, thinking, acting, and speaking in certain ways. Put simply, students and courses constitute a social structure. Similar to any game that subjects players to an existing set of rules, this social structure is a patterning of relations into which students *and* courses are projected. When students enter secondary school, for example, they do not encounter a randomized curriculum or enroll in courses willy-nilly. Rather, students "bump" into the

From "The Duality of Courses and Students: A Field-Theoretic Analysis of Secondary School Course-Taking," by Joseph J. Ferrare, 2013, *Sociology of Education, 86*(2). Published by Sage Publications on behalf of the American Sociological Association. Copyright © ASA/Sage.

residual tracings of socio-curricular configurations that have preceded them through historical struggles and compromises. In this sense, the social structure of students and courses is capable of shaping thought and action across individual schools, albeit with often disparate and unexpected results. This is not to say that this social structure determines student actions or outcomes or that students do not "push back" in meaningful ways. Rather, to persist as a social structure, courses must be continuously integrated and segregated through the assiduous work of students.

For most contemporary researchers in this area of the literature, the "shape" of this social structure is formed by vertically ordered course affiliations between students. Thus, students who share courses in common will occupy similar positions or "tracks" that form a vertical hierarchy. Researchers have developed sophisticated techniques for constructing these positions (for reviews, see Gamoran 1989, 2010), which have then been used to investigate a number of important questions. These questions have focused on the factors that predict students' position or track placement (e.g., Kelly 2004; Lucas and Gamoran 1993), as well as the implications this position has for their standardized test scores and postsecondary trajectories (e.g., Gamoran 1987; Sorensen and Hallinan 1986).

While researchers have made significant progress in this productive area of the literature (for reviews, see Gamoran 2010; Oakes, Gamoran, and Page 1992), there remains a gap in our understanding of the social structure of students and courses. Although much has been learned about how the organization of courses has meaningful consequences for students, very little attention has been paid to how the organization of students has meaningful consequences for courses and the content contained within and between them. That is, just as students are differentiated through the courses they share in common, courses, too, become integrated and segregated through the students they co-enroll. To speak of social structure in this context, then, is to specify a *duality* that is constituted by affiliations within and between a space of students and a space of courses. Yet—as a distinct unit of analysis—the space of courses has received limited attention within this area of the literature.

The following article attempts to address this aspect of the literature by illustrating that a more targeted analysis of the entire space of courses can contribute to a deeper sociological understanding of the social organization of a high school's curriculum. In particular, this article proceeds to make two distinct contributions. First, I will demonstrate how a secondary school's curriculum becomes organized in practice through a duality of student and course affiliations that take shape over a four-year period. The social organization of secondary school curriculum is thus conceptualized as courses—and the curricular discourses they contain—occupying positions in a multidimensional space. In addition, beyond considering only the vertical hierarchy of secondary school courses (e.g., advanced/general/remedial courses), I introduce a "horizontal" form of differentiation that serves as an important principle of organization within the curriculum.

Second, I examine the space of courses in relation to student attributes and postsecondary trajectories and argue that the different regions of this space represent relational strategies associated with students' position within this local social structure. That is, in addition to examining how the curriculum is organized through the social practice of course-taking, I also investigate "who" is organizing "which" particular segments of the curriculum. This contribution involves thinking theoretically about the duality of students and courses as a curricular "field," and to proceed with this work I draw from field theory and curriculum theory. Further, this theoretical work is undertaken in conversation with longitudinal course-taking, demographic, and postsecondary trajectory data collected from a large comprehensive secondary school in the midwestern United States. To model the duality of students and courses at this secondary school I use multidimensional scaling and multiple correspondence analysis. These techniques contain an inherent logic that is consistent with the overall theoretical logic of the analysis, a point that speaks to a subtext underlying the entire work. . . .

CURRICULAR TRACKS, POSITIONS, AND SPACES

Conventional research focusing on the social organization of secondary school curriculum has typically focused on discrete categories or "tracks" (e.g., academic/nonacademic, advanced placement/general/remedial, etc.). These categories have formed into a pervasive discourse, making it difficult to speak or think of the curriculum without them—even in the absence of an explicitly rigid tracking system. To be sure, many researchers have responded to the absence of an explicitly rigid system of tracking by developing a range of strategies for uncovering the more implicit system observed in secondary schools today. . . .

Another insightful strategy has been to construct "social positions" using techniques from social network analysis. . . . In network terms, an affiliation matrix is a two-mode data set consisting of a set of actors (e.g., students) and a set of events (e.g., courses). . . .

[While previous works] may vary in the way they derive students' positions within the sociocurricular order, they each similarly give primary attention to students and the way they are organized through the courses they share in common. Meanwhile, courses are only important insofar as they provide a medium through which students are grouped (or "tracked") and subsequently provided access to specific peer relations and learning opportunities. This emphasis on students is certainly reasonable given the sociological context of the work, and as noted earlier, this approach has yielded a number of important insights. However, the result of this student-centric focus has been a theoretical understanding that foregrounds students while drowning out

courses as a distinct unit of analysis. As a result, there have been few attempts to conceptualize—let alone analyze—students and courses as components comprising a distinct "whole."

Some sociologists of education have begun to think about course-taking in this way. . . . That is, while each student has a course profile specifying the courses they share in common with other students, each course has a student profile indicating the students that course shares in common with other courses. . . .

A key insight from this work is its recognition of the inherent "duality" between students and courses. That is, on the one hand, students who share similar courses in common will occupy spatially proximal (or "structurally equivalent" in network terms) positions. Courses, on the other hand, that co-enroll similar students will also occupy spatially proximal positions with other courses.

* * *

CASCADE HIGH SCHOOL

The primary source of data for this analysis comes in the form of longitudinal course enrollment and transcript data files for a comprehensive secondary school located in a suburban midwestern city with a population of approximately 57,000 (according to a 2009 census estimate). This suburb is adjacent to an urban city of approximately 200,000 residents and resides within a metropolitan area with a population of approximately 560,000. The median household income in this city is approximately $61,000 according to a 2009 census estimate, with 91.9 percent of the total population being white, 2.5 percent African American, 3.9 percent Asian, and 4.8 percent Latino/a (of any race).

The school—which I will refer to as Cascade High School (CHS)—has an enrollment of approximately 1,900 students and 125 certified staff members (of which approximately 75 percent hold at least a master's degree). The school offers a wide range of courses in art, business, computer science, language arts and reading, family and consumer sciences, mathematics, music, science, social studies, technology education, world languages, physical education, and a miscellaneous group of courses. There is also an extensive special education program available to those deemed to have special needs. Finally, a handful of students also take courses at an elite International Baccalaureate World School situated in the adjacent urban school district.

Students must have a minimum of 48 credits to graduate. The required distribution of credits includes 8 credits in language arts and reading, 1 credit in art, 6 credits in mathematics (including 2 credits in algebra), 4 credits in physical education, and 6 credits in both science and social studies. That is a total of 31 credits (61.4 percent of the total minimum to graduate). However, the actual number of required courses is a different matter. The only specific courses that are required are Language and Literature (2 credits, typically taken in grade nine), Speech Communication (1 credit), Fundamentals of Writing (1 credit), General Science (2 credits, typically taken in grade nine), U.S. History (2 credits) or American Heritage (2 credits), Economics (1 credit), and Government (1 credit). This means that only 10 of the 48 credits (20.8 percent) required to graduate are prespecified, and all others are "chosen." Thus, on paper, there is a considerable amount of flexibility in the range of courses that students are able to enroll.

* * *

Discussion

Toward a Field Theory for Sociology of Curriculum

At the outset of this article, I argued that a field-theoretic analysis of the duality of students and courses encourages us to consider the organization of students and courses concomitantly and as a distinct "whole." Thus, both students *and* courses occupy relational positions in a field of course-taking. By examining the dimensions underlying the space of courses on its own and in relation to student attributes and postsecondary trajectories, we were able to see that these positions have a conceptual coherence (or logic) that suggests a certain "causal texture" to course-taking at Cascade High School. This causal texture contains "information on how to construct meaningful trajectories of appropriate action" (Martin 2011:316). To apply Martin's (2011) metaphor to the present case, we might think of course-taking as similar to a scavenger hunt where each course or set of courses suggests to students which courses they should take next. At Cascade High School, this social organization of courses is not only differentiated by vertical positions of status, prestige, discursive forms, and course sequences, but also horizontal positions that oppose symbolic, artistic, and intrinsic knowledge to material, technical, and extrinsic knowledge.

We also saw that at Cascade High School the organization of course-taking corresponds to divisions of academic labor across racial, class, and sexual categories. Each student is positioned within these divisions in a way that makes certain course and student affiliations probable and improbable. At Cascade High School, this means for those intending to pursue the military, employment, or even the community college postsecondary trajectory, for example, their position does not include opportunities to think through many of the integrative and specialized discourses associated with music, language arts, mathematics, science, and world languages. In this sense, the social relations that constitute the field of course-taking differentially constrain and afford certain conceptual connections made available through specific courses and the forms of curricular discourse they offer. Note that there are no magical "mechanisms" at work here: it is the patterns of course-taking that afford some conceptual connections while making others more difficult. A student who enrolls in AP [Advanced Placement] Physics and Computer Science will be afforded very different potential conceptual linkages than a student who enrolls in AP Art and Anatomy.

The field of course-taking does not only differentiate the possible conceptual connections available to particular students. So often we limit our thought to the perspective of students and how the differential access to knowledge content and forms shapes their opportunities and identities. However, as a social structure that is constituted by a duality, it is also the case that the patterns of relations constituting this "field" differentiate the students available to particular courses. To take this aspect of the duality seriously means that we must be willing to think from the perspective of courses and the curricular discourses they contain and how the differential access to (raced, classed, and gendered) students—and their postsecondary trajectories—shapes curricular organization. Heretofore, the role of courses within this duality has been relegated to the passive medium through which students are grouped and provided disparate learning opportunities. Yet the curricular discourses made available in courses are also (at least potentially) grouped and subsequently integrated and segregated through the students they co-enroll. These curricular discourses are not only influential, then, but they are also influenced (again, at least potentially). That is, whether or not particular students enroll in (say) Advanced Contemporary Literature or Sports Marketing matters to those students as *well* as to the curricular discourses contained within these courses and those with which they share students in common.

[In] closing I will note that students do act as an important medium through which curricular discourses are integrated and segregated, making the construction of certain meanings possible (and others impossible). In this case, the production and organization of the curriculum is contingent upon those who are able to think and integrate its categories of thought and perception. "Socialization into knowledge," Bernstein (1977:97–8) says, "is socialization into order, the existing order, into the experience that the world's educational knowledge is impermeable."

Yet we must also acknowledge the other side of the duality: that knowledge, too, is brought into order, the existing *social* order(s). The field of course-taking, then, is not simply an ordering and positioning of students through the organization of courses or "tracks." Rather, it consists of the mutual constitution of these two spaces (i.e., a "field") that together allow us to examine what can be thought, who can think it, and—with further investigation—when, where, and how such thought takes place. Thus, the field of course-taking does not *explain* the pattern of relations between students and courses; it is the pattern of relations (Martin 2011).

Additional work needs to be done to link the phenomenological experiences of students directly to the positions in the field of course-taking. An important step toward this end is to learn how students draw upon their cultural resources to construct educational meanings and strategies from the curricular discourses affiliated with their positions. There is already evidence that many high school students are well aware of the variety of curricular trajectories and course configurations at their school. This fact has long been suggested in the literature (e.g., see Oakes [1985] 2005), and more recent evidence indicates that students cultivate academic strategies in relation to local course-taking patterns even in the absence of formal tracking contexts (see O'Connor el al. 2011). In addition, the underlying structure of course-taking at Cascade High School suggests that students are piecing together configurations of courses with a conceptual coherence that goes beyond course sequences and requirements. Exactly how—and to what effect—students weave together curricular discourses from these course configurations remains a pressing question for sociologists of curriculum.

Another important consideration is whether the patterning of this field of course-taking derives its logic entirely from its two constituent spaces. Recall that the logic within the space of courses is not a mere reflection of the logic organizing the space of students. Yet the properties of this duality are such that the organization of the space of courses must pass through the organization of the space of students (and dually). Since the field of course-taking is but one of many social fields and institutional layers that students and their families simultaneously traverse, some of the information they retrieve from those social environments is conceivably at work in the field of courses. Perhaps this is why we can observe a substantively familiar social hierarchy in the space of students while simultaneously observing substantively unique principles of organization in the space of courses that are, nonetheless, familiar in form.

REFERENCES

Bernstein, Basil B. 1977. *Class Codes and Control Volume 3: Towards a Theory of Educational Transmissions,* 2nd ed. London: Routledge and Kegan Paul.

Gamoran, Adam. 1987. "The Stratification of High School Learning Opportunities." *Sociology of Education* 60:135–55.

Gamoran, Adam. 1989. "Measuring Curriculum Differentiation." *American Journal of Education* 97:129–43.

Gamoran, Adam. 2010. "Tracking and Inequality: New Directions for Research and Practice." Pp. 213–28 in *The Routledge International Handbook of the Sociology of Education*, edited by M. W. Apple, S. J. Hall, and L. A. Gondin. London and New York: Routledge.

Kelly, Sean. 2004. "Do Increased Levels of Parental Involvement Account for Social Class Differences in Track Placement?" *Social Science Research* 33:626–59.

Lucas, Samuel R. 1990. "Course-based Indicators of Curricular Track Locations." Master's thesis, Department of Sociology, University of Wisconsin, Madison, Madison, WI.

Lucas, Samuel R. and Adam Gamoran. 1993. *Race and Track Assignment: A Reconsideration with Course-based Indicators of Track Locations.* Madison, WI: Center on Organization and Restructuring of Schools.

Martin, John Levi. 2011. *The Explanation of Social Action.* Oxford: Oxford University Press.

Oakes, Jeannie. [1985] 2005. *Keeping Track: How Schools Structure Inequality*, 2nd ed. New Haven, CT: Yale University Press.

Oakes, Jeannie, Adam Gamoran, and Reba Page. 1992. "Curriculum Differentiation: Opportunities. Outcomes, and Meanings." Pp. 570–608 in *Handbook of Research on Curriculum*, edited by P. W. Jackson. New York: Macmillan.

O'Connor, Carla, Jennifer Mueller, R. L'Heureaux Lewis, Deborah Rivas-Drake, and Seneca Rosenberg. 2011. "Being Black and Strategizing for Excellence in a Racially Stratified Academic Hierarchy." *American Educational Research Journal* 48:1232–57.

Sorensen, Aage B. and Maureen T. Hallinan. 1986. "Effects of Ability Grouping on Growth in Academic Achievement." *American Educational Research Journal* 23:519–42.

BEYOND THE SCHOOLYARD

The Role of Parenting Logics, Financial Resources, and Social Institutions in the Social Class Gap in Structured Activity Participation

Pamela R. Bennett, Amy C. Lutz, and Lakshmi Jayaram

Research supports the fact that the social environments in which children are raised affects their in-school achievement. Out-of-school and summer activities also affect children's achievement through the experiences they gain in sports, lessons in the arts, museum visits, vacation trips, camp programs, and academic or religious clubs and organizations, thus affecting children's future college and job opportunities. In this reading, Pamela R. Bennett, Amy C. Lutz, and Lakshmi Jayaram report findings from data gathered from semistructured interviews with parents at two racially and ethnically diverse middle schools located in a large northeastern city. One of these schools was located in a middle-class community and the other a working-class community. In all, the researchers interviewed 22 middle-class and 29 working-class parents of eighth-grade children. Unfortunately, given space constraints, we had to cut some of the quotes from parents in our presentation of their findings, but the following excerpt gives you the summaries of their data.

Questions to consider for this reading:

1. What differences in structured activity participation (after-school and school activities) of children were found by Bennett, Lutz, and Jayaram?

2. Why do these differences exist in structured activity participation, and do they perpetuate class differences?

3. If you were a policy maker in these communities, what would you do to equalize opportunities?

Prior research links participation in structured activities to social stratification through its effects on college attendance and destination (Kaufman and Gabler 2004; Karabel 2005; Gabler and Kaufman 2006; Soares 2007; Stevens 2007). To the extent that disadvantaged groups evidence lower participation than advantaged ones, organized activities become a mechanism through which social inequality is maintained and reproduced. A class

---

From "Beyond the Schoolyard: The Role of Parenting Logics, Financial Resources, and Social Class Gap in Structured Activity Participation," by Pamela R. Bennett, Amy C. Lutz, and Lakshmi Jayaram, 2013, *Sociology of Education*, 85(3). Published by Sage Publications on behalf of the American Sociological Association. Copyright © ASA/Sage.

gap in participation is well established, yet disagreement exists over explanations for its cause, with some authors focusing on cultural explanations and others on more structural ones (Furstenberg et al. 1999; Lareau 2002, 2003; Hofferth 2008; Hughes 2008; Lareau and Weininger 2008). We adopt an approach that allows us to explicitly recognize that social behavior often sits at the intersection of beliefs about what s*hould* occur (as informed by culture) and the *ability* to actualize those beliefs (as shaped by structure): Based on qualitative interviews with parents at two urban schools, we report findings on working- and middle-class children's level and type of activity participation, parents' expressed cultural logic regarding participation, and parents' reasons for enrolling their own children in structured activities.

We find that working-class parents use participation in organized activities as part of their parenting strategies and articulate many of the same reasons for doing so as their middle-class counterparts. Further, we find that the in-school activity profiles of working- and middle-class youth are strikingly similar, while the two groups differ in their out-of-school activities. That the class gap in activity participation is small within schools but substantial outside of schools suggests that schools play a critical role in equalizing access to activity participation opportunities across social class groups. What requires explanation, then, is not the lack of involvement in activities by working-class youth, but their low levels of participation in activities that are not organizationally tied to schools.

We argue that because of financial constraints, working-class families rely on social institutions for affordable participation opportunities, but have access to few such institutions beyond schools and churches, which are the ones prevalent in their neighborhoods. This is consistent with beliefs expressed by working-class parents regarding the value of activity participation for their children, the concentration of their children's participation in school and religious activities, as well as the virtual lack of participation outside of school in the kinds of elite activities

that colleges and universities value. Thus, almost a decade after publication of Lareau's (2002) influential study, we find that working-class parents in our sample are quite supportive of organized activities, but their children participate in fewer and different activities than their middle-class counterparts due to limited financial and institutional resources. We conclude that greater emphasis on organized activities by working-class parents is insufficient to close the class gap in activity participation because of structural constraints that they face.

SOCIAL CLASS AS CULTURE AND SOCIAL CLASS AS STRUCTURAL LOCATION

We argue that to fully understand class differences in youth participation in organized activities, we must extend our analytical lens beyond parenting logics to include the structural location of families. Doing so will help us distinguish between conceptualizing social behavior as the product of values, beliefs, and attitudes that people hold on the one hand and conceiving of behavior as structured by differential access to resources—the result of what Barry Wellman (1983:163) terms the "social distribution of possibilities." Only then can we identify the ways in which social class acts as culture and as structure in producing group differences in activity participation.

In *Unequal Childhoods: Class, Race, and Family Life,* Lareau ([2003] 2011) argues that divergent cultural logics exist among America's social classes, leading to differential management of children's time, including the time they spend in organized activities. In the middle-class homes in her study, she observed what she terms "concerted cultivation"—a cultural logic to parenting practices that emphasizes structure, language use, and interaction with dominant social institutions. In contrast, working-class and poor families displayed what she calls the "accomplishment of natural growth," which involves relatively unstructured days, use of directives with children, and general avoidance—even distrust—of dominant social institutions. Although middle-class parents use enrollment in extracurricular activities as a means to cultivate children's talents and skill, working-class parents, according to Lareau, are comfortable giving their children comparatively greater autonomy in how they spend free time and emphasize enrollment in activities less (Lareau [2003] 2011; Lareau and Weininger 2008). As a result, middle-class and working-class children evidence different levels of involvement in structured activities. When combined with other class differences in parenting strategies, class gaps in activity participation help to reproduce social class advantage and disadvantage across generations.

Chin and Phillips (2004) come to a different conclusion. They investigate the ways in which cultural, social, and "child" capital shape children's participation in organized activities in the summer. Findings from their research suggest that class differences in activities arise from differences in financial resources, knowledge of ways to develop children's interests, and information about how to connect children to activities.

An ecological perspective on social behavior implicates parenting practices in class gaps in structured activity participation, but in a different way than Lareau's work, by conceiving of parenting as the result of characteristics and processes that take place not only within the family (i.e., Lareau's focus) but also in neighborhoods and the wider community in which the family is embedded (Bronfenbrenner 1979; Luster and Okagaki 2005; Kotchick and Forehand 2002). Indeed, there is a growing literature on the relationship between neighborhood context and parenting, with much of it reporting negative relationships between disadvantaged neighborhood conditions (e.g., poverty, level of danger) and desirable parenting practices (e.g., demonstration of warmth, consistent discipline) (Klebanov, Brooks-Gunn, and Duncan 1994; Mohr, Fantuzzo, and Abdul-Kabir 2001; Pinderhughes et al. 2001; Letiecq and Koblinsky 2004). For example, Furstenberg et al. (1999) investigate neighborhood effects on parenting strategies in urban areas. They find two approaches to emerge: promotive strategies (which nurture and develop children's talents and opportunities) and preventive strategies (which attempt to reduce children's exposure to dangerous circumstances). Parents in high-resource neighborhoods are more likely to engage in promotive strategies by enrolling their children in structured activities, while parents in low-resource communities are more likely to use preventive strategies, primarily through keeping their children at home. . . .

Likewise, class differences in activity participation may reflect differences in the school context of working- and middle-class children, yet processes of social reproduction and leveling by schools have yet to be fully explored with respect to class gaps in structured activity participation. School systems in the United States are characterized by both racial and class segregation, which create the conditions under which working- and middle-class children attend separate and, often, qualitatively different schools (Kozol 1992, 2005; Orfield and Eaton 1996). Bourdieu (1977) most famously theorized the ways in which schools reproduce social inequalities. McNeal (1999) considers how school structure and composition impact students' participation in organized activities. He finds that school size and climate significantly affect participation, such that students in large schools and schools with difficult climates display lower levels of activity involvement. But size and climate are not the only features of schools that may matter. Teachers and administrators serve as gatekeepers to slots in extracurricular activities, recruiting students they perceive to be talented while restricting others who are disqualified by academic standards (McNeal 1998). Lower academic achievement among working- versus middle-class youth, in combination with teachers' evaluations that may fall along class lines, may contribute to social class gaps in activity participation.

Conversely, schools may serve to narrow class differences in activity participation by equalizing opportunities to participate. Several researchers have revealed how schools ameliorate social class differences in a variety of educational outcomes (Holloway and Fuller 1992; Entwisle and Alexander 1992; Downey, von

Hippel, and Broh 2004; Condron 2009). Because a myriad of structured activities are offered for little or no cost in public schools, schools may provide students with limited financial resources more opportunities to participate in activities than are available outside of school. To the extent that public schools that serve working-class youth offer a variety of organized activities, schools may have a "leveling" effect on class differences in participation much the same way they do with respect to other educational outcomes (Entwisle and Alexander 1992). Neighborhood institutions may play a similar role by offering low-cost activity options that are easily accessible, both financially and geographically, to working-class families. The leveling effect that schools and neighborhood institutions may have on organized activity participation has, thus far, been little explored in the literature.

* * *

Social Class Differences in Structured Activity Participation

Parents report a total of 189 nonunique activities in which their children participated during their eighth-grade year, ranging from as few as none to as many as 10 per child. Consistent with prior studies (Lareau [2003] 2011; Chin and Phillips 2004; Dumais 2006; Lareau and Weininger (2008), we observe class differences in participation, with the middle class having participated in the most activities (5.0 per child) and the working class having participated in the least (2.4 per child), on average. . . . Examining the frequency distribution for working- and middle-class families reveals further differences between them. Middle-class families are much more evenly distributed across the entire range of activity participation than are working-class families. . . . The majority of working-class families are concentrated at the lowest levels of participation, with three of them reporting no activities. Nevertheless, participation among working-class

children is not trivial. Collectively, working-class parents report 74 nonunique activities. Additionally, involvement in activities is widespread among working-class families; 26 of 29 families report activities in which their child(ren) participated.

Among the children in our sample who participated in multiple activities, it is typically the case that they were involved in different activities rather than multiple instances of the same activity. In other words, although some youth may have played, for example, the same sport both at school and on a neighborhood team, most youth became involved in myriad activities during the span of their eighth-grade year. Two examples illustrate the point: Quentin, a white child from a working-class family, participated in four activities: golfing at school, science club, serving as a library assistant, and participating in a program that teaches leadership skills to youth. Nathan, a white child from a middle-class family, participated in seven activities: street hockey, soccer, baseball, and private music lessons. He also attended synagogue and Hebrew school and participated in a youth group at the synagogue. . . .

There are, however, differences in the kinds of activities in which working- and middle-class families invested their time, money, and energies. Three are worth nothing. First, religious activities—often church attendance—account for a sizeable percentage of the activities of working-class children but only a small proportion of those of middle-class children (23.0 percent compared to 8.7 percent). Second, hobby activities, such as chess, were relatively popular among middle-class children but account for a much smaller percentage of the activities of their working-class peers (11.3 percent vs. 4.0 percent). And third, participation in youth-development activities is almost absent among middle-class children, though it accounts for 9.3 percent of the activities of working-class children.

Together, these findings reveal that while activity participation among working-class families is not as high as it is among their middle-class counterparts, participation is routine for them. Children from both social classes participated heavily in sports and cultural activities, which are precisely the kinds of activities that are expected to have implications for later educational outcomes. Kaufman and Gabler (2004), for example, find that participation in interscholastic sports is associated with increased likelihood of attending college. Such activities are expected to facilitate students' academic achievement by helping them create identities that are tied to their school and its mission. Likewise, cultural activities are associated with increased odds of attending elite colleges, as participation in such activities may signal to teachers and admissions officers that students are familiar with and appreciate middle-class norms and culture (Soares 2007). That working- and middle-class children heavily participate in such activities suggests that both groups of parents have positioned their children in activities that may pay educational dividends. These commonalities exist in the presence of an important difference, however. Despite meaningful participation in cultural activities by working-class children, adolescents from middle-class families have even greater involvement in such activities, in addition to higher participation in hobby clubs, both of which are associated with enrollment in elite colleges and universities (Kaufman and Gabler 2004; Gabler and Kaufman 2006), while working-class children make greater investments in religious activities.

PARENTS' EXPRESSED CULTURAL LOGIC

Parents' Responses to the Structured Activity Participation Scenario

For our first approach to assessing parents' beliefs about involving children in organized activities, we analyze their responses to our *structured activity participation scenario.* . . . The scenario is designed to free parents from the particular constraints in their personal lives so that they may express their "conceptions of the desirable" (Kohn [1969] 1977:7), unencumbered by what they feel is merely possible. In it, we

describe the activities and schedule of a fictional child. The scenario reads:

> Some children participate in many school and out-of-school activities. For example, let's take an 8th grader who plays in the school band, which means he/she has band practice for an hour and a half three times a week after school. He/She also plays on a neighborhood sports team and has practice every Saturday afternoon and has a game once a week. Sometimes the games are away and so he/she travels with the team.

After we read this scenario to parents, we invited their responses with the question: "What do you think of this child's level of participation in extracurricular activities?" . . .

There are several points to take away from this. . . . First, a similar percentage of working- and middle-class parents respond positively to the fictional child's level of activity participation—58.6 percent and 45.5 percent, respectively, indicated it was "good" or "great." Moreover, parents of both classes indicate caveats to their positive disposition toward the schedule of activities. Yet, those caveats reveal possible differences in concerns between the two groups. Working-class parents were concerned with whether the child's activities interfered with their ability to do well in school (17.2 percent) while proportionally fewer middle-class parents expressed that concern (9.1 percent). Veronica, a Latina immigrant working-class mother who was out of work but seeking employment at the time of the interview, says:

> I think [the fictional child's level of participation in activities is] excellent. Um . . . only if, if he can maintain his grades. If he can't . . . that's what I tell my daughter . . . my kids, "If you can maintain your grades, have good grades, then you can participate." If I see that the grades are slipping, then I tell them "no." . . .

Second, working- and middle-class parents are similar in their assessment that the amount of participation in our scenario is unequivocally too much for our fictional child (31.0 percent and 27.3 percent, respectively). Moreover, they arrive at that assessment for similar reasons. Both groups express concerns about (1) the lack of rest or downtime such a schedule would afford the child, (2) the complicated logistics and stress placed on parents inherent in such a schedule, and (3) the amount of time such a schedule requires. Working-class parents in this "too much" group differ from their middle-class peers only in their concern that a busy activity schedule might lower the amount of time the fictional child has available to do homework.

Perhaps working- and middle-class parents are similar in their assessment of the scenario, in part, because some middle-class parents, but no working-class parents, made their responses contingent on the child in question. Almost a fifth (18.2 percent) of middle-class parents indicate that they could only evaluate the level of participation of our fictional child in light of what the child wants or is capable of managing successfully. For example, Bette, a white, middle-class attorney, states:

> I think it depends on the kid. There are some kids that thrive on that and there are some kids who stress on that. So, it just really depends on the kid. . . .

Parents' Support for Their Children's Activity Participation

To understand parents' cultural logics, we also analyze their thoughts about and reasons for supporting their own children's participation (or nonparticipation) in structured activities. Although a variety of reasons for activity participation emerge within and across social classes, the majority of reasons fall into a relatively small set of categories. While other research finds that working-class parents support a parenting philosophy that does not emphasize enrollment in organized activities (Lareau [2003] 2011), we find much support for children's participation within the working-class sample. Moreover, working- and middle-class parents offer similar reasons for their children's participation, such as supporting their child's interest in an activity, keeping active, personal development, increasing the academic skills of their children, and providing a venue for children to socialize with peers. We find, nevertheless, that working-class parents offer a number of reasons that are scarcely mentioned by their middle-class counterparts. Both groups of reasons—common ones and those unique to working-class parents—are explored below.

Shared Reasons for Supporting Participation in Structured Activities

Child's interest. For many parents in both social classes, their child's interest in an activity is a primary reason for supporting it. . . .

Personal development. Both middle- and working-class parents cite personal development as a primary reason for their children's participation in activities. Personal development through organized activities can include the learning of values of the larger society or social group (e.g., learning to cooperate with others), the development of adolescents' personal qualities (e.g., overcoming shyness or gaining emotional well-being and maturity), or the learning of personal skills or lessons that may be useful or advantageous to have as children grow and transition into adulthood (e.g., how to persevere or handle rejection). . . .

Academic knowledge. Many parents across social class cite the acquisition of academic knowledge as an important reason for participation in extracurricular activities. This reason is primarily offered by parents whose children participate in tutoring programs or academic teams. . . .

Keeping active. Another reason for activity participation given by both working- and middle-class parents is that it keeps their children busy and active. For example, Grace says, "I don't see any drawbacks [to participation in activities]. The benefits—that it keeps her busy." Juliette, a working-class black Caribbean nurse's aide, says, "You know, that's me. Keep her busy, you know." . . .

Socializing. Both middle-class and working-class parents indicated that they appreciate extra-curricular activities because they give children an opportunity to get to know and socialize with other kids. For example. Holly, a white middle-class social worker whose son participates in basketball at school and basketball, baseball, and football outside of school, says, "the benefits are, you know, definitely socializing." . . .

Variation Across Social Class in Support for Participation in Structured Activities

While middle- and working-class parents share some reasons for supporting involvement in extra-curricular activities or viewing them as beneficial, other reasons for participation were particular to working-class parents.

Safety. Ten working-class parents (but no middle-class parents) cite keeping children safe and away from trouble as an important reason for their children's participation in structured activities. These parents describe their neighborhoods as dangerous places and prefer to see their children stay in the environment of school or other locations where organized activities take place. Among those who cite safety as a primary reason for their children's activity participation, 80 percent also articulate concerns about the level of danger in their neighborhood environment. . . .

Future opportunities. Another reason for supporting their child's involvement in structured activities given by some working-class parents (five), but no middle-class parents, is that structured activities are linked to future opportunities. In this sense, working-class parents see their children's activity participation as part of a plan for their children's social mobility. Some parents see a link between activities and educational success, while others see the activities themselves as pathways to future opportunities. . . .

For some of the working-class parents in our sample, structured activities are not only desirable for their intrinsic value, [but] they are important for their utility in securing future opportunities.

Making Sense of Parents' Support for Youth Participation in Structured Activities

Overall, parents of both social classes are overwhelmingly supportive of their children's participation in organized activities. Among those who view participation positively, 19 parents expressed some drawbacks to it, which for most (16) include concerns about time, rushing, transportation, and potential overscheduling that could reduce time for family, homework, and relaxation. These concerns are raised primarily by middle-class parents (12), particularly small business owners whose children are involved in more activities than children of other middle-class families. In only one case is a parent mostly unsupportive of activity participation; in this instance, a working-class father is unsupportive of his daughter's involvement in activities (sports, in particular) because of concerns about outside influences on her. However, even this father expresses that he would like his daughter to take voice lessons but cannot afford them.

Together, our findings raise questions about the extent to which cultural logics explain the class gap in involvement in structured activities. Working-class parents in our study show a great deal of support for participation in organized activities in general and for their children's participation in particular, as do middle-class parents. To the extent that working-class families voice concerns about active participation schedules, they do so with concerns for children's academic performance in mind. They also worry about coping with the logistics of getting children back and forth to activities given school and work schedules, along with the stress heavy participation places on parents themselves. These concerns are similarly voiced by middle-class parents.

Consistent with prior work, however, is evidence that middle-class parents are interested in customizing their children's experiences (Lareau [2003] 2011). Almost a fifth (18.2%) of middle-class parents, but no working-class parents, attempt to evaluate the activity schedule of our fictional child only from the perspective of the child's wishes, talents, and ability to handle the commitments that such a schedule entails. For this group of middle-class parents, there is no universal value placed on a highly active versus a somewhat inactive participation schedule that exists apart from the child's specific abilities.

Some of the reasons for supporting participation among the working-class [parents] are similar to those of middle-class parents (such as the child's interest, personal development, and the acquisition of academic knowledge). However, some working-class parents, but no middle-class parents, primarily cite a desire to keep their children safe and, to a lesser extent, shape future outcomes. In this way, working-class parents appear to use structured activities as part of a preventive parenting strategy (i.e., enrolling children in activities to keep them busy, out of the neighborhood, and safe) and as a promotive strategy (i.e., to open doors to future opportunities such as college or career entry) (Furstenberg et al. 1999). . . .

Our findings on parents' practices (i.e., enrollment of children in activities) combine with our findings on their expressed logic to reveal a puzzle—differences in the behavior of working- and middle-class parents but substantial overlap in their perspectives on activity participation. That is, class differences in behavior do not appear to reflect class differences in parenting logics regarding organized activities. In the next section, we attempt to shed light on the question that has emerged from our data: Why do working-class youth demonstrate less participation in structured activities than their middle-class counterparts given similarities in their parents' perspectives on the value and desirability of participation? The answer, we argue, lies in what our data reveal [about] the role that structure plays in the lives of working-class families.

SCHOOLS AS EQUALIZING INSTITUTIONS

We draw a distinction between school and out-of-school activities to investigate structural influences on activity participation. We find that a clear majority of the activities in which working-class children participate are school-based activities; more than half (60 percent) of their activities are organizationally tied to the school compared to only 40 percent of the activities of middle-class youth. Moreover, the class gap in activity participation is smaller in school activities than in out-of-school activities. Working-class youth participate in an average of 1.5 school activities, which compares favorably to the 2.0 school activities in which middle-class children participate. . . . Where working-class children fall short, and much shorter than their middle-class counterparts, is in participation in out-of-school activities. In these, they participate in less than one activity, on average, compared to 3.0 activities among the middle class.

These findings have at least three implications. First, schools serve as a critical avenue through which the children of working-class families become involved in organized activities. Second, where opportunities for participation are readily available, working-class parents demonstrate an interest in and commitment to supplementing the lives of their children by investing time, energy, and money in their children's involvement in activities. Finally, without the opportunities for participation that schools provide, the social class gap in activity involvement would likely be much larger than that previously documented.

That working- and middle-class children differentially become involved in school versus non-school activities has implications not just for their level of participation but also for the *kinds* of activities in which they participate. . . . The working-class and middle-class distributions for school-based activities are somewhat similar. Both groups display high levels of participation in sports and cultural activities and, to a lesser extent, academic and school service activities. Middle-class children have greater participation, however, in hobby activities while having no involvement in youth-development activities. These class differences, however, are rather small compared to those found in out-of-school activities.

Working- and middle-class families differ strikingly in their non-school activities. Middle-class children display heavy participation in cultural and sports activities, with less participation in academic and hobby activities. Thus, their investments in activities outside of school mirror, to some extent, those they make in school. In contrast, working-class children invest heavily in religious activities, often regular church attendance, church choir, or church youth group. Although these children also participate in cultural, sports, and academic activities outside of school, they do so to a much lower degree than they do in school. Thus, it appears that the decisions that working-class parents and children make about where to invest time, energy, and resources outside of school are rather different than the choices they make about which activities to pursue in school. . . .

Research on the academic consequences of participation in organized activities suggests that certain school-based activities may increase the odds that students will be admitted to college, while other activities may raise their chances of enrolling in selective colleges (Eccles and Barber 1999). Gabler and Kaufman (2006) find, for example, that participation in music, student government, and interscholastic sports is associated with an increased likelihood of attending college, while participation in hobby clubs, school yearbook, and school newspaper increases the chances of attending an elite university. Using these findings as an evaluative lens on the activity choice-set offered at our two schools, we find that the middle-class school offers its students somewhat greater opportunities to participate in activities that may pay educational dividends in terms of college attendance and selectivity.

Before reporting on the differences between the two schools, however, we describe their similarities. First, the two schools offer a similar number of structured activities. . . . Second, there is overlap in the choice-set of activities available to students at the two schools, particularly with regard to sports and school service activities. Both schools offer students the opportunity to participate in team sports (e.g., flag football, basketball, softball, and volleyball), serve on yearbook committees, publish literary magazines, and work in libraries alongside school librarians. Both schools also offer an array of academic activities. In sum, both schools offer students opportunities to participate in activities that have the potential to pay educational dividends.

However, there are meaningful differences in the range of activities available at the two schools. In particular, they offer markedly different hobby and cultural activities, which may have implications for the educational trajectories of students.

The most notable differences between the two schools reside in hobby and cultural activities. Although the working-class school offers a greater variety of hobby activities, the qualitative differences between them and those offered by the middle-class school are substantial. In one hobby activity, chess, the middle-class school is rather unique in that it offers its students expert-level instruction such that its team is able to compete nationally. There are no expert-level hobby activities at the working-class school. Moreover, the middle-class school offers a number of cultural activities that research suggests may serve as credentials that boost students' chances of attending college by signaling to teachers and college admissions officers that students either come from middle-class backgrounds or have elite cultural tastes. Activities such as jazz band, orchestra, choir and concert band are just such activities, yet they are only offered at the middle-class school. According to data obtained from the list of activities on the web site of the working-class school, students there can participate in only one cultural activity—the school chorus—though parents indicate that Drama Club and Dance Club are options. Were they interested in participating in other kinds of cultural activities in order to acquire cultural capital, they must do so outside of school and with, no doubt, greater financial and time investments than would be required were these activities offered at their school.

These findings illustrate that schools can serve as both levelers of class differences in structured activity participation as well as contributors to such differences. With respect to the types of activities in which children become involved, schools may contribute to class differences by offering to students qualitatively different activities even when they offer the same number of activities. Regarding level of participation, however, the schools in our data clearly serve to reduce class gaps in participation. Consequently, we are left with the question of what undergirds class differences in out-of-school activities.

FINANCIAL AND INSTITUTIONAL CONSTRAINTS ON NONSCHOOL ACTIVITIES AMONG THE WORKING CLASS

At least two possible explanations for social class gaps in nonschool activities emerge from our interview data: (1) fewer financial resources in working versus middle-class families and (2) weaker institutional capacity in working- versus middle-class neighborhoods. A classification of activities that emerged from the data (in contrast to the literature) suggests three groups of nonschool activities: elite activities, (nonelite) religious activities, and (nonelite) secular activities. Elite activities are ones often discussed in the literature as those that provide cultural capital to youth, as well as provide them with educational benefits like increased odds of attending college. They include activities such as chess, music and dance lessons, and summer programs at selective universities and other institutions. Religious activities are as we have previously defined them—those that are offered by religious institutions, such as church youth groups. Secular activities are nonelite activities that are unaffiliated with religious institutions or organizations,

such as sports in community leagues. This categorization of nonschool activities makes it strikingly clear just how different working- and middle-class children are in their out-of-school activities. . . . While middle-class children are involved in 4.3 times as many nonelite secular activities as working-class youth, they participate in *20 times* as many elite activities relative to their working-class peers. We suggest that class differences in financial resources undergird gaps in participation in elite activities, while the scarcity of secular institutions devoted to youth programs in working-class neighborhoods may undergird class gaps in secular activities.

Participation in elite activities often requires sizeable financial investments. Middle-class respondents report spending $400 a year on foreign language classes, $300 to $1,080 a year on music lessons, $90 to $3,337 a year on dance lessons, and $2,600 to $12,500 per year on chess lessons and competitions. Such financial commitments are possible for a group of parents that command substantial financial resources. The relevance of financial capital to participation is further illustrated by examining differences between upper-middle- and lower-middle-class families. Families that earn more than $75,000 annually participate in 2.6 times as many elite activities as middle-class families that earn less. No doubt, then, that participation in elite activities is more difficult for families with even more modest incomes.

Certainly, there are cases in which working-class youth are able to gain access to elite activities, such as when students obtain scholarships. Kenneth, for example, is a talented emerging artist whose mother has in the past been able to secure scholarships for art classes at a local art college where the instructors are professional artists. Other working-class children are able to attend private and university-based summer programs through scholarships. However, these represent exceptional experiences among the working class.

Indeed, the financial realities of working-class families are made clear by their responses to our question as to whether they had ever been prevented from doing something for their child because of financial limitations. Some working-class parents explicitly identify limits on their children's participation in activities. For example, Anne, a working-class black mother who is a caseworker, indicates that she was unable to send her daughter to a summer program at an elite university because of financial limitations. . . .

[The] literature on neighborhood organization and its relationship to youth development describes the relative absence of effective neighborhood institutions in disadvantaged urban neighborhoods (Wilson 1987, 1996; Quane and Rankin 2006). . . .

We investigated whether the incidence and types of social institutions in the neighborhood in which our working-class respondents live fit such a description. We attempted to identify activities in the neighborhood through web searches and communication with the following organizations: the city recreation department, a nonprofit organization that organizes volunteer-led activities in the city (which compiles and publishes a list of all structured activities in the city by zip code), and various organizations that offer youth activities in the vicinity of the neighborhood school. We found few secular activities other than those offered through religious organizations or schools. This is consistent with the neighborhood organization literature (Connell, Alber, and Walker 1995). Given that people with meager resources are disadvantaged in their efforts to create high-quality neighborhood institutions and services, as well as in their efforts to attract and retain external support for those that exist (Connell et al. 1995), it is unsurprising that our search for secular activities connected to neighborhood organizations bore such little fruit.

Discussion

In our investigation of the social class gap in structured activity participation, we relied on the strength of qualitative data analysis to identify elements in the lived experiences of individuals that hold potential for reframing the way we view social phenomena. Like other studies, we find greater participation in structured activities among middle-class children than working-class children. However, the ways in which their differences vary across social contexts point more toward a structural rather than a cultural explanation for them.

References

Bourdieu, Pierre. 1977. "Cultural Reproduction and Social Reproduction." Pp. 487–511 in *Power and Ideology in Education,* edited by J. Karabel and A. H. Halsey. New York: Oxford University Press.

Bronfenbrenner, Urie. 1979. *The Ecology of Human Development: Experiments by Nature and Design.* Cambridge, MA: Harvard University Press.

Chin, Tiffani and Meredith Phillips. 2004. "Social Reproduction and Child-rearing Practices: Social Class, Children's Agency, and the Summer Activity Gap." *Sociology of Education* 77:185–210.

Condron, Dennis J. 2009. "Social Class, School and Non-school Environments, and Black/White Inequality in Children's Learning." *American Sociological Review* 74:685–708.

Connell, James P., J. L. Alber, and G. Walker. 1995. "How Do Urban Communities Affect Youth? Using Social Services to Inform the Design and Evaluation of Comprehensive Community Initiatives." Pp. 93–125 in *New Approaches to Evaluating Community Initiatives: Concepts, Methods, and Contexts,* edited by J. P. Connell, A. C. Kubish, L. B. Schorr, and C. H. Weiss. New York: The Aspen Institute.

Downey, Douglas B., Paul T. von Hippel, and Beckett A. Broh. 2004. "Are Schools the Great Equalizer? Cognitive Inequality during the Summer Months and the School Year." *American Sociological Review* 69(5):613–35.

Dumais, Susan. 2006. "Elementary School Students' Extracurricular Activities: The Effects of Participation on Achievement and Teachers' Evaluations." *Sociological Spectrum* 26:117–47.

Eccles, Jacquelynne S. and Bonnie L. Barber. 1999. "Student Council, Volunteering, Basketball, or Marching Band: What Kinds of Extracurricular

Involvement Matters?" *Journal of Adolescent Research* 14(1):10–43.

Entwisle, Doris R. and Karl L. Alexander. 1992. "Summer Setback: Race, Poverty, and School Composition, and Mathematics Achievement in the First Two Years of School." *American Sociological Review* 57:72–84.

Furstenberg, Frank, Thomas D. Cook, Jacquelynne S. Eccles, Glen H. Elder Jr., and Arnold Sameroff. 1999. *Managing to Make It: Urban Families and Adolescent Success.* Chicago: University of Chicago Press.

Gabler, Jay and Jason Kaufman. 2006. "Chess, Cheerleading, Chopin: What Gets You into College?" *Contexts* 5:45–9.

Hofferth, Sandra. 2008. "Linking Social Class to Concerted Cultivation, Natural Growth and School Readiness." Pp. 199–205 in *Disparities in School Readiness: How Families Contribute to Transitions into School,* edited by A. Booth and A. C. Crouter. New York: Lawrence Erlbaum Associates.

Holloway, Susan D. and Bruce Fuller. 1992. "The Great Child Care Experiment: What Are the Lessons for School Improvement?" *Educational Researcher* 21(7):12–19.

Hughes, Diane. 2008. "Cultural versus Social Class Contexts for Extra-curricular Activity Participation." Pp. 189–98 in *Disparities in School Readiness: How Families Contribute to Transitions into School,* edited by A. Booth and A. C. Crouter. New York: Lawrence Erlbaum.

Karabel, Jerome. 2005. *The Chosen: The Hidden History of Admissions and Exclusion at Harvard, Yale, and Princeton.* Boston, MA and New York: Houghton Mifflin Company.

Kaufman, Jason and Jay Gabler. 2004. "Cultural Capital and the Extracurricular Activities of Girls and Boys in the College Attainment Process." *Poetics* 32(2):145–68.

Klebanov, Pamela Kato, Jeanne Brooks-Gunn, and Greg J. Duncan. 1994. "Does Neighborhood and Family Poverty Affect Mothers' Parenting, Mental Health, and Social Support." *Journal of Marriage and the Family* 56(2):441–55.

Kohn, Melvin L. [1969] 1977. *Class and Conformity: A Study in Values, with a Reassessment.* Chicago, IL: University of Chicago Press.

Kotchick, Beth A. and Rex Forehand. 2002. "Putting Parenting in Perspective: A Discussion of the Contextual Factors That Shape Parenting Practices." *Journal of Child and Family Studies* 11(3):255–69.

Kozol, Jonathan. 1992. *Savage Inequalities: The Children in America's Schools.* New York: HarperPerennial.

Kozol, Jonathan. 2005. *The Shame of the Nation: The Restoration of Apartheid Schooling in America.* New York: HarperPerennial.

Lareau, Annette. 2002. "Invisible Inequality: Social Class and Childrearing in Black Families and White Families." *American Sociological Review* 67:747–76.

Lareau, Annette. [2003] 2011. *Unequal Childhoods: Class, Race, and Family Life.* Berkeley: University of California Press.

Lareau, Annette and Elliot B. Weininger. 2008. "The Context of School Readiness: Social Class Differences in Time Use in Family Life." Pp. 155–87 in *Disparities in School Readiness: How Families Contribute to Transitions into School,* edited by A. Booth and A. C. Crouter. New York: Lawrence Erlbaum.

Letiecq, Bethany L. and Sally A. Koblinsky. 2004. "Parenting in Violent Neighborhoods: African American Fathers Share Strategies for Keeping Children Safe." *Journal of Family Issues* 25:715–34.

Luster, Tom and Lynn Okagaki. 2005. *Parenting: An Ecological Perspective.* Mahwah, NJ: Lawrence Erlbaum.

McNeal, Ralph B. 1998. "High School Extracurricular Activities: Closed Structures and Stratifying Patterns of Participation." *The Journal of Educational Research* 91:183–91.

McNeal, Ralph B. 1999. "Participation in High School Extracurricular Activities: Investigating School Effects." *Social Science Quarterly* 80(2): 291–309.

Mohr, Wanda K., John W. Fantuzzo, and Saburah Abdul-Kabir. 2001. "Safeguarding Themselves and Their Children: Mothers Share Their Strategies." *Journal of Family Violence* 16(1):75–92.

Orfield, Gary and Susan E. Eaton. 1996. *Dismantling Desegregation: The Quiet Reversal of* Brown v. Board of Education. New York: The New Press.

Pinderhughes, Ellen E., Robert Nix, E. Michael Foster, and Damon Jones. 2001. "Impact of Neighborhood Poverty, Residential Stability, Public Services, Social Networks, and Danger on

Parental Behaviors." *Journal of Marriage and Family* 63(4):941–53.

Quane, James M. and Bruce H. Rankin. 2006. "Does It Pay to Participate? Neighborhood-based Organizations and the Social Development of Urban Adolescents." *Children and Youth Services Review* 28:1229–250.

Soares, Joseph A. 2007. *The Power of Privilege: Yale and America's Elite Colleges*. Stanford, CA: Stanford University Press.

Stevens, Mitchell. 2007. *Creating a Class: College Admissions and the Education of Elites*. Cambridge, MA: Harvard University Press.

Wellman, Barry. 1983. "Network Analysis: Some Basic Principles." *Sociological Theory* 1:155–200.

Wilson, Julius. 1987. *The Truly Disadvantaged: The Inner City, the Underclass, and Public Policy*. Chicago, IL: University of Chicago Press

Wilson, Julius. 1996. *When Work Disappears: The World of the New Urban Poor*. New York: Vintage Books.

EXPLAINING RACIAL VARIATIONS IN EDUCATION

Caroline Hodges Persell

In this reading, Caroline Hodges Persell, a highly regarded sociologist of education, explores various theories to explain unequal educational outcomes for children of different races. She examines genetic, structural, and cultural explanations and proposes a new approach that incorporates structural, cultural, and interactional factors. Persell's argument is important because the explanations we give for racial differences in education influence how we approach solutions to these problems.

Questions to consider for this reading:

1. Do Persell's arguments help you to understand the different college completion rates listed by race in the introduction to this chapter?

2. Which of the reasons that Persell discusses for racial inequality in education do you think are most plausible?

3. Given Persell's arguments, what steps do you think should be taken to improve the educational experience of racial minority groups?

Racial differences exist in many aspects of education, including access, resources, experiences, and outcomes. This reading begins by considering educational outcomes such as achievement and completion, why they are important, and how they vary by race/ethnicity. It then examines existing explanations, proposes a new synthesis, and considers relevant evidence.

Much of the research on racial/ethnic differences has been based on black-white comparisons for several reasons. Historically and today, blacks[1] and Native Americans have been the most intensely "hyper-segregated" group, that is, isolated from other groups, clustered together in small concentrated areas. Moreover, slavery of blacks created a system of stratification based on

race where whites enjoyed political, economic, legal, and social rights that were denied to blacks on the basis of color. Thus, in the United States blackness and whiteness "are the symbolic anchors of our racial hierarchy" (Morning, 2007). Where data exist on other racial/ethnic groups it is included here. It is important to stress that race is a socially constructed, somewhat fluid, changeable, and complex concept, containing considerable variation within whatever categories are used (Omi, 2001). "Races are labels, not people," and some individuals and groups can change races over time (Morning, 2007). Boundary crossing varies widely between racial/ethnic groups, as does the extent of domination experienced by groups.

VARIATIONS IN EDUCATIONAL OUTCOMES

Of the possible educational outcomes, considerable research has focused on differences in educational achievement. Despite individual exceptions, there are variations in the educational achievement of African American, Latino/a, and Native American students, which, on average, is lower than that of whites and Asian Americans. Gaps occur in standardized test scores, grade point averages, rates of placement in gifted or special education programs, dropout rates, and college attendance and graduation rates (Hallinan, 2001; Kovach & Gordon, 1997; National Center for Education Statistics, 2001; Nettles & Perna, 1997). These differences in educational achievement outcomes are significant predictors of an individual's employment opportunities and wages, as is race.[2] Over the past 30 years, racial/ethnic differences in reading achievement declined until 1988 when they increased some until 1992 before leveling off through 2004. Math achievement gaps declined until 1990 and remained pretty level through 2004 (Berends, Lucas, & Penaloza, 2008).

EXPLANATIONS FOR DIFFERENT OUTCOMES

For a long time, no research could fully explain racial variations in academic achievement, although researchers[3] using different data sets found that a small number of social factors could statistically eliminate racial differences in achievement among young children. Black and white children of the same age and birth weight, whose mothers had the same test scores, education, occupation, income, and wealth, whose mothers were the same age when they had their first child, and who had the same number of children's books or similar cultural resources in their homes, scored the same on their reading and math tests. But, you may be thinking, black and white children are not equally likely to share these indicators of life chances, so we need to explain (or understand) why they do not. A second puzzle is why by the third grade the achievement gap between those same white and black children reappeared, and why the factors that explained it statistically among kindergarteners no longer fully explain the gap among older children. Scholars have considered genetic, cultural, and structural explanations for racial variations in achievement.

Genetic Explanations

There have been recurrent efforts to offer genetic explanations for racial/ethnic differences in educational achievement (e.g., Herrnstein & Murray, 1994; Jensen, 1969). In their 1994 book, *The Bell Curve*, Herrnstein and Murray presented evidence showing that when socioeconomic status was controlled, racial differences in educational achievement remained. Their measures of social factors were very incomplete, however. They then went on to suggest that the remaining difference must be due to genetic differences in intelligence (IQ) between the races since it was not explained by social factors. However, intelligence is not a simple, one-dimensional concept (Fischer et al., 1996; Gardner, 1983, 1993). Nor is intelligence unchanging through time and experience, as evidenced by Flynn's (2007) research showing a rise in western countries of roughly 15 IQ points in a single generation. Neither is intelligence rooted in a particular gene. In short, genetic explanations lack empirical support, and race is seen by social scientists as being a socially constructed concept, rather than a biological or genetic entity. Writing about the IQ test score gap, Nisbett (1998, p. 101) concluded, "The most relevant studies provide no evidence for the genetic superiority of either race, but strong evidence for a substantial environmental contribution to the IQ gap between blacks and whites. Almost equally important, rigorous interventions do affect IQ and cognitive skills at every stage of the life course." Studies of mixed-race children with one white and one black parent show that children with white mothers and black fathers have considerably higher IQs than those with black mothers and white fathers (Nisbett, 1998, p. 100). Although their genetic inheritance is similar, their social exposure to activities favored by a predominantly white society differs according to the race of their mothers. If environment, not genes, is central, what aspects of environment matter? Cultural explanations are frequently offered.

Cultural Explanations

Standing in apparent opposition to a genetic explanation for racial/ethnic differences in school achievement, sociocultural explanations tend to root the causes in the cultural values, parenting practices, and linguistic codes of families and children, and some research is consistent with such an explanation. A broader measure of family environment, including grandmother's education, explained two-thirds of the racial gap in achievement (Phillips, Crouse, & Ralph, 1998, p. 138), twice as much as earlier studies. Ogbu's (2003) observations of greater degrees of "disengagement" from school among black compared to white students are also a cultural explanation. While such cultural explanations—such as family environment, parenting practices, and student behavior—explain more of the achievement gap than do traditional measures of socioeconomic status (SES) alone, they fail to explain when and how such potentially important cultural differences arise.

Cross-cultural research suggests the importance of contextual factors for differences in the culture, IQ, and educational achievements of different racial/ethnic groups. For example in Japan, the ethnic-minority Buraku have lower IQs and educational achievement than the dominant, ethnic-Ippan group, even though the two groups are of the same race. However, when members of both groups migrate to the United States, they do equally well on standardized tests and in school (Ogbu, 2001, 2003; Ogbu & Stern, 2001). These cross-cultural findings are consistent with evidence that other social factors, which Herrnstein and Murray did not measure, affect different achievement levels (Fischer et al., 1996).

Both genetic and cultural explanations attribute the source of failure to children and their families, and unless the cultural explanation pushes beyond individuals to their social contexts, both may have self-fulfilling potency. That is, if people in the larger society come to believe these explanations, such beliefs may contribute to children being taught less. Both genetic and cultural explanations tend to legitimate inequalities and divert attention and reform efforts away from structural inequalities in society, which need to be considered as a source of racial differences in educational achievement.

Structural Explanations

The first structural condition to consider is race, which needs to be viewed not as an individual attribute, but as a system of social relationships that creates systematic advantages for members of one group while the members of another group are systematically disadvantaged (see the important work of critical race theorists such as Bonilla-Silva, 1996, 2001, 2003; Omi, 2001). They see race as a system of organized power in society.

A group's subordinate position in a racialized system of power relations affects its measured intelligence and school achievement through three processes according to Fischer et al. (1996, p. 174): (1) socioeconomic deprivation, (2) racial/ethnic segregation, which concentrates disadvantages and accentuates them, and (3) stigmatization as inferior by the wider society's perception of them. Recent research has statistically eliminated the racial gap in achievement among 10- to 14-year-olds by considering grandparents' characteristics and parenting behaviors (Mandara, Varner, Greene, & Richman, 2009). Another study statistically eliminated the racial gap among 10- to 18-year-olds, suggesting that intergenerational inequalities in wealth and education as well as structural inequalities in neighborhoods, schools, and friends statistically explain the achievement gap (Yeung, Persell, & Reilly, 2010).

TOWARD A FULLER EXPLANATION

The explanation proposed here links structural, cultural, and interactional elements. Structurally, it is important to measure the degree of racial stratification (i.e., structured inequality). This includes the historical social, symbolic, economic, educational, and political domination of one socially defined race over another either in different nations or in different regions of the same country. Those historical legacies are related to economic, cultural, social, and symbolic capital (Lewis, 2003), wealth (Conley, 1999; Oliver & Shapiro, 1997), and an individual's sense of efficacy.

Historical and current racial/ethnic stratification is related to *socialization contexts*, particularly neighborhoods, families, and schools. Racial stratification, ideologies, and socializing contexts shape and constrain *culture, interactions, and responses* that occur between parents and children, between teachers and students, between parents and teachers, and among peers. All three major components in the model are implicated in creating racial/ethnic differences in *educational outcomes*. The importance of multiple, interrelated factors is consistent with the evidence that relatively small educational differences between children in kindergarten grow in magnitude the longer they are in school. Since race/ethnicity and educational achievement are related to occupations, incomes, marital status, housing, social respect, and opportunities for the next generation, they have intergenerational consequences. One reason individuals may work hard in school is to help their children thrive. So the degree to which such "payoffs" of education vary for different races may undermine confidence in the system.

Historical and contemporary structural inequalities between races/ethnicities have been well documented in income, wealth, politics, prison populations, and social status.[4] When the degree of black-white inequality is measured, the achievement gap is greater in U.S. counties with more stratification by color. Including the local class context and the local racial context in which families, schools, and students were located revealed that family and school influences on educational achievement and attainment "are themselves embedded in, and partially a function of, broader structures and spatial variations in class- and race-based opportunity" (Roscigno, 1999, pp. 159–163). Class context (measured at the county level) is related to race, with blacks significantly more likely than whites to live in communities with larger numbers of families in poverty (Roscigno, 1999). What is really important to notice is the way that black educational achievement is depressed in areas of high racial inequality, above and beyond the effects of higher rates of absolute poverty (Figure 31.1). Greater racial inequality at the county level strongly depresses black student achievement, but not white student achievement. In counties where racial inequality in the local labor market is low, in the left portion of Figure 31.1, there are only small achievement differences between blacks and whites, compared to highly unequal counties where racial achievement differences are three times as large, in the right side of Figure 31.1. Not only the absolute level of poverty, but also the degree of racial inequality in an area, affects the racial gap by depressing the educational achievement of black students. Local racial inequality explains nearly half of the racial gap in achievement (Roscigno, 1999, p. 180). Longer-term exposure to the most disadvantaged neighborhoods is related to lower high school graduation rates (Wodtke, Harding, & Elwert, 2011).

Three recent changes negatively affect racial/ethnic achievement differences. First, the wealth gap between whites and blacks has widened dramatically (McKernan, Ratcliffe, Steuerle, & Zhang, 2013); second, "the rich-poor gap in test scores is about 40 percent larger now than it was 30 years ago" because of gains among the rich (Reardon, 2013); and third, blacks are more likely than whites to live in neighborhoods with concentrated poverty than in the past (Sharkey, 2013). This means that the structural situation of minority poor children is worse than it was in the past. How do these changes affect differences in

Figure 31.1   As Racial Inequality in the County Increases, So Does the Achievement Gap Between White and Black Children

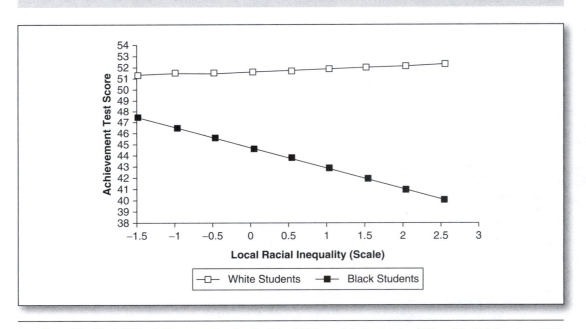

Note. From "The Black-White Achievement Gap, Family-School Links, and the Importance of Place," by V. J. Roscigno, 1999, *Sociological Inquiry, 69*(2), p. 179. Reprinted with permission.

educational achievement? Richer families are investing more in preparing their children for educational success through early childhood enrichment (even tutoring), hiring highly educated nannies, limiting TV time, and exposing their children to libraries, museums, and reading. "From 1972 to 2006 high-income families increased the amount they spent on enrichment activities for their children by 150 percent, while the spending of low-income families on enrichment grew by 57 percent" (Murnane & Duncan, 2011, p. 11). College-educated mothers and fathers are spending twice as much time with their children compared to less educated parents since 1975. The soaring investment in early childhood enrichment among the rich has been called "the rug rat race" by Ramey and Ramey (2010), which they suggest is related to increased competition for admission to selective colleges.

At the same time, Head Start and other early education programs for the poor have been cut. The fact that such rapid educational gains have been made among the wealthiest members of society in recent years underscores the importance of environmental and educational enrichment for school achievement rather than genetic factors. Children of color and white children also differ in their rates of attending private schools, socioeconomically advantaged schools, and smaller schools, as well as being in small classes.

Whites are considerably more likely than blacks to attend private school, and attending private school is related to higher chances of taking an academic curriculum, being in smaller schools, and having student bodies with higher socioeconomic status, greater discipline, and higher rates of attending college (Coleman & Hoffer, 1987). Public school students are much more likely to drop out of high school than are Catholic or other private school students (24%, 12%, and 13%, respectively) (Coleman, Hoffer, & Kilgore, 1982). Moreover, the strong academic curriculum and homework required in many private schools is important for student achievement (Bryk, Lee, & Holland, 1993; Coleman & Hoffer, 1987).

In public schools, blacks are more likely than whites to attend schools with larger numbers of low-income students and schools with more racial minorities. Many studies find correlations between the percent minority, or low income, in school and student achievement (e.g., Roscigno, 2000). School segregation, measured by the racial and socioeconomic composition of students in the school attended, varies by race and is related to educational achievement (Berends et al., 2008).

Black students are more likely than whites to attend large urban schools. Both school size and percent minority students in a school are related to the amount of tracking in it (Lucas & Berends, 2002), and blacks and Chicano/as are more likely than whites to attend schools with curricular tracking. Track placement is often related to what is taught, what is learned, test results, and continuing one's schooling (Oakes, 1985; Persell, 1977; Persell, Catsambis, & Cookson, 1992), but not always (Dreeben & Gamoran, 1986; Hallinan, 1987). Other potential contributing factors include the time teachers expect students to spend on homework (Oakes, 1985) and teacher-student interactions (Good, 1987; Oakes, 1985; Persell, 1977).

By 2004, blacks and whites were almost equally likely to be in academic tracks, although not necessarily at the highest levels (Berends et al., 2008). Between 1992 and 2004, blacks were increasingly more likely to attend schools with larger proportions of low-income and minority students, and even less likely to attend private schools compared to whites (Berends et al., 2008).

Schools with more low-income and racial minority students are more likely to have teachers who are not certified or are teaching out of their area of certification (Ingersoll, 2002), as well as teachers with lower achievement-test scores (Coleman, Campbell, Mood, Weinfeld, & York, 1966). Yet, teachers' test scores are related to students' test scores (Jencks & Phillips, 1998). Having a series of "high-achieving" teachers vastly increases the achievement of low-income and minority students. But, such students are more likely to get less experienced teachers (Kalogrides, Loeb, & Béteille, 2013). However, if black students attend schools with professional communities of teachers and high degrees of teacher collaboration, there are smaller achievement gaps than in schools without such professional communities (Moller, Mickelson, Stearns, Banerjee, & Bottia, 2013).

Because schools are supported by local property taxes and because there is so much housing segregation by social class and race in the United States, students who live in low-income areas are very likely to attend schools with lower per-pupil expenditures on instructional program. Such disparities in educational opportunities affect how much children learn, how long they stay in school, their graduation rates, and the rates at which they successfully pursue further education after high school.

STUDENT ATTITUDES AND BEHAVIORS

Despite all these structured inequalities in the types of education received by students of color, numerous researchers have found that black students value education as much as if not more than whites (Ainsworth-Darnell & Downey, 1998; Blau, 2003; Cook & Ludwig, 1998; Downey, Ainsworth, & Qian, 2009; Mickelson, 1990). Black students also value social goals and personal responsibility for achieving them more than white students do (Blau, 2003, p. 69). Among the differences in behavioral responses, black teens are less likely than whites but more likely than Asian or Latino students to report they have had discipline problems (Blau, 2003, p. 104). Blacks were more likely than whites, Asians, or Latinos, however, to report being unprepared for class and cutting classes (Blau, 2003, p. 104), reports that are consistent with higher rates of absenteeism among blacks in San Francisco high schools (Thernstrom & Thernstrom, 2003, p. 141). Overall, black students report doing fewer hours of homework per night and watching more TV or videos compared to other racial/ethnic groups. A panel analysis of a nationally representative sample of high school students found that extra time spent on math homework increased student test scores, while an extra hour of TV viewing negatively affected scores (Aksoy & Link, 2000).

Some of these behavioral responses have been taken as showing an "oppositional culture" among black or other minority race youths. A much contested cultural explanation, the concept of oppositional culture, emerged from a study of one all-black inner-city high school in Washington, DC (Fordham, 1988, 1993, 1996; Fordham & Ogbu, 1986). Subsequent researchers have found some (Downey & Ainsworth-Darnell, 2002; Farkas, Lleras, & Maczuga, 2002) or no empirical support (Cook & Ludwig, 1998; Ferguson, 2001; Kao, Tienda, & Schneider, 1996) for the concept. Overall, oppositional culture appears among some students of all races, is not uniform among all blacks, is class-linked, is most relevant for adolescents, and is more likely in schools where the race of students in each track does not reflect the racial composition of the school (Downey & Ainsworth-Darnell, 2002; Farkas et al., 2002; Horvat & O'Connor, 2006; Tyson, 2006).

We need to consider how racial inequalities in school practices may affect student responses including effort and achievement. Early academic performance and evaluations affect students' self-perceptions, and "these perceptions subsequently influence the decisions students make with respect to effort expended on schoolwork, course choices, and post high school plans, as well as how attached they feel to school" (Tyson, Darity, & Castellino, 2005, p. 16). The high value black students place on school and education may help to explain why doing poorly may be even more demoralizing for them than

for whites and, thus, even more consequential for their subsequent behavior (such as school disengagement). It may also be one reason why school characteristics have more impact on achievement of blacks compared to that of whites.

EDUCATIONAL PAYOFFS

Some students of color do complete higher education, despite the pitfalls of racial/ethnic inequalities in their neighborhoods, families, and schools. Do they receive the same "payoffs" from their educations as whites? Asian Americans have high levels of educational achievement. Do they earn the same as whites with similar education? The answer is yes, but only if they received that education in the United States, not if their degree is from another country (Zeng & Xie, 2004). Among blacks who attended selective colleges, Bowen and Bok (1998) found that, even among the most highly educated males, racial differences in income remained—although no earnings differences existed among women.

Education does not afford members of all racial groups the same payoff in housing choices or treatment by the police, the legal system, merchants, or restaurants, suggesting that educational achievement and attainment do not have the same "payoff" for blacks and whites in material, symbolic, or social terms. Such unequal effects might corrode trust and educational effort among some members of the next generation.

CONCLUSIONS

Racial differences in educational achievement—which some have tried to explain by genes or culture—are better understood by being rooted in historical and current systems of racial/ethnic inequality, which, in turn, affect the socializing contexts of neighborhoods, families, and schools, as well as individual responses and rewards. When social class and/or racial/ethnic differences are large, enduring, and institutionalized, they are consequential for the next generation and beyond, and they affect educational experiences and outcomes in some of the ways we have delineated here. Without understanding the larger social constellations in which race/ethnicity and education are embedded, we can never challenge and change them.

NOTES

1. While mostly the word *black* is used in this chapter, it is used interchangeably with *African-American* (see Tatum, 1999).

2. According to Moss and Tilly (2003) and Pager and Quillian (2005), among others.

3. Fryer and Levitt (2004); Yeung and Conley (2006); Yeung and Pfeiffer (2006).

4. See Persell and Hendrie (2005) for more details.

REFERENCES

Ainsworth-Darnell, J. W., & Downey, D. B. (1998). Assessing the oppositional culture explanation for racial/ethnic differences in school performance. *American Sociological Review, 63,* 536–553.

Aksoy, T., & Link, C. L. (2000). A panel analysis of student mathematics achievement in the U.S. in the 1990s: Does increasing the amount of time in learning activities affect math achievement? *Economics of Education Review, 19*(3), 261–277.

Berends, M., Lucas, S. R., & Penaloza, R. V. (2008). How changes in families and schools are related to trends in black-white test scores. *Sociology of Education, 81*(4), 313–344.

Blau, J. R. (2003). *Race in the schools: Perpetuating white dominance?* Boulder, CO: Lynne Rienner.

Bonilla-Silva, E. (1996). Rethinking racism: Toward a structural interpretation. *American Sociological Review, 62*(3), 465–480.

Bonilla-Silva, E. (2001). *White supremacy and racism in the post-civil rights era*. Boulder, CO: Lynne Rienner.

Bonilla-Silva, E. (2003). *Racism without racists*. Boulder, CO: Rowman & Littlefield.

Bowen, W. G., & Bok, D. C. (1998). *The shape of the river: Long-term consequences of considering race in college and university admissions.* Princeton, NJ: Princeton University Press.

Bryk, A. S., Lee, V. E., & Holland, P. B. (1993). *Catholic schools and the common good*. Cambridge, MA: Harvard University Press.

Coleman, J. S., Campbell, E. Q., Mood, A. M., Weinfeld, F. D., & York, R. L. (1966). *Equality of educational opportunity*. Washington, DC: U.S. Government Printing Office.

Coleman, J. S., & Hoffer, T. (1987). *Public and private high schools: The impact of communities*. New York: Basic Books.

Coleman, J. S., Hoffer, T., & Kilgore, S. (1982). *High school achievement*. New York: Basic Books.

Conley, D. (1999). *Being black, living in the red: Race, wealth, and social policy in America*. Berkeley: University of California Press.

Cook, P. J., & Ludwig, J. (1998). The burden of "acting white": Do black adolescents disparage academic achievement? In C. Jencks & M. Phillips (Eds.), *The black-white test score gap* (pp. 375–400). Washington, DC: Brookings Institution.

Downey, D. B., Ainsworth, J. W., & Qian, Z. (2009). Rethinking the attitude-achievement paradox among blacks. *Sociology of Education, 82*(1), 1–19.

Downey, D. B., & Ainsworth-Darnell, J. W. (2002). The search for oppositional culture among black students. *American Sociological Review, 67*(1), 156–164.

Dreeben, R., & Gamoran, A. (1986). Race, instruction, and learning. *American Sociological Review, 51*(5), 660–669.

Farkas, G., Lleras, C., & Maczuga, S. (2002). Does oppositional culture exist in minority and poverty peer groups? *American Sociological Review, 67*(1), 148–155.

Ferguson, R. F. (2001). Test-score trends along racial lines 1971 to 1996: Popular culture and community academic standards. In N. J. Smelser, W. J. Wilson, & F. Mitchell (Eds.), *America becoming: Racial trends and their consequences* (Vol. 1, pp. 348–390). Washington, DC: National Academies Press.

Fischer, C. S., Hout, M., Jankowski, M. S., Lucas, S. R., Swidler, A., & Voss, K. (1996). *Inequality by design: Cracking the bell curve*. Berkeley: University of California Press.

Flynn, J. R. (2007). *What is intelligence?* New York: Cambridge University Press.

Fordham, S. (1988). Racelessness as a factor in black students' school success: Pragmatic strategy or

Pyrrhic victory? *Harvard Educational Review, 58*(1), 54–84.

Fordham, S. (1993). "Those loud black girls": (Black) women, silence, and gender "passing" in the academy. *Anthropology & Education Quarterly, 24*(3), 3–32.

Fordham, S. (1996). *Blacked out: Dilemmas of race, identity, and success at capital high.* Chicago: University of Chicago.

Fordham, S., & Ogbu, J. (1986). Black students' school success: Coping with the "burden of acting white." *The Urban Review, 18*(3), 176–206.

Fryer, R. G., Jr., & Levitt, S. D. (2004). Understanding the black-white test score gap in the first two years of school. *The Review of Economics and Statistics, 86*(2), 447–464.

Gardner, H. (1983). *Frames of mind: The theory of multiple intelligences.* New York: Basic Books.

Gardner, H. (1993). *Multiple intelligences: The theory in practice.* New York: Basic Books.

Good, T. L. (1987). Two decades of research on teacher expectations: Findings and future directions. *Journal of Teacher Education, 38*(4), 32–47.

Hallinan, M. T. (1987). Ability grouping and student learning. In M. T. Hallinan (Ed.), *The social organization of schools: New conceptualizations of the learning process* (pp. 41–69). New York: Plenum.

Hallinan, M. (2001). Sociological perspectives on black-white inequalities in American schooling. *Sociology of Education* (extra issue), 50–70.

Herrnstein, R. J., & Murray, C. (1994). *The bell curve: Intelligence and class structure in American life.* New York: Free Press.

Horvat, E. M., & O'Connor, C. (Eds.). (2006). *Beyond acting white: Reframing the debate on black student achievement.* Boulder, CO: Rowman & Littlefield.

Ingersoll, R. M. (2002). *Out-of-field teaching, educational inequality, and the organization of schools* (Research Report No. R-02-1). Center for the Study of Teaching and Policy, University of Washington, Seattle.

Jencks, C., & Phillips, M. (1998). *The black-white test score gap.* Washington, DC: Brookings Institution Press.

Jensen, A. R. (1969). How much can we boost IQ and scholastic achievement? *Harvard Educational Review, 39*(1), 1–123.

Kalogrides, D., Loeb, S., & Béteille, T. (2013). Systematic sorting: Teacher characteristics and class assignments. *Sociology of Education*, 86(2), 103–123.

Kao, G., Tienda, T., & Schneider, B. (1996). Racial and ethnic variation in academic performance. In A. M. Pallas (Ed.), *Research in sociology of education and socialization* (Vol. 11, pp. 263–297). Greenwich, CT: JAI Press.

Kovach, J. A., & Gordon, D. E. (1997). Inclusive education: A modern day civil-rights struggle. *The Educational Forum, 61*(3), 247–257.

Lewis, A. E. (2003). *Race in the schoolyard: Negotiating the color line in classrooms and communities.* New Brunswick, NJ: Rutgers University Press.

Lucas, S. R., & Berends, M. (2002). Sociodemographic diversity, correlated achievement, and de facto tracking. *Sociology of Education, 75*(4), 328–348.

Mandara, J., Varner, F., Greene, N., & Richman, S. (2009). Intergenerational family predictors of the black-white achievement gap. *Journal of Educational Psychology, 101*(4), 867–878.

McKernan, S.-M., Ratcliffe, C., Steuerle, C. E., & Zhang, S. (2013). *Less than equal: Racial disparities in wealth accumulation.* Washington, DC: The Urban Institute.

Mickelson, R. (1990). The attitude-achievement paradox among black adolescents. *Sociology of Education, 63*(1), 44–61.

Moller, S., Mickelson, R. A., Stearns, E., Banerjee, N., & Bottia, M. C. (2013). Collective pedagogical teacher culture and mathematics achievement: Differences by race, ethnicity, and socioeconomic status. *Sociology of Education, 86*(2), 174–194.

Morning, A. (2007, August). *Teaching race.* Presentation at the American Sociological Association annual meeting, New York.

Moss, P., & Tilly, C. (2003). *Stories employers tell: Race, skill, and hiring in America.* New York: Russell Sage Foundation.

Murnane, R. J., & Duncan, G. J. (Eds.) (2011). *Whither opportunity: Rising inequality, schools and children's life chances.* New York: Russell Sage Foundation.

National Center for Education Statistics (NCES). (2001). *Bureau of the census, current population survey.* Washington, DC: Author.

Nettles, M. T., & Perna, L. W. (1997). *The African American education data book. Vol. I: Higher and adult education.* Fairfax, VA: Frederick D. Patterson Research Institute.

Nisbett, R. E. (1998). Race, genetics, and IQ. In C. Jencks & M. Phillips (Eds.), *The black-white test score gap* (pp. 86–102). Washington, DC: Brookings Institution.

Oakes, J. (1985). *Keeping track: How schools structure inequality.* New Haven, CT: Yale University Press.

Ogbu, J. (2001). Cultural amplifiers of intelligence: IQ and minority status in cross-cultural perspective. In J. M. Fish (Ed.), *Race and intelligence: Separating science from myth* (pp. 241–278). Mahwah, NJ: Lawrence Erlbaum.

Ogbu, J. (2003). *Black American students in an affluent suburb: A study of academic disengagement.* Mahwah, NJ: Lawrence Erlbaum.

Ogbu, J. U., & Stern, R. (2001). Caste and intellectual development. In R. J. Sternberg & E. L. Grigorenko (Eds.), *Environmental effects on cognitive abilities* (pp. 3–37). Mahwah, NJ: Lawrence Erlbaum.

Oliver, M. L., & Shapiro, T. M. (1997). *Black wealth/white wealth.* New York: Routledge.

Omi, M. A. (2001). The changing meaning of race. In N. J. Smelser, W. J. Wilson, & F. Mitchell (Eds.), *America becoming* (Vol. 1, pp. 243–263). Washington, DC: National Academies Press.

Pager, D., & Quillian, L. (2005). Walking the talk? What employers say versus what they do. *American Sociological Review, 70*(3), 355–380.

Persell, C. H. (1977). *Education and inequality: The roots and results of stratification in America's schools.* New York: Free Press.

Persell, C. H., Catsambis, S., & Cookson, P. W., Jr. (1992). Family background, high school type, and college attendance: A conjoint system of cultural capital transmission. *Journal of Research on Adolescence, 2*(1), 1–23.

Persell, C. H., & Hendrie, G. F. (2005). Race, education, and inequality. In M. Romero & E. Margolis (Eds.), *Blackwell companion to social inequalities* (pp. 533–612). London: Basil Blackwell.

Phillips, M., Crouse, J., & Ralph, J. (1998). Does the black-white test score gap widen after children enter school? In C. Jencks & M. Phillips (Eds.), *The black-white test score gap* (pp. 229–272). Washington, DC: Brookings Institution Press.

Ramey, G., & Ramey, V. A. (2010). *The rug rat race* (Working paper). National Bureau of Economic Research.

Reardon, S. F. (2011). The widening academic achievement gap between the rich and the poor: New evidence and possible explanations. In R. J. Murnane & G. J. Duncan (Eds.), *Whither opportunity: Rising inequality, schools and children's life chances* (pp. 91–116). New York: Russell Sage Foundation.

Reardon, S. F. (2013). No rich child left behind. *New York Times,* April 27. Retrieved from http://opinionator.blogs.nytimes.com/2013/04/27/no-rich-child-left-behind/?_r=0

Roscigno, V. J. (1999). The black-white achievement gap, family-school links, and the importance of place. *Sociological Inquiry, 69*(2), 159–186.

Roscigno, V. J. (2000). Family/school inequality and African-American/Hispanic achievement. *Social Problems, 47*(2), 266–290.

Sharkey, P. (2013). *Stuck in place: Urban neighborhoods and the end of progress toward racial equality.* Chicago: University of Chicago Press.

Tatum, B. D. (1999). *"Why are all the black kids sitting together in the cafeteria?" and other conversations about race.* New York: Basic Books.

Thernstrom, A., & Thernstrom, S. (2003). *No excuses: Closing the racial gap in learning.* New York: Simon & Schuster.

Tyson, K. (2002). Weighing in: Elementary-age students and the debate on attitudes toward school among black students. *Social Forces, 80*(4), 1157–1189.

Tyson, K. (2003). Notes from the back of the room: Problems and paradoxes in the schooling of young black students. *Sociology of Education, 76*(4), 326–343.

Tyson, K. (2006). The making of a "burden": Tracing the development of a "burden of acting white" in schools. In C. O'Connor and E. M. Horvat (Eds.), *Beyond acting white: Reframing the debate on black student achievement* (pp. 57–87). New York: Rowman & Littlefield.

Tyson, K., Darity, W., Jr., & Castellino, D. R. (2005). It's not "a black thing." Understanding the burden of acting white and other dilemmas of high achievement. *American Sociological Review, 70*(4), 582–605.

Wodtke, G. T., Harding, D. J., & Elwert, F. (2011). Neighborhood effects in temporal perspective: The impact of long-term exposure to concentrated disadvantage on high school graduation. *American Sociological Review,* 76(5), 713–736.

Yeung, W.-J. J., & Conley, D. (2006). *Black-white achievement gap and family wealth* (Unpublished working paper). New York University.

Yeung, W.-J. J., Persell, C. H., & Reilly, M. C. (2010, August). *Intergenerational stratification, child development, and the black-white achievement gap.* Paper presented at the American Sociological Association annual meeting, Atlanta, GA.

Yeung, W.-J. J., & Pfeiffer, K. (2006). *The black-white test score gap: Age and gender differentials* (Unpublished working paper). New York University.

Zeng, Z., & Xie, Y. (2004). Asian-Americans' earnings disadvantage reexamined: The role of place of education. *American Journal of Sociology, 109*(5), 1075–1108.

"Rednecks," "Rutters," and 'Rithmetic

Social Class, Masculinity, and Schooling in a Rural Context

Edward W. Morris

This reading by Edward W. Morris examines interactions in a white, poor, rural high school in Ohio. In ethnographic research (see Chapter 2) questions often emerge after you enter the field, as was the case for Morris. He found that girls did better in high school than boys and explains why this may be so based on one and a half years of observations in this school. He observed classrooms and after-school activities, conducted interviews with students, and collected school records and other documents such as newspapers. He argues that the definition of masculinity is a very strong factor in explaining boys' performance in school and that boys' definition of masculinity is very closely linked to the characteristics of the community in which they reside. One conclusion from this research is that we cannot examine race, gender, or social class separately from the social context—in this case a rural context—if we are to understand students' behaviors in school.

Questions to consider for this reading:

1. Look up the definition for hegemonic masculinity, or ask your professor. How does this concept fit the argument Morris is making in this reading?

2. What are the positive consequences of adhering to the above definition of masculinity for these young boys? What are the negative consequences?

3. How does social context, such as urban, suburban, or rural, impact educational outcomes? Use other readings from this book to help develop your answer.

I first entered Clayton High School[1] with the intention of studying school disconnection in a rural area. The school was located in a rural community once dominated by a booming coal industry, but now largely impoverished. Although it was not the original focus of my research, I soon discovered that girls outperformed boys academically and showed more interest in school . . . In this article I analyze this gender difference in academic perceptions and outcomes. My analysis illuminates contradictions of constructions of masculinity and demonstrates how social class and gender are intimately interwoven. My analysis also shines new light on the much-discussed academic "gender gap" favoring girls in disadvantaged contexts, suggesting that particular constructions of social class and gender are critical in producing these academic differences.

* * *

My analysis builds on the established tenet that men tend to seek historically specific outlets for asserting dominance over women and other men. But my analysis will also clarify and expand new directions in the theory. First, by focusing on a rural area that has undergone economic restructuring, the study will emphasize the interrelationship of global, regional, and local levels in contextual conditions and practices of masculinity (Connell & Messerschmidt, 2005). I will show, for example, how particular local history and concepts, broader regional categories such as "redneck," and global forces such as deindustrialization all shaped the enactment of masculinity among boys in this school. However, my analysis will stay primarily local and will, through the use of observational and interview data, emphasize individual action in the face of larger structural forces (see also Messerschmidt, 2004). This framework accounts for differences in local definitions of hegemonic masculinity, as well as different patterns of action based on interpretations of these definitions. Second, I will highlight a more intricate relationship between class and masculinity than many previous studies. My analysis does not just explain how pre-established factors such as class or race shape masculinity into subordinated or marginalized forms. Instead, it will demonstrate how social class and masculinity are constructed simultaneously (along with sexuality and whiteness), and how strategies of masculine dominance may actually reproduce class disadvantage. Finally, I will add to literature on hegemonic masculinity and latent costs for men. While past research has examined this phenomenon in areas such as crime (Messerschmidt, 1997) and sport (Messner, 1992), I focus here on education, which I discuss more below.

MASCULINITY AND SCHOOLING

Hegemonic masculinity reveals the ironies of the quest of many men to position themselves as different from and superior to women. Some of the more interesting views of the complications of masculinity have been shown in classic ethnographic studies in education. Although neither invoked hegemonic masculinity, Willis (1977) and MacLeod (1995) both demonstrated how for working-class boys "being a man" meant resisting school, engaging in risky, physically challenging behaviors such as fighting or drug use, and embracing manual or illegal labor. Such constructions of masculinity promoted opposition to school and other institutions. This only calcified the boys' working-class position, hindering their chances for upward mobility and greater social and economic power.

I examine whether similar processes might apply to constructions of masculinity among white working-class rural students, and what this can tell us about gendered differences in educational outcomes among disadvantaged youth in general. In contrast to Willis (1977) and MacLeod (1995), my analysis reveals how masculinity is not just an ancillary factor in the deeper dynamic of class reproduction. Instead, I position particular constructions of masculinity through social class as critical to this reproduction. I show how factors contributing to academic disconnection were seen as important resources for the expression of local hegemonic masculinity.

* * *

FINDINGS

Differences in Academic Achievement and Career Goals

Based on an analysis of school records, I found that girls overall outperformed boys academically and had greater ambitions for higher education. I obtained a listing from a guidance counselor of student grade point averages and class ranking at the beginning of the school year in 2006. Girls dominated the peaks of these rankings. For example, the top student in each grade level was a girl. In the senior class, eight of the top 10 were girls. Of the top 20 in the senior class, just five were boys. In the sophomore class, where I concentrated my observations, the top five students (with perfect 4.0 grade point averages) were girls. Nine of the top 10 and 17 of the top 20 in the sophomore rankings were girls. By contrast, many students with low grade point averages and those who were required to repeat a grade or repeat certain classes were boys. Of the 23 students who repeated ninth grade in 2006, 15 (65 percent) were boys. However, I should note that some girls were also low-performing. Of the eight students repeating tenth grade in 2006, for example, four were girls. And some girls appeared near the bottom of the class rankings in each grade. Overall, however, girls clearly performed better than boys.[2]

These differences in class rank corresponded to different ambitions for higher education. I obtained surveys regarding plans after graduation that a guidance counselor had distributed to the outgoing seniors in 2006. Of the students who reported that they had no plans for any sort of college, 84 percent were boys and 16 percent were girls. Of those reporting that they planned to attend four-year colleges, 33 percent were boys and 67 percent were girls. Many young men reported an interest in manual, blue-collar jobs typically done by men and requiring no college, such as auto mechanics, construction, and loading trucks. And some young men simply reported "no plans" or "nothing" after graduation. What caused such stark differences in career plans and academic achievement? Several themes appeared in my data.

Too Cool for School: Masculinity and Academic Nonchalance

Rather than gender having a specific effect on the educational behaviors of girls and boys, educational behavior itself became a vehicle for the construction of gender. The performance of gender in this setting employed educationally relevant behavior to accomplish masculine and feminine identities (Butler, 1999; Messerschmidt, 2000, 2004; West & Zimmerman, 1987), and this

shaped academic performance. For example, in my observations girls tended to direct considerable effort and attention to school. Boys, by contrast, took pride in their *lack* of academic effort. No boy I interviewed reported that he studied outside of school. Indeed, if boys achieved well academically, they had to do so without any overt sign of effort or planning. For instance, a boy named Preston was described by several teachers and students as the "smartest kid in the school." Yet Preston only had a 3.15 grade point average . . .

Preston reveals the ultimate goal of schoolwork for many boys at Clayton—to just "get by." My observations in classrooms mirrored what Preston described: Boys were more likely to sleep, less likely to turn in homework, and less likely to take notes.

Despite this, teachers and students frequently described boys as "smart." A science teacher named Mr. Deering told me, "I think the girls are more conscientious. They will work more, do more of what you ask them," [and] he then pointed to two boys in the class and said, "[T]hey're smart, but they don't do a whole lot." Similarly, girls at the school appeared to see boys as smart, while viewing their own abilities as more limited (see also AAUW, 1992; Luttrell, 1997). These gendered academic behaviors and perceptions emerged from a discourse that framed masculinity as something that should not include academic effort. Boys were understood by themselves and others as smart enough to "get by," but not expected to attend diligently to academic work. These actions were seen as representations of masculinity . . .

MASCULINITY, SEXUALITY, AND SCHOOL ENGAGEMENT

Perceptions of masculinity and educational engagement tended to show an interconnection between gender and sexuality. Similar to Pascoe (2007), I found that students at Clayton used terms charged with connotations of sexuality to police the boundaries of masculinity.

For example, boys (and to a lesser extent, girls) used the term "pussy," "gay," or "fag" to refer to boys whom they perceived as unmasculine (Eder, Evans, & Parker, 1995; Pascoe, 2007). While important in the everyday construction of gender, this discourse on feminized, lower-status masculinity also occurred through academics. Academically oriented behavior itself could be seen as not masculine. For example, boys perceived as "nerdy"—often those who put more effort into school and were involved in school activities such as band—were more likely to be called "gay" or "pussies." . . .

Masculinity and Perceptions of Academic Knowledge and Skills: "Booksmarts"

As the student career surveys demonstrated, many boys at Clayton valued manual labor. Gendered and classed views of work and education also emerged throughout my student interviews. One definitive gender difference concerned perceptions of "booksmarts." Virtually all the girls I interviewed responded that they thought "booksmarts"—the knowledge and competencies gained from books—were important to be successful. Few boys thought that booksmarts were as important. Instead, boys were more likely to value "common sense" and "working with your hands." . . .

To boys such as Robert, acquiring "book knowledge" required boring, inert activities such as reading or "listening to someone talk the whole time." In contrast, Robert and other boys perceived nonacademic, blue-collar work such as woodworking or construction as more active and enjoyable. In this way, these boys forged working-class identities. But such work was also perceived as more manly, as many boys referenced their fathers or other men in their family who did such work, and they praised the utility and vigor of manual labor. Thus, the boys simultaneously forged masculine identities.

In doing so, some boys disparaged academic work and "office jobs." . . . [A]cademic work was not seen as "hard work" and masculinity in this community had historically been defined through hard physical labor. Although the boys I interviewed tended to admit that "office jobs" could be lucrative, most did not see such careers as useful or gratifying. Much of this perception, however, stems from the local feminization of such work and the lower status placed on femininity in general. Academics and professions requiring "booksmarts" were feminized and considered lower status, while physical labor aligned with masculinity. This relationship undergirded local hegemonic masculinity, even though economic restructuring reduced manual labor jobs. As I show below, local views of masculine dominance in heterosexual relationships and work roles influenced such perceptions.

Gender, Work, and Power in the Community

Teachers at Clayton noted the irony of girls' high academic performance because they perceived the community (and most teachers lived in the community) as traditional and patriarchal . . .

These patriarchal views emerged in my student interviews. Boys and girls perceived family roles differently. Boys tended to see the man as the primary leader and provider within the family (all of the girls I interviewed thought it should be equal). A boy named Zack expressed this in an interview:

Do you think the man should be the main provider for the family? Oh yeah! I think it's just kinda stupid how girls have to go to work. It happens a lot around here. You have it so the girls have to go to work. I don't like that. *Ok, so you think it's kind of a problem that that has to happen?* Yeah. *And that happens a lot around here?* Happens quite a bit. Most of the time it happens around here, it's not because it has to happen. It's because people—the guys are too lazy. We got a lotta lazy people in our community.

Zack states an interest in the traditional breadwinner role for men, similar to other boys

I interviewed. But Zack adds a unique twist compared to other boys—he indicts men in the community as too lazy to fulfill this role properly. Zack was one of the highest-performing boys in his grade, and I suggest that this unique interpretation of local family life provoked him to work hard in school to obtain a good job (which he intended to do through going to college and the military). This example demonstrates the importance of viewing gender as a situated construction influenced by interpretation and agency. Zack's achievement is not an anomaly, rather it results from his interpretation of laziness and inability to support one's family as the true failure of masculinity, and his desire to construct his own (perceived stronger) masculinity through academic success. Many other boys, however, did not appear to see this same connection. They continued to eschew and feminize academics even as they revered a male-as-provider family role.[3] This stemmed from a strong local sense of masculine entitlement nested in industrial labor and familial economic power. Such traditionalism, however, was palpably fading economically. Thus, class-based concepts and practices in the peer culture offered regional and local springboards from which to assert and protect masculinity.

Constructing Masculinity, Class, and Whiteness: "Rednecks" and "Rutters"

Hegemonic practices of masculinity at Clayton focused on a carefree, almost rebellious attitude toward schoolwork, and physical toughness exemplified by manual labor. Both practices of masculinity were reflected, but also given new life, through a popular term and identity at the school: "redneck." The term "redneck" is a well-known popular culture identity that implies being blue-collar, rebellious, and southern (Hartigan, 2003; Shirley, 2003). On a more tacit level, "redneck" also strongly represents masculinity and whiteness. Shirley (2003) finds that "redneck" connotes more of a masculine than a feminine identity. Hartigan (2003) asserts that "redneck" reflects important internal dynamics of whiteness as a racial category. This identity is unabashedly white, but opposed to middle- and upper-class whiteness.

Such dynamics are important to recognize because economic decline in Clayton compromised whiteness as well as masculinity. White men, particularly in lower economic strata, may define themselves in opposition to nonwhites (particularly African Americans) through work and economic stability (Fine & Weis, 1998). When asked about race, the white boys I interviewed also defined whiteness through this sense of stability. When discussing differences between white and [b]lack people, a boy named Harry said: "[When thinking about white people] I think of people that . . . have better lives—live in good neighborhoods—stuff like that." Where economic situations are tenuous or declining such as in Clayton, however, this understanding of whiteness can be threatened (Fine & Weis, 1998; Kimmel & Ferber, 2006). The concept of "redneck" can reflect and respond to these tensions by reasserting a white blue-collar identity imbued with rebellious toughness. Such an identity fit well with hegemonic masculinity in Clayton.

For instance, I only heard the term "redneck" used at Clayton in reference to white men or boys. The boys I heard called this were most often in lower-level classes or vocational classes, indicating that the concept was not connected to sophistication and academic interest. Indeed, in popular culture "redneck" represents opposition to these ideals (Jarosz & Lawson, 2002). Similarly, some teachers used the term in a whimsically derogatory way to describe certain boys as blue-collar, uncouth, and brazenly macho. Although the term "redneck" is largely derogatory, many people in this community, especially men, embraced it. For example, several trucks in the area proudly displayed bright red "Redneck" stickers. Preston described the attitude in the following way: "Around here, it's like 'yeah I'm a redneck, what are you gonna do about it?' (laughs)."

As Preston implied, "redneck" at Clayton represented the stereotypically masculine trait of physical toughness. Harry mentioned this when I asked him to describe the school: "It's a rough school. It's ah, (laughs), it's a redneck school!" Uses of the term "redneck" captured a sense of pride embedded in living in this "rough," white working-class, rural location. Through the implication of toughness and opposition to elitist sophistication, this regional category offered a classed and raced template consistent with local hegemonic masculinity. This was an identity that could protect white working-class masculinity, but one that was not academically inclined.

While "redneck" served largely as a positive identity at the school, another class-based identity was not embraced: "rutter." Unlike the broader, regional category of redneck, "rutter" was a distinctively local term. "Rutter" denoted people who were extremely poor, dirty, and lowly, similar to the concept "white trash" (Hartigan, 2003; Wray, 2006). Students used this word as a class-based insult, and while "redneck" affirmed whiteness, "rutter" could impair it. (I analyze this further in a separate work: Morris, 2008.) For boys, using "rutter" as an invective often instigated fights . . .

Reclaiming Physically Tough Masculinity: Risk-Taking and Fighting

Several works discuss a "risk-taking" quality in masculinity (Connell, 1995; Connell & Messerschmidt, 2005; Messner, 1992). Ferguson (2000, p. 176) refers to a similar emphasis on "brinkmanship"—challenging rules, authority, and refusing to back down. Like the "redneck" identity, physical brinkmanship at Clayton provided avenues to reassert the power of masculinity.

Similar to Courtenay's (2006) research on injury and risk-taking for men in rural settings, I found that boys in Clayton often took bodily risks and incurred physical injuries. Boys were proud of their "battle scars" and excitedly regaled me with unadulterated stories of their accidents and pain . . .

The basic sense of risk-taking and physical bravery underlying such behavior could translate into challenging school rules and authority and the physical expression of power, both of which could hinder academic progress. These qualities can be seen through the example of fighting. There were several "girl fights" at the school, but students and adults tended to associate "real" fighting with masculinity. According to students, the purpose of fighting for boys was less complicated than for girls, and the goals intrinsic to the fight itself. As a girl named Jamie said, "Most of the girls have a purpose to fight, like the other girl makes them mad for a pretty good reason or something. And guys they just— 'you wanna fight, yeah, okay' [mimics punching motions]." For many boys fighting itself became the goal; it became an important method of cultivating and displaying masculinity. Fighting provided these boys a crucible that could demonstrate the superiority of masculinity to femininity. As Kevin and Roger stated, even boys perceived to not fight well could be branded as "pussies." This allowed some boys to prove superiority over other boys and over girls— something that they perceived could not be guaranteed through academics.

Some boys, particularly those from poorer backgrounds and those more disconnected from school, emphasized the freedom and closure they found in fighting (see also Ferguson, 2000). Fighting defied middle- to upper-class norms of comportment,[4] and also openly opposed school rules. In the second year of my research, the school enacted a stricter approach to fights, diligently policing the cafeteria (where most school fights occurred) and giving mandatory suspensions to those caught fighting. Several boys derided this "zero tolerance" approach as inhibiting a primary method of conflict resolution and self-expression . . .

Fighting conveyed a message of physical superiority consistent with hegemonic notions of masculinity. Perhaps because they felt marginalized in other ways, fighting gave these boys a sense of physical empowerment, freedom, and clarity lacking in other areas of their lives. But this entailed academic and bodily costs. Fighting not only led to suspensions, but negative judgments from teachers and school administrators that obstructed boys' attachment to school, and ultimately their achievement. Fighting was certainly detrimental to academic success, but resoundingly consistent with the physical toughness and power associated with local hegemonic masculinity.

CONCLUSION

This article develops a new view of the academic "gender gap," especially as it applies to disadvantaged students. I argue that gender should not be seen as a static cause of academic differences, but that academically relevant behavior is employed in the construction of gender. Despite the actual and potential inequalities faced by boys at Clayton and other disadvantaged contexts, I argue against a "boys as disadvantaged" perspective. I do this through applying and expanding the theory of hegemonic masculinity in relation to social class and education.

This research shows that definitions of hegemonic masculinity differ according to locale, and these differences might engender unique patterns of action and consequences. At Clayton, pursuing locally hegemonic practices of masculinity tended to hinder boys in school. Fighting as a display of physical masculine dominance, or viewing academic work and striving as feminized and lower status, are examples. Such perceptions and behaviors operated within local, as well as regional and global, patterns of masculinity and social class. Local history meant that hegemonic masculinity in this context stemmed (partly) from maintaining a "breadwinner" role within the family through physically demanding labor. But global dynamics of economic restructuring meant that such practices were difficult for men in Clayton to enact. Thus, I suggest that broader regional concepts such as the tough, rebellious "redneck," or displays of physical dominance such as fighting, were employed by

these boys as alternative means to forge and prove hegemonic masculinity.

The findings further demonstrate how class is produced through masculinity and how masculinity is produced through social class (and in a less elaborated way, how whiteness and sexuality are enmeshed in this process). Class privilege and gender privilege can be considered two separate, but interconnected systems of hegemony, further complicated by different (local, regional, and global) levels of practice. Local hegemonic masculinity entailed a sense of superiority tied to physical labor and displays of physical activity, risk, and power—not academics. While perceived to be advantageous locally, this masculinity was a disadvantage within the larger class structure, primarily because globalization has reduced opportunities for industrial labor in many pockets of the United States. This constraining class structure further compromised white working-class masculinity in Clayton, fueling a need to prove masculinity, along with class and race identities, in other ways. Some boys such as Zack crafted practices to accomplish this academically, but most saw academic behavior as inconsistent with local definitions of masculinity. Thus, interwoven processes of class and masculinity led to unexpected outcomes—specifically girls' academic advantage. Far from showing that girls have gender privilege, this outcome actually stems from boys seeking masculine privilege, but under a definition of masculinity that tended to hinder them academically.[5]

NOTES

1. All personal and place names are pseudonyms.
2. The only other achievement data I had access to were the Ohio Graduation Test results. Students in the state of Ohio are required to pass this curriculum-based achievement test before graduating from high school. There was no large difference in results by gender on this test, but it is difficult to use this as a gauge of performance because the results are reported as passing rates, not actual scores.

3. There were alternative enactments of masculinity at Clayton that demonstrated less traditional notions of gender, along with higher academic performance. The few boys already mentioned as "band kids" engaged in such practices, which again underscores the variability of masculinity. This constitutes an important area of further analysis; however, in this article I focus on hegemonic practices of masculinity to explain the academic "gender gap."

4. Fighting in school is related to family income. As income rises, it is less likely that a student will be involved in a physical fight in school. Perceptions of fighting among men also vary by class. Pyke (1996, p. 532) argues that higher-class men use the violence they associate with lower-class men as an example of brutality that "reemphasize[s] their superiority over lower-class men."

5. I am not arguing that these boys are responsible for their own disadvantage, but that local hegemonic masculinity promised a degree of relational power over women and other men. This local dynamic must be considered within larger relations of class and gender in which these boys face significant inequalities.

REFERENCES

American Association of University Women (AAUW). (1992). *The AAUW report: How schools shortchange girls.* Washington, DC: The AAUW Educational Foundation and National Educational Association.

Butler, J. (1999). *Gender trouble: Feminism and the subversion of identity.* New York: Routledge.

Connell, R. W. (1995). *Masculinities.* Berkeley: University of California Press.

Connell, R. W. (1996). Teaching the boys: New research on masculinity, and gender strategies for schools. *Teachers College Record, 98*(2), 206–235.

Connell, R. W., & Messerschmidt, J. W. (2005). Hegemonic masculinity: Rethinking the concept. *Gender & Society, 19*(6), 829–859.

Courtenay, W. H. (2006). Rural men's health: Situating risk in the negotiation of masculinity. In H. Campbell, M. Mayerfeld-Bell, & M. Finney (Eds.), *Country boys: Masculinity and rural life* (pp. 139–158). University Park: Pennsylvania State University Press.

Eder, D., Evans, C. C., & Parker, S. (1995). *School talk: Gender and adolescent culture.* New Brunswick, NJ: Rutgers University Press.

Ferguson, A. A. (2000). *Bad boys: Public schools in the making of black masculinity.* Ann Arbor: University of Michigan Press.

Fine, M., & Weis, L. (1998). *The unknown city: The lives of poor and working-class young adults.* Boston: Beacon Press.

Hartigan, J., Jr. (2003). Who are these white people? "Rednecks," "hillbillies," and "white trash" as marked racial subjects. In A. W. Doane & E. Bonilla-Silva (Eds.), *White out: The continuing significance of racism* (pp. 95–111). New York: Routledge.

Jarosz, L., & Lawson, V. (2002). Sophisticated people versus rednecks: Economic restructuring and class difference in America's West. *Antipode, 34*(1), 8–27.

Kimmel, M. S., & Ferber, A. L. (2006). White men are this nation: Right-wing militias and the restoration of rural masculinity. In H. Campbell, M. Mayerfeld-Bell, & M. Finney (Eds.), *Country boys: Masculinity and rural life* (pp. 121–138). University Park: The Pennsylvania State University Press.

Luttrell, W. (1997). *School-smart and mother-wise: Working-class women's identity and schooling.* New York: Routledge.

MacLeod, J. (1995). *Ain't no makin' it* (2nd ed.). Boulder, CO: Westview Press.

Messerschmidt, J. W. (1997). *Crime as structured action: Gender, race, class, and crime in the making.* Thousand Oaks, CA: Sage.

Messerschmidt, J. W. (2000). *Nine lives: Adolescent masculinities, the body, and violence.* Boulder, CO: Westview Press.

Messerschmidt, J. W. (2004). *Flesh and blood: Adolescent gender diversity and violence.* Lanham, MD: Rowman & Littlefield.

Messner, M. A. (1992). *Power at play: Sports and the problem of masculinity.* Boston: Beacon Press.

Morris, E. W. (2008). *"Rednecks" and "rutters": Constructions of social class and whiteness at a rural high school.* Paper presented at the North Central Sociological Association Meeting, Cincinnati.

Pascoe, C. J. (2007). *Dude, you're a fag: Masculinity and sexuality in high school.* Berkeley: University of California Press.

Pyke, K. D. (1996). Class-based masculinities: The interdependence of gender, class, and interpersonal power. *Gender & Society, 10*(5), 527–549.

Shirley, C. D. (2003). *"Rednecks" and "white trash": The gendering of whiteness.* Paper presented at the Southern Sociological Society Meetings, New Orleans.

West, C., & Zimmerman, D. (1987). Doing gender. *Gender & Society, 1*(2), 125–151.

Willis, P. (1977). *Learning to labor: How working class kids get working class jobs.* New York: Columbia University Press.

Wray, M. (2006). *Not quite white: White trash and the boundaries of whiteness.* Durham, NC: Duke University Press.

GENDER AND EDUCATION

Roslyn Arlin Mickelson

In 1989, Roslyn Arlin Mickelson published an article titled "Why Does Jane Read and Write So Well?" She revisits those premises in this reading, asking why women's achievement is an anomaly—being particularly successful in school but not being able to parlay their successes into occupational and financial returns. She also examines the recent concern about underachievement of boys. Mickelson addresses these questions using several different explanations and applies test score data to examine these theories.

Questions to consider for this reading:

1. Why does the article indicate that "Jane" reads and writes so well, and what are the concerns about her doing so?

2. How does the performance of girls in school compare to that of boys? What changes have occurred recently?

3. How are Mickelson's explanations for boys in schools similar to or different from those given by Morris in his reading in this chapter?

Contemporary gender trends in educational outcomes reveal recognizable patterns. Familiar gender differences can be summarized as follows: Net of race and social class, women do, on average, better in school and attain more education than do men; men's achievement and attainment patterns are somewhat bimodal in that men are more likely than women to be both academic stars and school failures; and women are less likely than men to excel in mathematics, science, and technical fields, while men are less likely to shine in reading, writing, social sciences, and humanities. Post–high school careers, college majors, and professional degrees reflect these similar gender patterns in choices of college majors.

Since the middle of the 20th century, the historic male advantages in access to schooling and educational outcomes have largely disappeared. Women's educational achievements have closed many of the gender gaps favoring men, and in some cases, new ones favoring women have emerged. To be sure, there are important social class and ethnic variations in gender differences. Nevertheless, overall, female students in the United States achieve at higher levels soon after they begin school and attain more education than their male counterparts at almost every degree level. However, at all education levels, men receive larger occupational and income returns to their education.

This reading begins with a more detailed description of gender differences in educational processes, outcomes, and returns to schooling from the opportunity structure. Gender differences suggest two dilemmas: The first dilemma involves why women do so well in school. In the face of continuing male income and occupational advantages in income returns for similar educational credentials, women's educational achievements and attainments appear anomalous. The second one concerns the underperformance of male students, especially males from disadvantaged ethnic minority backgrounds.

K–12 EDUCATIONAL PROCESSES AND OUTCOMES

The years between children's birth and entry into kindergarten are critically important for readying them for school. There are very few gender differences in young children's access to preprimary school. Nonetheless, by kindergarten, females have a slight advantage in word recognition. By fourth grade males begin to perform slightly better in mathematics (U.S. Department of Education, 2013). These early, small gender differences in academic performance foreshadow the achievement patterns that continue through high school and postsecondary education.

TRACKING AND GROUPING

Ability grouping within elementary school classrooms and tracking of academic courses in secondary school are two of the most common organizational features of U.S. public education that shape educational outcomes. A student's gender alone rarely has a large effect on ability group or track placement, but elementary school placements in special education and gifted programs often reflect an intersection of students' gender, social class, and racial background. For example, although a majority of students are not identified for any special programs during elementary school, middle-class and white students are more likely to be identified as academically gifted, while ethnic minority and working-class students are more likely to be identified for special education. Disadvantaged minority males (especially African Americans, Latinos, and Native Americans) are disproportionately placed in special education classes for learning, behavioral, or emotionally disabled students while white, middle-class females are disproportionately identified for gifted education programs (Oakes, 2005). These placements are consequential because elementary school ability groupings launch students onto educational trajectories that influence outcomes from elementary through postsecondary education (Lucas, 1999; Oakes, 2005).

ACADEMIC PERFORMANCE K–12

A key reason that tracking and ability grouping are important is because they influence students' exposure to the formal curriculum. The National Assessment of Educational Progress (NAEP) is widely recognized as a measure of how well students learned the formal curriculum. NAEP assesses student academic performance in a given school at Grades 4, 8, and 12 in a variety of subjects. NAEP results since 2000 show gender gaps exist in reading, writing, and mathematics. Overall, at each grade level, females outperform males in reading and writing. Males slightly outperform females in mathematics; however, when 12th-grade NAEP performance is broken down into subject areas, males' performance exceeds females' in only two of four mathematics content areas (U.S. Department of Education, 2013, p. 16). Males outperform females in science during the early grades, but by 12th grade, their advantage disappears. Overall, the gender gaps in math and science have narrowed since the 1970s, but the ones in reading and math persist.

SAT

College entrance exams such as the SAT are highly influential. The majority of SAT takers are females (53.3%), and overall scores reflect a large gender gap in favor of males (1486 compared to 1511) (College Board, 2012). It is worth noting that gender differences in SAT scores are dwarfed by ethnic differences in them, with Asians and whites scoring higher than other racial and ethnic groups. Males' SAT math scores exceed those of females by 33 points. On average, males' scores in critical reading fall slightly above those of females (5 points), which is the opposite of the pattern found in NAEP scores where females do better than males in reading. Women's SAT writing scores exceed those of men by 13 points. The population of students who take the SAT includes those planning to attend college whereas NAEP tests reflect the overall population of students. This may be one reason that SAT scores do not reflect gender patterns found in NAEP results.

HIGH SCHOOL CURRICULA

Students cannot learn what they have not been taught. Pallas and Alexander (1983) demonstrated that 30 years ago a major factor in SAT score gaps was students' differential enrollment rates in key high-level courses; students enrolling in higher-level courses in math and science generally score better on their college entrance exams. Analyses of high school transcripts reveal that large proportions of male and female students enroll in geometry, algebra II, chemistry, and biology (Institute of Education Sciences, 2007). In fact, compared to the gender gaps of the 1970s, contemporary enrollment gaps in these courses are relatively small. With the exception of calculus and physics, females are slightly more likely than males to enroll in these math and science courses.

Today, there are few official systematic gender differences in curricular offerings for public school students. That was not always the case. Until the early 20th century, female students were unlikely to enroll in certain courses because of pervasive gender stereotypes about the proper kinds of knowledge for males and females. Curricula in coed schools varied but always reflected the local community's social construction of gender, especially the gendered nature of men's and women's public and private roles. Historically, some secondary science electives offered gendered curricula. For example, in a physics course for girls, students learned about the mechanics of vacuum cleaners and sewing machines (Tyack & Hansot, 1990). Observable gender differences in math and science enrollments that grew out of the ways that schools organized access to the curricula resulted in females taking far fewer advanced math and science courses than males. Tyack and Hansot (1990) conclude that this historical gendering of the science curricula contributed to few if any females being prepared for college science or engineering courses during the early decades of the 20th century.

At present there are no gender differences in the likelihood of students' placements in higher-level math and science secondary tracks once their prior achievement and previous track placements are taken into account. Research identifies persistent race and social class effects in track placements, though. Ethnic differences in higher-level course enrollments are related to many factors, including the fact that disadvantaged minority students, especially males, were disproportionately placed in special education during elementary school. By high school, relatively few disadvantaged minority males are prepared to enroll in top-level academic courses.

ADVANCED PLACEMENT COURSES

Advanced Placement (AP) courses offer the most rigorous, college-level coverage of subject matter. Compared to other high-track courses, AP courses provide students with several advantages including exposure to college-level course work. If they pass the AP exam, students may receive college course credit. To pass the AP exam, students must score a 3 or 4 on the exam (depending on the institution in which they enroll). Males are more likely than female students to score a 3 or higher (61% compared to 54%) on biology, calculus A/B, U.S. history, chemistry, English literature, and composition (Ross et al., 2012).

Females are the majority of exam takers in social studies, English, and foreign languages; males were the majority of exam takers in calculus, computer science, and sciences. Nevertheless, compared to males, females fare relatively poorly in most AP exam subjects. Males' average AP scores in social studies, English, calculus, computer science, and sciences exceeded those of females. Females' average AP scores exceeded males' average scores only in foreign languages (U.S. Department of Education, 2005, p. 6). In fact, foreign languages is the only subject area in which females' average scores exceeded the threshold of 3.0 necessary for college credit, whereas males' average scores exceeded the 3.0 threshold in all other subject areas. The gendered patterns of achievement favoring male students in AP exam results are more similar to SAT scores than to NAEP gender patterns. It is important to remember that the college-bound population of students taking AP or SAT exams is not the same as the general population that takes NAEP tests.

EXTRACURRICULAR AND COCURRICULAR ACTIVITIES

For most students, high school is much more than academic courses. Extracurricular and cocurricular activities are important components of students' social lives as well as key contributors to their cognitive development, especially activities considered as cocurricular. Sociological research indicates that positive school outcomes are correlated with participation in extracurricular and cocurricular activities.

There are clear gender differences in the degree and type of participation in extracurricular activities. Females are more likely than males to participate in extracurricular and cocurricular activities, a fact that may be related to their overall higher academic performance. With the exception of student government, where participation rates are comparable among males and females, other activities are clearly gendered. Athletics are the only activity in which more males (45%) than females (32%) are involved. Females are much more likely than male students to participate in yearbook, newspaper, music and performing arts, and academic clubs (Freeman, 2004).

RISKY BEHAVIOR IN HIGH SCHOOL

Students who dislike school or who engage in risky behavior are less likely to succeed academically, and they are more likely to drop out of high school. NAEP data suggest that while most students are not involved in risky behavior, male students are more likely than female peers to have engaged in drug or alcohol use, to have carried a weapon to school, or to have been a participant in or victim of school violence. Childbearing has a negative effect on females' likelihood of completing high school, although young mothers from higher socioeconomic status (SES) are more likely to graduate than young mothers from low-SES backgrounds (Freeman, 2004).

High school graduation is an important indicator of many future life course outcomes. The proportion of public high school freshmen who graduate with a regular diploma four years after beginning Grade 9 is estimated by the average freshman graduation rate (AFGR). The overall AFGR in 2009 was 75.5%, but the male rate (71.8%) was lower than the rate for females (78.9%). The rates indicate that one-fourth of those who began public high school fail to graduate within four years (Ross et al., 2012).

Nationally, an estimated 78% of whites, 72% of Asian Americans, 55% of African Americans, and 53% of Latinos graduated from high school in 2003 (Greene & Winters, 2006). Gender differences in dropout rates exist in all ethnic groups: Among whites, 5% fewer males (78.9%) than females (84.0%) graduate from high school; among African Americans, males (57.3%) are 12% less likely to graduate than females (69.3%); among Asian American males, the graduation rate of 88% is 4% lower than for females (93.1%); among American Indian students, males (60.5%) are 5.2% less likely to graduate than females (67.7%); and among Latinos, males (60.3%) are less likely to graduate than females (69.7%), reflecting a 9.4% female graduation advantage (Ross et al., 2012). Dropout rates are declining for all male ethnic groups, except Latinos for whom rates are holding steady (Freeman, 2004).

POSTSECONDARY OUTCOMES

Postsecondary Enrollments

Postsecondary education is becoming increasingly important in the information age. In 2010, 43% of Americans 18–24 years of age were enrolled in higher education. Although 40 years ago men were the majority of students at all levels of postsecondary education, since 1980, females have been more likely to enroll in college and to graduate than their male peers. In 2010, 39% of males in the "18–24 years of age" cohort compared to 47% of females were enrolled in postsecondary education. Currently, the gender imbalance among those who are enrolled is stark: Fifty-six percent of undergraduates and 58% of graduate students are women.

According to Ross et al. (2012), the pattern of gender imbalance holds for whites, among whom 43% of males compared to 51% of females aged 18–24 are enrolled in college; the figures are, for blacks, 31% compared to 43%; for Latinos, 26% compared to 36%; for American Indian youth, 24% compared to 33%, and for multiracial students between the ages of 18 and 24, 40% compared to 49%.

Although men are still a majority of students in first-professional degree programs (medicine, dentistry, law, optometry, pharmacy, medicine, podiatry, and theology), women have made striking progress in first-professional degree enrollment since the 1970s when only 9% of students were women. In 1970, for instance, women received 5% of law degrees, 8% of medical degrees, and 1% of dentistry degrees (Freeman, 2004). By 2001, the percentages were 47%, 43%, and 39%, respectively. In some fields, like veterinary medicine and pharmacy, a majority of recent recipients are women (Wright, 2006).

Postsecondary Attainment

Enrollment is the first step to obtaining a higher education. Persistence to graduation is the final and most important step. Males are less likely than females to persist in higher education. Among students who entered postsecondary educational institutions in the 2003–2004 academic year, 49% attained some type of degree by 2009 (this includes certificates as well as AA and BA degrees). Those attending two-year schools were more likely than those attending four-year schools to receive their degrees by 2009. Among full-time four-year degree students who began their college educations in 2003–2004, 51% of blacks, 52% of Latinos, 66% of multiracial individuals, 73% of whites, and 76% of Asians obtained their degrees by 2009 (Ross et al., 2012).

While 59% of undergraduate degrees are awarded to female students, race-by-gender variations in undergraduate degree attainment remain. Among white bachelor's degree recipients, 57% are female; among blacks, 66%; and among Latinos, 60%. There are notable gender differences (about ±10% in degree attainment across all racial groups), but the magnitude of the gender discrepancies is dwarfed by the much larger between-race differences in time to degree among full-time students (Ross et al., 2012).

There are persistent gender differences in college majors. About one-fourth of the bachelor's degrees conferred each year are in science, technology, engineering, and mathematics (STEM).

Males continue to be more likely than females to receive a STEM degree. Not unexpectedly, there are race differences in STEM degree attainment, but there is little difference across race in the gender difference in STEM attainment (Ross et al., 2012). Table 33.1 presents data on majors by gender. Although it is over a decade old, the table shows that students majoring in engineering, computer and information systems, and agriculture are disproportionately male; those majoring in biology and life sciences, accounting,

education, psychology, and health fields are largely females. The only majors that approach gender balance are mathematics, business administration, and the social sciences and history.

These patterns both reflect and deviate from earlier trends in academic outcomes. Accounting, social science, mathematics, biology, and history were fields historically dominated by males, but increasingly women are choosing the field as a major. At the same time, the disproportionate enrollment of males in engineering and computer and information systems majors is inconsistent with the minor gender disparities in high school course-taking and academic achievement. The virtual monopoly that men once enjoyed in engineering and computer and information sciences has been broken, but the fields of study are far from gender parity (Huang, Taddese, & Walter, 2000). Gender differences in fields of study have implications for labor force participation.

Table 33.1 Percentage of Bachelor's Degrees Granted by Field and Gender (2001)

	Female	Male
Engineering	20	80
Computer and Information Systems	28	72
Physical Sciences	41	59
Agriculture and Natural Resources	45	55
Mathematics	48	52
Business Administration	49	51
Social Sciences and History	52	48
Biology and Life Sciences	60	40
Accounting	61	39
Education	77	23
Psychology	78	22
Health and Related Services	84	16

Note. From *Trends in Educational Equity of Girls and Women: 2004* (p. 78), by C. E. Freeman, 2004, Washington, DC: U.S. Department of Education, National Center for Educational Statistics. Reprinted with permission.

LABOR FORCE PARTICIPATION

Labor market outcomes for men and women have changed during the past 35 years in ways that reflect many of the trends in education. During the past half-century as the U.S. economy transformed from one based upon manufacturing to one dominated by services, gender roles became less rigid, more women obtained educational credentials, and greater proportions of women entered the labor force.

Women today are much more likely to work outside the home across all levels of educational attainment, and the occupational structure is much less sex segregated than it was a generation ago. Nonetheless, at every level of education, women's labor force participation rates are lower than men's. For example, in 2010 among 25- to 64-year-olds with less than a high school diploma, 64% of men compared to 40% of women were employed or looking for work. Labor participation rates for men and women increase as their educational credentials increase. Among those with a high school education, 72% of men compared to 60% of women participated in the labor force; among those with a bachelor of arts degree, 89% of men and 82% of women were employed (Ross et al., 2012).

INCOME RETURNS TO EDUCATIONAL CREDENTIALS

Just as labor force participation rates increase with educational attainment levels, so do earnings. Both females and males enjoy a positive relationship between their educational credentials and income at every level of education; those with more education earn more. Still, even with comparable education levels, females continue to earn less than males. The 2010 U.S. Census shows that for all year-round full-time workers, overall females earned 69% of what males earned. The gap in the female–male earnings ratio tends to narrow as occupations require greater education. Women in retail sales earn 65.5% of what males in retail sales earn, while women in computer programming earn 88.5% of what males in the same occupation earn (Hegewisch, Williams, & Henderson, 2011). The U.S. Bureau of Labor Statistics reports that in 2010 females in medicine earned 71.1% of the income of male physicians, most likely because they specialize in less lucrative fields such as family medicine as compared to orthopedic surgery, a specialty dominated by males (U.S. Census Bureau, 2004).

There is a gender gap in income returns at every level of educational attainment. In 2000, women without a high school diploma earned 80% of what men with similar education earned; in 2010, women from all racial groups with a high school diploma earned 83% of what comparably educated men earned; women with bachelor's degrees received 88% of men's income. Notably jobs in STEM fields pay women 86% of what they pay men in comparable jobs (Ross et al., 2012). This gender gap in pay is found among all racial groups.

Economists and sociologists offer several possible reasons for the education-to-earnings gender gap. Structural explanations include the tendency for women to major in fields that are less lucrative (teaching vs. engineering), sex-composition

bias—whereby people who work in female-dominated fields or subspecialties are paid less (Bellas & Reskin, 1994), the likelihood that women will drop in and out of the labor force to have children, and the relatively higher rate of part-time employment among women (Freeman, 2004, p. 98). Sociologists also recognize that sexist norms that devalue women's work may contribute to the income gap.

None of these explanations adequately accounts for gender gaps within occupations. Women's median earnings are lower than men's in nearly all occupations. This is true for the female-dominated, male-dominated, and gender-neutral occupations. Occupations are considered largely sex segregated if they are dominated by men or women. Four of 10 women work in traditionally female occupations while 5 of 10 men work in traditionally male occupations. Typically male-dominated occupations pay more than female ones requiring similar skills and educational credentials. Men even earn more than women in traditionally female jobs like nursing (men's $1,201 per week compared to women's $1,037) and teaching (men's $1,024 per week compared to women's $931) (Hegewisch et al., 2011).

In 2010, the Bureau of Labor Statistics (BLS) calculated the weekly earnings for men and women in 111 occupations. In only 4 of 111 did women's median weekly earnings exceed those of men employed in the same occupation (Hegewisch et al., 2011). Although the actual size of the gender wage gap has fallen since 2000, of 534 occupations listed by the BLS, women earn more than men in only 7 of them. Together these 7 occupations account for 3% of full-time working women in the labor force. Thus, the remaining 97% of full-time working women earn less than their male counterparts for the same job (Glynn & Wu, 2013).

THE FEMALE QUESTION: WHY DO FEMALES DO SO WELL IN SCHOOL?

Exploring the structural reasons women earn less for their educational credentials is useful for understanding income differences by gender, but it does not help to account for *why* women continue to achieve so well and attain so much education in the face of the education-to-earnings gender gap. Given that American society is purportedly a meritocracy that rewards those who accomplish more, the academic success of women relative to men in the face of such income disparities seems anomalous.

Mickelson (1989) proposed several hypotheses to account for the apparent anomaly of women's educational accomplishments. The various hypotheses draw from social scientific theories of human behavior that build upon the intersection between structural forces and individual components of achievement motivation.

The first one challenges the notion that discrimination in the labor force still exists. The Pollyanna hypothesis proposes that contemporary women believe men and women are rewarded equally by the opportunity structure based on their merit, not gender. For the young women who believe discrimination in labor force returns to women's education is a thing of the past, doing well in school is the rational course of action. Under this scenario, the achievement by women is not anomalous because they expect to be equally rewarded for their efforts and accomplishments.

Even the young women who accept that gender discrimination still exists in the occupational structure do well in school. The differential reference group hypothesis proposes that they gauge fairness of rewards to education by comparisons among women with different levels of education, not necessarily between men and women with the same education. Women with more education work in more lucrative, higher-status occupations than women with less education; therefore, women's growing educational accomplishments make perfect sense. In her memoir, Supreme Court Justice Sonia Sotomayor explained her decision to join the New York district attorney's office after graduating from Yale Law School instead of taking a lucrative position with a law firm:

[M]y starting salary would still be more than what my mother ever made as a nurse, which to Titi Aurora, who worked as a seamstress, had always seemed lavish. (Sotomayor, 2013, p. 194)

Third, the social-powerlessness perspective rests on the premise that young women are keenly aware that the sex-segregated occupational structure and lower wages paid to women mean their educational efforts will not necessarily be rewarded based on merit. The social-powerlessness hypothesis proposes that well-educated young women expect to obtain returns on their own schooling through their future husbands' occupational successes. Given this reality, they expect academic achievement will reap the greatest rewards from the marriage market, not the labor market. Hence they do well in school because better-educated women make more desirable wives and mothers, and educational achievements will better position them to compete in the marriage market.

The next hypothesis rests on theories of gender-role socialization. According to this view women do well in school because they have been socialized to respond to external validation for their efforts, whereas males are more likely to have an internal orientation. "Good girls" comply with directives from authority figures like parents and teachers because they desire the praise of these significant others. Because their motivation to excel in school is not necessarily linked to external rewards such as occupational prestige or high incomes, the weaker returns to education they receive do not render their achievement anomalous. Educational achievement is not about getting good jobs and high salaries; rather, it is about doing the right thing—what the teacher or professor asks.

The fifth hypothesis proposes that women are more likely than men to evaluate returns to education in terms not only of the income, status, and careers they may lead to, but also of education's potential to enhance the quality of their personal, familial, and community lives. Feminist theory challenges the traditional views that labor market rewards are the primary measure of returns to educational successes. Feminist theory suggests that there are fluid boundaries between women's public and private spheres. From a young age, women are socialized to approach their lives by weaving public and private roles into a single tapestry. For women, the public (the economy and the polity) and the private (family and community) exist as a continuum, rather than as a dichotomy. Thus, educational accomplishments that are useful to a woman for her roles in the private sphere are highly valuable.

Dumais (2002) observed that each of Mickelson's hypotheses for women's school success reflects a different habitus, one of three core components of Bourdieu's theory of practice, more commonly referred to as a theory of social action. According to Bourdieu, cultural capital, habitus, and field operate together to generate social action—in this case school success. The concept of cultural capital refers to objects that require special cultural abilities to appreciate, such as art; educational credentials and the credentialing system; and the capacity to appreciate and understand cultural goods (Dumais, 2002, p. 46). Schools reward students with greater cultural capital. Consequently, those who possess cultural capital excel in school. Middle-class girls are likely to possess more cultural capital than are boys. An important source of middle-class females' cultural capital edge is their greater participation in private music, dance, or art lessons and cocurricular activities, all of which contribute to their stock of cultural capital (Dumais, 2002).

Bourdieu's concept of habitus refers to dispositions that influence a person's actions. The gendered nature of habitus is a consequence of the different possibilities that women and men perceive as available to them. Habitus is developed during childhood as a person grows to understand her or his place in the social structure. A student's habitus expresses perceived aspects of the gendered structure of opportunity that awaits her or him (race and social class are also relevant). Habitus plays a large role in school success because students' decisions to invest in their education, whether or not to study hard, and what college major and career

to pursue depend on their expectations of whether people like themselves can and should be academically successful.

The research of sociologists like Dumais and Mickelson offers various theories to account for the female portion of the dilemma of gendered patterns in academic achievement, specifically the anomalous achievement of females in the face of relatively inequitable rewards for their accomplishments. While none of the theories provides a definitive explanation for women's academic successes, each one sheds some light on the ways that social structure and individual agency contribute to school outcomes. We now turn to the dilemma raised by male patterns of academic underperformance.

THE MALE QUESTION: IS THERE A MALE CRISIS IN EDUCATION?

The previous sections of this chapter described how, on average, beginning in elementary school males fall behind females on a number of measures of academic achievement. Even taking into account the striking ethnic and social class differences in these outcomes, overall, males demonstrate lower verbal skills and are more likely to be identified for special education, to engage in more risky behaviors, to have lower high school graduation rates, and to attend and graduate from college at lower rates than females.

The gender gaps in primary, secondary, and postsecondary enrollments, performance, and outcomes have gained attention from policy makers, parents, and educators. Adherents to one school of thought consider the gender gaps as indicators that American society is leaving boys behind. Many of the observers who perceive "a boy crisis" believe that the societal focus on females' educational disadvantages (American Association of University Women, 1992; c.f., Sadker & Sadker, 1995) during the past 30 years has resulted in neglect of the genuine problems of male students (Sommers, 2000). Some argue that the presence of so many female teachers in elementary school and behavioral norms that require students to sit still for extended periods of time, in combination with a curriculum that emphasizes reading and verbal skills, create learning environments that are less conducive to boys' early educational successes. Consequently, these critics argue, males fall behind their female counterparts beginning in the early grades, and they are launched on less positive educational trajectories than females with similar backgrounds and cognitive strengths.

Many educators, parents, and scholars find the situation of black male students particularly troubling (Brown, 2011; Holzman, 2012; Jackson & Moore, 2006; Kunjufu, 1985). Ferguson (2000) proposes that widely held negative societal images of black masculinity result in many educators, primarily whites, "seeing" black boys as adults. Educators' responses to black boys, especially the harsh discipline they dole out, contribute to the early educational failures that later become the high rates of special education placement, low test scores, high rates of dropping out, and consequent low rates of college attendance and graduation among black males. Lopez (2003) makes a similar argument about immigrant Caribbean males' negative educational experiences. She describes the toxic race–gender stigma that accompanies immigrant Caribbean male students to urban schools and educators' harsh responses to the stereotypes of them as "hoodlums."

A second school of thought, while acknowledging the existence of gender gaps, rejects the notion of a boy crisis. Those who hold this view note that when educational outcomes are broken out by social class and ethnicity, a much more nuanced view of the gender and education landscape appears. There is more within-gender variation in educational outcomes by ethnicity and social class than variation in outcomes between the genders. From this perspective, each gender faces unique problems, but the gender gap is dwarfed by race, ethnic, and social class gaps. Cynthia Fuchs Epstein (1988) calls this phenomenon a deceptive distinction, because gaps appear to be about gender when, in fact, they are about something else.

Those who reject the existence of a boy crisis in education point to evidence that contradicts the sweeping generalization that male students are being left behind. They note that wealthy males do not lag behind females in middle or high school. Poor and inner-city males—primarily blacks, Latinos, and American Indian males—have significantly less educational success than females from their ethnic group (Kimmel, 2006). Throughout K–12 schooling, males tend to perform better than females in math and science, a long-standing pattern according to historians of education (Tyack & Hansot, 1990). On achievement tests, especially the important AP exam and SAT college entrance exams, males still outperform females.

As previously discussed, because males are less likely to matriculate to postsecondary education, postsecondary enrollment gaps by gender are stark. And once again, ethnicity and social class complicate the picture. For example, at most elite private institutions including Stanford, Harvard, Princeton, Duke, Yale, and Chicago, there is no gender imbalance in enrollment. At the University of California–Berkeley, the California Institute of Technology, and the Massachusetts Institute of Technology the gender balance in enrollment favors males (Kimmel, 2006). College majors continue to reflect social stereotypes of gender roles. With the exception of biology, male undergraduates are more likely than females to major in the STEM disciplines that lead to lucrative careers. Importantly, irrespective of college majors, labor force data indicate that, compared to females, males earn more at all educational levels and all levels of the occupational structure.

Whether or not one considers the relative underachievement of males to be evidence of a crisis, patterns of male underperformance require an explanation. Social conservatives, like Sommers (2000), argue that the educational system operates in ways that are destructive to boys. For example, the overwhelmingly female elementary teacher force means boys have little access to adult male role models during a critical period in their early development. She finds that schools are organized in ways that devalue or actually work against males' innate strengths. Moreover, she maintains, progressive educators and feminists have ignored boys' educational problems while focusing on girls' needs.

Kimmel (2006) and Lopez (2003) suggest that the nature of some school subjects either work in support of or against certain norms of masculinity. From this perspective, succeeding in the humanities, reading, English, and foreign language requires "feminine" ways of thinking; Kimmel (2006) argues that boys hate English for the same reasons that girls love it—there is no single correct answer to most questions in that discipline. Science, mathematics, and technology, all of which have discrete correct answers, are more in tune with stereotypical masculine norms. Willis (1977) proposed a variation of this argument to explain why British working-class males rejected working hard in school. He found that working-class males defined schoolwork and other forms of intellectual labor as feminine in contrast to physical labor, which they considered to be masculine. These arguments are consistent with the data showing that working-class and low-income males, rather than elite males, are the most likely to underperform in school relative to females of the same social class background.

Sociologists also have proposed a more obvious reason that boys do less well in school. Essentially, why should men work so hard? School underperformance can be considered rational behavior given the fact that males at every level of educational attainment will likely obtain greater occupational and income rewards than females even with less education. Males have less incentive to achieve and attain their full educational potentials considering that in some labor markets male high school graduates earn as much as or more than female college graduates.

Conclusion

Without doubt, gender differences in educational processes and outcomes exist. Because gender patterns in academic outcomes are consequential, they require continued attention by educators, parents, and policy makers. Nevertheless, it is important to consider the fact that there are greater within-gender variations by social class and ethnicity than there are differences between the genders. The ways that gender shapes a given student's educational experiences and eventual outcomes are intimately tied to her or his social class and ethnicity and to the larger social structural context in which she or he lives.

The twin dilemmas of female achievement in the face of uncertain rewards and male underachievement are more than flip sides of the same coin. They raise important issues for sociologists trying to understand how the processes involved in the gendered aspects of educational stratification contribute to social stratification more generally.

References

American Association of University Women. (1992). *How schools shortchange girls.* Washington, DC: Author.

Bellas, M., & Reskin, B. (1994). On comparable worth. *Academe* (September/October), 83–85.

Brown, A. L. (2011). "Same old stories": The black male in social science and educational literature, 1930s to the present. *Teachers College Record, 113*(9), 2047–2079.

College Board. (2012). *2012 college-bound seniors: Total group profile report.* Princeton, NJ: Author.

Dumais, S. (2002). Cultural capital, gender, and school success: The role of habitus. *Sociology of Education, 75*(1), 44–68.

Epstein, C. F. (1988). *Deceptive distinctions: Sex, gender, and the social order.* New Haven, CT: Yale University Press.

Ferguson, A. A. (2000). *Bad boys: Public schools in the making of black masculinity.* Ann Arbor: University of Michigan Press.

Freeman, C. E. (2004). *Trends in educational equity of girls and women: 2004.* Washington, DC: U.S. Department of Education, National Center for Education Statistics, U.S. Government Printing Office.

Glynn, S., & Wu, N. (2013, April). *Gender wage gap differs by occupation.* Washington, DC: Center for American Progress. Retrieved from www .americanprogress.org/issues/labor/news/2013

Greene, J. P., & Winters, M. A. (2006, April). *Leaving boys behind: Public high school graduation rates* (Civil Report 48). New York: Manhattan Institute.

Hegewisch, A., Williams, G., & Henderson, A. (2011, April). *Gender wage gap by occupation fact sheet* (IWPS#C350a). Washington, DC: Institute for Women's Policy Research.

Holzman, M. (2012). *The urgency of now: The Schott 50 state report on public education and black males.* Cambridge, MA: Schott Foundation for Public Education.

Huang, G., Taddese, N., & Walter, E. (2000). Entry and persistence of women and minorities in college science and engineering education. *Education Statistics Quarterly, 2*(3), 59–60. Retrieved from http://nces.ed.gov/pubsearch/pubsinfo.asp?pubid=2000601

Institute of Education Sciences. (2007). *America's high school graduates: Results from the 2005 NAEP high school transcript study* (NCES2007-467). Washington, DC: U.S. Department of Education. Retrieved from http://nationsreportcard.gov

Jackson, J. F. L., & Moore, J. L. (2006). African American males in education: Endangered or ignored? *Teachers College Record, 108*(2), 201–205.

Kimmel, M. (2006). A war against boys? *Dissent* (Fall). Retrieved from http://www.dissentmagazine.org/article/?article=700

Kunjufu, J. (1985). *Countering the conspiracy to destroy black boys.* Chicago: African American Images.

Lopez, N. (2003). *Hopeful girls, troubled boys: Race and gender disparity in urban education.* New York: Routledge.

Lucas, S. R. (1999). *Tracking inequality: Stratification and mobility in American high schools.* New York: Teachers College Press, Columbia University.

Mickelson, R. A. (1989). Why does Jane read and write so well? The anomaly of women's achievement. *Sociology of Education, 62*(1), 47–63.

Oakes, J. (2005). *Keeping track: How schools structure inequality.* New Haven, CT: Yale University Press.

Pallas, A. M., & Alexander, K. L. (1983). Sex differences in quantitative SAT performance: New evidence on the differential coursework hypothesis. *American Educational Research Journal, 20*(2), 165–182.

Ross, T., Kena, G., Rathbun, A., KewalRamani, A., Zhang, J., Kristapovich, P., & Manning, E. (2005). *Higher education: Gaps in access and persistence study.* Washington, DC: Institute of Education Sciences, National Center for Education Statistics, U.S. Department of Education.

Sadker, M., & Sadker, D. (1995). *Failing at fairness: How our schools cheat girls.* New York: Simon & Schuster.

Sommers, C. H. (2000). *The war against boys: How misguided feminism is harming our young men.* New York: Simon & Schuster.

Sotomayor, S. (2013). *My beloved world.* New York: Knopf.

Swanson, C. B. (2004). *Graduation rates: Real kids, real numbers.* Washington, DC: Urban Institute.

Tyack, D., & Hansot, E. (1990). *Learning together: A history of coeducation in American public schools.* New Haven, CT: Yale University Press.

U.S. Census Bureau. (2004). *Population estimates.* Washington, DC: Author.

U.S. Department of Education. (2005). *National Center for Education Statistics: 2005 mathematics assessment.* Washington, DC: Institute of Education Sciences.

U.S. Department of Education. (2013). *National Center for Education Statistics: 2011 mathematics assessment.* Washington, DC: Author, Institute of Education Sciences.

Willis, P. (1977). *Learning to labor.* New York: Columbia University Press.

Wright, D. (2006, January). Animal attraction: Women in contemporary veterinary medicine. *S&T.* Retrieved from http://www.brynmawr.edu/sandt/2006_january

Projects for Further Exploration

1. Using an academic database, look up the topics of "race" and "academic achievement" to see what other research has been done in this area. How does this compare to the arguments made by Caroline Hodges Persell and Roslyn Arlin Mickelson in this chapter?

2. Try to replicate the data used by Joseph J. Ferrare in this chapter by collecting information on what courses are offered at the schools on which you are collecting data. This information may be on the webpages for those schools, or you could get a list of courses available from the school offices. Identify vertical courses and horizontal courses. Which courses do you suspect are the most popular among students in your schools? Why are the courses popular, or why not?

3. Using the U.S. Census website, collect information about the poverty level of the school districts you are studying. Are there patterns between socioeconomic classes of districts and the measures of achievement on which you previously collected data?

8

EDUCATION AND OPPORTUNITY

Attempts at Equality and Equity in Education

Why is there inequality in the educational system, and what can we do about it? As suggested by this book's introduction and the readings in Chapter 7, the U.S. educational system is rife with problems of inequality. Many programs to bring about change have been designed to remedy these inequalities. This chapter contains descriptions and analyses of some of these efforts, most of which are current issues in education today. Although we cannot cover all attempts at equality and equity, we focus on those most salient, both historically and at the present time. We do not cover general educational reforms in this part of the book, but leave the discussion of those efforts to Chapter 11 and other chapters.

In studying broad changes in education of any kind, we notice that the impetus for these changes comes from many different directions, with the most far-reaching changes generated at the federal level, either through judicial decisions or via massive funding efforts. This should not be surprising, given the preceding readings about the organization of schools in the United States (Chapter 4) and the way schools are financed (Reyes and Rodriguez, Chapter 3). In fact, loose coupling combined with local financing of schools makes broad-based reform efforts very difficult in the United States, as the readings in this chapter suggest.

School systems across the United States and other countries are very difficult organizations in which to introduce change, as illustrated by the many stakeholders in the open systems model. One of the most significant pieces of legislation to impact schools was targeted directly at increasing equality in education—*Brown v. Board of Education*. In 1954, the Supreme Court decision of *Brown v. the Board of Education of Topeka, Kansas* ruled that separate but equal education was unconstitutional. This decision set in motion many changes in public school education today and is thought to be responsible for changing the composition of cities and their schools as whites fled from cities to avoid sending their children to desegregated schools. In 1964, James Coleman was commissioned by the U.S. Congress to assess changes in schools 10 years after this ruling. Coleman found that the 1954 decision had little impact on the segregation of America's schools. Pressure began to mount as school districts were "encouraged" to desegregate. These changes sometimes meant closing all-black schools and moving those students into formerly all-white schools (Cecelski, 1994). White residents also worked to alter the shape and structure of school districts during this period in an attempt to keep from sending their children to desegregated schools (Rubin, 1972).

The early 1970s were active times, with courts mandating school desegregation across the country in a climate of outright racial conflict, particularly in the South. Policies of both desegregation and affirmative action have been challenged and overturned in the courts. Focus on both minority status and social class is important because poverty is not distributed evenly across racial and ethnic households. In 2009, far more black (42.1%) and Hispanic (33.0%) households with children under the age of 18 were living below the poverty level than white (13.4%) households (U.S. Census Bureau, 2012).

Issues of segregation, desegregation, and resegregation are addressed in the first two readings in this chapter. The first reading by Gary Orfield discusses the legal history of school desegregation and the current state of "resegregation" in American schools. The second reading by Megan M. Holland describes what happens when minority students are integrated into a majority white high school. She describes the process of integration from the perspective of the students being integrated.

Two more recent attempts by the federal government to achieve equality in education are No Child Left Behind (NCLB) and Race to the Top. These two pieces of legislation designed to improve schools focused on increasing educational opportunities and experiences for *all* children. A series of federal reform efforts culminated in 2002 in the NCLB legislation, and in 2010, President Obama introduced his Blueprint for Reform; both of these focus on accountability and innovation. One reform effort that is gaining momentum as a result of NCLB and the Blueprint for Reform is the charter school movement. Both pieces of legislation saw charter schools as an opportunity to provide alternative educational opportunities in public school systems and put more pressure on existing schools to improve the educational experiences they provide. Charter schools share many similarities with the earlier magnet schools; however, charter schools operate outside of most regulation by federal, state, and local authorities. The reading in this chapter by Linda A. Renzulli and Vincent J. Roscigno describes the rise of charter schools in the United States and considers the future of this recent school movement. The reading by Linda Darling-Hammond uses her experience and background in researching school reform efforts to consider how charter schools, and all schools, can be more successful in educating children from disadvantaged backgrounds.

Although only briefly discussed in readings in this chapter, magnet schools, the precursors to charter schools, were one way that school districts attempted to desegregate without busing students involuntarily from one school to another. Magnet schools were organized in districts to attract students from different backgrounds around particular subject areas such as math and science or the arts. Successful magnet schools should have desegregated school districts; however, this was not always the case. In many cases, magnet schools enrolled only white students because those students had the cultural resources to both learn about and qualify for admittance to these specialized schools. Another problem was that teachers in magnet schools were trained in the particular area of the magnet, not necessarily in working with children from diverse racial backgrounds, as would be the case in desegregated schools (Metz, 1994).

A little background may be useful to understand the controversy surrounding the idea of parents choosing schools for their children. School choice became a political issue in the 1970s. At that time Americans were concerned about desegregation and the quality of education their children were receiving. Choice was seen as a way of improving education without increasing costs and getting parents more involved in the education of their children. Models of school choice, however, varied considerably; some were statewide, and some only involved a single district, while others included private schools. Whereas some people argue that school choice gives lower-class families an opportunity to get their children out of inferior educational settings and send them to better schools, others believe that lower-class parents will not have the "cultural capital" necessary to find their way through the system to the best schools (Saporito & Lareau, 1999) or to broker the best education for their children. Unfortunately, the first criterion for white parents in making a school choice is the racial composition of the school their children will attend (Johnson, 2006; Saporito & Lareau, 1999). The result of such choices reinforces the resegregation of schools, as described in this chapter.

Attempts to achieve equality and equity in education face an uphill battle. The problems faced by schools are considerable, and setting standards alone does not make up for inequality in society. As Douglas B. Downey and Benjamin G. Gibbs remind us in their reading in this chapter, the achievement gap is rooted as much in the context of children's lives as it is in the structure of our schools.

You will soon see that changing schools to make them more equal is clearly political. We include a selection by Michael W. Apple to explicitly discuss the politics of school reform. In the last reading in this chapter, Apple considers the conservative strategy toward education and suggests that liberals must think more politically if they are to effect change in schools.

All of these efforts to achieve equity and equality are very different; none are without controversy, but some are more controversial than others. It could be argued that none have been entirely successful because the condition of education for poor and minority children has not improved significantly. The readings in this chapter point to the problems of achieving equality, especially when doing so can affect the privilege of those who benefit from the unequal conditions.

References

Cecelski, D. S. (1994). *Along freedom road: Hyde County, North Carolina, and the fate of black schools in the south*. Chapel Hill: University of North Carolina Press.

Johnson, H. B. (2006). *The American Dream and the power of wealth: Changing schools and inheriting inequality in the land of opportunity*. New York: Routledge.

Metz, M. H. (1994). Desegregation as necessity and challenge. *Journal of Negro Education, 63*(1), 64–76.

Rubin, L. B. (1972). *Busing and backlash: White against white in an urban school district*. Berkeley: University of California Press.

Saporito, S., & Lareau, A. (1999). School selection as a process: The multiple dimensions of race in framing educational choice. *Social Problems, 46*(3), 418–439.

U.S. Census Bureau. (2012). Table 712. Children below poverty level by race and Hispanic origin: 1980 to 2009. *Statistical Abstract of the United States: 2012*. Retrieved from http://www.census.gov/compendia/statab/2012/tables/12s0712.pdf

Lessons Forgotten

Gary Orfield

Gary Orfield is a leading scholar on issues of civil rights and racial segregation in U.S. schools. He is currently codirector of the Civil Rights Project/Proyecto Derechos Civiles, a center that was originally at Harvard University and renamed when it moved to the University of California at Los Angeles in 2007. In this reading, Orfield describes the history of school desegregation in the United States. In addition to the legislation, critical to the desegregation and subsequent resegregation of American schools, he examines the political climate and factors that influenced the attempts to provide more equal educational opportunities across race. Based on his research on school segregation and desegregation over time, this analysis and his other work suggest little hope that the current state of segregation in American schools will be reduced in the future.

Questions to consider for this reading:

1. According to Orfield, how did court cases fall short in ensuring desegregation of American schools?

2. What societal responses to the 1970s legislation made the resegregation of America's schools inevitable?

3. What difference does it make if schools are segregated?

I n an era of great hope for this country's racial transformation from the mid-1960s to the early 1970s, we committed ourselves to creating integrated schools. There was a brief period in our history in which there was serious policy and research attention on how to devise racially diverse schools to achieve integration and equal opportunity. Civil rights leaders and participants in the hundreds of demonstrations demanding integrated education knew the sorry history of "separate but equal" and fought for access to the opportunities concentrated in White schools.

The desegregation experience has often been described by critics as little more than a mechanistic transfer of students, but it was often much more than that. From thousands of desegregation plans implemented around the nation we learned about the ways to operate successful integrated schools and classrooms. Now, as we deal both with resegregation, where court orders are

From *Lessons in Integration: Realizing the Promise of Racial Diversity in American Schools* (pp. 1–6), edited by E. Frankenberg and G. Orfield, 2007, Charlottesville: University of Virginia Press. Copyright 2007 by the Rector and Visitors of the University of Virginia. Reprinted with permission.

dropped, and with the emergence of racial diversity in thousands of other schools, not as the result of court orders, but as the product of a great increase in the non-White population and of diversification of growing sectors of suburbia, that experience and the unfinished agenda of the civil rights era are relevant again. Too many hard-earned lessons have been forgotten.

Most of the public struggle for desegregation involved opening the doors of White schools to students who had been historically excluded—Black and, in some cases, Latino students who attended segregated schools that were commonly inferior on many dimensions.[1] There was a fierce, two-decade struggle after *Brown v. Board of Education of Topeka* to desegregate the South, followed, in the 1970s, by a brief and usually losing struggle to desegregate northern cities. The Supreme Court's 1974 decision in the metropolitan Detroit case of *Milliken v. Bradley* rejected the only remedy that could have produced substantial and lasting school desegregation in much of the North, and instead built a massive legal barrier between city school districts and the surrounding suburban districts, where most White children resided and where typically the best schools were located. President Richard Nixon, who ran on the "southern strategy" promising to roll back desegregation, had dismantled much of the civil rights machinery of the federal government by this time (Panetta & Gall, 1971).

Critics often describe this period as one of mandatory race mixing with no educational components. Many educational experts, civil rights advocates, and officials, however, understood early that more must be done. Simply letting some minority students into previously White schools operated by the same district officials was not likely to solve the problems of inequality. In fact, these officials often found new ways to discriminate within schools.

The deeper changes, in educational and social terms, involved going from the reality of desegregation—the fact that children of different racial and ethnic groups were now in the same school and faculties had been ordered to be desegregated—toward real integration, which required fair and equal treatment of each racial and ethnic group. Gordon Allport's classic book, *The Nature of Prejudice* (1954), published the year of the *Brown* decision, had concluded that creating desegregated settings could produce either positive or negative outcomes, which depended on how desegregation was done. The key, he said, was creating "equal status interaction" between the previously segregated groups. Allport wrote: "It required years of labor and billions of dollars to gain the secret of the atom. It will take a still greater investment to gain the secrets of man's irrational nature. It is easier, someone has said, to smash an atom than a prejudice" (as cited in Clark, 1979).

In the early days of desegregation there were too many reports of segregated classes, removal of minority teachers and principals, failure to integrate school activities, segregated classroom seating, discriminatory counseling, curricula that ignored minority history, and many other conditions that limited or prevented full access for minority students. Additionally, these conditions limited positive diversity experiences for White and minority students. Many educators, advocates, and researchers realized that factors influencing the nature of the transition from segregation to desegregation, and ultimately to integration, could shift the academic and social outcomes of students in these schools (Schofield, 1981). Most school staff members, who themselves attended segregated schools and were trained to work in one-race schools, did not have the knowledge and tools to address these issues.

Desegregation orders and plans by the late 1960s often went far beyond simply transferring students. The Supreme Court ended token desegregation that had been occurring through "freedom of choice" plans in 1968 and ordered "root and branch" desegregation to eliminate "dual school systems" organized on the basis of race (*Green v. County School Board of New Kent County,* 1968). To fulfill the constitutional requirement to create "unitary" school systems that were fully integrated, school desegregation plans had to include desegregation of teachers and students, and equalization of educational opportunities, facilities, and curriculum. The plans usually included strategies for informing the public of the plan, managing crises, retraining teachers and staff, developing new educational materials, and implementing policies for fair discipline and participation in student activities among the various groups of students.

Following the Supreme Court's decision in *Swann v. Charlotte-Mecklenburg Board of Education* (1971), there was massive controversy over court orders using tools such as busing to more thoroughly desegregate urban schools. Despite disagreements, both critics and supporters of desegregation recognized that help was needed in the suddenly integrated schools in hundreds of cities. Government responded, for a time. The Emergency School Aid Act was a bipartisan law initially intended to smooth the crises caused by sudden desegregation of urban school systems. In this act, negotiated between the Nixon White House and Senate liberals led by Senator Walter Mondale,[2] Congress enacted a policy of giving money to schools to support successful desegregation. Regardless of whether they supported desegregation plans, both sides could agree that if the plans must be implemented, schools required help to prevent dangerous cleavages in communities, such as those that did such severe damage to several cities, including Little Rock, Birmingham, and Boston, after racial violence flared. The programs funded under the desegregation assistance law did not provide money for busing itself, but they did provide hundreds of millions of dollars for helping the schools adapt.

The Emergency School Aid Act (Orfield, 1978, chap. 9) lasted from 1972 until 1981, when the Reagan administration ended it (Orfield & Eaton, 1996). While in operation, the law funded training, intervention programs, new curricula development, magnet schools for voluntary desegregation, and large-scale research or ways to improve race relations. Because courts were actively requiring desegregation, there was interest in obtaining help, and, as a result, school districts eagerly applied for these funds. The funding was so enthusiastically sought, in fact, that districts were often willing to do additional desegregation of students and teachers, not required by their own plan, to get it. Many magnet schools began and spread rapidly under this program, as school choice became a significant element in American education for the first time. The law required that magnets be desegregated—choice was designed to combine equity with educational options.

During the Carter administration, the law was rewritten to incorporate the lessons of the major evaluation studies, which showed that aid made a substantial difference for both achievement and race relations, and was needed for at least several years to facilitate successful change. At the same time, the National Institute of Education supported research on desegregated schools and developed a research agenda for the field. Research on the effects of the programs and changes funded by the desegregation assistance law produced important findings about the conditions under which race relations and educational achievement gains were most likely to occur in interracial schools. During the desegregation era the Black-White gap declined sharply. Major studies documented the benefits of certain classroom techniques in mixed-race classrooms. Teachers and administrators facing racial change were given a great deal of inservice preparation.[3]

During this same period, education schools across the country and their national accreditation agencies made significant efforts to require training of teachers in multicultural education. Sensing a large new market, publishers supported substantial revisions of texts that had an exclusively White perspective. Many districts commissioned new curriculum about local minority contributions. At the same rime, the spread of bilingual education requirements and funding under the 1968 Bilingual Education Act, as well as the 1974 *Lau v. Nichols* Supreme Court decision about the rights of non-English-speaking students, brought into the schools an increasing number of Latino teachers and supported beginning education in a child's native language. Several desegregation orders, including those in school districts in Denver, Boston, and Texas, contained specific programs for language-minority students and their teachers.

The need for these efforts did not cease, but the support did. Training, school district programs, and research withered away. The Reagan administration in its first months opposed desegregation orders and eliminated the desegregation assistance program that had made desegregation plans work better; the research operation was shut down, and for the next quarter century there would be no significant federal funding for research or policy on effective race relations in diverse schools (Orfield & Eaton, 1996). The Reagan administration did, however, support research on "White flight," which it used to oppose desegregation in federal courts.

The country turned in a different direction when the standards movement emerged in the aftermath of the Reagan administration's *A Nation at Risk* report in 1983. The basic ideas of standards-based reform were that the social context of schools could be overlooked—both the problems of racial and economic inequality and the positive possibilities of racial diversity—and that standards, requirements, and sanctions would produce more equal outcomes in and of themselves or, if necessary, with the additional pressure of market competition from charter and private schools. Part of the basic analysis of the "excellence" movement was that schools had been diverted from traditional education responsibilities to counterproductive social reform efforts.

Virtually all states adopted this agenda, which was reinforced by the agreement between President George H. W. Bush and the nation's governors in 1989. At the Charlottesville Educational Summit, the National Governors Association's chair, Governor Bill Clinton of Arkansas, led the governors to agreement with the president on six national education goals to which the country should aspire by 2000, from school readiness to increasing high school graduation rates. Goal 3 (U.S. students should be first in the world in mathematics and science achievement) and goal 4 (all students should demonstrate achievement in core subjects) in particular spurred the bipartisan standards agenda (National Governors Association, 1989, 2000). The program to achieve the national goals became known as the America 2000 program, but it was not until the Goals 2000: Educate America Act passed in 1993 during Clinton's first presidential term that the six goals were adopted as part of federal education law. In addition, the 1994 reauthorization of the Elementary and Secondary Education Act (known as the Improving America's Schools Act, or IASA) further drove the standards movement by requiring that all states adopt a system of standards, assessments, and accountability to measure student performance in order to qualify for Title I funding. The IASA also required states to disaggregate student performance data for schools' annual yearly progress by race, gender, and socioeconomic status, but sanctions were not seriously enforced. Ultimately, none of the goals for closing the racial gap were realized and the gaps widened in some dimensions.

The No Child Left Behind Act of 2001 (NCLB), however, imposed more demanding goals and deadlines on all American schools. NCLB had strong goals and sweeping sanctions for equalizing achievement among minority and White children, but had no requirement to equalize the very unequal schooling opportunities or take any action to end segregation of minority students in inferior schools and improve race relations. By insisting on equal outcomes from patently unequal schools highly segregated by race and poverty, the 2001 law's sanctions tended to strongly penalize minority schools and teachers (Sunderman, Kim, & Orfield, 2005).

The effects of segregated education cannot be cured by merely enacting strong demands for achievement gains and changing nothing else in schools that are usually unequal in every major dimension relating to student achievement, including the quality of teachers, curriculum offered, and the level of competition (peer group). In fact, enforcing rigid standards without equalizing opportunity can exacerbate the inequalities by stigmatizing minority schools as failures, narrowing their curriculum to endless testing drills, and leading strong, experienced teachers to transfer to less pressured situations. The massive publicity given to test scores may also help destabilize residentially integrated communities, as realtors use test scores to steer White buyers to outlying White communities. Thus, the ironic impact of ignoring the inequality of the segregated schools in the name of standards is to worsen them.

In the past quarter century of incredible demographic transformation of the American school-age population there has been virtually no investment in either determining the best policies for extraordinarily complex school communities or even in applying well-documented programs and policies that are likely to make things better. Federal funding of desegregation research and experiments ended in the early 1980s, and private foundations do not generally support research about these topics, which has drastically limited the development of new knowledge that could assist schools with the racial transformation. This myopia makes school communities less effective internally and much weaker as anchors for multiracial communities dealing with pressures of racial stratification, fear, and racial transformation.

NOTES

1. The right for Latinos to desegregate was not acknowledged by the Supreme Court until 1973, after most active desegregation efforts had already ended. In striking contrast to the Johnson administration's role in the South, the Nixon administration did virtually nothing to enforce this policy.

2. Mondale, who became Jimmy Carter's vice president, chaired the Senate select Committee on Equal Educational Opportunity, which compiled 30 volumes of congressional hearings on all aspects of desegregation and issued a comprehensive report in 1972 that included a chapter on conditions for successful integration (U.S. Senate, 1972, chapter 17).

3. Much of that research is summarized in Hawley, Crain, Rossell, Schofield, & Fernandez (1983).

REFERENCES

Allport, G. W. (1954). *The nature of prejudice.* Reading, MA: Addison-Wesley.

Brown v. Board of Education of Topeka. 347 U.S. 483 (1954).

Clark, K. (1979). Introduction. In G. Allport, *The nature of prejudice* (pp. ix–xi). Cambridge, MA: Perseus.

Green v. County School Board of New Kent County. 391 U.S. 430 (1968).

Hawley, W. D., Crain, R. L., Rossell, C. H., Schofield, J. W., & Fernandez, R. (1983). *Strategies for effective desegregation: Lessons from research.* Lexington, MA: Lexington/D.C. Heath.

Lau v. Nichols. 414 U.S. 563 (1974).

Milliken v. Bradley. 418 U.S. 717 (1974).

National Governors Association. (1989). *Charlottesville summit.* Retrieved from http://www.nga.org/portal/sitc/nga/menuitem

National Governors Association. (2000). *America 2000 program.* Retrieved from http://govinfo.library.unt.ed/negp/reports/nego30.pdf

Orfield, G. (1978). *Must we bus? Segregated schools and national policy.* Washington, DC: Brookings Institution Press.

Orfield, G., & Eaton, S. E. (1996). *Dismantling desegregation: The quiet reversal of "Brown v. Board of Education."* New York: New Press.

Panetta, L., & Gall, P. (1971). *Bring us together: The Nixon team and the civil rights retreat.* Philadelphia: Lippincott.

Schofield, J. W. (1981). Complementary and conflicting identities: Images and interaction in an interracial school. In S. R. Asher & J. M. Gottman (Eds.), *The development of children's friendships* (pp. 53–90). Cambridge, England: Cambridge University Press.

Sunderman, G. L., Kim, J., & Orfield, G. (2005). *NCLB meets school realities: Lessons from the field.* Thousand Oaks, CA: Corwin Press.

Swann v. Charlotte-Mecklenburg Board of Education. 402 U.S. 1 (1971).

United States Senate, Select Committee on Equal Educational Opportunity. (1972). *Toward equal educational opportunity,* 92d Cong., 2nd Sess. Washington, DC: Government Printing Office.

READING 35

Only Here for a Day

Social Integration of Minority Students at a Majority White High School

Megan M. Holland

Integrating schools has been a challenge in the United States despite court orders as described by Gary Orfield in the first reading in this chapter. Megan M. Holland describes a program in which city youths, primarily African American and Latino, attend a school in a nearby suburb. She observed at the suburban school for approximately five months with one other researcher and conducted 14 small group interviews with 26 students from the voluntary desegregation program (VDP) and 17 students from the hosting high school. As you read this piece, you will find that gender made a difference in how the VDP students were received in this high school.

Questions to consider for this reading:

1. What hardships did the VDP students face in participating in the voluntary desegregation program?

2. How did gender influence how well VDP students were received at this high school?

3. What benefits and problems associated with voluntary desegregation programs are apparent from this reading?

When the Supreme Court handed down the *Brown* decision in 1954, the hope was that desegregated schools would lead to increased educational achievement for African American students as well as improved race relations for the country. Since then, hundreds of studies have examined desegregation, particularly its effects on interracial friendship and relations (see Schofield 1991 for a review). However, much of this work has focused on outcomes, with less attention paid to understanding the process of integration within schools. Therefore, we lack a deep knowledge of what the experience of integration is like for students and how the organizational and cultural context of a school affects this, particularly in contemporary desegregation programs.

In this article, I use observational and interview data to understand how the context of one school that participates in a desegregation program shapes the integration process for the African American and Latino students who are

---

bussed in, identifying gender differences in their social experiences. I argue that the boys are more socially integrated than the girls due to two interacting processes: (1) At the interpersonal level, suburban white youth value the status characteristics attributed to African American and Latino males, which facilitates integration according to Blau's (1960) theory of social integration, and (2) at the organizational level, the organizational practices of the school facilitate participation for the boys in extracurricular activities, which lead to interracial contact under ideal conditions (Allport 1954), while blocking the girls from such participation. I argue that these two processes occur simultaneously on different levels of interaction, creating a cycle whereby the school provides opportunities for minority boys to make friends with whites and participate in athletics, which gives them status and positive social experiences, which makes them more likely to make more friends. In contrast, the school provides little opportunity outside of class time for minority girls to interact and make friends with white students, which makes them little known at the school, which leads to negative social experiences, which makes them less likely to make friends. Although I do not make claims as to the exact origins of these processes, I do show how they reinforce each other and result in very different experiences for males and females. . . .

LITERATURE

Social Integration

Most studies on integrated schools use network or survey data to identify the amount of interracial contact, the interracial friendship choices, or the racial attitudes of students. Consequently, we know a great deal about the patterns of these attitudes and friendships but little about the depth of these friendships, how they play out on a day-to-day basis, or how they affect the perceptions students have of their place in a school. While other studies on diverse or desegregated schools have used qualitative methods, they have tended to focus more on the construction of racial or gender identity within groups (Bettie 2003; Hemmings 1996; Lewis 2003; Tatum 2003) and less on how intergroup dynamics develop and affect students' feelings of integration into the school community.

As I am studying the process of integration at one school, I focus on students' subjective perceptions of the school climate, and I therefore will be looking at the social integration of students rather than friendship patterns or the development of racial or gender identities. Work among social psychologists has focused on understanding both the factors contributing to and the effect of "a sense of belonging" among students, which tends to be conceptualized as feeling a part of and supported by the school community (see Osterman 2000 for a review). This concept is similar to how I define *social integration* in this study, although I also consider how incorporated a student is into the social structure of the school. Therefore, while I conceptualize social integration as feeling a part of, and equally valued and supported in, a school community, I also consider the extent to which a student has social connections outside of his or her racial in-group. In this way, I build on past studies of interracial friendship by analyzing the feelings and understandings of individual students about how they fit into the community as well as their social incorporation or isolation. As such, I use Blau's (1960:546) theory of social integration as it focuses on the individual-level processes that create social bonds within groups and help individuals form a cohesive social structure. He conceptualizes social integration as a process whereby individuals must make themselves attractive to a larger group and at the same time approachable. Higher social status usually makes an individual more attractive; however, in making oneself attractive, one can also be seen as unapproachable. Blau discusses how using a self-deprecating modesty can make one more approachable.

This theory of social integration is useful because it considers two elements often left out of research on desegregated schools—status and process. Studies of friendship patterns tend to neglect the role of status as a multidimensional concept in determining a student's position in the social network. Status, when included, is usually operationalized as academic ability or racial minority status (see Kitsner et al. 1993). Status among youth can be seen as a reflection of parents' socioeconomic status (Gaines 1991; Hollingshead 1950), but many other elements can affect a student's status within his or her peer culture, such as athleticism and participation in extracurricular activities (Adams and Bettis 2003; Coleman 1961; Eder and Kinney 1995; Goto 1997; Kinney 1993) as well as attractiveness, social skills, and personality (Coleman 1961; Kinney 1993).

In considering how cultural conceptions of status may influence perceptions of African American males and females, we can see that they yield some divergent predictions. African American males may have higher social status than females for a number of reasons that are dependent on the school's context. For instance, young African American males are typically stereotyped as athletic, which may help them gain status in schools that value sports, and participating in sports typically brings more status to boys than to girls (Eder and Parker 1987). In addition, minority girls may be less likely to join high-status girls' sports, such as cheerleading, because they are so strongly associated with white girls (Bettis and Adams 2003). Many white suburban males are also increasingly listening to rap and hip-hop music and becoming fascinated with images that this music represents (see Rodriquez 2006). This may allow African American males in a majority white context to gain status. In contrast, African American females do not have the same kinds of cultural signals to trade on for status.

However, African American males also have to contend with stereotypes that paint them as violent and aggressive. Blau's (1960) theory of social integration predicts that an individual will be accepted by his [or her] peers based on both his or her attractiveness to the group and his or her approachability. Studies in the workplace have found that African American females are better able to cross cultural boundaries than males as they are less threatening (Epstein 1973). Considering this, we might then expect African American females to make more cross-race friends due to their approachability.

Therefore, it is unclear how social integration according to Blau (1960) may vary for African American males and females in terms of status valuation and approachability. However, it is important to understand how these gender differences affect social integration as this may influence a student's general social and academic experience as well as his or her experience with students of other races. This experience may affect whether students will choose to segregate or integrate themselves in the future (Braddock 1980; Dawkins and Braddock 1994).

School Organizational Effects on Integration

Previous researchers have usually focused on two ways that the organizational structure of a school can influence race relations and friendship patterns—through the interaction opportunities available and through the conditions under which interaction takes place.

Blau's (1977) macrostructural theory posits that relations can develop only when people have the opportunity to interact. In schools, chances of interaction are largely a function of the classes students are in. Many schools engage in curricular tracking, placing students in different classes according to ability. Tracking plays an important role in students' friendship choices, with students tending to make more friends within their tracks (Hallinan and Williams 1989; Kubitschek and Hallinan 1998; Moody 2001). Furthermore, students placed into ability groups within classrooms in middle school are more likely to make friends within those groups (Hallinan and Sørenson 1985).

Other organizational characteristics of the school and classroom influence the kinds of opportunities students have to interact and form friendships. For instance, separating students by grade level in the lunchroom in middle and high school, rather than grouping all grades together (Moody 2001), and the type of classroom—open or traditional in elementary and middle school—have been found to influence the development of interracial friendships (Hallinan 1976). Other studies of within-race peer-group segregation have found that school organization influences friendship formation. For example, Levinson (1998), in studying a Mexican secondary school, identified how school practices led students to feel connected to an academically and socioeconomically diverse group, while Flores-Gonzalez (2005) showed how academic tracking and use of school space in an inner-city high school created segregated groups—the "school kids" and the "street kids."

The racial composition of both the school and individual classrooms can also affect students' friendship choices. Macrostructural theory would predict that the more diverse a school is, the more opportunity there is for cross-race interaction and therefore the more likely it is that interracial friendships will form. Some studies confirm this; for example, Quillian and Campbell (2003), in studying cross-race friendship among white, Asian, Latino, and African American high school students, found that friendships between students of different races increased with the diversity of the school. However, Moody (2001) found a "tipping point" of diversity in that once an individual middle or high school became racially balanced (i.e., having a racial heterogeneity score between .30 and .65), the number of interracial friendships decreased. Similarly, Hallinan (1982) found both African American and white elementary school students made the most interracial friendships in majority white classrooms. Other studies in middle schools have found that opportunity for interaction does not necessarily lead to interaction and is not sufficient to lead to friendships, changes in attitudes, or feelings of solidarity (Schofield 1979).

Contact Theory

While macrostructural theory focuses on the structural conditions that influence the opportunity to interact, contact theory specifies the conditions of interaction most likely to lead to positive racial sentiment. Allport (1954) set out specific conditions under which contact is ideal: when individuals are of equal status; they are working toward a common, cooperative goal; and there is institutional support. Multiple studies have followed up on Allport's theory (see Pettigrew and Tropp 2006) and refined and extended it (Pettigrew 1998, 2008).

The school context is important to understand to test Allport's (1954) theory under his conditions (Moody 2001; Schofield 1991). The size, population, and organization of the school are all factors that influence not only the opportunity for contact but also the conditions under which contact takes place (Khmelkov and Hallinan 1999; Moody 2001). Simple opportunity for interaction does not mean that friendships will be made when conditions that are likely to lead to positive interactions are not in place (Pettigrew and Tropp 2006; Rodkin, Wilson, and Ahn 2007).

Academic tracking influences status differences, which can lead to fewer interracial friendships if students of one race are disproportionately assigned to a lower track (Schofield 1979). In many schools, African Americans are disproportionately placed in lower-ability tracks (Noguera and Wing 2006; Oakes 1985), which can lead to African American and white students' being of unequal academic status. Extracurricular activities fulfill Allport's (1954) first condition of equal status better than academic activities due to the ability tracking that occurs in most schools (Braddock, Dawkins, and Wilson 1995; Khmelkov and Hallinan 1999). Allport's other criteria, for both groups to be working toward a common, cooperative goal, is also better realized in a setting outside the classroom where students are concerned with the performance or product of the group rather than their own individual grades. Indeed, African American and white students who participate in extracurricular activities together usually have more cross-race friendships than those who do not (Hallinan and Teixeira 1987; Moody 2001; Zweigenhaft and Domhoff 1991). However, status hierarchies can still develop within teams, which may lead to racial conflict (Greenfield 2002).

Allport's (1954) last condition, that there is support by authorities, is rarely met in most studies of cross-race interaction in schools. It is usually assumed to be true in schools; however, schools can vary widely in their commitment to encouraging interracial friendship. Most past studies, in focusing on large national data sets, have failed to look at this condition. However, Schofield and Sager (1977), in studying one middle school with a high commitment to fostering diversity and integration, found that over time the school's efforts lead to more interracial interaction.

Gender Differences in Integration

Very few of the hundreds of studies on integration in schools have focused on gender differences in friendship patterns, and those that have identified gender differences have not always been able to identify the mechanisms behind them. Studies of gender differences across both races have been somewhat contradictory. Some have found that males of both races are more likely to interact across racial lines (Schofield 1982; Schofield and Sager 1977), while others have found that it is white females who are most likely to do so (Damico and Sparks 1986). Some studies have found that African American females are less likely to have interracial interactions or friendships in comparison to African American males (Damico and Sparks 1986; Eaton 2001; Ispa-Landa 2009; Kitsner et al. 1993), while studies focusing more broadly on crossing social boundaries have tended to find that African American females are more willing and/or able to engage in different interaction styles to facilitate this crossing. African American females were found to be most likely compared to white females and African American and white males to act as "go-betweens" in elementary classrooms, interacting across race, age, and

gender boundaries (Grant 1984). African American and Latina females are also more likely than their male counterparts to act as "cultural straddlers," code switching between non-dominant and dominant forms of cultural capital (Carter 2005). However, when looking at such gender differences in code switching, it is important to keep in mind that the cultural context of the school may play an important role. For example, Mehan, Hubbard, and Villanueva (1994) found that both male and female minority high school students were able to switch between a school and neighborhood identity with ease, and the authors suggest that this was due to institutional mechanisms within the school that facilitated the development of a critical consciousness.

The literature on gender differences in integration in multiracial contexts is somewhat inconclusive. While studies on interracial contact and friendships seem to find that African American females are less likely to cross racial lines than others, studies on cultural boundary crossing have found more fluidity in the cultural and interactional styles and identities of African American females, although Mehan, Hubbard, and Villanueva's (1994) study suggests that this may be influenced by the context of the school. It is necessary then to further investigate how the social and organizational context of the school may influence these gender differences. In this article, I shed light on the perceptions of African American and Latina/Latino females and males as they experience being minorities in a majority white school and identify how the organizational features of the school influence the experiences of these students.

* * *

FINDINGS

The Setting

The Village community. Village is a small, historically quaint, and very well-to-do suburb approximately 20 miles outside of NCC [Northeast Capital City]. In Village, the median home price according to the 2000 census was $453,000 compared to $191,000 in NCC. The median household income in Village was $96,000 compared to $40,000 in NCC. Of the 17,000 residents of Village, approximately 92 percent were white, 2 percent African American, 3 percent Asian, 2 percent Other, and 3 percent ethnically identified as Latino. VHS [Village High School] serves both Village and another smaller town demographically similar to Village.

The school. VHS is an academically successful school. Of its students, 94 percent scored proficient or above on the State Achievement Test in English, compared to 58 percent from NCC. A total of 98 percent of its students graduate, with 100 percent of those students going on to college. In NCC, 58 percent of students graduate, with 52 percent of those students going on to college. The student-teacher ratio at VHS is 14:1. Of the 88 teachers at the school, one is African American, one is Asian, and the rest are white.

Only classes in math and science are academically tracked by ability in VHS. However, this did not lead to racially segregated classes as the VDP [voluntary desegregation program] students were such a small minority. Even in lower-tracked math classes that I sat in on, VDP students were never more than a quarter of the students in the class. Very few, if any, VDP students were in honors or advanced placement classes, so the majority of these classes were more segregated than others.

Issues of race—visible and invisible. During my time at the school, I talked to both VDP and VHS students. In informal discussions with VDP students, issues of race almost always entered the conversation. In contrast, VHS students usually did not bring up race or VDP unless explicitly asked. However, the administration and teachers of VHS were very concerned with race relations within the school, especially with the racial achievement gap. An achievement task force was set up, and meetings were conducted with VDP parents. Our presence in the school was greatly supported by this task force for any

light we could shed on the issue. During my time at VHS, I also observed the school host a special diversity program that sought to bring down race, gender, class, and status barriers among teens. On the surface then, there would seem to be support for cross-race friendships by authorities, one of Allport's (1954) conditions for positive racial contact.

While the school made visible attempts to address issues of race and had many concerned teachers and administrators with good intentions, during our observations we noted how some attempts to foster diversity only served to highlight the ambivalence of VHS students, teachers, and the community concerning integration. As part of a senior project, one of the VDP students organized a bus tour of NCC neighborhoods for VHS teachers. Later, while discussing reactions to the tour, the teacher who helped organize it mentioned that someone had said how "surprised they were that drugs were sold so openly" during the tour. In the same meeting, teachers involved in VDP were troubled that VHS teachers were overly concerned with having security at an event that was going to be held in NCC and that few VHS students had bought tickets to it. Also, at a "peace" walk held in Village in honor of a former VDP student killed by gunfire in NCC, VDP students commented that there was still racial segregation at this event by both students and staff.

In many ways, there were clear racial divides within the school—in attitudes and perceptions as well as physically in the cafeteria or in classrooms, where groups usually segregated by race. However, after conducting interviews with groups of VDP students, it was clear that there also were many internal differences among the VDP students in how they integrated into the school.

The Social Experience of Being a Minority at VHS

The experience of being a minority and a VDP student at VHS was very different for males and females. In general, the females were less satisfied with their experiences at VHS. In an interview with a group of 11th-grade African American females, when asked if there was anything they liked about school, one girl replied,

> I value my education and I like coming here because I see my friends and stuff, but when you're in an environment that really isn't . . . you don't really feel comfortable, then it's kind of hard to focus on one thing to learn. . . . Sometimes it makes me want to just be like I don't even know why I'm here. I'd rather just go to school in NCC.

This student valued the academic advantages of VHS but struggled with an uncomfortable "environment" in the school. The other girls in this interview echoed a similar feeling. Later on in the interview, the girls indicated that they felt uncomfortable due to racism at VHS as well as conflicting academic pressures. They felt that there was an expectation from the Village community that they would not do well academically, but this expectation of failure was coupled with a pressure from the Village community to succeed as well as to represent all VDP students. In the same interview, another 11th-grade female commented, "And they [the Village community] put us in a group and it's hard because they expect us all to . . . come here and goof off and not do well and those kids who do, it's like, it's such a big surprise." Her friend, another 11th-grade female, followed up by saying, "As a group, VDP, we have to live up to certain expectations that the community or Village has for us as a group of VDP kids."

The girls felt their individual performance reflected on VDP students as a whole and discussed how they almost wished they could attend school in NCC where their own performance would not represent the group. . . .

[They] resented the spotlight that was put on VDP students for not doing well in school, such as instituting academic contracts. She also felt that this pressure actually weighed her down when she came out to Village.

Females at VHS appeared to be very affected by the racism they perceived on the part of the community and the students. Another 11th-grade minority female described what she thought the white students at VHS were thinking about VDP students:

> I'm not going to sit here and say I know what they [the Village community] say but it's like they [VHS students] basically look . . . it's like, oh, yeah, we can be friends and stuff but knowing that you're a VDP student, I probably know that you're failing all of your classes.

This student felt her academic identity was discounted at VHS and that the students and the community considered her, and VDP students as a whole, a failure.

The girls had negative associations with VHS students, and this led to limited contact with students who were not in VDP. More minority females than males hung out exclusively with other VDP students. In an interview with 10th-grade African American and Latina females, an African American female discussed being ambivalent about how integrated she felt into the school and how she did not feel the need to make an extra effort to make friends with VHS students. . . .

In this group interview, both of the African American females felt that they had more friends in VDP, while the Latina female felt her friendships were about equally split between VDP and VHS. In a focus group with two 9th-grade females, one African American and one Latina, both females acknowledged that they had friends outside of VDP, especially in classes in which they were the only VDP students, but indicated that most of their friends were in VDP and that VDP students were whom they would choose to hang out with socially. In an interview with 12th-grade minority females, those students felt that their true friends were in VDP and not among the VHS students. When they graduated, they thought they would keep in contact only with their VDP friends. In fact, when three of the students were asked to name one good friend from VHS, they all named the same girl, indicating how small their social circles were. The VDP girls also felt that they were not known at the school in many ways and were resentful that very few minority students were nominated for the Superlatives section in their yearbook (such as Class Clown and Class Flirt) and that the only VDP student (a female) who won was for "Loudest Person."

Overall, the minority girls had negative impressions of the school, the community, and the students. The VDP girls felt a weight on their backs when they took the bus out to Village and felt uncomfortable in an environment where they thought that students, teachers, and the community had low expectations for them.

The males' experiences at VHS were very different from the females'. In stark contrast to the way the females felt when they headed to school each day, the males interviewed frequently described a weight lifting off of their shoulders when they took the bus ride out. For example, an 11th-grade African American male, when asked what he did and did not like about VHS, answered,

> Something I like is I like any time I come out here, I get to be normal. I can just like relax and be cool about things and back home I've got to be like, looking over my shoulder and stuff like that. You see everybody just expressing who they really are. . . . So, you know, you get to express your individuality without worrying about other people judging you [at VHS].

While the girls felt the pressure of different expectations, this young man actually felt that coming to Village, he could be in a place where he was not being judged. He felt very at ease and comfortable in the surroundings. While boys and girls were asked the same initial questions, it was girls who brought up academics and boys who brought up relating to people socially. An African American 12th-grade male, in his interview, also brought up the social aspect of school right away and mentioned how much he liked it, and other boys in his interview agreed. He elaborated by describing how sports played a role in the "atmosphere" at school that he enjoyed:

> People seem to know you [when you play sports]. There are definitely cliques and if you're in the right clique, you have a good time. When you're in class, you're with your friends all the time, and there's people you see every day so it's just . . . it's nice to have inside jokes and just hang with friends all of the time.

While the females felt that the atmosphere at school was uncomfortable and burdening, the males felt free and accepted by friends.

Researchers have documented that minority boys tend to spend a lot of time hanging out on the street in their neighborhoods (Clampet-Lundquist et al. 2011; Dance 2002; Lopez 2002), which can result in being more exposed to street culture, which requires a constant maintenance of respect and the presentation of a "street" image (Anderson 1990, 1999). As a result, boys mentioned appreciating Village because they did not have to worry about what they said or how they looked at someone. They could relax and did not have to worry about "looking over their shoulder" all the time. Even though the boys engaged in code-switching techniques that required them to change how they acted in Village (which I discuss later), the lack of pressure to constantly be on the lookout for potentially dangerous situations led boys to feel more comfortable in Village.

Minority males in VDP not only felt more comfortable in the school but also had more friends from VHS as well as contacts with the larger Village community. A few boys talked about going to parties in Village or coming out to play basketball with their Village friends on the weekends. . . .

Many boys also participated in sports, which allowed them to have "host families." Host families were created in a variety of ways. Sometimes coaches informally set up arrangements with Village families who had children on the team, or boys became friends with VHS students and grew friendly with the families. Many students spoke about being very close with their host families. For example, a 12th-grade Latino male and a 12th-grade African American male, in their interview, both discussed how much they appreciated their host families and all they had done for them during their high school careers. . . .

Host families provided the boys places to stay and also support systems. [One] Latino student said his host father came to the school to talk to his guidance counselor at times. Having host families also allowed the boys to stay overnight in Village, which gave them the opportunity to more easily participate in sports and go to parties with Village students. They had more time to be social with VHS students, which led to contacts with the students and their parents. In contrast, girls did not mention any relationships with host families.

Although the boys had a better impression of Village and had more white friends than did the girls, this was not because they did not experience any racism or discrimination. Males recounted incidents wherein their friends said the "N" word in front of them or wherein teammates automatically blamed VDP students when things were stolen and asked the boys to "ask on their bus" if anyone had a missing iPod. Although the boys were angered by these incidents and frustrated by the ignorance of their friends, this did not lead them to develop a negative overall impression of Village, as the girls did. The boys were aware of the stereotypes that whites might have about them but felt that this could be overcome once people got to know them. . . .

Socially Integrating into the School

In analyzing integration at VHS, we can think about both the VDP students' attempting to become accepted by the VHS students and the VHS students' attempting to become accepted by the VDP students. It is important to consider that both processes may have been going on in some cases. However, in the next section, I will argue that for the most part VHS students did not attempt to integrate into the VDP students' worlds.

Integration—a one-way street. One issue that upset many VDP students was their feeling that VHS students had little interest in understanding their lives. The VDP students expressed a desire for the VHS students to be open to coming to NCC and getting to know who they were rather than just relying on stereotypes. A 12th-grade African American female said in her interview,

> I have some friends from Village and . . . they don't mind inviting me over to like dinner and like to their house so I enjoy that, but I'm also like, "Okay, come where I live. Like it's okay. Like you won't get shot." And I think it should be like . . . it should be something that's shared, you know, not just I come out to your town where it's safe and secure but like [they should] just come out [to my town].

The VDP students did not think the VHS students were open to learning about other communities outside of Village, and this student wished that that were part of her friendships with VHS students. Similarly, in an interview with 11th-grade Latina and African American females, when asked what accounted for the separation between the communities, one student responded with the observation that there "isn't enough knowledge." The girls then went on to describe the ideas that the VHS students had of NCC and the VDP students' lives, assuming that they were all constantly exposed to violence, lived in the "ghetto," and did not participate in traditional activities such as trick-or-treating on Halloween. The 11th-grade girls frequently referred to the "box theory," which according to one African American female was the idea that "they [VHS students] live in this box and their parents just feed them these ideas and the media is over here. It's hard and I feel like it's . . . at times, it's not their fault but there are actually some people that are just ignorant." For the most part, these girls felt that integration at the school was difficult because it was not up to just the VDP students to integrate into the Village community; rather, there needed to be an effort on the part of the VHS students. In another interview with 10th- and 11th-grade African American males, a 10th-grade male also expressed the idea that integration was not up to just the VDP students by saying, "VDP is not just about coming out to suburban schools, doing the homework and going back to our own homes. VDP is about teaching suburban schools, suburban students what it's like to live in the inner city, what it feels like to be a person of color."

Although the VDP students did not think that integration should be solely their responsibility, for the most part the process was one-sided. The interviews and observations I conducted shed light on some of the ways the VDP students attempted, or did not attempt, to integrate with the VHS students and how this varied by gender.

Strategies of social integration—status. Blau (1960) posits that to integrate into a community, one must be attractive to those in that community and that usually we are attracted to those of higher status. While status is usually associated with socioeconomic class, in the world of adolescence, many other elements can confer social status, such as athleticism, physical attractiveness, personality, or participation in extracurricular activities (Adams and Bettis 2003; Coleman 1961; Eder and Kinney 1995; Goto 1997; Kinney 1993). While most VDP students were below VHS students in socioeconomic status, they did have other kinds of status characteristics that were valued at VHS. The VDP males, in particular, were able to use their status as athletes to socially integrate with the VHS students as well as the status attributed to hip-hop and rap stars, whose style they physically represented, to gain friends.

Many of the males interviewed cited friendships formed through sports. Being a part of sports teams helped make them more known at school, and increased visibility, especially through athletics, usually increases a student's popularity (Eder 1985; Flores-Gonzalez 2005; Kinney 1993). An 11th-grade African American male explained how sports helped him make friends by saying,

> I got to know a lot of kids through sports. You know, baseball kind of boosts up a lot of your confidence, a lot of your friends and stuff like that. So just, I mean, sometimes when you're practicing with the varsity guys and, you know, that's how you know your name starts to circulate. . . . You

start to meet some of their friends, and they start to meet some of your friends and then your whole fan base . . . or your whole, you know, friend base just expands.

Participating in sports teams facilitated making friends with VHS students, and it also brought social status to the boys. As the above student stated, sports made him more known among boys on the team and then later in the school as a whole. Being involved with sports and being seen as athletic (a masculine characteristic) usually brings more social rewards for males than it does for females (Coleman 1961; Eder and Parker 1987). Girls' sports in general, aside from cheerleading, tend to have less visibility than male athletics (Eder and Kinney 1995). Being involved with sports gave boys both status and the opportunity to interact with VHS students. In fact, when VHS males were asked to discuss segregation between VHS and VDP students, they frequently talked about sports as a way that they crossed those racial boundaries. In an interview with Caucasian and Asian 11th-grade males from VHS, when asked what could account for the racial separation in the cafeteria, one of the Caucasian males responded, "I think the one thing that really does bring us together is sports, the VDP kids and Village. I mean, I think most of the friends I've made from VDP were through like track or other sports." As I will discuss later, females did not participate in sports to the same degree as did males. . . .

The males were able to gain social status based on suburban ideas of the urban hip-hop culture. This allowed them to present a certain masculine image that gained them status (Majors and Billson 1992). The males' physical appearance and clothing personified this hip-hop image, although the males did not act in a way that might frighten or alienate the white males. The females contend that in the context of NCC, the VDP boys are not actually the tough youth but that they use that image of black male masculinity to gain status with males in suburbia. Perry (2002:109) suggests that white suburban males may listen to hip-hop and embrace aspects of the culture because they want to be associated with "characteristics of blackness, namely being cool, tough and hip."

The girls had fewer opportunities to participate in sports and other school activities that might have brought them status. While athleticism usually brings status to males, being friends with other popular girls, such as cheerleaders, can contribute to increasing girls' status, so popularity for females is based on not only what they do but also whom they know (Eder 1985; Eder and Kinney 1995). As I will discuss in the next section, the females in VDP had less opportunity to participate in activities and therefore less opportunity to make connections with other girls.

In addition, the females were not able to trade on stereotypes of their femininity that would have value at VHS. While we did not collect direct data on the rates of interracial dating, observations suggest that this mostly occurred between VDP males and VHS females. This mirrors the findings of other studies, which have attributed the lack of interracial dating between African American girls and white boys to the status hierarchy, which tends to put African American females in particular at the bottom (Schofield 1982). In an interview with 10th-grade African American and Latina females, the Latina female mentioned that she had had a crush on a VHS boy. When she told him he had "nice legs" and hung out outside his class to say "hi," she felt he went out of his way to then avoid her. Her friends, somewhat jokingly, agreed that the boy was "scared" of her. In contrast, I observed VDP males flirting and hanging out with VHS females on multiple occasions, and at least one steady relationship occurred between an African American male and a white female during my observations. These differences in interactions with the opposite sex may also have prevented the VDP females from gaining status as girls gain status through their popularity with the opposite sex (Schofield 1982). In addition, as evidenced previously by the nomination in the Superlatives section of the yearbook, the females tended to be seen as loud, obnoxious, hostile, or

having other negative characteristics associated with African American females (Fordham 1993).

Strategies of social integration—approachability. The males also attempted to socially integrate into the Village community by making themselves more approachable. VDP males appeared to change how they acted depending on whether they were at home or at school more than the females. While Blau (1960) argued that being approachable meant using self-deprecating modesty to play down one's status, I argue that for the VDP boys, being approachable meant changing their speech and behavior to play down stereotypes of minority males that painted them as aggressive, violent, and unintelligent. In a group interview of 10th- and 11th-grade minority males, students talked about how they changed some of their behaviors:

> AFRICAN AMERICAN MALE 1: They . . . I hold my speech every day.
>
> AFRICAN AMERICAN MALE 2: You've got to be . . . I change up.
>
> AFRICAN AMERICAN MALE 3: They change up to become more intellectual with the other Village kids.
>
> AFRICAN AMERICAN MALE 1: It works better like . . .
>
> AFRICAN AMERICAN MALE 3: Yeah. It does. It does. They gain more white friends.
>
> AFRICAN AMERICAN MALE 2: It helps you interact.

Here, the males are consciously aware of what they say in VHS and note that what they say and how they say it affects how students treat them. The boys also changed their behavior in other ways. In the same interview, a student said,

> Let's say a white kid called me an idiot. I'm not going to do the whole rah, rah, I'm going to try to beat you up type thing. It's just . . . you got to know when and where to do that as for if I was in NCC, I'd be like, "Let's fight right now then." Compared to here [VHS] where you're just like, no.

Researchers have noted the highly aggressive and violent "code of the street" (Anderson 1999) that is prevalent in many inner-city neighborhoods. This code is based on respect, an element that must be maintained and defended at all costs. This student states how if he were at home in NCC, he would not be able to shrug off an insult and instead would become aggressive. In VHS, he can leave that persona behind and become a part of a culture that does not require hypervigilance of respect. In the same interview, another male commented, "It's like, they're white people. You try not to be obnoxious because like he said, they get scared. There's just a bunch of other things you have to . . . you can't do what you would do in NCC and vice versa."

In contrast, the females claimed they did not change how they acted when in VHS. One female stated that she did not want to change herself because this was her last year, and she just did not care anymore about the school or how people saw her. In another interview, a Latina female also indicated that she did not change her dress, her speech, her tastes, or her behavior. However, some admitted that they changed when they were at home in their neighborhoods. For example, one 12th-grade female said, "When I get home [to NCC] I'm making sure I don't have my book bag." She also said that she would not tell her NCC friends that she did her homework.

The minority males who were interviewed also claimed that the females did not change how they acted. In an interview with minority males in 10th and 11th grades, when asked what sort of issues the females had to deal with in adjusting to VHS, the males stated, "When they [females in VDP] come here, they bring that little hood mentality here as well which is 100 percent bad." Another male agreed, stating, "I don't know how they feel because I haven't asked them about that, but I just know they act ghetto sometimes and it's not called for."

From the VDP students' interviews, it appears that the VDP girls did not attempt to make themselves more approachable to the Village community. This is also reflected in interviews with VHS girls, where they seem to attribute any separation between VHS and VDP students to the VDP students' being "hostile" or being very close-knit and therefore not welcoming of VHS students. . . .

[One] student attributes the majority of the barriers to the VDP students themselves and their lack of approachability. In another interview with 12th-grade African American and Caucasian females, a Caucasian female, who was dating an African American male in VDP, discussed how intimidated she felt sometimes around VDP students since they were so close to each other and such a tight community.

Although the VHS females do not directly mention the VDP females in their responses, as students tend to make friends within their own gender, it is likely that their ideas about VDP students were influenced by their experiences with female VDP students. In addition, when interracial dating did occur, it was between an African American male and a white female, so it is unlikely that the VHS girls viewed the VDP males as hostile. While this is evidence that the VDP females were not viewed as very approachable by the VHS community, it is difficult to interpret the sequence of cause and effect. It could be the VDP females were in fact reacting to the ignorance of the VHS students, which the VHS students interpreted as hostility, which led to a lack of social integration among the VDP females. The VDP females also may have realized that they lacked the status characteristics necessary to gain social acceptance at VHS and so may not have put in the same effort the boys did into being approachable, as it would have little effect on their social integration, thereby leading the VHS girls to interpret this as hostility.

Organizational Aspects of the School Affecting Integration

In the previous section, I discussed the gender differences in the strategies of social integration among the VDP students and also identified the perceptions of the VHS students concerning the integration of the VDP students. The perceptions of racial friendliness on both sides, however, were intricately related to the opportunities available for interaction and the conditions under which interaction did occur. In this section, I contend that the lack of social integration and the perceptions of hostility and ignorance among the VHS and VDP females were in part due to school practices that limited the amount of contact these girls had with each other and structured the contact they did have to be under less favorable conditions than the boys'.

Both macrostructural theory and contact theory suggest integration is largely a function of the organization and structure of the school day. The organization of the school affected the opportunities for cross-race interaction differently for females in VDP than for males, giving males more opportunity in general to interact and more opportunities under the conditions necessary for positive contact (Allport 1954; Pettigrew and Tropp 2006).

The school's transportation practices and host family provisions for students were set up to provide for both male and female VDP students; however, this interacted with differences in parental supervision of sons versus daughters and gender differences in students' own preferences concerning staying overnight in someone else's home, which led to differential effects. According to the interview data, parents of VDP girls worried about their daughters and were protective over them. The logistics of being a VDP student required a great deal of travel, with students getting up very early to catch the bus to school and having a long ride home in the evening. One bus left right after school at 3:15 and another left at 5:15. After the last bus, the only option was to walk to the train station in the center of Village and take a train to the center of NCC, which would then require multiple other transfers for the students to arrive at their homes. This meant that for the students to participate in many after-school activities, including sports teams, they either needed to be picked up by their parents or needed to stay with a host family. While the males embraced this idea and gained

access to important contacts through their host families, females did not. In an interview, a 12th-grade minority female explained that she quit basketball, even though she was quite good, because the practices ended so late and she did not like taking the train home. When I was talking with her informally during my observations, she explained to me that she did not like to stay at other people's homes. Other females mentioned quitting sports teams with their parents' support because parents worried about how their girls would get home at night. . . .

In contrast, no males mentioned a parent's worry about their whereabouts when they would stay over in Village.

Being unable to participate in sports or other after-school activities prevented the girls from forming friendships with VHS students and from feeling a part of the school. Girls felt that because the school did not attempt to make it easier for them to participate in activities, they were not valued. In an interview with 12th-grade African American females, the girls expressed anger and bitterness about the lack of attention paid to their dilemma and cited examples of trying to participate in fencing and student government with little success.

Of course, not all males participated in sports, and these exceptions help illuminate how school practices that valued the VDP students for certain characteristics, such as athleticism, served to devalue students who did not fit that ideal. For example, a 10th-grade African American male shared with me his disappointment with and anger at the school. In my field notes that day I wrote,

> He also felt like it was hard at Village to get involved in interesting clubs like the Model UN or Amnesty International because they meet at 6:30 and the last bus leaves at 5:00. If you can't find someone to sleep over with, it's hard. Most parents can't come and pick up their kids, and the [train] is unreliable. He compared it though to sports teams—if a coach needed a good VDP player to stay, he would arrange for him to spend the night with a Village student, even if the two weren't great friends. He said this showed what they valued VDP students for. . . .

Not being as able to participate in after-school activities prevented VDP students from having the simple opportunity to meet and interact with more VHS students and also prevented them from being in situations that fulfilled Allport's (1954) conditions for ideal contact (equal status; common, cooperative goals; and institutional support). Academic tracking can prevent interracial contact due to lack of opportunity and differences in status. While VHS did not track all of its classes, some were tracked, so general academic performance was not hard to determine. From interviews, it appeared that the girls did not think the VHS students thought of them as equally intelligent, so the VDP girls most likely did not perceive that there were equal status conditions in classes. Sports and other cooperative group activities, however, did put students on equal levels and also had them working toward a common goal. Other studies have supported the finding that participating in integrated extracurricular activities leads to improved race relations (Moody 2001; Steams, Buchmann, and Bonneau 2009). This may partly explain why boys seemed to have a more positive view of VHS and a better social experience.

In addition to structural barriers to participation in extracurricular activities, other school practices that were in place to support VDP students academically only served to further distance the girls from the school community. The school set aside a special room for tutoring during study periods for VDP students and hired an African American woman to supervise and help the students. Although the room and the supports were intended for all VDP students, mostly female minority students took advantage of the study room. The males did not feel supported by the supervisor and felt that she gave preference to the females, so fewer males spent time in there. As a result, they interacted more with other VHS students while the girls secluded themselves in the VDP room. This resulted in disadvantages for both minority males and minority females—the males did not get the help they needed academically since they felt uncomfortable in such a feminine space, and the females were even more socially isolated in the school.

REFERENCES

Adams, Natalie and Pamela Bettis. 2003. "Commanding the Room in Short Skirts: Cheering as the Embodiment of Ideal Girlhood." *Gender & Society* 17(1):73–91.

Allport, Gordon. 1954. *The Nature of Prejudice*. Cambridge, MA: Addison-Wesley.

Anderson, Elijah. 1990. *Streetwise: Race, Class and Change in an Urban Community*. Chicago: University of Chicago.

Anderson, Elijah. 1999. *Code of the Street: Decency, Violence, and the Moral Life of the Inner City*. New York: Norton.

Bettie, Julie. 2003. *Women without Class: Girls, Race and Identity*. Berkeley: University of California Press.

Bettis, Pamela and Natalie Adams. 2003. "The Power of the Preps and a Cheerleading Equity Policy." *Sociology of Education* 76(2):128–42.

Blau, Peter M. 1960. "A Theory of Social Integration." *American Journal of Sociology* 65(6):545–56.

Blau, Peter M. 1977. *Inequality and Heterogeneity: A Primitive Theory of Social Structure*. New York: Free Press.

Braddock, Jomills H. 1980. "The Perpetuation of Segregation across Levels of Education: Behavioral Assessment of the Contact-hypothesis." *Sociology of Education* 53(3):178–86.

Braddock, Jomills H., Marvin P. Dawkins, and George Wilson. 1995. "Intercultural Contact and Race Relations among American Youth." Pp. 237–56 in *Toward a Common Destiny: Improving Race and Ethnic Relations in America*, edited by W. D. Hawley and A. W. Jackson. San Francisco: Jossey-Bass.

Carter, Prudence L. 2005. *Keepin' It Real: School Success beyond Black and White*. New York: Oxford University Press.

Clampet-Lundquist, Susan, Kathryn Edin, Jeffrey R. Kling, and Greg J. Duncan. 2011. "Moving At-risk Teenagers Out of High-risk Neighborhoods: Why Girls Fare Better Than Boys." *American Journal of Sociology* 116(4):1154–89.

Clement, Dorothy C. and Joe R. Harding. 1978. "Social Distinctions and Emergent Student Groups in a Desegregated School." *Anthropology & Education Quarterly* 4:272–82.

Coleman, James S. 1961. *The Adolescent Society: The Social Life of the Teenager and Its Impact on Education*. New York: Free Press.

Damico, Sandra Bowman and Christopher Sparks. 1986. "Cross-group Contact Opportunities on Interpersonal Relationships in Desegregated Middle Schools." *Sociology of Education* 59(2):113–23.

Dance, L. Jannelle. 2002. *Tough Fronts: The Impact of Street Culture on Schooling*. New York: Routledge Falmer.

Dawkins, Marvin P. and Jomills H. Braddock. 1994. "The Continuing Significance of Desegregation: School Racial Composition and African American Inclusion in American Society." *Journal of Negro Education* 63(3):394–405.

Eaton, Susan. 2001. *The Other Boston Busing Story: What's Won and Lost across the Boundary Line*. New Haven, CT: Yale University Press.

Eder, Donna. 1985. "The Cycle of Popularity: Interpersonal Relations among Female Adolescents." *Sociology of Education* 58(3):154–65.

Eder, Donna and David A. Kinney. 1995. "The Effect of Middle School Extracurricular Activities on Adolescents' Popularity and Peer Status." *Youth & Society* 26:298–98.

Eder, Donna and Stephen Parker. 1987. "The Cultural Production and Reproduction of Gender: The Effect of Extracurricular Activities on Peer Group Culture." *Sociology of Education* 60(3):200–13.

Epstein, Cynthia Fuchs. 1973. "Positive Effects of the Multiple Negative: Explaining the Success of Black Professional Women." *American Journal of Sociology* 78(4):912–35.

Flores-Gonzalez, Nilda. 2005. "Popularity versus Respect: School Structure, Peer Groups and Latino Academic Achievement." *International Journal of Qualitative Studies in Education* 18(5):625–42.

Fordham, Signithia. 1993. "'Those Loud Black Girls': (Black) Women, Silence, and Gender 'Passing' in the Academy." *Anthropology & Education Quarterly* 24(1):3–32.

Gaines, Donna. 1991. *Teenage Wasteland*. New York: Harper Perennial.

Goto, Stanford T. 1997. "Nerds, Normal People, and Homeboys: Accommodation and Resistance among Chinese American Students." *Anthropology & Education Quarterly* 28(1):70–84.

Grant, Linda. 1984. "Black Females' 'Place' in Desegregated Classrooms." *Sociology of Education* 57(2):98–111.

Greenfield, Patricia. 2002. "Understanding Intercultural Relations on Multiethnic High School Sports Teams." Pp. 141–57 in *Paradoxes of Youth and Sport*, edited by M. Gatz, M. A. Messner, and S. J. Ball-Rokeach. Albany: State University of New York Press.

Hallinan, Maureen T. 1976. "Friendship Patterns in Open and Traditional Classrooms." *Sociology of Education* 49:254–65.

Hallinan, Maureen T. 1982. "Classroom Racial Composition and Students' Friendships." *Social Forces* 61(1):56–72.

Hallinan, Maureen T. and Aage Sørenson. 1985. "Ability Grouping and Student Friendships." *American Educational Research Journal* 22:495–99.

Hallinan, Maureen T. and Ruy A. Teixeira. 1987. "Students Interracial Friendships: Individual Characteristics, Structural Effects, and Racial Differences." *American Journal of Education* 95:563–83.

Hallinan, Maureen T. and Richard A. Williams. 1989. "Interracial Friendship Choices in Secondary Schools." *American Sociological Review* 54:67–78.

Hemmings, Annette. 1996. "Conflicting Images? Being Black and a Model High School Student." *Anthropology & Education Quarterly* 27(1):20–50.

Hollingshead, A. B. 1950. *Elmstown's Youth*. New York: John Wiley.

Ispa-Landa, Simone. 2009. "Social and Academic Effects of Participation in an Urban to Suburban Desegregation Program." Paper presented at the Race, Culture and Inequality Graduate Student Workshop, April 27, Cambridge, MA.

Johnson, Monica Kirkpatrick and Margaret Mooney Marini. 1998. "Bridging the Racial Divide in the United States: The Effect of Gender." *Social Psychology Quarterly* 61(3):247–58.

Khmelkov, Vladimer T. and Maureen T. Hallinan. 1999. "Organizational Effects on Race Relations in Schools." *Journal of Social Issues* 55:627–45.

Kinney, David A. 1993. "From Nerds to Normals: The Recovery of Identity among Adolescents from Middle School to High School." *Sociology of Education* 66:21–40.

Kitsner, Janet, Amy Merzler, Deborah Gatlin, and Susan Risi. 1993. "Classroom Racial Proportions and Children's Peer Relations: Race and Gender Effects." *Journal of Educational Psychology* 85(3):446–52.

Kubitschek, Warren N. and Maureen T. Hallinan. 1998. "Tracking and Students' Friendships." *Social Psychology Quarterly* 61(1):1–15.

Levinson, Bradley A. 1998. "Student Culture and the Contradictions of Equality at a Mexican Secondary School." *Anthropology & Education Quarterly* 29(3):267–96.

Lewis, Amanda E. 2003. *Race in the Schoolyard: Negotiating the Color Line in Classrooms and Communities*. New Brunswick, NJ: Rutgers University Press.

Longshore, Douglas and Jeffrey Prager. 1985. "The Impact of School Desegregation: A Situational Analysis." *Annual Review of Sociology* 11:75–91.

Lopez, Nancy. 2002. *Hopeful Girls, Troubled Boys: Race and Gender Disparity in Urban Education*. New York: Routledge.

Majors, Richard and Janet Mancini Billson. 1992. *Cool Pose: The Dilemmas of Black Manhood in America*. New York: Simon & Schuster.

Mehan, Hugh, Lea Hubbard, and Irene Villanueva. 1994. "Forming Academic Identities: Accommodation without Assimilation among Involuntary Minorities." *Anthropology & Education Quarterly* 25(2):91–117.

Moody, James. 2001. "Race, School Integration, and Friendship Segregation in America." *American Journal of Sociology* 107:679–716.

Noguera, Pedro A. and Jean Yonemura Wing. 2006. *Unfinished Business: Closing the Racial Achievement Gap in Our Schools*. San Francisco: Jossey-Bass.

Oakes, Jeannie. 1985. *Keeping Track: How Schools Structure Inequality*. New Haven, CT: Yale University Press.

Osterman, Karen F. 2000. "Students' Need for Belonging in the School Community." *Review of Educational Research* 70:323–67.

Perry, Pamela. 2002. *Shades of White: White Kids and Racial Identity in High School*. Durham, NC: Duke University Press.

Pettigrew, Thomas F. 1998. "Intergroup Contact Theory." *Annual Review of Psychology* 49(1): 65–85.

Pettigrew, Thomas F. 2008. "Future Directions for Intergroup Contact Theory and Research." *International Journal of Intercultural Relations* 32(3):187–99.

Pettigrew, Thomas F. and Linda R. Tropp. 2006. "A Meta-analytic Test of Intergroup Contact Theory." *Journal of Personality and Social Psychology* 90(5):751–83.

Quillian, Lincoln and Mary E. Campbell. 2003. "Beyond Black and White: The Present and Future of Multiracial Friendship Segregation." *American Sociological Review* 68:540–66.

Rodkin, Philip C., Travis Wilson, and Hai-Jeong Ahn. 2007. "Social Integration between African American and European American Children in Majority Black, Majority White, and Multicultural Classrooms." *New Directions for Child and Adolescent Development* 118:25–42.

Rodriquez, Jason. 2006. "Color-blind Ideology and the Cultural Appropriation of Hip-hop." *Journal of Contemporary Ethnography* 35(6):645–68.

Schofield, Janet W. and H. Andrew Sager. 1977. "Peer Interaction Patterns in an Integrated Middle School." *Sociometry* 40(2):130–38.

Schofield, Janet Ward. 1979. "The Impact of Positively Structured Contact on Intergroup Behavior: Does It Last under Adverse Conditions?" *Social Psychology Quarterly* 42:280–84.

Schofield, Janet Ward. 1982. *Black and White in School: Trust, Tension, or Tolerance?* New York: Praeger.

Schofield, Janet Ward. 1991. "School Desegregation and Intergroup Relations: A Review of the Literature." *Review of Research in Education* 17:335–409.

Steams, Elizabeth, Claudia Buchmann, and Kara Bonneau. 2009. "Interracial Friendships in the Transition to College: Do Birds of a Feather Flock Together Once They Leave the Nest?" *Sociology of Education* 82(2):173–95.

Tatum, Beverly D. 2003. *Why Are All the Black Kids Sitting Together in the Cafeteria? And Other Conversations about Race*. New York: Basic Books.

Wells, Amy Stuart and Robert L. Crain. 1997. *Stepping over the Color Line: African-American Students in White Suburban Schools*. New Haven, CT: Yale University Press.

Zweigenhaft, Richard L. and G. William Domhoff. 1991. *Blacks in the White Establishment? A Study of Race and Class in America*. New Haven, CT: Yale University Press.

READING 36

CHARTER SCHOOLS AND THE PUBLIC GOOD

Linda A. Renzulli and Vincent J. Roscigno

In this reading, Linda A. Renzulli and Vincent J. Roscigno examine the growth and possible outcomes of the increase in the number of charter schools. These schools provide a radical approach to traditional schooling in the United States because they operate outside of many regulations that dictate the structure of schooling across the country. The idea of charter schools, embedded in a "market economy" framework, also involves parents in the selection of schools for their children. Yet, as the authors argue, by changing the focus of accountability in schools these new freedoms for school administrators, teachers, and parents come with problems as well as hopes for the future of education.

Questions to consider for this reading:

1. How and when did the charter school movement begin?

2. How do charter schools differ from public schools?

3. Do you think changes in accountability described in this reading will lead to improved education for the nation's poorest children? Why or why not?

According to the U.S. Department of Education, "No Child Left Behind is designed to change the culture of America's schools by closing the achievement gap, offering more flexibility, giving parents more options, and teaching students based on what works." Charter schools—a recent innovation in U.S. education—are one of the most visible developments aimed at meeting these goals. Although they preceded the 2002 No Child Left Behind (NCLB) Act, charter schools are now supported politically and financially through NCLB. Charter schools are public schools set up and administered outside the traditional bureaucratic constraints of local school boards, with the goal of creating choice, autonomy, and accountability.

Unlike regular public schools, charter schools are developed and managed by individuals, groups of parents, community members, teachers, or education-management organizations. In exchange for their independence from most state and local regulations (except those related to health, safety, and nondiscrimination), they must uphold their contracts with the local or state school board or risk being closed. Each provides its own guidelines for establishing rules and procedures, including curriculum, subject to evaluation by the state in which it resides.

Charter schools are among the most rapidly growing educational institutions in the United States today. No charter schools existed before 1990, but such schools are now operating in

40 states and the District of Columbia. According to the Center for Education Reform, 3,977 charter schools are now educating more than a million students.

Charter schools have received bipartisan support and media accolades. This, however, is surprising. The true academic value of the educational choices that charter schools provide to students, as well as their broader implications for the traditional system of public education, are simply unknown—a fact that became obvious in November 2004, when voters in the state of Washington rejected—for the third time—legislation allowing the creation of charter schools. Driven by an alliance of parents, teachers, and teacher unions against sponsorship by powerful figures such as Bill Gates, this rejection went squarely against a decade-long trend. Reflecting on Washington's rejection, a state Democrat told the *New York Times,* "Charter schools will never have a future here now until there is conclusive evidence, nationwide, that these schools really work. Until the issue of student achievement gets resolved, I'd not even attempt to start over again in the Legislature."

these new public educational options. Opponents contend that charter schools cannot fix broader educational problems; if anything, they become instruments of segregation, deplete public school systems of their resources, and undermine the public good.

Given the rationales for charter schools before and after the NCLB Act, it is surprising how few assessments have been made of charter school functioning, impacts on achievement, or the implications of choice for school systems. Only a handful of studies have attempted to evaluate systematically the claims of charter school effectiveness, and few of these have used national data. The various justifications for charter schools—including the desire to increase achievement in the public school system—warrant attention, as do concrete research and evidence on whether such schools work. The debate, however, involves more than simply how to enhance student achievement. It also involves educational competition and accountability, individual choice and, most fundamentally, education's role in fostering the "public good."

THE RATIONALE

Most justifications for charter schools argue that the traditional system of public schooling is ineffective and that the introduction of competition and choice can resolve any deficiencies. The leading rationale is that accountability standards (for educational outcomes and student progress), choice (in curriculum, structure, and discipline), and autonomy (for teachers and parents) will generate higher levels of student achievement. The result will be high-quality schools for all children, particularly those from poor and minority backgrounds, and higher levels of student achievement.

While wealthy families have always been able to send their children to private schools, other Americans have historically had fewer, if any, options. Proponents suggest that charter schools can address such inequality by allowing all families, regardless of wealth, to take advantage of

IS THERE PROOF IN THE PUDDING?

Do students in charter schools do better than they would in traditional public schools? Unfortunately, the jury is still out, and the evidence is mixed. Profiles in the *New Yorker, Forbes, Time,* and *Newsweek,* for example, highlight the successes of individual charter schools in the inner cities of Washington, DC, and New York, not to mention anecdotal examples offered by high-profile advocates like John Walton and Bill Gates. While anecdotes and single examples suggest that charter schools may work, they hardly constitute proof or even systematic evidence that they always do. In fact, broader empirical studies using representative and national data suggest that many charter schools have failed.

One noteworthy study, released by the American Federation of Teachers (AFT) in 2004, reports that charter schools are not providing a better education than traditional public schools. Moreover, they are not boosting student achievement. Using fourth- and eighth-grade test scores from the National Assessment of Educational Progress across all states with charter schools, the report finds that charter-school students perform *less* well, on average, in math and reading than their traditional-school counterparts. There appear to be no significant differences among eighth-graders and no discernable difference in black-white achievement gaps across school type.

Because the results reported in the AFT study—which have received considerable media attention—do not incorporate basic demographic, regional, or school characteristics simultaneously, they can only relate average differences across charter schools and public schools. But this ignores the huge effects of family background, above and beyond school environment. Without accounting for the background attributes of students themselves, not to mention other factors such as the race and social-class composition of the student body, estimates of the differences between charter schools and traditional public schools are overstated.

In response to the 2004 AFT report, economists Carolyn Hoxby and Jonah Rockoff compared charter schools to surrounding public schools. Their results contradict many of the AFT's findings. They examined students who applied to but did not attend charter schools because they lost lotteries for spots. Hoxby and Rockoff found that, compared to their lotteried-out fellow applicants, students who attended charter schools in Chicago scored higher in both math and reading. This is true especially in the early elementary grades compared to nearby public schools with similar racial compositions. Their work and that of others also shows that older charter schools perform better than newly formed ones—perhaps suggesting that school stability and effectiveness require time to take hold. Important weaknesses nevertheless remain in the research design. For example, Hoxby and Rockoff conducted their study in a single city—Chicago—and thus it does not represent the effect of charter schools in general.

As with the research conducted by the AFT, we should interpret selective case studies and school-level comparisons with caution. Individual student background is an important force in shaping student achievement, yet it rarely receives attention in this research or in the charter school achievement debate more generally. The positive influence of charter schools, where it is found, could easily be a function of more advantaged student populations drawn from families with significant educational resources at home. We know from prior research that parents of such children are more likely to understand schooling options and are motivated to ensure their children's academic success. Since family background, parental investments, and parental educational involvement typically trump school effects in student achievement, it is likely that positive charter school effects are simply spurious.

More recently, a report by the National Center for Education Statistics (NCES), using sophisticated models, appropriate demographic controls, and a national sample, has concurred with the AFT report—charter schools are not producing children who score better on standardized achievement tests. The NCES report showed that average achievement in math and reading in public schools and in charter schools that were linked to a school district did not differ statistically. Charter schools not associated with a public school district, however, scored significantly *less* well than their public school counterparts.

Nevertheless, neither side of the debate has shown conclusively, through rigorous, replicated, and representative research, whether charter schools boost student achievement. The NCES report mentioned above has, in our opinion, done the best job of examining the achievement issue and has shown that charter schools are not doing better than traditional public schools when it comes to improving achievement.

Clearly, in the case of charter schools, the legislative cart has been put before the empirical horse. Perhaps this is because the debate is about more than achievement. Charter school debates and legislation are rooted in more fundamental disagreements over competition, individualism, and, most fundamentally, education's role in the public good. This reflects an important and significant shift in the cultural evaluation of public education in the United States, at the crux of which is the application of a market-based economic model, complete with accompanying ideas of "competition" and "individualism."

COMPETITION AND ACCOUNTABILITY

To whom are charter schools accountable? Some say their clients, namely, the public. Others say the system, namely, their authorizers. If charter schools are accountable to the public, then competition between schools should ensure academic achievement and bureaucratic prudence. If charter schools are accountable to the system, policies and procedures should ensure academic achievement and bureaucratic prudence. In either case, the assumption is that charter schools will close when they are not successful. The successful application of these criteria, however, requires clear-cut standards, oversight, and accountability—which are currently lacking, according to many scholars. Indeed, despite the rhetoric of their advocates and legislators, charter schools are seldom held accountable in the market or by the political structures that create them.

In a "market" view of accountability, competition will ultimately breed excellence by "weeding out" ineffectual organizations. Through "ripple effects," all schools will be forced to improve their standards. Much like business organizations, schools that face competition will survive only by becoming more efficient and producing a better overall product (higher levels of achievement) than their private and public school counterparts.

Social scientists, including the authors of this article, question this simplistic, if intuitively appealing, application of neoliberal business principles to the complex nature of the educational system, children's learning, and parental choice for schools. If competition were leading to accountability, we would see parents pulling

their children out of unsuccessful charter schools. But research shows that this seldom happens. Indeed, parents, particularly those with resources, typically choose schools for reasons of religion, culture, and social similarity rather than academic quality.

Nor are charter schools accountable to bureaucrats. Even though charter schools are not outperforming traditional public schools, relatively few (10 percent nationally) have actually been closed by their authorizers over the last decade. Although we might interpret a 10 percent closure rate as evidence of academic accountability at work, this would be misleading. Financial rather than academic issues are the principal reasons cited for these closures. By all indications, charter schools are not being held accountable to academic standards, either by their authorizers or by market forces.

In addition to measuring accountability through student performance, charter schools should also be held to standards of financial and educational quality. Here, some charter schools are faltering. From California to New York and Ohio, newspaper editorials question fiscal oversight. There are extreme cases such as the California Charter Academy, a publicly financed but privately run chain of 60 charter schools. Despite a budget of $100 million, this chain became insolvent in August 2004, leaving thousands of children without a school to attend.

More direct accountability issues include educational quality and annual reports to state legislatures; here, charter-school performance is poor or mixed. In Ohio, where nearly 60,000 students now attend charter schools, approximately one-quarter of these schools are not following the state's mandate to report school-level test score results, and only 45 percent of the teachers at the state's 250 charter schools hold full teaching certification. Oversight is further complicated by the creation of "online" charter schools, which serve 16,000 of Ohio's public school students.

It is ironic that many charter schools are not held to the very standards of competition, quality, and accountability that legislators and advocates used to justify them in the first place. Perhaps this is why Fredrick Hess, a charter school researcher, recently referred to accountability as applied to charter schools as little more than a "toothless threat."

INDIVIDUALISM OR INEQUALITY?

The most obvious goal of education is student achievement. Public education in the United States, however, has also set itself several other goals that are not reducible to achievement or opportunity at an individual level but are important culturally and socially. Public education has traditionally managed diversity and integration, created common standards for the socialization of the next generation, and ensured some equality of opportunity and potential for meritocracy in the society at large. The focus of the charter school debate on achievement—rooted in purely economic rationales of competition and individual opportunism—has ignored these broader concerns.

Individual choice in the market is a key component of neoliberal and "free-market" theory— a freedom many Americans cherish. Therefore, it makes sense that parents might support choice in public schooling. Theoretically, school choice provides them market power to seek the best product for their children, to weigh alternatives, and to make changes in their child's interest. But this power is only available to informed consumers, so that educational institutions and policies that provide choice may be reinforcing the historical disadvantages faced by racial and ethnic minorities and the poor.

We might expect that students from advantaged class backgrounds whose parents are knowledgeable about educational options would be more likely to enroll in charter schools. White parents might also see charter schools as an educational escape route from integrated public schools that avoids the financial burden of private schooling. On the other hand, the justification for charter schools is often framed in terms of an "educational fix" for poor, minority concentrated districts in urban areas. Here, charter schools may appear to be a better opportunity for aggrieved parents whose children are attending poorly funded, dilapidated public schools.

National research, at first glance, offers encouraging evidence that charter schools are providing choices to those who previously had few options: 52 percent of those enrolled in charter schools are nonwhite compared to 41 percent of those in traditional public schools. These figures, however, tell us little about the local concentrations of whites and nonwhites in charter schools, or how the racial composition and distribution of charter schools compares to the racial composition and distribution of local, traditional public schools.

African-American students attend charter and noncharter schools in about the same proportion, yet a closer look at individual charter schools within districts reveals that they are often segregated. In Florida, for instance, charter schools are 82 percent white, whereas traditional public schools are only 51 percent white. Similar patterns are found across Arizona school districts, where charter school enrollment is 20 percent more white than traditional schools. Amy Stuart Wells's recent research finds similar tendencies toward segregation among Latinos, who are underrepresented in California's charter schools. Linda Renzulli and Lorraine Evans's national analysis of racial composition within districts containing charter schools shows that charter school formation often results in greater levels of segregation in schools between whites and nonwhites. This is not to suggest that minority populations do not make use of charter schools. But, when they do, they do so in segregated contexts.

Historically, racial integration has been a key cause of white flight and it remains a key factor in the racial composition of charter schools and other schools of choice. Decades of research on school segregation have taught us that when public school districts become integrated, through either court mandates or simple population change, white parents may seek alternative schools for their children. Current research suggests that a similar trend exists with charter schools, which provide a public-school option for white flight without the drawbacks of moving (such as job changes and longer commutes). While those from less-privileged and minority backgrounds have charter schools at their disposal, the realities of poor urban districts and contemporary patterns of racial residential segregation may mean that the "choice" is between a racially and economically segregated charter school or an equally segregated traditional school, as Renzulli's research has shown. Individualism in the form of educational choice, although perhaps intuitively appealing, in reality may be magnifying some of the very inequalities that public education has been attempting to overcome since the *Brown v. Board of Education* decision in 1954.

Regarding equality of opportunity and its implications for the American ideal of meritocracy, there is also reason for concern. Opponents have pointed to the dilution of district resources where charter schools have emerged, especially as funds are diverted to charter schools. Advocates, in contrast, argue that charter schools have insufficient resources. More research on the funding consequences of charter school creation is clearly warranted. Why, within a system of public education, should some students receive more than others? And what of those left behind, particularly students from disadvantaged backgrounds whose parents may not be aware of their options? Although evidence on the funding question is sparse, research on public schools generally and charter school attendance specifically suggests that U.S. public education may be gravitating again toward a system of separate, but not equal, education.

The Future of Public Education

Variation across charter schools prevents easy evaluation of their academic success or social consequences for public education. Case studies can point to a good school or a bad one. National studies can provide statistical averages and comparisons, yet they may be unable to reveal the best and worst effects of charter schools. Neither type of research has yet fully accounted for the influence of family background and school demographic composition. Although conclusions about charter school effectiveness or failure remain questionable, the most rigorous national analyses to date suggest that charter schools are doing no better than traditional public schools.

Certainly some charter schools are improving the educational quality and experience of some children. KIPP (Knowledge Is Power Program) schools, for example, are doing remarkable things for the students lucky enough to attend them. But for every KIPP school (of which there are only 45, and not all are charter schools), there are many more charter schools that do not provide the same educational opportunity to students, have closed their doors in the middle of the school year, and, in effect, isolate students from their peers of other races and social classes. Does this mean that we should prevent KIPP, for example, from educating students through the charter school option? Maybe. Or perhaps we should develop better program evaluations—of what works and what does not—and implement them as guideposts. To the dismay of some policymakers and "competition" advocates, however, such standardized evaluation and accountability would undercut significant charter school variations if not the very nature of the charter school innovation itself.

Student achievement is only part of the puzzle when it comes to the charter school debate; we need to consider social integration and equality as well. These broader issues, although neglected, warrant as much attention as potential effects on achievement. We suspect that such concerns, although seldom explicit, probably underlie the often contentious charter school and school choice debate itself. We believe it is time to question the logic pertaining to competition, choice, and accountability. Moreover, we should all scrutinize the existing empirical evidence, not to mention educational policy not firmly rooted in empirical reality and research. As Karl Alexander eloquently noted in his presidential address to the Southern Sociological Society, "The charter school movement, with its 'let 1,000 flowers bloom' philosophy, is certain to yield an occasional prize-winning rose. But is either of these approaches [to school choice] likely to prove a reliable guide for broad-based, systemic reform—the kind of reform that will carry the great mass of our children closer to where we want them to be? I hardly think so." Neither do we.

FURTHER READINGS

[Editors' Note: No references were provided for this article; however, the authors recommend the following for further research into the subject.]

Fusarelli, L. D., & Crawford, J. R. (Eds.). (2001). Charter schools and the accountability puzzle (Special issue). *Education and Urban Society, 33*(2), 107–215. Eight articles examine different models of charter school accountability.

Hening, J. R. (1994). *Rethinking school choice: Limits of the market metaphor.* Princeton, NJ: Princeton University Press. In this early work on school choice, Hening discusses market-oriented choice programs, suggesting they may not work and are likely to make education worse in terms of segregation and outcomes.

Hoxby, C., & Rockoff, J. (2004). *Impact of charter schools on student achievement.* Unpublished manuscript. Retrieved from http://post.economics .harvard.edu/faculty/hoxby/papers/hoxbyrockoff .pdf. Hoxby and Rockoff analyze the achievement of charter school students in Chicago, Illinois, compared to the achievement of students who do not attend charter schools.

Nelson, F. H., Rosenberg, B., & Van Meter, N. (2004). *Charter school achievement on the 2003 national assessment of educational progress.* Washington, DC: American Federation of Teachers. The authors compare the math and reading scores of charter school and non–charter school students.

Renzulli, L. A., & Evans, L. (2005). School choice, charter schools, and white flight. *Social Problems, 52*(3), 398–418. Renzulli and Evans show that integration in public school leads to increased proportions of white students in local charter schools.

Vergari, S. (2002). *The charter school landscape.* Pittsburgh, PA: Pittsburgh University Press. Vergari examines charter school politics and policies in eleven states and the province of Alberta to show how charter schools are affecting public education.

ORGANIZING FOR SUCCESS

From Inequality to Quality

Linda Darling-Hammond

Linda Darling-Hammond elaborates on innovative schools, particularly charter schools as discussed in the previous reading. She brings to this discussion considerable experience working in schools to bring about change for low-income students. This excerpt from her book, *The Flat World and Education: How America's Commitment to Equity Will Determine Our Future,* illustrates what she has found does and does not work for low-income students in schools. This reading focuses more on the things that work, practices that she and her team of researchers have found to be effective in schools. While she echoes some of the concerns and problems with schools today that Linda A. Renzulli and Vincent J. Roscigno discussed in their reading, this one offers some structural and organizational changes that can make any school more effective for those students who need it the most.

Questions to consider for this reading:

1. Does Darling-Hammond believe that charter schools are sufficient in and of themselves to provide the innovation we need in the organization of our schools?

2. What suggestion offered by Darling-Hammond do you think would be most effective in changing the type of education we offer to our children?

3. What factors do you think will inhibit change or make the changes she recommends in the structure of schools less likely to occur?

CREATING SYSTEMS OF SUCCESSFUL SCHOOLS

Designing schools that serve low-income students of color well is not impossible. Since the ground-breaking research of Ron Edmonds more than 3 decades ago,[1] many studies have documented the practices of unusually effective schools and have uncovered similar features of those that succeed with students who are historically underserved.[2] However, to create such schools on a much wider scale, a new policy environment must be constructed that routinely encourages such schools to be developed and sustained.

From *The Flat World and Education: How America's Commitment to Equity Will Determine Our Future* (pp. 264–277), by Linda Darling-Hammond, 2010, New York: Teachers College Press. Copyright 2010 by Teachers College Press, Columbia University. Reprinted with permission.

Supporting Successful Innovation

Creating new schools and innovations is a great American pastime. Waves of reform producing productive new school designs occurred at the turn of the 20th century when John Dewey, Ella Flagg Young, Lucy Sprague Mitchell, and others were working in Chicago, New York, and other Northern cities, and African American educators such as Anna Julia Cooper, Lucy Laney, and Mary McLeod Bethune were creating schools in the South. A wave of new school designs swept the country in the 1930s and 1940s when the Progressive Education Association helped redesign and study 30 "experimental" high schools that were found, in the famous Eight-Year Study, to perform substantially better than traditional schools in developing high-achieving, intellectually adventurous, socially responsible young people able to succeed in college and in life.[3] Urban school reform movements occurred in the 1960s and 1970s, producing schools such as the Parkway Program in Philadelphia and Central Park East Elementary in New York, for example; and in the 1990s when the impulse for innovation returned once again. . . .

Despite more successful and more equitable outcomes than most traditional schools, few of these innovative schools were sustained over time. Any educator who has been in the field for any period of time has participated in what former Seattle teacher union leader, Roger Erskine, has dubbed "random acts of innovation"[4] that have come and gone, regardless of their success. Generally, this is because, like bank voles and wolf spiders, urban districts often eat their young. Changes in superintendents and school boards create swings in policies, including efforts to standardize instruction, go "back to the basics," and bring innovators to heel. Even when they achieve better outcomes, distinctive school models confront long-standing traditions, standard operating procedures, and expectations, including, sometimes, the expectation that the students who have traditionally failed should continue to do so, so that the traditionally advantaged can continue in their position of privilege. Indeed,

Anna Julia Cooper's progressive M Street School in segregated Washington, D.C., which offered a "thinking curriculum" to Black students and outperformed two of the three White high schools in the city, was attacked for both of these reasons in the early 20th century.[5]

Sometimes, successful schools and programs fade because special foundation or government money has dried up, and the district does not have the foresight or wherewithal to preserve what is working. Other times, the challenges of replenishing the capable, dynamic teachers and leaders who have created a successful school prove too great to sustain the model. Historian Lawrence Cremin argued that the successes of progressive education reforms did not spread widely because such practice required "infinitely skilled teachers" who were never prepared in sufficient numbers to sustain these more complex forms of teaching and schooling.[6]

New York City's unusual renaissance was facilitated by the creation of an innovation silo in the form of the Alternative Schools Superintendency—which buffered schools from many regulations and forged new solutions to old bureaucratic problems, and by a rich array of professional resources in support of reforms, including expert practitioners who created networks of learning and support, a large set of public and private universities offering expertise and intellectual resources, and philanthropists and researchers who provided additional professional and political support to these efforts. The United Federation of Teachers (UFT) ran its own Teachers Center, and many of the teachers active in this professional development were involved in the new schools initiatives. Over time, the UFT incorporated many supports for reform-oriented schools into its contracts—first through waivers and later through changes in collective bargaining agreements—and, in some cases, became part of the protection for further reforms. Even when frequent changes in leadership might have led to abandonment of the new schools initiative, these forces kept the reform momentum going.

In most places, however, the lack of investment in professional education that would allow teachers and school leaders to acquire the knowledge they need to undertake sophisticated practices has proved to be an ongoing problem. Another recurring problem is the lack of policy development that could encourage the growth of such schools rather than keeping them as exceptions, on waiver, and at the margins . . .

In the current environment, some, including Hill,[7] suggest that charters, contract schools, or performance schools that are essentially licensed by school boards to provide a particular model or approach may provide a way to spark innovation and protect it from the vicissitudes of district politics and changes of course. This strategy has the potential virtue of enabling continuity of educational direction and philosophy within schools—where, arguably, coherence is most important—and holding schools accountable for results, rather than for bureaucratic compliance.

Certainly, some important new school models have been launched through charters. In California, where the state has used chartering as a major lever for innovation, three of the five high schools we studied—Animo, Leadership, and New Tech—were charters. This allowed them to outline a specific approach to education and hold onto it, without being buffeted by changing district views or intruded upon by curriculum, testing, and management mandates. Although collective bargaining agreements from the industrial era often create cumbersome constraints in many districts, new approaches to bargaining have also begun to emerge, and two of these three charters employ unionized teachers.

Many other successful new small school models have been started and expanded through special arrangements for autonomy from district regulations or through charter organizations. Some, like Envision Schools, Asia Society, High Tech High, Uncommon Schools, and others, have introduced substantially new educational approaches, including performance assessments, exhibitions of learning, curriculum focused on global understandings, advisory systems, and more. Odds are that, within many districts, without formal protection, their adventurousness would have been quashed by some school board or superintendent's insistence on introducing a new standardized curriculum or testing system, or pressuring the schools to grow in size and revert to factory-model designs, or requiring the hiring of teachers or leaders who are not prepared for or bought into the model. (Both district practices of centralized assignment and collective bargaining agreements that require seniority transfers can be culpable in this problem.) Even when there are good intentions to support innovation, local districts are subject to a geological dig of laws, regulations, precedents, and standard operating procedures that can be enormously difficult to untangle before they strangle change efforts.

For these reasons and others, Hill suggests an entirely new role for school districts as managers of a portfolio of relatively autonomous schools, rather than as school operators:

> Today, boards oversee a central bureaucracy which owns and operates all the schools in a given district. It is time to retire this "command-and-control" system and replace it with a new model: portfolio management. In this new system, school boards would manage a diverse array of schools, some run by the school district and others by independent organizations, each designed to meet the different needs of students. Like investors with diversified portfolios of stocks and bonds, school boards would closely manage their community's portfolio of educational service offerings, divesting less productive schools and adding more promising ones. If existing schools do not serve students well, boards would experiment with promising new approaches to find ones that work.

This notion of a portfolio of schools—also advocated by the Gates Foundation—has many potential virtues to recommend it. Certainly, choice is better than coercion in the management of education. Students and families could find better fits with their interests and philosophies, and make a greater commitment to schools they have chosen. Choice could make schools more accountable and attentive to student needs. Schools that create successful designs should benefit from more autonomy to refine and maintain their good work. If a portfolio strategy works well it should "ensure a supply of quality school options that reflects a community's needs, interests, and assets . . . and [ensure] that every student has access to high-quality schools that prepare them for further learning, work, and citizenship."[8] A portfolio structure is essentially what has emerged in New York City within the regular district structure (now divided into sets of school zones and networks) and, on a smaller scale, in Boston, which has launched a set of Pilot Schools—alternatives that provide a variety of educational options sharing the features described earlier in this chapter, which are succeeding at rates far above those of many other schools serving similar students.[9]

However, neither choice nor charters alone is a panacea. And not all innovations are useful ones. Although some public schools of choice have been successful, others have made little difference. For example, a recent evaluation of Chicago's Renaissance 2010 initiative, which replaced a group of low-performing schools with charters and other autonomous schools of choice run by entrepreneurs and the district, found that the achievement of students in the new schools was no different from that of a matched comparison group of students in the old schools they had left, and both groups continued to be very low-performing.[10]

Results for charters nationally have also been mixed. Reviews of the evidence have found positive impacts in some places and insignificant or negative impacts in others.[11]

A study of 16 states, covering 70% of all charter schools, found that only 17% of charters produced academic gains that were significantly better than traditional public schools serving demographically similar students, while 37[%] performed worse than their traditional public school counterparts, and 46% showed no difference from district-run public schools. The fact that outcomes differ across states suggests that different approaches to regulation and funding may be important. For example, in Ohio, where an unregulated market strategy created a huge range of for-profit and nonprofit providers with few public safeguards, charter school students were found to achieve at consistently lower levels than their demographically similar public school counterparts. Studies have also found lower average performance for charter students in the poorly regulated charter sectors in Washington, D.C., and Arizona, where charters can be granted for 15 years and fewer safeguards for students are required.[12] . . .

[T]he pressures under recent accountability regimes to get test scores up have led to growing concerns that some new schools—charters and otherwise—have sought to exclude those students who are the most challenging to teach, either by structuring admissions so that low-achieving students and those with special education or other needs are unlikely to be admitted, or by creating conditions under which such students are encouraged to leave. Studies of new schools created in New York City after 2000, for example, have found that these schools, unlike the earlier pioneers, enrolled more academically able students and fewer English language learners or students with disabilities than the large comprehensive schools they replaced. This enabled them to show better outcomes.[13]

Thus, it is not the governance mechanism or the degree of autonomy alone that determines whether schools will succeed. In places where new school models and redesigned schools have done well without ignoring or pushing out struggling students, attention has been paid both to sparking new educational possibilities and building schools' capacities for good instruction, and to removing unnecessary constraints and creating appropriate safeguards for students.

Sustaining Change

The goal, ultimately, is not just to support a vanguard group of unique schools, but to enable all schools to adopt practices that will be more successful for all of their students. For this to happen, districts must find ways to foster innovation and responsiveness without compromising equity, access, and the public purpose of schools to prepare citizens who can live, work, and contribute to a common democratic society. This will require redesigning districts as well as schools, rethinking regulations and collective bargaining, while building capacity and allocating resources in smarter and more equitable ways.

Redesigning Districts. For successful schools to become the norm, districts must move beyond the pursuit of an array of ad hoc initiatives managed by exception to fundamental changes in district operations and policy. Throughout the 20th century most urban districts adopted increasingly bureaucratic approaches to managing schools. They created extensive rules to manage every aspect of school life—from curriculum, instruction, and testing to hiring, purchasing, and facilities—along with complex, departmentalized structures to manage these rules and procedures. Siloed bureaucrats have had the mission of administering procedures that often get in the way of practitioners' instructional efforts, rather than managing quality by being accountable for figuring out ways to support success. To create a new paradigm, the role of the district must shift

- From enforcing procedures to building school capacity
- From managing compliance to managing improvement
- From rewarding staff for following orders and "doing things right" to rewarding staff for getting results by "doing the right things"
- From rationing educational opportunities to expanding successful programs
- From ignoring (and compounding) failure in schools serving the least powerful to reallocating resources to ensure their success

To a large extent, these changes represent a switch from bureaucratic accountability—that is, hierarchical systems that pass down decisions and hold employees accountable for following the rules, whether or not they are effective—to professional accountability—that is, knowledge-based systems that help build capacity in schools for doing the work well, and hold people accountable for using professional practices that enable student success.

In a new paradigm, the design of the district office should also evolve from a set of silos that rarely interact with one another to a team structure that can integrate efforts across areas such as personnel, professional development, curriculum and instruction, and evaluation, with the goal of creating greater capacity in a more integrated fashion. These supports should include

- Recruiting a pool of well-prepared teachers and leaders from which schools can choose—and building pipelines to facilitate their training and availability
- Organizing access to high-quality, sustained professional development and resources, including skilled instructional mentors and coaches that schools can call upon and that can be deployed to diagnose problems and support improvements in schools that are struggling
- Ensuring that high-quality instructional resources—curriculum materials, books, computers, and texts—are available
- Providing services, such as purchasing and facilities maintenance, to school consumers in effective and efficient ways—if schools choose to acquire them from the district

If they incorporate choice, districts will need to ensure that all schools are worth choosing and that all students have access to good schools. This means they must continuously evaluate how schools are doing, seeking to learn from successful schools and to support improvements in struggling schools by ensuring that these schools secure strong leadership and excellent teachers, and are supported in adopting successful program strategies. Districts will need to become learning organizations themselves—developing their capacity to investigate and learn from innovations in order to leverage productive strategies, and developing their capacity to support successful change. Where good schools and programs are oversubscribed, districts will have to learn how to spread good models rather than rationing them, and where schools are failing, they will need to learn how to diagnose, address problems, and invest resources to improve them. These capacities are needed in all systems, whether or not they adopt choice strategies.

If education is to serve the public good, it is critical to guard against the emergence of a privatized system in which schools are separated by their ability to choose their students, rather than by the ability of students and families to choose their schools. For choice to work, districts must not only provide information and transportation to parents; they must also manage parents' and schools' choices so that schools recruit and admit students without regard to race, class, or prior academic achievement, both to preserve the possibilities for integrated, common schools and to ensure that some schools do not become enclaves of privilege while others remain dumping grounds. Managed choice arrangements in cities such as Cambridge, Massachusetts, and (in some eras) New York City have created strategies for doing this, allowing parents to state several preferences and requiring schools to admit a diverse student body from all parts of the achievement range. However, these districts have also learned that such strategies require constant vigilance and are not by themselves enough to guarantee access to quality schools for all students. In particular, without the right support and incentives, many schools will seek to recruit the most advantaged students and deflect or push out the least advantaged ones. These incentives, as I discuss below, have to do with the level of capacity to serve students well, with resources, and with accountability measures.

Building Professional Capacity. [B]uilding professional capacity ultimately requires investments in effective preparation, hiring, mentoring, evaluation, and professional development for school leaders, as well as teachers and other staff. In addition, systems need to develop strategies for sharing good practice across schools, ranging from research that is widely disseminated to the establishment of networks of schools, teachers, and principals that develop and share practice with one another, to the creation of strategies such as school quality reviews that allow educators to examine one another's practice and get feedback that can help them grow.

Growing successful new schools or improving existing ones is not likely to be accomplished merely by a replication strategy in which external agents seek to transplant programs or designs from one school into another. Replication efforts have an inglorious history, largely because they quickly run up against differences in staff knowledge and capacity resources, and contexts of receiving schools. Unless they are accompanied by intensive, long-term professional development support, schools can rarely attend to the nuances and implications of new strategies in ways that would permit strong implementation over the long run. When the purportedly effective techniques don't work immediately, especially for students who are challenging to teach, staff will tend to revert to old approaches and/or focus on reaching those who are easiest to teach given what teachers already know how to do and have the resources to support.

Another approach was used to achieve the surprisingly consistent and sophisticated practices we found across the Coalition Campus Schools we studied, which allowed them to be successful with normally low-achieving students. Following what might be called a birthing and parenting strategy, many of the new school "launchers" had been teachers in the older, successful schools. They were mentored by expert veteran principals and teachers while belonging to a set of networks that facilitated ongoing sharing of practice and supported problem solving.

Networking strategies have increasingly been found to be powerful for sharing practitioner knowledge. Teacher-to-teacher networks such as the National Writing Project help teachers develop effective pedagogical practices; principal networks have become critically important within many districts seeking to support stronger instructional leadership and create opportunities for shared problem solving; and, in both the United States and abroad . . . , school networks are enabling educators to share departmental and schoolwide practices through collective professional development, observational visits, and pooling of intellectual resources.

Managing and Allocating Resources. For schools to succeed with all students, they also must be adequately resourced to do so. As we have seen, disparities in funding between states, districts, and schools often leave those working with the neediest students with the fewest resources. States can begin to change this by costing out what would be required to provide an adequate education to graduate all students, having met the state standards, and then allocating resources equitably to each student on a per pupil basis adjusted for regional cost-of-living differentials and pupil needs. The weighted student formula approach, advocated by many school finance reformers and adopted in some cities to equalize within-district funding, is intended to provide an added increment for students with disabilities, new English language learners, and low-income students, determined by estimating the costs of educating these students to the state's standards. Schools serving large concentrations of high-need students would receive additional funds to provide the services that so many of their students require.

Schools and districts also need the flexibility to spend their funds in optimal ways. Among the distinctive features of successful, redesigned schools is the fact that they use the resources of people and time very differently from traditional systems in order to provide more intense relationships between adults and students and to ensure collaborative planning and learning time for teachers, as schools in other nations do. [T]he United States spends much less of its educational budget on classroom instruction and on teachers—just over 50%, as compared to 70 to 80% in other countries.[14] This weakens instruction.

In part, this is because the United States spends more on several layers of bureaucracy between the state and the school, made necessary in part by the dizzying array of federal and state categorical programs schools are expected to manage because they are not trusted to make good decisions about resources. These categorical programs themselves create inefficiencies in spending, requiring administrative attention and audit trails, as well as fragmenting programs and efforts in schools in ways that undermine educational outcomes. Often, these programs and other regulations prescribe staffing patterns and other uses of resources that reduce focus and effectiveness.

In addition, the United States spends more of its personnel budget on a variety of administrative staff and instructional aides rather than on teachers directly, implementing the outdated model that added a variety of pull-out programs and peripheral services to make up for the failures of a factory-model system, rather than investing in the instructional core of expert teachers given time to work productively with students whom they know well. Thus, whereas full-time teachers engaged in instruction comprise about 70 to 80% of education employees in most Asian and European nations, they are only about half of education employees in the United States.[15] In 2003, for example, whereas only 51% of school district employees in the United States were classroom teachers, the proportion of full-time classroom teachers in Japanese schools was 89% of all educational staff. The proportion is 72% of all employees, if one also includes the large number of doctors, dentists, and pharmacists who are based in Japanese schools.[16] . . . Indeed, Japanese schools had, proportionately, as many doctors as there were instructional aides in U.S. schools, but only one-third the proportion of administrative staff.

Successful, redesigned schools often invest more of their resources in classroom teachers and organize teachers in teams that share students over longer periods of time, to create more sharing of knowledge, as well as to focus on accountability for student needs and success. They consolidate their resources to offer a strong, common core curriculum and key supports, resisting the temptation to diffuse their energies or spend on peripherals at the expense of the central goals of the school. The implications for staffing patterns, resource allocations, and the uses of teachers' and students' time are even more distinctive for schools that engage students in extended internships outside the school, as the Met and its network of schools do; for schools that are engaging students in a range of college courses while they are in high school; and for schools that are embracing technology-based approaches to project work as the New Tech network of schools does.

States and districts will need to encourage more thoughtful and inventive uses of resources by resisting the temptation to prescribe old factory-model requirements for staffing and uses of time and funds, and by providing supports for school leaders to learn how to design organizations that use resources in ways that are likely to produce the desired outcomes.

Deregulating Strategically. As I have suggested, a challenge in scaling up more effective school designs is that the century-old model of school organization that has shaped most schools is now reinforced by layers of regulations that often do not produce the most effective forms of education. Most state regulatory frameworks for schools have not yet shifted to accommodate or encourage the design choices made by new school models.

Where innovations are made possible by relief from regulations, they cannot spread unless the same regulatory relief is applied to other parts of the system. Few states have examined ways to deregulate public schools strategically in ways that would permit greater focus and success while preserving core public values. In recent years, as charters and other relatively autonomous schools have been created to permit flexibility in one part of the system, heavy-handed regulation has often increased in the remainder of the system.

The Boston Pilot Schools and the New York City alternative schools are proof that large public organizations can create organizational firewalls that allow space for successful innovation. But to do so, they must always be conscious of the impact of their policies on school-level practice, and they must, over time, allow innovators to help change the rules as well as avoid them. Regulations protecting access and providing equitable allocations of resources should provide the foundation of a redesigned system, while professional standards and investments in

professional capacity that allow educators to be trusted should replace efforts to micromanage teaching and the design of schools.

Changing Contracts. Over time, many of the features of the factory model have been incorporated into collective bargaining agreements by both unions and school boards. Among the most problematic aspects for school reforms are constraints on how time and work are structured and procedures for faculty hiring and assignment that have assumed, in the assembly-line era, that teachers are interchangeable parts.

The success of schools committed to a set of educational principles depends on their ability to hire faculty who believe in those principles and have the capacity to enact them. Thus, centralized assignments of teachers can be a problem, whether in the initial hiring of teachers or due to seniority transfers that give teachers rights to transfer into schools where their skills and philosophy may not fit. Some districts have begun to change these traditions by taking on the responsibility to build a strong pool of well-prepared personnel from which schools can then recruit, and by placing teachers who want to transfer schools into this pool when openings are available, with rights to an early interview but not to placement in a specific school.

In New York, for example, the new school development process triggered important system reforms, including in the key area of selecting teachers. With the cooperation of the Board of Education, the United Federation of Teachers (UFT) and the CCS Project negotiated a process for selecting staff in which a committee of teachers reviews resumes, interviews prospective candidates—and often observes them teaching or planning collaboratively—and selects those most qualified for the available positions. Where teachers are equally qualified, seniority is the decisive variable. UFT representatives participated in these hiring committees, and were so pleased with the outcomes that the union introduced the process into contract negotiations and recommended its adoption more broadly. The contract now includes a peer selection process for teachers in all nontraditional schools, illustrating how innovation can be used as a lever to transform system policies.

In addition, in any New York school where 55% of teachers vote to do so, the school can trigger a School-Based Option that relieves it from many contract constraints and allows new arrangements to be substituted. Many innovative schools have created their own contracts for teachers which, for example, may recognize teachers' roles as advisors and acknowledge different uses of time during the day and week in return for smaller pupil loads and greater autonomy.

Rethinking Accountability. Finally, policymakers must learn new ways to manage the tension between fostering innovation and holding schools accountable to the other purposes of public education—equity, access, development of citizenship, and progress in learning. One critical aspect of the state's role is to ascertain that students are being adequately taught to become productive citizens of society. In recent years, accountability in the United States has largely come to mean tracking test scores on increasingly limited measures, rather than ensuring access to adequate and equitable learning opportunities and the achievement of a broader set of outcomes. As we have seen, the allocation of sanctions to schools based on these high-stakes measures also creates disincentives for schools to admit and keep the neediest students.

Some states, such as Nebraska and Rhode Island, have allowed schools to develop and implement broader, more ambitious assessments of student learning that are approved by the state and examined for accountability purposes along with other documented student outcomes. In New York, 31 schools in the Performance Standards Consortium, including many of those we studied, have developed their own graduation portfolio of challenging research papers and exhibitions. This collection of required products treats both academic outcomes and civic and social responsibility—the latter demonstrated through community service and contributions to the school—and is approved for use in lieu of

some of the New York State Regents examinations, with the expectation that schools also track evidence of college admission and completion.

In the long run, accountability systems that provide the right incentives for school quality and equity will need to examine student growth and school progress on a range of high-quality measures, not just their status at a moment in time on one limited measure, include evidence of students' opportunities to learn as well as their outcomes, and enforce professional standards of practice that assure parents their children will be well taught, not just well tested.

CONCLUSION

A growing number of schools have disrupted the status quo by providing opportunities for low-income students of color to become critical thinkers and leaders for the future. Unless policy systems change, however, these schools will remain anomalies, rather than harbingers of the future. Creating a system that supports the learning of all students is not impossible. It will take clarity of vision and purposeful, consistent action to create a web of supportive, mutually reinforcing elements. In particular, dismantling the institutionalized inequities that feed the racial, socioeconomic, and linguistic achievement gap will require substantive policy changes in redesigning schools, developing teachers and principals, expanding our conceptions of curriculum and assessment, rethinking funding strategies, and reconceptualizing accountability.

NOTES

1. Edmonds (1979).
2. For a review; see Levine & Lezotte (1990).
3. Eight-year study.
4. Erskine (2002).
5. Robinson (1984).
6. Cremin (1961).
7. Hill (2006).
8. Gates Foundation (2005), p. 3.

9. French (2008).

10. Young et al. (2009).

11. Imberman (2007); Miron & Nelson (2001), p. 36.

12. Carnoy, Jacobsen, Mishel, & Rothstein (2005).

13. Advocates for Children (2002).

14. Darling-Hammond (1997); NCTAF (1996).

15. NCTAF (1996).

16. Japanese statistics are for elementary and lower secondary schools, as reported in Japanese Ministry of Education, Culture, Sports, Science, and Technology (2004); U.S. statistics are from National Center for Education Statistics (2005), Table 79.

References

Advocates for Children. (2002). *Pushing out at-risk students: An analysis of high school discharge figures—a joint report by AFC and the public advocate.* Retrieved from http://www.advocates forchildren.org/pubs/pushout-11-20-02.html

Carnoy, M., Jacobsen, R., Mishel, L., & Rothstein, R. (2005). *The charter school dust-up: Examining the evidence on enrollment and achievement.* Washington, DC: Economic Policy Institute.

Cremin, L. (1961). *The transformation of the school: Progressivism in American education, 1876–1957.* New York: Vintage Books.

Darling-Hammond, L. (1997). *The right to learn: A blueprint for creating schools that work.* San Francisco: Jossey-Bass.

Edmonds, R. (1979). Effective schools for the urban poor. *Educational Leadership, 37*(1), 15–18, 20–24.

Erskine, R. (2002, February). *Statement on school reform and the Seattle contract.* Society for the Advancement of Excellence in Education. Retrieved from http://www.saee.ca/index.php?option=com_content&task=view&id=319&Itemid=90

French, D. (2008). Boston's pilot schools: An alternative to charter schools. In L. Dingerson, B. Miner, B. Peterson, & S. Walters (Eds.), *Keeping the promise? The debate over charter schools* (pp. 67–80). Milwaukee, WI: Rethinking Schools.

Gates Foundation. (2005). *High performing school districts: Challenge, support, alignment, and choice.* Seattle: Bill & Melinda Gates Foundation.

Hill, P. (2006). *Put learning first: A portfolio approach to public schools.* Washington, DC: Progressive Policy Institute.

Imberman, S. (2007). *Achievement and behavior in charter schools: Drawing a more complete picture* (Occasional paper no. 142). New York: National Center for the Study of Privatizations in Education.

Japanese Ministry of Education, Culture, Sports, Science, and Technology. (2004). *Japan's education at a glance, 2004: School education.* Tokyo: Author.

Levine, D., & Lezotte, L. (1990). *Unusually effective schools: A review and analysis of research and practice.* Madison, WI: The National Center for Effective Schools Research & Development.

Miron, G., & Nelson, C. (2001). *Student achievement in charter schools: What we know and why we know so little* (Occasional paper no. 41). New York: Teachers College, Columbia University, National Center for the Study of Privatization in Education.

National Center for Education Statistics (NCES). (2005). *Digest of education statistics, 2005.* Washington, DC: U.S. Department of Education. Retrieved from http://nces.ed.gov/programs/digest/d05/tables/dt05_079.asp?referrer=list

National Commission on Teaching and America's Future (NCTAF). (1996). *What matters most: Teaching for America's future.* New York: Author.

Robinson, H. S. (1984). The M Street School. *Records of the Columbia Historical Society of Washington, D.C.: 1891–1916, 51,* p. 122.

Young, V. M., Humphrey, D. C., Wang, H., Bosetti, K. R., Cassidy, L., Wechsler, . . . Schanzenbach, D. W. (2009). *Renaissance schools fund-supported schools: Early outcomes, challenges, and opportunities.* Menlo Park, CA: Stanford Research International and Chicago: Consortium on Chicago School Research. Retrieved from http://ccsr.uchicago.edu/publications/RSF%20FINAL%20April%2015.pdf

How Schools Really Matter

Douglas B. Downey and Benjamin G. Gibbs

The current era of school reform policy tends to blame schools and/or teachers for the low academic achievement of some students. Douglas B. Downey and Benjamin G. Gibbs take a different orientation for trying to understand the impact of schooling on children, particularly children from families of low socioeconomic status. Their emphasis is not on what happens in schools but rather on the context within which schooling occurs. They argue that this context needs to be taken into account when we assess the success or failure of schools, regardless of the socioeconomic groups the schools serve.

Questions to consider for this reading:

1. What arguments do Downey and Gibbs make to support their point that schools are more the solution than the problem today?

2. What features of social context do they think we need to attend to when evaluating the effectiveness of our schools?

3. What reforms to schools are they proposing in this piece?

There's an old joke about a man on a street corner, down on his hands and knees searching for his lost wallet. A passerby stops to help, asking, "So you lost it right around here?" "Oh no," the man replies, "I lost the wallet several blocks ago. I'm just looking on this street corner because this is where the lighting is good."

It's tempting to look for the source of a problem in places where the lighting is good even if we're not in the right place. When we hear about high dropout rates; persistent black/white gaps in test scores; low American reading, math, and science scores; dramatic differences in resources among schools; and even growing childhood obesity, it's sort of easy to ascribe these negative outcomes to schools. In fact, this is the "traditional" story we hear about American schools.

The Traditional Tale of Schools

The tendency to view schools as the source of so many problems is especially true when we consider equality of opportunity, an important American value. There are many good reasons to believe that schools are the primary engines of inequality. First, children attending schools with lots of high-income children tend to perform better on standardized tests than kids at schools with lots of low-income children. Second, there are clear resource differences between these schools, rooted in the fact that, in most states, local tax revenues constitute a significant portion of the school's budget. For example, Ohio's local taxes constitute about half of a school's budget (state taxes constitute 43% and federal taxes about 7%). As a result of the heavy emphasis on local taxes, some schools are able to spend substantially more money per student than others. This means schools located in areas with expensive houses and successful businesses can spend more on new textbooks, teacher pay, recreational facilities, extracurricular activities, and help for students with special needs. Third, in high-resource schools, teachers encounter fewer children with behavioral problems and more parents engaged in their children's education, factors that can attract and retain better teachers. Based on these patterns, it seems obvious that if we want to improve the quality of life for the disadvantaged in the U.S., the best place to start is schools.

But this traditional story has developed largely without understanding the way in which children's academic outcomes are shaped by many factors outside of schools. Simply look at the amount of time children spend outside of school. If we focus on the 9-month academic year only, the proportion of time children spend in school is about *one-third*. And if we include the non-school summer, children spend just one-quarter of their waking hours in school each year. Now if we also include the years before kindergarten—which certainly affect children—we find that the typical 18-year-old American has spent just 13% of his or her waking hours in school. For most of us, it's surprising to learn that such a large percentage of children's time is spent outside of school, but it's important to keep in mind if we're serious about understanding how schools really matter.

A contextual perspective reminds us to look at the rest of kids' lives. For instance, not every student comes to school with the same economic, social, or cultural resources. Even with the same educational opportunities, some students benefit from home environments that prepare them for school work and so they are better able to take advantage of education.

Moving away from the traditional, narrow view of schools that forgets the importance of children's time outside the classroom, we endorse adopting a contextualized (or impact) view of schools. This new emphasis can really change how we think about what schools can—and can't—do for our kids.

PIANOS AND PARENTS

Imagine that we want to compare the effectiveness of two piano instructors who will both teach 10-week piano classes for beginners. We flip a coin and assign one instructor to place A and the other to place B. Our goal is complicated, however, by the fact that in place B, due to cost, almost no students come from a home with a piano, whereas in place A, whose parents have more disposable income, most students have a piano at home. As a result, place A's students have already had some practice time on a piano, whereas place B's students have had little to none. In addition, while both instructors teach a session once a week, place A's students practice on their own several times a week, whereas in place B—where few have pianos at home—students have a much harder time finding a way to practice.

Obviously, if we just compared the piano students' skills at the end of the 10-week program we couldn't accurately assess the quality of the two instructors—the two groups' skills differed before the lessons began. And if we compared how much the students' skills improved during the instructional period, it would still be hard to know which instructor was more effective because place A's students practiced more often than place B's students did. Given that these two instructors face different challenges, is there a way to evaluate them fairly? Can we isolate how the piano teachers really mattered?

This is the quandary we have when trying to understand how schools (or teachers) matter for children's lives; the same kinds of complicating factors are at work. First, children begin schooling with very different levels of academic skills. For example, the black/white gap in math and reading skills is roughly a standard deviation at the end of high school, but half of this gap is evident at the beginning of kindergarten, before schools have had a chance to matter. And the differences in 8 skills between high- and low-socioeconomic status (SES) students at the start of kindergarten are even larger. Obviously, these variations aren't a consequence of differences in school quality, but of the different kinds of students schools serve.

Thinking contextually, some home environments complement what occurs at school as parents help with homework, communicate with teachers, reinforce school concepts, provide a safe and stable environment for study, and attend to children's medical needs (by, for instance, providing consistent visits to doctors and dentists). In her book *Home Advantage,* sociologist Annette Lareau gives a poignant description of just how important parents can be, getting involved in their child's coursework and with their teachers in ways that promote academic success and instilling in their children a kind of academic entitlement. She wrote that these parents "made an effort to integrate educational goals into family life including teaching children new words when driving by billboards, having children practice penmanship and vocabulary by writing out shopping lists, practicing mathematics during baking projects, and practicing vocabulary during breakfast time." Interacting with instructors, the upper-middle class parents Lareau observed requested specific classroom teachers or asked that their child be placed in school programs for the gifted, for speech therapy, or with the learning resource center. In contrast, low-SES parents tended to have less time for involvement with their children's schoolwork, leaving educational experiences in the hands of the "experts." Much like having a piano at home, these contexts of advantage and disadvantage play a critical role in shaping how children gain academic skills during their school years.

BRINGING IN CONTEXT

By using a contextual perspective, sociologists have contributed considerably to our understanding of how schools matter. One of the most influential studies was the 1966 Coleman Report, a massive analysis of American schools that was commissioned by the Federal Department of Education. James Coleman, the lead author of the report, directed the collection of data from 4,000 schools and more than 645,000 American school children in the early 1960s. The researchers were interested in why some children had high math and reading skills and others did not. They measured many characteristics of schools (including school curriculum, facilities, teacher qualities, and student body characteristics) and many characteristics of children's home lives (like parents' SES—education, income, and occupation level) to see which were more closely related to academic skills. Surprisingly, school characteristics were only weakly related to academic skills. It turned out that differences between schools in terms of quality played only a small role in understanding the variation in students' academic skills while home life (parents' SES showed the strongest relationship) mattered much more. Skeptics of this conclusion, such as sociologist Christopher Jencks, re-evaluated Coleman's conclusion with new data, but ended up finding similar patterns.

Of course, one limitation of this approach is that it depends heavily on whether Coleman and Jencks were measuring the right things about schools. Maybe they were missing what really mattered. While they were measuring per pupil expenditures, teacher/student ratios, and racial composition, they missed critical factors like teacher quality. If they failed to measure a lot of important things about schools, then their conclusions that schools play only a minor role in explaining inequality of skills might be wrong.

SEASONAL COMPARISON RESEARCH

What researchers need is a way to untangle the role of school and non-school influences. Observing student learning during the school year tells us little about how schools matter because students are exposed to both school and non-school environments. When we compare annually-collected test scores, for example, it becomes very difficult to know why some students fall behind and some get ahead. Sociologist Barbara Heyns pointed out that during the summer children are influenced by non-school factors only. The best way to understand how schools matter, she reasoned, was to observe how things change between the non-school period (summer) and the school period. This strategy works like a natural experiment, separating the "treatment" from the treated. Knowing what happens to group-level differences in achievement by race, class, or gender when school is in session (the treatment) compared to when it is not (the control) is a good way to know if schools make educational gaps bigger or smaller.

This important insight led Heyns to collect a different kind of data. She evaluated fifth, sixth, and seventh grade students at the beginning and end of the academic years in Atlanta. By testing them both in the fall and spring, she was able to tell how much they learned during the summer, when school was out. This study design allowed her to uncover a provocative pattern—high- and low-SES students gained academic skills at about the same rate during the nine-month academic year. Gaps in skills developed during the summers. Although schools did not close achievement gaps between groups, these results bolstered Coleman and Jencks's initial conclusions that schools were not the primary reason for group-level inequalities. Heyns's provocative findings were replicated by sociologists Doris Entwisle and Karl Alexander in Baltimore and, more recently, by myself [Douglas Downey] with colleagues at Ohio State. With nationally representative data, we found that low- and high-SES children learned math and reading at similar rates during the 9-month kindergarten and first grade periods, but that gaps in skills grew quickly during the summer in between, when school was out.

Taken together, the overall pattern from this seasonal research supports Coleman's conclusion: schools are not the source of inequality. The seasonal approach to understanding schools gives us a much more accurate understanding of how schools influence inequality. This research consistently produces an unconventional conclusion—if we lived in a world with no schools at all, inequality would be much worse. In other words, when it comes to inequality, schools are more part of the solution than the problem.

This contextual way of thinking about schools and inequality is difficult to reconcile, however, with the "traditional" story—that wide variations in school quality are the engine of inequality. By adopting a more contextual perspective on schools, we can understand this counterintuitive claim: despite the fact that some schools have more resources than others, schools end up being an equalizing force. The key is that the inequalities that exist outside of school are considerably larger than the ones students experience in school.

SCHOOLS, CONTEXT, AND POLICY

At the beginning of this article, we pointed out that it's natural to look to schools for the source of many of our kids' problems—they're the corner with the best "lighting." The often-unexplored terrain *outside* of schools, though, remains shadowy and seemingly inaccessible. This doesn't need to be the case. And, though extending the light beyond schools reveals that group-level inequality would be much worse if not for schools, it doesn't mean that schools are off the hook. In fact, using school impact as a guide, many "successful" schools in the traditional view are revealed as low-impact—good students don't always signal good instructors. In these schools, children pass proficiency exams, but since they started off in a better position, it's arguable that the schools didn't actually serve their students.

Clearly, when we employ a contextual perspective, we think about school policy, child development, and social problems in a new light. A contextual approach to schools promotes sensible policy, efficiently targeted resources, and reasonable assessment tools that recognize that some schools and teachers face very different challenges than others.

For example, a tremendous amount of energy and money is directed toward developing accountability systems for schools. But recall the analogy of the two piano instructors. It's difficult to determine which instructor is best, given that place A has students that start with more skills and practice more outside of instruction. Now suppose that we knew one more piece of information: how fast each group of piano players gained skills when not taking lessons. Suddenly, we could compare the rate of improvement outside of instruction with the rate observed during the instructional period. We could see how much instruction mattered.

This "impact" view has recently been applied to schools. In 2008, with fellow sociologists Paul T. von Hippel and Melanie Hughes, I [Douglas Downey] constructed impact measures by taking a school's average difference between its students' first-grade learning rate and the learning rate observed in the summer prior to first grade. The key finding was that not all the schools deemed as "failing" under traditional criteria were really failing. Indeed, three out of four schools had been incorrectly evaluated. That's not to say that there were no variations in school quality, but many schools did much better than expected when we took a contextual approach to measurement. And some did much worse. If impact evaluations are more accurate, then teachers serving disadvantaged children are doing a better job than previously thought and current methods of school evaluation are producing substantial errors.

With its contextual orientation, seasonal research has also provided insights into other ways that schools matter. For example, researchers have

considered whether "summer setback" can be avoided by modifying the school year so that there is no long gap in school exposure. Von Hippel has compared math and reading learning in schools with year-long calendars versus those with traditional school-year/summer break calendars. In both conditions, children attended school for about 180 days a year, but the timing of those days was spread more evenly in year-round schools. It turned out that, once a calendar year was up, both groups had learned about the same. The policy lesson is that increasing school exposure is probably more important than fiddling with how school days are distributed across the year.

Given that school exposure appears critical, many have viewed summer school (restricted to academically struggling children) as an attractive option for reducing inequality. It turns out, though, that children attending summer school gain fewer academic skills than we would expect. This may be because the academic programs in the summer are of lower quality, but it may also be because the kinds of students who typically attend summer school are also the kind who would typically suffer a "summer setback" without it. Viewed in this light, just treading water or maintaining the same academic skills during the summer could be viewed as a positive outcome.

And in other research employing seasonal comparisons, researchers have shown that children gain body mass index (BMI) three times faster during the summer than during the school year. Obviously, schools shouldn't abandon attempts to improve the quality of lunches or the schooling environment, but research suggests that attention should be paid to non-school factors as the primary sources of childhood obesity.

In the end, looking at schools through a contextual lens provides exciting insights. When we forget how other aspects of children's lives figure into their development, we create a distorted view of schools. The contextual perspective corrects this error and produces a more accurate understanding of how schools really matter. It suggests that if we are serious about improving American children's school performance, we will need to take a broader view of education policy. In addition to school reform, we must also aim to improve children's lives where they spend the vast majority of their time—with their families and in their neighborhoods.

RECOMMENDED RESOURCES

[Editors' Note: No references were provided for this article; however, the authors recommend the following for further research into the subject.]

James S. Coleman. "Equality of Educational Opportunity," United States Office of Education and National Center for Education Statistics (1966). The classic large-scale study of American schools and factors related to test score performance.

Douglas B. Downey, Paul T. von Hippel, and Melanie Hughes. "Are 'Failing' Schools Really Failing? Using Seasonal Comparisons to Evaluate School Effectiveness." *Sociology of Education* (2008), 81(3):242–270. Introduces impact evaluation, which isolates school from non-school factors in child achievement via seasonal comparisons.

Doris R. Entwisle, Karl L. Alexander, and Linda S. Olson. *Children, Schools & Inequality* (Westview Press, 1997). Uses data from Baltimore to show how social context shapes children's early schooling experiences.

Barbara Heyns. *Summer Learning and the Effects of Schooling* (Academic Press, 1978). Describes the seminal use of "seasonal comparisons" to report the results of summer versus school-time learning.

Annette Lareau. *Home Advantage: Social Class and Parental Intervention in Elementary Education* (Rowman & Littlefield, 2000). A vivid ethnographic account of the different ways working and middle-class families prepare their children for school and interact with teachers.

CAN SCHOOLING CONTRIBUTE TO A MORE JUST SOCIETY?

Michael W. Apple

In this excerpt from a larger piece, Michael W. Apple, a well-known critical theorist, examines the attempts at equality from a political framework. This excerpt, which is based in critical theory, examines both the politics of educational reform and the motivations driving conservative social movements in education. He looks at what makes these movements successful and suggests that liberals should consider such strategies in their attempts to change the educational process. This piece moves the issue of equality and equity in education to a new level, far outside the schools, to that of the politics of education.

Questions to consider for this reading:

1. Are politics important in deciding what happens in classrooms? If so, why?

2. According to Apple, why has the Right been successful in mobilizing people, even when participation is against their better interests?

3. What strategy for educational reforms is Apple suggesting as an alternative to the agenda for political reform put forth by conservative groups?

[W]hen a nation and its government and major institutions do not deliver on their promises and on the sets of values they officially profess in education and elsewhere, then substantive criticism is the ultimate act of patriotism. Such criticism says that "We are not just passing through. This is our country and our institutions as well, built by the labor of millions of people such as ourselves. We take the values in our founding documents seriously and demand that you do so too."

Of course, the arguments [I am] making in this article are quite political. But that is the point. Over the past three decades, many committed and critical educators have argued that education must be seen as a political act. They have suggested that in order to do this, we need to think *relationally*. That is, understanding education requires that we situate it back into both the unequal relations of power in the larger society and into the relations of dominance and subordination—and the conflicts to change these things—that are generated by these relations. Thus, rather than simply asking whether students have mastered a particular subject matter and have done well on our all too common tests, we should ask a different set of questions: Whose knowledge is this? How did it become "official"? What is the relationship between this knowledge and who has cultural, social and economic capital in this society? Who benefits from these definitions of legitimate knowledge and who does not? What can we do as critical educators and activists to change existing educational and social inequalities and to create curricula and teaching that are more socially just (Apple, 1996, 2000; Apple & Beane, 2007)?

These are complicated questions and they often require complicated answers. However, there is now a long tradition of asking and answering these kinds of critical challenges to the ways education is currently being carried on, a tradition that has grown considerably since the time when I first raised these issues in *Ideology and Curriculum* (Apple, 1979; see also the more recent 3rd ed., Apple, 2004). Perhaps the best way of documenting why we need to keep these political issues at the forefront of our vision of what schools now do and what they should do is to focus on the life of a student, someone I knew very well. I hope that you will forgive me if at times throughout this article I use personal narratives to make larger points. But it seems to me that sometimes such a writing style can bring home points in ways that more abstract ways of presenting things cannot. Such a style also makes the politics of education not something "out there" in some abstract universe very far away, but puts it "right here" in terms of our personal choices inside and outside of education.

Remembering Real Schools and Real Children

Joseph sobbed at my desk. He was a tough kid, a hard case, someone who often made life difficult for his teachers. He was all of nine-years-old and here he was sobbing, holding on to me in public. He had been in my fourth-grade class all year, a classroom situated in a decaying building in an east coast city that was among the most impover-

ished in the nation. There were times when I wondered, seriously, whether I would make it through that year. There were many Josephs in that classroom and I was constantly drained by the demands, the bureaucratic rules, the daily lessons that bounced off of the kids' armor. Yet somehow it was satisfying, compelling and important, even though the prescribed curriculum and the textbooks that were meant to teach it were often beside the point. They were boring to the kids and boring to me.

I should have realized the first day what it would be like when I opened that city's "Getting Started" suggested lessons for the first few days and it began with the suggestion that "as a new teacher" I should circle the students' desks and have them introduce each other and tell something about themselves. It's not that I was against this activity; it's just that I didn't have enough unbroken desks (or even chairs) for all of the students. A number of the kids had nowhere to sit. This was my first lesson—but certainly not my last—in understanding that the curriculum and those who planned it lived in an unreal world, a world *fundamentally* disconnected from my life with those children in that inner city classroom.

But here's Joseph. He's still crying. I've worked extremely hard with him all year long. We've eaten lunch together; we've read stories; we've gotten to know each other. There are times when he drives me to despair and other times when I find him to be among the most sensitive children in my class. I just can't give up on this kid. He's just received his report card and it says that he is to repeat fourth grade. The school system has a policy that states that failure in any two subjects (including the "behavior" side of the report card) requires that the student be left back. Joseph was failing "gym" and arithmetic. Even though he had shown improvement, he had trouble keeping awake during arithmetic, had done poorly on the mandatory city-wide tests, and hated gym. One of his parents worked a late shift and Joseph would often stay up, hoping to spend some time with her. And the things that students were asked to do in gym were, to him, "lame."

The thing is, he had made real progress during the year. But I was instructed to keep him back.

I knew that things would be worse next year. There would still not be enough desks. The poverty in that community would still be horrible; and health care and sufficient funding for job training and other services would be diminished. I knew that the jobs that were available in this former mill town paid deplorable wages and that even with both of his parents working for pay, Joseph's family income was simply insufficient. I also knew that, given all that I already had to do each day in that classroom and each night at home in preparation for the next day, it would be nearly impossible for me to work any harder than I had already done with Joseph. And there were another five children in that class whom I was supposed to leave back.

So Joseph sobbed. Both he and I understood what this meant. There would be no additional help for me—or for children such as Joseph—next year. The promises would remain simply rhetorical. Words would be thrown at the problems. Teachers and parents and children would be blamed. But the school system would look like it believed in and enforced higher standards. The structuring of economic and political power in that community and that state would again go on as "business as usual."

The next year Joseph basically stopped trying. The last time I heard anything about him was that he was in prison.

This story is not apocryphal. While the incident took place a while ago, the conditions in that community and that school are much worse today. And the intense pressure that teachers, administrators, and local communities are under is also considerably worse (Kozol, 1991; Lipman, 2004). It reminds me of why large numbers of thoughtful educators and activists mistrust the incessant focus on standards, increased testing, marketization and vouchers, and other kinds of educational "reforms" which may sound good in the abstract, but which often work in exactly the opposite ways when they reach the level of the classroom (see Apple, 2006; Lipman, 2004; McNeil, 2000; Valenzuela, 2005). It is exactly this sensibility of the contradictions between proposals for reform and the realities

and complexities of education on the ground that provides one of the major reasons so many of us are asking the questions surrounding how education can make a more serious contribution to social justice. I want to say more about this in the next section of this article.

THE POLITICS OF EDUCATIONAL REFORM

Critical educators have long demonstrated that policies often have strikingly unforeseen consequences. Reforms that are instituted with good intentions may have hidden effects that are more than a little problematic. We have shown for instance that the effects of some of the favorite reforms of neo-liberals and neo-conservatives—voucher plans, national or state-wide curricula, and national or state-wide testing can serve as examples—quite often reproduce or even worsen inequalities. Thus, we should be very cautious about accepting what may seem to be meritorious intentions at face value. Intentions are too often contradicted by how reforms may function in practice. This is true not only for large scale transformations of educational policies and governance, but also about moves to change the ways curriculum and teaching go on in schools.

The framework politically and educationally progressive educators have employed to understand this is grounded in what in cultural theory is called the act of repositioning. It in essence says that the best way to understand what any set of institutions, policies, and practices does is to see it from the standpoint of those who have the least power. Speaking personally, growing up poor myself made this almost a "natural" perspective for me to take. That is, every institution, policy, and practice—and especially those that now dominate education and the larger society—establish relations of power in which some voices are heard and some are not. While it is not preordained that those voices that will be heard most clearly are also those who have the most economic, cultural and social capital, it is most likely that this will be the case. After all, we do not exist on a level playing field. Many economic, social and educational policies when actually put in place tend to benefit those who already have advantages.

These points may seem overly rhetorical and too abstract, but unfortunately there is no small amount of truth in them. For example, in a time when all too much of the discourse around educational reform is focused on vouchers and choice plans on the one hand and on proposals for national or state curricula, standards, and testing on the other, as I have shown in a number of volumes (Apple, 1995, 1996, 2000, 2006, 2009; Apple et al., 2003), there is a good deal of international evidence now that such policies may actually reproduce or even worsen class, gender and race inequalities. Thus, existing structures of economic and cultural power often lead to a situation in which what may have started out in some educators' or legislators' minds as an attempt to make things better, in the end is all too usually transformed into another set of mechanisms for social stratification.

While much of this is due to the ways in which race, gender, class and "ability" act as structural realities in this society and to how we fund (and do not fund) schools, some of it is related to the hesitancy of policy makers to take seriously enough the complicated ways in which education is itself a political act. These very politics and the structurally generated inequalities that stand behind them provide much of the substance underpinning the organizational principles of my work.

A key word in my discussion above is *reform*. This concept is what might be called a "sliding signifier." That is, it has no essential meaning and, like a glass, can be filled with multiple things. As Wittgenstein (1953) reminded us, it is always wise not to accept the meaning of a concept at face value. Instead, one must contextualize it. The meaning is in its *use*. Let us look at this in a bit more detail.

The language of educational reform is always interesting. It consistently paints a picture that what is going [on] in schools now needs fixing, is outmoded, inefficient or simply "bad." Reforms will fix it. They will make things "better." Over the past decades certain language systems in particular have been mobilized. Not only will specific reforms make things better, [but] they will make schools more democratic. Of course, the word democracy is one of the best examples of a sliding signifier. It carries with it an entire history of conflicts over its very meaning (Foner, 1998). Like reform, democracy does not carry an essential meaning emblazoned on its head so to speak. Instead it is one of the most contested words in the English language. Indeed, one of the major tactics of dominant groups historically and currently is to cement particular meanings of democracy into public discourse. Thus, under current neo-liberal policies in education and elsewhere, there are consistent attempts to redefine democracy as simply consumer choice. Here democracy is not a collective project of building and rebuilding our public institutions. It becomes simply a matter of placing everything that was once public onto a market. Collective justice will somehow take care of itself as the market works its wonders.

As Mary Lee Smith and her colleagues have recently demonstrated in their powerful analysis of a number of educational reforms, the nice sounding and "democratic" language used to promote reforms is often totally at odds with the actual functioning of these reforms in real schools in real communities (Smith, 2004). A significant number of things that were advertised (and that is often the appropriate word) as making schools more responsive and "better" (increased testing and parental choice through marketization may serve as examples) may have exacerbated problems of inequality. (Think of Joseph and what happened to him in an earlier round of increased testing and "raising standards.")

One of the reasons this is the case is because the formation of a good deal of educational policy is actually a form of "symbolic politics," basically a kind of theater (Smith, 2004). This is not to claim that policy makers are acting in bad faith. Rather, because of the distribution (or not) of resources, tragic levels of impoverishment, the ways policies are implemented (or not), and the cleverness of economically and cultural[ly] dominant groups in using reforms for their own advantage, the patterns of benefits are not anywhere near the supposedly democratic ends envisioned by some of their well-meaning proponents. (Some reforms as well may simply be the result of cynical manipulation of the public for electoral advantage; but that's a topic for another essay.)

Understanding Conservative Social Movements in Education

The arguments I made above are related to a particular claim that is important to make. Many of us have spent a good deal of time showing that it is social movements, *not* educators, who are the real engines of educational transformations (Anyon, 2005; Apple, 2000, 2006, 2009). And the social movements that are the most powerful now are more than a little conservative. I want to argue in fact that unless we think very tactically about what the Right has been able to accomplish and what the balance of forces now are, all too much of our attempts at putting in place more critically democratic reforms may be less powerful than we would like.

Over the past decade, a good deal of concerted effort has been devoted to analyzing the reasons behind the rightist resurgence—what I have called "conservative modernization"—in education and to try to find spaces for interrupting it (see Apple, 2006; Apple & Buras, 2006). My own aim has not simply been to castigate the Right, although there is a bit of fun in doing so. Rather, I have also sought to illuminate the dangers, and the elements of good sense, not only bad sense, that are found within what is an identifiable and powerful new "hegemonic bloc" (that is, a powerful set of groups that provides overall leadership to and pressure on what the basic goals and policies of a society are). This new rightist alliance is made up of various factions—neo-liberals, neo-conservatives, authoritarian populist religious conservatives

and some members of the professional and managerial new middle class. These are complicated groups, but let me describe them briefly.

This power bloc combines multiple fractions of capital who are committed to neo-liberal marketized solutions to educational problems, neo-conservative intellectuals who want a "return" to higher standards and a "common culture," authoritarian populist religious fundamentalists who are deeply worried about secularity and the preservation of their own traditions, and particular fractions of the professionally oriented new middle class who are committed to the ideology and techniques of accountability, measurement and "management." While there are clear tensions and conflicts within this alliance, in general its overall aims are in providing the educational conditions believed necessary both for increasing international competitiveness, profit and discipline and for returning us to a romanticized past of the "ideal" home, family and school (Apple, 1996, 2006).

I have had a number of reasons for focusing on the alliance behind conservative modernization. First, these groups are indeed powerful, as any honest analysis of what is happening in education and the larger society clearly indicates. Second, they are quite talented in connecting to people who might ordinarily disagree with them. For this reason, I have shown in a number of places that people who find certain elements of conservative modernization relevant to their lives are not puppets. They are not dupes who have little understanding of the "real" relations of this society. This smacks of earlier reductive analyses within the critical tradition that were based in ideas of "false consciousness."

My position is very different. I maintain that the reason that some of the arguments coming from the various factions of this new hegemonic bloc are listened to is because they *are* connected to aspects of the realities that people experience (Apple, 1996; Apple & Pedroni, 2005). The tense alliance of neo-liberals, neo-conservatives, authoritarian populist religious activists and the professional and managerial new middle class only works because there has been a very creative articulation of themes that resonate deeply with the experiences, fears, hopes and dreams of people as they go about their daily lives. The Right has often been more than a little manipulative in its articulation of these themes. It has integrated them within racist nativist discourses, within economically dominant forms of understanding, and within a problematic sense of "tradition." But, this integration could only occur if they were organized around people's understanding of their real material and cultural lives.

The second reason I have stressed the tension between good and bad sense and the ability of dominant groups to connect to people's real understandings of their lives—aside from my profound respect for Antonio Gramsci's (1968, 1971) writings about this—has to do with my belief that we have witnessed a major educational accomplishment over the past three decades in many countries. All too often, we assume that educational and cultural struggles are epiphenomenal. The real battles occur in the paid workplace—the "economy." Not only is this a strikingly reductive sense of what the economy is (its focus on paid, not unpaid, work; its neglect of the fact that, say, cultural institutions such as schools are also places where paid work goes on, etc.) (Apple, 1986), it also ignores what the Right has actually done.

Conservative modernization has radically reshaped the commonsense of society. It has worked in every sphere—the economic, the political and the cultural—to alter the basic categories we use to evaluate our institutions and our public and private lives. It has established new identities. It has recognized that to win in the state, you must win in civil society. That is, you need to work at the level of people's daily experiences, not only in government policies. The accomplishment of such a vast educational project has many implications. It shows how important cultural struggles are. And, oddly enough, it gives reason for hope. It forces us to ask a number of significant questions. What can we learn from the Right about how to build movements for social transformation? If the Right can do this, why can't we?

I do not mean these as rhetorical questions. As I have argued repeatedly in my own work, the Right has shown how powerful the struggle over meaning and identity—and hence, schools, curricula, teaching and evaluation—can be. While we should not want to emulate their often cynical and manipulative processes, the fact that they have had such success in pulling people under their ideological umbrella has much to teach us. Granted there are real differences in money and power between the forces of conservative modernization and those whose lives are being tragically altered by the policies and practices coming from the alliance. But, the Right was not as powerful 30 years ago as it is now. It collectively organized. It created a decentered unity, one where each element sacrificed some of its particular agenda to push forward on those areas that bound them together. Can we not do the same?

I believe that we can, but only if we face up to the realities and dynamics of power in unromantic ways—and think tactically about what can be done now even under conditions that we may not always control. And this means not only critically analyzing the rightist agendas and the effects of their increasingly mistaken and arrogant policies, but engaging in some serious criticism of some elements within the progressive and critical educational communities as well. Thus, as I argue in *Educating the "Right" Way* (Apple, 2006), the romantic, possibilitarian rhetoric of some of the writers on critical pedagogy is not sufficiently based on a tactical or strategic analysis of the current situation nor is it sufficiently grounded in its understanding of the reconstructions of discourse and movements that are occurring in all too many places. Here I follow Cameron McCarthy (2000), who wisely reminds us, "We must think possibility within constraint; that is the condition of our time."

We need to remember that cultural and educational struggles are not epiphenomenal. They *count*, and they count in institutions throughout society. In order for dominant groups to exercise leadership, large numbers of people must be convinced that the maps of reality circulated by those with the most economic, political, and cultural power are indeed wiser than other alternatives. Dominant groups do this by attaching these maps to the elements of good sense that people have and by changing the very meaning of the key concepts and their accompanying structures of feeling that provide the centers of gravity for our hopes, fears, and dreams about this society. The Right has been much more successful in doing this than progressive groups and movements, in part because it has been able to craft—through hard and lengthy economic, political, and cultural efforts—a tense but still successful alliance that has shifted the major debates over education and economic and social policy onto its own terrain. And the sometimes mostly rhetorical material of critical pedagogy simply is unable to cope with this. Only when it is linked much more to concrete issues of educational policy and practice—and to the daily lives of educators, students, and community members— can it succeed. This, of course, is why journals such as *Rethinking Schools* and books such as *Democratic Schools* (Apple & Beane, 2007) that connect critical educational theories and approaches to the actual ways in which they can be and are present in real classrooms become so important. Thus, while we should support the principles of critical theory and critical pedagogy in the USA and elsewhere, we also need to act as internal critics when it has forgotten what it is meant to do and has sometimes become simply an academic specialization at universities.

REFERENCES

Anyon, J. (2005). *Radical possibilities*. New York: Routledge.

Apple, M. W. (1979). *Ideology and curriculum*. Boston: Routledge Kegan Paul.

Apple, M. W. (1986). *Teachers and texts*. New York: Routledge.

Apple, M. W. (1995). *Education and power* (2nd ed.). New York: Routledge.

Apple, M. W. (1996). *Cultural politics and education*. New York: Teachers College Press.

Apple, M. W. (2000). *Official knowledge* (2nd ed.). New York: Routledge.

Apple, M. W. (2004). *Ideology and curriculum; 25th anniversary* (3rd ed.). New York: Routledge Falmer.

Apple, M. W. (2006). *Educating the "right" way: Markets, standards, God, and inequality* (2nd ed.). New York: Routledge.

Apple, M. W. (Ed.). (2009). *Global crises, education, and social justice*. New York: Routledge.

Apple, M. W., Aasen, P., Cho, M. K., Gandin, L. A., Oliver, A., Sung, Y.-K. . . . Wong, T.-H. (2003). *The state and the politics of knowledge*. New York: Routledge Falmer.

Apple, M. W., & Beane, J. A. (2007). *Democratic schools: Lessons in powerful education* (2nd ed.). Portsmouth, NH: Heinemann.

Apple, M. W., & Buras, K. L. (Eds.). (2006). *The subaltern speak: Curriculum, power, and educational struggles*. New York: Routledge.

Apple, M. W., & Pedroni, T. (2005). Conservative alliance building and African American support of voucher reform. *Teachers College Record, 107,* 2068–2105.

Foner, E. (1998). *The story of American freedom*. New York: Norton.

Gramsci, A. (1968). *The modern prince and other writings*. New York: International Publishers.

Gramsci, A. (1971). *Selections from the prison notebooks*. New York: International Publishers.

Kozol, J. (1991). *Savage inequalities*. New York: Crown.

Lipman, P. (2004). *High stakes education*. New York: Routledge Falmer.

McCarthy, C. (2000, January). Presentation at the International Sociology of Education Conference, University of Sheffield, England.

McNeil, L. (2000). *The contradictions of school reform*. New York: Routledge.

Smith, M. L. (with Miller-Kahn, L., Heinecke, W., & Jarvis, P. F.). (2004). *Political spectacle and the fate of American schools*. New York: Routledge Falmer.

Teitelbaum, K. (1993). *Schooling for good rebels*. New York: Teachers College Press.

Valenzuela, A. (Ed.). (2005). *Leaving children behind*. Albany: State University of New York Press.

Wittgenstein, L. (1953). *Philosophical investigations*. New York: Macmillan.

Projects for Further Exploration

1. Find the school report cards (part of the No Child Left Behind Act) for three school districts in your area (one from a rural area, one from a suburban area, and one from an urban area) and compare the data for each district on factors such as graduation rate, percentage of students going on to college, and racial composition.

2. Using an academic database, look for the most recent studies on charter schools and compare the findings from these studies to those presented in the readings by Linda A. Renzulli and Vincent J. Roscigno and by Linda Darling-Hammond.

3. Read your local newspaper for articles about education and schools, paying particular attention to political dimensions of the issues being discussed. Can you tell if those articles are coming from conservative or liberal political groups? Who is being blamed in the articles for the problems in our schools?

9

HIGHER EDUCATION

Educational systems provide knowledge and skills from basic literacy to professional training. Higher education is part of that system in most countries, providing specialized professional and vocational preparation. In this chapter, we include readings that examine the various issues faced by institutions of higher education. Some of these issues are similar to those at other levels of education—pressures from the environment for external funding, demands from businesses and communities, negotiating roles and relationships, interactions between students and teachers, and the role of higher education in maintaining inequality in society.

With more and more students seeking postsecondary educational experiences, higher education has become an important part of the structure of education, particularly in the United States. College enrollments in the United States are at an all-time high, with 21.58 million students enrolled in fall 2011, representing steady increases in full-time enrollment over the past several years (National Center for Education Statistics, 2012a, table 200).

In the United States, higher education institutions vary considerably. A brief history of the development of higher education in the United States helps to explain where we are today. Harvard University, the first institution of higher learning in America, was founded in 1643, followed in 1693 by the College of William and Mary. By 1770, there were only nine colleges in colonial America. The growth of colleges during the next 90 years was spotty, with over 700 colleges failing to survive prior to 1860 (Rudolph, 1990, p. 219). Lawrence Veysey (1965) described college life prior to 1865 as "archaic" (p. 2), one in which the task of education was to instill discipline and piety. Despite the fact that postsecondary education was faltering and intended for white males only, three black colleges were established before the Civil War (Willie, 2003), and two women's colleges were opened in 1855 (Miller-Bernal, 2006).

The end of the Civil War and nascent industrialization in this country, however, revitalized higher education. This growth included new colleges for blacks and women; these colleges were the only option for blacks and women as only a few blacks or women were allowed into colleges serving white, elite males (Miller-Bernal, 2006). Indeed, the greatest growth was in those colleges for white, elite men. According to Frederick Rudolph (1990, p. 244), "the movement for technological and scientific education, which had been underway before the war, spawned new and more popular colleges and institutes." Federal and state aid and bequests by wealthy industrialists led to the chartering of newer, more practical institutions such as the Massachusetts Institute of Technology (MIT) and Cornell, both in 1865. Changes in society also prompted changes in many of the older, established colleges. For instance, Princeton added its engineering school in 1871 (Rudolph, 1990).

In addition to the considerable growth in the number of colleges and universities, the post–Civil War era saw enrollments increase with the first waves of immigration in the 1890s. Higher education during this period continued to be limited to the wealthy, who at that time recognized the advantages of educating their children as a means of distinguishing themselves as a class above the newly arrived immigrants. Indeed, the enrollments in higher education grew at 4.7 times the rate of growth of the population during the years from 1890 to 1925 (Rudolph, 1990, p. 442). Higher education, however, was not necessarily focused around academics. According to Veysey (1965), the college experience at the end of the 19th century "meant good times, pleasant friendships, and, underneath it all, the expectation of life-long prestige resulting from the degree" (p. 269) at the most elite colleges.

The turn of the century saw a blending of worldly issues into the university, as business and academics mingled more so than in the past. Among the changes in higher education that occurred after the Civil War was the introduction of an elective curriculum in which students could choose from an array of courses; this curriculum replaced the rigid classical curriculum previously in use. However, at the same time that colleges worked to attract more students, they also raised standards (Veysey, 1965). In addition, the development of advanced programs in graduate studies transformed universities during this period (Rudolph, 1990).

Drawing on the ideas of progressivism at the early part of the 20th century, the ideal of service was introduced as a goal of higher education. During this period, universities developed extension courses and programs that attempted to serve community needs and provide expertise to the country (Rudolph, 1990). Scholarship, however, did not drop in significance as college and university professors formed learned societies, and the role of higher education was solidified in the early 20th century. Rudolph argues that the turn of the century was accompanied by a push toward more "organized" colleges and universities, with changes such as no longer installing only members of the clergy as college presidents.

World War I brought a counterrevolution, with pressures to return to a course of study that produced a well-rounded and academically grounded graduate. Thus, there was a push toward a general education or core curriculum. Service and practical learning, however, was still evident in land-grant universities and colleges of business administration (Rudolph, 1990).

The period from the depression of the 1920s through World War II was a time that tested higher education's resilience. Colleges and universities struggled to survive. With money scarce, college was a luxury neither society nor students could easily afford. Many students attending college during this period freely admitted to being "broke" (Rudolph, 1990, p. 466). The end of World War II brought enormous changes to college campuses previously enrolling only white, upper-class men. The GI Bill, which provided the means for many soldiers to attend college, was responsible for an enormous increase in the size of campuses, including what were once called "normal schools" that evolved into teachers' colleges. Across the country, temporary classrooms and housing were hastily constructed to accommodate the returning soldiers. This growth in higher education continued through the end of the 20th century. In 1960, 3.5 million students attended higher education in the United States, a figure that doubled by 1970 (Rudolph, 1990, p. 486). As Kevin J. Dougherty and Vanessa S. Morest note in their reading in this chapter, the demand for community colleges grew in response to the massive growth in higher education during the decade of the 1960s. Community colleges were not only cheaper than residential campuses, but they could accommodate weaker students, thus permitting existing colleges and universities to continue to be more selective. Dougherty and Morest also describe the role that community colleges play today, including close ties to business communities. Public colleges and universities were also an important opportunity for students who could not afford tuition at private institutions (see discussion in Gaye Tuchman's reading in this chapter).

In contrast to the ideal of service to the community, higher education in the United States did not contribute to the development of new knowledge until they were called on during World War II

(Graham & Diamond, 1997). Shortly after the war ended, the federal government created the National Science Foundation to fund scientific research. The funding was primarily in the physical sciences and engineering and used merit-based competition to distribute the research funds to universities and professors. The Department of Defense also provided support for research during the war and thereafter (Graham & Diamond, 1997).

The launching of Sputnik by the Soviet Union in 1957 unleashed even more federal funds for universities, as the United States raced to catch up in the new space-age technologies. The amount of federal funding to universities has waxed and waned over the years since World War II. Tuchman describes how important research, rather than teaching, has become in evaluating faculty in colleges and universities.

Colleges and universities continue to receive pressure from the business community to make education useful. The push today is to focus more on preparing students to enter an increasingly global economy, evidenced by Europe's Bologna Process described by Fiona Hunter in the last reading in this chapter. Dougherty also states that American community colleges are responding to the business community's desire to educate workers for a global economy. And, the readings by Tuchman and Laura Hamilton and Elizabeth A. Armstrong note the desire of students to obtain "practical" knowledge from their college years.

More than the direction in higher education is changing as we move into the 21st century. Indeed, the very structure of the institution is changing. The readings by Tuchman, Dougherty and Morest, and Hunter illustrate some of the most recent changes, but other changes are happening as well. We can now find universities online, where students complete a degree through distance learning. The increase in the use of automation in higher education have led one scholar to call these universities "digital diploma mills" (Noble, 1998). And, the recent introduction of MOOCs (Massive Open Online Courses) by major universities has opened learning opportunities to many individuals who would not otherwise be able to access college courses in elite universities. In both of these cases, campuses are no longer as necessary as they once were.

Along with changes in the structure and purpose of college come changes in the composition of the student body. Among the most significant post–World War II changes in student composition are the increases in the numbers of women attending college in the United States, a change that began dramatically in the 1970s according to Miller-Bernal (2006). The numbers of women getting a bachelor's degree have grown considerably from 43.1% of all bachelor's degrees awarded in 1969–1970 (National Center for Education Statistics, 1996) to 57.4% in 2009–2010 (National Center for Education Statistics, 2012b). A similar shift upward occurred in the percentage of degrees awarded for racial and ethnic minorities with blacks earning 6.4% of the bachelor's degrees in 1976–1977 to 10.3% of the degrees in 2009–2010 and for Hispanics from 2.0% in 1976–1977 to 8.8% in 2009–2010 (National Center for Education Statistics, 2012b). In contrast, white males earned 47.7% of bachelor's degrees awarded in 1976–1977 and 44.0% in 2009–2010 (National Center for Education Statistics, 2012b). These numbers are not surprising since women and minority groups were kept out of most institutions of higher education, which were primarily all white and predominantly male, until the 1970s. Therefore, women's and historically black colleges and universities were basically the only avenue for higher education if you were not a white male prior to 1970. Although what were called "Negro colleges" were established in the South after the Civil War, and occasionally a black man graduated from college prior to the Civil War, the education of blacks and women in the United States continued to be an issue throughout the 20th century. Higher education was one of the issues that the civil rights movement of the 1960s addressed. By then, some strong black colleges had evolved and had graduated many people who went on to become early civil rights leaders. Those leaders, however, demanded access to primarily white colleges and universities. It wasn't until affirmative action legislation of the mid-1960s that there was legal support to enforce the admittance of women and minorities to attend previously all-white, all-male colleges and universities.

Despite the gains in access in recent years, life on college campuses continues to be difficult for black students. Feagin, Vera, and Imani (1996, p. 17) refer to "educational apartheid" when describing the position of black students at white colleges and universities. Issues for other minority groups in higher education are also of concern, not only in terms of access but also in terms of quality of academic and social life once they are on campus.

The women's rights efforts of the 1970s opened up colleges and universities for women in many ways, and women have been quite successful in gaining postsecondary degrees, except in some areas as discussed in the introduction to Chapter 7 and the reading by Mickelson in that chapter. However, the growth in women's enrollment in higher education has led to a decline in the number of women's colleges in the United States (Miller-Bernal, 2006).

Public colleges and universities have been important in providing pathways to higher education for people who might not otherwise have been able to afford college, with major expansion of public institutions of higher education occurring between 1960 and 1985 (Tobin, 2009; see also Tuchman in this chapter). Many obstacles must be overcome for lower-income students to achieve a college degree. Alejandro Portes and Patricia Fernández-Kelly describe factors in the lives of disadvantaged immigrant children that contributed to their success in college. Although the cases described are only a small portion of the children they studied, these stories help us to consider what things we might be able to change to help disadvantaged children achieve higher education degrees.

The system of higher education in America differs from the patterns and practices of advanced education in other countries. In Europe today, countries are working together to standardize higher education and ensure colleges and universities provide the same high standard of education across member countries. The Bologna Process, introduced in 1999 has generated considerable change across member countries and is continuing to affect higher education in Europe, as Hunter describes in her reading.

As you can see, institutions of higher education have undergone and will continue to undergo many changes. The growth of private, for-profit institutions of higher education and the flexibility of technology in providing degrees are likely to lead to many more changes. This chapter is intended to familiarize you with some of the issues in higher education in the United States today and help you understand how the institution that you are currently attending fits into a history of higher education. All of the parts of the open systems model can be applied to understanding higher education in the readings that follow—organization, input and output, and feedback and influences from the surrounding environment.

References

Feagin, J. R., Vera, H., & Imani, N. (1996). *The agony of education: Black students at white colleges and universities.* New York: Routledge.

Graham, H. D., & Diamond, N. (1997). *The rise of American research universities: Elites and challengers in the postwar era.* Baltimore: Johns Hopkins University Press.

Miller-Bernal, L. (2006). Changes in the status and function of women's colleges over time. In L. Miller-Bernal & S. L. Poulson (Eds.), *Challenged by coeducation: Women's colleges since the 1960s* (pp. 1–20). Nashville, TN: Vanderbilt University Press.

National Center for Education Statistics. (1996). *Degrees conferred by institutions of higher education, by level of degree and sex of student: 1949–50 to 1993–94.* Washington, DC: U.S. Department of Education. Retrieved from http://nces.ed.gov/pubs98/yi/y9632a.asp/

National Center for Education Statistics. (2012a). *Digest of education statistics*. Washington, DC: U.S. Department of Education. Retrieved from http://nces.ed.gov/

National Center for Education Statistics. (2012b). *Fast facts: Degrees conferred by sex and race.* Washington, DC: U.S. Department of Education, Institute of Education Sciences. Retrieved from http://nces.ed.gov/fastfacts/display.asp?id=72

Noble, D. F. (1998). *Digital diploma mills: The automation of higher education.* Retrieved from http://www.firstmonday.dk/issues/issue3_1/noble/

Rudolph, F. (1990). *The American college and university: A history*. Athens: University of Georgia Press.

Tobin, E. M. (2009). The modern evolution of America's flagship universities. In W. G. Bowen, M. M. Chingos, & M. S. McPherson (Eds.), *Crossing the finish line: Completing college at America's public universities* (Appendix A, pp. 239–264). Princeton, NJ: Princeton University Press.

Veysey, L. R. (1965). *The emergence of the American university*. Chicago: University of Chicago Press.

Willie, S. S. (2003). *Acting black: College identity and the performance of race.* New York: Routledge.

THE UNINTENDED DECENTERING OF TEACHING AND LEARNING

Gaye Tuchman

In her review of Richard Arum and Josipa Roksa's book, *Academically Adrift* (2011), Gaye Tuchman provides a thoughtful and critical overview of higher education today. Her book, *Wannabe U: Inside the Corporate University* (2009), criticizes the changes in higher education. She bases her conclusions on six years of observations at a university in the United States. Her concerns cover the entire university, including changes in management, values, faculty orientation, and even student expectations and behavior. It will likely surprise you to view your collegiate experience from this perspective.

Questions to consider for this reading:

1. What does it mean to view higher education as a private good versus a public good?

2. Why does she argue that the "privatization" of higher education has led to some of the problems with colleges and universities today?

3. What is the effect of the new managerialism on students' collegiate experiences?

Once upon a time in a land not so far away, higher education was a public good and state colleges and universities were virtually free. Students paid for books and fees. When a school was far from home, they also paid for room and board. By 1970, admission at some colleges was quite competitive.

Over the years, I have heard colleagues talk about a golden age, when the City University of New York did not charge tuition—not the 1920s and 30s, when City College was the school of choice for future Nobel laureates, but the 1960s and early 70s, when academically striving and upwardly mobile second-generation Americans headed to City, Brooklyn, Hunter and Queens Colleges. "I never could have gone to college if Brooklyn weren't free," said one social scientist, who had been reared in a housing project. "Hunter cost $100 in fees and even that was a lot for me," a daughter of Latino immigrants, told me. Each emphasized that she was able to go to college, because the City University of New York did not charge tuition.

The financing of higher education is quite different now; so is the meaning of a college degree. Today, it is defined as a private good. Also, as students' costs have escalated and the state has paid less, there have been serious unintended consequences. Richard Arum and Josipa Roksa (2011) have provided a great service by identifying some of them in *Academically Adrift*. They tell us, "Neoliberal policy makers who

From "The Unintended Decentering of Teaching and Learning," by Gaye Tuchman, from *Society*, 2011, Copyright © Springer.

have advocated for increased privatization and market-based educational reforms have produced a system that has expanded opportunity for all. What conservative policy makers have missed, however, is that market-based educational reforms that elevate the role of students as 'consumers' do not necessarily yield improved outcomes in terms of student learning" (2011: 137). Instead, [Arum and Roksa's] data indicate, students spend less time studying and also less time studying alone. At every sort of higher-education institution—selective and nonselective, public and private—they are learning less than students did twenty years ago. Furthermore, the gap between the educational accomplishments of rich and poor undergraduates and also the gulf between those of whites and underrepresented minorities is growing.

I believe that the privatization of higher education explicit in current neoliberal financial arrangements has encouraged educational institutions to imitate corporations, the professoriate to behave like ambitious entrepreneurs (many of whom are often oblivious to the undergraduates populating their classrooms, lecture halls and labs), and students to act like consumers intent on receiving "elaborate and ever-expanding services" (p. 15). These include dormitory suites with kitchens, mall-like student unions with food courts, as well as fitness centers replete with the latest elliptical exercisers, and even Olympic pools. Additionally, the transformation of higher education has introduced an accountability regime—a politics of surveillance, control, and market management disguising itself as the value-neutral and scientific administration of individuals and organizations. It has not served well either the faculty or the students.

My argument draws on data gathered at the pseudonymous Wannabe University, a rather typical northern flagship university with over 20,000 students where I conducted participant observation for over six years. (I named it Wannabe University, because it satisfies the characteristics listed by *The Chronicle of Higher Education*; to wit, ambition to be a national university, aspirations to increase its national ranking, increased

funding of famous faculty and expanded construction, self-identification as an economic engine for its region, a slick advertising campaign about its potential greatness, and dreams of becoming the next Silicon Valley.)

I talked about City University of New York, because its history captures the national pattern. Initially it did not charge tuition and it was the first university system to announce open admission—anyone graduating in the top half of a New York high school could attend a four-year college and any graduate could enroll at a community college. It even committed itself to remediation at all of its campuses; as a result, underprepared students swarmed to CUNY. Initially more whites than underrepresented minorities reaped the benefits, according to David Lavin, Richard Alba and Richard Silberstein's (1981) now classic *Right versus Privilege: The Open University Experiment at the City University of New York*, though the media continued to say that the open admissions policy was aimed at the city's underrepresented minorities. In 1975, when bankruptcy threatened the city, CUNY was forced to abandon its expensive idealistic policies and instead became one of the first universities to adopt the neoliberal policies of expanded admissions, increased tuition, and decreased public funding. (By the new century, it had discontinued remedial programs at the senior campuses.) Public higher education was no longer to be defined as a public good.

Wannabe U has also responded to neoliberal pressures, albeit more subtle ones. Here are two of the many reasons that it has joined the competition to satisfy the student consumerism that is now rampant in higher education. Increasingly, both federal and state governments have turned from financing institutions to financing students. Although some programs introduced in the 1970s, such as Pell Grants and New York State's Tuition Assistance Program (TAP), subsidize the needy rather than the affluent, they nonetheless embody the neoliberal emphasis. By funding students, not institutions, they inadvertently decrease institutional control; [b]luntly, such programs push students to decide where they will spend their tuition dollars and leave colleges to figure out how to attract them. (These programs also regulated how many remedial courses funded students could take and so contributed to the turn of-the-century demise of remedial education at CUNY's senior colleges.) Simultaneously, decreased state financing has forced colleges and universities to raise their own funds, to engage in what (in the book of the same name) Sheila Slaughter and Gary Rhoades (2004) call "academic capitalism." Responding to these and other financial pressures, colleges have constituted themselves as competing brands. Not only does one college play Coca-Cola to another's Pepsi (many colleges' viewbooks include pictures of their gleaming fitness centers as if flaunting their superiority in the latest taste test); but also both Coke and Pepsi will pay a university over $1,000,000 to be the only firm whose soft drinks are sold on campus.

During the past decades, a double movement has been occurring within educational institutions. Teaching matters less. In the late 1930s, when Clark Kerr was studying economics at Berkeley, the professors with the most prestige were the best teachers. After World War II, the expansion of the National Institutes of Health, the establishment of the National Science Foundation, and even the redirection of private foundations to tackle national priorities led higher education to emphasize research. When the American Association of University Professors had pressed for the institution of tenure in 1915, it had intended to protect free speech so as to promote classroom inquiry and debate. By 1960, after the expansion of the funding agencies and universities' identification of research as a revenue stream, tenure had become a reward for the production of scholarship. Today, the professors with the most prestige are the publishers and grant-getters; at some research universities, many faculty members pay so much attention to the prestige garnered by scholarship that they don't even know who the best teachers are. Kerr himself put it this way: "There appears to be a point of no return . . . after which research, consulting and graduate instruction become so absorbing that faculty efforts can no

longer be concentrated on undergraduate instruction as they once were" (quoted in Tobin, 2009: 255). When some major public universities receive as little as 8% of their general fund from their legislature and so must scrounge for monies, teaching is decentered. When most students think that the only purpose of education is to get a diploma that yields a job, students will be "academically adrift," to use Richard Arum and Josipa Roksa's (2011) term, and their learning will be decentered, too.

Like the undergraduates in Arum and Roksa's (2011) study, Wannabe University's students have also come to define college in social and occupational terms rather than as an opportunity to explore intellectual possibilities. One can chart how Wannabe's evolution has affected them. In 1970, Wannabe University was free, too. As costs rose, well-prepared upper-middle class students left for more prestigious pastures until the state legislature decried the brain drain resulting from Wannabe's identity as a safety school. (As at CUNY, potential applicants seemed to think that since they were paying, they might as well aim for a more selective school. Wan U became the place for good in-state students to go if they couldn't get in elsewhere.) To attract better students, Wannabe U bought them. In the 1990s, it instituted special merit scholarships for salutatorians and valedictorians, though it continued to award funds to those in need. It entered the "amenities race": it built dormitories with suites; it revised cafeteria menus; it emphasized sports. And, like other higher-education institutions, it pushed its professoriate, especially its science faculty, to accumulate grants and contracts and, as provided by the Bayh-Dole Act of 1980, to patent their findings whenever possible. By the 1990s and early twenty-first century, when Wannabe U expressed a serious commitment to the national push for better classroom teaching, its instructors had already responded to the nation's neoliberal emphasis on research. As had professors elsewhere, they had embraced research as the path to professional prestige and personal success. Wan U encouraged them to do so. Especially at the research universities, many scholars looked at undergraduate teaching with condescension. Their employers also encouraged them to do so. Needing money, colleges and universities could not abandon the emphasis on funded research.

A new doctrine of professional responsibility and more detailed merit forms to assess individual accomplishments were among the policies that increased the accountability of tenure-line faculty and encouraged professors to audit themselves. They were to monitor the expansion of the lists of publications and grants on their curriculum vitae much as they weighed themselves in the morning. Even as Wannabe's central administrators initiated programs to increase student retention and graduation rates, it pushed faculty to tackle more funded research. "Non-instructional staff" ran those new programs, not professors. One ex-dean claimed that it was easier to fire non-instructional staff if a program did not work out. Moreover, the academic departments were to attract and create potential revenue streams. (The School of Agriculture taught horse-back riding in the summer and even marketed its campus-made ice cream.) Advising one another of the experiences on their end of campus, scientists told humanists, "If you think that the people in the humanities feel pressure, you should see what it's like in the sciences."

At Wan U, as elsewhere, research had trumped teaching. As I describe in *Wannabe U: Inside the Corporate University*, both central administrators and departments placed so much emphasis on scholarship, especially funded research, that sometimes they even construed instructing undergraduates as a punishment. At Wannabe, as elsewhere, professors who do not produce enough scholarship are assigned to teach more courses than their well-published or well-funded colleagues. Four-year colleges mimic the universities. Although their faculties are not expected to devote as much time and effort to scholarship, research matters—both to bring in needed monies and to garner prestige. At such prestigious colleges as Wellesley, Hamilton, and Vassar, publishers are more likely than acclaimed teachers to be distinguished professors and to hold named chairs.

I read the recent histories of both CUNY and Wannabe University, as well as Arum and Roksa's (2011) *Academically Adrift*, as stories about the unintended consequences of neoliberalism. No one had meant the stress on research and consumerism to diminish teaching; but one can trace the processes by which it did so. Neoliberalism encouraged the introduction of corporate management techniques, especially of what Michael Power (1999) has called the new managerialism—an emphasis on efficiency, effectiveness, and economy. In higher education, the new managerialism was to be achieved in part by

- the centralization of authority in the staff of presidents and provosts,

- the introduction of vision statements, mission statements, and business plans ("An academic plan is simply a business plan," one Wannabe president informed "his" faculty),

- an emphasis on hiring non-instructional staff to provide the services that choosy students were demanding, and so the hiring of fewer full-time instructors, and thus

- a shift to at-will instructors who could not even pretend to have a say in the governance of their departments, let alone the university. (Currently only 35% of faculty are tenured (25%) or tenure-track (10%) instructors; the rest, the contingent faculty, are mainly adjuncts who commute from one college to another to earn a meager living.)

The power of the accountability regime helps to explain many professors' disenchantment with teaching. As I describe in Wannabe U, the new managerialism introduced significant changes in work conditions without consulting the professoriate (the workers). Under the guise of investing their assets wisely, deans and central administrators encouraged some forms of research, but not others. They played an increasingly active role in establishing how research should and would be conducted at their institution. Sometimes they assumed the right to define the appropriate parameters of scholarly fields. Small wonder that many full-time professors grew disheartened, almost inert, and that previously peaceful academic departments experienced significant conflict, while departments in which faculty had frequently squabbled were virtually rent asunder. And how are the adjuncts running from job to job supposed to be dedicated to their students and institutions, when many have little contact with one another, let alone their full-time colleagues? When a complex organization consistently pushes each individual worker to achieve for his or her own benefit while it simultaneously seeks status and minimizes the welfare of the collectivity, the very notion of the common good may melt into a puddle and evaporate.

Teaching suffers. It is difficult to dedicate oneself to teaching students who do not want to take one's course and sometimes make it clear that they don't care a fig about it—though they do care about the grade. (Following the reasoning of the accountability regime, students seem to feel that scoring well on tests is more important than learning.) It is especially difficult to give one's classes a high priority, when one's profession lauds scholarship, not teaching. At Wannabe University, the Institute for Teaching and Learning (ITL), established in the 1990s, is supposed to address this problem by teaching teachers how to teach, but it cannot make them care. The head of one of the ITL's programs explained a problem he faces. Department heads order faculty who receive poor ratings on student evaluations to go to the institute. "They don't want to be here," he told me. He finds it difficult to help these "faculty-learners" who don't give a fig either. Some professors justify their distrust of the ITL by saying that it is more responsive to the central administration than to the instructors whom the institute supposedly serves.

However, one cannot simply blame colleges, universities, administrators, middle-managers, and professors for the decreased learning that Arum and Roksa (2011) document. When students study less, they learn less. I believe that their retreat from studying, especially studying alone, is a response to contemporary conditions, including the growing schism between the wealthy and everyone else that is associated with the current version of globalization, the mediatization of politics, religion, and daily life, and the commodification that has resulted as increased conformity masquerades as individualization.

Our students' comparatively poor study habits and their dedication to having fun are reminders that they have bought into contemporary norms about what they should be doing. Commodification has taught them to judge others by their possessions. The changing distribution of jobs—and the associated growing schism between the wealthy and the rest of us—has intensified the feeling that they must train to find a stable job. As Philip Kasinitz, Mary Waters, John Mollenkopf, and Jennifer Holdiaway (2008) document in *Inheriting the City: The Children of Immigrants Come of Age*, at CUNY many upwardly mobile second-generation Americans aim for a practical career. So do some Wan U students. Others have no idea why they are in college, except for their conviction that a college degree will somehow bring a good and (with luck) stable job. (Over the past four decades—from the New York City fiscal crisis to the Great Recession—my classrooms have been peopled by a goodly percentage of students who raised their hands when I asked if they know people who were fired in the most recent recession.)

To be sure, these concerns are not new. Earlier generations of upwardly mobile undergraduates sought training. In a bygone era wealthy students attended elite institutions without really knowing why they were there—except, of course, they felt sure that members of their social class were supposed to spend time in college. Many of the undergraduates of yesteryear also dedicated themselves to enjoying what they were certain were the best years of their life—the time without responsibility. But contemporary social conditions, including the expansion of higher education, have exacerbated these themes.

Today's undergraduates are filled with contradictions. They want both social acceptance and private goods. They want to get through their coursework; they want jobs that pay well, but not the solitary learning necessary to stretch the mind. They want to have fun. They want to be recognized as individuals. They stand at the campus bus stops, cell phone glued to ear, stance announcing that they have a friend to talk with and so are not alone. Like the members of David Riesman's (1950) *Lonely Crowd*, they are most themselves when they are in a group.

The problem facing both educators and policymakers is not simply what has happened to America's higher-education institutions. Rather, colleges and universities cannot be fixed without analyzing what has happened to our youngsters, too. We must reconsider the impact of contemporary neoliberalism and its accountability regime on both students and schools.

REFERENCES

Arum, R., & Roksa, J. 2011. *Academically adrift: Limited learning on college campuses.* Chicago: University of Chicago Press.

Attewell, P., Lavin, D. E., Thurston, D., & Levey, T. 2009. *Passing the torch: Does higher education for the disadvantaged pay off across the generations?* New York: Russell Sage.

Evans, M. 2004. *Killing thinking.* New York: Continuum.

Kasinitz, P., Waters, M., Mollenkopf, J., & Holdiaway, J. 2008. *Inheriting the city: The children of immigrants come of age.* New York: Russell Sage Foundation and Cambridge, MA: Harvard University Press.

Lavin, D. E., Alba, R. D., & Silberstein, R. A. 1981. *Right versus privilege: The open university experiment at the City University of New York.* New York: Free Press

Power, M. 1999. *The audit society: Rituals of verification.* New York: Oxford University Press.

Riesman, D. 1950. *The lonely crowd: A study of the changing American character.* New Haven, CT: Yale University Press.

Slaughter, S., & Rhoades, G. 2004. *Academic capitalism and the new economy.* Baltimore: Johns Hopkins University Press.

Tobin, E. M. 2009. Appendix A: The modern evolution of America's flagship universities. In W. G. Bowen, M. M. Chingas, & M. S. McPherson (Eds.), *Crossing the finish line* (pp. 238–264). Princeton: Princeton University Press.

Tuchman, G. 2009. *Wannabe U: Inside the corporate university.* Chicago: University of Chicago Press.

THE COMMUNITY COLLEGE

The Impact, Origin, and Future of a Contradictory Institution

Kevin J. Dougherty and Vanessa S. Morest

Kevin J. Dougherty and Vanessa S. Morest discuss the development of the community college and its role in American society. In doing so, they explore what they call "the contradictory roles" of community colleges and consider the future of this important, but often neglected, part of higher education. As you read through this reading, consider how community colleges came to be and how educational trajectories and future work careers are shaped by the type of educational institution you attend.

Questions to consider for this reading:

1. What are the functions of community colleges? In what sense are they contradictory?

2. What is the role of community colleges in maintaining inequality in society?

3. How did business and government affect the growth of community colleges, and how was their impact different from that on research universities?

Community colleges are one of the most important sectors of U.S. higher education. They are important because of their great number, their critical role in providing college opportunity (especially for nontraditional students), and the essential role that they play in providing postsecondary vocational training. These public two-year colleges—numbering 967 in 2011—comprise nearly one-quarter of all higher educational institutions in the United States (National Center for Education Statistics, 2012, table 306). Community colleges enroll over one-third of all college students (some 7.1 million in fall 2011). This enrollment share is even greater for nontraditional students, whether older, part-time, minority, or disadvantaged (National Center for Education Statistics, 2012, tables 223, 227, 264). Finally, community colleges are important as key sources of postsecondary vocational education. Vocational enrollees at community colleges comprise over half of all students in all forms of postsecondary vocational training and provide a large share of our nation's graduates in such important occupations as nursing, computer operations, and auto repair (Cohen & Brawer, 2008; Dougherty & Bakia, 2000; Grubb, 1996, pp. 54–56).

Yet, because of this very importance, community colleges are contradictory institutions. Community colleges have taken on a host of different social functions, but some of these functions are partially incompatible. In this piece I explore these contradictory functions in closer detail and trace their historical origins.

CONTRADICTORY FUNCTIONS AND IMPACTS

Most community colleges are "comprehensive" institutions, offering a wide variety of programs to a diverse clientele. In most community colleges, a majority of students are enrolled in workforce preparation and economic development programs. However, three-quarters of all first-time community college students (including adults) aspire to get at least a baccalaureate degree, and one-quarter transfer to a four-year college within five years of entering a community college (McCormick, 1997, pp. 32, 41).[1] In addition, community colleges operate sizable programs in remedial education, adult education, and community services (such as concerts and day camps) (Cohen & Brawer, 2008). Examining these functions in greater detail allows us to better understand the ways in which they are compatible or incompatible, synergistic, or contradictory.

COLLEGE ACCESS AND OPPORTUNITY

The community college is a central avenue into higher education and toward the baccalaureate degree, particularly for working class, nonwhite, and female students. Many baccalaureate recipients, particularly in states such as California and Florida, got their start at community colleges. In fact, several studies find that states and localities that are highly endowed with community colleges have significantly higher rates of college attendance and baccalaureate attainment than states and localities with a smaller community college presence (Dougherty, 1994, pp. 50–51; Rouse, 1998).

Several features of community colleges make them great avenues of college access. Community colleges are widely distributed across the country and located in urban, suburban, and rural areas. They are cheaper to attend than four-year colleges. Their tuitions are usually low, and dormitory residence is not necessary because the colleges are nearby. And because of their open-door admissions ideal, they are more willing to take "nontraditional" students: high school dropouts, vocational aspirants, and adults interested in leisure education.

However, despite the community college's success in widening college access, there is concern about its role in providing college success. Many students entering the community college do not leave it either with a degree in hand or having transferred to another institution. Among students who entered a community college in fall 2003 and were followed up three years later, 45% had left higher education without a degree of any kind or transferring to a four-year institution (Horn, 2009, pp. 22–23).

In explaining this high dropout rate, it is important to acknowledge that community college students tend to come from less advantaged backgrounds and be less prepared academically than four-year college entrants. However, it is also important to acknowledge the important role of *institutional* factors. Community colleges are less able to academically and socially integrate their students into the life of the college through such means as on-campus housing (Dougherty, 1994, chap. 4; 2002, pp. 317–318). Moreover, community college faculty are less able to engage students because so many are part-time. In fall 2007, 69% of all faculty in public two-year colleges were part-timers (National Center for Education Statistics, 2009, table 245). In studies that control for various student and institutional characteristics, there is evidence that higher proportions of part-time faculty in community colleges are associated with lower rates of student retention (Calcagno, Bailey, Jenkins, Kienzl, & Leinbach, 2008; Jaeger & Eagan, 2009). Finally, community colleges often do not adequately meet the needs of their students for extensive program and career advice (Rosenbaum, Deil-Amen, & Person, 2006).

PREPARATION FOR THE
BACCALAUREATE (COLLEGE TRANSFER)

Historically, one of the leading roles of the community college has been to provide access to the baccalaureate. Originally, this took the role of fostering transfer to four-year colleges, but in recent years, community colleges have begun increasingly to offer their own baccalaureate degrees (Floyd, Skolnik, & Walker, 2005). But despite the long-standing nature of this role of the community college, it has been fraught with controversy.

Many different studies find that entering a community college rather than a four-year college significantly lowers the probability that a student will attain a baccalaureate degree. Clearly, this gap in baccalaureate attainment could be simply due to the fact that community college students *on average* tend to be less well off, less prepared academically, and less ambitious educationally and occupationally than are four-year college entrants. But even when we compare community college entrants and four-year college entrants with the same family background, academic aptitude, high school grades, and educational and occupational aspirations, the community college entrants on average attain about 15% *fewer* baccalaureate degrees than their four-year college peers. This baccalaureate gap even holds in studies that systematically address issues of selection bias through the use of instrumental variable analysis or propensity score analysis (Alfonso, 2006; Dougherty, 1994, pp. 52–61; Doyle, 2008; Long & Kurlaender, 2009; Pascarella & Terenzini, 2005, p. 376). How do we explain this?

On closer inspection we find that—quite apart from the qualities students bring to college—entering the community college puts obstacles in the way of the pursuit of the baccalaureate degree. All other things being equal, baccalaureate aspirants who begin at a community college are more likely than comparable four-year college entrants to drop out during the first two years of college and not move on to become juniors at a four-year college.[2] As we have seen above, community college students more often drop out in the first two years of college because community colleges are less able to academically and socially integrate their students into the life of the college. In addition, fewer community college students go on to the junior year at four-year colleges because, in comparison to four-year college entrants, they receive weaker encouragement to pursue a bachelor's degree, less adequate financial aid, and less interest by four-year colleges in admitting them to popular campuses and programs (Dougherty, 2002, pp. 315–323). This lack of transfer to universities is more pronounced among students who are lower in socioeconomic status, nonwhite, and older (Cabrera, Burkum, & LaNasa, 2005; Dougherty & Kienzl, 2006). Moreover, transferability of college credits is complicated for community college students because the equivalency of curriculum often is determined on a course-by-course basis, meaning that in many instances there is little guarantee that the courses completed at the community college will fulfill the degree requirements of a bachelor's degree. Increasingly, transfer articulation is becoming a state mandate (Morest, 2013; Kisker, Wagoner, & Cohen, 2011), which may eventually strengthen the outcomes of transfer students. However, there is also evidence that even statewide articulation agreements have little impact on transfer rates (Roksa, 2009).

WORKFORCE PREPARATION
AND ECONOMIC DEVELOPMENT

The community college role in workforce preparation and economic development ranges from preparing students for their first job to retraining unemployed workers and welfare recipients, upgrading the skills of employed workers, assisting owners of small businesses, and helping communities with economic development planning (Dougherty & Bakia, 2000; Cohen & Brawer, 2008, chap. 8; Grubb, 1996; Jacobs & Dougherty, 2006).

In terms of initial job preparation, community colleges play a central role in supplying trained workers for "middle level" or "semiprofessional" occupations such as nurses, computer operators, and auto mechanics. In fact, about one-fifth of recent labor force entrants began at a community college (Grubb, 1996, pp. 54–56). These vocational graduates receive substantial economic payoffs. For example, students earning a vocational associate's degree from a community college earn 15% to 30% more in annual income than high school graduates of similar race and ethnicity, parental education, marital status, and job experience (Grubb, 2002; Marcotte, Bailey, Borkoski, & Kienzl, 2005).[3] In fact, there are community college vocational programs—particularly in nursing and certain technical fields—whose graduates earn more than many bachelor's degree holders. As a result, for many less privileged students who are only able to pursue short-term degrees, vocational education has emerged as a viable path to success (Deil-Amen & Deluca, 2010).

Still, the economic payoffs to community college degree holders are, on average, not as good as those for baccalaureate degree holders. Looking across all fields of study, the average baccalaureate degree holder earns about 40% to 50% more than the average high school degree holder, considerably more than the average vocational or academic associate's degree holder (Grubb, 2002; Marcotte et al., 2005). Moreover, community college students who pursue a vocational degree are significantly less likely to eventually transfer to pursue a baccalaureate degree, even when one controls for family background, educational aspirations, and high school preparation (Dougherty & Kienzl, 2006).

The community college's role in job retraining, small business assistance, and economic development planning—though less heralded than its role in job preparation—is important. Today, almost all community colleges retrain workers for new jobs or new tasks in existing jobs. In addition, many colleges assist small business owners by sponsoring small business development centers or simply offering courses that

provide advice and training in management and personnel practices, marketing, finance, procuring contracts with government agencies, introducing new production technologies and work practices, and adapting to new government regulations. Finally, community colleges promote economic development by assisting local economic development planning efforts (Dougherty & Bakia, 2000).

While the community college's role in workforce preparation and economic development is very useful, it also can cause the community college considerable difficulties. Community colleges with very active workforce preparation programs can lose money on unpopular or expensive training programs, flood the market with too many graduates, provoke criticism by competing training providers, and give employers too much influence over the college curriculum (Dougherty, 1994; Dougherty & Bakia, 2000). Moreover, an active workforce preparation effort can interfere with other functions of the community college such as preparing students for transfer to four-year colleges and providing students with a general education.

REMEDIAL EDUCATION

From the beginning, community colleges have been gateways into higher education for students whom four-year colleges would turn away as unprepared for college. As a result, community colleges have long provided remedial education to many of their students (Cohen & Brawer, 2008). In 2000, 42% of freshmen in public two-year colleges were officially enrolled in remedial courses in either reading, writing, or arithmetic, as compared to 28% of college students generally (National Center for Education Statistics, 2003, p. 18). This remedial role grew during the 1990s as state legislators and four-year college boards pushed to have remedial education reduced or even eliminated at four-year colleges and relegated instead to community colleges (Shaw, 1997). This diversion of remediation into the community college poses a deep dilemma, one rooted in the contradictory effects of the community college. On the one hand, academically unprepared students pushed into community colleges may attain more education by perhaps receiving easier access to remediation and occupational education than they would at four-year colleges. (However, there is no conclusive evidence that this is the case.[4]) But on the other hand, their long-run educational attainment may be harmed by receiving less assistance in pursuing a baccalaureate degree.

A growing body of literature indicates that the remedial education programs offered by community colleges may present students with significant barriers to academic success (Attewell, Lavin, Domina, & Levey, 2006; Bailey, 2009; Bettinger & Long, 2005). Placement into remediation is typically done on the basis of standardized testing, which may not be sufficient to accurately identify students' academic levels (Scott-Clayton, 2012). A typical program of remediation involves a sequence of courses. These courses have high failure rates, and as a result, many students leave college prior to completing the remedial sequences. During the past decade, community college remedial education became a major focus of national reform efforts. New models and policies are beginning to emerge that seek to increase student success in remediation by using technology to alter the delivery of remedial course work; accelerating entry into college-level courses; or contextualizing the remedial content of courses by integrating it with occupational or applied learning (Morest, 2013).

ADULT, CONTINUING EDUCATION, AND COMMUNITY EDUCATION

Adult, continuing, and community education (ACCE) is a catchall including vocational improvement and retraining for those already working, high school completion and adult literacy improvement, personal development and recreational courses, and community services such as arts events.

Adult-education students are a key community college constituency. Many adult students enter the community college to take high school equivalency (GED), adult basic education (ABE), and English as a second language (ESL) courses. It is estimated that 33% of adult-education enrollees are in community colleges, and such students make up 7% of total credit and noncredit full-time equivalent (FTE) enrollments in community colleges. About three-quarters of these community college adult-education students are in the bottom half in socioeconomic status, and about half are nonwhite (Grubb, Badway, & Bell, 2003, p. 223; Prince & Jenkins, 2005). Despite the hopes for adult-education programs, there is little evidence that they bring significant income benefits if they do not lead to a degree (Grubb et al., 2003, pp. 229–233; Prince & Jenkins, 2005, pp. 5–6, 21). A study of first-time adult students entering Washington State community colleges in the late 1990s (the majority of whom did not have high school diplomas) found that the income payoff only becomes significant if students accrue at least a year's worth of credits and a credential. Unfortunately, the same study found that five years after entering the community college only 58% of adult-education students had acquired *any* college credits (with only 13% of ESL entrants doing so) (Prince & Jenkins, 2005, pp. 13–16, 23).

The ACCE divisions of community colleges are often their most dynamic because community colleges can more easily develop new course offerings in this area because the courses usually do not carry credit and therefore are less subject to state regulation. Community colleges can use noncredit offerings to learn more about the demands of the labor market, particularly in fast changing technology fields, and then develop similar credit-bearing courses (Dougherty & Bakia, 2000; Downey, Pusser, & Turner, 2006; Van Noy, Jacobs, Korey, Bailey, & Hughes, 2008). However, ACCE divisions of community colleges usually are not well funded, with state funding often being absent or paying less per student than state funding for regular, credit-bearing academic and occupational programs

(Cohen & Brawer, 2008, chap. 10; Grubb et al., 2003; Van Noy et al., 2008). In part because of this, ACCE courses, particularly in adult education, are often criticized for being of poor quality because they rely on too many part-time faculty and provide inadequate student support services (Grubb et al., 2003).

GENERAL EDUCATION

Community colleges have made a major commitment to general education, whether defined as transmitting a common culture or fostering skills of broad utility in a person's life, such as critical thinking and communication skills (Higginbotham & Romano, 2006). Unfortunately, this commitment is partially contradicted by the community college's other commitments, particularly to occupational education. An analysis of the catalogs of 32 community colleges found that all of them had some kind of general education requirement for their transfer programs and at least 90% had a general education requirement for their nontransfer programs. But though these figures are impressive, they also exaggerate the actual degree to which community college students receive a general education. For example, among the 90% of those 32 community colleges that had core curriculum requirements for their nontransfer programs, only half required taking even one course in U.S. government, and only one-fifth required a course in ethnic studies or multiculturalism (Zeszotarski, 1999).

These apparent gaps in the provision of general education are not surprising because community colleges face great difficulties in providing general education for all their students. The rise of occupational education has meant that community colleges now enroll many students whose primary purpose is likely to be preparation for a job rather than preparation for a variety of life roles. Since an associate's degree consists of approximately 20 courses, occupational programs are sometimes extended in length and reframed as occupational transfer programs with a more robust general education core curriculum included. Some research has concluded that this overly complicated curriculum negatively impacts student success (Person & Rosenbaum, 2006). The problem of offering a balanced curriculum is exacerbated if employers are paying for the training. Contract training programs typically are narrowly focused on providing skills and usually devote little or no attention to broader social knowledge and life skills. Finally, it is easier for public authorities to hold community colleges accountable for inculcating work skills than general learning (Dougherty, 2002, pp. 333–338; Higginbotham & Romano, 2006).

THE ORIGINS AND LATER DEVELOPMENT OF COMMUNITY COLLEGES

Befitting their multiple and contradictory functions, community colleges have had equally mixed and contrasting origins. This is rarely acknowledged in the standard accounts of how community colleges were founded and later developed. Typically, these conventional accounts state that the community college was founded in response to calls by students, parents, and publicly interested educators and government officials for more college opportunities. And later, community colleges moved from an emphasis on academic education to a stress on occupational education primarily in response to the needs of students and employers for vocational training (Cohen & Brawer, 2008).

But other observers—particularly sociologists—have pointed out how these conventional chronicles miss much of the real history of the community college. For example, while these accounts mention the key role of state universities, they often misanalyze it. The state universities pushed the founding of community colleges not just to expand college opportunity, as is typically claimed, but also to keep the universities academically selective by channeling less able students toward the community colleges. Moreover, the universities unwittingly spurred the vocationalization of the community college by monopolizing greater status as "senior" colleges that trained for the most prestigious professional and managerial occupations. In order to escape the status of "junior" colleges, community colleges began in the 1920s to carve out an independent role as suppliers of a distinct training market of their own, the "middle level" or semiprofessional occupations such as technicians, nurses, and others (Brint & Karabel, 1989; Dougherty, 1994).

Local and state government officials also played a key role in the establishment and later vocationalization of community colleges, motivated not just by a sincere belief in educational opportunity but also by self-interest. At the local level, school superintendents and high school principals were the prime instigators of local drives to found community colleges. While they were certainly moved by a commitment to expand college opportunity, they were also driven by the desires to earn prestige as college founders and to secure jobs as presidents of the new colleges (Dougherty, 1994).

At the state level, governors, state legislators, and state education departments strongly pushed the expansion and later vocationalization of community colleges. Again, their support was prompted by more than just a desire to widen college access. State officials were mindful that building more community colleges, rather than expanding existing four-year colleges, could meet the great demand for college access in the 1960s and 1970s at a much lower cost to state government. Unlike the four-year colleges, community colleges would not require expensive dormitories, libraries, and research facilities. These savings would translate either into lower taxes or more state funds for other politically popular programs, both of which would make elected government officials more popular. In addition, community colleges, because of their strong commitment to vocational and technical education, could help stimulate the growth of state economies by attracting business firms with the carrot of publicly subsidized training of employees. This economic growth in turn would enhance the reelection chances of officials when they ran again for political office (Dougherty, 1994).

Business firms usually did not play a powerful *direct* role in founding or vocationalizing community colleges. But business played a powerful *indirect* role, based on business's central position within the economic and ideological systems in the United States. Economically, business controls jobs and investment capital. Hence, in order to get their graduates access to the jobs employers control, community college officials on their own initiative will develop occupational programs that employers find useful, even without business demand for such programs (Brint & Karabel, 1989; Dougherty, 1994). Business also owns investment capital and thus largely controls the pace and distribution of economic growth. Realizing that capital investment is key to economic growth and therefore their own political prospects, elected officials have taken the initiative to offer business publicly subsidized vocational education in order to secure business investment in their jurisdictions. Ideologically, business influences government officials because those officials subscribe to values and beliefs—such as that economic growth is vital and that this growth must come primarily through an expansion of jobs in the private rather than public sector—that have made them ready to serve business interests (Dougherty, 1994).[5]

FROM COMPLEX ORIGINS TO CONTRADICTORY EFFECTS

An awareness of the community college's complex origins allows us to see how community colleges have come to powerfully hinder the baccalaureate opportunities of their students without this necessarily being an intended result. Because they lack dormitories, community colleges are less likely to keep their students in college by enmeshing them in a vibrant campus social life. But the reason community colleges lack dormitories is because this made the colleges cheaper to operate, a potent consideration in the minds of the local educators founding them and the state officials financing them. Because community colleges are heavily vocational, this may lead their transfer rate to be lower than it might otherwise be.[6] But a major reason community colleges are so strongly vocational is that this was a means of meeting elected officials' desire for economic investment and community college officials' desire for political support from business and jobs for their graduates. Finally, because community colleges are two-year schools, students are discouraged from pursuing a baccalaureate degree because they have to transfer to separate four-year institutions with different academic standards. But the reason community colleges are two-year schools is largely because university heads did not want the competition of many more four-year schools, state officials did not want the financial burden of myriad four-year colleges, and local educators felt two-year colleges would be easier to establish and be staffed by local educators. The precipitate of these many different interests is an institutional structure that, unfortunately and largely unintentionally, often subverts the educational ambitions of baccalaureate aspirants entering community college, even as it opens up opportunities for students with nonbaccalaureate ambitions. In short, the complex origins of the community college have created a contradictory institution: one serving many, often conflicting, missions.

What Can Community Colleges Do to Improve Student Success?

Many of the difficulties the community college encounters are out of its control, lying in the nature of its students (who typically are less well off and less prepared than four-year college students) and the community college's very structure as a two-year nonresidential institution. Still, there is much community colleges can do to improve success rates for their students. They can reduce the number who leave without a degree by improving the academic and social integration of students and their academic achievement by creating learning communities and freshman seminars, employing more

full-time faculty, improving advising and retention services particularly for minority students, working with high schools to improve the skills students enter college with, and developing more effective and transparent remedial education (Bailey, 2009; Bailey, Calcagno, Jenkins, Leinbach, & Kienzl, 2006; Dougherty, 2002, pp. 324–325; Jenkins, 2006; Kirst & Venezia, 2006; O'Gara, Karp, & Hughes, 2009; Rosenbaum et al., 2006; Scrivener et al., 2008; Zeidenberg, Jenkins, & Calcagno, 2007). Community colleges can increase transfer rates by encouraging transfer aspirations through better transfer advising, working to facilitate the transfer of course credits (especially for occupational students), and pushing state governments to provide financial aid specifically for transfer students (Bahr, 2008; Dougherty, 2002, pp. 325–328; Ignash & Kotun, 2005; Moore, Shulock, & Jensen, 2009).[7] In addition to these operational reforms, community colleges can also consider more far-reaching structural reforms, particularly themselves offering baccalaureate degrees rather than requiring students to engage in the often difficult process of transferring to a four-year college (Dougherty, 2002, pp. 328–330; Floyd et al., 2005).[8]

The Future of the Community College

The community college will not remain static. It will continue to change, perhaps sharply, due to its diffuse institutional mission and high responsiveness to its economic, social, and political environments (Townsend & Dougherty, 2006). As our economy globalizes, skilled and semi-skilled jobs in offices and factories continue to be eliminated or moved abroad, and class inequality increases. In response, community colleges are being asked to revamp their job preparation and economic development efforts to put more emphasis on high-skill jobs, including ones requiring baccalaureate degrees (Levin, 2001). Yet at the same time, community colleges still feel they should meet the needs of the many people who require remedial and adult basic education and preparation for semiskilled jobs (Jacobs & Dougherty, 2006). Meanwhile, as states conclude that their economies need more baccalaureate degree holders, community colleges are increasingly being asked by state officials to replace the more expensive public universities as the main site for the first two years of baccalaureate education (Wellman, 2002). But even as they respond to these demands, community colleges face increasing difficulties getting enough funds from state governments and rising competition from other colleges, whether four-year colleges offering continuing education or for-profit colleges offering occupational education with higher placement rates than community colleges typically produce (Bailey, 2006; Kenton, Huba, Schuh, & Shelley, 2005; Rosenbaum et al., 2006). As the focus for these many cross-pressures emanating from a socially stratified and conflictual society, the community college will continue to be an important, but also contradictory, institution.

Authors' Note: I would like to thank Regina Deil-Amen, Floyd Hammack, James Jacobs, Vanessa Smith Morest, and Joan Spade for their comments on this chapter as it has evolved over the years.

NOTES

1. These figures overstate the baccalaureate ambitions of community college students. Many of those holding baccalaureate ambitions are in no hurry to realize them. Moreover, for a good many, this ambition is not founded on a very solid basis. However, it is still important to realize that many students who enter community college, even if it is with the intention of securing vocational training, do hope to eventually get a baccalaureate degree.

2. Data from the 1980s indicate that baccalaureate attainment of community college transfer students was undercut as well by higher rates of attrition in the junior and senior years than was the case for students who had started at four-year colleges as freshmen. However, studies based on data from the 1990s find that this is no longer the case (Melguizo & Dowd, 2009; Melguizo, Kienzl, & Alfonso, 2011). However, see Kienzl, Wesaw, & Kumar (2012).

3. Those who hold lower degrees receive smaller payoffs. Students receiving one-year certificates outpace high school graduates by only about 10% in annual earnings, and students who attend community college but do not receive a certificate or degree lead high school graduates by only 5% to 10% in earnings for every year of community college. Moreover, the payoff to the holder of a given community college credential varies by the student's social background, major, and job placement. For example, women who have associate's degrees and certificates make more than do men but make less when they have secured no credential. The payoff is considerably higher for those with associate's degrees in engineering and computers, business, and (for women) health than in education or humanities. Finally, community college students get much better returns if they find employment in fields related to their training than if they do not (Grubb, 1996, pp. 90, 95, 99, 102; 2002).

4. Despite the importance of remedial education, we have little hard data on how well community colleges actually remediate. A number of studies have found small positive impacts of community college developmental education, but the areas of impact (whether grades on subsequent nonremedial courses, completing a degree, or transferring to a four-year college) are not consistent across studies. In addition, there is no consensus on what forms of developmental education are most effective (Bailey, 2009; Dougherty, 2002, pp. 311–312; Perin, 2006).

5. The argument laid out in the preceding paragraphs is indebted to the theory of the state in political sociology and institutional theory in the sociology of organizations. For more on these theoretical roots, see Dougherty (1994) and Brint and Karabel (1989).

6. There is some debate over how much transfer rates are negatively affected by whether a community college is high in the proportion of its students and degrees that are in vocational fields. Compare Roksa (2006) and Dougherty and Kienzl (2006). In any case, the growing push to facilitate the transfer of occupational credits and degrees will help reduce any negative impact of the vocational emphasis of community colleges on transfer rates.

7. It bears noting that studies of the impact of state policies to facilitate transfer and articulation do not find that seemingly stronger policies lead to higher rates of transfer or even lesser credit loss. However, the studies conducted so far have had to cope with less than ideal data, so there is a need for further studies in this area (Roksa, 2009).

8. Community colleges in 14 states have begun to offer their own baccalaureate degrees (Dougherty, 2002, pp. 329–330; Floyd et al., 2005). In Florida, over a third of community colleges offer baccalaureate degrees, primarily in education, business management, nursing, and health care administration (Community College Baccalaureate Association, 2010). See also the literature on the applied baccalaureate (Ruud, Bragg, & Townsend, 2009).

References

Alfonso, M. (2006). The impact of community college attendance on baccalaureate attainment. *Research in Higher Education, 47*(8), 873–903.

Attewell, P., Lavin, D., Domina, T., & Levey, T. (2006). New evidence on college remediation. *Journal of Higher Education, 77*(5), 886–924.

Bahr, P. R. (2008). Cooling out in the community college: What is the effect of academic advising on students' chances of success? *Research in Higher Education, 49*(8), 704–732.

Bailey, T. (2006). Increasing competition and the growth of the for profits. In T. Bailey & V. S. Morest (Eds.), *Defending the community college equity agenda* (pp. 87–109). Baltimore: Johns Hopkins University Press.

Bailey, T. (2009). Challenge and opportunity: Rethinking the role and function of developmental education in community college. In C. P. Harbour & P. L. Farrell (Eds.), *Contemporary issues in institutional ethics: New directions for community colleges #148* (pp. 11–30). San Francisco: Jossey-Bass.

Bailey, T., Calcagno, J. C., Jenkins, D., Leinbach, T., & Kienzl, G. (2006). Is student right-to-know all you should know? An analysis of community college graduation rates. *Research in Higher Education, 47*(3), 491–519.

Bettinger, E., & Long, B. T. (2005). *Addressing the needs of under-prepared students in higher education: Does college remediation work?* Cambridge, MA: National Bureau of Economic Research.

Brint, S. G., & Karabel, J. B. (1989). *The diverted dream*. New York: Oxford University Books.

Cabrera, A. F., Burkum, K. R., & LaNasa, S. M. (2005). Pathways to a four-year degree. In A. Seidman (Ed.), *College student retention: Formula for student success* (pp. 155–214). Westport, CT: Praeger.

Calcagno, J. C., Bailey, T., Jenkins, D., Kienzl, G., & Leinbach, T. (2008). Community college student success: What institutional characteristics make a difference? *Economics of Education Review, 27*(6), 632–645.

Cohen, A. C., & Brawer, F. B. (2008). *The American community college* (5th ed.). San Francisco: Jossey-Bass.

Community College Baccalaureate Association. (2010). *Baccalaureate conferring locations*. Fort Myers, FL: Author. Retrieved from http://www.accbd.org/resources/baccalaureate-conferring-locations/

Deil-Amen, R., & Deluca, S. (2010). The underserved third: How our educational structures populate an educational underclass. *Journal of Education for Students Placed at Risk, 15*(1/2), 27–50.

Dougherty, K. J. (1994). *The contradictory college: The conflicting origins, impacts, and futures of the community college*. Albany: State University of New York Press.

Dougherty, K. J. (2002). The evolving role of the community college: Policy issues and research questions. In J. Smart & W. Tierney (Eds.), *Higher education: Handbook of theory and research* (Vol. 17, pp. 295–348). Dordrecht, Netherlands: Kluwer.

Dougherty, K. J., & Bakia, M. F. (2000). Community colleges and contract training: Content, origins, and impacts. *Teachers College Record, 102*(1), 198–244.

Dougherty, K. J., & Kienzl, G. (2006). It's not enough to get through the open door: Inequalities by social background in transfer from community colleges to four-year colleges. *Teachers College Record, 108*(3), 452–487.

Downey, J., Pusser, B., & Turner, K. (2006). Competing missions: Balancing entrepreneurialism with community responsiveness in community college continuing education divisions. In B. T. Townsend & K. J. Dougherty (Eds.), *Community college missions in the 21st century: New directions for community colleges #136* (pp. 75–82). San Francisco: Jossey-Bass.

Doyle, W. R. (2008). The effect of community college enrollment on bachelor's degree completion. *Economics of Education Review, 28*(2), 199–206.

Floyd, D. F., Skolnik, M., & Walker, K. (Eds.). (2005). *The community college baccalaureate*. Sterling, VA: Stylus Press.

Grubb, W. N. (1996). *Working in the middle*. San Francisco: Jossey-Bass.

Grubb, W. N. (2002). Learning and earning in the middle: Part I. National studies of pre-baccalaureate education. *Economics of Education Review, 21*(4), 299–321.

Grubb, W. N., Badway, N., & Bell, D. (2003). Community colleges and the equity agenda: The potential of non-credit education. *Annals of the American Academy of Social and Political Science, 586*(1), 218–240.

Higginbotham, G. H., & Romano, R. M. (2006). Appraising the efficacy of civic education at the community college. In B. T. Townsend & K. J. Dougherty (Eds.), *Community college missions in the 21st century: New directions for community colleges #136* (pp. 23–32). San Francisco: Jossey-Bass.

Horn, L. (2009). *On track to complete? A taxonomy of beginning community college students and their outcomes 3 years after enrolling: 2003–04 through 2006. Statistical analysis report* (NCES 2009-152). Washington, DC: Government Printing Office.

Ignash, J. M., & Kotun, D. (2005). Results of a national study of transfer in occupational/technical degrees: Policies and practices. *Journal of Applied Research in the Community College, 12*(2), 109–120.

Jacobs, J., & Dougherty, K. J. (2006). The uncertain future of the workforce development mission of community colleges. In B. T. Townsend & K. J. Dougherty (Eds.), *Community college missions in the 21st century: New directions for community colleges #136* (pp. 53–62). San Francisco: Jossey-Bass.

Jaeger, A. J., & Eagan, M. K. (2009). Unintended consequences: Examining the effect of part-time faculty members on associate's degree completion. *Community College Review, 36*(3), 167–194.

Jenkins, D. (2006). *What community college management practices are effective in promoting student success?* New York: Columbia University, Teachers College, Community College Research Center. Retrieved from http://ccrc.tc.columbia.edu/Publication.asp?UID=419

Kenton, C. P., Huba, M. E., Schuh, J. H., & Shelley, M. C. (2005). Financing community colleges: A longitudinal study of 11 states. *Community College Journal of Research and Practice, 29*(2), 109–122.

Kienzl, G. S., Wesaw, A., & Kumar, A. (2012). *Understanding the transfer process*. Washington, DC: Institute for Higher Education Policy.

Kirst, M., & Venezia, A. (Eds.). (2006). *From high school to college: Improving opportunities for success in post-secondary education*. San Francisco: Jossey-Bass.

Kisker, C. B., Wagoner, R. L., & Cohen, A. M. (2011, April). *An analysis of transfer associate degrees in four states*. Los Angeles, CA: Center for the Study of Community Colleges.

Levin, J. (2001). *Globalizing the community college*. New York: Palgrave.

Long, B. T., & Kurlaender, M. (2009). Do community colleges provide a viable pathway to a baccalaureate degree? *Educational Evaluation and Policy Analysis, 31*(1), 30–53.

Marcotte, D. E., Bailey, T., Borkoski, C., & Kienzl, G. S. (2005). The returns of a community college education: Evidence from the national education longitudinal survey. *Educational Evaluation and Policy Analysis, 27*(2), 157–175.

McCormick, A. (1997). *Transfer behavior among beginning postsecondary students: 1989–94* (NCES 97-266). Washington, DC: National Center for Education Statistics.

Melguizo, T., & Dowd, A. C. (2009). Baccalaureate success of transfers and rising 4-year college juniors. *Teachers College Record, 111*(1), 55–89.

Melguizo, T., Kienzl, G., & Alfonso, A. (2011). Comparing the educational attainment of community college transfer students and four-year college rising juniors using propensity score matching methods. *Journal of Higher Education, 82*(3), 265–291.

Moore, C., Shulock, N., & Jensen, C. (2009). *Creating a student-centered transfer process in California: Lessons from other states*. Sacramento: California State University, Institute for Higher Education Leadership & Policy.

Morest, V. S. (2013). *Community college student success: From boardrooms to classrooms*. New York: Rowman & Littlefield.

National Center for Education Statistics. (2003). *Remedial education at degree granting postsecondary institutions in fall 2000* (NCES 2004-010). Washington, DC: U.S. Government Printing Office.

National Center for Education Statistics. (2009). *Digest of education statistics, 2009*. Washington, DC: U.S. Government Printing Office.

National Center for Education Statistics. (2012). *Digest of education statistics, 2011*. Washington, DC: U.S. Government Printing Office.

O'Gara, L., Karp, M. M., & Hughes, K. L. (2009). Student success courses in the community college:

An exploratory study of student perspectives. *Community College Review, 36*(3), 195–218.

Pascarella, E. T., & Terenzini, P. T. (2005). *How college affects students* (2nd ed.). San Francisco: Jossey-Bass.

Perin, D. (2006). Can community colleges protect both access and standards? The problem of remediation. *Teachers College Record, 108*(3), 339–373.

Person, A., & Rosenbaum, J. E. (2006). Student planning and information problems in different college structures. *Teachers College Record, 108*(3), 374–396.

Prince, D., & Jenkins, D. (2005). *Building pathways to success for low-skill adult students: Lessons for community college policy and practice from a statewide longitudinal tracking study*. New York: Columbia University, Teachers College, Community College Research Center.

Roksa, J. (2006). Does the vocational focus of community colleges hinder students' educational attainment? *Review of Higher Education, 29*(4), 499–526.

Roksa, J. (2009). Building bridges for student success: Are higher education articulation policies effective? *Teachers College Record, 111*(10), 2444–2478.

Rosenbaum, J. E., Deil-Amen, R., & Person, A. E. (2006). *After admission: From college access to college success*. New York: Russell Sage Foundation.

Rouse, C. E. (1998). Do two-year colleges increase overall educational attainment? Evidence from the states. *Journal of Policy Analysis and Management, 17*(4), 595–620.

Ruud, C., Bragg, D. D., & Townsend, B. (2009). The applied baccalaureate degree: The right time and place. *Community College Journal of Research and Practice, 34*(1–2), 136–152.

Scott-Clayton, J. (2012). *Do high-stakes placement exams predict college success?* New York: Columbia University, Teachers College, Community College Research Center.

Scrivener, S., Bloom, D., LeBlanc, A., Paxson, C., Rouse, C. E., & Sommo, C. (2008). *A good start: Two-year effects of a freshmen learning community program at Kingsborough Community College*. New York: MDRC. Retrieved from http://www.mdrc.org/publications/473/full.pdf

Shaw, K. M. (1997). Remedial education as ideological battleground: Emerging remedial education policies in the community college. *Educational Evaluation and Policy Analysis, 19*(3), 284–296.

Townsend, B. T., & Dougherty, K. J. (Eds.). (2006). *Community college missions in the 21st century: New directions for community colleges #136*. San Francisco: Jossey-Bass.

Van Noy, M., Jacobs, J., Korey, S., Bailey, T., & Hughes, K. L. (2008). *The landscape of noncredit workforce education: State policies and community college practice* (Issue Brief 38). New York: Community College Research Center, Teachers College, Columbia University. Retrieved from http://ccrc.tc.columbia.edu/Publication.asp?uid=634

Wellman, J. V. (2002). *State policy and community college-baccalaureate transfer*. San Jose, CA: National Center for Public Policy and Higher Education.

Zeidenberg, M., Jenkins, D., & Calcagno. J. C. (2007). *Do student success courses actually help community college students succeed?* (CCRC Brief #36). New York: Community College Research Center, Teachers College, Columbia University. Retrieved from http://ccrc.tc.columbia.edu/Publication.asp?uid=667

Zeszotarski, P. (1999). Dimensions of general education requirements. In G. Schuyler (Ed.), *Trends in community college curriculum: New directions for community colleges #108* (pp. 39–48). San Francisco: Jossey-Bass.

THE (MIS)EDUCATION OF MONICA AND KAREN

Laura Hamilton and Elizabeth A. Armstrong

Laura Hamilton and Elizabeth A. Armstrong collected considerable data over more than five years in their qualitative study of college dormitory life. This reading looks at the fit between the background of students, their college experiences, and their expectations for their futures. The authors' description of Monica's and Karen's experiences during their first year at a large Midwestern university helps to highlight the pressures and supports that colleges may or may not provide to incoming students. Consider the "fit" between your own background and expectations for college and your college career as you read this piece.

Questions to consider for this reading:

1. What factors did Monica and Karen share that made this large, Midwestern university a poor fit for them both?

2. Why did some students succeed at this large, Midwestern university when Monica and Karen did not?

3. After reading this article, what recommendations would you make for increasing completion rates at this university? What changes would you make at your own university or college to improve completion rates there?

Monica grew up in a small, struggling Midwestern community, population 3,000, that was once a booming factory town. She was from a working-class family, and paid for most of her education at Midwest U, a "moderately selective" residential university, herself. She worked two jobs, sometimes over 40 hours a week, to afford in-state tuition. Going out-of-state, or to a pricey private school, was simply out of the question without a large scholarship. Attending MU was even a stretch; one year there cost as much as four years at the regional campus near her hometown.

Karen grew up in the same small town as Monica, but in a solidly middle-class family. Her college-educated parents could afford to provide more financial assistance. But even though MU was only three hours away, her father "wasn't too thrilled" about her going so far from home. He had attended a small religious school that was only 10 minutes away.

Neither Karen nor Monica was academically well prepared for college. Both had good, but not stellar, grades and passable SAT scores, which made admission to a more selective school unlikely. Given the lower cost, ease of admission, and opportunity to commute from home, they might have started at the regional campus. However, MU offered, as Monica's mother put it, a chance to "go away and experience college life." Karen refused to look at any other school because she wanted to leave home. As she noted, "I really don't think I'm a small town girl." Monica's family was betting on MU as the best place for her to launch her dream career as a doctor.

Karen and Monica's stories offer us a glimpse into the college experiences of average, in-state students at large, mid-tier public universities. Though they struggled to gain entrance to the flagship campus, they soon found that the structure of social and academic life there served them poorly—and had deleterious effects.

THE GREAT MISMATCH

Most four-year residential colleges and universities in the United States are designed to serve well-funded students, who have minimal (if any) caretaking responsibilities, and who attend college full-time after they graduate from high school. Yet only a minority of individuals who pursue postsecondary education in the United States fit this profile. There is a great gap between what the vast majority of Americans need and what four-year institutions offer them.

This mismatch is acutely visible at Midwest U, where Karen and Monica started their college careers. Almost half of those attending four-year colleges find themselves at schools like this one. Students from modest backgrounds who have above average, but not exceptional, academic profiles attend state flagship universities because they believe such schools offer a surefire route to economic security.

Public universities were founded to enable mobility, especially among in-state populations of students—which contributes to their legitimacy in the eyes of the public. In an era of declining state funding, schools like Midwest U have raised tuition and recruited more out-of-state students. They especially covet academically accomplished, ambitious children of affluent families.

As sociologist Mitchell Stevens describes in *Creating a Class*, elite institutions also pursue such students. While observing a small, private school, Stevens overheard an admissions officer describe an ideal applicant: "He's got great SATs [and] he's free [not requiring any financial aid]. . . . He helps us in every way that's quantifiable." Once private colleges skim off affluent, high-performing students, large, middle-tier, public universities are left to compete for the tuition dollars of less studious students from wealthy families.

How, we wondered, do in-state students fare in this context? To find out, for over five years we followed a dormitory floor of female students through their college careers and into the workforce, conducted an ethnography of the floor, and interviewed the women and their parents. What we found is that schools like MU only serve a segment of their student body well—affluent, socially-oriented, and out-of-state students—to the detriment of typical in-state students like Karen and Monica.

"I'M SUPPOSED TO GET DRUNK"

Monica and Karen approached the housing application process with little information, and were unprepared for what they encountered when they were assigned to a room in a "party dorm." At MU, over a third of the freshman class is housed in such dorms. Though minimal partying actually took place in the heavily policed residence halls, many residents partied off-site, typically at fraternities, returning in the wee hours drunk and loud. Affluent students—both in and out-of-state—often requested rooms in party dorms, based on the recommendations of their similarly social siblings and friends.

Party dorms are a pipeline to the Greek system, which dominates campus life. Less than 20 percent of the student body at MU is involved in a fraternity or sorority, but these predominately white organizations enjoy a great deal of power. They own space in central campus areas, across from academic buildings and sports arenas. They monopolize the social life of first-year students, offering underage drinkers massive, free supplies of alcohol, with virtual legal impunity. They even enjoy special ties to administrators, with officers sitting on a special advisory board to the dean of students.

Over 40 percent of Monica and Karen's floor joined sororities their first year. The pressure to rush was so intense that one roommate pair who opted out posted a disclaimer on their door, asking people to stop bugging them about it. The entire campus—including academic functions—often revolved around the schedule of Greek life. When a math test for a large, required class conflicted with women's rush, rather than excusing a group of women from a few rush events, the test itself was rescheduled.

Monica, like most economically disadvantaged students, chose not to rush a sorority, discouraged by the mandatory $60 t-shirt, as well as by the costly membership fees. Karen, who was middle class, had just enough funds to make rushing possible. However, she came to realize that Greek houses implicitly screened for social class. She pulled out her boots—practical rain boots that pegged her as a small town, in-state girl instead of an affluent, out-of-state student with money and the right taste in clothing. They were a "dead give-away," she said. She soon dropped out of rush.

Like all but a few students on the 53-person floor, Monica and Karen chose to participate in the party scene. Neither drank much in high school. Nor did they arrive armed with shot glasses or party-themed posters, as some students did. They partied because, as a woman from a similar background put it, "I'm supposed to get drunk every weekend. I'm supposed to go to parties every weekend." With little party experience, and few contacts in the Greek system, Monica and Karen were easy targets for fraternity men's sexual disrespect. Heavy alcohol consumption helped to put them at ease in otherwise uncomfortable situations. "I pretty much became an alcoholic," said Monica. "I was craving alcohol all the time."

Their forced attempts to participate in the party scene showed how poorly it suited their needs. "I tried so hard to fit in with what everybody else was doing here," Monica explained. "I think one morning I just woke up and realized that this isn't me at all; I don't like the way I am right now." She felt it forced her to become more immature. "Growing up to me isn't going out and getting smashed and sleeping around," she lamented. Partying is particularly costly for students of lesser means, who need to grow up sooner, cannot afford to be financially irresponsible, and need the credentials and skills that college offers.

ACADEMIC STRUGGLES AND "EXOTIC" MAJORS

Partying also takes its toll on academic performance, and Monica's poor grades quickly squelched her pre-med dreams. Karen, who hoped to become a teacher, also found it hard to keep up. "I did really bad in that math class, the first elementary ed math class," one of three that were required. Rather than retake the class, Karen changed her major to one that was popular among affluent, socially-oriented students on the floor: sports broadcasting.

She explained, "I'm from a really small town and it's just all I ever really knew was jobs that were around me, and most of those are teachers." A woman on her floor was majoring in sports broadcasting, which Karen had never considered. "I would have never thought about that. And so I saw hers, and I was like that's something that I really like. One of my interests is sports, watching them, playing them," she reasoned. "I could be a sportscaster on ESPN if I really wanted to."

Karen's experience shows the seductive appeal of certain "easy majors." These are occupational and professional programs that are often housed in their own schools and colleges. They are associated with a higher overall GPA and, as sociologists Richard Arum and Josipa Roksa report in *Academically Adrift*, lower levels of learning than majors in the more challenging sciences and humanities housed in colleges of arts and sciences.

In many easy majors, career success also depends on personal characteristics (such as appearance, personality, and aesthetic taste) that are developed outside of the classroom—often prior to entering college. Socially-oriented students flock to fields like communications, fashion, tourism, recreation, fitness, and numerous "business-lite" options, which are often linked to sports or the arts, rather than the competitive business school. About a third of the student body majored in business, management, marketing, communications, journalism, and related subfields.

Karen's switch to sports broadcasting gave her more time to socialize. But education is a more practical major that translates directly into a career; hiring rests largely on the credential. In contrast, success in sports broadcasting is dependent on class-based characteristics—such as family social ties to industry insiders. Several of Karen's wealthier peers secured plum internships in big cities because their parents made phone calls for them; Karen could not even land an unpaid internship with the Triple-A baseball team located 25 minutes from her house.

No one Karen encountered on campus helped her to assess the practicality of a career in this field. Her parents were frustrated that she had been persuaded not to graduate with a recognizable marketable skill. As her mother explained, "She gets down there and you start hearing all these exotic sounding majors. . . . I'm not sure quite what jobs they're going to end up with." Her mother was frustrated that Karen "went to see the advisor to make plans for her sophomore year, and they're going, 'Well, what's your passion?'" Her mother was not impressed. "How

many people do their passion? To me, that's more what you do for a hobby. . . . I mean most people, that's not what their job is."

Halfway through college, when Karen realized she could not get an internship, much less a job, in sports broadcasting, her parents told her to switch back to education. The switch was costly: it was going to take her two more years to complete. As her mother complained, "When you're going through the orientation . . . they're going, 'oh, most people change their major five times.' And they make it sound like it's no big deal. But yeah, they're making big bucks by kids changing."

Leaving Midwest U Behind

Monica left MU after her first year. "I was afraid if I continued down there that I would just go crazy and either not finish school, or get myself in trouble," she explained. "And I just didn't want to do that." She immediately enrolled in a beauty school near her home. Dissatisfied with the income she earned as a hairstylist she later entered a community college to complete an associate degree in nursing. She paid for her nursing classes as she studied, but had 10,000 dollars in student loan debt from her time at MU. Still, her debt burden was substantially smaller than if she had stayed there; some of her MU peers had amassed over 50,000 dollars in loans by graduation.

Because her GPA was too low to return to elementary education at MU, Karen transferred to a regional college during her fourth year. Since the classes she took for sports broadcasting did not fulfill any requirements, it took her six years to graduate. Karen's parents, who reported that they spent the first 10 years of their married life paying off their own loans, took out loans to cover most of the cost, and anticipated spending even longer to finance their daughter's education.

Monica and Karen were not the only ones on their dormitory floor to leave MU. Nine other in-state women, the majority of whom were from working-class or lower-middle-class backgrounds, did as well. The only out-of-state student who transferred left for a higher-ranked institution. While we were concerned that the in-state leavers, most of whom were moving down the ladder of prestige to regional campuses, would suffer, they actually did better than in-state women from less privileged families who stayed at MU. Their GPAs improved, they selected majors with a more direct payoff, and they were happier overall.

The institutions to which women moved played a large role in this transformation. As one leaver described the regional campus to which she transferred, it "doesn't have any fraternities or sororities. It only has, like, 10 buildings." But, she said, "I just really love it." One of the things she loved was that nobody cared about partying. "They're there just to graduate and get through." It prioritized the needs of a different type of student: "Kids who have lower social economic status, who work for their school."

Without the social pressures of MU, it was possible to, as Karen put it, "get away from going out all the time, and refocus on what my goal was for this part of my life." Few majors like sports broadcasting and fashion merchandising were available, reducing the possible ways to go astray academically. Those who attended regional or community colleges trained to become accountants, teachers, social workers, nurses or other health professionals. At the conclusion of our study, they had better employment prospects than those from similar backgrounds who stayed at MU.

THE IMPORTANCE OF INSTITUTIONAL CONTEXT

It is tempting to assume that academic success is determined, in large part, by what students bring with them—different ability levels, resources, and orientations to college life. But Monica and Karen's stories demonstrate that what students get out of college is also organizationally produced. Students who were far more academically gifted than Monica or Karen sometimes floundered at

MU, while others who were considerably less motivated breezed through college. The best predictor of success was whether there was a good fit between a given student's resources and agendas, and the structure of the university.

Monica and Karen's struggles at MU can be attributed, in part, to the dominance of a "party pathway" at that institution. These organizational arrangements—a robust, university-supported Greek system, and an array of easy majors—are designed to attract and serve affluent socially-oriented students. The party pathway is not a hard sell; the idea that college is about fun and partying is celebrated in popular culture and actively promoted by leisure and alcohol industries. The problem is that this pathway often appeals to students for whom it is ill suited.

Regardless of what they might want, students from different class backgrounds require different things. What Monica and Karen needed was a "mobility pathway." When resources are limited, mistakes—whether a semester of grades lost to partying, or courses that do not count toward a credential—can be very costly. Monica and Karen needed every course to move them toward a degree that would translate directly into a job.

They also needed more financial aid than they received—grants, not loans—and much better advising. A skilled advisor who understood Karen's background and her abilities might have helped her realize that changing majors was a bad idea. But while most public universities provide such advising support for disadvantaged students, these programs are often small, and admit only the best and brightest of the disadvantaged—not run-of-the-mill students like Monica and Karen.

Monica, Karen, and others like them did not find a mobility pathway at MU. Since university resources are finite, catering to one population of students often comes at a cost to others, especially if their needs are at odds with one another. When a party pathway is the most accessible avenue through a university, it is easy to stumble upon, hard to avoid, and it crowds out other pathways.

As Monica and Karen's stories suggest, students are not necessarily better served by attending the most selective college they can get into. The structure of the pathways available at a given school greatly influences success. When selecting a college or university, families should consider much more than institutional selectivity. They should also assess whether the school fits the particular student's needs.

Students and parents with limited financial resources should look for schools with high retention rates among minority and first-generation students, where there are large and accessible student services for these populations. Visible Greek systems and reputations as party schools, in contrast, should be red flags.

Families should investigate what majors are available, whether they require prerequisites, and, to the extent it is possible, what additional investments are required to translate a particular major into a job. Are internships required? Will the school link the student to job opportunities, or are families expected to do so on their own? These are some questions they should ask.

Collectively, the priorities of public universities and other higher education institutions that support "party pathways" should be challenged. Reducing the number of easy majors, pulling university support from the Greek system, and expanding academic advising for less privileged students would help. At federal and state levels, greater commitment to the funding of higher education is necessary. If public universities are forced to rely on tuition and donations for funding, they will continue to appeal to those who can pay full freight. Without these changes, the mismatch between what universities offer and what most postsecondary students need is likely to continue.

RECOMMENDED RESOURCES

[Editors' Note: No references were provided for this article; however, the authors recommend the following for further research into the subject.]

Arum, Richard, and Josipa Roksa. *Academically Adrift: Limited Learning on College Campuses* (University of Chicago Press, 2011). Uses survey data from 24 institutions to offer an evaluation of what students are really learning during their time at college.

Bowen, William G., Matthew M. Chingos, and Michael S. McPherson. *Crossing the Finish Line: Completing College at America's Public Universities* (Princeton University Press, 2009). Offers a systematic analysis of the factors shaping college completion at American public universities.

Brint, Steven (ed.). *The Future of the City of Intellect: The Changing American University* (Stanford University Press, 2002). Provides an assessment of how postsecondary education is changing, the forces behind such change, and the future prospects for the sector from top scholars of higher education.

Deil-Amen, Regina. "The 'Traditional' College Student: A Smaller and Smaller Minority and Its Implications for Diversity and Access Institutions," paper prepared for the Mapping Broad-Access Higher Education conference (2011). Available online at cepa.stanford.edu. Discusses the diverse group of non-traditional college students who are marginalized despite forming a majority of the college-going population.

Stevens, Mitchell. *Creating a Class: College Admissions and the Education of Elites* (Harvard University Press, 2007). Provides an inside perspective on how admissions officers at elite private colleges construct an incoming class.

Stuber, Jenny. *Inside the College Gates: How Class and Culture Matter in Higher Education* (Lexington Books, 2011). Offers a comparison of how college social life and extracurricular activities contribute to social class inequities at a large public and small private institution.

READING 43

No Margin for Error

Educational and Occupational Achievement Among Disadvantaged Children of Immigrants

Alejandro Portes and Patricia Fernández-Kelly

This reading by Alejandro Portes and Patricia Fernández-Kelly provides a deep look into the background conditions of immigrant children that facilitate achievement in higher education. From their sample of 5,262 immigrant children who grew up in very disadvantaged conditions, they identified 50 individuals who went on to achieve a college degree or degrees. While this is a small percentage (less than 1%) of their original sample, they argue that understanding what factors influenced these individuals to achieve is important. In this reading, Portes and Fernández-Kelly use what they call the segmented assimilation theory to examine what features of four individuals' lives may have taken them on a different trajectory. They focus on three major factors: (1) human capital in the form of skills and education that their families brought with them from their home countries; (2) how they and their families are incorporated into their new culture by the government, society, and the community; and (3) the structure of their immigrant families.

Questions to consider for this reading:

1. How does having human capital help individuals to achieve higher levels of education? Do you think this could be true for nonimmigrants as well, such as in the previous reading about Monica and Karen?

2. What do the authors mean by "modes of incorporation"? Give examples from the reading.

3. If you were a policy maker or person in a powerful role in your community, what changes would you make to ensure the successful college completion of disadvantaged youth?

Immigration since the 1960s has transformed the United States. Today, close to one-fourth of the American population is of immigrant stock—immigrants themselves or children of immigrants. The same rough proportion holds among young Americans, aged 18 or younger. Children of immigrants and immigrant children exceed 30 million and are, by far, the fastest growing component of this population. Hence, their destiny as they reach adulthood and seek to

From "No Margin for Error: Educational and Occupational Achievement Among Disadvantaged Children of Immigrants," by A. Portes and P. Fernández-Kelly, 2008, *The ANNALS of the American Academy of Political and Social Science, 620*(1), pp. 12–36. Copyright 2008 by Sage Publications. Reprinted with permission.

integrate socially and economically into the mainstream is of more than academic interest.

Past research into this bourgeoning population has shown that a conventional assimilation model based on a unilinear process of acculturation followed by social and economic ascent and integration does not work well in depicting what takes place on the ground. Instead, several distinct paths of adaptation have been identified, some of which lead upwards as portrayed by the conventional assimilation model; other paths, however, lead in the opposite direction, compounding the spectacle of poverty, drugs, and gangs in the nation's cities. *Segmented assimilation* is the concept coined to refer to these realities. This alternative model has both charted the main alternative path of contemporary second generation adaptation and identified the main forces at play in that process ([Portes & Rumbaut, 2006]; Portes & Zhou, 1992; Zhou & Bankston, 1998).

Specifically, three major factors have been identified: the human capital that immigrant parents bring with them, the social context in which they are received in America, and the composition of the immigrant family. Human capital, operationally identified with formal education and occupational skills, translates into competitiveness in the host labor market and the potential for achieving desirable positions in the American hierarchies of status and wealth. The transformation of this potential into reality depends, however, on the context into which immigrants are incorporated. A receptive or at least neutral reception by government authorities, a sympathetic or at least not hostile reception by the native population, and the existence of social networks with well-established coethnics pave the ground for putting to use whatever credentials and skills have been brought from abroad. Conversely, a hostile reception by authorities and the public and a weak or nonexistent coethnic community handicap immigrants and make it difficult for them to translate their human capital into commensurate occupations or to acquire new occupational skills. The mode of incorporation is the concept used in the literature

to refer to these tripartite (government/society/community) differences in the contexts that receive newcomers ([Hirschman, 2001]; Portes & Rumbaut, 2001, chap. 3).

Lastly, the structure of the immigrant family has also proved to be highly significant in determining second generation outcomes. Parents who stay together and extended families where grandparents and older siblings play a role in motivating and controlling adolescents, keeping them away from the lure of gangs and drugs, play a significant role in promoting upward assimilation. Single-parent families experiencing conflicting demands and unable to provide children with proper supervision have exactly the opposite effect (Fernández-Kelly & Konczal, 2005; [Portes, Fernández-Kelly, & Haller, 2005]).

* * *

Research Questions

Sociology deals with social facts, expressed in rates or averages, rather than with individuals. There are times, however, when the study of individual cases can say something important about how social outcomes come to be or how they can be modified. Segmented assimilation in the second generation offers a case in point. The structural forces leading to alternative paths of adaptation are clear and have been well documented. Yet, not all children advantaged by their parents' human capital, favorable contexts of reception, and stable families manage to succeed educationally, and not all growing up under conditions of severe disadvantage end up in permanent poverty or in jail. Some among the latter even make it to the top, achieving a college degree and moving into the professions. Those individual cases have sociological significance for the lessons they offer in how to overcome the power of structural forces. Put differently, exceptions and outliers are important insofar as they point to alternative social processes obscured in sample averages that, when present, can lead to unforeseen outcomes.[1] . . .

First Narrative:
Miguel Morales, Mexican,
Aged Twenty-Eight, San Diego

Miguel was born and grew up in Inglewood, a working-class neighborhood close to South Central Los Angeles.[2] His mother has a seventh-grade education and never worked after marriage. His father has a fourth-grade education and, for most of his adult life, has worked as a food preparer in the kitchen of the Los Angeles Airport Hyatt Hotel. Miguel has a B.S. with honors in physics from the University of California, San Diego (UCSD), and a master's in physics from San Diego State University. He will soon join a PhD program in computational science at Claremont. His strength is math. He works as a high school and junior college instructor in math and physics.

Miguel's parents were born in rural Mexico, met and married in Tijuana, and managed to obtain legal U.S. residence through family ties. In Inglewood, Miguel grew up in a sheltered, Spanish-only community. Although born in the United States, he did not speak English when entering elementary school and suffered accordingly. On the other hand, his father was so committed to his son's education that he spent a third of his meager salary on tuition so that Miguel could attend a Catholic grammar school. The child eventually overcame his language deficit and started to get good grades.

Not only was Inglewood a Mexican cultural enclave, but the parents did not tolerate anything that escaped their reach. No sleepovers, no strange friends. Miguel Sr. took his sons everywhere he went. When Miguel rebelled in early adolescence, wanting to wear baggy clothes, he had a serious encounter with his dad's belt. Later on, at age eighteen, he tried to sneak out of the house through a window to attend a party, only to be physically dragged back into the house by his father.

This kind of isolation and discipline focused Miguel's attention on his studies but also left him woefully unprepared to cope with the world outside. He successfully completed his studies at St. Joseph's School and transferred to Stanley Junior High. The confrontation with the multi-ethnic environment of a public school and the embarrassment of having to take showers naked in front of others in the gym proved too much for the Mexican Catholic boy. He begged his father to pull him out. Miguel Sr. agreed. He sold his van, his only possession of value outside of the house, so that his son could attend South Port Christian Academy in National City.

By then, the family had moved to San Diego to be closer to relatives on the other side of the border. After completing junior high, Miguel moved to Point Loma High School, close to La Jolla, a school frequented mostly by children of affluent white families. He was the only Mexican taking advanced courses at Point Loma, and he succeeded in graduating with As and Bs. Through AVID (Achievement via Individual Determination), a program designed to facilitate admittance to college for poor minority students, he gained access to several summer internships doing research in biochemistry at the University of California, San Diego (UCSD), under a faculty member. That was the single most important experience of his high school days and oriented him decisively toward medical school.

After high school, he was admitted to UCSD, sponsored, among others, by Percy Russell, dean of UCSD's Medical School. An African American, Russell was an active supporter of AVID and organized the summer internship program in which Miguel took part. At UCSD, Miguel accumulated a 3.7 GPA in the sciences and an overall 3.5 GPA, graduating with honors. In his junior year, he shifted his major to physics. Before leaving UCSD, Miguel became an AVID tutor teaching other minority students in nearby high schools.

After receiving his B.S., Miguel went straight for his master's at San Diego State. As a high school and junior college physics instructor, he earns $67,000 a year. Despite his high income, he is determined to join a doctoral program in computational sciences in the fall. He lives on his own, but several times a week he visits his parents' home, where the interview was conducted, with Miguel Sr. arriving just as the conversation was about to end. Having told his life history, our respondent turned toward his father and told him, "*Gracias, Papa, porque me disciplinaste; me enseñaste bien.*" ("Thanks, Dad, because you disciplined me; you educated me well.")

STERN FAMILIES; SELECTIVE ACCULTURATION

The childrearing and educational psychology literatures in the United States have converged in preaching to parents a tolerant, patient, nonauthoritative attitude toward their offspring and in promoting openness to new experiences and intensive socializing among the young.[3] In parallel fashion, schools and other mainstream institutions pressure immigrants and their children to acculturate as fast as possible, viewing their full Americanization as a step toward economic mobility and social acceptance.

A recurring theme in our interviews was the presence of stern parental figures who controlled, if not suppressed, extensive external contacts and who sought to preserve the cultural and linguistic traditions in which they themselves were reared. Talking back to such parents is not an option, and physical punishment is a distinct possibility when parental authority is challenged. These family environments have the effect of isolating children from much of what goes on in the outside world; they are expected to go to school and return home with few distractions in between. While such rearing practices will be surely frowned upon by many educational psychologists, they have the effect of protecting children from the perils of street life in their immediate surroundings and of keeping them in touch with their cultural roots.

In other words, while freedom to explore and tolerant parental attitudes may work well in protected suburban environments, they do not have the same effect in poor urban neighborhoods where what there is to "explore" is frequently linked to the presence of gangs and drugs. Furthermore, and contrary to conventional wisdom, full Americanization has the effect of disconnecting youth from their parents and depriving them of a cultural reference point on which to ground their sense of self and their personal dignity. As we shall see, this reference point is also an important component of success stories.

Maintenance of parental authority and strong family discipline has the effect of inducing *selective acculturation*, as opposed to the full-barreled variety advocated by public schools and other mainstream institutions. Selective acculturation combines learning of English and American ways with preservation of key elements of the parental culture, including language. Previous studies based on CILS [the Children of Immigrants Longitudinal Study] show that fluent bilingualism is significantly associated with positive outcomes in late adolescence, including higher school grades, higher educational aspirations, higher self-esteem, and lesser intergenerational conflict (Portes & Rumbaut, 2001, chaps. 6, 9; Portes & Rumbaut, 2006, chap. 8). CILS-IV interviews confirm this result, indicating that instances of success-out-of-disadvantage are almost invariably undergirded by strong parental controls, which leads to selective acculturation. By early adulthood, young people like Miguel Morales can recognize the benefits of such practices and thank their parents, in their parents' own language, for having educated them well.

Second Narrative: Raquel Torres, Mexican, Aged Twenty-Nine, San Diego

Raquel is the oldest daughter of a Mexican couple that emigrated illegally to San Diego after living for years in Tijuana. Her mother has a ninth-grade education and did not work outside the home while her three children were growing up; her father has a sixth-grade education. While living in Tijuana, he commuted to San Diego to work as a waiter. At some point, his commuter permit was confiscated and the family decided to sneak across the border. They settled in National City, a poor and mostly Mexican neighborhood where Raquel grew up monolingual in Spanish. As a result of her limited English fluency, she had problems at El Toyon Elementary, but she was enrolled in a bilingual training program where children were pulled out of classes for intensive English training. "My teachers were wonderful," she says.

It was while attending elementary school that she realized how poor her family was. She wanted jeans, tennis shoes, and popular toys that she saw other children have, but her parents said no, stating that they did not have the money. On the other hand, discipline at home was stern: "My parents, they brought us up very strict, very traditional, there was no argument; you just got the look and knew better than to insist." In middle school, she made contact with the AVID program. While she was still struggling with English, AVID provided her with a college student tutor and took her on field trips to San Diego State University: "It was a fabulous field trip; we were paired up with other students and sat in class. Mine was on biology. Still, I hadn't thought of going to college."

The decisive moment came in her first year at Sweetwater Senior High in National City after she enrolled in Mr. Carranza's French class. Carranza, a Mexican American himself and a Vietnam veteran, took a keen interest in his students: "I mean, it wasn't so much the French that he taught, but he would also bring Chicano poetry, and within the first month, I remember he asked me, 'Where are you going to college?'" At Open House that year, Carranza took her mother aside, "Usted sabe que su hija es muy inteligente?" (Do you know that your daughter is very intelligent?) "De veras, mi hija?" (Really, my daughter?), asked the mother. "Yes," the teacher replied, "she can go to college." "All of a sudden, everything made sense to me; I was going to college."

Raquel graduated with a 3.5 GPA from Sweetwater and applied and was admitted at UCSD. At the time, her family had moved to Las Vegas in search of better work, but Raquel wanted to be on her own. She had clearly outgrown parents who, at this time, had started to become an obstacle. "When I was studying late at night in senior high, my mother would come and turn off the light. She would say, 'Go to sleep, you'll go blind reading so much.'" Raquel entered UCSD in the last year of the Affirmative Action Program in California. While she was criticized by several fellow students for getting an unfair advantage, she strongly defended the program: "Without Affirmative Action, I probably would not have made it into UCSD. Besides, the program made me work harder. Other students took their education for granted and didn't study as much, instead going to parties and fooling around."

Raquel graduated from UCSD with a 3.02 GPA and immediately went for a master's degree in education at San Diego State. After graduating, she took a job as a counselor in the Barrio Logan College Institute, a private organization helping minority students like herself attend college. She is planning to enroll in a doctoral program in education. Her advice to immigrant students: "Stop making excuses; there's always going to be family drama, there's always gonna be many issues. But it's what you want to do that matters."

REALLY SIGNIFICANT OTHERS; OUTSIDE HELP

Despite these "where there's a will, there's a way" parting words, it is clear that Raquel moved ahead by receiving assistance in multiple ways. First, the same strict upbringing that we saw in the case of Miguel Morales kept her out of trouble, although it set her back in English. Her own selective acculturation had to be nudged along by those "wonderful" language teachers at El Toyon Elementary. Then, like Morales, she encountered the AVID program, which provided her with personalized educational assistance and the first inklings of what college life would be like. Finally, she encountered Carranza and her future took a decisive turn. The French teacher went beyond motivating her to recruiting her mother to support Raquel's new aspirations. Stern immigrant parents may instill discipline and self-control in their children, but they are often helpless in the face of school bureaucracies and can even become an obstacle.

A constant in our interviews, in addition to authoritative, alert parents, is the appearance of a *really* significant other. That person can be a teacher, a counselor, a friend of the family, or even an older sibling. The important thing is that they take a keen interest in the child, motivate him or her to graduate from high school and to attend college, and possess the necessary knowledge and experience to guide the student in the right direction. Neither family discipline nor the appearance of a significant other is by itself sufficient to produce high educational attainment, but their *combination* is decisive.

The second element that Raquel's story illustrates is the important role of organized programs sponsored by nonprofits to assist disadvantaged students. Whether it is AVID; the PREUSS Program, also organized by UCSD; Latinas Unidas; the Barrio Logan College Institute; or other philanthropic groups, such organizations can play a key supplementary role by conveying information that parents do not possess: how to fill out a college application, how to prepare for SATs and when to take them, how to present oneself in interviews, how college campuses look and what college life is like, and so on. The creation and support of such programs is within the power of external actors and can be strengthened by policy. While the character of family life or the emergence of a significant other is largely in the private realm, the presence and effectiveness of special assistance programs for minority students is a public matter, amenable to policy intervention. The programs and organizations that proved effective were grounded, invariably, in knowledge of the culture and language that the children brought to school and in respect for them. They are commonly staffed by coethnics or bilingual staff.

Unlike the full assimilation approach emphasized by public school personnel, these programs convey the message that it is not necessary to reject one's own culture and history to do well in school. On the contrary, such roots can provide the necessary point of reference to strengthen the children's self-esteem and aspirations for the future. In this sense, programs like AVID both depend on and promote selective acculturation as the best path toward educational achievement.

Third Narrative:
Martin Lacayo, Nicaraguan,
Aged Twenty-Nine, Miami

Martin's mother, Violeta, was a businesswoman in her native Nicaragua until the Sandinista regime confiscated her properties. His father was a professional and, for a time, mayor of the city of Jinotega. The Sandinistas jailed him as a counterrevolutionary, and he left prison a broken man. When Violeta made the decision to leave the country to escape the conscription of her sons in the Sandinista army, Martin's father refused to leave. Violeta managed to send her two oldest sons to Miami to the care of relatives. She then used her savings to buy tickets to Mexico City for Martin, her younger daughter, and herself. They then traveled by land to the border and crossed illegally with the help of two *coyotes* (smugglers).

Arriving in Miami, they found themselves without money, without knowledge of the language, and without access to government help because of their illegal status. To survive, Violeta started cleaning houses for wealthy Cuban families. She rented an apartment in the modest suburb of Sweetwater, and Martin enrolled in the local junior high school. Having studied at the private Catholic La Salle School in Jinotega, he found the *One Potato, Two Potato* book he was assigned to read offensive. "It seemed that the teacher wanted us all to go work at the Burger King," Martin said.

At Sweetwater Junior High, he finally came under the protection of Mrs. Robinson, an

African American teacher who took an interest in the boy. She managed to have him receive a "Student of the Week" award, and his picture was displayed prominently in the school's office. That meant the world to Martin, who had never received any distinction in the United States. Eventually, the family regularized its legal status under the NACARA law, engineered by Miami Cuban American congressmen for the benefit of Nicaraguan refugees. Violeta found a job as a janitor at Florida International University and combined it with her private maid service. The family's economic situation improved, although Violeta never rose above the status of a janitor and her husband never rejoined her.

Martin venerates his mother for the strength and decisiveness that she displayed in those difficult years and for her unwavering support of her children. After the family moved to a better part of town, he attended Ruben Darío Senior High School where he excelled, graduating with honors and immediately enrolling at the University of Miami. There, he completed a bachelor's degree in economics and accounting. He currently works as an accountant for Merrill Lynch and has just bought a luxury condominium in Miami Beach.

THE IMPORTANCE OF CULTURAL CAPITAL

Aside from the elements already noted, the most important feature illustrated by Martin Lacayo's story is the transferability of social class assets and their use in overcoming extremely trying conditions. The son of separated parents, with a cleaning woman as a mother, and living as an illegal migrant, Martin still managed to avoid the lures of gangs and street life, stayed in school, graduated from high school, and then swiftly completed his college education.

The La Salle School that he attended as a young child and the memory of the middle-class life that he and his brother[s] enjoyed before escaping to Miami provided key points of reference as he confronted poverty and the prospect of going no further than a fast-food job. He knew the meaning of the dull books put in the hands of limited-English students in public school and set his sights on escaping that environment. His mother not only supported him in that goal but also never allowed him to forget his family's origins. She could be a cleaning woman in Miami, but she remained, despite appearances, an educated, middle-class person.

A recurrent theme in our interviews is the importance of a respectable past, real or imaginary, in the country of origin. Parents repeat stories of who they or their ancestors "really were" as a way to sustain their dignity despite present circumstances. Children exposed to such family stories often internalize them, using them as a spur to achievement. We heard references to uncles and grandparents who were "doctors" or "professors" in Mexico, to ancestors who were "landowners in California and put down an Indian rebellion," and to parents who were high government officials before having to leave to escape political persecution. . . .

The "cultural capital" (Bourdieu, 1979, 1985) brought from the home country has actually two components. The first is the motivational force to restore family pride and status. Regardless of whether the achievements of the past are real or imaginary, they can still serve as a means to instill high aspirations among the young. The second is the "know-how" that immigrants who come from the upper or middle classes possess. This know-how consists of information, values, and demeanor that migrants from more modest origins do not have. Regardless of how difficult present circumstances are, formerly middle-class parents have a clear sense of who they are, knowledge of the possible means to overcome difficult situations, and the right attitude when opportunities arise. These two dimensions of cultural capital converge in cases like Martin Lacayo's where both family lore and the *habitus* of past middle-class life are decisive in helping second-generation youth overcome seemingly insurmountable obstacles. . . .

Fourth Narrative: Ovidio Cardenas, PhD; Cuban, Aged Twenty-Eight, Stanford, California

Ovidio Cardenas's family came from Cuba during the chaotic Mariel exodus of 1980 and settled in Union City, New Jersey. He was a young child then and barely remembers life in Cuba. His mother promptly separated from her wayward husband and eventually moved to Florida, settling with her son in the working-class city of Hialeah, next to Miami. With a grade-level education, she could not go far and eventually settled for a job as a seamstress in a local factory. She eventually remarried another Cuban man who worked as a janitor.

Ovidio attended public schools in Hialeah, some of the worst in Miami. Gang fights, the open sale of drugs, and a prison-like environment at school were everyday experiences. "Most students were lazy. I was different because my mom and stepdad drilled into me the idea that I should not end up like them." The parents worked long hours, often at two jobs. The stepfather was a strict, traditional Cuban man who spoke little but strongly supported Ovidio in his studies. At Hialeah High, an English teacher, a white American woman, also made a deep impression on the young man. She conveyed to him the fact that "Hialeah was not the world" and eventually took time to work with him on his college applications and personal statement.

Ovidio focused on the sciences, especially biology, and graduated with a near-perfect GPA. He was one of the few among his graduating class at Hialeah High to go on to college and the only one to gain admission to an Ivy League institution. He was seriously depressed during his first days at Cornell. Hialeah may not have been the world, but it was the only world that he knew. He felt himself torn from his roots and certain that he would fail. He even attempted suicide on one occasion. After that event, somehow Ovidio pulled himself together and focused on his work. "All I did was study, morning, afternoon, and night. No sports, little recreation." After four years, he graduated from Cornell with a major in biology with honors and was admitted to Johns Hopkins Medical School. Originally, motivated by the suffering of his grandmother who died of cancer, he wanted to be a doctor. Eventually, however, he shifted to the biological sciences and, after completing his dissertation research, received his PhD in cellular and molecular biology. He is currently a postdoctoral fellow at Stanford Medical School.

Ovidio's career aspiration is to pursue research on leukemia at a private lab and eventually make a contribution to eradicate that disease. He also wants to help "Hispanics" (meaning young Hialeah Cubans) improve their education and their careers, but he does not know quite how. A devout Catholic, he makes sizable donations to the church. He is single, but he lives with a partner, also a PhD student.

Ovidio's advice to young Hispanics: "Stay focused; education is everything." He does not agree, however, that in life you get what you deserve: "There is too much variation in the situations surrounding people; some good people face dire problems and many who don't deserve success prosper." Another of his projects is to complete his family tree through genealogical research on his ancestors in Cuba. His mother never tired of telling him that his family had deep roots and that her ancestors had been among the founders of the city of Cardenas, which was named after them.

THE MOTIVATING FEAR OF FAILURE

The story of Ovidio Cardenas is included here for several reasons. First, he is arguably the most successful member of our disadvantage-to-achievement sample, having reached the doctorate and attained a substantial income before age thirty. Second, his case summarizes all the themes explored previously: traditional authoritative parenting, a really significant other encountered in adolescence, and a cultural memory from the home country on which to base his self-esteem and reinforce ambition. While Ovidio has never been back to Cuba, his sense of self is inextricably linked to the hometown that he barely remembers from his early childhood. He plans to return to the ancestral land to complete the family tree to establish firmly who his ancestors were.

The new dimension illustrated by this story is a final theme common to many respondents: fear of remaining in the same class position as parents. Along with stern discipline, immigrant parents often dispense the advice that education is the only way to rise above the menial jobs, long hours, and modest housing that has been their own fate—a message that youth absorb. While it can lead to downward assimilation among those dropping out of school and seeking alternatives to poverty in deviant activities, a more common result is to spur youngsters to higher achievement. Theirs is a *defensive success* that owes as much to personal ability as to rejection of their present status.

Thus, if memories of a real or imagined exalted past in the home country lead *proactively* to higher ambition and effort, fear of stagnating into the lower classes strengthens resolve *reactively*. Both mechanisms are privy to the internal dynamics of immigrant families and, hence, less amenable to external intervention than others noted previously.

* * *

CONCLUSION

While our interviews raised additional themes showing the complexity and diversity of individual adaptation paths, the cases highlighted above represent common threads running through the lives of successful young men and women who faced daunting obstacles as children. Given the smallness of the sample and the retroactive character of our interviews, the causal factors identified by the study can be read as hypotheses in need of further validation.

As noted earlier, several of the factors identified are internal to immigrant families and, hence, not readily amenable to external intervention. The presence of authoritative parents capable of controlling

children and protecting them from outside perils; the existence of family retrospectives and middle-class cultural capital brought from the home country; the motivational messages that parents transmit to children; and the number, order, and gender of siblings are all dimensions about which little can be done from the outside.

On the other hand, organized voluntary programs to assist and inform minority students in inner-city schools, the presence of teachers and counselors who take a direct interest in these children and drive them to pursue their studies, and the availability of community colleges that provide skills for decent employment and serve as stepping stones to four-year institutions are all factors that can be strengthened by policy, including incentive schedules for school personnel and financial support for effective outside programs.

Finally, even with the best-intentioned policies and the most effective interventions in place, not all immigrant children who grew up in conditions of severe disadvantage will make it to college. Even fewer will repeat Ovidio Cardenas's feat of converting a Hialeah High education into an entrance ramp for an Ivy League degree. In addition to helping other exceptional students follow the path of these high achievers, it is necessary to understand and address the needs of others not so motivated and not so gifted. A good vocational education, such as that dispensed by many community colleges, is probably the most feasible path for immigrant youths who may manage to avoid downward assimilation but who lack the skills or drive for a university degree. We suspect that the average educational achievement registered by the CILS sample in our last survey—fourteen years—is indicative that this path has been the one followed by a large number of immigrant children.

NOTES

1. This is a clear case of "sampling on the dependent variable," a research strategy adopted deliberately in this case. Results of this exercise cannot be

used to "test" particular propositions but can be valuable in suggesting patterns and relationships testable in future studies.

2. Most of the names of persons in this article are fictitious.

3. The educational and social psychological literatures on this point are too extensive to cite. They start with followers of various brands of psychoanalysis, such as Bettelheim, Fromm, Erikson, and Redl and Wineman, and culminate in a veritable library of practical, how-to books addressed to parents. See Bettelheim (1955), Erikson (1959), Fromm (1945), and Redl and Wineman (1951). For an example of a recent practical guide, see P. Portes (1995).

REFERENCES

Bettelheim, B. (1955). *Paul and Mary: Two case studies of truants from life*. Garden City, NY: Anchor Books.

Bourdieu, P. (1979). Les trois etats du capital culturel. *Actes de la Recherche en Sciences Sociales, 30* (novembre), 3–6.

Bourdieu, P. (1985). The forms of capital. In J. G. Richardson (Ed.), *Handbook of theory and research for the sociology of education* (pp. 241–258). New York: Greenwood.

Erikson, E. (1959). *Childhood and society*. New York: Free Press.

Fernández-Kelly, P., & Konczal, L. (2005). "Murdering the alphabet": Identity and entrepreneurship among second generation Cubans, West Indians, and Central Americans. *Ethnic and Racial Studies, 28*(6), 1153–1181.

Fromm, E. (1945). *Escape from freedom*. New York: Free Press.

Hirschman, C. (2001). The educational enrollment of immigrant youth: A test of the segmented assimilation hypothesis. *Demography, 38*(3), 317–336.

Portes, A., Fernández-Kelly, P., & Haller, P. (2005). Segmented assimilation on the ground: The new second generation in early adulthood. *Ethnic and Racial Studies, 28*(6), 1000–1040.

Portes, A., & Rumbaut, R. G. (2001). *Legacies: The story of the immigrant second generation*. Berkeley: University of California Press and Russell Sage Foundation.

Portes, A., & Rumbaut, R. G. (2006). *Immigrant America: A portrait* (3rd ed.). Berkeley: University of California Press.

Portes, A., & Zhou, M. (1992). Gaining the upper hand: Economic mobility among immigrant and domestic minorities. *Ethnic and Racial Studies, 15*(4), 491–522.

Portes, P. (1995). *Making kids smarter*. Louisville, KY: Butler Books.

Redl, F., & Wineman, D. (1951). *Children who hate*. New York: Free Press.

Zhou, M., & Bankston, C. (1998). *Growing up American: How Vietnamese immigrants adapt to life in the United States*. New York: Russell Sage Foundation.

Bologna Beyond 2010

Looking Backward, Looking Forward

Fiona Hunter

This reading by Fiona Hunter provides a brief look into the changes in higher education that are being made across European countries. The Bologna Process, begun in 1999, had barely gotten off the ground when she wrote this in 2010. However, member countries are cooperating in accepting degrees and higher education credits from other member countries and applying strict standards and assessment criteria to build a solid system of higher education across Europe. The Bologna Process likely will have an impact on higher education around the world. This reading reviews some of the changes that have already been implemented and some changes yet to come. In addition, we include a list of websites from this article for future exploration of the topic. Although this is a little old, Hunter provides an excellent overview of the changes in higher education in Europe.

Questions to consider for this reading:

1. What is the Bologna Process, and what are the advantages to European countries who participate in the agreement?

2. What are the advantages to individuals who attend college under this system?

3. How might the Bologna Process impact higher education in other countries?

A couple of years ago, I was discussing the Bologna Process and what it would be like in 2010, "when we would all wake up one cold January morning and discover life in the brand new European Higher Education Area (EHEA)." That morning has arrived (and it is cold) and since the word January comes from Janus, the two-headed Roman god of beginnings and endings, it seems an appropriate moment to look back to what has been achieved and look forward to what still lies ahead.

A Quick Reminder

Let's remind ourselves quickly about how the Bologna Process came about in 1999 when higher education systems all over Europe were struggling to modernize in response to a changing environment. Shared problems called for shared solutions, and the Bologna Process developed into an unprecedented landmark reform with 10 action lines and a 2010 deadline to restructure and harmonize historically diverse systems. The

From "Bologna Beyond 2010: Looking Backward, Looking Forward," by F. Hunter, 2010, *International Educator, 19*(2), pp. 60–63. Copyright 2010 by NAFSA: Association of International Educators. Reprinted with permission.

29 signatory countries became 46, representing 5,600 institutions and 31 million students.

The main goal of the Bologna Process is to establish the European Higher Education Area (EHEA) and to promote the European system of higher education worldwide through tools that enhance the employability and mobility of people and boost global attractiveness. While it was undoubtedly inspired by the Erasmus experience[1] of interuniversity cooperation, it also introduced the idea of competition in the very early stages, a reality that still sits uncomfortably in many university environments.

GLOBAL BOLOGNA

While the principal focus in the beginning was on the internal dimension and putting the European house in order, the Bologna Process has very quickly acquired an important external dimension as other countries across the world have taken a strong interest in the European response. International competitiveness is now accompanied by international dialogue and connections to other world regions.

The Bologna Process has given an identity to European higher education, although that identity may not yet be completely formed or understood, and to that end, a new information and promotion strategy is currently being developed to communicate Bologna outside the EHEA both for the purposes of cooperation and competition.

The growing interest in Bologna worldwide has also led to the creation of a global policy dialogue that took place back to back with the 2009 ministerial meeting in Leuven/Louvain-La-Neuve in Belgium. It included 15 countries from all over the world that gathered to discuss the effects of Bologna in their countries as well as the broader role and identity of higher education in the new environment: Australia, Brazil, Canada, China, Egypt, Ethiopia, Israel, Japan, Kazakhstan, Kyrgyzstan, Mexico, Morocco, New Zealand, Tunisia, and the United States. The dialogue will continue . . .

In many ways, the Bologna Process is offering new instruments and models for other world regions seeking collaborative agreements and solutions. If Erasmus has been hailed as the most successful European initiative ever, the Bologna Process has achieved in 10 years what many national governments failed to achieve in decades, a policy for reform and a framework of reference, that is now not only transforming European higher education but is having tangible impacts beyond its own borders.

The domino effect of reform in the different countries has been activated by the mechanisms of this voluntary intergovernmental agreement. The reform process is driven by the different stakeholder groups and structured via communiques announced at biannual ministerial meetings where results of the previous period are evaluated and priorities for the next two years set. The priorities are transformed into national reform and implemented by the institutions but it is essential to remember that this happens in different ways and at different speeds in each of the signatory countries and individual institutions will interpret and implement the reform according to their capacity and ambition. As has been said many times before, it is a process of harmonization not homogenization.

MASSIVE CHANGES

There can be no doubt that there have been massive changes and the most important to date has been structural reform. European higher education has converged into three cycles—bachelor's, master's, and doctoral degrees—but with diversification in length of study. Bachelor's degrees last between three and four years, master's between one and two years, and doctoral studies between three and four years.

The European Credit Transfer System (ECTS) has not only been adopted as the standard but has since been linked to learning outcomes, which have been collaboratively developed to create a common language and frame of reference at the level of both cycles and disciplines. Learning outcomes do not sound particularly exciting or powerful, but they have the potential to revolutionize the way in which universities organize educational delivery as well as bring greater transparency, recognition and flexibility across the Bologna agenda. They transform approaches to curricular design and assessment, provide building blocks for qualifications frameworks and transmit valuable information to employers or professional bodies. They act as a tool for greater integration across the sectors in lifelong learning and make an important contribution to mobility both for study and employment purposes. Credits and learning outcomes are key tools for the development of student-centered learning, which has the potential to revolutionize the way in which universities organize educational delivery.

The Diploma Supplement, a standard template to describe qualifications, is increasingly being issued along with the final qualification and progress is being made in all countries to develop a qualifications framework that describes national qualifications according to a commonly defined set of descriptors and these will be inserted into an overarching European framework, connecting the different national education systems.

The last 10 years have seen a convergence of degree structures, credit frameworks, learning outcomes, and descriptors, but there has never been the objective of standardised qualifications. As has been often repeated, there is no single Bologna degree, but a range of Bologna-compliant degrees that fit the overall structures but have emerged in line with national and institutional preferences and traditions.

The Bologna Process has often accelerated internationalization processes in the institutions resulting in stronger institutional cooperation in integrated curricula for double and joint degrees. There has also been a significant increase in teaching in English in European universities, particularly at master's level, to facilitate mobility for both student exchange and student recruitment, as the new European master's degrees begin to establish themselves on the global higher education market.

In a Europe where many higher education systems had no quality assurance systems in place, there is now extensive European cooperation in quality assurance that has led to the development of European standards and guidelines providing a framework for the creation of the different national systems. And in a Europe where mobility was often hampered by lack of recognition principles, the Lisbon Recognition Convention gives the right to fair recognition and provides transparent and coherent criteria.

There can be no doubt that European higher education has undergone significant transformation in the space of one decade.

Messy Realities

So, the new European university has readable and comparable degrees, operates a credit system linked to learning outcomes, places the student at the centre of the educational process, issues the Diploma Supplement to all its graduates, has its own internal quality assurance mechanisms, is externally accredited by a quality assurance agency, is part of a system that has developed a national qualifications framework, and has fully implemented the Lisbon Recognition convention.

However, 46 countries and 5,600 institutions with a wide range of higher education traditions across the EHEA are all at different phases of implementation and there is significant diversity in national and institutional contexts and response capacities. Reality at ground level is much messier than the official government reports and declarations.

While the structural reforms are in place across Europe, there are a number of issues that need to be addressed in the next decade. The first objective will be completion of the reforms not only at legislative level, but ensuring they are properly implemented and firmly embedded in the institutions.

It must be said that in many institutions there has often been only a cosmetic introduction of the reforms. They may have been forced to adopt the new structures, but have then failed to rework their programs, design new curricula in line with new professions and interact with employers. The bachelor's degrees are not universally accepted as an entry point to the labor market and while many consider the master's degree as the real exit point, there is much confusion in the proliferation and variety of master's degrees. Doctoral reform is at the very early stages. Cramming old courses into new structures has also had the effect of reducing mobility and the next decade will focus on guaranteeing mobility at all levels of study.

ECTS as a tool for measuring student workload and linking to student outcomes is often misunderstood and seen as a bureaucratic requirement rather than an opportunity to innovate. Issuing the Diploma Supplement to all graduates has not yet become standard practice and national qualifications frameworks are still to be implemented in most countries. Quality assurance mechanisms may be in place but a quality assurance culture for institutional learning and improvement is not yet embedded. The Lisbon recognition principles are not always in line with national legislation and recognition of degrees is often a long and cumbersome process.

Reaching the Bologna goals at institutional level requires culture change and that is the biggest challenge of all. Culture change takes time, it requires energy and commitment from leadership, but it also calls for professional development and financial resources, which have often been lacking.

It cannot be ignored that the Bologna Process has also generated confusion and hostility. Overcoming these challenges and maintaining momentum will be essential to avoid the risk of "Bologna burnout" among stakeholders that have been instrumental in driving the process forward.

Beyond the internal and external dimension, the social dimension of the Bologna Process is mentioned less frequently in international discussions, but it is gaining in importance and sense of urgency. The questions of access to higher education and lifelong learning are not yet high priorities in most European institutional agendas and will become a major policy challenge in the next decade to ensure higher education is meeting societal needs.

BOLOGNA 2020

It is clear that, despite the remarkable progress of the last decade, there is still a long way to go before the Bologna goals of employability, mobility, and global competitiveness are reached and the EHEA becomes a reality. The Bologna Process represents a major modernization agenda for Europe and it is destined to go deeper and broader in the next decade.

An important new tool decided at the 2009 ministerial meeting is data collection and evaluation which will increase understanding of the changes and inform future decisions. An independent assessment of the last decade will be presented at the next ministerial conference and policy forum March 11–12, 2010, in Budapest, Hungary, and Vienna, Austria. Indicators to measure mobility and the social dimension will be in place by 2012.[2]

Future institutional reforms will need to move from structural change to enhancement and modernization of the curricula and much emphasis will be put on ensuring optimisation in use of ECTS and learning outcomes, introduction of student-centered learning, employability especially at bachelor's level, and access and quality of mobility.

One target for mobility has already been set and that is 20 percent of graduates should have had a study or placement abroad by 2020. Mobility studies should provide data on mobility between cycles and countries, mobility and employability, mobility in and beyond Europe, and instruments for quality of and access to mobility.

Data collection and evaluation should also provide input for the social dimension to ensure Europe's student bodies reflect the diversity of its populations. Universities will be called upon to develop action plans for more flexible educational delivery accessible to a wider range of students and to realise lifelong learning through better recognition of prior learning and development of adult learning. Each country will be required to set measurable targets for increasing the participation of underrepresented groups by 2020.

The external dimension will focus on enhancing relationships between the EHEA and the rest of the world and preparing its institutions to face global challenges. A strategy will be put in place to promote the EHEA around the world and create the EHEA brand but also to ensure international dialogue and cooperation. International reputation is closely tied to international rankings and European pilot projects are being developed to create new approaches and encourage institutional diversity. Quality assurance and recognition will take on stronger international dimensions and include transnational education.

Research and innovation have also been identified as a priority and there will be emphasis on creating strong links between the EHEA and the ERA (the European Research Area). Doctoral education will receive greater attention for reform to improve careers for young researchers and enhance opportunity for mobility. Diversity in institutional research profiles will be encouraged.

An open debate that will continue throughout the next decade will be the issue of funding higher education. Higher education has been declared a public good and public responsibility and governments have made commitments to maintaining investment levels in the current global crisis. Nevertheless, European higher education funding is low compared to the United States and has often decreased in the past decade. Discussions on the levels and balances of public and private funding, in particular student fee structures, will continue in the search for a sustainable funding model for Europe.

SEEING OPPORTUNITY

The Bologna Process has been considered the greatest higher education reform ever implemented in Europe, bringing about unprecedented change, and yet as it draws to its 10-year conclusion it already appears insufficient to provide the solutions that are required to make European higher education a truly global player.

Significant structural reform has been carried out and important tools for convergence have been introduced. But as the next decade begins, Europe will need to develop an even more ambitious reform agenda, driving forward and interlinking the internal, external, and social dimensions while creating the conditions for effective institutional implementation of the reforms.

Success will lie in the institutional capacity and ambition to change. Those institutions that see the Bologna Process as an opportunity rather than a threat will not only implement the changes but go beyond them to craft their own agenda to become active players in the new environment. For those who continue to resist and remain nostalgic about the past, the words of Eric Shinseki come to mind, "If you don't like change, you're going to like irrelevance even less." That is surely not an option for European universities.

BOLOGNA PROCESS WEB RESOURCES

Official Bologna Process Website

http://www.ond.vlaanderen.be/hogeronderwijs/Bologna/

European Qualifications Framework

http://www.ond.vlaanderen.be/hogeronderwijs/bologna/qf/qf.asp

European Credit Transfer and Accumulation System

http://ec.europa.eu/education/lifelong-learning-policy/doc48_en.htm

Diploma Supplement

http://ec.europa.eu/education/lifelong-learning-policy/doc1239_en.htm

European Quality Assurance

http://www.eqar.eu/

Information on quality assured and accredited higher education institutions (in progress)

http://www.qrossroads.eu/about-qrossroads

Study in Europe

http://ec.europa.eu/education/study-in-europe/

Notes

1. Editors' Note: The Erasmus program, begun in 1987, is a European Union cooperation and mobility initiative to promote European higher education in which students can take and transfer courses across countries in the European Union.

2. Editor's Note: The March conference met in March 2010 and welcomed Kazakhstan to the countries already participating in the Bologna Process. Member countries committed themselves to future implementation, recognizing the variable implementation rates across countries and need for continued development in strengthening the educational experiences across members of this group. To review the entire Declaration developed at that forum, see http://www.enqa.eu/files/Budapest-Vienna_Declaration.pdf. Further documentation is available at the official website (see websites listed in this reading).

Projects for Further Exploration

1. Go online to get national data to compare the percentage of African American, Hispanic, Asian American, and Native American men and women graduates (BA/BS, MA/MS, and PhD) of college to the percentage of Caucasian college graduates. How does this compare to the arguments in the readings in this chapter?

2. Using the web, compare the number and size of institutions of higher education in your area. Go to the webpages of two or three of these colleges and compare their missions and criteria for acceptance. How does this information compare with the arguments made by Tuchman; Hamilton and Armstrong; and Dougherty and Morest?

3. Use a search engine to get the most recent news stories on higher education in Europe to find out how the Bologna Process has changed patterns of higher education there.

10

GLOBALIZATION AND EDUCATION

Comparing Global Systems

rom Afghanistan to Zimbabwe, children around the world attend schools, but their access, goals, and experiences vary greatly. For some, the goal is a university education and professional degrees. For others, basic literacy is all children can hope to achieve, regardless of their ability. Not long ago in human history, education of children was carried out informally; during the socialization process, parents, relatives, and elders taught children the skills they would need to survive. Early scholars were primarily religious figures who studied to read and interpret religious texts. However, with industrialization, globalization, and advances in technology, new forces are driving education and educational reform. The growth of industry, trade, business, and demand for an educated workforce is now heard around the world (Stewart, 2005).

The term *globalization* means many things to many people. Attempts at a concise definition are difficult because some scholars define its historical beginnings; others look at the political, economic, or sociocultural aspects of the process; and still others use interdisciplinary analysis including business and economics. Some studying globalization focus on "globalization from above" and "globalization from below." Globalization from above looks at the big picture—major world patterns and trends related to globalization such as Westernization, internationalization, marketization, and educational needs (Singh, Kenway, & Apple, 2005). This top-down globalization generally starts from two points. The first is scholars who consider historical shifts and cultural patterns resulting in globalization. The second considers the role of multinational corporations and global political and economic organizations in globalization. Globalization from below, on the other hand, focuses on fragmentation and inequalities caused by globalization, and what is happening in traditional and local communities, some of which are being hard hit by effects of globalization and the rich-poor divide. This is where the educational divide is very apparent.

Theories of educational change today assume that global political, economic, and social change affects educational systems around the world in numerous ways. New theories are emerging to view this ongoing process of change (Carnoy & Rhoten, 2002). *Institutional theory*, for example, is concerned with influence from the global social environment and broader cultural norms on educational systems. Several questions guide the studies of researchers who take this approach: Why do educational organizations located in different communities and even countries have similar practices and structures? How do these organizations adapt to changing conditions in their environments? How do broader forces in individual countries and internationally result in change across organizations? (Ballantine & Hammack, 2012; Meyer, 2009).

Understanding the impact of globalization on educational systems is critical to understanding education in today's world. Major theoretical perspectives proposed to help us understand globalization and education include world systems theory and postcolonialism, among others (Spring, 2008). For example, just as countries are divided by economic systems and wealth into center core areas and poorer peripheral areas (world systems theory), so too do educational systems reflect the economic and political institutions of a given society and its place in the world system. Within and between countries, educational levels reflect the economic status of families, communities, and societies. Distinctions between countries lie at the base of many comparative studies and sometimes reflect the former colonial status of countries (postcolonial theory).

Sociologists of education are particularly interested in the differences in world educational systems because those differences help to put their own national systems into perspective. The following paragraphs summarize several areas of study in comparative education that are discussed in the readings in Chapter 10.

Influences on curricula: Sociologists of education have traced the origins of modern educational systems and curricula to former colonial systems. For instance, former British colonies often include classical British literature in their curriculum and require the British O-level and A-level (vocational and university entrance) examinations at the completion of high school and for entrance to university. However, critics argue that this type of system is not preparing all citizens for the realities of their world because O-level students do not always receive the same amount or quality of education (Ramirez & Boli-Bennett, 1987). Some former colonized countries have developed educational systems that meet the needs of the majority of their populations, often including information on agricultural practices, health care, and other essential subjects for their societies.

Although there are commonalities in educational systems around the world, many researchers question whether that convergence is good for all members of all societies, especially students from peripheral third world countries. These scholars suggest that learning to read materials relevant to the needs of rural farmers, for example, would be more appropriate for some members of society than learning Latin. This is a key point made by educational reformers Ivan Illich (see Chapter 11) and Paulo Freire (1973; also Freire & Macedo, 1995) with regard to Latin America and other developing regions.

Comparison of educational systems: Most countries provide free education for basic literacy skills, and many require schooling to the age of 16. Some countries even provide free education through the university level for those who qualify. However, the world's children do not have equal opportunity to attend schools, as discussed in the first two articles in this chapter. Although variations in educational systems around the world are great, there are also areas of similarity (Boli, Ramirez, & Meyer, 1985; Zhao, 2005). Comparisons of systems take many approaches including reviewing curricula, test results, structures of educational systems, access to education, and other variables. There are attempts to copy strategies of successful countries, or sometimes to impose educational systems on others. However, cultures and, therefore, educational systems cannot be transported easily from one nation to another. Each country must meet its own needs based in its unique situation. Still, similarities in curricular content around the world have evolved because of global educational demands, even as these systems provide education to meet their national needs.

Educating all children: In the first reading in this chapter, Joel E. Cohen, David E. Bloom, Martin B. Malin, and Helen Anne Curry discuss the necessity of educating all children for today's world. They point out the status of educational systems today—the good, the bad, and the ugly; what changes need to take place; and the challenges that lie ahead. Countries of the world are becoming more interdependent and sharing ideas about effective curricula and structures of educational systems in today's interdependent world. This means that there will be a need for continued study of the processes of globalization, urbanization, development, and change around the world as they impact educational systems.

Race, class, gender, and different school experiences: Continuing the discussion of educating all, children have very different experiences in schools. Race, class, and gender all affect what chances a child has to achieve in school. Most poignant are the cases of girls in some Middle Eastern, Asian, and African countries who have limited opportunities in life, face female genital mutilation, and receive much less education than their brothers (King, 1999; Lewis & Lockheed, 2006). Although many children from poor families in poor villages are at an educational disadvantage, girls are most severely affected (Sperling, 2005)—yet girls are the ones who raise and feed the children and often need to support the family. A measure of the development of a country is often seen in the statistics on education of girls.

The Reading by Maureen A. Lewis and Marlaine E. Lockheed provides a picture of the situation for girls in many poorer countries, especially in rural areas. Due to poverty, political or religious beliefs, lack of infrastructure to accommodate all children, and a host of other problems, girls and some minority children may not have the opportunity to attend school, even primary school, to reach basic literacy. Lewis and Lockheed lament the status of girls in some countries and regions. They point out the benefits of educating girls and the costs to society and girls when there is a lack of educational opportunity.

International comparative testing: In this chapter, David H. Kamens and Connie L. McNeely review national assessments of educational systems and comparative educational testing. They also discuss the global trends in curriculum and testing that have brought similarities in educational expectations across the globe. Findings generally support a convergence of curricular themes across nations, reflecting the social, political, economic, and educational interdependence of nations (Chabbott & Ramirez, 2000; McEneaney & Meyer, 2000). The National Assessment of Educational Progress (NAEP) and the International Association for the Evaluation of Educational Achievement (IEA) are two international tests that compare scores of children around the world in literacy, mathematics, science, civic education, and foreign language. These rankings provide information on the similarities, differences, and effects of development on educational systems. The comparatively low scores of U.S. students are of concern to U.S. educators and government officials. However, it is necessary to exercise caution when interpreting international data, because, despite United Nations guidelines, data gathered in countries are not always standardized. Therefore, when reporting results, comparative studies must take this into account (Baker & LeTendre, 2005).

Transition from school to work: A major purpose of schools is to train students for their future occupations and contributions to society. Every society expects schools to help prepare young people for the transition from school to work. This school-to-work transition has stimulated research in recent years as societies transition from industrial to postindustrial information nations, and as globalization changes the economic systems. Much of this research is coming from Europe and South America. by

Rachel Brooks explores the education-to-work transition and its effect on students, stratification systems, and societies. Brooks compares education-to-work plans of several European countries, the United States, and other countries, and discusses different patterns that have emerged due to global social, political, and economic changes.

With the ubiquity of globalization and the impact on educational needs and patterns around the globe, no nation seems able to ignore education for the contemporary needs of society. This chapter addresses some of the issues in this growing field of international education.

REFERENCES

Baker, D. P., & LeTendre, G. K. (2005). *National differences, global similarities*. Stanford, CA: Sanford University Press.

Ballantine, J. H., & Hammack, F. M. (2012). *The sociology of education: A systematic approach* (7th ed.). Upper Saddle River, NJ: Prentice Hall.

Boli, J., Ramirez, F. O., & Meyer, J. W. (1985). Explaining the origins and expansion of mass education. *Comparative Education Review, 29*(2), 145–170.

Carnoy, M., & Rhoten, D. (2002). What does globalization mean for educational change? A comparative approach. *Comparative Education Review, 46*(1), 1–6.

Chabbott, C., & Ramirez, F. O. (2000). Development and education. In M. T. Hallinan (Ed.), *Handbook of sociology of education* (pp. 163–187). New York: Kluwer Academic/Plenum.

Freire, P. (1973). *Pedagogy of the oppressed*. New York: Herder and Herder.

Freire, P., & Macedo, D. P. (1995). A dialogue: Culture, language, and race. *Harvard Education Review, 65*(3), 377–402.

King, E. W. (1999). *Looking into the lives of children: A worldwide view*. Melbourne, Australia: James Nicholas.

Lewis, M. A., & Lockheed, M. E. (2006). *Inexcusable absence: Why 60 million girls still aren't in school and what to do about it*. Washington, DC: Center for Global Development.

McEneaney, E. H., & Meyer, J. W. (2000). The content of the curriculum: An institutionalist perspective. In M. T. Hallinan (Ed.), *Handbook of the sociology of education* (pp. 189–211). New York: Kluwer Academic/Plenum.

Meyer, J. W. (2009). Reflections: Institutional theory and world society. In G. Krücken & G. S. Drori (Eds.), *World society: The writings of John W. Meyer* (pp. 36–63). Oxford, England: Oxford University Press.

Ramirez, F. O., & Boli-Bennett, J. (1987, August). *The political construction of mass schooling: European origins and worldwide institutionalization*. Paper presented at the meeting of the American Sociological Association, Chicago.

Singh, M., Kenway, J., & Apple, M. W. (2005). Globalizing education: Perspectives from above and below. In M. W. Apple, J. Kenway, & M. Singh (Eds.), *Globalizing education: Policies, pedagogies, and politics* (pp. 1–29). New York: Peter Lang.

Sperling, G. B. (2005). The case for universal basic education for the world's poorest boys and girls. *Phi Delta Kappan, 87*(3), 213–216.

Spring, J. (2008). Research on globalization and education. *Review of Educational Research, 78*(2), 330–363.

Stewart, V. (2005). A world transformed: How other countries are preparing students for the interconnected world of the 21st century. *Phi Delta Kappan, 87*(3), 229–232.

Zhao, Y. (2005). Increasing math and science achievement: The best and worst of the east and west. *Phi Delta Kappan, 87*(3), 219–222.

EDUCATING ALL CHILDREN

A Global Agenda

Joel E. Cohen, David E. Bloom, Martin B. Malin, and Helen Anne Curry

The first reading in this chapter discusses the current state of universal mass education in the world, including a discussion of the obstacles to global education and how we might move beyond them. The good news is that formal education has been spreading around the globe, encompassing more and more eligible and eager learners. Literacy rose from 25% to more than 75% in the 20th century, and access to education continues to increase rapidly. However, there are still millions of uneducated children without the opportunity to move ahead. Those who can attend school may not receive quality education. The largest problem for would-be school attendees is that in some regions of the world, lower-income groups, girls, and minorities do not have equal opportunity. Spending on education varies widely as well. Why provide all children with quality educations? Here, the authors point to the advantages that accrue to those individuals and societies with strong educational systems: economic benefits, strong societies, better health for students and their families, and fulfillment of what many believe is a basic human right. Yet to reach the goal of universal education, societies must deal with obstacles such as corruption and lack of infrastructure supporting schools. Pressure on countries to increase educational opportunities in order to participate in the 21st-century world is great, thus generating growing demand and educational enrollments.

Questions to consider for this reading:

1. What is the current status of world educational opportunities?

2. Describe some challenges that poor countries face in trying to improve their educational systems. What does the future for educating all children look like?

3. What are the benefits of universal education for recipients and for countries?

O ver the past century, three approaches have been advocated to escape the consequences of widespread poverty, rapid population growth, environmental problems, and social injustices. The *bigger pie* approach says: use technology to produce more and to alleviate shortages. The *fewer forks* approach says: make contraception and reproductive health care available to eliminate unwanted fertility and to slow population growth. The *better manners* approach says: eliminate violence and corruption; improve the operation of markets and government provision of public goods; reduce the unwanted after-effects of consumption; and achieve greater social and political equity between young and old, male and female, rich and poor (Cohen, 1995). Providing all the world's children with the equivalent of a high-quality primary and secondary education, whether through formal schooling or by alternative means, could, in principle, support all three of these approaches. Universal education is the stated goal of several international initiatives. In 1990, the global community pledged at the World Conference on Education for All in Jomtien, Thailand, to achieve universal primary education (UPE) and greatly reduce illiteracy by 2000. In 2000, when these goals were not met, it again pledged to achieve UPE, this time at the World Education Forum in Dakar, Senegal, with a target date of 2015. The UN Millennium Development Conference in 2000 also adopted UPE by 2015 as one of its goals, along with the elimination of gender disparities in primary and secondary education by 2015.

Educational access increased enormously in the past century. Illiteracy fell dramatically and a higher proportion of people are completing primary, secondary, or tertiary education than ever before. Despite this progress, huge problems remain for providing universal access and high-quality schooling through the secondary level of education. The UPE goal looks unlikely to be achieved by 2015 at the current rate of progress. An estimated 299 million school-age children will be missing primary or secondary school in 2015; of these, an estimated 114 million will be missing primary school. These statistics suggest that providing every child between the approximate ages of 6 and 17 with an education of high quality will require time, resources, and colossal effort. Should the international community commit the necessary economic, human, and political resources to the goal of universal education? If so, how should it deploy these resources, and how much will it cost?

THE CURRENT SCENE

Current educational data indicate that the world has made significant progress in education, though shortfalls and disparities remain.

The Good

Over the past century, formal schooling spread remarkably, as measured by the primary gross enrollment ratio (GER)—the ratio of total primary enrollment, regardless of age, to the population of the age group that officially belongs in primary education. In 1900, estimated primary GERs were below 40 percent in all regions, except that in northwestern Europe, North America, and Anglophone regions of the Pacific, collectively, the ratio was 72 percent (Williams, 1997, p. 122). Within the past few years, the estimated global primary net enrollment ratio (NER)—the number of pupils in the official primary school-age group expressed as a percentage of the total population in that age group—reached 86 percent (Bloom, chapter one [of *Educating All Children*], Appendix A). The NER is a stricter standard (i.e., it gives lower numbers) than the GER, so the achievement is all the more remarkable. Secondary-school enrollment shows similar progress. The number of students enrolled in secondary school increased eight-fold in the past 50 years, roughly from 50 million to 414 million (calculations by Bloom, based on UNESCO online data).

Measures distinct from enrollment round out this picture. Over the twentieth century, literacy tripled in developing countries, from 25 percent to 75 percent. The average years of schooling in these countries more than doubled between 1960 and 1990, increasing from 2.1 to 4.4 years (Bloom & Cohen, 2002). That figure has risen further since 1990. This growth in enrollment and literacy was supported by more global spending on primary and secondary education than at any previous time. According to Glewwe and Zhao [in chapter seven of *Educating All Children*], developing countries spent approximately $82 billion on primary schooling in 2000; Binder, in chapter eight, estimates that spending for secondary education in developing countries in 2000 was $93 billion per year. Although the data and methods of estimation underlying these figures differ, they both indicate large expenditures.

As access to education and literacy increased, global monitoring of students, schools, and educational systems also increased. Developing countries are participating in international measurements of educational status in greater numbers. More statistical measures of schooling have been defined (for example, net and gross enrollment ratios, attendance rates, completion rates, average years of attainment, and school life expectancy). Though not all are well supported by reliable, internationally comparable, comprehensive data, several organizations are working toward this goal. The UNESCO Institute of Statistics, Montreal, maintains the highest-quality data (for example, UNESCO, 2000; [UNESCO-UIS,] 2004).

The Bad

This progress is considerable, but large deficits remain. Roughly 323 million children are not enrolled in school (23 percent of the age group 6–17); roughly 30 percent of these children are missing from primary school, the rest from secondary school (Bloom, chapter one) [of Educating All Children]. In developing countries, 15 percent of youth aged 15 to 24 are illiterate, as are about one in every four adults (UNESCO, 2005).

Moreover, enrollment does not necessarily mean attendance, attendance does not necessarily mean receiving an education, and receiving an education does not necessarily mean receiving a good education. High enrollment ratios may give the mistaken impression that a high proportion of school-age children are being well educated. Some 75–95 percent of the world's children live in countries where the quality of education lags behind—most often far behind—the average of OECD countries, as measured by standardized test scores. That standard may not be universally appropriate. However, it is uncontested that educational quality is too often poor.

In addition, indicators of educational quality are scarce. Though participation in international and regional assessments of educational quality has increased, countries most in need of improvements are least likely to participate. As a result, important comparative data on quality continue to be lacking for the developing world. The problem of inadequate or missing data is pervasive.

The Ugly

Gross disparities in education separate regions, income groups, and genders. The populations farthest from achieving UPE are typically the world's poorest. Net primary enrollment ratios have advanced in most of the developing world but remain low in Sub-Saharan Africa. . . .

Girls' education falls short of boys' education in much of the world. Although enrollment rates sometimes do not differ greatly, many more boys than girls complete schooling, especially at the primary level. Although we know that gender, proximity to a city, and income level interact in influencing educational deficits, a systematic global analysis remains to be done of how much each contributes to differences in children's educational opportunities and achievements. In India in 1992–93, the enrollment rate of boys aged 6–14 exceeded that of girls by 2.5 percentage points among children of the richest households; the difference in favor of boys was 24 percentage points among children from poor households (Filmer, 1999). The study also shows that wealth gaps in enrollment greatly exceeded sex gaps in enrollment. The boys from rich households had enrollment rates 34 percentage points higher than those of boys from poor households; the gap in favor of rich girls compared to poor girls was 55.4 percentage points.

Developing countries differ widely in spending on primary education, ranging from $46 per student per year in South Asia and $68 in Sub-Saharan Africa to $878 in Europe and Central Asia (see Table 45.1). Spending per student in secondary education shows a similar range, from $117 per student per year in South Asia and $257 in Sub-Saharan Africa to $577 in Latin America and the Caribbean.

Table 45.1   Recent Public Current Expenditures on Primary Schooling in Developing Countries

Region	Public Spending per Student (U.S. $)	Total Public Spending (millions U.S. $)	Fraction of Population with Public Spending Data*
South Asia	46	6,910	0.98
Sub-Saharan Africa	68	6,100	0.98
East Asia and Pacific	103	21,200	0.96
Latin America and the Caribbean	440	28,200	0.90
Middle East and North Africa	519	14,200	0.60
Europe and Central Asia	878	5,210	0.22
All developing regions	151	81,800	0.88

Source: Glewwe and Zhao, chapter seven [*Educating All Children*].

Note. *Public spending figures are more reliable in regions where public spending data are available for a higher fraction of the population.

CHALLENGES

Closing the gap between the current state of global education and the goal of providing all children with high-quality primary and secondary education schooling requires meeting several distinct challenges.

- Educate the roughly 97 million children of primary-school age who are not currently enrolled in school. As a majority of these students are female and most live in absolute poverty, the underlying conditions that create disparities in educational access will likely need to be addressed.
- Educate the 226 million children of secondary-school age not in school. Improved access to primary education fuels the demand for secondary education. As more and more children attend school, more and more teachers—who should have at least a secondary education—will also be needed (UNESCO[-UIS], 2006).
- Develop the capacity to educate the 90 million additional children 5–17 years old in developing countries in the next 20 years (United Nations, 2004).

- Improve the quality of primary and secondary education, assessed according to constructive goals and clear standards.
- Provide policymakers with clear, empirically supported rationales for why education matters.

Achieving these goals requires a realistic appraisal of the obstacles that have thus far prevented educational opportunity for all children. It requires fresh thinking about what the goals of education should be, and how best to pursue those goals. And it demands an assessment of the costs, which are likely to be significant, as well as an assessment of the consequences of educational expansion and the returns on this investment, which are essential to securing societal and political support . . .

WHY UNIVERSAL PRIMARY AND SECONDARY EDUCATION?

Although education is not available to hundreds of millions of children, neither are health care, adequate nutrition, employment opportunities, and other basic services available to these children or their families. Why should universal primary and secondary education be a development goal of high priority?

Several rationales support the pursuit of universal primary and secondary education. Education provides economic benefits. Education builds strong societies and polities. Education reduces fertility and improves health. Education is a widely accepted humanitarian obligation and an internationally mandated human right. These rationales are commonly offered for universal primary education, but many benefits of education do not accrue until students have had 10 or more years of education. Completion of primary education is more attractive if high-quality secondary education beckons.

Economic Benefits

. . . Extensive sociological and economic studies have found that education generally enables individuals to improve their economic circumstances. Although the benefits of education for the individual are clear, the aggregate effects on economic growth are more difficult to measure and remain a matter of dispute (Krueger & Lindahl, 2001; Pritchett, 1997; Bloom & Canning, 2004).

It is clear, however, that more education contributes to a demographic transition from high fertility and high mortality to low fertility and low mortality, and Bloom and colleagues (2003) find this change is associated with accelerated growth. When fertility rates fall, the resulting demographic transition offers countries a large working-age population with fewer children to support, although only for a transient interval before population aging begins. In this interval, the large fraction of the population that is of working age offers an exceptional opportunity for high economic growth (Bloom et al., 2003).

Women who attend school, particularly at the secondary or tertiary level, generally have fewer children than those who do not. An increase by 10 percent in primary GERs is associated with an

average reduction in the total fertility rate of 0.1 children. A 10 percent increase in secondary GERs is associated with an average reduction of 0.2 children. In Brazil, women with a secondary education have an average of 2.5 children, compared to 6.5 children for illiterate women. In some African societies, total fertility is reduced only among girls who have had 10 or more years of schooling (Jejeebhoy, 1996).

Education contributes to reduced fertility through numerous pathways. Maternal education can lead to increased use of contraceptives. Education can enable women more easily to work outside the home and earn money. This improvement in status leads to empowerment and increased decision-making authority in limiting fertility. Educated women tend to delay marriage and childbearing, perhaps because of the increased opportunity costs of not participating in the paid labor force. Education and income may also become intertwined in a virtuous spiral: as incomes grow, more money is available to finance the spread of education, which leads to further increases in income.

Strong Societies and Polities

Although the evidence is not definitive, education has been shown to strengthen social and cultural capital. Absolute increases in educational attainment can shift disadvantaged groups, such as ethnic minorities or females, from absolute deprivation to relative deprivation compared to more advantaged groups. Educated citizens may be more likely to vote and to voice opposition. Among states, higher enrollment ratios at all levels of education correspond to increases in indicators of democracy. If the content of the education encourages it, education can promote social justice, human rights, and tolerance. As the percentage of the male population enrolled in secondary school goes up, the probability of civil conflict goes down (Collier & Hoeffler, 2001). These desirable effects depend on the content of education and do not flow from the fact of education per se (Cohen, [in press]).

Health

Controlling for income, educated individuals have longer, healthier lives than those without education. Children who are in school are healthier than those who are not, though causation could flow in either direction or both.

Many effects of education on health are indirect effects through increased income. Education increases economic status, and higher-income individuals have better access to health care services, better nutrition, and increased mobility. Education also has direct impacts on health, unrelated to income. It can provide vital health knowledge and encourage healthy lifestyles. For example, the offspring of educated mothers have lower child and infant mortality rates and higher immunization rates, even when socioeconomic conditions are controlled statistically . . .

Improved health may in turn enhance education . . . Randomized evaluations of school-based health programs in Kenya and India suggest that simple, inexpensive treatments for basic health problems such as anemia and intestinal worms can dramatically increase the quantity of schooling students attain . . .

A Basic Human Right

Universal education is justified on ethical and humanitarian grounds as right, good, and fair. Education enables people to develop their capacities to lead fulfilling, dignified lives. High-quality education helps people give meaning to their lives by placing them in the context of human and natural history and by creating in them an awareness of other cultures. Article 26 of the United Nations' Universal Declaration of Human Rights, adopted in 1948, asserts: "Everyone has the right to education." It maintains that primary education should be free and compulsory. The Convention on the Rights of the Child, which entered into force in 1990, obliges governments to make universal primary education compulsory and also to make different forms of secondary education accessible to every child.

OBSTACLES

The rationales for continued educational expansion are powerful, but the barriers too are numerous and formidable. The cost to governments of providing universal primary and secondary schooling, discussed later in this introduction and in chapters seven and eight [of *Educating All Children*], are significant. The cost of education to individuals and families is sometimes a strong disincentive. Because governments face competing demands for the allocation of state resources, education is often pushed down the list of priorities. And even if financial resources for education were plentiful, then politics, corruption, culture, poor information, and history among other factors would conspire to block or slow the achievement of access to high-quality education for all children.

Economic Disincentives

Millions of children have access to schooling but do not attend. Some families may place greater value on the time children spend in other activities, such as performing work for income or handling chores so other household members are free to work in market activities. In developing countries, a troubled household economic situation may more often be a deterrent to enrollment than lack of access to a school. For example, in Ghana, almost half of parents, when asked why their children were not in school, answered, "school is too expensive" or "child needed to work at home"; another 22 percent believed that education was of too little value (World Bank, 2004).

Economic barriers disproportionately harm girls. Some parents perceive the costs—direct, indirect, and opportunity costs—of educating daughters to be higher than that of educating sons (Herz & Sperling, 2004).

Political Obstacles

Education competes for scarce national resources with many worthy projects such as building roads, providing medical care, and strengthening a country's energy system. Limited resources can hamper educational expansion in many ways. Organized interest groups may divert funding from education to their own causes. When social crises, such as crime, unemployment, or civil war, demand the time and resources of the government, citizens are perhaps unlikely to focus on education. Popular demand for education is frequently weakest in poor regions or countries where it is most needed.

Directing adequate funds to education requires a national commitment to education that many countries lack. Government decisions guided by the short-term interests of those in power are unlikely to reflect the importance of education, as educational returns accrue over much longer time horizons. When politicians devote funds to education, the funding sometimes flows to political supporters rather than to programs and regions where it is most needed. Moreover, a limited capacity to oversee the implementation of education programs and the limited political status of education ministries within many governments may blunt reforms as they are enacted.

Corruption

As with any large public sector, the education sector is rife with opportunities for corruption. When funds are diverted for private gain at any level, educational expansion and improvement may be harmed. At the highest levels of government, corruption can affect the allocation of funds to the education budget; at the ministry level, it can influence the distribution of funds to individual schools; and at the school level, it can involve the diversion of money from school supplies, and the payment of bribes by parents to ensure their children's access to or success in school and by teachers to secure promotions or other benefits (Meier, 2004).

International donors may be deterred by a recipient's history of poor spending accountability, and may curtail funding or impose accountability measures that are themselves costly. The loss of financial resources is always harmful. It is most detrimental at the local level, where the poorest children may be denied access to education because they are not able to afford bribes or where systems of merit—both for students and teachers—are distorted through the widespread use of bribes to secure advancement (Chapman, 2002). Heyneman (2003) argues that if pervasive corruption leads to the public perception of education as unfair or not meritocratic, then this distrust of the school system may lead to distrust of the leaders it produces. As a result, he says, a country's "sense of social cohesion, the principal ingredient of all successful modern societies," may be undermined.

Lack of Information

Reliable, internationally comparable, useful data on many aspects of primary and secondary education are lacking. For example, the mechanisms that keep children out of school are poorly understood in quantitative (as opposed to qualitative) detail. Most routine data focus on measures of "butts-in-seats" such as enrollment, attendance, and completion. Data on educational processes, such as pedagogical techniques and curricula, and on learning outcomes, are inadequate.

Political incentives sometimes work against accurate reporting on even basic quantitative measures. In Uganda, enrollment was historically under-reported because schools were required to remit private tuition receipts to the government in proportion to the number of students they reported. When schools became publicly funded on the basis of enrolled pupils, the incentive for schools to report higher numbers resulted in a leap in official enrollments. In addition, governments may be reluctant to publish potentially unflattering data on their school systems, for fear of political consequences.

Failing to provide data on education feeds a vicious circle. Lack of accurate data impairs the formulation of effective education policy; citizens lack the information they need to hold their school administrators and elected officials accountable; unaccountable officials have few incentives to collect information that would help them to improve the system. Improving educational data could help to transform this vicious circle into a virtuous one by providing necessary information to citizens, administrators, and officials to monitor and improve the quality of schooling.

Historical Legacies

The history of efforts to expand education provides a rich source of models and lessons. These historical legacies can also present impediments to those who underestimate their importance. Benavot and Resnik examine in chapter two [of *Educating All Children*] the emergence of compulsory education laws, the transformation of diverse educational frameworks into formal school systems, the problems of inequality that have arisen, and the role played by international organizations in creating an increasingly interconnected global education system.

Despite the apparent uniformity in contemporary schooling, past educational models took many forms and motivations for educational expansion varied widely. Because national contexts differ, international organizations seeking to facilitate educational expansion need to be attuned to this varied history if their interventions are to succeed. Solutions that ignore the history of education in a particular country are likely to be less effective than solutions tuned to context. For example, when leaders advocated the decentralization of public schools in Latin American countries in the 1980s, they ignored the specific social and political purposes for which those schools had been founded, which included ending severe socio-economic segregation. Decentralization led to a growth of private schools and renewed fragmentation along socioeconomic lines, which exacerbated the social divide that school centralization was initially intended to correct.

Though the past must not be ignored, it is not always a useful guide to present educational reform. Past state motivations to provide education—to consolidate national identity, win citizen loyalty, or neutralize rival political groups—were most prominent when nationalist, revolutionary, and totalitarian ideologies drove political development. Today, these rationales are less relevant.

REFERENCES

Bloom, D. E., & Canning, D. (2004). *Reconciling micro and macro estimates of the returns to schooling* (Working Paper of the Project on Universal Basic and Secondary Education). Cambridge, MA: American Academy of Arts and Sciences.

Bloom, D. E., Canning, D., & Sevilla, J. (2003). *The demographic dividend: A new perspective on the economic consequent of population change.* Santa Monica, CA: RAND.

Bloom, D. E., & Cohen, J. E. (2002). Education for all: An unfinished revolution. *Daedalus, 131*(3), 84–95.

Chapman, D. (2002, November). *Corruption and the education sector.* Sectoral Perspectives on Corruption Series. Washington, DC: USAID/ MIS.

Cohen, J. E. (1995). *How many people can the earth support?* New York: W.W. Norton.

Cohen, J. E. (Ed.). (in press). *Education for all, but for what? International perspectives on the goals of primary and secondary education.*

Collier, P., & Hoeffler, A. (2001, October). *Greed and grievance in civil war.* Washington, DC: World Bank. Retrieved from http://www.worldbank.org/research/conflict/papers/greedgrievance_23oct.pdf

Filmer, D. (1999). The structure of social disparities in education: Gender and wealth. In *Engendering development through gender equality in rights, resources, and voice* (World Bank Background Paper). Washington, DC: World Bank. Retrieved from http://www.onlinewomeninpolitics.org/beijing12/g%26w.pdf

Herz, B., & Sperling, G. B. (2004). *What works in girls' education: Evidence and policies from the developing world.* New York: Council on Foreign Relations.

Heyneman, S. P. (2003). *Education and corruption.* Retrieved from http://tistats.transparency.org/index

.php/content/download/23772/355754/file/heynemann_education_2003.pdf

Jejeebhoy, S. J. (1996). *Women's education, autonomy, and reproductive behaviour: Experience from developing countries.* New York: Oxford University Press.

Krueger, A. B., & Lindahl, M. (2001). Education for growth: Why and for whom? *Journal of Economic Literature, 39*(4), 1101–1136.

Meier, B. (2004). *Corruption in the education sector: An introduction.* Working Paper, Transparency International, July.

Pritchett, L. (1997). *Where has all the education gone?* (World Bank Policy Research Working Paper 1581). Washington, DC: World Bank.

UNESCO. (2000, April). *Education for all 2000 assessment: Statistical document.* Prepared for the International Consultative Forum on Education for All, World Education Forum, Dakar, Senegal. Retrieved from http://unesdoc.unesco.org/images/0012/001204/120472e.pdf

UNESCO. (2005). *Education for all: Literacy for life.* Paris: Author.

UNESCO-UIS. (2004). *Global education digest 2004: Comparing education statistics across the world.* Montreal: Author.

UNESCO-UIS. (2006). *Teachers and educational quality: Monitoring global needs for 2015.* Montreal: Author.

United Nations. (2004). *World population prospects: The 2004 revision.* Retrieved from http://esa.un.org/unpp

Williams, J. H. (1997). The diffusion of the modern school. In W. K. Cummings & N. F. McGinn (Eds.), *International handbook of education and development: Preparing schools, students and nations for the twenty-first century* (pp. 119–136). New York: Pergamon, Elsevier Science.

World Bank. (2004). *Books, buildings and learning outcomes: An impact evaluation of World Bank support to basic education in Ghana.* Washington, DC: Author.

Inexcusable Absence

Who Are the Out-of-School Girls—and What Can Be Done to Get Them in School?

Maureen A. Lewis and Marlaine E. Lockheed

In rich global north (developed) countries, girls generally have the same chance to obtain an education as boys. In fact, they attend university at higher rates than males, although the typical fields women pursue may not pay as well as fields males pursue. The picture is different in poor global south countries. Many girls, especially those from rural areas and minority groups, have no opportunities to pursue even primary-level education, leaving them illiterate. Maureen A. Lewis and Marlaine E. Lockheed discuss some of the reasons for this lack of opportunity for girls and what it means for the girls, their families, their communities, and their countries. Their discussion focuses on the sources of the problem for girls and the types of exclusions they experience. In addition, they look at the number of girls who do not receive education in different parts of the world and the cost to society and girls due to their lack of educational opportunity. Finally, the authors indicate some strategies for advancing educational opportunities for excluded girls.

Questions to consider for this reading:

1. Why are girls in some countries excluded from educational opportunity, what are patterns of girls' exclusion, and how many girls are excluded?

2. What are the consequences of excluding girls from educational opportunity?

3. What can be done to increase the educational opportunities for girls?

Impressive strides have been made in bringing girls into primary school over the past 25 years, with many countries achieving universal primary education and gender parity. But considerable disparity exists within and across countries, with intracountry differences stemming largely from the lagging involvement of excluded groups—rural tribes in Pakistan, lower castes in India, Roma in Europe, indigenous peoples in Latin America. Of the 60 million girls not in primary school, almost 70 percent are from excluded groups. If further progress is to be realized, educating these girls must be a priority.

Who are the 60 million girls who remain out of school nearly two decades after the worldwide declaration on Education for All? These are their faces:

Meera, 8, *lives with her family on a sidewalk in New Delhi, India. During the day she roams major intersections, her infant sister hanging from her hip, begging drivers for coins in the few words of English she knows. She does not go to school. In a few years she will be married off to a stranger. She will have six children, one of whom will go to school. Or she will die young, possibly immolated in a kitchen fire for having brought with her an insufficient dowry.*

Sonia, 10, *lives on the outskirts of a capital city in Eastern Europe. Like her siblings, all of whom speak only Romani, she does not attend school. Instead, Sonia spends her days committing petty theft to support her family. Adults in the town spit at her and warn visitors to watch their purses when they see her.*

Lia, 12, *went to school for a few years in her remote hill village in Thailand. Then her family sent her to the capital to earn a respectable living in a factory, but she was sold into the sex trade instead. She lives in a brothel and services dozens of clients a day. She will die young, most likely from HIV/AIDS.*

Wambui, 14, *goes to boarding school because no secondary school is available in her Kenyan village. But she will soon be expelled from school because she is pregnant, having been raped at school by boy students from another tribe, who considered it a mere prank.*

Many developing countries have achieved gender equity in education, with near-universal girls' participation converging with that of boys:

Indrani, 10, *is the daughter of illiterate parents living in rural Bangladesh. She goes to school. Her older sister is finishing secondary school and plans to work in the garment factory in the market center. While her mother was betrothed at 12, her parents have decided that their daughters must finish school before marrying.*

Monique, 12, *is excelling in secondary school in Tunisia. She and her siblings have finished primary school with the exception of her eldest sister, whose arranged marriage interrupted her schooling. She expects to work before she marries and plans to have two children.*

Are excluded girls simply the daughters of the poor, or are other, more subtle factors at work? Why do some countries make better progress? School participation figures from six low- and middle-income countries offer some clues:

- In Laos, a low-income country, Lao-Tai girls living in rural communities complete five years of school, whereas hill tribe girls living in comparable communities complete fewer than two years of school.
- In Bangladesh, a low-income country, 86 percent of primary school–age girls attend school and 69 percent complete primary school. There is no significant difference between girls living in urban and rural communities.
- In Guatemala, a lower middle-income country, 62 percent of Spanish-speaking girls but only 26 percent of indigenous, non-Spanish-speaking girls complete primary school.
- In Tunisia, a lower middle-income country, 95 percent of all girls complete primary school and 68 percent are enrolled in secondary school.
- In the Slovak Republic, an upper middle-income country, 54 percent of Slovak girls but only 9 percent of minority girls attend secondary school.
- In Botswana, an upper middle-income country, 95 percent of all girls complete primary school and 57 percent attend secondary school.

Sources, Forms, and Levels of Exclusion

What accounts for these differences? Most obvious is the presence or absence of significant subgroups. Bangladesh, Botswana, and Tunisia are largely homogeneous, while Guatemala, Laos, and the Slovak Republic have excluded subgroups.[1] In homogeneous countries higher shares of girls complete primary school, enroll in secondary school, and see higher achievement than those in heterogeneous countries.

Excluded subgroups are based on tribal, ethnic, linguistic, or traditional occupational classifications, such as the "untouchable" occupations of the lowest caste groups in India. But ethnic or linguistic diversity within a country does not necessarily lead to a failure to educate girls. The Basques in Spain, for example, are linguistically diverse but have high levels of female education. It is diversity accompanied by derogation and discrimination that leads to exclusion. The main driver of the remaining gender inequalities in education is the existence of subgroups within countries, accompanied by social stratification and cultural norms that seclude women. This driver operates both culturally and structurally to exclude girls from school. It is thus a particularly pernicious barrier.

Exclusion can take many forms—the more severe, the greater its effect on school opportunities . . . At one end are extreme forms of exclusion leading to genocide. Only somewhat less severe is the exclusion associated with ethnically based slavery (not slavery as an outcome of conflict), where education is denied to children of slaves, as was the case for African slaves in the southern United States or Brazil in the 1800s. The shunning of a group, such as the Dalits in India or the Roma in Europe, is less severe. It can result in lack of schools, inaccessible schools, segregated or "special" schools, corporal punishment of students, teacher absenteeism, and generally poor-quality schools. Moderate exclusion can result in schooling that is poorly matched with the needs of students. Consider the conditions faced by Berber children in Morocco before 2005; . . . teaching and school materials were not in their mother tongue, mild corporal punishment and ability tracking were used, and early qualifying exams excluded poorly performing children from further education.

A mild form of exclusion is that associated with individual social preferences, whereby teachers may overlook students from excluded groups or children from a minority group may not be included in social events. Exclusion can also result in decreased demand for education or for autonomy in the provision of education.

Severe exclusion has structural consequences: schools are not built, curricular materials are not supplied, roads to schools are not paved, and teachers are often absent. Milder exclusion is cultural. It can affect the behavior of teachers and schoolmates, making teachers insensitive to excluded students' needs.

Language and ethnicity are only two of the sources of exclusion. Children living in remote rural communities face structural barriers to education due to distance, and these barriers are most pronounced for girls. Poor children face barriers to education due to the direct and indirect costs of education. Because the poor in developing countries often show a strong preference for sons, education investments are biased toward boys. Residential segregation often results in access to poorer quality schools.

The cultures of subgroups can differ with respect to the status and roles accorded to women. Where women are secluded, or expected to work long hours performing domestic chores or agricultural labors, cultural beliefs and norms limit girls' educational opportunities. Girls face special cultural barriers associated with their roles in the home and as future wives. As a result, social exclusion from these multiple sources has severe consequences for girls' education and will require different, more tailored policies to remedy them. The degree and nature of exclusion dictates the approach and scope of interventions; often multiple efforts are needed.

How Many Girls Are Excluded?

How many girls are affected by exclusion due to multiple causes? No formal estimates of the numbers of excluded out-of-school girls are available, because most developing countries do not systematically collect or report data on school participation disaggregated by all of the subgroups subject to exclusion. Data from various sources can be used to estimate the figure, however. These data reveal a staggering finding: nearly three-quarters of girls who do not go to school come from excluded groups, while these groups represent only about 20 percent of the developing world's population.

Most out-of-school girls live in Africa and South Asia, which together account for 78 percent of all girls not in school (UIS, 2005). [See Table 46.1.] In some large countries a small share of girls are out of school, but the size of the country means that large numbers of girls are affected. In some small countries the share of out-of-school girls is high, which represents a huge national challenge but adds little quantitatively to the global problem. For example, in Guinea-Bissau 55 percent of school-age girls never attend school, but because the total population of the country is little more than 1.2 million, only about 60,000 school-age girls are not in school. By contrast, in India 20 percent of school-age girls are not in school, but with a national population exceeding 1 billion, 27.7 million girls (ages 7–14) are not in school (Census of India, 2001 [Government of India, 2011]).

Data on excluded girls are limited. But recent Indian census data document how multiple exclusions can deter girls' participation in school. Of the nearly 50 million children 7–14 years old not enrolled in school in India, 55 percent are girls. This figure is disproportionately high, with girls representing just 48 percent of all children 7–14 years old. Of the 27.7 million girls 7–14 years old not enrolled in school, 33 percent come from scheduled castes or scheduled tribes.[2] This figure is also disproportionately high, because only 26 percent of girls this age come from scheduled tribes or scheduled castes.

The cost of excluding girls from school is high, and the benefits of inclusion significant . . . The social benefits of educating girls have been widely documented, and studies have also found economic benefits from educating girls.

Mild forms of exclusion often affect girls once they enter school, but the evidence suggests that when girls from excluded groups are given

the opportunity to go to school, they tend to go—and to succeed—at least through primary school. Their achievement is often comparable to that of girls from nonexcluded groups and equal to or better than that of excluded boys. Given that the quality of primary schools attended by excluded children is often poor, this is remarkable.

A concatenation of sources of exclusion—gender, ethnicity, area of residence—greatly reduces overall achievement by the time girls reach lower secondary school. Designing interventions and proposing solutions thus require assessing the demand for and supply of education and examining the school practices that affect girls and other excluded subgroups . . .

Lessons from developed countries can guide donors and policymakers in developing countries. But even developed countries grapple with exclusion. In some, failure to establish a level playing field early on has resulted in a backlash that exacerbates rather than mitigates differences. In developing countries, the diversity of subgroups and the specificities of the cultural contexts make building a new body of knowledge essential . . .

Ensuring that excluded girls go to school is a major challenge, requiring targeted interventions that address both the structural and cultural dimensions of discrimination in education. The costs of failing are tremendous in terms of lives lost and development opportunities missed.

ADVANCING EXCLUDED GIRLS' EDUCATION

Strategies for advancing excluded girls' education do not apply in all contexts—what works in one country may prove disastrous in another, and "one size does not fit all." Consider busing. In Bulgaria the largely urban and peri-urban Roma community benefited greatly from being bused to better schools. In rural Turkey, busing led parents to pull their daughters out of school over concern for their safety because the new school was in another village. Context is critical . . .

Table 46.1   Most Primary School-Age Girls Out of Schools Are From Excluded Groups, 2000

Region	Girls out of school (thousands)	Excluded girls out of school[a] (thousands)	Excluded girls as percent of all girls out of school	Excluded subgroups
Sub-Saharan Africa	23,827	17,870[b]	75	Members of nondominant tribes
South Asia	23,552	15,780[c]	67	Rural people in Afghanistan, scheduled castes and tribes in India, lower castes in Nepal, rural tribes in Pakistan
Middle East and North Africa	5,092	1,680[d]	33	Berbers, rural populations
East Asia and the Pacific	4,870	4,383[e]	90	Hill tribes, Muslim minorities, other ethnic minorities
Eastern Europe and Central Asia, Commonwealth of Independent States	1,583	1,425[f]	90	Roma, rural populations in Turkey
Latin America and the Caribbean	1,497	1,482[g]	99	Indigenous and Afro-Latino populations
Total	60,421	42,620	71	

Source: UIS, 2005; India census, 2001 [Government of India, 2011]; Pakistan household survey, 2001–02 [Pakistan Bureau of Statistics, 2001–2002]; Vietnam Living Standard Measurement Survey, 1998 [Scott, Steele, & Temesgen, 1998]; Ringold, Orenstein, & Wilkens, 2003; Winkler & Cueto, 2004.

Note. Data are for girls 7–12 years old, unless otherwise noted.

a. Estimated. The percentages in column 3 provide the basis for estimating the total number of out-of-school girls by region reported in column 2.

b. Based on the density of heterogeneity and the assumption that most out-of-school children are from minority groups.

c. Based on 2001 census data from India for the number of girls 7–14 years old from scheduled castes and scheduled tribes, on tribal breakdowns in the Pakistan Integrated Household Survey, a household survey of Nepal, and linguistic and ethnic data from non-urban girls in Afghanistan.

d. Percent of Berbers used to determine the number of out-of-school children.

e. Assumes all children out of school come from excluded groups.

f. Includes Roma and Turkish girls out of school.

Policies to spark progress with the remaining out-of-school populations will require actions on various fronts:

- Altering education policies and addressing discrimination by changing laws and administrative rules.
- Expanding options for educating out-of-school children, especially girls.
- Improving the quality and relevance of schools and classrooms by ensuring that excluded girls receive basic educational inputs and providing professional development to help teachers become agents of change.
- Supporting compensatory preschool and in-school programs that engage and retain excluded children, particularly girls.
- Providing incentives for households to help overcome both the reluctance to send girls to school and the costs of doing so. Donors could spearhead innovation by:

  o Establishing a trust fund for multilateral programs targeted at excluded girls that supports experimentation, innovative programs, alternative schooling options, and the basic inputs for effective schools.
  o Expanding the knowledge base about what works to improve the school participation and achievement of excluded girls through a girls' education evaluation fund. The fund could finance a range of evaluations to build the knowledge base for policy. It could also assist more heterogeneous countries in participating in international assessments of learning achievement to monitor changes over time.
  o Creating demand by financing the compensatory costs associated with reaching excluded children; promoting outreach programs for parents; building partnerships for conditional, cash transfers; and providing school meals, scholarships for girls, and school stipend programs for books and supplies.

ALTERING EDUCATION POLICIES AND ADDRESSING DISCRIMINATION

Changes in policies and rules can help determine the environment in which excluded groups function and increase the credibility of government efforts to reach out-of-school children. Policies alone ensure little, however. Establishing clear mandates against discrimination, a legal system that enforces both entitlements and rights of all citizens, administrative rules that foster the completion of basic education for all children, and an articulated education policy for excluded groups are needed to strengthen the credibility of government, establish a foundation for action, and bring together target populations. These actions also provide a context for engaging donors in advocating for marginalized groups, particularly marginalized girls, and in reaching under-served regions with education programs.

Antidiscrimination laws undergird both legal and policy efforts in fighting exclusion. Clear legal protection offers a beginning in reversing implicit and explicit discrimination against minorities. It has proved critical in Canada, New Zealand, and the United States, where official and public discrimination against minorities was once widespread. South African blacks suffered similarly during apartheid, as did Cuban blacks prior to the revolution of 1958. Unless discrimination is aggressively addressed in the labor market, returns to education will not materialize, reducing the demand for schooling, particularly by girls. Barring trained workers from jobs on the basis of ethnicity, language, or cultural differences has adverse consequences for education because it reduces demand for education by groups that believe the returns will not be positive.

Affirmative action—and the less controversial "preferential" action, which emphasizes bolstering the performance of disadvantaged students while maintaining common standards—has been effective in many countries. Summer math programs and after-school enrichment can strengthen the skills of disadvantaged children. Compensatory programs assume that the minority groups suffer from deficits that can be remedied through tutoring, behavioral guidance, or other compensatory interventions. Brazil, India, Malaysia, South Africa, and Sri Lanka use a combination of affirmative action and compensatory investments to mitigate the effects of discrimination.

Administrative rules often prevent girls from attending schools. In some communities, separate schools for boys and girls are required, which often results in too few schools for girls. Rules preventing children from studying in their mother tongue keep some children who do not speak the language of instruction out of school or make it harder for them to learn. Early ability-based tracking allows schools to provide unequal education programs and produces dropouts. Expulsion of pregnant girls from school and lack of flexibility in school hours for young mothers attempting to continue their schooling after giving birth severely limit their educational opportunities. Changes in all of these rules could increase the number of excluded girls attending school.

Donors could expedite integration by fostering alternative forms of positive discrimination and expanding opportunities for girls who would otherwise have no options. The Open Society Institute assisted local nongovernmental organizations and governments in their efforts to initiate laws and regulations to protect the Roma and make schools safe havens for Roma children. Donor initiatives could also help countries analyze the educational regulations in place that act as barriers to girls.

EXPANDING OPTIONS FOR SCHOOLING

One of the lessons from the high-income OECD [Organisation for Economic Co-operation and Development] countries is that targeted, tailored programs are essential to complement overall schooling investments in order to reach excluded populations and keep excluded children in school. A first step in improving access is making schools or school equivalents locally available. Increasing the number of local schools typically results in greater access for children who are historically excluded.

One way of increasing the number of locally available schools is to allow communities to establish their own schools. Community schools are formal schools that provide the basic elements of the school curriculum, adapted to local conditions, including variations in language of instruction and hours of operation. They are designed to shape schooling to meet the needs and ensure the involvement of community members. They are the ultimate means of giving parents voice in the running of schools. South Asia pioneered the approach in 1987 with its *Shiksha Karmi* Project in Rajasthan, India, which uses paraprofessional teachers, allows the community to select and supervise teachers, and hires part-time workers to escort girls to school.

Two alternatives to formal schooling are nonformal schools and distance education. Nonformal schools address gaps or compensate for limitations of existing schools, particularly for children who never started school or who dropped out early and are older than primary school students. In some cases nonformal schools provide basic literacy training. In others they serve as preparation for re-entry into mainstream schools. Nonformal schools can be highly important in preparing disadvantaged children academically and in developing appropriate social skills and self-discipline. Such schools have contributed to progress in primary education in Bangladesh, which has recently achieved gender parity in primary school.

When expansion of schooling requires the use of teachers with less education, radio or television can help provide better quality lessons. Primary education programs that combine radio delivery of a high-quality curriculum with local monitoring of children's progress have been rigorously evaluated and found to boost learning. The most widely used are interactive radio instruction programs, which use professionally developed curricula broadcast to children in remote regions. Thirteen countries have successfully applied such programs.

At the secondary level, distance education programs such as Mexico's *Telesecondaria* offer a full range of courses, which would be difficult to provide in schools serving small communities. For girls with limited access to information or learning outside the immediate community, such programs vastly increase educational opportunities.

What has not succeeded, though, is providing separate schools for children from ethnic, cultural, and linguistic minorities—often tried in earlier periods, as in the United States, Canada, and New Zealand. Separate schools, for example for the Roma throughout Eastern Europe or blacks in the United States pre-1954, are inherently unequal and suffer from poor quality. Similarly, creating separate schools for girls may fail to improve girls' educational outcomes. Separate schools for girls can also limit their access and, because of poor quality, their performance. Indeed, the lagging performance of Pakistan in girls' education can be attributed in part to the need for double investments in schooling, one for girls, the other for boys. Bangladesh, which has coeducational primary schools, has sped ahead while Pakistan continues to struggle with expanding separate access for both genders.

Lack of funding often prevents experimentation with innovative means of expanding schooling to difficult-to-reach groups or adapting effective programs to new contexts. A trust fund for multilateral programs targeting excluded girls could provide the financial basis for expanding successful efforts of donors and governments.

Donors could also play a catalytic role in devising and financing alternative schooling options, particularly for innovative programs for adolescent girls. Programs such as English language immersion classes or computer training provide an alternative to secondary school that equips girls with marketable skills. Creation of a girls' education evaluation fund to finance bilateral, multilateral, and nongovernmental organization evaluations of new or ongoing programs aimed at reaching girls would help fill a major gap and offer guidance to both policymakers and donors eager to use their resources to promote girls' education . . .

CREATING INCENTIVES FOR HOUSEHOLDS TO SEND GIRLS TO SCHOOL

Cultural taboos, the opportunity cost of labor, low demand for education, and reluctance to allow children, especially girls, to enter mainstream schools contribute to low enrollment, low completion rates, and below-average achievement among excluded groups. Three types of programs—conditional cash transfers, girls' scholarships, and school feeding programs—have shown promise in meeting these challenges.

Conditional cash transfers provide resources to households to defray the costs of sending their children to school. They tie social assistance payments to desirable behaviors, in this case enrolling and keeping children in school. Although challenging to administer, conditional cash transfers provide financial incentives to families and put the onus on them to ensure that children actually go to school, something that school officials often find impossible to do. Robust evaluations have shown that conditional cash transfers increase both school enrollment and retention rates. Excluded groups, who are often more difficult to attract to these programs, have not been identified in these evaluations, so the impact on those groups is not yet known.

Scholarships for girls offer financing for primary and secondary school. They also encourage girls to stay in school. Scholarships compensate families for the direct and indirect costs of education. They are effective when households view cost as the impediment to girls' schooling. Scholarships also provide an additional revenue stream for secondary schools. They have been effective for girls at the secondary level in several countries, notably Bangladesh.

Various types of school feeding programs have been associated with higher attendance, higher enrollment, and, in some cases, lower dropout and higher student achievement. School feeding programs are most effective in meeting school attendance objectives. They are particularly successful where attendance is relatively low at the outset and children come from poor households. A concern, however, is whether school feeding provides additional nutrition or simply substitutes for home meals, particularly for girls; this issue deserves attention.

Governments and multilateral donors have forged partnerships for conditional cash transfers in many countries in Latin America. Expanding those initiatives to other countries and to difficult-to-reach groups could increase the number of excluded girls who attend school. How successful such programs can be in attracting excluded girls, especially adolescent girls, to school remains an open question. Donors could finance and manage household stipend components of conditional cash transfers for low-income countries that lack the managerial capacity and resources to conduct a conditional cash transfer program.

Scholarships for girls have demonstrated enormous promise. Donor initiatives to expand such programs to lower secondary, higher secondary, and tertiary education would increase the number of educated women in low-income countries. Educated women from disadvantaged households could serve as both community leaders and role models for excluded girls.

Stipends could be used to finance uniforms, school supplies, and books for girls—items parents often cannot afford or refuse to pay for because they do not appreciate their value. Providing assistance through stipends avoids the bureaucratic management problems of subsidizing inputs.

Financing school meals can attract children to school. It can also provide employment for adults and help involve parents in school, reinforcing the school as a focus of community life. Such initiatives offer an entry point to help upgrade schools and provide the potential for additional help to children with faltering attendance or performance. School feeding programs have not been tested specifically among excluded groups. Donor funding could help determine whether these programs are effective among excluded children.

Notes

1. The excluded subgroups are: indigenous peoples in Guatemala, hill tribes in Laos, and Roma in the Slovak Republic.

2. Scheduled castes are the lowest caste populations in India and include the "untouchables." Scheduled tribes include indigenous people. They are both on a government schedule of disadvantaged groups, hence the name.

References

Government of India. 2011. *Census—2001 Data Summary*. India Ministry of Home Affairs. www .censusindia.gov.in/2011-common/Census DataSummary.html.

Pakistan Bureau of Statistics. 2001–2002. *Household integrated economic survey 2001–2002*. www.pbs .gov.pk/content/household-integrated-economic-survey-2001-2002.

Ringold, D., M. Orenstein, & E. Wilkens. 2003. *Roma in an expanding Europe? Breaking the poverty cycle*. Washington, DC: World Bank.

Scott, K., D. Steele, & T. Temesgen. 1998. *Household sample surveys in developing and transition countries: Chapter XXII: Living standards measurement study surveys*. Washington, DC: World Bank. http://unstats.un.org/unsd/hhsurveys.

UIS (UNESCO Institute for Statistics). 2005. *Children out of school: Measuring exclusion from primary education*. Montreal: UNESCO.

Winkler, D., & S. Cueto. (Eds.). 2004. *Etnicidad, raza, género y educación en América Latina*. Washington, DC: Inter-American Dialogue, Partnership for Educational Revitalization in the Americas (PREAL). www.preal.org/public-IpeLIBROSindex.php. January 2006.

GLOBALIZATION AND THE GROWTH OF
INTERNATIONAL EDUCATIONAL TESTING AND ASSESSMENT

David H. Kamens and Connie L. McNeely

Along with the spread of educational practices and curricula have come assessments of educational systems around the world. Key to comparative assessment is "international benchmarking," identifying what is considered necessary educational knowledge for a nation's needs, improvement, and global competitiveness. The measurement of student achievement with the use of national educational assessment and international testing indicates an agreement about the importance of testing and what is to be tested. The authors, David H. Kamens and Connie L. McNeely, point out that the significance of testing is the agreement that high levels of educational achievement, national assessment, and international testing are important in order for nations to compete in the global economy and the global "race to the top." In addition, it means that there is an agreed-upon body of knowledge to test globally. The implications are that nations are moving toward similar educational systems and standards.

Questions to consider for this reading:

1. Why are national assessment and international testing important for educational systems, and why has international testing spread rapidly throughout the world?

2. What can be done to increase international assessment, and what are the results of increased global assessment and testing?

3. How do the global assessment and testing movements relate to this chapter's first reading, "Educating All Children"?

Education has long been characterized as a central requirement for national economic development and political democratization in the contemporary world. Moreover, international benchmarking has been identified as the "basis for improvement. . . . It is only through such benchmarking that countries can understand relative strengths and weaknesses of their education systems and identify best practices and ways forward" (OECD 2006, 18). Statements such as this example signal an international consensus that has emerged—at least among "developed" countries—about the legitimacy and, even more so, the necessity of international testing and

From "Globalization and the Growth of International Education Testing and National Assessment," by David H. Kamens and Connie L. McNeely, 2010, *Comparative Education Review, 54*(1), pp. 5–9; 19–22. Copyright University of Chicago Press Journals/Rightslink.

national assessment. As David P. Baker and Gerald K. LeTendre (2005) observe, both international testing and national assessment are linked to efforts to reform educational systems and are often themselves stimuli for further cycles of reform. The results of international testing, they note, will fuel further interest in national assessment.

Here we develop an argument about the global forces that have led to the explosive growth of national educational assessment and international testing. In particular, we argue that the international acceptance of testing comes from key ideological forces in the world polity that are associated with the accelerating globalization of national and international cultural, economic, and political structures. As we develop and warrant this argument, we also qualify it by pointing out that national adaptations to this larger world culture may vary depending on the presence and capacities of international organizations and regional associations that act to mediate and adapt these changes to conditions in individual countries. In addition, we consider the effects of subnational movements in introducing pressures for change that may favor more national assessment.

THE SPREAD OF INTERNATIONAL TESTING AND NATIONAL ASSESSMENT

During the past 40 years, the number of countries participating in international testing for learning in mathematics, science, and reading has increased dramatically, with participation growing among both developed and developing countries (Kamens and McNeely 2007). Indeed, by the end of the first decade of the twenty-first century, over a third of the world's countries will be using standardized tests to assess their middle school and high school student achievement. Still, 65 percent of the countries in the world are not yet involved in international testing, so we must also address the possibilities of limits to this trend.

Two other facts about participation are especially telling. First, countries that score poorly in early rounds of international testing typically continue to participate in later rounds. Second, low-scoring countries that drop out often turn to international governmental organizations (IGOs) and nongovernmental organizations (NGOs) to assist them in conducting national assessments (McNeely and Cha 1994; McNeely 1995; Martens 2005). Thus, the "need" to test or assess student populations is spreading as a taken-for-granted assumption. Moreover, an expanding number of donor agencies and multilateral organizations are mandating some form of learning assessment to accompany their loans and other aid support.[1] Often involving cooperation with organizations that provide technical advice and support, testing is increasingly viewed as an obligation of nation-states. National ministries of education typically act as the agents imposing this activity on schools and education systems.

In addition to the growth of international testing, national learning assessment is growing rapidly, especially in mathematics and language and more so at the primary and lower secondary levels. This trend is occurring not only among the more affluent countries but also among the poorer ones. For example, the Dominican Republic has engaged in a long-term assessment project with the help of the Educational Evaluation Research Consortium and with funding from the United States Agency for International Development (USAID). Similarly, both Latin American and African countries have regional assessment programs funded by UNESCO. The Latin American Association for the Assessment of the Quality of Education, founded in 1994, now has 19 members. The Southern and Eastern African Consortium for Monitoring Educational Quality (SACMEQ), started in 1990, has 15 member countries; seven of them participated in its first assessment study in 1995–97, and 14 were involved in 2000–2003 studies. Similarly, Francophone Africa has the Conference des Ministres de l'Éducation des Pays Ayant le Français en Partage (CONFEMEN), which encourages and assists member states in performing national assessments. Also, some of these associations sponsor regionwide assessments that are more highly standardized than national ones and that resemble international tests.

In 2006 and 2007, UNESCO gathered the most authoritative data to date on the spread of national learning assessments, which tend to focus on how well the intended curriculum is taught and learned. These data show that, across virtually all world regions, national assessments are a rapidly growing phenomenon (Benavot and Tanner 2007). From 1995 to 2005, the number of countries carrying out learning assessments more than doubled, from 28 to 67. And although developed countries continue to have the highest rates, developing countries have almost doubled their rates of learning assessments (from 28 to 51 percent). While "in transition" countries have the lowest levels of assessments, they too, increased in participation over the 10-year span, from 0 to 17 (43 percent).[2] Even "fragile states" have begun to carry out national assessments, with 15 of 35 (43 percent)—half located in East Asia and the Pacific—having done so by 2005.[3]

Nevertheless, there are regional differences in conducting national assessments. In the 1990s, the lowest rates were in sub-Saharan Africa and Central Asia. During the same period, much of southeastern sub-Saharan Africa began conducting national assessments. As of 2005, North America and Western Europe had the highest rates of assessments, followed by Central and Eastern Europe, East Asia, and Latin America. Most of Latin America began national assessment testing in the 1990s. Between 1995 and 2006, the Middle East Arab states, together with South and West Asia, had particularly dramatic increases in their rates (from 15 to 55 percent and from 11 to 44 percent, respectively).

The rapid pattern of growth of national learning assessments looks similar to that of international testing. For instance, while developed countries are leading the use of learning assessments, developing countries—including the most fragile states—are catching up. Additionally, even in regions where almost no international testing has been done, large proportions of countries conduct

national assessments.[4] Countries in Francophone Africa and the Caribbean are particularly striking examples of this pattern—few participate in international testing, but all have conducted national assessments. Finally, the subjects covered in national assessments have been almost identical to those addressed in international testing: mathematics, language, and civics or social studies. This pattern is not surprising since these subjects and science constitute the bulk of the curriculum of grades 1–6, in which much international testing and most national assessments are done (Meyer et al. 1992; Benavot and Tanner 2007).

Despite critics and controversies, it appears that international testing and national assessment have become relatively commonplace across different countries. These initiatives are works in progress, however, and one can expect the related methodology, as well as the breadth of the testing subject matter, to evolve. While comparative interest in national examination systems actually dates back to the late nineteenth century (Meyer et al. 1992; Eckstein and Noah 1993; McNeely and Cha 1994), formal international testing is largely a post–World War II project based in part on technological advances and the availability of sophisticated testing methods and computing capabilities that have made large-scale data collection and analysis possible.

Technological capability is only part of the story. Consider the following scenario: in a world where national educational systems are viewed as unique in structure, history, and purpose, international testing would have little plausibility. In fact, this view was the dominant perspective when Torsten Husén and the International Association for the Evaluation of Educational Achievement (IEA) first conducted international math and science testing in the 1960s. Husén (1967) himself saw the purpose of these studies as investigating national differences in educational systems, which he argued were due to unique educational and cultural histories. Since that time, there has been a change in perspective; testing and assessment no longer seem like a case of comparing apples to oranges (UNESCO 1986).

For example, in the past, countries with centralized educational systems were most likely to implement national examination systems. These examination systems, however, were designed to select students for further education, not to assess the curriculum and its implementation (Eckstein and Noah 1993). Times have changed, and now the emphasis is more typically on the use of testing and assessment to judge the adequacy of educational systems to deliver desired outcomes (Travers and Westbury 1989). In this new environment, it is not clear that distinctions among nation-states and among their educational systems will have such strong impacts on the spread of national assessment and testing. Among the most developed countries, for instance, we have seen that almost all—ranging from those with highly centralized education systems, like France, to those with more decentralized systems, like the United States—do a lot of international testing and national assessment (Baker and LeTendre 2005; Benavot and Tanner 2007). In spite of differences in state structure and the organization of education, the pressure and tendency to test and assess seem equally prevalent. The trend cuts across different types of educational systems—for example, a class-based educational system in France (see discussions in Bowles and Gintis [1976]; Kamens, Meyer, and Benavot [1992]; Rubinson and Fuller [1992]; and Prasad [2005]) and a mass-credentialing system like that in the United States (Collins 1979).

* * *

CONCLUSIONS

It seems clear that international testing is increasing, and the limited data on national assessment suggest that it has also expanded since the 1990s. It seems that fewer and fewer countries imagine that they will achieve the status of the "good society" without high levels of formal education and accompanying efforts at national assessment and/or international testing. Thirty-five percent of

countries now do international testing, but many more are conducting some form of national assessment. According to Benavot and Tanner (2007), 81 percent of developed countries have conducted national assessments as of 2006, and 51 percent of developing countries have also done so. Most of the former also have participated in international achievement testing. About 43 percent of the poorest countries have not done international testing but have completed one or more national assessments. Thus, national assessments are the major growth sector of international testing and will probably continue to expand.

While there may be debates about the forms that education should take, evidence on rising national enrollment levels across the world indicate that no country's elites can envision a successful future without high levels of popular education. Moreover, with notions of education for all come increased pressures for educational accountability. Accordingly, we expect that national assessment will spread and that international testing also will continue to expand in keeping with increasing globalization and world polity cultural dynamics and social relations.

In particular, we have posited the diffusion of international educational testing and national assessment on the basis of three principal cultural features of the world polity: (1) ideologies of education as a source of national and world progress, (2) the hegemony of science as a critical means to development, and (3) the idea that educational systems—and, indeed, society in general—can be managed to produce desirable outcomes. . . . [I]ncreased testing and assessment result from pressures to rationalize education and schooling, with IGOs, NGOs, regional associations, and subnational movements operating as agents of diffusion.

As societal rationalization proceeds and education expands, new domains of assessment are likely to become common. The difficulty will lie in deciding the limits on learning that students should be expected to master (World Bank 2005). Also, given the worldwide expansion of higher education (Schofer and Meyer 2005), it is very likely that the urge to assess will expand to cover additional levels of education. For example, countries might seek information on how their systems of higher education compare with one another (cf. OECD 2008).

National assessment is also likely to expand. Both political elites and external organizations, such as IGOs and NGOs, will facilitate the process as well as demand accountability and evidence of educational effectiveness in exchange for resources. Moreover, since the biggest differences in test scores are linked to issues of democracy within countries, such as access and equality, assessments and comparisons could help in evaluating school policies, constructing models of schooling and teacher practices, and providing educators and the public with contextually sensitive accounts of exposure and learning levels (e.g., Downey et al. 2008).

As previously mentioned, constraints on testing and assessment also exist. While constraints may weaken in the world polity environment, they will not necessarily disappear. In the case of international testing, we have noted at least two practical impediments that must be considered. First, an important problem is the fundamental lack of resources and lack of organizational capacity to administer this complex activity. As more standardization of testing regimes is required, more administrative capability and expertise are also needed to carry out related activities. Sampling designs, test construction, translation, and so on all become complex and important issues. Poor countries simply may not have the necessary resources to coordinate and undertake these activities. Thus, to date, many developing countries have been absent from the populations of countries in which international testing has occurred. Second, engaging in testing opens a country to external scrutiny and may also intensify internal conflicts over perceived responsibilities for inadequate or unequal educational outcomes. Even the most amenable elites in such societies may feel that such comparisons are premature and dangerous at a time when they may be trying to devise school systems and curricula that bridge gaps among groups in their countries.

Nevertheless, the spread of international testing has produced its own dynamic in shaping educational systems, and the modern obsession with education produces intense interest in testing and assessment around the world (McKnight et al. 1987; Stevenson and Stigler 1992; Baker and LeTendre 2005). This is one of the institutionalizations of education and of its "transcendental" character. No matter how well students perform on international tests, educators and political elites are constantly looking for ways to improve their educational systems (Baker and LeTendre 2005). In the context of a globalizing economy, every country is looking for an edge that makes it more competitive. Accordingly, all countries have the urge to compare and compete.

In this global environment, it is difficult to imagine what forces would restrain the urge among national elites to assess and test. World polity culture will continue to spread, even in the face of global economic downturn. This perspective privileges education as integral to democracy and human rights, stimulating demands for both educational expansion and educational accountability. Thus, the drive to assess and test is built into modern education, and both assessment and testing are likely to increase as more countries become more fully integrated into the world polity.

NOTES

1. Aaron Benavot, personal communication, July 2009.

2. "In transition" or "transitional" countries are those attempting to change their basic constitutional elements toward market-style fundamentals (IMF 2000). Countries and territories in transition include the Czech Republic, Estonia, Hungary, Latvia, Lithuania, Poland, Romania, Russia, Slovakia, and Ukraine, plus the more "advanced" developing countries, namely, the Bahamas, Bermuda, Brunei, the Cayman Islands, Cyprus, the Falkland Islands, Hong Kong, Israel, Kuwait, Qatar, Singapore, Taiwan, and the United Arab Emirates. Some World Bank studies also include Mongolia (IMF 2000; DFID 2009).

3. States are considered "fragile" when their governments cannot or will not deliver core functions to their people, with a focus on the "weak capacity and/or lack of political will to provide services and to sustain a development partnership with the international community" (Vallings and Moreno-Torres 2005, 4).

4. National assessment may be a widely respected substitute for participation in international "high-stakes" testing because the former (*a*) has higher utility for policy elites, providing useful national and subnational evidence on the functioning of teachers and regional school systems; (*b*) is more relevant in given countries' curricula; and (*r*) may avoid problems associated with international testing and comparison (e.g., potential political humiliation and high costs).

REFERENCES

Baker, D. P., and G. K. LeTendre. 2005. *National Differences, Global Similarities: World Culture and the Future of Schooling*. Stanford, CA: Stanford University Press.

Benavot, A., and E. Tanner. 2007. "The Growth of National Learning Assessments in the World, 1995–2006." Background paper prepared for the *Education for All Global Monitoring Report, 2008*, UNESCO, Paris.

Bowles, S., and H. Gintis. 1976. *Schooling in Capitalist America*. New York: Basic.

Chabbott, C. 2003. *Constructing Education for Development: International Organizations and Education for All*. New York: Routledge/Falmer.

Collins, R. 1979. *The Credential Society*. New York: Academic Press.

Comber, L. C., and J. P. Keeves. 1973. *Science Education in Nineteen Countries*. New York: Wiley.

DFID (Department for International Development). 2009. "DFID Glossary." http://www.dfid.gov.uk/About-DFID/Glossary/

Downey, D., P. von Hippel, and M. Hughes. 2008. "Are 'Failing' Schools Really Failing? Using Seasonal Comparison to Evaluate School Effectiveness." *Sociology of Education* 81 (July): 242–70.

Eckstein, M., and H. Noah. 1993. *Secondary School Examinations*. New Haven, CT: Yale University Press.

Husén, T. 1967. *International Study of Achievement in Mathematics: A Comparison of Twelve Countries*. New York: Wiley.

International Monetary Fund. 2000. *Transition Economies: An IMF Perspective on Progress and Prospects*. Washington, DC: IMF.

Kamens, D. H., and C. L. McNeely. 2007. "International Benchmarking and National Curricular Reform: Educational Goal Setting and Assessment Effects." Paper presented at the Annual Conference of the Comparative and International Education Society, March 13, Baltimore.

Kamens, D. H., J. W. Meyer, and A. Benavot. 1992. "The Changing Content of World Secondary Education Systems, 1920–1990." Policy, Planning, and Research Working Paper, Education and Employment, World Bank, Washington, DC.

Martens, K. 2005. *NGOs and the United Nations*. New York: Macmillan.

McKnight, C. C., F. J. Crosswhite, and J. A. Dossey. 1987. *The Underachieving Curriculum: Assessing U.S. Mathematics from an International Perspective*. Champaign, IL: Stipes.

McNeely, C. L. 1995. "Prescribing National Education Politics: The Role of International Organizations." *Comparative Education Review* 39 (4): 483–507.

McNeely, C. L., and Y. K. Cha. 1994. "Worldwide Educational Convergence through International Organizations: Avenues for Research." *Education Policy Analysis Archives* 2 (14): 1–17.

Meyer, J. W., D. H. Kamens, and A. Benavot. 1992. *School Knowledge for the Masses: World Models and Curricular Categories in the Twentieth Century*. London: Falmer.

OECD (Organisation for Economic Co-operation and Development). 2006. *Education at a Glance, 2006*. Paris: OECD.

OECD (Organisation for Economic Co-operation and Development). 2008. *Education at a Glance, 2008*. Paris: OECD.

Prasad, M. 2005. "Why Is France So French? Culture, Institutions, and Neoliberalism, 1974–1981." *American Journal of Sociology* 111 (September): 357–408.

Rubinson, R., and B. Fuller. 1992. "Specifying the Effects of Education on National Economic Growth." In *The Political Construction of Education: The State, School Expansion, and*

Economic Change, ed. B. Fuller and R. Rubinson. New York: Praeger.

Schofer, E., and J. W. Meyer. 2005. "Worldwide Expansion of Higher Education." *American Sociological Review* 70 (December): 898–920.

Stevenson, H., and J. Stigler. 1992. *Why Our Schools Are Failing and What We Can Learn from Japanese and Chinese Education.* New York: Summit.

Travers, K., and I. Westbury, eds. 1989 *The IEA Study of Mathematics I: Analysis of Mathematics Curricula.* New York: Pergamon.

UNESCO. 1986. *The Place of Science and Technology in School Curricula: A Global Survey.* Paris: UNESCO Division of Science, Technical, and Environmental Education.

Vallings, C., and M. Moreno-Torres. 2005. "Drivers of Fragility: What Makes States Fragile?" Poverty Reduction in Difficult Environments (PRDE) Working Paper no. 7, Department of International Development, London.

World Bank. 2005. *Expanding Opportunities and Building Competencies for Young People.* Washington, DC: World Bank.

TRANSITIONS FROM EDUCATION TO WORK

An Introduction

Rachel Brooks

This reading by Rachel Brooks focuses on the end goal of education: graduating a productive working member of society. Graduation signifies a rite of passage from youth to adulthood. In today's world, however, increased complexity has made this transition anything but straightforward. Changes in social, political, and economic institutions in societies result in a variety of often complex transition models; for instance, many youth begin work before finishing school or are in and out of school before settling into a career. Brooks discusses factors that influence transitions including education-to-work policies and complexities of the transitions in various regions of the world.

Questions to consider for this reading:

1. Why are nations' governments concerned about the transition from education to work?

2. What are some complications discussed by Brooks in making this transition?

3. What are some ways to accomplish this transition?

CHANGING PATTERNS OF TRANSITION?

The concept of a "transition" from full-time education to full-time work is one with a long history in youth studies, sociology, psychology and education. However, along with other transitions typically associated with the period of "youth" (i.e. from the parental home into independent housing and from the "family of destination" to the "family of origin"), it has been subjected to considerable critical scrutiny over recent years. . . . [S]ome researchers have argued that it now offers little theoretical purchase on the experiences of young people in the twenty-first century and the increasing complexity of the choices they are required to make as they move towards adulthood. While acknowledging the changes to the social, political and economic context within which young people now live, other scholars have suggested that it is more helpful to discuss changes to the nature of transitions, rather than assume that the concept is now obsolete. Indeed, in mapping some of these changes over recent decades, youth researchers have highlighted three significant trends in young people's transition from education to work, which have been identified in many parts of the world. First, it is clear that young people are remaining in full-time education for longer periods of time and, as a consequence, entering the labour market (as full-time employees) at a correspondingly older age. This is evident not only in Western Europe, the United States and Australia, but also in Asian and post-communist countries (France, 2007). In the United Kingdom, 82 per cent of 16-year-olds and 69 per cent of 17-year-olds were in full-time post-compulsory education or government-supported training in 2005/2006 (DCSF, 2007), compared with around a third of this cohort in the early 1970s. Across all OECD (Organisation for Economic Co-operation and Development) countries, the average educational enrollments amongst 15- to 19-year-olds reached a similar level (of 82 per cent) in 2005, with some countries such as Belgium, the Czech Republic, Greece and Poland having reached 90 per cent or more (OECD, 2007).

Second, the youth labour market remains stagnant. For many countries in Europe, this stagnation has its roots in the early 1980s when youth employment collapsed as a reaction to a more general economic downturn. As Furlong and Cartmel (2007) note, youth unemployment is typically more sensitive to economic pressures than adult employment, and thus suffers disproportionately during periods of recession. Although a large number of countries experienced a collapse in the youth labour market in the last three decades of the twentieth century, there has been considerable variation in both the time at which this occurred and the magnitude of the decline. For example, whereas youth unemployment in European countries typically peaked in the mid-1980s and early 1990s, it was not experienced in Japan until the mid-1990s. Even within Europe disparities were seen, with higher levels of unemployment and sharper rises in the rate of unemployment occurring in southern European countries than in their northern counterparts (ibid.). This clearly had an impact on

extending the period of education, discussed above: with fewer jobs available for school leavers, educational opportunities came to be perceived as increasingly attractive. Although some of the more pessimistic predictions about the future of youth employment did not come to fruition (namely that levels of youth unemployment would remain very high permanently), structural changes to the labour market over the last part of the twentieth century have had a significant impact on the type of work that is available to school leavers and other young people in search of employment. Young workers are now typically employed in small-sized firms in the service sector and, like many older adults, are increasingly employed on temporary contracts and on a part-time basis (du Bois Reymond and Chisholm, 2006). It is also the case that we are witnessing more variation in patterns of transition, as young people increasingly "blend" periods of education and work, moving backwards and forwards between the two and engaging in significant elements of paid work whilst being a fuller- or part-time student. Indeed, reflecting on changes witnessed in the last few decades of the twentieth century, Chisholm (2006) notes:

> Transitions to the labour market were taking place not only later but also in more differentiated and gradual ways as young people mixed study and work in a combination between practical economic necessity, tactical career planning, and personal choices. (p. 15)

Third, alongside the extension of full-time education, we have witnessed the emergence of what some researchers have called the "training state" as a major pathway for school leavers since the 1980s (Mizen, 2004). Indeed, offering more extensive training packages to young people as they leave school has been one way in which national governments have tried to manage unemployment and skills shortages. This has been replicated at a regional level: for example, the European Union (EU) Summit on Employment held in Luxembourg in 1997 established a common set of principles to underpin provisions for young people who had been unemployed for a period of six months or more—which included a guarantee of education, training or employment (Chisholm, 2006; Furlong and Cartmel, 2007).

Though the nature of young people's transition from education to work has changed in the ways outlined above, there are also important elements of continuity, which should not be overlooked. For example, in their comparison of the transitions of British young people in the 1970s and the 1990s, Schoon et al. (2001) argue that, although the latter cohort demonstrates more fluidity in its transition patterns, gender continues to play a central role in shaping the pathways taken by young people, with more young women than young men outside the labour force—involved either in education or in family care. Similar gender differences are apparent in other parts of the world. On the basis of their analysis of data from the European Labour Force Survey, Iannelli and Smyth (2008) suggest that gender has a significant impact on transitions in most European countries, as a result of the different pathways taken by young men and young women through education and training (and, in particular, the different fields of study they choose) rather than because of differentials in the level of qualification attained. Schoon et al. also demonstrate persistent inequalities across time in the fortunes of those with the lowest level of qualification. Indeed, they contend that as a result of the more general trend towards staying on longer in education those who leave "early" with few or no qualifications are increasingly adversely affected by the disappearance of traditional entry-level jobs and the polarisation of the labour market (p. 19). Similar arguments are advanced by Dwyer and Wyn (2001) in their analysis of young people's transitions to employment within the Australian labour market. Such differences also continue to be quite strongly associated with social class, with young people from working-class backgrounds over-represented amongst early labour market entrants, while the nature and type of work-based training taken up by young people also continue to be highly stratified by socio-economic status

(as well as gender and "race"/ethnicity) (Furlong and Cartmel, 2007, p. 29).

These trends in young people's transitions from education to work are inextricably related to wider economic changes in Europe and other parts of the world over recent decades. The changing structure of the labour market, periods of recession and the increasing dominance of the so-called "knowledge economy" have all had considerable impact on the experiences of young people as they come towards the end of their full-time education. However, within Europe in particular, youth researchers have argued that young people's transitions from education to work have been altered, not only by the changing economic structures around them, but also by the considerable shifts in the political environment that occurred in the last couple of decades of the twentieth century—namely the demise of communist regimes in central and eastern Europe and the drive towards further European integration across the continent. Indeed, Chisholm (2006) goes as far as to suggest that, as a result of these changes, "Young Europeans could now think of their lifestyles and futures in different ways; new options for realization became practically available" (p. 15). . . .

THE IMPACT OF POLICY

Over recent years, many scholars have argued that state autonomy in relation to education policy-making has become increasingly limited by trends and initiatives at the European and international level. For example, Stephen Ball has contended that "the nation state is no longer adequate on its own as a space within which to think about policy" (2008, p. 25), maintaining that policies are now made largely in response to globalisation and tend to be driven by supranational agencies, practical policy "fads" and the flow of policies between countries. In relation to Europe, in particular, Martin Lawn has suggested that, as a result of both the Bologna Process and the Lisbon Strategy, a new "European learning space" has opened up, which "stands in sharp contrast to the older, central roles played by organisations, rigid borders and national sites" (2006, p. 272). The Lisbon Strategy (European Parliament, 2000) aims to make the EU the most competitive and dynamic knowledge-based society in the world . . . through measures such as encouraging the mobility (for both learning and working) of European citizens; creating an "information society" for all; promoting employability through investment in citizens' knowledge and competences; and the adaptation of education and training to enable individuals to be offered tailored learning opportunities at all stages of life. The Bologna Process (Commission of the European Communities, 1999) is an inter-governmental initiative which aims to create a European "higher education area" . . . and to promote the European system of higher education worldwide.

Initiatives such as these, it is argued, have had considerable impact on young people's transitions from education to work. Indeed, Walther and Plug (2006) outline a number of concepts which, they suggest, have gained widespread currency across Europe through processes of European integration and European policy-making. These include "employability," which, they argue, is based on an individualised understanding of disadvantage—in which unemployed young people (and older adults) are viewed as insufficiently adapted to the demands of potential employers; "lifelong learning," which "reflects the fact that education and employment are no longer linked directly within post-Fordist labour markets" (p. 85); and "activation" employment policies—which rely on motivating individuals to look for a job. More specifically, mechanisms have been put in place to drive forward the "Europeification" of education and training policies: the definition by the EU of a matrix of policies to be developed by member states in the field of education and training; the establishment of inter-governmental platforms to take decisions about measures to be implemented in individual countries; and the development of an EU community agenda and

policy for education and training (Antunes, 2006). These have underpinned the Open Method of Co-ordination, which has attempted to promote convergence in vocational education and training across Europe.

Despite these trends, however, the nation state retains considerable autonomy in relation to education. It is notable that the Open Method of Co-ordination aims for convergence (i.e. moving closer together) rather than harmonisation in this area, and even this aim has been subject to criticism from European politicians, on the grounds that it may well compromise national diversity (Fredriksson, 2003). Moreover, various empirical studies have demonstrated the enduring differences in education policies, educational systems and education-to-work transitions across Europe. While acknowledging the various pressures from the EU to further the co-operation between universities and the world of work, Dahlgren et al. (2007), for example, point to considerable variation in the extent to which this was implemented in the four European countries in which they conducted research. Similarly, Furlong and Cartmel (2007) outline significant national differences in responses to the widespread unemployment of young people across Europe in the 1990s (and despite the establishment of a common set of principles for tackling youth unemployment, outlined during the EU summit on employment held in Luxembourg in 1997).

Recent scholarship has also emphasised the influence of the nature of national welfare regimes in determining education-to-work policies and, as a result, young people's experiences as they reach the end of their full-time education (Iannelli and Smyth, 2008). Drawing on Esping-Anderson's work (1990), Pohl and Walther (2007) identify five types of "transition regime" operating in Europe. These are broadly related to the more general welfare regimes operating in the individual countries (or clusters of countries), but are also underpinned by the differences in policies that impact young people's transitions from education to work and, perhaps most fundamentally, different ways in which "youth" is conceptualised. The "universalistic" transition regime of the Nordic countries is, Pohl and Walther argue, based on assumptions about the importance of collective welfare—and the citizenship rights of all young people, irrespective of their social background. Here, labour market activation measures focus on opening up access and developing individuals' orientations towards mainstream jobs, rather than damping down aspirations and encouraging take-up of low-status careers. In contrast, the "liberal" transition regime typical of the United Kingdom and Ireland is characterised by Pohl and Walther as valuing individual rights and responsibilities above collective provisions, and understanding youth as a transition phase that should be replaced as quickly as possible by economic independence. Policy responses place more responsibility on the individual for maximising his/her own "employability." The "employment-centred" transition regime is evident in continental countries such as Austria and Germany. Here, youth is understood as a process of socialisation into allocated social positions—through a selective schooling system and a limited range of labour market options for young people experiencing unemployment. The "sub-protective" transition regime is found, according to Pohl and Walther, in southern European countries including Spain, Greece and Italy. Young people in these countries have no distinct status, and youth transitions are characterised by a long "waiting phase" during which young people are dependent on their families. Labour market segmentation and a lack of training opportunities are argued to contribute to high levels of youth unemployment. Finally, countries included within the "post-communist" regime of eastern Europe have mixed understandings of "youth." Transition policies vary accordingly, with some sharing significant elements with the liberal regime, whereas others have more in common with the employment-centred, universalistic or sub-protective regimes. These differences highlight the important variations between the experiences of young people across Europe and the close interaction between the way in which youth is understood in a particular society and its youth-related policies.

REFERENCES

Antunes, F., "Globalisation and Europeification of education policies: routes, processes and metamorphoses," *European Educational Research Journal,* 5 (1) (2006) 38–55.

Ball, S., *The Education Debate* (Bristol: The Policy Press, 2008).

Brooks, R., ed., *Transitions from Education to Work: New Perspectives from Europe and Beyond* (Palgrave, 2009).

Chisholm, L., "European youth research: Developments, debates, demands," *New Directions for Child and Adolescent Development,* 113 (2006) 11–21.

Commission of the European Communities, *The Bologna Declaration on the European Space for Higher Education, a Joint Declaration of the European Ministers of Education* (Luxembourg: Office for Official Publications of the European Communities, 1999).

Dahlgren, L., Handal, G., Szkudlarek, T., and Bayer, M., "Students as journeymen between cultures of higher education and work: A comparative European project on the transition from higher education to working life," *Higher Education in Europe,* 32 (4) (2007) 305–316.

Department for Children, Schools and Families (DCSF), *Education and Training Statistics for the United Kingdom* (2007 edition) http://www.dcsf.gov.uk/rsgateway/DB/VOL/v000761/Vweb02-2007final.pdf (accessed 27 June 2008).

du Bois Reymond M. and Chisholm, L., "Young Europeans in a changing world," *New Directions for Child and Adolescent Development,* 113 (2006) 1–9.

Dwyer, P. and Wyn, J., *Youth, Education and Risk: Facing the Future* (London: Routledge, 2001).

Esping-Anderson, G., *The Three Worlds of Welfare Capitalism* (Cambridge: Polity Press, 1990).

European Parliament, *Presidency Conclusions, Lisbon European Council (23 and 24 March 2000).* http://www.europarl.europa.eu/summits/lis1_en.htm#c (accessed 5 July 2007).

France, A., *Understanding Youth in Late Modernity* (Maidenhead: Open University Press, 2007).

Fredriksson, U., "Change of education policies within the European union in the light of globalisation," *European Educational Research Journal,* 2 (4) (2003) 522–546.

Furlong, A. and Cartmel, F., *Young People and Social Change*: *Individualisation and Risk in Late Modernity* 2nd edn (Milton Keynes: Open University Press, 2007).

Iannelli, C. and Smyth, E. E., "Mapping gender and social background differences in education and youth transitions across Europe," *Journal of Youth Studies,* 11 (2) (2008) 213–232.

Lawn, M., "Soft governance and the learning spaces of Europe," *Comparative European Politics,* 4 (2006) 272–288.

Mizen, P., *The Changing State of Youth* (Basingstoke: Palgrave, 2004).

Organisation for Economic Co-operation and Development (OECD), *Education at a Glance 2007: OECD Indicators* (Paris: OECD, 2007).

Pohl, A. and Walther, A., "Activating the disadvantaged: Variations in addressing youth transitions across Europe," *International Journal of Lifelong Education,* 26 (5) (2007) 533–553.

Schoon, I., McCulloch, A., Joshi, H. E., Wiggins, R. D., and Bynner, J., "Transitions from school to work in a changing social context," *Young,* 9 (4) (2001) 4–22.

Walther, A. and Plug, W., "Transitions from school to work in Europe: Destandardization and policy trends," *New Directions for Child and Adolescent Development,* 113 (2006) 77–90.

Projects for Further Exploration

1. Various tests are used to compare academic achievement across countries. Using an academic database, search *international*, *test results*, and *education* to find a listing of test results across countries. How do students from the United States compare with those from other countries?

2. Using the web, look up at least two colleges or universities from three countries in different regions of the world. Compare the criteria for admission, curriculum offerings, methods for funding education, and format for instruction in these three different countries.

3. Interview a student or person from another country. Ask the interviewee about the structure of educational systems in his or her country and how the educational system there prepares students for entry into the workforce.

11

CAN SCHOOLS CHANGE?

Educational Reform and Change

We have examined various parts of the open systems model throughout this book. Many of these readings point to places in the model where change and reform are desirable. In this chapter, we conclude by focusing on the "whole" education system and looking at the possibility of change. These four readings include historical analyses of change, comparative studies of educational reforms, and recommendations for the future.

Why even discuss change in education when sociologists define institutions as stable clusters of roles, norms, and values? It would seem that the tendency is for education to remain "as is" rather than to change rapidly. In studying the history of change in schools, Tyack and Cuban (1995) found that change in the structure of schooling is complicated and likely to be rejected because interest in change may conflict with other interests in keeping things as they are. Many changes from the past are all too familiar and form the basis of what we consider to be "real schools" today. One example is the graded school, which began in 1860, and another the school calendar. It can be baffling at times to try to understand why change is so difficult.

However, there is a history of broader-based reform efforts in the United States. A brief review of these reform efforts since the 1980s helps us to understand the patterns inherent in these attempts at change. Race to the Top and No Child Left Behind (NCLB) are the most recent in a series of reform strategies. Looking back, the publication of *A Nation at Risk* by the National Commission on Excellence in Education began what some called the first wave of reform in 1983. This report called for tightening requirements for students and qualifications for teachers. This was followed by calls from the National Governors Association for school restructuring, including school-based management and school choice. When these efforts did not produce results by the late 1980s, the National Governors Association defined goals for American schools. These goals called for systemic reform at all levels of education using both top-down and bottom-up strategies for implementation, including outcome-based education (Dougherty & Hall, 1997). The next wave of reform was initiated in 1989 with the specification of eight goals that were set for the year 2000. Goals 2000 focused on outcomes such as higher graduation rates and improved performance, including higher achievement in mathematics and science. Not surprisingly, these goals were accompanied by a focus on evaluation and assessment. The year 2000 arrived, and clearly these goals had not been reached.

The current focus on educational standards and testing, discussed in this chapter's first reading by Ben Levin, Robert B. Schwartz, and Adam Gamoran, is a natural outgrowth of these reform efforts and is specified clearly in NCLB and Race to the Top. These authors use international assessment measures, TIMSS and PISA, to identify countries that have been particularly successful in increasing academic achievement. They then make recommendations for school reforms in the United States by examining patterns of schooling that have been successful in other countries. Interestingly, they find that countries that are successful do not use assessments in the same way they are used in the United States.

All too often we get caught up on issues within schools and forget why they became issues in the first place. The reading by Douglas B. Downey and Benjamin G. Gibbs in Chapter 8 reminds us to consider contextual factors and the things schools can't control when developing school reforms. Many of these factors are related to the burdens of living in poverty. In the second reading in this chapter, Jean Anyon describes the role of social movements in effecting educational change. She argues that change in schools comes from connections of overlapping networks, including parents, unions, minority groups, academics, and others—all working together to call for change in the way schools work. Anyon believes that social movements, or the merging of interests of multiple groups, can create a context for change in schools and promote equity in education.

We include in this chapter a classic piece by Ivan Illich that proposes an entirely different system of schooling and challenges the need for traditional forms of schooling. In his classic piece, published in 1971, Illich does not propose educational reform; rather he calls for radical changes in the way we "do" education. Illich argues for abolishing traditional schooling and replacing it with an entirely elective system in which individuals can learn whenever they wish from whomever they wish. Although his proposals may not stand a chance of implementation in the near or even distant future, it is useful in raising questions about what we are really trying to accomplish in our schools.

Yet, society is changing rapidly, with technology leading the way. We close this book with a reading by Paul Hill and Mike Johnston; the latter is a former teacher, high school principal, and state senator in Colorado. They see "a new landscape of public schooling" that depends less on classrooms and teachers who teach in traditional ways. The changes they describe rely less on classrooms and more on technology and innovations in the way students connect to learning.

We, of course, are only providing a brief glimpse into the area about which many studies and reports proposing educational reform have been written. As you read this chapter, recall the open systems model in the introduction to this book. Think about how all these elements of the open systems model facilitate as well as inhibit change. We hope these readings stoke your creative juices and provide a framework for you to look at the parts of the educational system and envision the future of education in new and productive ways.

References

Dougherty, K., & Hall, P. M. (1997). Implications of the Goals 2000 legislation. In K. M. Borman, P. W. Cookson, Jr., A. R. Sadovnik, & J. Z. Spade (Eds.), *Implementing educational reform: Sociological perspectives on educational policy* (pp. 459–467). Norwood, NJ: Ablex.

Tyack, D., & Cuban, L. (1995). *Tinkering toward utopia: A century of public school reform.* Cambridge, MA: Harvard University Press.

Learning From Abroad

Ben Levin, Robert B. Schwartz, and Adam Gamoran

As described in the introduction to this chapter, educational reform is hardly a new concept. Gradually over time, educational reforms have tended to focus on assessments used to evaluate schools, teachers, and students, with the ultimate goal of dismantling "bad" schools and giving students who attend those schools or their parents an opportunity to choose a "better school." Ben Levin, Robert B. Schwartz, and Adam Gamoran take a very different tactic in this reading. They turn their focus to countries that have better records at improving academic achievement than the United States and describe seven patterns that likely contribute to higher achievement in the diverse countries.

Questions to consider for this reading:

1. Of the seven reforms the authors recommend, which do you think would be easiest to implement in the United States?

2. Why do they think the patterns of education that work in other countries could be effective in the United States?

3. Why do they think U.S. schools don't have high expectations for all students?

[I]deas abound for the best ways to improve the U.S. public education system. In this chapter, we propose an approach that builds on strategies that have been successful in other parts of the world but are not yet central in the U.S. education debate. . . .

Our starting point is this: for the past two decades, the U.S. has been engaged in a sustained effort to improve academic achievement and to reduce persistent racial and socioeconomic gaps in achievement in its schools. While some states and large urban districts have made significant progress during this period, overall improvement in performance has been disappointingly modest.[1]

Meanwhile, international assessments such as the Trends in International Mathematics and Science Study (TIMSS) and Program for International Student Assessment (PISA) allow U.S. policy makers to compare the performance of our schools and students with those in other countries.[2] These assessments leave no doubt that there are nations (or in some cases, states or provinces) whose education systems achieve both higher overall performance and more equitable

From "Learning From Abroad: Rapid Improvement Is Possible, Even in a System Like Ours," by Ben Levin, Robert B. Schwartz, and Adam Gamoran, 2012, pp. 13–26 in *The Futures of School Reform,* edited by Jal Mehta, Robert B. Schwartz, and Frederick M. Hess. Cambridge, MA: Harvard Education Press. Copyright © President and Fellows of Harvard University; Harvard Education Press.

outcomes than the United States. The studies also highlight the fact that some countries have shown dramatic improvement in educational outcomes over relatively short periods; for example, Korea and Singapore have gone from having very low levels of education to very high levels for large numbers of people in only two or three decades.[3]

But while these international rankings tend to get most of the media attention, they are only a small part of the TIMSS and PISA findings, and in many ways the least interesting element. If one digs deeper, one finds sophisticated studies that look behind the achievement levels to understand the dynamics driving them. The tests themselves are carefully designed to ensure that they are not culturally biased, and they factor in data on related matters such as students' motivation and sense of belonging as well as teachers' and principals' ideas about good policy and practice.[4] Moreover, the consistency in results across multiple administrations, especially in PISA, suggests that these studies are indeed capturing important dynamics of the various systems.

Of course, countries cannot simply imitate one another's policies, whether in education or in other fields. Each context is different, which means that policies have to be adapted to fit local conditions. Education policy does not travel easily from Alaska to Alabama or Massachusetts to Montana, so one cannot simply copy what's been done elsewhere and expect it to work. Teaching Finnish to all U.S. children, for example, would likely not reproduce Finland's high levels of literacy. However, it is possible to understand this need for adaptation of policy and still believe that one can gain important ideas from systems in other places. Understanding the policy framework that is successful in one place does not mean adopting it entirely in another, but equally, differences in context should not mean that there is nothing to learn.

In fact, the United States itself has been a major exporter of ideas and policies around the world, and has advocated their adoption in places with different cultures and histories. Moreover, the education policy lessons from other countries that we emphasize in this chapter are not just those of one place, but those that appear to be effective in a number of diverse settings. Just as we should not blindly accept the results of one research study but look for similar results across a number of studies, we should also ensure that potential policy approaches have proven effective in several places, not just one, before they are the subject of serious interest.

Our approach is to look at some of the common elements in countries that have yielded very high levels of education performance or have made large improvements in recent years, or both. The countries that fit this definition include some that are quite different from the U.S., such as Finland, Singapore, Japan, and Korea, and others that are much more similar, such as Canada and Australia. Those six systems differ in many ways—in basic structural features, size, homogeneity, culture, and so on. Some have unitary systems, while others, such as Australia and Canada, are federal states like the United States. Canada and Australia also have high levels of population diversity like the U.S. The fact that all these jurisdictions share some common features lends weight to the contention that it is these features, more than the peculiarities of each country, that have produced improvement.

And, again, in a few cases this improvement has taken place in a relatively short time. Some of these jurisdictions have shown very substantial improvement in educational outcomes—catching up to or surpassing those in the United States—over only the last twenty or thirty years. Finland, for example, saw a very large upturn in performance when it changed its approach twenty or so years ago.[5] And as we noted earlier, some countries, like Korea and Singapore, have gone in less than fifty years from being very poorly educated countries to being among the best educated in the world. Several studies have also cited the province of Ontario in Canada for its significantly improved outcomes in the last few years, while Quebec and Alberta have been high performing in all rounds of PISA and in TIMSS.[6]

These countries do not employ a common recipe. They embody many differences that reflect their varied histories, values, and institutional structures. However, there are some core features that distinguish them, that are closely connected to their excellent results, and that could richly inform U.S. education policy.

INTERNATIONAL LEADERS' COMMON ELEMENTS

Let's start with what these jurisdictions do *not* do. Several of the most significant features of recent education policy debate in the U.S. are simply not found in any of these countries—for example, charter schools, pathways into teaching that allow candidates with only several weeks of training to assume full responsibility for a classroom, teacher evaluation systems based on student test scores, and school accountability systems based on the premise that schools with low average test scores are failures, irrespective of the compositions of their student populations. Nor is choice or competition a main driver in any of these countries, though several have some degree of parent choice.

Instead, these countries share seven common elements:

1. A focus on attracting, retaining, and developing talented people as educators.

2. Priority attention to requiring—and helping— all schools and educators improve their work, not through the imposition of practice but through the development of common approaches based on research and evidence.

3. Careful attention to developing leaders.

4. High expectations for all students coupled with real efforts to keep students on track for success from the very beginning of their schooling.

5. Strong efforts to connect secondary education to the economy and employment as well as to post-secondary education.

6. National policies and resources that focus on minimizing disparities in outcomes and on

helping most [of] those schools that face the greatest challenges in terms of student demographics.

7. A positive approach that builds trust and commitment while engaging all partners in efforts toward further improvement.

This list may seem rather prosaic. There are no dramatic steps here, no measures that will single-handedly produce transformation. Indeed, we take the view that it is precisely the steady pursuit of improvement, rather than the desire for the single dramatic change, that is key to better education, just as it has been in many other fields of human activity. In developing this list, we are drawing on several sources of knowledge about high performing education systems.[7]

In the following pages, we'll say a little more about each element, noting that space permits only a very brief discussion of these complex issues.

1. A focus on attracting, retaining, and developing talented people as educators

Successful education systems focus intensively on what happens in schools and classrooms between students and teachers. These systems understand that teachers need to be well prepared, and consequently, that the programs that prepare educators need to be rigorous. In Finland, for example, all prospective teachers must go through a five-year, university-based program that culminates in a master's degree. Finland, like most high performing countries, recruits aspiring teachers from the top third of the talent pool, and its university training programs now have ten applicants for every available position. In Canada, there are typically three or four applicants for every teacher training place, while teacher education programs in Singapore and Korea are also highly selective.

Legislators and policy makers in high performing countries understand that to attract top talent into teaching, the work must be seen as professional, and schools must be organized to support the continuous learning and development of teachers. In Japan, this takes the form of setting aside substantial time during the school day for teachers to have collaborative planning opportunities and lesson study. Strong education systems give their highest priority to helping their teachers and principals get better at their work. This means more than professional development workshops; it involves creating a school culture where the adults, just like the students, are encouraged and expected to think about their work and to continue improving their skills. Recent studies in the U.S. suggest that these supports are no less important in our context.[8]

Some high performing systems also provide career opportunities for teachers so they can advance in the profession without having to leave the classroom entirely, unless they choose to. In Singapore, for example, teachers can choose among three pathways once they have established themselves as highly effective teachers. They can move onto an administrative track, heading toward the principalship. They can become specialists in areas like research, assessment, or technology. But they can also choose a pathway leading them to successive levels of responsibility as teachers. The pay scales in each pathway are comparable, so a master teacher can make as much as a senior administrator.

2. Priority attention to requiring—and helping—all schools and educators improve their work, not through the imposition of practice but through the development of common approaches based on research and evidence

Most high performing countries begin with some form of national curriculum that provides overall coherence and direction to students' studies across the entire system. However, their curriculum documents are often thinner and less structured than those in the United States. They highlight a few key topics in each subject and grade level that are essential for students to master, and provide guidance to teachers on how these topics might be approached, but they leave a substantial amount of discretion for teachers—at the local level—to account for local preferences and students' needs. Again, unlike most of the U.S., assessments are closely linked to the curriculum, including attention to higher-order skills. Where assessments reflect the breadth of curriculum goals, teaching to the test is also teaching to the curriculum, so the whole emphasis on test preparation is much diminished. In many successful systems, the assessments are also designed to provide diagnostic and instructional [information], in addition to—or even instead of—student or school accountability information.

A common curriculum allows for both initial teacher preparation and ongoing professional development programs to focus on helping teachers develop the capacity to teach the curriculum. In Japan, for example, lesson study enables teachers to share best practices for teaching key topics or lessons in the national curriculum. Primary reading instruction in Ontario, to take another example, is much more consistent across classrooms and schools, a major factor in improved results there. In the U.S., by contrast, one can never be entirely sure that two teachers in the same subject area in the same school are working on the same assignments and lessons, so this form of professional development rarely occurs.

High performing countries typically put into place thoughtful processes for the periodic revision of their curriculum, systematically collecting evidence from the analysis of student performance data and the testimony of teachers about areas for improvement. In Finland, for example, the only national assessments that are administered before the end of secondary school are designed to produce system-level data at two grade levels to inform policy makers about the strengths and weaknesses of the system as a whole, not for school or student accountability. Australia uses state and national data to identify schools that need additional support, as well as areas that require more attention across the system. A key aspect of this approach to improvement is the expectation that all schools are involved in improvement, not just a small proportion seen as struggling or failing.

3. Careful attention to developing leaders

School systems also require high-quality leadership from people who understand the core business of teaching and learning, and who focus their attention on teachers and classrooms.

Singapore provides perhaps the best international example of a system that gives substantial attention to the identification and development of school leaders. Singapore explicitly models its leadership development strategy on the best practices of large private corporations. Vivien Stewart, an experienced observer of Asian educational systems, recently described this strategy in an Organisation for Economic Co-operation and Development (OECD) report as follows:

> In Singapore young teachers are continuously assessed for their leadership potential and given opportunities to demonstrate and learn, for example, by serving on committees and then being promoted to head of department at a very young age. Some are transferred to the Ministry of Education for a time. After these experiences are monitored, potential principals are selected for interviews and go through leadership situational exercises. If they pass these, then they are eligible to go to the National Institute of Education for six months of executive leadership training, with their salaries paid. The process is comprehensive and intensive and includes a study trip and a project on school innovation in another country.[9]

Contrast this talent identification and development approach with U.S. practice, where any teacher can enroll in an administrative certification program and then seek a position as principal. While districts may be supporting leadership development, as with curriculum and teaching, a more systematic approach will yield greater consistency and better results.

Other countries are also investing in leadership development as a system activity, including leadership institutes in several Australian states and a national organization, and a leadership framework and strategy in several Canadian provinces. Moreover, in these systems leadership development is closely linked to better instruction and school improvement, and highly connected to system goals and strategies.

4. High expectations for all students coupled with real efforts to keep students on track for success from the very beginning of their schooling

What we know from much research is that virtually all students have the potential to perform at higher levels given enough motivation and support. Systems that give students additional supports as needed and offer many routes for them to return to standard or better levels of progress are more likely to generate success for more students.

High expectations for all students is a mantra in the U.S., but the rhetoric is not matched by the reality. There are still many situations in which the responsibility for poor performance is seen to lie with students or their families, and schools feel unable to change that. The reality is that high expectations are of no use unless they are matched by the necessary skills.

Here, too, there is much we can learn from the Finns. After a long public debate, Finland abolished its two-tiered middle school system in the mid-1960s and moved to a single comprehensive education system for all students from grades one through nine. Two decades later, the country abolished within-school tracking. In doing this, it understood that its teachers would require a different level of training to serve all students effectively, regardless of family background or perceived academic ability. Consequently, Finland placed much greater emphasis on its upgraded teacher preparation programs in equipping teachers to recognize and respond to learning difficulties, and it decided to create a new position in each school, called the "special teacher," for someone with an additional year of training. While Finland does have separate special education programs for severely handicapped children, the special teacher's job is to work closely with the regular class teachers to provide individual or small-group support to students who may at any given point be struggling to keep up with the rest of the class. Because most students at some point in their schooling careers will receive help from the special teacher—perhaps because they were ill and missed a few days of school, or because they just need some extra tutoring to understand a particular mathematics concept—there is no stigma attached to receiving such help. The goal is to ensure that no student falls between the cracks, and that virtually all students are able to stay in the mainstream program and keep up with their peers. This focus on providing early intervention and support helps explain why Finland, in addition to its consistent high performance, is the country with the least variation in within-school and between-school performance. This pattern stands in stark contrast to the U.S., where a student's socioeconomic background is highly predictive of academic achievement.

There is a lively debate about how much difference schools can make in the areas of inequality and achievement in a society.[10] Clearly, schools are not solely responsible for inequality, but that does not mean they are powerless to respond to the challenges of diverse student populations. We have evidence that schools with very similar demographics vary greatly in outcomes, and also lots of evidence that individual schools or groups of schools can generate significant improvement given the right supports. We do not, therefore, accept the view that schools will inevitably mirror or necessarily exacerbate inequalities in the larger society.

At the same time, there is no reason to think that schools are immune from larger social forces, or that they can, no matter how heroic the efforts, compensate for vast inequalities in society. Children who start school—or life—with few or no positive factors face a much harder struggle than do the more fortunate. Children with health problems, poor nutrition, unstable housing, fetal alcohol syndrome, or other such issues are not playing on level ground with children who don't have these challenges. Education policy cannot be divorced from social policy more broadly.

The United States is one of the richest countries in the world, and among the most unequal of all wealthy countries.[11] There is clearly a link between high levels of child poverty, huge inequalities in wealth, poor health care for millions, lack of any system of child care, and the gaps in achievement in American schools. Indeed, the entire gap between the U.S. and other countries is accounted for by poor performance at the bottom of the achievement distribution, and these are overwhelmingly young people growing up in poverty. In our view, the United States cannot solve its educational challenge by focusing only on schools. Schools should not be let off the hook for doing their share, of course, but if the rest of the nation is unwilling to do its part, we cannot expect them to remedy all the problems created outside their walls. . . .

5. Strong efforts to connect secondary education to the economy and employment as well as to post-secondary education

At the end of lower secondary school (grade nine or ten), most high performing systems, especially those in northern Europe, provide students with a choice between a pathway leading to university and one leading more directly to a career.[12] The career-oriented pathways are well developed, cover a broad range of occupations (high-tech, low-tech; white-collar, blue-collar), and have strong employer involvement in shaping curriculum and qualifications. These programs typically provide a mix of work-based and classroom-based learning, extend over three or four years, and culminate in a certificate with real currency in the labor market. These are mainstream systems, serving between 40 and 70 percent of young people in countries like Denmark, Finland, Germany, the Netherlands, and Switzerland.

If one converses with young people in these European apprenticeship systems, it is easy to understand the appeal. After nine or ten years of sitting in classrooms, many (perhaps most) young people are eager for an opportunity to learn by doing, to be learning and working alongside adults who are skilled and knowledgeable, and to earn while they are learning so they can begin to establish their independence. Because these countries have built pathways that enable young people to continue on to some form of advanced education after they have completed their upper secondary vocational program, students are not closing off options by entering the vocational pathway. These systems recognize that skilled occupations are increasingly integrated with various aspects of post-secondary education.

Despite the checkered past of vocational education in the U.S., recent advances in career and technical education suggest that the groundwork is being laid for a more robust articulation between the education system and the work force. The 2006 reauthorization of the Perkins Act, the primary federal funding program for career and technical education at both the secondary and post-secondary levels, required each district to develop at least one program of study aimed at work force preparation through a coherent sequence of courses across levels.[13] At the secondary level, curricular innovations demonstrate the feasibility of integrating academic content with technical studies in a manner that elevates academic performance without detracting from the growth of students' technical knowledge.[14] Numerous examples of sophisticated technical education programs are now available that, if implemented widely, would mirror their productive European counterparts.[15]

6. National policies and resources that focus on minimizing disparities in outcomes and on helping most [of] those schools that face the greatest challenges in terms of student demographics

High performing systems invest significant attention and resources in prevention and early intervention rather than remediation. The goal is to keep all students on track with their peers, not to build separate treatment systems for students who are behind (and from which students rarely escape). In Finland, as indicated previously, teachers are well trained to diagnose learning difficulties, and every school has a special teacher whose job it is to work closely with regular classroom teachers.

Successful systems quickly mobilize support from all available sources for students and families

in need of specialized help, and generally work hard to make sure that no student falls through the cracks. The special education system is less formal: providing the right supports for learning is more important than giving students a label. There is little or no emphasis on "diagnosis." In Finland, as in other Scandinavian countries, all students are in a common, untracked curriculum through lower secondary school (the U.S. equivalent of ninth or tenth grade), and there is a strong preference for inclusion rather than separate special education classes. In Ontario, all high schools have systems to identify students who are in danger of failing courses, leading to early intervention to prevent that failure.

Similarly, high performing systems respond to struggling schools early with intervention and support, not punishment. Ontario and other high performing states and nations do not close low performing schools. Instead, the ministry of education in Ontario works closely with school district leaders to ensure that low performing schools receive intensive technical assistance and support. The process is collaborative and based on support rather than blame. As a result, the number of struggling schools in the province has dropped from 110 to 18 in two years, and high school graduation rates rose by nearly 20 percent.[16]

While these steps are important, the ability of the schools to keep students on track is also closely related to the overall state of the society; a country with greater economic and social inequality is likely to have those challenges in the schools as well. . . .

7. A positive approach that builds trust and commitment while engaging all partners in efforts toward further improvement

This point is stated last but is perhaps most important. Indeed, if we could identify only one change for the U.S., it would be to move away from a culture of blame to one of mutual support and effort.

Successful systems and countries build a positive approach to education improvement. They are not engaged in bashing teachers, attacking teacher unions, denigrating parents, or blaming problems on someone else. In fact, blame is not important at all in these settings; instead, these systems make an effort to have all partners work together in support of better outcomes for all students. They do this through a good balance of clear overall goals and standards coupled with significant school and district autonomy, and by directing resources to supporting better teaching and learning rather than to administrative processes. In successful systems, individual schools or districts do not have independent goals, but they do have considerable scope as to how they pursue various communal goals. Progress is based on strong partnerships in which every level of the system has a genuine sense of respect and engagement.

This work is accomplished through "large and small *p*" political processes. In many European countries, there are regular mechanisms for educators, employers, students, and education authorities to discuss key education issues. Ontario created a "partnership table" that brings all the stakeholders together to review major policy initiatives before they are finalized and implemented. Finland uses a highly consensual process to develop education policy, and the same approach is characteristic of Asian countries. Also, these education systems have high alignment at the school, district, regional, and national levels, unlike the fractured system in the U.S., with its many small but independent districts and weak states. It is not a question of centralization (though Canada has many fewer districts relative to size than does the U.S.), but a matter of bringing people together to agree on courses of action and approaches to implementation.

As a consequence of these features, high performing systems generally have a more collaborative and trust-based school culture than what typically characterizes the U.S. system. Their administrative leaders are relentlessly positive and optimistic in their communications, stressing capabilities and contributions, not deficiencies. They focus on improvement, not blame. They try not to divide people or to declare winners and losers, but

to keep everyone—students, parents, teachers, and others—engaged in a positive way. This kind of cooperation is characteristic of all high performing systems. U.S. research on trust in schools—among educators, as well as between educators and parents and community members—suggests that the same benefits could accrue here if such cooperation were more widespread.[17]

Notes

1. Bobby D. Rampey, Gloria S. Dion, and Patricia L. Donahue, *NAEP 2008: Trends in Academic Progress* (Publication No. NCES 2009-479) (Washington, DC: U.S. Department of Education, 2009), http://nces.ed.gov/nationsreportcard/pdf/main2008/2009479.pdf.

2. Michael O. Mullis, Ina V. S. Martin, and Pierre Foy, *TIMSS 2007 International Mathematics Report* (Chestnut Hill, MA: TIMSS & PIRLS International Study Center, Boston College, 2008), http://timss.bc.edu/timss2007/intl_reports.html; Organisation for Economic Co-operation and Development, *Strong Performers and Successful Reformers in Education: Lessons from PISA for the United States* (Paris: Organisation for Economic Cooperation and Development Publishing, 2011), http://www.oecd.org/dataoecd/32/50/46623978.pdf.

3. Yossi Shavit, Richard Arum, and Adam Gamoran, eds., *Stratification in Higher Education: A Comparative Study* (Palo Alto, CA: Stanford University Press, 2007); Vivien Stewart, "Singapore: A Journey to the Top, Step by Step," in *Surpassing Shanghai,* ed. Marc S. Tucker (Cambridge, MA: Harvard Education Press, 2011), 113–140.

4. Andrew C. Porter and Adam Gamoran, *Methodological Advances in Cross-National Surveys of Educational Achievement* (Washington, DC: National Academies Press, 2002), http://www.nap.edu/catalog.php?record_id=10322.

5. Pasi Sahlberg, *Finnish Lessons: What Can the World Learn from Educational Change in Finland?* (New York: Teachers College Press, 2011).

6. Organisation for Economic Co-operation and Development, *PISA 2009 Results: What Students Know and Can Do—Student Performance in Reading, Mathematics and Science I* (Paris: Organisation for Economic Co-operation and Development, 2010); Mona Mourshed, Chinezi Chijioke, and Michael Barber, *How the World's Most Improved School*

Systems Keep Getting Better (London: McKinsey & Company, 2010).

7. Ben Levin and Michael Fullan, "Learning About System Renewal," *Journal of Educational Management, Administration and Leadership* 36, no. 2 (2008): 289–303; Ben Levin, *How to Change 5000 Schools* (Cambridge, MA: Harvard Education Press, 2008); Mourshed, Chijioke, and Barber, *World's Most Improved School Systems*; Organisation for Economic Co-operation and Development, *PISA 2009 Results*; Sahlberg, *Finnish Lessons*.

8. Adam Gamoran et al., *Transforming Teaching in Math and Science: How Schools and Districts Can Support Change* (New York: Teachers College Press, 2003); Anthony S. Bryk et al., *Organizing Schools for Improvement: Lessons from Chicago* (Chicago: University of Chicago Press, 2010).

9. Organisation for Economic Co-operation and Development, *Lessons from PISA for the United States* (Paris: Organisation for Economic Cooperation and Development, 2011), 170, http://www.oecd.org/datao ecd/32/50/46623978.pdf.

10. Richard Rothstein, *Class and Schools: Using Social, Economic, and Educational Reform to Close the Black-White Achievement Gap* (New York: Teachers College Press, 2004).

11. Richard Wilkinson and Kate Pickett, *The Spirit Level: Why Greater Equality Makes Societies Stronger* (London: Penguin, 2009).

12. Organisation for Economic Co-operation and Development, *Learning for Jobs* (Paris: Organisation for Economic Co-operation and Development, 2010), http://www.oecd.org/edu/learning forjobs.

13. Programs of Study Joint Technical Working Group, *Programs of Study: Year 3 Joint Technical Report* (Louisville, KY: National Research Center for Career and Technical Education, 2011).

14. James R. Stone III, Corinne Alfeld, and Donna Pearson, "Rigor and Relevance: Testing a Model of Enhanced Math Learning in Career and Technical Education," *American Education Research Journal* 45 (2008): 767–795; W. Norton Grubb, *Leadership Challenges in High Schools: Multiple Pathways to Success* (Boulder, CO: Paradigm Publishers, 2011).

15. William C. Symonds, Robert B. Schwartz, and Ronald Ferguson, *Pathways to Prosperity: Meeting the Challenge of Preparing Young Americans for the 21st Century* (Cambridge, MA: Harvard Graduate School of Education, 2011), http://www.gse .harvard.edu/news_events/features/2011/Pathways_ to_Prosperity_Feb2011.pdf.

16. Levin, *How to Change*.

17. Anthony S. Bryk and Barbara L. Schneider, *Trust in Schools: A Core Resource for Improvement* (New York: Russell Sage Foundation, 2002); Anthony S. Bryk et al., *Organizing Schools*.

PROGRESSIVE SOCIAL MOVEMENTS AND EDUCATIONAL EQUITY

Jean Anyon

In this excerpt from a longer article, Jean Anyon discusses educational reforms resulting from pressure by grass-roots social movements. In addition to defining social movements, she uses previous educational reforms to illustrate their role in changing schools. Anyon's approach is that the problem of attaining educational equity extends far beyond school walls and requires a coalition of community groups who can identify the barriers to educational equity.

Questions to consider for this reading:

1. In your own words, describe how Anyon defines a social movement.

2. How does Anyon's approach to educational change in this article differ from the discussion of possible educational reforms in the reading by Ben Levin, Robert B. Schwartz, and Adam Gamoran in this chapter?

3. Consider how the three recent organizing efforts Anyon describes in this article—Southern Echo, Logan Square Neighborhood Association, and Community Collaborative for District 9—fit her definition of social movements. What types of change are they likely to achieve?

A social movement connects what may feel like personal, individual exclusion or subordination to social structure and political causes. Social movements also provide a way of connecting with other individuals and groups across neighborhoods, cities, regions, and states to forge collective solutions to social problems. They offer a forum for working together to develop community power and to collaborate with others in making fundamental shifts in the political and social arrangements that have caused inequities, exclusions, and subordination. Thus, social movements are not symptoms of a "dysfunctional" political system, as some earlier scholars argued (e.g., Neil Smelser, 1962). Rather, in a healthy democracy, social movements are part and parcel of the process of change.

The concept of a social movement does not apply just to workers in struggle for unions and higher wages. The concept applies to all people and groups struggling for what political philosopher Nancy Fraser (2000) calls recognition or redistribution—for racial rights, economic justice, women's reproductive freedom, or educational opportunities. Social movements can also strive for negative goals like ending unpopular wars or seemingly unwarranted invasion of other countries.

There have of course been movements on the political Right (e.g., the "Right to Life" movement). But this chapter concerns progressive social movements and what those involved in school reform and public engagement can learn from them (to garner lessons from the Right, see Apple, 2006. [An excerpt from another article by Apple is in Chapter 8.]).[1]

A comprehensive definition of social movements, summarizing several decades of sociological research, is as follows: We have a social movement in process when individuals and organizations are involved in "collective conflictual relations with clearly identified opponents" (Della Porta & Diani, 2006, p. 20). The conflict involves "an oppositional relationship between actors who seek control of the same stake—be it political, economic or cultural power—and in the process make . . . claims on each other which, if realized, would damage the interests of the other actors" (Tilly, 1978, as cited in Della Porta & Diani, 2006, p. 21). Thus, the conflict can be cultural and/or political-economic. The conflict typically has as a goal to promote or oppose social change. In a social movement, the actors engaged in the collective action are linked by dense informal networks of organizations and individuals. They share a collective identity or sense of shared mission. The networks and interactions between groups and members yield social and cultural capital, which are important to bridging locales, groups, and opportunities, and provide the skills involved in planning, mobilizing, and executing actions and campaigns. People involved in a social movement typically feel a collective identity. They feel connected by a common purpose and share commitment to a cause; they feel linked or at least compatible with a broader collective mobilization (Della Porta & Diani, 2006; Touraine, 1981).

It is important to note that one organization, no matter how large, does not make a movement. The dense and sometimes overlapping networks that constitute a social movement are made up of multiple organizations, all of which are in pursuit of a common goal (Della Porta & Diani, 2006; see also Tilly, 2004; Touraine, 1981).

Nor are social movements isolated protest events or short-lived temporary coalitions that form around an issue. They involve episodes of action that are perceived as components of longer lasting action, over time—typically multiple years of effort. Social movements use various forms of protest against the specified targets and may also involve cultural expressions of belief as in group singing and the production of art and music that contain a social message.

In sum, when people feel excluded or subordinated, when people face governments or other groups whose actions they believe are unjust, and when they belong to networks or organizations that share goals and collaborate over long periods of time to attempt to increase equity through protest and sustained political and social contention against the targeted groups, they are engaged in a social movement, or social movement building.

* * *

PAST IMPACTS OF SOCIAL MOVEMENTS ON EDUCATIONAL EQUITY

Although not the only source of equity—upper class reformers, business groups, and politicians have at times advocated successfully for new educational resources or opportunities—progressive social movements have made substantial gains in increasing educational equity in America. Although we do not usually think of social movements as characterizing U.S. educational history in the early/mid-19th century, one can document substantial pressure from below that contributed to important educational change during those years.

The 19th Century

Horace Mann and his colleagues were not the only force pressing for the establishment of common schools in America in the 19th century. Historian Joel Spring (2008) points out that

> [t]raditional labor history . . . stresses the key role of working men's parties in the late 1820s and 30s in fighting for common school reforms. This interpretation places the American worker at the forefront of the battle for common schools. Of particular importance . . . is the opposition of workers to the . . . charity schools, which they felt reinforced social-class distinctions. (p. 100)

Active in the northeastern states of the United States, the Workingmen's Parties believed that "kept in ignorance, workers could be deprived of their rights, cheated in their daily business, and 'gulled and deceived' by . . . 'parasitic politicians,' 'greedy bank directors,' and 'heartless manufacturers'" (Russell, 1981, as cited in Spring, 2008, p. 100). These early union members believed that knowledge was power. Knowledge, to be acquired in schools available to everyone, was essential to protect workers' rights in the economic system.

Irish Catholics also fought against the public schools they faced. Between 1850 and 1900, Irish church officials and Catholic parishioners fought tenaciously against the public schools created by upper class reformers. Catholics rebelled against the Protestantism and anti-Catholic sentiment expressed in reading materials and personnel of the public schools. By 1900, they had established a wide network of Catholic schools for their children (Ravitch, 2000; Spring, 2008). In addition to providing opportunities for Irish families around the turn of the 20th century, the establishment of a system of Catholic schools in America provided opportunities later for children of color in cities as an alternative to public schools deemed deficient by parents. The existence of a system of religious schools had ramifications as well on federal education policy that continues to this day.

Foreshadowing later Civil Rights struggles, in the 1820s Boston's African American community, led by Black Abolitionist David Walker, began a 30-year fight against segregated public schools in that city. Their contestation ultimately led to a formal decision by the Massachusetts governor to end legal segregation in the state. In September 1855, the Boston public schools were legally integrated "without any violent hostilities" (Spring, 2008, p. 121). As we are aware, there would be more struggle necessary in the next century.

The 20th Century

During the Progressive Era, labor organizations, settlement house reformers, and immigrant families all put pressure on public school administrators to respond to the needs of the immigrant working-class population. Although there was a substantial effort in these reforms to "Americanize" newcomers, the schools were also responding to the pressures of the working-class majority in cities like New York. Schools as social centers with services enjoyed by many thousands of students and immigrant adults were the result; the school as a social center soon developed throughout the country at the turn of the 20th century (Spring, 2008).

The movement to establish teachers' unions radically changed the politics of U.S. public education and increased equity for the teaching force. Unionization of teachers increased their salaries and removed the most egregious forms of administrative control over their employment.

Most teachers' associations in the early part of the 20th century were politically conservative. But teacher organizations in those years in New York and Chicago had a radical ideology and developed out of the Labor Movement (in the case of Chicago, there were close ties to the early women's movement as well). The teacher federations in both cities fought openly with conservative business interests and school administrators (Spring, 2008). Out of these struggles—and in concert with less radical pressures exerted by the more cautious teachers' organizations—policies regulating the teaching force were instituted that made teachers' salaries and working conditions considerably more equitable than they had been.

The 20th-century Civil Rights Movement, of course, achieved many educational victories for minorities. Although the *Brown* decisions in the 1950s did not initially bring about education integration in the South, they did renew and strengthen activist organizing toward that end, and ultimately, the decision delegitimated separate but equal accommodations in the civil sphere. As a consequence of the national social movement for political rights of Black Americans, this decision and others following it produced vastly increased opportunities in education for people of color—in educational admissions, the availability of administrative positions, K–16 curriculum offerings, expanded programs for students of color in public school, and in federal, state, and local policies and programs that supported these and other advances.[2]

The Head Start program, for instance, was a product of pressure from the Civil Rights Movement. Black and White Civil Rights workers, most of whom were involved in the 1960s in building Freedom Schools and the 1964 "Freedom Summer" (when scores of Northern college students went South to assist in voter registration drives), developed a program in rural Mississippi that provided education and services for poor children. Funded with War on Poverty money, the centers were staffed by Civil Rights activists and local people. After 2 years, in 1966, southern White politicians in Congress succeeded in defunding these early Head Start centers in Mississippi. With money from wealthy Northern supporters, activists and families took two busloads of preschool children to Washington in protest.

There, with their teachers and teacher's aides, they would show what Head Start in Mississippi was all about. "A romper lobby from Mississippi petitioned Congress today for a redress of grievances," was *The New York Times*' lead in its February 12 story on what others were calling "the children's crusade." Forty-eight Black children and their teachers turned the hearing room of the House Education and Labor Committee into a kindergarten, complete with pictures and children dragging "quacking Donald Ducks across the floor" (Dittmer, 1994, pp. 374–375).

Two weeks later, the Office of Economic Opportunity awarded the group a grant to continue operations. Head Start moved to center stage in the Johnson administration's efforts to support the education of low-income minorities and has remained a major source of opportunity for the education of young low-income children.

The women's movement of the 1960s and 1970s also was responsible for increased opportunities in education, specifically for female students. A confluence of Civil Rights and feminist organizing during these decades yielded not only laws and programs to protect and support people of color but women as well . . .

On June 23, 1972, 2 years after the hearings, Title IX of the Education Amendments of 1972 was passed by the Congress and on July 1 was signed into law by President Richard Nixon.

The historic passage of Title IX was hardly noticed (by the press). I remember only one or two sentences in the Washington papers.

But Title IX would have a huge impact on education. It protects students, faculty, and staff in federally funded education programs at all levels. Title IX also applies to programs and activities affiliated with schools that receive federal funds (such as internships or School-to-Work programs) and to federally funded education programs run by other entities, such as correctional facilities, health care entities, unions, and businesses. The act covers admissions, recruitment, educational programs and activities, course offerings and access, counseling, financial aid, employment assistance, facilities and housing, health and insurance benefits and services, scholarships, and athletics. It also protects from discrimination against marital and parental status. Both male and female students are protected from harassment regardless of who is committing the harassing behavior.

A further example of increases in opportunities and resources resulting from social movement pressure is the right to learn and be taught in one's native language. Federal legislation creating bilingual programs was implemented in most parts of the nation originally as a result of organizing by Puerto Ricans in New York City and Chinese residents of San Francisco (Miguel & Miguel, 2004) . . .

RECENT ORGANIZING FOR EDUCATIONAL EQUITY

The past 15 years have witnessed the appearance and rapid growth across the nation of community organizing specifically for school reform, or education organizing. This type of advocacy involves the actions of parents and other community residents to change neighborhood schools through an "intentional building of power" (Mediratta, Fruchter, & Lewis, 2002, p. 5). Education organizing aims to create social capital in communities and to encourage parents and other residents to use their collective strength to force system change. Education organizing attempts to build leadership in parents by providing skill training, mentoring, and opportunity for public actions. Parents conduct community and school surveys, speak at rallies, mobilize other parents and community residents, and plan and enact campaigns aimed at school and district personnel and practices.

Because education organizing gives parents a base outside of school—typically in alliance with other community groups—parents are not dependent on school personnel for approval or legitimacy. When successful, parent organizing in poor communities yields the clout that parents create among themselves in affluent suburbs—where, with their skills and economic and political influence, they closely monitor the actions of district educators and politicians.

Several studies of parent organizing groups in low-income neighborhoods around the country document their rapid increase in number and influence, especially since the early 1990s (Mediratta et al., 2002).[3] Moreover, 80% of 66 parent organizing groups studied by the Collaborative Communications Group are working not only in local neighborhoods but also in regional or state coalitions formed to improve district or state education policy. One such group is Mississippi-based Southern Echo, which has grassroots community organizations in Tennessee, Arkansas, Louisiana, South Carolina, Kentucky, Florida, North Carolina, and West Virginia.

Southern Echo is an exemplar in several ways: It is regional, multigenerational, and led by former Civil Rights and labor union activists. The group describes itself as a "leadership development, education and training organization working to develop new, grassroots leadership in African American communities in Mississippi and the surrounding region." Until 1992, their work focused on jobs, affordable housing, and rebuilding community organizations. When they shifted their attention to education in the early 1990s, they began to organize around minority rights in education.

Southern Echo worked to create a force that could put pressure on state education officials. They provided training and technical assistance to help community groups carry out local campaigns, created residential training schools that lasted 2 days or more, and published training manuals and delivered hundreds of workshops in communities. One result of the work of Southern Echo and an affiliate, Mississippi Education Working Group, is that on October 23, 2002, the Mississippi State Board of Education agreed to fully comply with federal requirements for providing services to special education students—for the first time in 35 years. Echo leaders report that this was "the first time the community came together to force legislators, the state board of education, superintendents, special education administrators and curriculum coordinators to sit down together."

A particularly impressive education organizing group in the North is the Logan Square Neighborhood Association (LSNA) in Chicago—founded in the 1960s to work with the variety of problems local residents faced in their community. In 1988, when the Chicago School Reform Law created local schools councils, LSNA began to assist parents and community members [with their] work to improve their schools (Mediratta et al., 2002, p. 27). Among the accomplishments of the LSNA and parents are construction of seven new school buildings, evening community learning centers in six schools, mortgage lender programs to offer incentives for educators to buy housing in the area, parent training as reading tutors and cultural mentors of classroom teachers, the establishment of bilingual lending libraries for parents, a new bilingual teacher-training program for neighborhood parents interested in becoming teachers, and collaboration with Chicago State University to offer courses at the neighborhood school at no cost to participants (Mediratta et al., 2002, p. 28). . . .

The final example of education organizing comes from South Bronx, New York. This group, Community Collaborative for District 9 (CC9), is an important instance of coalition building—between parents, community-based organizations (CBOs), the teachers' union, and a university partner (Mediratta et al., 2002, p. 29). Organizational members include ACORN (which has been organizing parents in Districts 7, 9, and 12 for a decade), the New York City American Federation of Teachers, Citizens Advice Bureau (a local CBO providing educational services to residents for 30 years), High Bridge Community Life Center (a CBO providing job training and educational services since 1979), Mid-Bronx Senior Citizens Council (one of the largest CBOs in the South Bronx), parents from New Settlement Apartments, Northwest Bronx Community and Clergy Coalition (which unites 10 neighborhood housing reform groups), and the Institute for Education and Social Policy (which conducts research and evaluation and provides other technical assistance to community organizing groups).

The CC9 coalition researched educational best practices to determine what reform it was going to pursue. It decided that stabilizing the teaching force was critical and that increased staff development and lead teachers at every grade level in the schools would give teachers skills to be more successful with their students and thus encourage them to remain in district classrooms. The coalition then organized residents, petitioned, demonstrated, and engaged in other direct action campaigns to obtain New York City Department of Education funding to pay for the reforms. At every step, neighborhood parents were in the forefront. In April 2004, New York City provided $1.6 million for lead teachers and staff development throughout the 10-school district. Since that time, CC9 has expanded to include collaborations across the city and has been engaged in efforts to improve middle school education system wide.

But these efforts have been confined to education. Although that is of course important for educational equity, it may be necessary to collaborate across social sectors, if we are to build the power to make changes that will be fundamental and sustainable . . .

I have been arguing that progressive social movements are an important force for increasing equity in education, but it may be that to wring sustainable, systemic change from the education system, we will have to work with groups active on other fronts as well. Indeed, we would not have to build a collaborative social movement for economic and educational rights from scratch.

* * *

Late 20th- and 21st-century globalization has indeed made the problems that public engagement efforts seek to solve no longer purely local. The causes of neighborhood problems like poorly funded education or lack of jobs often lie outside of the neighborhood and city in regional, state, and often national and global developments and policies. But although the problems people face may not be local, Tilly (2004) points out that most organizing is still local. The vast majority of organizing, he notes, still takes place in communities rather than on the global stage.

It may be that the important challenge of globalization for social movement building efforts in education (and economic) justice is that our organizing campaigns need to transcend neighborhoods. By this, I mean to suggest that the issues public engagement groups develop campaigns around need to be those that affect people in most or all of the neighborhoods of a city and in most or all of the cities of the state and nation. And the analysis that informs public advocacy needs to make the link to global causes. In this regard, analyses ought to transcend local power sources as causes and be supplemented by the identification of national and global developments and policies that affect neighborhoods. For instance, a local campaign against an underfunded urban school or district might connect the lack of public monies available for education to 25 years of diminished state and federal tax rates on corporations or to the huge federal spending on foreign wars. And as I have suggested earlier, we could expect synergy if we connected this local effort for increased education funding to alliances across sectors and indeed across the nation, in this case by joining education funding struggles to national antiwar and other alliances.

NOTES

1. As Tom Pedroni (2007) importantly points out, however, there are some social movements (like the Nation of Islam, for example) that are not clearly of the Left or the Right, in that they exhibit characteristics of both.

2. It is interesting to note here that, as Jack Dougherty (2003) demonstrates in *More Than One Struggle*, many African Americans in the South supported desegregation to obtain better educational quality but did not support integration as a social goal. Indeed, as Vanessa Siddle Walker (1996) has pointed out, the desegregation of Southern schools removed from Black communities the embeddedness of their educational institutions.

3. As Pedroni (2007) demonstrates, some of this organizing can have complex relationships with both the Left and the Right—as in the case of vouchers and some charter school movements.

REFERENCES

Apple, M. (2006). *Educating the "right" way: Markets, standards, God, and inequality* (2nd ed.). New York: Rutledge.

Della Porta, D., & Diani, M. (2006). *Social movements: An introduction.* Oxford, England: Blackwell.

Dittmer, J. (1994). *Local people: The struggle for civil rights in Mississippi.* Urbana: University of Illinois Press.

Dougherty, J. (2003). *More than one struggle: The evolution of black school reform in Milwaukee.* Chapel Hill: University of North Carolina Press.

Fraser, N. (2000). Rethinking recognition. *New Left Review, 3,* 107–120.

Mediratta, K., Fruchter, N., & Lewis, A. (2002). *Organizing for school reform: How communities are finding their voices and reclaiming their public schools.* Providence, RI: Annenberg Institute for School Reform.

Miguel, G., & Miguel, G., Jr. (2004). *Contested policy: The rise and fall of federal bilingual education in the United States, 1960–2001.* Denton: University of North Texas Press.

Pedroni, T. (2007). *Market movements: African American involvement for school voucher reform.* New York: Routledge.

Ravitch, D. (2000). *The great school wars: A history of the New York City public schools.* Baltimore: Johns Hopkins University Press.

Russell, W. (1981). *Education and the working class: The expansion of public education during the transition to capitalism* (Unpublished doctoral dissertation). University of Cincinnati.

Siddle Walker, V. (1996). *Their highest potential: An African American school community in the segregated South.* Chapel Hill: North Carolina University Press.

Smelser, N. (1962). *Theory of collective behavior.* New York: Free Press.

Spring, J. (2008). *The American school* (7th ed.). Boston: McGraw-Hill.

Tilly, C. (1978). *From mobilization to revolution.* Reading, MA: Addison-Wesley.

Tilly, C. (2004). *Social movements, 1768–2004.* Boulder, CO: Paradigm.

Touraine, A. (1981). *The voice and the eye: An analysis of social movements.* Cambridge, England: Cambridge University Press.

Descshooling Society

Ivan Illich

It is appropriate to include in this final part a reading by one of the more creative educational reformers of the 20th century. In this excerpt from his book of the same title, Ivan Illich proposes a totally different educational system that does not rely on schooling as we know it. The book from which this reading was taken is a classic in educational literature. Published in 1971, it provides an interesting way to rethink the function and structure of schools. Illich's idea of deschooling society provides a totally different approach to what we know as "real school." May this reading trigger your imagination and raise many questions as you consider changes in education.

Questions to consider for this reading:

1. What parts of education does Illich find to be most harmful?

2. Describe the type of education Illich would like to see in society.

3. What do you know about schools as educational organizations from other readings in this book that would make Illich's reforms difficult to implement?

Equal educational opportunity is, indeed, both a desirable and a feasible goal, but to equate this with obligatory schooling is to confuse salvation with the Church. School has become the world religion of a modernized proletariat, and makes futile promises of salvation to the poor of the technological age. The nation-state has adopted it, drafting all citizens into a graded curriculum leading to sequential diplomas not unlike the initiation rituals and hieratic promotions of former times. The modern state has assumed the duty of enforcing the judgment of its educators through well-meant truant officers and job requirements, much as did the Spanish kings who enforced the judgments of their theologians through the conquistadors and the Inquisition.

Two centuries ago the United States led the world in a movement to disestablish the monopoly of a single church. Now we need the constitutional disestablishment of the monopoly of the school, and thereby of a system which legally combines prejudice with discrimination. The first article of a bill of rights for a modern, humanist society would correspond to the First Amendment to the U.S. Constitution: "The State shall make no law with respect to the establishment of education." There shall be no ritual obligatory for all.

From *Deschooling Society* (World Perspectives Vol. 44), by I. Illich, 1971, London: Calder and Boyers, 1971. Copyright 1970 by Ivan Illich. Reprinted with permission of Marion Boyars Publishers.

To make this disestablishment effective, we need a law forbidding discrimination in hiring, voting, or admission to centers of learning based on previous attendance at some curriculum. This guarantee would not exclude performance tests of competence for a function or role, but would remove the present absurd discrimination in favor of the person who learns a given skill with the largest expenditure of public funds or—what is equally likely—has been able to obtain a diploma which has no relation to any useful skill or job. Only by protecting the citizen from being disqualified by anything in his career in school can a constitutional disestablishment of school become psychologically effective.

Neither learning nor justice is promoted by schooling because educators insist on packaging instruction with certification. Learning and the assignment of social roles are melted into schooling. Yet to learn means to acquire a new skill or insight, while promotion depends on an opinion which others have formed. Learning frequently is the result of instruction, but selection for a role or category in the job market increasingly depends on mere length of attendance.

Instruction is the choice of circumstances which facilitate learning. Roles are assigned by setting a curriculum of conditions which the candidate must meet if he is to make the grade. School links instruction—but not learning—to these roles. This is neither reasonable nor liberating. It is not reasonable because it does not link relevant qualities or competences to roles, but rather the process by which such qualities are supposed to be acquired. It is not liberating or educational because school reserves instruction to those whose every step in learning fits previously approved measures of social control.

Curriculum has always been used to assign social rank. However, instead of equalizing chances, the school system has monopolized their distribution.

To detach competence from curriculum, inquiries into a man's learning history must be made taboo, like inquiries into his political affiliation, church attendance, lineage, sex habits, or racial background. Laws forbidding discrimination on the basis of prior schooling must be enacted. Laws, of course, cannot stop prejudice against the unschooled—nor are they meant to force anyone to intermarry with an autodidact [a self-taught individual]—but they can discourage unjustified discrimination.

A second major illusion on which the school system rests is that most learning is the result of teaching. Teaching, it is true, may contribute to certain kinds of learning under certain circumstances. But most people acquire most of their knowledge outside school, and in school only insofar as school, in a few rich countries, has become their place of confinement during an increasing part of their lives.

Most learning happens casually, and even most intentional learning is not the result of programmed instruction. Normal children learn their first language casually, although faster if their parents pay attention to them. Most people who learn a second language well do so as a result of odd circumstances and not of sequential teaching. They go to live with their grandparents, they travel, or they fall in love with a foreigner. Fluency in reading is also more often than not a result of such extracurricular activities. Most people who read widely, and with pleasure, merely believe that they learned to do so in school; when challenged, they easily discard this illusion.

But the fact that a great deal of learning even now seems to happen casually and as a by-product of some other activity defined as work or leisure does not mean that planned learning does not benefit from planned instruction and that both do not stand in need of improvement. The strongly motivated student who is faced with the task of acquiring a new and complex skill may benefit greatly from the discipline now associated with the old-fashioned schoolmaster who taught reading, Hebrew, catechism, or multiplication by rote. School has now made this kind of drill teaching rare and disreputable, yet there are many skills which a motivated student with normal aptitude can master in a matter of a few months if taught in this traditional way. This is as true of codes as of their encipherment; of second and third languages as of reading and writing; and equally of special languages such as algebra, computer programming, chemical analysis, or of manual skills like typing, watch-making, plumbing, writing, TV repair; or for that matter dancing, driving, and diving.

In certain cases acceptance into a learning program aimed at a specific skill might presuppose competence in some other skill, but it should certainly not be made to depend upon the process by which such prerequisite skills were acquired. TV repair presupposes literacy and some math; diving, good swimming; and driving, very little of either. . . .

At present schools pre-empt most educational funds. Drill instruction which costs less than comparable schooling is now a privilege of those rich enough to bypass the schools, and those whom either the army or big business sends through in-service training. In a program of progressive deschooling of U.S. education, at first the resources available for drill training would be limited. But ultimately there should be no obstacle for anyone at any time of his life to be able to choose instruction among hundreds of definable skills at public expense.

Right now educational credit good at any skill center could be provided in limited amounts for people of all ages, and not just to the poor. I envisage such credit in the form of an educational passport or an "edu-credit card" provided to each citizen at birth. In order to favor the poor, who probably would not use their yearly grants early in life, a provision could be made that interest accrued to later users of cumulated "entitlements." Such credits would permit most people to acquire the skills most in demand, at their convenience, better, faster, cheaper, and with fewer undesirable side effects than in school.

Potential skill teachers are never scarce for long because, on the one hand, demand for a skill grows only with its performance within a community and, on the other, a man exercising a skill could also teach it. But, at present, those using skills which are in demand and do require a human teacher are discouraged from sharing these skills with others. This is done either by teachers who monopolize the licenses or by unions which protect their trade interests. Skill

centers which would be judged by customers on their results, and not on the personnel they employ or the process they use, would open unsuspected working opportunities, frequently even for those who are now considered unemployable. Indeed, there is no reason why such skill centers should not be at the work place itself, with the employer and his work force supplying instruction as well as jobs to those who choose to use their educational credits in this way.

In 1956 there arose a need to teach Spanish quickly to several hundred teachers, social workers, and ministers from the New York Archdiocese so that they could communicate with Puerto Ricans. My friend Gerry Morris announced over a Spanish radio station that he needed native speakers from Harlem. Next day some two hundred teen-agers lined up in front of his office, and he selected four dozen of them—many of them school dropouts. He trained them in the use of the U.S. Foreign Service Institute (FSI) Spanish manual, designed for use by linguists with graduate training, and within a week his teachers were on their own—each in charge of four New Yorkers who wanted to speak the language. Within six months the mission was accomplished. Cardinal Spellman could claim that he had 127 parishes in which at least three staff members could communicate in Spanish. No school program could have matched these results.

Skill teachers are made scarce by the belief in the value of licenses. Certification constitutes a form of market manipulation and is plausible only to a schooled mind. Most teachers of arts and trades are less skillful, less inventive, and less communicative than the best craftsmen and tradesmen. Most high-school teachers of Spanish or French do not speak the language as correctly as their pupils might after half a year of competent drills. Experiments conducted by Angel Quintero in Puerto Rico suggest that many young teen-agers, if given the proper incentives, programs, and access to tools, are better than most schoolteachers at introducing their peers to the scientific exploration of plants, stars, and matter, and to the discovery of how and why a motor or a radio functions.

Opportunities for skill-learning can be vastly multiplied if we open the "market." This depends on matching the right teacher with the right student when he is highly motivated in an intelligent program, without the constraint of curriculum.

Free and competing drill instruction is a subversive blasphemy to the orthodox educator. It dissociates the acquisition of skills from "humane" education, which schools package together, and thus it promotes unlicensed learning no less than unlicensed teaching for unpredictable purposes.

There is currently a proposal on record which seems at first to make a great deal of sense. It has been prepared by Christopher Jencks of the Center for the Study of Public Policy and is sponsored by the Office of Economic Opportunity. It proposes to put educational "entitlements" or tuition grants into the hands of parents and students for expenditure in the schools of their choice. Such individual entitlements could indeed be an important step in the right direction. We need a guarantee of the right of each citizen to an equal share of tax-derived educational resources, the right to verify this share, and the right to sue for it if denied. It is one form of a guarantee against regressive taxation.

The Jencks proposal, however, begins with the ominous statement that "conservatives, liberals, and radicals have all complained at one time or another that the American educational system gives professional educators too little incentive to provide high quality education to most children." The proposal condemns itself by proposing tuition grants which would have to be spent on schooling.

This is like giving a lame man a pair of crutches and stipulating that he use them only if the ends are tied together. As the proposal for tuition grants now stands, it plays into the hands not only of the professional educators but of racists, promoters of religious schools, and others whose interests are socially divisive. Above all, educational entitlements restricted to use within schools play into the hands of all those who want to continue to live in a society in which social advancement is tied not to proven knowledge but to the learning pedigree by which it is supposedly acquired. This discrimination in favor of schools which dominates Jencks's discussion on refinancing education could discredit one of the most critically needed principles for educational reform: the return of initiative and accountability for learning to the learner or his most immediate tutor.

The deschooling of society implies a recognition of the two-faced nature of learning. An insistence on skill drill alone could be a disaster; equal emphasis must be placed on other kinds of learning. But if schools are the wrong places for learning a skill, they are even worse places for getting an education. School does both tasks badly, partly because it does not distinguish between them. School is inefficient in skill instruction especially because it is curricular. In most schools a program which is meant to improve one skill is chained always to another irrelevant task. History is tied to advancement in math, and class attendance to the right to use the playground.

Schools are even less efficient in the arrangement of the circumstances which encourage the open-ended, exploratory use of acquired skills, for which I will reserve the term "liberal education." The main reason for this is that school is obligatory and becomes schooling for schooling's sake: an enforced stay in the company of teachers, which pays off in the doubtful privilege of more such company. Just as skill instruction must be freed from curricular restraints, so must liberal education be dissociated from obligatory attendance. Both skill-learning and education for inventive and creative behavior can be aided by institutional arrangement, but they are of a different, frequently opposed nature.

Most skills can be acquired and improved by drills, because skill implies the mastery of definable and predictable behavior. Skill instruction can rely, therefore, on the simulation of circumstances in which the skill will be used. Education in the exploratory and creative use of skills, however, cannot rely on drills. Education can be the outcome of instruction, though instruction of a kind fundamentally opposed to drill. It relies on the relationship between partners who already have some of the keys which give access to memories stored in and by the community. It relies on the critical intent of all those who use memories creatively. It relies on the surprise of the unexpected question which opens new doors for the inquirer and his partner.

The skill instructor relies on the arrangement of set circumstances which permit the learner to develop standard responses. The educational guide or master is concerned with helping matching partners to meet so that learning can take place. He matches individuals starting from their own, unresolved questions. At the most he helps the pupil to formulate his puzzlement since only a clear statement will give him the power to find his match, moved like him, at the moment, to explore the same issue in the same context.

Matching partners for educational purposes initially seems more difficult to imagine than finding skill instructors and partners for a game. One reason is the deep fear which school has implanted in us, a fear which makes us censorious. The unlicensed exchange of skills—even undesirable skills—is more predictable and therefore seems less dangerous than the unlimited opportunity for meeting among people who share an issue which for them, at the moment, is socially, intellectually, and emotionally important.

The Brazilian teacher Paulo Freire knows this from experience. He discovered that any adult can begin to read in a matter of forty hours if the first words he deciphers are charged with political meaning. Freire trains his teachers to move into a village and to discover the words which designate current important issues, such as the access to a well or the compound interest on the debts owed to the patron. In the evening the villagers meet for the discussion of these key words. They begin to realize that each word stays on the blackboard even after its sound has faded. The letters continue to unlock reality and to make it manageable as a problem. I have frequently witnessed how discussants grow in social awareness and how they are impelled to take political action as fast as they learn to read.

They seem to take reality into their hands as they write it down.

I remember the man who complained about the weight of pencils: they were difficult to handle because they did not weigh as much as a shovel; and I remember another who on his way to work stopped with his companions and wrote the word they were discussing with his hoe on the ground: "agua." Since 1962 my friend Freire has moved from exile to exile, mainly because he refuses to conduct his sessions around words which are preselected by approved educators, rather than those which his discussants bring to the class.

The educational matchmaking among people who have been successfully schooled is a different task. Those who do not need such assistance are a minority, even among the readers of serious journals. The majority cannot and should not be rallied for discussion around a slogan, a word, or a picture. But the idea remains the same: they should be able to meet around a problem chosen and defined by their own initiative. Creative, exploratory learning requires peers currently puzzled about the same terms or problems. Large universities make the futile attempt to match them by multiplying their courses, and they generally fail since they are bound to curriculum, course structure, and bureaucratic administration. In schools, including universities, most resources are spent to purchase the time and motivation of a limited number of people to take up predetermined problems in a ritually defined setting. The most radical alternative to school would be a network or service which gave each man the same opportunity to share his current concern with others motivated by the same concern.

Let me give, as an example of what I mean, a description of how an intellectual match might work in New York City. Each man, at any given moment and at a minimum price, could identify himself to a computer with his address and telephone number, indicating the book, article, film, or recording on which he seeks a partner for discussion. Within days he could receive by mail the list of others who recently had taken the same initiative. This list would enable him by telephone to arrange for a meeting with persons who initially would be known exclusively by the fact that they requested a dialogue about the same subject.

Matching people according to their interest in a particular title is radically simple. It permits identification only on the basis of a mutual desire to discuss a statement recorded by a third person, and it leaves the initiative of arranging the meeting to the individual. Three objections are usually raised against this skeletal purity. I take them up not only to clarify the theory that I want to illustrate by my proposal—for they highlight the deep-seated resistance to deschooling education, to separating learning from social control—but also because they may help to suggest existing resources which are not now used for learning purposes.

The first objection is: Why cannot self-identification be based also on an idea or an issue? Certainly such subjective terms could also be used in a computer system. Political parties, churches, unions, clubs, neighborhood centers, and professional societies already organize their educational activities in this way and in effect they act as schools. They all match people in order to explore certain "themes"; and these are dealt with in courses, seminars, and curricula in which presumed "common interests" are prepackaged. Such theme-matching is by definition teacher-centered: it requires an authoritarian presence to define for the participants the starting point for their discussion.

By contrast, matching by the title of a book, film, etc., in its pure form leaves it to the author to define the special language, the terms, and the framework within which a given problem or fact is stated; and it enables those who accept this starting point to identify themselves to one another. For instance, matching people around the idea of "cultural revolution" usually leads either to confusion or to demagoguery. On the other hand, matching those interested in helping each other understand a specific article by Mao, Marcuse, Freud, or Goodman stands in the great tradition of liberal learning from Plato's Dialogues, which are built around presumed statements by

Socrates, to Aquinas's commentaries on Peter the Lombard. The idea of matching by title is thus radically different from the theory on which the "Great Books" clubs, for example, were built: instead of relying on the selection by some Chicago professors, any two partners can choose any book for further analysis.

The second objection asks: Why not let the identification of match seekers include information on age, background, world view, competence, experience, or other defining characteristics? Again, there is no reason why such discriminatory restrictions could not and should not be built into some of the many universities—with or without walls—which could use title-matching as their basic organizational device. I could conceive of a system designed to encourage meetings of interested persons at which the author of the book chosen would be present or represented; or a system which guaranteed the presence of a competent adviser; or one to which only students registered in a department or school had access; or one which permitted meetings only between people who defined their special approach to the title under discussion. Advantages for achieving specific goals of learning could be found for each of these restrictions. But I fear that, more often than not, the real reason for proposing such restrictions is contempt arising from the presumption that people are ignorant: educators want to avoid the ignorant meeting the ignorant around a text which they may not understand and which they read only because they are interested in it.

The third objection: Why not provide match seekers with incidental assistance that will facilitate their meetings—with space, schedules, screening, and protection? This is now done by schools with all the inefficiency characterizing large bureaucracies. If we left the initiative for meetings to the match seekers themselves, organizations which nobody now classifies as educational would probably do the job much better. I think of restaurant owners, publishers, telephone-answering services, department store managers, and even commuter train executives who could promote their services by rendering them attractive for educational meetings.

At a first meeting in a coffee shop, say, the partners might establish their identities by placing the book under discussion next to their cups. People who took the initiative to arrange for such meetings would soon learn what items to quote to meet the people they sought. The risk that the self-chosen discussion with one or several strangers might lead to a loss of time, disappointment, or even unpleasantness is certainly smaller than the same risk taken by a college applicant. A computer-arranged meeting to discuss an article in a national magazine, held in a coffee shop off Fourth Avenue, would obligate none of the participants to stay in the company of his new acquaintances for longer than it took to drink a cup of coffee, nor would he have to meet any of them ever again. The chance that it would help to pierce the opaqueness of life in a modern city and further new friendship, self-chosen work, and critical reading is high. (The fact that a record of personal readings and meetings could be obtained thus by the FBI is undeniable; that this should still worry anybody in 1970 is only amusing to a free man, who willy-nilly contributes his share in order to drown snoopers in the irrelevancies they gather.)

Both the exchange of skills and matching of partners are based on the assumption that education for all means education by all. Not the draft into a specialized institution but only the mobilization of the whole population can lead to popular culture. The equal right of each man to exercise his competence to learn and to instruct is now pre-empted by certified teachers. The teachers' competence, in turn, is restricted to what may be done in school. And, further, work and leisure are alienated from each other as a result: the spectator and the worker alike are supposed to arrive at the work place all ready to fit into a routine prepared for them. Adaptation in the form of a product's design, instruction, and publicity shapes them for their role as much as formal education by schooling. A radical alternative to a schooled society requires not only new formal mechanisms for the formal acquisition of skills and their educational use. A deschooled society implies a new approach to incidental or informal education.

Incidental education cannot any longer return to the forms which learning took in the village or the medieval town. Traditional society was more like a set of concentric circles of meaningful structures, while modern man must learn how to find meaning in many structures to which he is only marginally related. In the village, language and architecture and work and religion and family customs were consistent with one another, mutually explanatory and reinforcing. To grow into one implied a growth into the others. Even specialized apprenticeship was a by-product of specialized activities, such as shoemaking or the singing of psalms. If an apprentice never became a master or a scholar, he still contributed to making shoes or to making church services solemn. Education did not compete for time with either work or leisure. Almost all education was complex, lifelong, and unplanned.

Contemporary society is the result of conscious designs, and educational opportunities must be designed into them. Our reliance on specialized, full-time instruction through school will now decrease, and we must find more ways to learn and teach: the educational quality of all institutions must increase again. But this is a very ambiguous forecast. It could mean that men in the modern city will be increasingly the victims of an effective process of total instruction and manipulation once they are deprived of even the tenuous pretense of critical independence which liberal schools now provide for at least some of their pupils.

It could also mean that men will shield themselves less behind certificates acquired in school and thus gain in courage to "talk back" and thereby control and instruct the institutions in which they participate. To ensure the latter we must learn to estimate the social value of work and leisure by the educational give-and-take for which they offer opportunity. Effective participation in the politics of a street, a work place, the library, a news program, or a hospital is therefore the best measuring stick to evaluate their level as educational institutions.

I recently spoke to a group of junior-high school students in the process of organizing a resistance movement to their obligatory draft into the next class. Their slogan was "participation—not simulation." They were disappointed that this was understood as a demand for less rather than for more education, and reminded me of the resistance which Karl Marx put up against a passage in the Gotha program which—one hundred years ago—wanted to outlaw child labor. He opposed the proposal in the interest of the education of the young, which could happen only at work. If the greatest fruit of man's labor should be the education he receives from it and the opportunity which work gives him to initiate the education of others, then the alienation of modern society in a pedagogical sense is even worse than its economic alienation.

The major obstacle on the way to a society that truly educates was well defined by a black friend of mine in Chicago, who told me that our imagination was "all schooled up." We permit the state to ascertain the universal educational deficiencies of its citizens and establish one specialized agency to treat them. We thus share in the delusion that we can distinguish between what is necessary education for others and what is not, just as former generations established laws which defined what was sacred and what was profane.

Durkheim recognized that this ability to divide social reality into two realms was the very essence of formal religion. There are, he reasoned, religions without the supernatural and religions without gods, but none which does not subdivide the world into things and times and persons that are sacred and others that as a consequence are profane. Durkheim's insight can be applied to the sociology of education, for school is radically divisive in a similar way.

The very existence of obligatory schools divides any society into two realms: some time spans and processes and treatments and professions are "academic" or "pedagogic," and others are not. The power of school thus to divide social reality has no boundaries: education becomes unworldly and the world becomes noneducational.

IN THE FUTURE, DIVERSE APPROACHES TO SCHOOLING

Paul Hill and Mike Johnston

In the last reading, Paul Hill and Mike Johnston suggest other ways that do away with schooling as we know it, changes that are related to technology and the way students and their teachers "connect" to each other and school. They depict ways that change schooling in this country, and they challenge us to get out from behind desks and do things differently.

Questions to consider for this reading:

1. How does what Hill and Johnston describe in this reading change the relationship between teacher and student in our schools?

2. Do you think that the changes in the way we deliver education that they discuss will be more or less effective in improving academic achievement?

3. How are the changes Hill and Johnston propose similar to or different from those proposed in the previous reading by Ivan Illich?

Critics of U.S. K–12 education often complain that the basic structure of public schools hasn't changed in a hundred years. That criticism doesn't fit the facts today—there are many exceptions to the generalization that all instruction is delivered by a lone teacher in a sealed-off classroom—and it will be more dramatically wrong in the future.

Over the next few decades, public schooling will evolve and diversify much further. Though many children will continue to attend conventional schools, an increasing number of children will attend schools that deliver instruction, use time, and define the work of teachers and students very differently. Moreover, the idea that a school's primary identity is linked to the building that it and it alone occupies is already an anachronism.

In the past, public schools were buildings where students were housed from 8 a.m. to 3 p.m. In the future, public schools will become a broad and diverse mechanism for helping young people access, master, and use information. This change will be as radical as what has happened to public libraries over the past 30 years: Originally, public libraries were the physical buildings where people went to gather information. Now, the process of information gathering is diffuse, infinite, and without any physical home; it is managed entirely by the user and not the physical provider. The notion that in the year 2040, all American 12-year-olds will be boarding a school bus and riding to a comprehensive public school building to learn how to read and write from 8 a.m. to 3 p.m. is now as preposterous as presuming that in the year 2040 that same student would be riding a bus to the public library to flip through the card catalog for books on snakes.

Schooling alternatives are emerging or will soon emerge, and new approaches to government funding and oversight are also likely to emerge as public education diversifies.

THE NEW LANDSCAPE OF PUBLIC SCHOOLING

In the future, large numbers of children, up to half of those whose education is paid for with government funds, could attend schools that differ from the dominant model in which students and career teachers are in all-day contact with one another and in which teachers are fully responsible for assigning, explaining, and enriching the materials to be learned; assessing students' learning; and remedying deficiencies.

New forms of education are emerging for four reasons. First, the explosion of technology: Entrepreneurs and technology developers are experimenting with new forms of instruction that provide high-quality content with ongoing support for students at reduced costs.

Second, recession: States and localities, faced with severe revenue declines, are searching for ways to make the best use of their costliest and scarcest asset, excellent teachers. If current cutback scenarios continue (pink-slipping large numbers of junior teachers in order to maintain salaries for smaller numbers of senior teachers), many districts will find themselves with too few teachers to provide all the needed instruction and will look to technology for ways to increase the numbers of students one person can teach.

Third, public sector innovation: Districts such as New York City and Denver are searching for forms of schooling that might be more effective with groups that now experience low rates of success, and they're developing accountability systems based on school performance, allowing much more flexible use of public funds. New York is also formally experimenting with combinations of online and face-to-face instruction and intends to expand the number of schools making new uses of teachers, technology, time, and student work.

Fourth, a new commitment to attaining standards: This national focus on learning outcomes has changed the entire sector from one focused on how and where students learn to a system focused on what they learn. Now, when a policy maker, superintendent, or academic is confronted with a novel school concept, the question is no longer whether this model allows students to meet certain seat-time requirements or ensures that teachers are qualified or guarantees that students have a sports program. The first and only question is: Does this model help students meet standards?

At least three new forms of schooling are likely to become common enough to be recognized by teachers and parents as "normal."

1. Virtual schools in which teachers' sole contact with students is by monitoring progress on technology-based courses, assigning technology-based remedial and enrichment materials, assessing, and grading.

2. Hybrid schools that mix full-time teachers, contractors, and technology-driven instruction. Students learn at the school building and in other places. Full-time teachers manage online learning by monitoring an individual student's progress, assigning remedial work whenever a student falls behind, assigning enrichment materials and paper writing, and convening discussion groups. Students have some combination of virtual and face-to-face support, some from licensed teachers, some from subject-matter experts who aren't certified teachers, and some from tutors or paraprofessionals.

3. Schools that operate as brokers of instructional services, providing some courses by hiring contractors instead of unionized classroom teachers. For example, a school may contract with hourly rate music teachers who already

work in the community or firms that provide classes in the hard sciences and advanced math (taught by advanced graduate students or people working in industry); or they may partner with community college or university teachers to provide instruction under pay-per-course arrangements.

These different forms of schooling each have different implications for the use of time and the day-to-day work of school administrators, teachers, and students. . . .

These alternatives aren't common now, but examples of them exist. Several states have online schools, and many states accept credits from a national vendor (K–12). Many school districts offer assessment and enrichment courses for students who take most of their instruction online. A new charter school operator, Rocketship, is committed to using technology-based methods to individualize instruction and focus teachers' work on what only they can do. These are the first examples of "hybrid" schools and are prevalent by necessity in some rural districts where online courses are the only way students can access foreign language or upper-level math and science courses.

"Broker" schools are also emerging, though mostly at the secondary level. New York City has led the way in developing "multiple pathways to graduation," which include schools that assign students to learning alternatives, both inside and outside the school building, depending on students' learning needs and their schedules.

The fact that these alternative approaches to schooling exist now doesn't mean they'll become prevalent. Most parents will continue to want their children supervised and mentored by adults and like the social interaction that comes from the traditional school structure, so the demand for purely online schools will be limited. However, hybrid and broker schools, which offer flexibility and individualization yet can maintain close contact between students and professional adults, could appeal to parents who think their children could benefit from both individualization and direct adult oversight. They could also appeal to districts that need to find ways to serve students who can't or won't journey to school every day or to maintain quality course offerings on a shrinking budget.

How Common Will These Schools Be?

Whether these new forms of schooling become common or remain rare depends in part on their performance and in part on the removal of regulatory and funding barriers. In an era of performance accountability, districts or charter operators are unlikely to adopt new approaches to schooling if they're not, at least for some students and compared to conventional schools, effectiveness-neutral. One important dimension of effectiveness is citizenship preparation. Though parochial, private, and charter schools are generally as likely as public schools to produce students who endorse First Amendment principles and vote (Campbell 2006), there can be exceptions, and the results for virtual schools are not known.

Full exploitation of technology in hybrid and broker schools won't just happen. In theory (though not yet in fact) it should be possible to build schools around *new integrated instructional systems* that combine adult and student work with technology to cover whole subjects or entire school curricula. Integrated instructional systems for hybrid and broker schools would merge individually paced presentation of material with teacher work, that is, diagnosis, enrichment, and leadership of group interactions. Most material would be presented individually to students by technical means, but teachers would track students' work and intervene when needed. Consistent with the design of the instructional system, teachers also could suggest enrichment work, assign projects, lead discussions, and present materials not covered by technical means.

New integrated instructional systems would redefine teaching. Significant components of instructional delivery, assessment of results, and feedback on performance could be done with technology, offering students more individualization than is possible under the current classroom structure. The teacher would rely on technology to organize and deliver routine instruction whenever possible and reserve his own time and attention for intervention that only an expert human can do, for example, to explain an idea in a way not provided by the text or digital materials, intervene with an individual student, frame group work, or call attention to productive differences in ways different students approach a task. This also creates a new role in the teaching space for an adult who can help students navigate the technological supports, a role that might need different combinations of skills than do current teacher duties.

Integrated instructional systems would also transform teacher preparation. Teachers would need to interpret assessments, know what technology-based supplementary resources were available and what they were good for, and decide when to use supplementary resources and when to provide personal tutoring or coaching. If students are to benefit from teacher use of supplementary technologies, teachers must be clear about their instructional objectives and understand what resources are most useful as remedies to particular student performance problems.

There's no guarantee that any new form of schooling will be particularly efficient or meet the needs of students for whom it's designed. States and local school districts should closely track the performance of these schools, as we will suggest below.

Public Regulation and Oversight

Though there are existing examples for all these kinds of schools, the virtual, hybrid, and broker models all strain against the current structure of funding mechanisms, regulations, labor contracts, and accountability systems.

All, for example, require much more flexible use of money than state funding programs allow. Schools need cash—not people and resources purchased elsewhere and allocated to them—so they can buy services and products and pay for nontraditional teachers working part time or under contract.

Current state or local requirements that set class sizes, require that funds be used only to pay salaries, mandate hours of school operation, or set minimums for student seat time all militate against these new forms of instruction. Similarly, labor contracts and teacher licensing rules privilege individuals with skills and training needed by conventional schools and complicate the hiring of people with skills needed by different forms of schooling. We could envision a system where money not only follows the child in a pure form of student-based budgeting, but where even the dollars allocated to an individual child are broken up by standards, so that a given unit of information the state owed to an individual child has a specific price tag. This would empower the school or family to contract with multiple providers for different components of a child's education.

The existing virtual, hybrid, and broker schools almost all rely on special exemptions or alternative regulatory mechanisms that are by design limited to a few instances. In many states, virtual schools are often funded from separate and strictly limited state appropriations. When students transfer to virtual schools, state dollars held by school districts (and the regulations that accompany them) do not move. Similarly, hybrid and broker schools are often based on charters, which allow novel approaches to hiring and funds use but are limited in number by state-legislated "caps." Charters and virtual schools are also generally exempt from collective bargaining agreements that limit hiring, teacher work assignment, and pay scales that base compensation on seniority.

There are, however, emerging opportunities for broader experimentation with new forms of schooling. The states of New York, Louisiana, Colorado, Illinois, California, Pennsylvania, and Connecticut have allowed their largest urban districts to develop new schools and attract new independent school providers. In New York, the United Federation of Teachers has cooperated with the city school district's experimentation with new schools, and the union is itself running some modestly innovative charter schools.

The districts thus empowered are experimenting with both new forms of schooling and new institutions to support school quality. For example, teacher training and school improvement efforts in New York City are no longer constrained by the capacities of the district central office. Schools can choose among dozens of sources, including some staffed by district employees and others run by nonprofits.

Nationally and in key cities (New York, New Orleans), new charter management organizations (CMOs) are being formed to develop distinctive approaches to schooling and reproduce these at scale. As these organizations develop, creating additional schools of the new kinds will be easier, both in the cities where they first developed and elsewhere.

Other states (Wisconsin, Minnesota, Ohio, and Indiana) might follow suit, either putting schools under state or mayoral control or exempting specific localities from key regulations. As these governance reforms spread among districts and states, new forms of schooling are likely also to spread.

Virtual schools also have appeal outside major cities, especially in remote areas where students might not be able to get to school every day or in small districts that can't find qualified instructors in key subjects such as science and mathematics. Virtual schooling materials developed for rural and small town use might also be adapted for city schools and vice versa, thus accelerating the spread of new forms of schooling everywhere.

New forms of schooling might also prosper under a voucher system that welcomes almost any private or public entity to open a school and allows families to choose almost any instructional program. However, under those circumstances, cautious entrepreneurs might avoid highly innovative schools, preferring to reassure parents with familiar methods and assurances of conventional custodial arrangements. As long as entrepreneurs could fill their schools, they might not be concerned about students whose needs remain unmet.

On the other hand, school districts responsible for improving options for the most disadvantaged students might be more willing to take risks and develop multiple new options. Thus, a more conventional governance arrangement, under which a public agency is responsible to ensure that every student has a school, might lead to more development and experimentation with schooling options than would a wide-open voucher system. As long as high levels of accountability continue to require districts to help every student meet standards, and as long as open and competitive marketplaces exist where multiple providers can enter, we can expect that districts and families will continue to pursue innovative strategies that deliver results regardless of how that content is delivered or the physical structure of the building.

CONCLUSION

These diverse forms of schooling challenge the idea that the defining attributes of public education are uniformity and adherence to exhaustive rules. Standards-based reform encouraged some diversity of practice in pursuit of common student outcomes, but its early supporters scarcely imagined the diversity of approaches now emerging.

The new forms make it even more important for states and localities to determine what minimum skills all students need to attain and what, if any, common experiences they must all have. Their task is not easy: Prescription that is not based on evidence about what all children truly need will stifle innovation, yet too little clarity invites questions about what common interest schools serve.

States and school districts will also need to clarify how to measure student outcomes—including how tests will be combined with longer-term measures of student and school performance—and what will be done about schools, however defined, where students do not learn. Ducking these questions was easy when public education was defined in terms of the body of rules made over time to control it. New possibilities for diversification and individualization of instruction put new burdens on those who define the public purposes of education.

REFERENCE

Campbell, David E. *Why We Vote: How Schools and Communities Shape Our Civic Life.* Princeton. N.J.: Princeton University Press, 2006.

Projects for Further Exploration

1. Use an academic database (with no restrictions to refereed journals) to look up *educational reform*. What reform efforts are most cited in nonacademic journals? How do they differ from the reforms discussed in this book?

2. Using an academic database (with no restrictions to refereed journals), look up *"assessment"* and *education*. What is the current discussion around assessment, and how does it relate to the arguments made in the reading by Ben Levin, Robert B. Schwartz, and Adam Gamoran in this chapter?

3. Using a web search engine, look up community efforts to improve education and compare these efforts with those described in the Jean Anyon reading.

CONCLUDING REMARKS

Many people hang their hopes on the institution of education and the schools and classrooms within that institution. Ivan Illich, however, is not alone in his frustration with the educational systems in many countries. Other individuals also criticize components of the educational systems, and some offer solutions. Governments wrestle with these problems and look for research that proposes reforms. A number of articles in this book discuss possible reforms (see Chapters 8 and 11 in particular), and yet they only begin to describe the various reforms that have been attempted or speculate on those that will be tried in the future.

The purpose of this book has not been to propose solutions or reforms, although some of the readings do just that. Instead, we intended to provide readers with an overview of the theories, methods, and issues in sociology of education today. Sociologists provide a rather unique view of institutions, one that places institutions such as education, family, religion, and politics within a societal context. Although few sociologists set out with the goal of school reform, by raising questions about educational issues, they encourage critical analyses of schools. Sociological studies can inform debates and provide scientific findings to guide policymakers. Sociological researchers provide a unique perspective that can help those involved in decisions about our children's education to see schools in a new light.

Why haven't some of the major educational problems been solved? Many of the readings in this book point to reasons why things remain the same or, if changed, why schools still do not meet the needs of many students. We hope that by reading the articles in this book you have come to understand how complex educational systems are. We hope that you have come to understand that one person's sense of frustration can be another's sense of accomplishment. We hope that you now have a better sense of both the structure and the processes within schools and the many variations and permutations both structure and process have within educational systems. We hope that you now know that schools both mirror and reinforce existing social patterns in society. And, we hope you understand that schools do not exist in a vacuum, that educational systems respond to many external conditions, in addition to internal factors, in shaping how we educate young people.

APPENDIX

Web Resources for Continued Exploration of the Topics in This Book

Research Literatures

ERIC can be searched online to find research and reflections on a wide variety of educational topics: http://www.eric.ed.gov/. When at this site, you can search the literature data base.

Jstor: http://www.jstor.org/ (found at college and university libraries that subscribe). Jstor contains electronic versions of journal articles more than 5 years old in such journals as *Sociology of Education, American Journal of Sociology, American Sociological Review,* and others.

National Library of Education: ies.ed.gov/ncee/projects/nle

Online journals and/or abstracts

Anthropology and Education Quarterly: onlinelibrary.wiley.com/journal/10.1111/(ISSN)1548-1492

Chronicle of Higher Education: http://chronicle.com

Education Week: http://www.edweek.org

Educational Leadership: http://www.ascd.org/publications/educational-leadership.aspx

Harvard Education Letter: hepg.org/main/hel/Index.htmlHarvard Education Review: http://www.hepg/org/her

Journal of Blacks in Higher Education: www.jbhe.com

Phi Delta Kappan: http://www.pdkintl.org/publications/kappan

Rethinking Schools: http://www.rethinkingschools.org

Teachers College Record at: http://www.tcrecord.org

Free Online News Sources

Boston Globe: http://www.boston.com/bostonglobe

LA Times: http://www.latimes.com

New York Times: http://www.nytimes.com

Libraries

Library of Congress: http://lcweb.loc.gov/homepage/lchp.html

New York Public Library: www.nypl.org

Professional Associations

American Association of School Administrators: http://www.aasa.org

American Educational Research Association: http://www.aera.net

American Federation of Teachers: http://www.aft.org

American Sociological Association (ASA): http://www.asanet.org

Association for Supervision and Curriculum Development: http://www.ascd.org

Council for Aid to Education: http://www.cae.org

Council of Chief State School Officers: http://www.ccsso.org/intasc

Council of Great City Schools: http://www.cgcs.org

Education Commission of the States: http://www.ecs.org

Institute for Educational Leadership: http://www.iel.org

National Board for Professional Teaching Standards: http://www.nbpts.org

National Education Association: http://www.nea.org

Sociology of Education Section, ASA: http://www.asanet.org/ (go to sections, then Education)

Research Organizations

AACTE Education Policy Clearinghouse: aacte.org

Center for Social Organization of Schools: http://web.jhu.edu/csos

Consortium for Policy Research in Education: http://www.cpre.org

Key National Education Indicators: www.nap.edu/catalog.php?record_id=13453

National Center for Research in Vocational Education: ncrve.berkeley.edu

National Center for Research on Evaluation, Standards, and Student Testing (CRESST): www.cse.ucla.edu/index.htm

Office of Educational Research and Improvement: http://www2.ed.gov/pubs/TeachersGuide/oeri.html

Office of Postsecondary Education: http://www2.ed.gov/about/offices/list/ope/index.html

RAND Organization: http://www.rand.org.

U.S. Department of Education: http://www.ed.gov.

U.S. Department of Education Nation's Report Card: http://nces.ed.gov/nationsreportcard

Educational Reform Organizations And Information

ASA Trails: Teaching Resources and Innovations: trails.asanet.org

Accelerated Schools Project: http://www.acceleratedschools.net

Achieve, Inc. (an organization of governors and business leaders): http://www.achieve.org

American Youth Policy Form: www.aypf.org

Annenberg Institute on Educational Reform: http://www.annenberginstitute.org

Center for Educational Reform: http://www.edreform.com

Center on Reinventing Public Education: http://www.crpe.org

Center on School, Family and Community Partnerships: http://www.csos.jhu.edu/p2000/center.htm

Coalition for Essential Schools: http://www.essentialschools.org

Comer School Development Program: http://medicine.yale.edu/childstudy/comer

Edison Schools: http://www.edisonproject.com

The National Center for Fair & Open Testing: http://www.fairtest.org

National Charter School Research Project: http://www.crpe.org/cs/crpe/view/projects/1

Network for Public Education: http://www.networkforpubliceducation.org

New American Schools Network (merged with American Institutes for Research): http://www.air.org

Success for All Foundation: http://www.successfulforall.org

Higher Education Resources

American Association of College and Universities: http://www.aacu.org

American Association of Community Colleges: http://www.aacc.nche.edu

Association for Institutional Research: http://www.airweb.org

Association for the Study of Higher Education http://www.ashe.ws

Center for International Higher Education: http://www.bc.edu/research/cihe

Community College Research Center: http://ccrc.tc.columbia.edu

Fund for the Improvement of Postsecondary Education: http://www2.ed.gov/about/offices/list/ope/fipse/index.html

Historically Black Colleges and Universities: http://edonline.com/cq/hbcu

League for Innovation in the Community College: http://www.league.org

Learning Alliance for Higher Education: http://www.thelearningalliance.info

National Center for Postsecondary Improvement: http://www.stanford.edu/group/ncpi

National Center for Public Policy and Higher Education: http://www.highereducatio.org

Review of Higher Education: http://www.press.jhu.edu/journals/review_of_higher_education

Society for College and University Planning: http://www.scup.org

Western Interstate Commission for Higher Education: http://www.wiche.edu

International Materials

International Bureau of Education: http://www.ibe.unesco.org

International Sociological Association: http://www. isa-sociology.org

United Nations Educational, Scientific and Cultural Organization – UNESCO: http://www.unesco.org/new/un/education

U.S. Government – Comparative Statistics: http://nces.ed.gov

Data

General Social Survey (GSS) is available online, and simple analyses may be conducted online at: http://www.icpsr.umich.edu

National Center for Educational Statistics (NCES): http://nces.ed.gov

NCES Encyclopedia of Education Statistics and Annual Reports: http://nces.ed.gov/annuals

NCES Surveys: http://nces.ed.gov/surveys

Roper Center for Public Policy Research: http://www.ropercenter.unconn.edu

School Report Cards: Go to your State Education website and search from there

U.S. Census Bureau, Home Page: http://www.census.gov

U. S. Census State, County, and Community data: http://quickfacts.census.gov/qfd/states/00000.html

U. S. Census Statistical Abstract of the U.S.: www.census.gov/compendia/statab

The preceding information is an updated list of Internet Resources originally compiled by Caroline Hodges Persell and Floyd M. Hammack and originally published in *Teaching Sociology of Education* by the American Sociological Association, 2001.

⑤SAGE research**methods**

The essential online tool for researchers from the world's leading methods publisher

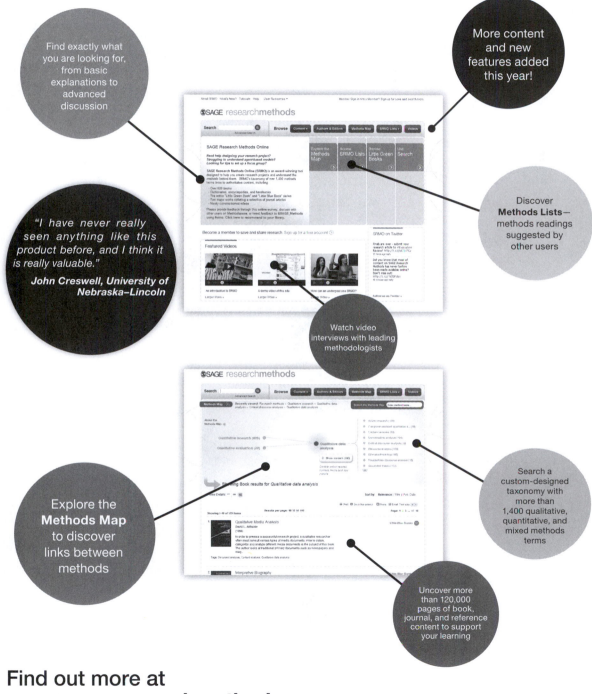

Find exactly what you are looking for, from basic explanations to advanced discussion

More content and new features added this year!

"I have never really seen anything like this product before, and I think it is really valuable."

John Creswell, University of Nebraska–Lincoln

Discover **Methods Lists**—methods readings suggested by other users

Watch video interviews with leading methodologists

Explore the **Methods Map** to discover links between methods

Search a custom-designed taxonomy with more than 1,400 qualitative, quantitative, and mixed methods terms

Uncover more than 120,000 pages of book, journal, and reference content to support your learning

Find out more at
www.sageresearchmethods.com